SOUTHEAST ASIAN AFFAIRS 2017

SOUTHEAST ASIAN AFFAIRS 2017

EDITED BY

DALJIT SINGH
MALCOLM COOK

ISEAS YUSOF ISHAK INSTITUTE

First published in Singapore in 2017 by
ISEAS Publishing
ISEAS – Yusof Ishak Institute
30 Heng Mui Keng Terrace
Singapore 119614
E-mail: publish@iseas.edu.sg
Website: http://bookshop.iseas.edu.sg

The responsibility for facts and opinions in this publication rests exclusively with the authors and their interpretations do not necessarily reflect the views or the policy of the publisher or its supporters.

ISEAS Library Cataloguing-in-Publication Data

Southeast Asian affairs.
1974–
Annual
1. Southeast Asia—Periodicals.
I. ISEAS–Yusof Ishak Institute.
DS501 S72A

ISSN 0377-5437
ISBN 978-981-47-6286-1 (hard cover)
ISBN 978-981-47-6287-8 (E-book PDF)

Typeset by Superskill Graphics Pte Ltd
Printed in Singapore by Mainland Press Pte Ltd

Contents

VIETNAM

Foreword

It is my pleasure to present the forty-fourth edition of *Southeast Asian Affairs*. The information and analysis in this forward-looking annual review will be useful for all interested in contemporary developments in Southeast Asia.

On the security front, the election of Donald Trump has deepened questions about the role of the United States in Southeast Asia, while the election of Rodrigo Duterte in the Philippines has sharply altered Southeast Asian approaches to the South China Sea disputes. The 12 July arbitral tribunal ruling that comprehensively undercut China's claims in the Spratlys, while precedent-setting for international maritime law, has had little effect on China's assertiveness.

Domestic politics in 2016 again underlined the region's diversity and different political cycles. In Singapore and Indonesia, consolidation and stability featured after recent national elections. In Thailand, Malaysia, Cambodia and Timor-Leste, positioning for upcoming elections took precedence. For the Philippines, Vietnam, Myanmar and Laos, new governments took office.

The regional economic picture was similarly diverse, though all economies were affected by the regional ramifications of longer-term global economic changes. Exports' contribution to growth continued to weaken, with many Southeast Asian economies suffering from slower GDP growth. Southeast Asia's demographic picture highlights the very different long-term economic challenges facing Southeast Asian countries and their impact on labour migration within the region.

I would like to thank the authors, the editors as well as others who have helped to make this publication possible. The chapters in the volume contain a wide variety of views and perspectives. They do not necessarily reflect the views of the Institute. The authors alone are responsible for the facts and opinions presented in their contributions.

Tan Chin Tiong
Director
ISEAS – Yusof Ishak Institute
January 2017

Introduction

Vandana Prakash Nair and Malcolm Cook

In the post–Cold War era, 2016 could well stand out as a watershed year for the global order, the Southeast Asian region, and many Southeast Asian states. Events in 2016 saw sharp new changes that may create new continuities going forward within Southeast Asian states and changes within long-term structural continuities that will have important ramifications for Southeast Asia.[1] As suggested by the title of this volume, the events of 2016 covered in the twenty-four chapters by twenty-eight authors will have a determining influence on the trajectories of Southeast Asia and the countries of the region in 2017 and beyond.

Structural Factors

U.S.-China Rivalry

The first regional chapter, by Alice Ba, focuses on a defining post–Cold War strategic continuity for Southeast Asian security and states' foreign and security policies: the strategic rivalry between the United States as the declining status quo power and China as the rising revisionist power. As Ba discusses, Donald Trump's victory in the November 2016 U.S. presidential election is a significant change on the U.S. side of this rivalry with unknown but likely profound importance for the U.S. role in Southeast Asia and Southeast Asian states' relations with the United States. At the same time, the author analyses how 2016 saw China become more assertive in its push to develop an alternate China-centred regional order and against obstacles to the pursuit of its national interests in Southeast Asia. These include the 12 July Arbitral Tribunal ruling invalidating most of China's maritime rights claims in the South China Sea.

VANDANA PRAKASH NAIR is Research Officer at the ISEAS –Yusof Ishak Institute, Singapore.

MALCOLM COOK is Senior Fellow at the ISEAS – Yusof Ishak Institute, Singapore.

The chapter by Andrew Shearer on the future of U.S.–Japan–Australia trilateral security cooperation delves deeper into the strategic ramifications of the U.S.–China rivalry and the common threat of terrorism. Shearer agrees that the Trump victory is a watershed moment for the United States in Asia. Australia and Japan will be under renewed U.S. pressure to contribute more to their respective alliance relationships with the United States. These relationships and the Trilateral Strategic Dialogue process provides Tokyo and Canberra unique communication channels to Washington DC.

Leo Suryadinata's chapter in the Region section looks at an element of China's rising power and regional and global interests of particular concern for most Southeast Asian states. Suryadinata argues that over the last decade the Chinese government has become more proactive in engaging with Chinese overseas to advance Chinese state and commercial interests. This runs the risk of aggravating long-held fears and prejudices in many Southeast Asian countries towards their respective Chinese overseas communities.

The U.S.–China rivalry and the 2016 changes affecting this rivalry were major considerations for the foreign and security policies of all Southeast Asian states. Donald Weatherbee's chapter on Indonesian foreign policy under the Jokowi administration looks at Indonesian responses in depth. The Malaysia country review chapter by Helena Varkkey, the Philippine one by Aries Arugay, and the Vietnam one by Phuong Nguyen each canvass this issue as well.

Terrorism

The year 2016 saw heightened concerns about the threat of terrorism in the region aided and abetted by strengthening ties between local terrorist groups and ISIS (Islamic State of Iraq and Syria). The thematic chapter for Singapore by Kumar Ramakrishna focuses on the Singapore state's proactive response to this threat and the difficulties of countering it. The thematic chapter for the Philippines by Joseph Franco focuses on the Duterte government's approach to the stop-start peace process in Muslim Mindanao. As noted by Franco and Ramakrishna, Muslim Mindanao has long been a safe haven for terrorists in Southeast Asia due to its stateless nature and the lack of an effective peace deal between the Philippine government and the main insurgency groups.

The Economic New Normal

Building on trends identified by Cassey Lee in *Southeast Asian Affairs 2016*, the regional economic outlook chapter by Tham Siew Yean and Andrew Kam Jia Yi looks at key economic trends in Southeast Asia and more broadly those routinely packaged under the term the "new normal". These include a slowdown in global and regional trade, slower economic growth and softer, if recovering, commodity prices. Tham and Kam analyse how the effects of these global trends are not common but rather quite varied across the individual Southeast Asian economies.

The chapter on the ASEAN Economic Community by Tan Sri Munir Majid reflects how the "new normal" and the election of Donald Trump increase the importance of regional economic integration and the ASEAN Economic Community for Southeast Asia and more broadly. Yet, Tan Sri Munir does not shy away from the implementation challenges facing this nascent Community.

Demographics

The chapter on demographic trends in Southeast Asia by Tey Nai Peng, as with the Tham and Kam one, reflects the diversity of economic challenges across Southeast Asian economies and societies and how regional statistics can be misguiding. While Southeast Asia as a whole is enjoying a demographic dividend with a growing working-age population, Singapore and Thailand are aging societies with worsening dependency ratios. Demographic trends are extremely difficult to alter and have a significant impact on government spending, growth rates, and labour migration flows within Southeast Asia.

Tension and Transition: Southeast Asia in 2016

Leadership was the name of the game in Southeast Asia in 2016. While most states in the region underwent some form of internal transition, each state's ability to respond to external and internal tensions depended upon the inherent stability of its leadership and governance model. International forces favouring populism also reached Southeast Asia's shores, auguring even greater uncertainty in 2017.

Enduring Models: Consolidation and Accommodation

In Singapore in 2016, the People's Action Party (PAP) government's eye was on the future as it focused on the twin tasks of regime consolidation and leadership renewal. In their review on Singapore, Kenneth Paul Tan and Augustin Boey identify key measures taken by the government to achieve both objectives, including a constitutional amendment to ensure minority representation in the Elected Presidency, revamping the education system to address a widening inequality gap, and an extensive economic restructuring programme. Despite the stability of Singapore's governance model, Tan and Boey point out that the PAP's uncharacteristic tardiness in identifying and grooming Prime Minister Lee Hsien Loong's potential successor will mean greater unpredictability as the nation-state grapples with growing hostility from China and the increasing risk of a terrorist attack. In fact, in his exposition on the threat that Islamic extremism poses to Singapore, Kumar Ramakrishna lists a number of planned attacks in 2016 where the authorities managed to uncover the plots in advance. Ramakrishna stresses the dual importance of effectively engaging non-violent extremist ideologues and battling "Islamaphobia" in the fight against physical terrorism.

Leadership renewal was also the focus for Laos in 2016, as the ruling Lao People's Revolutionary Party held its Tenth Party Congress in January, which was particularly significant for the retirement of several members of the revolutionary generation, including Secretary-General and State President Choummaly Sayasone. Soulatha Sayalath and Simon Creak consider the renewal process an exercise in preserving "the status-quo" in Laos. Indeed, the party's structures and processes had been designed both to maintain party stability and to ensure that elite prerogatives remain unchallenged. They predict that the Lao system is unlikely to change in the foreseeable future.

Meanwhile, in order to effect a similar level of regime stability, the Cambodian People's Party (CPP)-led government adopted both hard and soft approaches in 2016 to strengthen its credibility while simultaneously undermining the growing popularity of the opposition Cambodian National Rescue Party (CNRP). Thearith Leng posits that these efforts were generally successful, resulting in a tamed CNRP. However, he warns that the CPP cannot rest easy, as the growing discontent of the middle class is certain to pose more governance challenges in the future.

Brunei's governance model endured in 2016 along with its government's pursuit of economic sustainability. The oil and gas sector continues to disproportionately ballast the country's economy, accounting for eighty per cent of exports in 2016. Even so, Asiyah az-Zahra Ahmad Kumpoh believes that the government is on the "right track" with its extensive economic diversification programme which includes increased emphasis on infrastructure investment and improving Brunei's business environment. Certainly, as Kumpoh points out, some of the government's efforts have borne fruit, as Brunei climbed the World Bank's Ease of Doing Business Index in 2016, reaching 72nd out of 190 countries from its previous rank of 84th.

Transitioning Models: Stress and Instability

By and large, while predictability prevailed in Singapore, Laos, Cambodia, and Brunei, traditionally stable systems in Malaysia, Thailand, Vietnam, and Timor-

Leste contended with leadership challenges largely caused by unresolved political and economic problems.

In Malaysia, the 1MDB corruption saga continued to pose problems for Prime Minister Najib Razak's government in 2016. In her review chapter on Malaysia, Helena Varkkey narrates that in response Najib employed the twin strategies of removing dissenting individuals from his party, the United Malays National Organisation (UMNO), and consolidating his government's authority over public spaces through the increasing use of laws such as the Sedition Act and the Security Offences (Special Measures) Act 2012. Far from quelled, however, Malaysia's civil society is slowly building momentum. In November 2016, 25,000 Malaysians participated in the Bersih 5 rally, an annual anti-corruption demonstration. In a more formidable leadership challenge, former Prime Minister Mahathir Mohamad quit UMNO to form his own new opposition party, Parti Pribumi Bersatu Malaysia. Despite the efforts of the opposition, Varkkey contends that "[i]t is a race against the clock as to whether the opposition parties can organize themselves to stand as a united front before the next general election". The potent mix of political drama, the ringgit's sustained slide, and increasing social tension arising from growing Islamization means that instability will characterize Malaysian politics well into 2017.

Governance models in Thailand and Vietnam also came under particular stress in 2016 due to leadership transitions in both countries. In the case of Thailand, transition took the form of the passing of King Bhumibol Adulyadej, hitherto the world's longest-reigning monarch. In Chookiat Panaspornprasit's view, 2016 was a year of "shock and unpredictability" for Thailand, largely due to King Bhumibol's passing but also because there was no clear sign that democracy would be restored even after the national referendum held in August saw sixty-one per cent of the population vote in favour of the new draft constitution. In Panaspornprasit's opinion, "the military establishment in Thailand is still poised to hold on to power.... Democratization in Thailand is therefore … in indefinite transition".

Meanwhile the 12th Congress of the ruling Vietnamese Communist Party was held in January 2016, where former Prime Minister Nguyen Tan Dung failed to secure the post of General Secretary despite his best efforts. Instead, Dung was outmanoeuvred by his rival Nguyen Phu Trong who was re-elected General Secretary. In his analysis of the long-term implications of the leadership transition, Alexander Vuving demonstrates that the influence of rent-seekers and conservatives in Vietnamese politics has decreased, while moderates and modernizers have become more powerful. In effect this means that the party-state will have to rely more on legitimacy to stay in power. Beyond politics, Phuong Nguyen relates in her review chapter that Vietnam is still searching for a new growth model after thirty years of market-reforms, or *doi moi*. While Vietnam's leaders have achieved the main goal of turning the country into a "basic industrialized country", they are unsure of how to build a socialist-oriented market economy, which Phuong anticipates will be a major fault line in Vietnamese policymaking in the years to come.

In the words of Dennis Shoesmith, "Timor-Leste in 2016 occupied a seriously ambivalent political space". This ambivalence has been brought about by the country's ongoing transition to a "consociational democracy" where the opposition agreed to effectively surrender its role in return for a share of government. Former Prime Minister and founding father Xanana Gusmão bears responsibility for this unique transition, maintaining his powerful influence over the country's politics. In 2016 Timor-Leste was also brought to the brink of a constitutional crisis due to the machinations of President Taur Matan Ruak, an opponent of Gusmão's, who unilaterally appointed the Vice Chief of Staff of the Defense Forces. Shoesmith argues that Timor-Leste's new governance model has undermined an already underdeveloped party system, questioning its ability to survive the 2017 elections. Certainly, more change is in the offing for Timor-Leste.

Transitioned Models: Consolidation and Disruption

The year 2016 saw leaders of transitioned models in Indonesia and Myanmar consolidate their power. This process was not without its challenges. For Dirk Tomsa, 2016 was the year in which political outsider Joko "Jokowi" Widodo matured into his role as President of Indonesia and managed to consistently consolidate his power through a series of political manoeuvres. His efforts were disrupted, however, near the end of the year when his political opponents and Islamist hardliners like the Islamic Defenders Front (FPI) teamed up to demonstrate against Jakarta governor Basuki Tjahaja Purnama (Ahok), Jokowi's ally, who faced blasphemy charges. The demonstrations and Ahok's blasphemy trial were not only manifestations of the FPI's growing political clout but were reportedly sponsored by powerful political interests who sought to undermine Jokowi's position. The anxiety and uncertainty produced by the demonstrations have only been exacerbated by what Tomsa labels as Jokowi's failure to shape a consistent and coherent policy agenda.

Incoherence is echoed in Indonesia's foreign policy agenda. Using the Garuda as a metaphor to represent Indonesian foreign policy, Donald Weatherbee is lyrical in his appraisal that under Jokowi's leadership "the Garuda has been hovering, circling a more self-restricted flight zone while casting about for direction, still unsettled on a course". Taking the example of the Indonesia–China fisheries confrontation in March 2016, Weatherbee maintains that there is no single voice speaking authoritatively from Jakarta to the world or providing a rational, cross-government foreign policy agenda, often provoking the question, "Who's in charge?"

In Myanmar, the newly elected National League for Democracy (NLD) led by Daw Aung San Suu Kyi spent the year slowly finding its footing. Ardeth Thawnghmung and Gwen Robinson note that early signs were positive, with the NLD transforming its relationships with the military and the former ruling party, the Union Solidarity and Development Party, into a workable dynamic with compromises on all sides. The NLD dropped charges for or released 235 political prisoners, broadened anti-corruption rules for officials, and increased agricultural loans to farmers, amongst other progressive measures. In a surprise move, the two NLD-dominated houses of parliament passed a bill appointing Aung San Suu Kyi as State Counsellor, averting constitutional restrictions that prevent her from assuming the Presidency. By holding the two portfolios of State Counsellor and Minister of Foreign Affairs, a post that carries with it membership of the National Defense and Security Council, Suu Kyi has established herself as the most powerful member of the NLD government.

Perhaps the biggest obstacle to democratic consolidation in Myanmar is the Tatmadaw's (Myanmar Armed Forces) entrenched role in the political life of the country, with its constitutionally mandated right to occupy twenty-five per cent of seats in the national and regional parliaments. Maung Aung Myoe makes it clear that Myanmar does not enjoy democratic civil–military relations, but the Tatmadaw's position has been tempered by a gentle shift from direct involvement in state administration to a more consultative role. Instead of challenging constitutional limits, the NLD is attempting to reduce the Tatmadaw's influence by bypassing it in the policy process. On the whole, Myoe believes that the NLD and the Tatmadaw are "learning to live with each other".

Perhaps the most disruptive transition of 2016 occurred in the Philippines, which, contrary to earlier expectations, witnessed the presidential election of maverick political outsider Rodrigo Duterte, with 16.6 million out of the 44 million votes cast. Aries Arugay describes the circumstances surrounding his election thus: "Coming from Mindanao, Duterte's unprecedented triumph is an important rebuke of the elites who have dominated politics for decades." Not known for mincing his words, Duterte's populist sentiments and hard-line policies have caused ripples within the Philippines and across the region. Within his first hundred days in office, Duterte had implemented a war on drugs which resulted in more than three thousand deaths, sparking condemnation from international human rights groups. In Arugay's assessment, Duterte has delivered on his campaign promise of "Change is coming!", proving that actual change can occur within a year. Even so, Duterte's promises to make constitutional amendments aimed at transforming the Philippines into a federal republic could end up polarizing the country, leading to political instability and a lost chance to create meaningful change.

State–Centre Relations

Leadership transitions and resulting tensions have also made an impact on the ability of national governments to navigate state–centre relations, particularly in the Philippines, Myanmar, Thailand, and Malaysia.

Reflecting the uncertainty introduced by President Duterte's election, Joseph Franco provides insight into the current situation in Mindanao and the new President's approach to the challenges of secessionism and terrorism in that region. In a positive development, Duterte's government appears to have adopted former President Aquino's peace paradigm in relation to the Moro Islamic Liberation Front. His government has been concurrently pursuing a security-centric strategy to defeat terrorists in Mindanao. Even so, in Franco's estimation, Duterte's policies towards terrorist groups can be characterized as ambivalent at best, and generally volatile. Of particular concern to regional stability is the Basilan-based faction of the Abu Sayyaf extremist group in Mindanao that has pledged allegiance to ISIS, providing a base from which ISIS can operate in the region. Duterte's conflicting messages could exacerbate the security situation in Mindanao, with regional implications.

Similarly, Myanmar's peace initiative under the NLD government has come to naught. Fighting between the Tatmadaw and armed ethnic groups in Shan and Kachin states intensified towards the latter half of the year, and in October the Tatmadaw responded aggressively to a series of attacks on police units in Rakhine state. Thawnghmung and Robinson recount that widespread reports of human rights abuses by the military fuelled questions about Aung San Suu Kyi's lack of control over the army. The unabating conflict in these areas provides one explanation for the Tatmadaw's lasting prominence in the political life of Myanmar.

Thailand and Malaysia offer less violent examples of state–centre relations. Porphant Ouyyanont provides a historical analysis of Thailand's northeast region and how it evolved to become a thorn in the ruling military government's side with its overwhelming support for Thaksin Shinawatra and political parties associated with the former prime minister. Ouyyanont points to the development of a unique northeastern identity, separate from the dominant and cohesive Thai identity propagated by the government, based on the region's distinct historical development, ethnic makeup, religion, social structure, and economy. The region's relative poverty and the superior attitude which colours the Bangkok elite's interactions with it have also served to aggravate challenges in state–centre relations.

In the case of Malaysia, Neilson Ilan Mersat uses political developments in the state of Sarawak to illustrate how a strong, charismatic Chief Minister can negotiate the boundaries of state power within a federal system. According to Ilan Mersat, "When Adenan Satem took over from Taib Mahmud as the new Chief Minister in early 2014, centre–state relations changed and business as usual ended." Through his willingness to work unceasingly to advance the interests of the state by negotiating with the opposition, advocating for change in the education system, repeatedly pushing for an increase in the state's share of oil and gas royalties, and promoting the use of English in Sarawak, Adenan Satem managed to increase his state's leverage vis-à-vis a federal government mired in a corruption scandal. Adenan Satem's untimely death in early 2017, post the writing of this chapter, has cast doubt on the hopeful expectation that "the voice of Sarawak and its state interests will grow louder in Malaysia".

The Road to 2017

The authors of this volume have shown that the dynamics of disruption characterized Southeast Asian politics in 2016, setting the stage for even greater unpredictability in 2017. As leaders and governments across the region consolidate power and undertake reform in 2017, their interactions with international forces will test their political dexterity and the region's unity. States will need to engineer unilateral and multilateral strategies to manage growing Chinese assertiveness coupled with the possibility of an ambivalent U.S. presence in the region under a Donald Trump presidency. The United States' withdrawal from the Trans-Pacific Partnership (TPP) agreement will have negative ramifications, particularly in countries like Vietnam and Brunei where the prospect of participating in the TPP had driven economic reform. The threat of violence from extremist groups will not diminish, while the status of the Rohingya will continue to be a question mark.

There is still cause for optimism. ASEAN will commemorate the fiftieth anniversary of its establishment in 2017 with much to celebrate as it perseveres in providing a platform for regional engagement. Regional states will unceasingly pursue economic integration through the Asian Economic Community and the Regional Comprehensive Economic Community. Governments will have more opportunity to harness the power of disruptive technologies to boost domestic economies if they introduce policies to soften any adverse social consequences.

With the prospect of elections in 2017–18, the leaders of Cambodia, Malaysia, Thailand, and Timor-Leste will be obliged to steady their respective ships. And it is hoped that in the midst of international anxiety, Southeast Asia in 2017 will be a region of peace, if not stability.

Note

1. *Southeast Asian Affairs 2017* reflects the speed and breadth of these two sources of change. Authors were required to submit their chapters for editing and preparation for publishing in early December 2016 with little scope to revise them to take into consideration new changes or the unfolding consequences of changes identified. ISEAS would like to thank the authors and the readers for their appreciation of this unavoidable situation.

Acknowledgements

We would like to thank the large number of people who contributed to this volume. First, to the twenty-eight authors of the book's chapters for their diligence. Special mention must go to Vandana Prakash Nair, the Institute's Research Officer who has spent the most time helping bring the volume to print. On the publication side, thanks to Stephen Logan for overseeing the project and preparing the drafts for publication and to Betty Tan for assisting in this process. We would also like to acknowledge the contributions of colleagues and friends of ISEAS whose advice and views were sought and always provided. They include Gao Jiankang, Michael Montesano, Robert Taylor, Pushpa Thambipillai, and Cassey Lee. Finally, we would like to thank for their support ISEAS – Yusof Ishak Institute Director Ambassador Tan Chin Tiong, Deputy Director Ooi Kee Beng, and Head of Publishing Ng Kok Kiong.

Apologies to anyone inadvertently omitted.

Daljit Singh
Malcolm Cook
Editors
Southeast Asian Affairs 2017

The Region

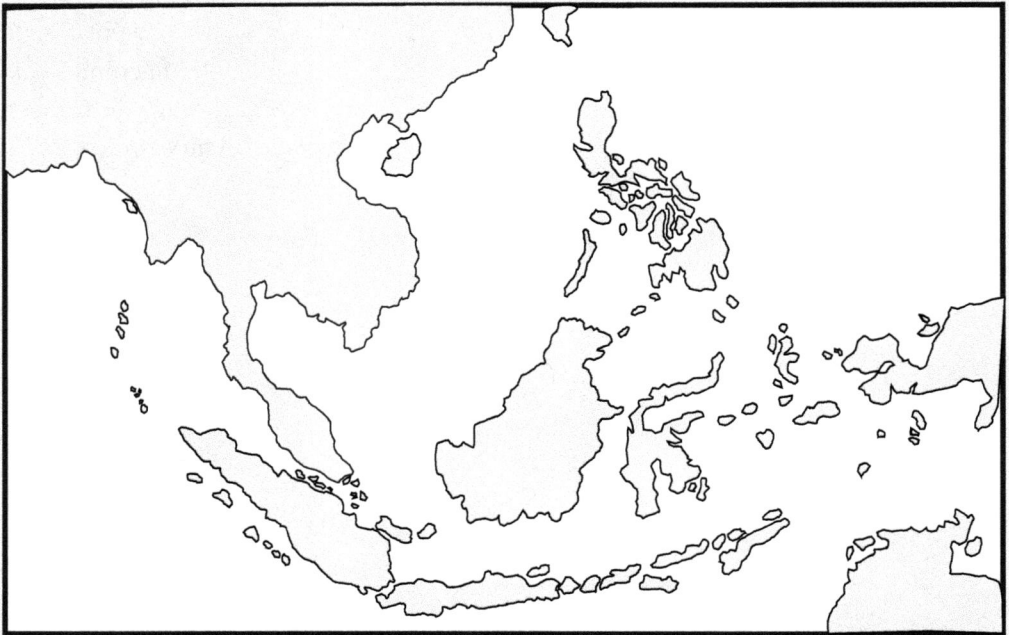

SOUTHEAST ASIA IN AN AGE OF STRATEGIC UNCERTAINTY: Legal Rulings, Domestic Impulses, and the Ongoing Pursuit of Autonomy

Alice D. Ba

Growing strategic uncertainty has defined much of the Southeast Asian context for the last decade. Much of this has been due to changing great power dynamics created, on the one hand, by the growing capacities and confidence of China as a rising power in Asia, and, on the other, the intensified anxieties of the United States and Japan as the region's status quo powers. Developments of 2016 were unlikely to change that basic structural condition, but it did prove to be a year of some notable developments nonetheless. Among the most anticipated was the 12 July ruling on the South China Sea by an Arbitral Tribunal housed at the Permanent Court of Arbitration in The Hague, which unanimously ruled in favour of the Philippines on almost all the fifteen points brought to the court. In a different region such a development might be more decisive, but this is Southeast Asia, where uncertainty remains a defining feature of the strategic environment, where mixed incentives associated with large states produce forces of both repulsion and attraction, and where hedging and the pursuit of autonomy remain the hallmarks of security strategies. Moreover, domestic developments in 2016 may prove to be as, if not more, defining in their implications for regional security and strategic trends.

In the face of heightened flux, three related dangers and imperatives that have long defined the Southeast Asian predicament remained outstanding in 2016: (1) how to ensure that Southeast Asian states are not made casualties of great

ALICE D. BA is Professor of Political Science and International Relations at the University of Delaware, USA.

power conflict; (2) strategies of hedging in defence of Southeast Asian autonomy; and (3) the future of the ASEAN project as a means to greater comprehensive security and in defence of Southeast Asian voice and institutional centrality.

The South China Sea Arbitration Ruling: Dramatic and Not?

After a decade of intensified tensions in the South China Sea, 2016 stands out as the year that the Arbitral Tribunal issued a devastating ruling against China's position and activities in the South China Sea. Among its most notable points, the tribunal ruled that China's nine-dash-line claim based on historic rights had no standing under UNCLOS, which China had signed and ratified and which now "superseded any historic rights, or other sovereign rights or jurisdiction" beyond those set by UNCLOS. Similarly, under UNCLOS, China's activities in the Philippines' exclusive economic zone (EEZ) — its large-scale land reclamation and construction of artificial islands; its interference with Philippine exploration and fishing activities; and its constructions on Mischief Reef, which sits on the Philippines' continental shelf — were found to have violated the Philippines' sovereign rights. Further, it ruled that none of the Spratlys' land features in contention constituted "islands" deserving of an EEZ of two hundred nautical miles. This includes Itu Aba, the largest of the Spratlys' natural features, which, along with other large features, were assessed to be mere "rocks" unable to sustain "a stable community of people" and thus eligible to no more than a twelve-nautical-mile territorial sea.[1]

In a sharp rebuke to China, the tribunal additionally concluded that China had knowingly failed to meet its international obligations to protect and preserve the maritime environment when it allowed large-scale harvesting of endangered species and giant clams and that China's construction activities had not only caused "severe and irreparable" environmental degradation in violation of its responsibilities as a ratifier of UNCLOS, but also its continued construction activities following Manila's legal submission "undermined the integrity of ... proceedings and rendered the task before the tribunal more difficult".[2] Further, its harassment of Philippine fishing vessels had "created serious risk of collision and danger to Philippine ships and personnel", violating China's obligations as a signatory to the International Maritime Organization's 1972 Convention on the International Regulations for Preventing Collisions at Sea.

Predictably, China denounced the tribunal's findings as "biased", "null and void", and as political instruments employed by colluding states (the Philippines and the United States) against China. It also approached Manila with an offer to hold talks "outside of and in disregard of the arbitral ruling".[3]

At the same time, in an apparent acknowledgement of the heightened reputational stakes associated with the ruling, it also moved to identify states that supported its position, at one point claiming that over sixty states agreed that the tribunal's proceedings were illegitimate. In fact, as the CSIS Asian Maritime Transparency Initiative found, only thirty-one states publicly protested the legitimacy of the tribunal prior to the ruling; moreover, that number dropped to six once the ruling was made.[4] While the states identified were mostly geopolitically insignificant, China's action seemed to acknowledge that legitimacy requires more than unilateral declaration.

To the extent that China has created what the tribunal calls "a *fait accompli*" at Mischief Reef — that China's constructions (as the tribunal, itself, concluded) are unlikely to be reversed, and that China's efforts to establish effective control through patrols and other activity continue — it remains unclear what effect the tribunal's ruling has in terms of the current material and physical position of claimants in contested areas.

Southeast Asian and ASEAN Reactions

Notably, Southeast Asian reactions to the tribunal's ruling were relatively cautious. In their official statements, only the Philippines and Vietnam explicitly welcomed the tribunal's ruling, but both remained circumspect. Myanmar, in its first public statement on the dispute, urged collective effort in support of the ASEAN–China Declaration of Conduct of Parties in the South China Sea (DOC) and a future Code of Conduct (COC) and joined Singapore and others in urging full respect for legal processes. Malaysia and Indonesia, despite heightened concerns, emphasized self-restraint in their statements, but did not comment on the ruling itself. Thailand, in a statement issued hours before the ruling, also did not mention the anticipated ruling, and emphasized mutual trust and confidence as well as equal benefit as the ways forward. Other states did not issue an official statement.[5]

Meanwhile, ASEAN as a collective chose not to explicitly reference the tribunal's ruling in either their July foreign ministers' communique or September leaders' statement, opting instead to underscore, as they did prior to the ruling, the rule of law, UNCLOS, non-militarization, the lawful rights of freedom of navigation and overflight, the pursuit of "full and effective implementation of the DOC in its entirety", and "the early adoption of an effective Code of Conduct". These same principles, minus the references to the DOC and COC, were also underscored in the seventeen-point joint U.S.–ASEAN statement following a historic U.S.–ASEAN Special Leaders' Summit held in February 2016 at Sunnylands in California. Unlike the others, the Sunnylands statement, however, never cited the "South China Sea" by name.

ASEAN states' strongest statement may have come a month before the ruling in the form of a retracted ASEAN press statement following a Special ASEAN–China Foreign Ministers Meeting in Kunming in June. Reportedly, China took offense at ASEAN explicitly citing the South China Sea "as an important issue in the relations and cooperation between ASEAN and China".[6] It was also notable that ASEAN ministers chose to issue a media statement of their own that moreover separated out the South China Sea from the many other issues covered in the ASEAN–China meeting. Otherwise, the language and their expression of collective "serious concerns over recent and ongoing developments" in the South China Sea as threats to "trust and confidence", with the potential to "undermine peace, security, and stability", was consistent with previous statements that ASEAN had made in 2015 and 2016.

Partly, the muted reactions from Southeast Asian states on the arbitral ruling likely reflected states' broadly shared disposition that China be allowed what just-sworn-in Philippine President Rodrigo Duterte referred to as a "soft landing" so as to not create political incentives for China to harden its position or retaliate with additional actions in the South China Sea. Partly, also, muted reactions likely reflected states' interest not to allow the South China Sea to damage other domestic and economic aspects of their relations with China. However, as Southeast Asian states know all too well, much depends on the reactions of other states, especially the United States. While the United States is not a claimant in the dispute, the South China Sea remained in 2016 as much about U.S.–China relations as China–Southeast Asia relations.

The United States and the South China Sea

At the end of 2015 the United States resumed limited freedom of navigation operations (FONOPs) in the South China Sea. In 2016 the United States conducted at least two FONOPs in the South China Sea — USS *William P. Lawrence* around Fiery Cross Reef in May and the USS *Decatur* in October (the United States also conducted a FONOP near Triton Island in the Paracels in January).

While the United States has commonly employed FONOPs as a means to challenge what it sees to be excessive claims that potentially challenge its right to innocent passage under UNCLOS Article 17, its recent operations in the South China Sea were nevertheless distinct for the "uncommon and unusual publicity" attached to them.[7] Such publicity is not only contrary to U.S. past practice but also contrasts with the approach taken by other states like Australia that have conducted airborne surveillance patrols (under Operation Gateway), including a possible overflight FONOP in December 2015,[8] but have chosen to do so with less fanfare. In addition, despite Washington's public request that Australia exercise FONOPs within twelve nautical miles of Chinese occupied features, Australia, as of November 2016, had yet to do so, leaving Washington mostly alone in its operations. China's Defence Ministry used the opportunity to issue post-hoc justifications of its construction activities. Washington's more confrontational approach, which practically seems to invite a reaction from China, also contrasts with the low-key approach of ASEAN states, which seems designed to avoid exactly that.

This said, China's response to both the tribunal's ruling and U.S. FONOPs appears to display some potentially interesting shifts. As detailed in one analysis by Andrew Chubb, a statement issued by China's State Council a day after the ruling suggested an effort to "separate [China's] nine-dash line from the claim to 'historic rights' and other maritime rights claims'" — though a subsequent Central Party School article in the *PLA Daily* re-established some links. But both statements suggest "little or no support to the expansionist reading of the line that has underpinned many provocative PRC actions in recent years".[9] Similarly, in contrast to the Defence Ministry, China's Foreign Affairs Ministry turned to legal arguments challenging what it sees as Washington's expansive reading of "innocent passage" and specifically whether it applies to warships. The advantage of the legal argument is that China's interpretation that activity by military vessels in another's EEZ requires prior consent is shared by some other states, including Indonesia, Malaysia, Myanmar, and Thailand in Southeast Asia.[10] The Philippines has also expressed similar objections.[11] China's view that innocent passage by military ships through another's twenty-four nautical mile contiguous zone requires prior consent is also shared by Vietnam and Cambodia.[12]

These efforts suggest some attempt to move to a more complex approach that acknowledges China's politically isolated position as regards to its maritime claims and activities, and, more broadly, the pressures created by the structure of international maritime law (even if contested). To the extent that such moves suggest efforts to widen the space that China had cornered itself into, they may also expand ways forward.

In the meantime, China and ASEAN states were able to agree to the initiation of an "MFA-to-MFA" (Ministry of Foreign Affairs) hotline, as well as a Code for Unplanned Encounters at Sea.

Other Maritime Engagements and Responses

While ASEAN states generally opted for a low-key response to the arbitration ruling, some states also pursued cooperation with various partners. Perhaps most notably, the Philippine Supreme Court, in a ten to four vote, affirmed the constitutionality of the ten-year Enhanced Defence Cooperation Agreement concluded by Washington and Manila under the Obama and Aquino administrations. While critical statements by incoming U.S. and Philippine Presidents raised questions about the alliance, the Supreme Court decisions nonetheless allowed the implementation of the 2014 agreement, under which U.S. military forces and weapons would be stationed in as many as eight locations on Philippine territory on a temporary, rotating basis. In addition to substantiating Philippine defence capabilities, the agreement also importantly supports U.S. strategic mobility in Southeast Asia and the South China Sea.

The United States also continued to support and expand efforts to develop Southeast Asian maritime capacities through its Southeast Asian Maritime Law Enforcement Program and Southeast Asian Maritime Security Initiative, as well as bilateral support specific to individual states. In 2016 the United States also completely lifted arms export restrictions on Vietnam.

Southeast Asian states also pursued cooperation with others in apparent efforts to diversify their security relations and resources beyond the United States. The Aquino government, which has made modernization of its air and naval capabilities a priority, received two light fighters (with the possibility of ten more) from South Korea and contracted the construction of two brand new frigates with a South Korean firm. Also delivered in 2016 was the last of three landing craft promised by Australia.

Japan, which has expressed "serious concern" about China's maritime activities, has been especially forthcoming in its defence assistance.[13] In 2016 the Philippines received the first of ten new multi-role response vessels under a Japanese Official Development Assistance loan agreement made soon after the Scarborough Shoal standoff in 2012. In February the two states also signed a defence agreement — the first such agreement Japan has signed with an Asian state — providing for "joint research and development, and even joint production, of defence equipment and technology".[14] Japan also agreed to lease to the Philippines five second-hand reconnaissance aircraft to support its ability to patrol the South China Sea.[15]

Incoming President Duterte also affirmed his appreciation for Japan's assistance.[16] Consistent with Manila's pursuit of defence acquisitions through multiple sources, Duterte's visit to Tokyo, which followed his much-publicized criticisms of the United States and the U.S. alliance, as well as a visit to China, has been interpreted as an effort to assert autonomy vis-à-vis both China and the United States through his cultivation of additional partners. Japan, for its part, made its first submarine port call to the Philippines in fifteen years, as well as an unprecedented visit by Japanese naval ships to Cam Ranh Bay in Vietnam, with whom Tokyo hopes to expand maritime cooperation. During a visit of Japan's Foreign Minister to Vietnam, Japan promised additional patrol ships towards supporting Vietnam's maritime patrol capabilities.[17] In addition to agreements with the Philippines and Vietnam, Japan also worked with Indonesia to launch a cooperation framework that included maritime security and economic development in remote islets.

In 2016 heightened pressure from Chinese maritime activities in Indonesia and Malaysia may have also factored into other partnerships. In March the appearance of Chinese fishing boats in Malaysian and Indonesian waters — Malaysian maritime authorities reported around a hundred boats near Luconia Shoals (Beting Patinggi Ali)[18] — prompted both governments to express objections, while also playing down the incidents. Those boats were accompanied by Chinese coastguard escorts, one of which rammed into an Indonesian vessel that had attempted to tow in a Chinese fishing boat after its crew was arrested for illegal fishing. Despite the incident being characterized as China's "most provocative by far" vis-à-vis Indonesia, and though Indonesian authorities did adopt a "stronger tone of protest", especially in its public criticism of China's actions, Indonesia, like Malaysia, continued to downplay the significance of events.[19] Ristian Supriyanto characterizes Jakarta's position as pragmatic (a desire not to harm economic relations and opportunities), domestic (a desire to avoid stoking anti-ethnic Chinese sentiment and, in turn, upsetting Indonesia's interracial relations), and strategic/ideological (a desire to avoid pressure to align more closely with the United States and violating its long-time commitment to a "free and active" foreign policy).[20]

Developments may, however, have increased Jakarta's receptiveness to working with Australia. At their 2+2 Dialogue meeting in October, Indonesia's Defence Minister Ryamizard Ryacudu reportedly proposed that the two states consider "peace patrols" in the Eastern part of the South China Sea. The sensitivity of the proposal for both Indonesian foreign policy and its relations with China was immediately apparent in the "awkward silence" from Indonesian authorities, as well as the backpedalling that followed soon after.

Still, Australia, whose 2016 White Paper affirmed the importance of strengthened defence engagements with Southeast Asian states, has been a receptive partner. In 2016, Australia and Singapore also expanded their already strong security relations. At their inaugural annual summit of the Comprehensive Strategic Partnership in October, the two states finalized agreements that included Memoranda of Understanding (MOU) on Military Training and Training Area Development in Australia, on Cooperation in Innovation and Science, and on Combating Transnational Drug Crime and Developing Cooperation, as well as an Agreement to Amend the Singapore–Australia Free Trade Agreement.

Meanwhile, Malaysia agreed to buy an initial four littoral mission ships from China, following Prime Minister Najib's November visit to China that produced fifteen business-to-business MOUs and sixteen government-to-government MOUs. While Malaysia is far from alone among Southeast Asian states in its willingness to pursue defence acquisitions or defence development from China, the "landmark" agreement may also have been given additional incentive by Najib's 1MDB scandal, against which the U.S. Justice Department has filed suit.[21]

Other Security Developments

All the attention given to the maritime front can make it easy to forget that the year began with a terrorist attack in central Jakarta. Linked to local, militant jihadists, it was also the first attack on Southeast Asia in which the so-called Islamic State of Iraq and Syria (ISIS) claimed responsibility. The summer saw additional ISIS-linked attacks on Kuala Lumpur and the city of Davao in the Southern Philippines, where Manila has long fought with separatist militants. Their cause has been cited as a source of inspiration for some Southeast Asian jihadists who have been encouraged to "go to the Philippines" if they cannot go to Syria.[22] Such developments, combined with the general lack of governing control there, have heightened fears that the Southern Philippines might become a sanctuary, if not a stronghold, for ISIS sympathizers and other radicalized groups to train, network, and organize — or, in the words of Indonesia's coordinating minister for political, legal, and security affairs, Luhut Binsar Panjaitan, "the next Somalia".[23]

While the numbers of actual ISIS recruits in Southeast Asia remain relatively small, uncoordinated, and motivated primarily by local grievances than by any global cause,[24] attacks in 2016 have nevertheless heightened concerns about violent extremism and radicalized Islam, especially in Indonesia and Malaysia where domestic electoral politics can also complicate stronger responses. In general, attacks highlighted increased concerns about three potential sources of vulnerability — recently returned fighters from Syria and Iraq (even if their numbers are small), militants recently released from jail and that require reintegration, and women and children who may be vulnerable to various propaganda efforts through social media, as well as religious and educational outlets.[25]

In response to the situation in the Southern Philippines, where piracy and hostage-taking have become important sources of revenue for both radicalized groups and various criminal ones, Indonesia, Malaysia, and the Philippines, following trilateral meetings of foreign and defence ministers in May and July, also agreed in August to a framework that included three-way communication hotlines, three command posts in support of intelligence-sharing and other coordination, and a trilateral working group towards the creation of trilateral air and sea maritime patrols — the "Sulu Seas Patrol Initiative (SSPI)" — which takes as its model the Malacca Straits Patrols between Indonesia, Malaysia, and Singapore, as well as Thailand.[26] Multiple incidents involving the kidnapping of Indonesian, Malaysian, and other foreign nationals by Abu Sayyaf and other groups throughout 2016 provided both immediate and ongoing impetus for the framework.

Affirmed at the ASEAN Defence Ministers Meeting in November, the three states agreed to begin joint counterterrorism training and drills in January 2017; however, other outstanding operational details of the SSPI continued to be negotiated. Also in 2016, the ADMM-Plus Maritime and Counter-Terrorism Exercise held its largest exercise to date.

Geostrategic Implications of Domestic and Economic Developments

In 2016, domestic transitions and changes were also geopolitically consequential. Among the more notable was the election of Rodrigo Duterte in the Philippines. His geopolitical inclinations and certainly his statements have stood in marked contrast to that of his very pro-U.S. predecessor. While Duterte expressed greater support for the U.S. alliance when elected, he quickly reverted to a more critical stance following U.S. criticisms of his violent "war on drugs", a campaign that has resulted in over 5,900 deaths (2,086 by police and 3,841 by vigilantes and extrajudicial actors, according to Philippine National Police) since his taking office.[27] Washington's criticisms provoked Duterte to announce his "separation from the United States" and the end of U.S.–Philippine joint military exercises.

While perhaps more rhetoric than policy, Duterte's vocal criticisms of the U.S. alliance, combined with his greater interest in courting China, nevertheless seemed to undercut U.S. efforts to impress upon both partners and rivals its enduring commitment and presence in Asia. This was a particular blow to the Obama administration, which suffered more than one setback in its efforts to consolidate and affirm U.S. rebalancing policies in its last months in office. Moreover, while the election of Donald Trump in the United States did lead to a more conciliatory tone from Manila, the Duterte administration nevertheless continued to express a strong position on Philippine autonomy. At a minimum, his preference for a more conciliatory approach towards China may constrain the strategic value of the alliance for the United States. For example, despite Trump's election, defence officials stated in December that the Philippines would be "unlikely" to allow the U.S. military to conduct FONOPs from the Philippines so as "to avoid any provocative actions that can escalate tensions in the South China Sea".[28]

Moreover, with U.S.–Thai relations still challenged since the 2014 military coup there, the turn in U.S.–Philippine relations meant that Washington's only two official allies in Southeast Asia could be counted among its less-dependable relations in Asia as a result of differences over domestic policies and human rights. In the case of Thailand, strategic and diplomatic relations continued to suffer in 2016 with additional sharp exchanges over Thailand's *lèse majesté* laws and policies (under which the U.S. Ambassador to Thailand remained under investigation for comments made in late 2015). In addition to the continued suspension of U.S. arms sales and military assistance under the U.S. Foreign Assistance Act, U.S. participation in annual Cobra Gold exercises was also significantly reduced to less than forty per cent of what it had been in 2013. Meanwhile, the passage of a constitutional referendum giving more power to the military, along with the death of Thailand's beloved, long-time monarch King Bhumibol Adulyadej, who had provided a unifying national figure for over six decades, suggests additional domestic and foreign policy challenges ahead.

Domestic politics, especially as regards economic developmental priorities, also have other geopolitical effects. In particular, and as illustrated by some states' responses to the South China Sea, China-linked economic incentives and opportunities also have implications for regional security. Moreover, 2016 saw expanded economic opportunities through China's "One Belt, One Road" initiatives that promised support for national and regional integration projects, as well as the China-led multilateral Asian Infrastructure Investment Bank (AIIB), which began operation in January. For many, Washington's failure to ratify the Trans-Pacific Partnership (TPP) — not to mention the bipartisan opposition to similar agreements — makes those Chinese initiatives more important. Still, it is not lost on Southeast Asian states that China's boldest economic initiatives to date should also coincide with China's expansive maritime activities.

In Vietnam, the 12th Party Congress' contest for the top General Secretary position resulted in a conservative win. But in addition to pragmatism on the domestic front, the leadership is expected to maintain its "three no's" stance (no foreign base, no military alliance, no siding with one country against another) and to continue pursuing relations with the United States, as well as Japan and Europe, in support of "diversifying and multilateralizing" its external relations.[29] Term limits also produced a transition at the April 2016 meeting of the Lao National Assembly that suggests a similar interest in autonomy — in this case, maintaining its close ties with Vietnam to offset growing economic relations with China.

For some states, like Myanmar, relations with China in 2016 saw new openings as a result of interdependent economic and domestic security concerns. While the National League for Democracy's historic November 2015 victory initially raised questions that it would pursue policies more autonomous from China, diplomatic exchanges between the two governments over the course of 2016, including Chinese Foreign Minister Wang Yi's visit to Naypyitaw in April and Aung San Suu Kyi's visit to Beijing in August, indicate willingness on both sides to cooperate on the challenges that have recently complicated relations, in particular, tensions over existing Chinese projects (e.g., in the Sagaing Region and Kachin State) and ethnic conflicts along the border.

Perhaps the domestic development with potentially the largest impact on Southeast Asian security came not from within the region but from without — namely, the November election of Donald J. Trump to the Presidency of the United States. On the one hand, Trump is likely to make human rights less an issue in bilateral relations, thus easing some of the irritations that have plagued, for example, recent U.S. relations with Thailand and the Philippines. As widely reported, Duterte and Trump appear to share similar propensities for disregarding laws when it suits their purposes, offensive comments, and impulsive retaliations against their critics (what Duterte referred to as their inclination to "curse at the slightest of reasons"). On the other hand, while Duterte may have moderated his hostile tone, Trump's expressed policy positions suggest substantive differences that are likely to complicate U.S. relations with most Southeast Asian states. Not least of these are Trump's transactional approach to security and other relations, as well as his highly confrontational and combative approach to all those he takes issue with, including China.

Indeed, policy preferences proclaimed on the campaign trail have the potential to affect regional security in Southeast Asia in both direct and indirect ways. While much remains unknown about the incoming U.S. President's priorities towards Southeast Asia, at least four potential security challenges might be discerned from statements. The most obvious regards Trump's well-publicized criticisms of U.S. alliance partners for not doing enough. While he did not mention Southeast Asian partners by name, the message sent is that Washington should not be relied upon to support its partners and allies. At a minimum, if Trump follows through on comments made as a candidate, it seems likely that there will be greater pressure on Japan to pick up some of the security burden. While all Southeast Asian states have welcomed Japanese assistance, a Japan unanchored by the United States also creates potentially more difficult challenges with respect to China, given the higher Chinese domestic stakes and sensitivities associated with the Sino–Japanese relationship. For those looking for strategic reassurance and certainty from the United States, they likely did not find it in the Trump election.

The second regards the power of economics and diplomacy in a region where concerns about economics and national and regional autonomy have proven critical to a host of strategic issues. While the TPP was given much more significance than it deserved by the Obama administration, Washington's failure to ratify the TPP nevertheless has strategic implications. At a minimum, for those in Southeast Asia it creates incentives for expanded relations with other partners, perhaps, especially, China, and gives heightened importance to regional integration efforts like the Regional Comprehensive Economic Partnership (RCEP). Regional integration is not a bad outcome for Southeast Asia, but its parameters — as with the TPP's for China — do have potentially important effects for U.S. regional standing and U.S. strategic priorities. Meanwhile, Trump's charges of currency manipulation and threats of import and value-added taxes, while targeted at China, have economic implications for all, given the production networks that tie much of Asia together, as well as potential consequences for both domestic and less traditional aspects of security.

One of the less discussed security implications of the Trump election regards his statements and professed policies towards Muslim populations. As the "War on Terror" under President George W. Bush demonstrated, perceptions of the United States as "anti-Islam" can complicate the ability of some Southeast Asian leaders to work more closely and, at least, publicly with the United States. Trump's anti-Muslim tweets and arguments can also be a source of inspiration for radicalized groups at a time when all states — Southeast Asian states and the United States — have an interest in working together to stem and limit the size and effects of extremist groups.

Last but not least, it seems highly likely, given Trump's statements and temperament displayed on the campaign trail, that his administration will depart from the Obama administration's diplomatic-institutional engagement of ASEAN, which had been a defining feature of Obama's rebalance policies and given particular expression in the U.S.–ASEAN Sunnylands summit at the start of 2016. If Trump would withdraw from NATO, it seems he would have even less patience for ASEAN and other Asian frameworks where regional norms of consensus rule.

For ASEAN states, U.S. downgrading of ASEAN challenges states' interest in "ASEAN centrality", which has provided an important means of defending and asserting Southeast Asian voice and interests amidst larger powers. Further, the inclusive engagement that has typified ASEAN institutionalism has also offered Southeast Asian states opportunities to moderate some of the more fragmenting effects of major power competition. At a minimum, diminished U.S. institutional engagement puts at risk a more multidimensional strategic picture of Southeast Asia, allowing Washington's China-centric narratives and insecurities to drive policy — the result likely being more, not less, strategic tension.

Notes

1. Other land features categorized as rocks were Cuarteron Reef, Fiery Cross Reef, Gaven Reef (North), Johnson Reef, and McKennan Reef. Further, Gaven Reef (South), Hughes Reef, Mischief Reef, Second Thomas Shoal, and Subi Reef were determined to be low tide elevations.
2. For two overviews of the tribunal's ruling, see Ankit Panda, "5 Takeaways: A Closer Look at the Historic South China Sea Arbitration Award", *The Diplomat*, 13 July 2016; Carlyle Thayer, "After the Ruling: Lawfare in the South China Sea", *The Diplomat*, 3 August 2016.
3. "Philippines Rejects China's Offer to Talk 'Outside of' Court's Ruling on South China Sea", Associated Press, 18 July 2016.
4. "Who is Taking Sides after the South China Sea Ruling?", *Asian Maritime Transparency Initiative*, 15 August 2016 <https://amti.csis.org/sides-in-south-china-sea/>.
5. For overviews of Southeast Asian states' initial reactions to the tribunal's ruling, see Ian Storey, "Assessing Responses to the Arbitral Tribunal's Ruling on the South China Sea", *ISEAS Perspective* 2016, no. 43, 28 July 2016; Termsak Chalermpalanupap, "No ASEAN Consensus on the South China Sea", *The Diplomat*, 21 July 2016; See also, Nyan Lynn Aung, "Myanmar Wades in to South China Sea Ruling with a Balancing Act", *Myanmar Times*, 19 July 2016.
6. The retracted statement can be found at "Press Statement of ASEAN FMs at Meeting with China FM", Vietnam News Agency, 16 June 2016.
7. See commentary by Taylor Fravel in Julian G. Ku, M. Taylor Fravel, and Malcolm Cook, "Freedom of Navigation Operations Are Not Enough", *Foreign Policy*, 16 May 2016.
8. "Australia Conducting 'Freedom of Navigation' Flights in South China Sea", BBC, 15 December 2015.
9. Andrew Chubb, "Did China Just Clarify The Nine-Dash Line?", *East Asia Forum*, 14 July 2016 <http://www.eastasiaforum.org/2016/07/14/did-china-just-clarify-the-nine-dash-line/>.

10. Other states that say prior consent is necessary are India, the Maldives, Pakistan, Bangladesh, Brazil, Cape Verde, North Korea, Iran, Kenya, Mauritius, and Uruguay.

11. See Paul Pedrozo, "Military Activities in the Exclusive Economic Zone: East Asia Focus", *International Law Studies* 90 (2014): 521–22; Chuah Meng Soon, "Restrictions on Foreign Military Activities in the Exclusive Economic Zone: Major Powers' 'Lawfare' ", *Pointer: Journal of the Singapore Armed Forces* 42, no. 1 (February 2016).

12. Julian Ku, "Why 'Following International Law' Won't Necessary Solve the South China Sea Conflict over Freedom of Navigation", *Opinio Juris*, 15 October 2015.

13. "The Philippines to Lease Planes from Japan to Patrol Disputed Sea", Reuters, 9 March 2016; "Abe Tells Asian Leaders of 'Serious Concern' with China Posturing in South China Sea", Kyodo, 7 September 2016.

14. Renato Cruz De Castro, "The Philippines and Japan Sign New Defence Agreement", *Asian Maritime Transparency Initiative*, 15 March 2016.

15. Ibid.

16. "Philippines Accepts First of 10 Japan-funded Patrol Vessels to Beef Up Coast Guard", Kyodo, 18 August 2016; "New Rescue Ship Arrives in PH from Japan", *Rappler*, 18 August 2016; Rosette Adel, "Duterte Thanks Japan for Coast Guard Ship, Past Aid", *Philippine Star*, 12 October 2016.

17. Tan Qiuyi, "Japan 'Looking into' New Ships for Vietnam Coast Guard", Channel NewsAsia, 5 May 2016.

18. Lee Seok Hwai, "Malaysia Monitoring 100 Chinese Fishing Boats Encroaching into Malaysian Waters in South China Sea", *Straits Times*, 25 March 2016; Prashanth Parameswaran, "Around 100 China Ships Encroaching Malaysia's Waters: Minister", *The Diplomat*, 25 March 2016.

19. Ristian Atriandi Supriyanto, "A View from Indonesia (National Commentary)", *ASAN Forum*, 28 April 2016.

20. Ibid.

21. Cheng-Chwee Kuik "A View from Malaysia", *ASAN Forum*, 12 December 2016.

22. Malaysian militant Mohd Rafi Udin quoted in "ISIS to Followers in SE Asia: 'Go to the Philippines' ", *Rappler*, 25 June 2016.

23. Kusumasari Ayuningtyas, "Indonesia, Malaysia and the Philippines Vow to Combat Sea Piracy Together", *Jakarta Post*, 5 May 2016.

24. Joseph Liow, for example, notes that "the greater, long-term threat" comes not from ISIS but "from a rejuvenated Jemaah Islamiyah, which has a larger network and is better funded than the pro-ISIS groups in the region". Joseph Chinyong Liow, "ISIS Threat in Southeast Asia: An Assessment", *RSIS Commentary*, no. 099/2016, 29 April 2016. See, also, Shannon Tiezzi, Huang Nan, and Zhang Juan, "Interview with Zachary Abuza on ISIS in Asia", *The Diplomat*, 3 August 2016.

25. See, for example, comments of Francis Chan, Barry Desker, and Sydney Jones

in Rehme Ahmad, "Alleged Mastermind of Jakarta Blasts Now 'Most Dangerous Ideologue' ", *Straits Times*, 25 February 2016.

26. Coordinated sea patrols began in 2004 and air patrols in 2005. Thailand, which borders the opening to the Malacca Strait, joined as a fourth member and participant in late 2008.

27. Sherwin Alfaro and Elizabeth Roberts, "More than 5,900 Deaths in 'War on Drugs' Since July", CNN, 12 December 2016.

28. "No Help for US on South China Sea Patrols: Manila", Associated Press, 10 December 2016.

29. Nguyen Manh Hung, "Continuity and Change under Vietnam's New Leadership", *ISEAS Perspective* 2016, no. 50, 13 September 2016.

SOUTHEAST ASIAN ECONOMIES:
In Search of Sustaining Growth

Tham Siew Yean and Andrew Kam Jia Yi

The year 2016 will be remembered for its extraordinary events. It started on a promising note with the signing of the Trans Pacific Partnership (TPP) Agreement in February 2016, after prolonged years of negotiations. This was followed by the unexpected United Kingdom vote in favour of leaving the European Union (Brexit) in June and Donald Trump's stunning victory in the U.S. presidential election in November. The latter event has now cast doubt over whether the TPP will be ratified. In Southeast Asia the death of Thailand's revered King Bhumibol Adulyadej, the world's longest-reigning monarch, in October, also marked another historical moment. China's launching of the Asian Infrastructure Investment Bank (AIIB) in January 2016 signalled a new era in global finance, as the new international bank is perceived to rival the U.S.-led World Bank. All ten economies in Southeast Asia have signed on to be members, although the ratification of Malaysia and the Philippines had not been completed at the time of writing.

Within the region there have been several changes that may affect its internal cohesiveness, as well as the region's economic and political relations with external powers. These include changes in political leadership in Laos, the Philippines, and Vietnam, while rising tensions over territorial disputes in the South China Sea have strained relations between China and some countries in the region. The signing of the TPP has also been perceived by some members of ASEAN as disruptive to ASEAN integration.

Amidst such changes, how did the Southeast Asian economies fare in 2016? The main objective of this chapter is to examine the growth of the ten Southeast Asian economies over the year and the main factors that have contributed to this

THAM SIEW YEAN is Senior Fellow at the ISEAS – Yusof Ishak Institute, Singapore.

ANDREW KAM JIA YI is Fellow at the Institute of Malaysian and International Studies (IKMAS), Universiti Kebangsaan Malaysia.

growth. It also discusses the issues that have the potential to affect economic growth of these countries in 2017 and beyond.

Economic Performance in 2016

Overall Growth Performance

Global growth is projected to fall from 2015 to 2016 due to the uncertainties associated with Brexit and the global impact of the U.S. election results of November 2016. Even in the Asia Pacific, the growth rate for the region is forecast to stagnate from 2015 to 2016.[1] Five of the Southeast Asian economies are expected to have slower growth in 2016 compared to 2015 (Table 1). Open economies,[2] especially small economies like Malaysia and Singapore, have continued their downward trend in growth since 2014. Apart from its exposure to external trade, the slowdown in Vietnam's growth trajectory was also caused by some unexpected shocks in its domestic agricultural sector, such as the drought and the pile-up of dead fish in the first half of the year.[3]

TABLE 1
Real GDP Annual Growth Rates, 2013–17

	2013	2014	2015	2016*	2017**
World	2.2	2.6	2.6	2.2	2.4
China	7.8	7.3	6.9	6.7	6.2
EU-15	0.2	1.6	2.1	1.6	1.0
Japan	1.4	−0.1	0.6	0.5	0.4
United States	1.7	2.4	2.6	1.6	2.3
Brunei Darussalam	−1.7	−2.7	−0.5	0.5	0.9
Cambodia	7.0	7.5	7.0	6.5	7.6
Indonesia	5.6	5.0	4.8	5.2	5.1
Laos	8.5	7.8	7.3	6.8	7.9
Malaysia	4.7	6.0	5.0	4.3	4.4
Myanmar	8.4	8.7	6.8	7.8	9
Philippines	7.0	6.2	5.9	6.4	6.3
Singapore	4.7	3.2	2.0	1.0	2.2
Thailand	2.6	0.8	2.8	3.0	3.1
Vietnam	5.5	6.0	6.6	6.0	6.6

Notes: * Estimates by EIU
          ** Forecasts by EIU
Source: EIU DataServices.

Trade-dependent Cambodia is also expected to witness a modest decline in its growth rate, unlike Thailand, where a small improvement is expected. Brunei is estimated to see a slight rebound in its economy due to improved consumer confidence. Indonesia's projected upturn in 2016 can be attributed to the increase in government spending and the relative success of the first phase of its tax amnesty programme — from September 2016 to March 2017 — to assist the state in bringing home money that Indonesians have kept outside the country. Myanmar and the Philippines are expected to have a rebound in their growth as the former continues its economic reforms after recovering from the negative supply shocks in 2015,[4] while infrastructure spending, improved infrastructure, and remittances continue to support growth in the latter economy.[5] A downturn is forecast for Laos.

Overall, inflationary pressures in terms of changes in the consumer price index have been modest for most Southeast Asian economies (Table 2), with the

TABLE 2
Inflation,[a] 2013–17 (%)

	2013	2014	2015	2016*	2017**
World*	3.9	3.6	3.2	3.9	4.2
China	2.6	2.1	1.5	2.1	2.0
EU-15*	1.5	0.6	n.a.	0.3	1.4
Japan	0.3	2.8	0.8	−0.1	0.4
United States	1.5	1.6	0.1	1.1	2.1
Brunei Darussalam	0.4	−0.2	−0.4	−0.7	0.4
Cambodia	2.9	3.9	1.2	3.0	3.6
Indonesia	6.4	6.4	6.4	3.7	4.5
Laos	6.4	4.1	1.3	1.3	2.1
Malaysia	2.1	3.1	2.1	1.9	2.3
Myanmar	5.5	5.5	10.8	7.0	8.8
Philippines	3.0	4.2	1.3	1.7	2.9
Singapore	2.4	1.0	−0.5	−0.7	0.8
Thailand	2.2	1.9	−0.9	0.2	0.7
Vietnam	6.6	4.1	0.6	2.6	3.4

Notes: *   Estimates by EIU
        **   Forecasts by EIU
        a   Percentage change in consumer price index in local currency (period average) over previous year.
        n.a. Not available
Source: EIU DataServices.

exceptions of Myanmar, Indonesia, and Cambodia. In the case of Myanmar, inflation has moderated compared to 2015 due to the agricultural sector's recovery from the 2015 floods, which has had a moderating impact on food prices.[6] Inflation also eased in Indonesia and Malaysia from 2015 to 2016. Since producer price deflation can also affect economic growth, it is important to note that changes in the producer price index indicating deflationary pressures have eased from 2015 to 2016 for five of the Southeast Asian economies that have available data (Table 3).

Table 4 indicates that unemployment eased in 2016 for Myanmar and Vietnam, which incidentally have relatively higher unemployment rates compared to the other countries in Southeast Asia. However, it increased slightly in two other Southeast Asian economies that also have relatively high unemployment; namely, Indonesia and the Philippines. Unemployment also increased slightly in Malaysia and Singapore.

The main drivers of growth are examined in the next section.

TABLE 3
Change in Producer Price Index[a] (%)

	2013	2014	2015	2016*	2017**
World*	1.4	1.7	−1.0	1.0	3.0
China	−1.4	−3.3	−5.9	−1.9	1.2
EU-15*	0.0	−1.1	−2.6	−2.3	2.1
Japan	1.3	3.2	−2.3	−3.5	1.5
United States	1.4	1.6	−0.9	0.2	1.8
Brunei Darussalam	n.a.	n.a.	n.a.	n.a.	n.a.
Cambodia	n.a.	n.a.	n.a.	n.a.	n.a.
Indonesia	7.7	10.7	4.4	7.0	8.0
Laos	n.a.	n.a.	n.a.	n.a.	n.a.
Malaysia	−1.7	2.5	−7.5	−2.1	0.3
Myanmar	n.a.	n.a.	n.a.	n.a.	n.a.
Philippines	−7.6	−0.9	−6.7	−4.9	−1.5
Singapore	−2.7	−3.4	−15.3	−9.9	0.9
Thailand	0.1	0.1	−4.1	−1.1	0.9
Vietnam	3.3	3.3	−0.6	−0.5	2.5

Notes: *   Estimates by EIU
        **   Forecasts by EIU
        [a]   The producer price index rebased to 2005=100 by the EIU.
        n.a. Not available
Source: EIU DataServices.

TABLE 4
Unemployment,[a] 2013–17 (%)

Country	2013	2014	2015	2016*	2017**
China	4.1	4.1	4.0	4.2	4.4
EU-15*	10.9	10.4	9.7	9.0	8.6
Japan	4.0	3.6	3.4	3.1	2.9
United States	7.4	6.2	5.3	4.8	4.5
Brunei Darussalam	n.a.	n.a.	n.a.	n.a.	n.a.
Cambodia	n.a.	n.a.	n.a.	n.a.	n.a.
Indonesia	6.2	5.9	6.2	6.3	6.2
Laos	1.3	1.4	n.a.	n.a.	n.a.
Malaysia	3.1	2.9	3.1	3.2	3.1
Myanmar*	5.2	5.1	5.0	4.8	4.7
Philippines	7.1	6.8	6.3	6.4	6.1
Singapore	1.9	2.0	1.9	2.1	2.0
Thailand	0.7	0.8	0.9	0.9	0.9
Vietnam	3.6	3.4	3.4	3.3	3.3

Notes: *   Estimates by EIU
       **   Forecasts by EIU
       a   Recorded official unemployment as a percentage of total labour force.
       n.a. Not available
Source: EIU DataServices.

Sources of Growth

A major concern that emerged in the wake of the global financial crisis of 2008 is the need to rebalance the source of growth from exports to domestic demand. This is due to the subsequent slowdown in global trade (aside for the uptick in 2010), as economic recovery in the United States and the EU is taking longer than expected, while the ongoing economic restructuring in China has further dented global trade. It is therefore important to decompose the GDP of each country to ascertain the main sources of growth in 2016.

The increasing contribution of domestic private consumption compared to net trade in the growth performance of Southeast Asian economies can be seen for all the years shown in Table 5. In fact the external balance in eight out of the ten economies subtracted from growth in 2016, compared to six countries in 2015, indicating a decline in the contribution of exports to growth (Table 6). The contribution of net balance to economic growth in 2016 has only increased for

TABLE 5
Contribution of Private Consumption[a] to Economic Growth, 2013–17

	2013	2014	2015	2016	2017
World	1.2	1.4	1.4	1.4	1.5
China	2.6	3.0	3.3	3.2	3.2
EU-15	0.0	0.6	1.1	1.0	0.4
Japan	1.0	−0.6	−0.7	0.4	0.3
United States	1.0	1.9	2.2	1.9	2.0
Brunei Darussalam	1.0	−0.5	0.8	1.7	1.6
Cambodia	4.9	3.8	6.4	4.6	5.0
Indonesia	3.0	2.9	2.7	3.0	2.8
Laos	4.1	5.2	3.3	4.2	3.8
Malaysia	3.6	3.6	3.1	2.6	2.6
Myanmar	4.2	1.4	1.0	1.5	1.7
Philippines	4.0	3.8	4.3	4.6	4.5
Singapore	1.1	0.7	1.5	0.9	0.9
Thailand	0.6	0.3	1.1	1.3	1.5
Vietnam	3.4	4.0	6.1	3.9	4.3

Notes: * Estimates by EIU
          ** Forecasts by EIU
          [a] Change in private consumption as a percentage of real GDP in the previous period.
Source: EIU DataServices.

five out of the ten economies (Brunei, Laos, Malaysia, Thailand, and Vietnam). However, the contribution of private consumption for four of the economies has weakened from 2015 to 2016 (Cambodia, Malaysia, Singapore, and Vietnam), while it increased for the other six (Table 5).

As for gross fixed investment, its contribution to growth is also less than that of domestic consumption for all Southeast Asian economies, with the exception of Laos and Myanmar (Table 7). Nevertheless, its contribution increased for five of the economies (Cambodia, Indonesia, Laos, Myanmar, and Vietnam) from 2015 to 2016.

In summary, the main driver for growth in 2016 continued to be private consumption in most Southeast Asian economies, followed by gross fixed investment, while the contribution of exports to growth decreased for the majority

TABLE 6
Contribution of External Balance[b] to Economic Growth, 2013–17

	2013	2014	2015	2016	2017
World	0.2	0.2	0.2	0.0	−0.1
China	−0.1	0.3	−0.2	−0.7	−0.3
EU-15	0.1	−0.1	0.2	0.0	0.3
Japan	−0.3	0.3	0.4	0.0	−0.1
United States	0.3	−0.1	−0.7	−0.2	−0.2
Brunei Darussalam	−9.9	16.1	−2.6	−1.1	−1.2
Cambodia	−3.3	−0.5	1.4	−0.4	0.3
Indonesia	0.6	−0.3	0.9	−0.1	0.0
Laos	0.2	−1.1	−8.3	−2.0	−2.2
Malaysia	−1.0	1.2	−0.4	−0.1	0.0
Myanmar	−0.1	−0.1	−0.1	−0.1	−0.1
Philippines	−2.5	0.8	−2.4	−2.4	−1.3
Singapore	1.9	1.8	1.3	1.3	1.1
Thailand	0.9	4.1	0.4	1.3	−0.2
Vietnam	0.2	−1.0	−5.3	−1.5	−1.3

Notes: * Estimates by EIU
        ** Forecasts by EIU
        b Change in net exports as a percentage of real GDP in the previous period.
Source: EIU DataServices.

of these economies. The economic performance in 2016 therefore continued the trend of economic rebalancing in the region as a whole.

Key Factors That Affected Growth in 2016

External Environment

The economic growth of China, Japan, the United States, and the EU continues to exert an influence on the economic performance of Southeast Asian economies through the trade and investment channel, as these are the top four trading and investment partners of the region (Appendix Tables A1 and A2).

China's growth (Table 1) has continued its downward trend since 2007 as it continues its economic restructuring in an effort to overcome the challenges of excess productive capacity, environmental degradation, and unbalanced growth from

TABLE 7
Contribution of Gross Fixed Investment[c] to Economic Growth, 2013–17

	2013	2014	2015	2016	2017
World	0.7	0.9	0.7	0.3	0.7
China	4.2	3.1	2.7	2.8	2.1
EU-15	−0.1	0.9	0.5	0.3	0.1
Japan	0.5	0.2	0.1	0.0	0.1
United States	0.8	0.9	0.7	−0.1	0.4
Brunei Darussalam	5.7	−15.2	2.1	−0.3	0.7
Cambodia	3.6	2.3	0.7	1.2	0.9
Indonesia	1.7	1.5	1.6	1.7	1.8
Laos	0.1	3.2	3.6	5.4	6.2
Malaysia	2.1	1.3	1.0	1.0	1.1
Myanmar	4.0	7.0	5.4	6.0	7.0
Philippines	2.4	1.3	3.2	3.0	2.2
Singapore	1.6	−0.7	−0.3	−0.2	0.5
Thailand	−0.3	−0.7	1.2	0.9	1.1
Vietnam	1.5	2.5	2.6	2.8	3.0

Notes: *   Estimates by EIU
       ** Forecasts by EIU
       c   Change in gross fixed investment as a percentage of real GDP in the previous
           period.
Source: EIU DataServices.

three decades of high growth. It is also trying to rebalance its sources of growth towards consumption and, at the same time, navigate a shift to an innovation and services-driven economy. The contribution of domestic consumption to China's growth exceeded that of gross fixed capital formation in 2015 and 2016 (Tables 5 and 7), while a shift to the services sector based on its contribution to employment has taken place since 2012.

The impact of China's growth on individual Southeast Asian economies depends on the nature of its trade and investment links with each of them, which is generally varied due to the different stages of development and the economic characteristics of these economies. In the case of Myanmar and Indonesia, their exports to China are mainly concentrated in fuels and minerals,[7] while regional production networks link Malaysia, Thailand, Singapore, and the Philippines with China through trade in intermediate goods.[8] Vietnam is increasingly drawn into these production networks, as it revised its investment laws and regulatory landscape in 2015[9] to draw in more foreign direct investment for the development of its manufacturing sector. Laos and Cambodia are mainly exporters of natural resources to China rather than manufactured goods, though they are dependent on imports of manufactured goods from China.

But Southeast Asia's trade in intermediate goods with China is also dependent on the growth of the United States, the EU, and Japan, as these are the ultimate destination countries of the goods that are assembled in China. Thus, the continued slowdown in each of these economies in 2016 (Table 1) and their cumulative impact on their respective direct trade and investment links with Southeast Asia, as well as their demand for final goods from China, have also affected the growth performance of each country in the region.

There is also increasing evidence that China is progressively producing more inputs domestically. Empirical studies on trade in value added indicate an increase in the domestic content of China's exports. Data at the firm level and customs-transactions level suggest that the substitution of domestic for imported materials by individual exporters has contributed to an increase in the domestic content of China's exports from 65 to 70 per cent for the period 2000–2007.[10] This will inevitably affect the trade in intermediate goods between China and Malaysia, Singapore, Thailand, and the Philippines, as more onshoring displaces China's imports of these goods.

China's slowdown has also affected such Southeast Asian economies as Malaysia and Indonesia that are exporting commodities such as palm oil to China. In as much as China's boom in the 2000s contributed to the unusually high global demand and high commodity prices, its current transition and contraction in demand has also contributed to the current slump in commodity prices. Recent estimates by the International Monetary Fund (IMF) indicates that China's impact on commodity prices has been significant since 2013.[11]

In particular, the price of palm oil peaked in 2011 but has declined steadily in subsequent years (Figure 1). The export pattern of palm oil in Southeast Asia mirrors the falling price due to the fall in demand (Figure 1). Excess supply and decreased demand from Egypt, Pakistan, and the Philippines, along with the increase in Chinese imports of soya bean oil, have contributed to the decline in price.[12] Weather changes continue to affect the price of palm oil. The impact of El Niño increased the price of palm oil in 2016 over that of 2015, while the 2017 forecast of La Niña rain may improve fruit yields, as it will bring an important source of water to palm plantations in Southeast Asia.

The price of crude oil has also affected the economic performance of the Southeast Asian economies that depend on oil revenues. Exports of petroleum, petroleum products, and related materials generally follow the trend of the oil

Tham Siew Yean and Andrew Kam Jia Yi

FIGURE 1
Price of Palm Oil (USD per tonne) and ASEAN-10 Palm Oil Exports[a]
as a Percentage of Total Exports to World

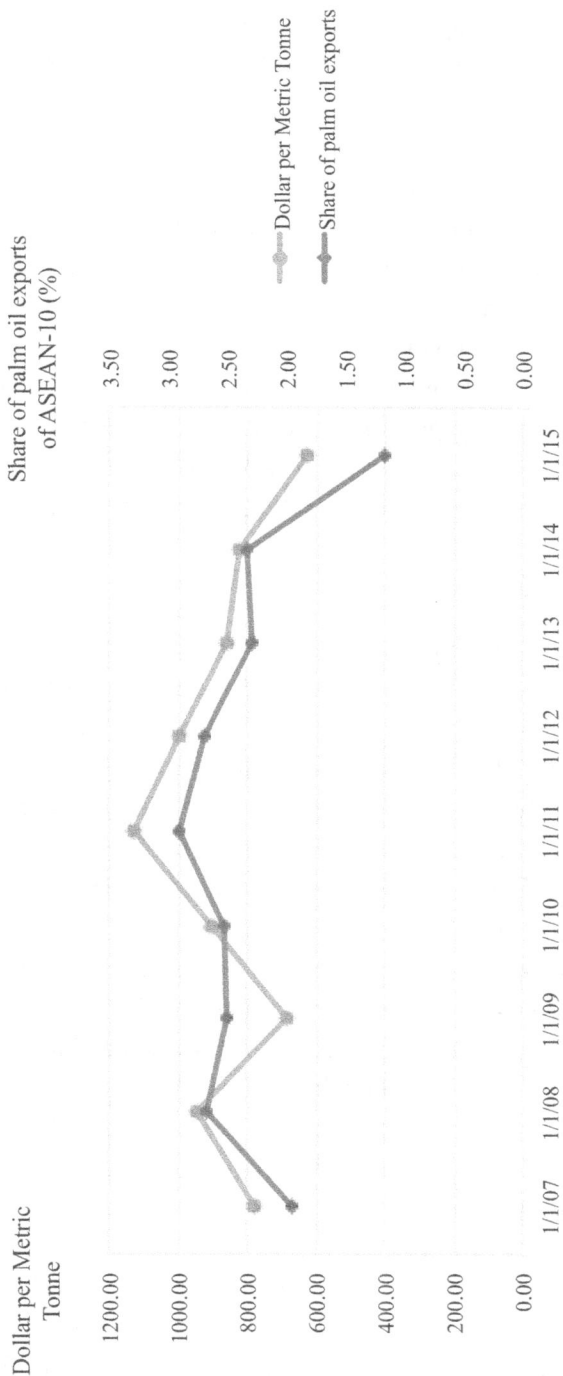

Notes: [a] HS 1996 – Code 1511 – Palm oil and its fractions, not chemically modified.
Source: World Bank Global Economic Monitor (GEM) Commodities and UNComtrade data.

price (Figure 2). For example, the decline in Southeast Asian oil exports to the world is in line with the drop in global demand during the global financial crisis. After a short rally around 2011 to 2013, oil prices began to fall again as supply increased faster than demand. In response to the slowdown in China's factory output, oil prices declined in 2014. Although falling demand should trigger a cut in production, major oil producers led by OPEC, Russia, and U.S. oil-fracking firms have maintained the flow of crude oil to the world market,[13] further pushing the prices down due to oversupply. The expansion of U.S. oil and shale gas production has created price competition between OPEC countries and the United States, exerting a further downward pressure on prices. The drop in exploration investment and the disruption in Nigeria marginally increased the oil price in early 2016, but its monthly price had receded up to the last reported month in September 2016 at the time of writing. The World Bank has, however, raised its 2017 oil-price forecast in anticipation of OPEC countries cutting their production.[14]

Internal Factors

How did the countries fund the continued shift to demand-driven growth in 2016? Table 8 shows that there is a general trend for household debt to increase over time, with the exception of Singapore and Thailand. Malaysia had the highest household debt to GDP in Southeast Asia in 2015, followed by Thailand and Singapore. Incidentally, the household debt to GDP in Malaysia was also higher than China, the EU, Japan, and the United States (Table 8). These three Southeast Asian economies also had the lowest Central Bank interest rate among the ASEAN-5 economies in 2016.[15]

Fiscal stimulus was used in almost all the Southeast Asian economies in 2016 (Table 9). Moreover, all these economies had increasing fiscal deficits in 2016 compared to 2015, with the exception of Myanmar. Singapore is an outlier in that it has a fiscal surplus, although this has also been narrowing over time. The increase in Brunei's budget deficit can be attributed to lower oil prices and increased government spending, especially on infrastructure projects. The IMF reports that there are ongoing efforts to adjust to the lower oil prices and improve spending through better prioritizing.[16]

Overall for the region, public debt as a share of GDP also shows an increasing trend, with the exception of Laos, Myanmar, and the Philippines (Table 10). The relatively high public debt in Singapore is less likely to be a problem as it could be for the other Southeast Asian countries, since its fiscal position indicates it has the fiscal strength to pay off its debts.

Tham Siew Yean and Andrew Kam Jia Yi

FIGURE 2
Oil Price (USD per barrel) and ASEAN-10 Petrol Exports[a]
as a Percentage of Total Exports to World

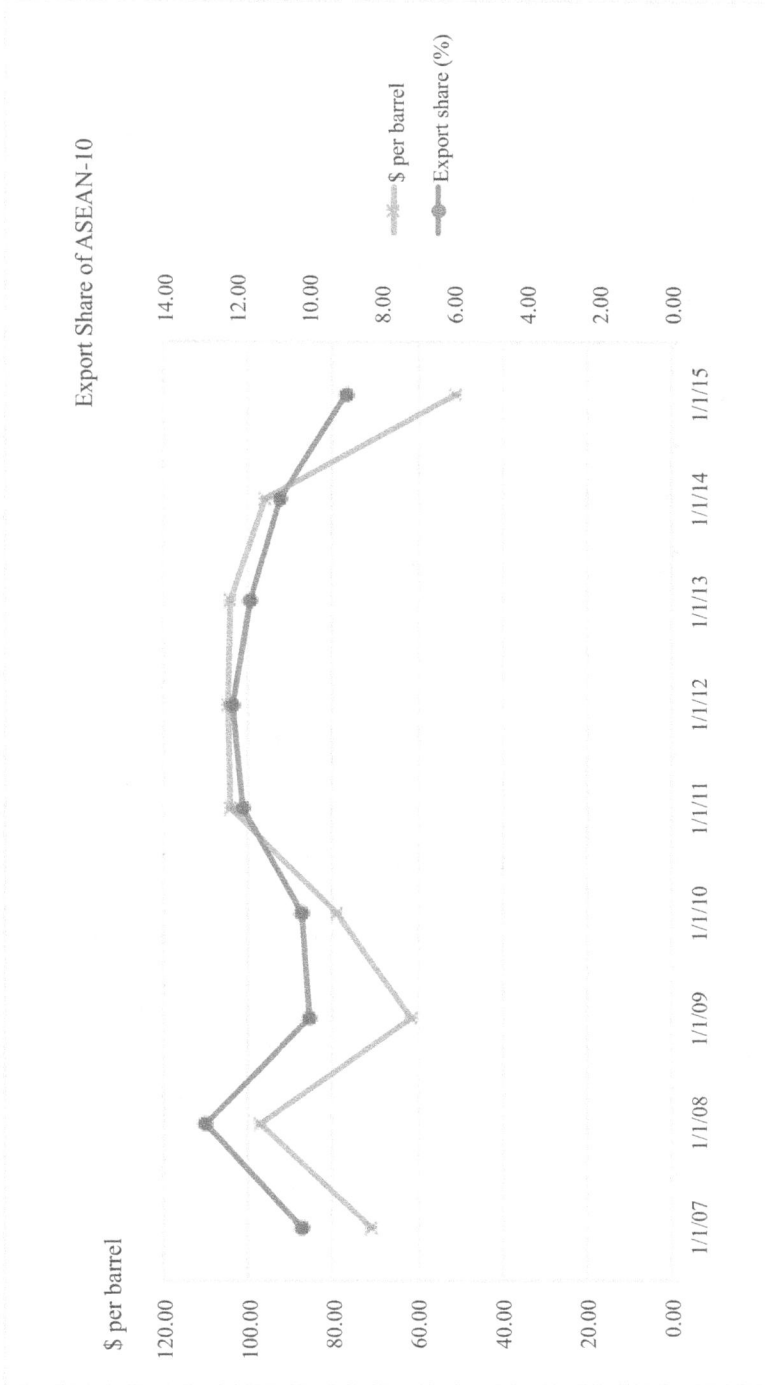

Notes: [a] SITC rev 3 – Code 33 – Petroleum, petroleum products, and related materials
Source: World Bank Global Economic Monitor (GEM) Commodities and UNComtrade data.

TABLE 8
Household Debt to GDP (%)

	2013	2014	2015
China	33.3	35.9	39.4
EU	53.0	51.6	50.8
Japan	74.5	75.4	76.2
United States	82.6	81.5	80.4
Brunei Darussalam	13.5	13.7	17.4
Cambodia	4.7	6.3	8.3
Indonesia	8.5	9.5	9.6
Malaysia	86.2	86.8	89.1
Philippines	6.3	7.1	8.0
Singapore	59.9	60.9	60.3
Thailand	74.2	79.7	78.3

Note: Data is not available for Laos, Myanmar, or Vietnam.
Source: CEIC database.

TABLE 9
Fiscal Deficit (% GDP)

	2012	2013	2014	2015	2016
Brunei Darussalam	15.7	13.0	3.6	−14.5	−26.2
Cambodia	−3.8	−2.1	−1.3	−1.6	−2.6
Indonesia	−1.6	−2.2	−2.2	−2.6	−2.5
Laos	−0.5	−5.6	−4.5	−2.9	−3.0
Malaysia	−3.8	−4.1	−2.7	−3.0	−3.4
Myanmar	−1.9	−2.1	−0.6	−4.8	−4.6
Philippines	−0.3	0.2	0.9	0.2	−0.4
Singapore	7.9	6.7	5.5	2.6	2.4
Thailand	−1.0	0.4	−0.9	0.3	−0.4
Vietnam	−6.8	−7.4	−6.2	−5.9	−6.5

Source: IMF World Economic Outlook Database.

TABLE 10
Public Debt to GDP (%)

	2011	2012	2013	2014	2015	2016*	2017**
Cambodia[c]	29.9	31.9	32.6	35.6	38.1	38.7	42.1
Indonesia[a]	21.4	22.0	22.8	25.9	29.4	30.5	31.1
Laos[a]	57.2	59.4	59.5	60.4	63.2	58.7	57.5
Malaysia[b]	50.0	51.6	53.0	52.7	54.5	55.3	55.4
Myanmar[b]	49.4	43.1	34.8	31.6	31.3	29.9	29.4
Philippines[b]	51.0	51.5	49.3	45.4	44.8	42.8	42.4
Singapore[a]	102.3	106.5	103.9	99.8	104.7	110.9	111.6
Thailand[b]	38.0	40.2	42.3	42.8	46.0	49.4	53.4
Vietnam[a]	49.7	50.0	53.7	57.1	58.2	58.4	58.4

Notes:
There is no data for Brunei.
* estimates
** forecasts
[a] Total of domestic, external, and IMF debt owed by central government as a percentage of GDP.
[b] Total debt (both local and foreign currency) owed by government to domestic residents, foreign nationals, and multilateral institutions such as the IMF, expressed as a percentage of GDP.
[c] Total of domestic, external, and IMF government debt as a percentage of nominal GDP. Usually, but not exclusively, central government.
Source: EIU database.

Moving Forward in 2017 and Beyond

Overall, the global economy is not expected to improve much in 2017 (Table 1). While the restructuring of the Chinese economy will doubtless continue, there are still many internal challenges to overcome, including debt overhangs, property bubbles, and reforming inefficient state-owned enterprises and banks. These are structural issues that will take time to change, even with proactive and appropriate government policies. Growth in China is expected to decrease, as has been the case for the EU and Japan. The Economist Intelligence Unit (EIU), however, forecasts an improvement in U.S. economic growth for 2017.

The election of Donald Trump has heightened global uncertainty, as it is unclear the extent to which some of his campaign statements will be translated into policy actions, such as increasing trade protectionism, especially towards China, and increasing interest rates. It has also raised questions over the future of trade liberalization and trade governance, since multilateral liberalization is no longer feasible as the Doha Round has been declared dead, while the future of the TPP at the time of writing remains unclear.[17] Hence, the policy actions of the United States in 2017 are expected to affect its trade and investment ties, in particular for the trade-dependent countries of Southeast Asia and the region as a whole. It remains to be seen whether bilateral free trade agreements — which are suboptimal compared to regional and multilateral liberalization due to their greater trade and investment diversion effects — will rule the future of global trade. Hence, at the regional level, the completion of ongoing negotiations for the Regional Comprehensive Economic Partnership Agreement (RCEP) by 2017 is critical. But its completion will only serve to realize the region's potential if the agreement turns out to be a substantial one.

The increase in interest rates by the U.S. Federal Reserve in late 2015 triggered capital outflows from emerging markets in Asia, including Southeast Asia, to U.S.-denominated assets with higher yields. This created a stronger dollar and, as seen in Figure 3, most Southeast Asian currencies plunged following increasing demand for U.S. dollars. The slowdown in China further exacerbated currency depreciation, especially in export-dependent and commodity-linked countries. Countries with high external financing (that is where external financing requirements exceed official reserves), such as Indonesia and Malaysia, will encounter severe challenges in coping with changes in U.S. monetary policy in 2017.

In moving forward to 2017, an important question to consider is the sustainability of consumption-driven growth for Southeast Asia, since it is expected that the external environment will still be dampened. EIU forecasts the public debt to increase marginally or to remain the same for 2017 for all countries,

FIGURE 3
Change in Exchange Rate, LCU:USD (% of change)

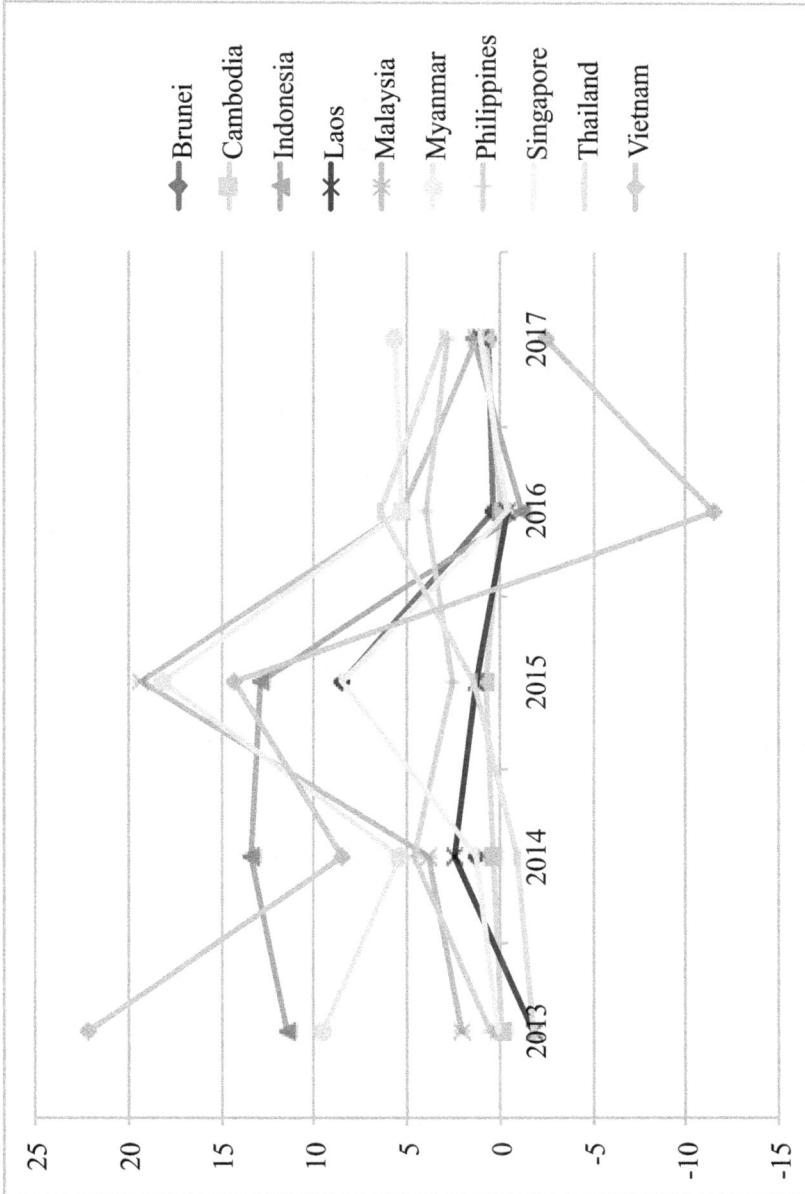

Source: Calculated from EIU database.

TABLE 11
Productivity (growth in output per labour), 2013–17 (%)

	2013	2014	2015	2016	2017
China	6.9	7.1	6.5	6.1	5.9
Japan	0.9	−1.0	0.9	1.3	0.8
United States	0.8	0.8	0.9	1.7	2.0
Brunei Darussalam	−2.9	4.9	−2.6	2.1	2.3
Cambodia	6.5	5.3	4.8	5.1	5.3
Indonesia	4.4	3.3	3.1	3.6	3.8
Laos	6.1	5.3	4.7	5.3	5.0
Malaysia	0.3	3.7	2.4	2.7	3.1
Myanmar	6.9	7.3	7.1	6.9	6.8
Philippines	5.3	3.6	4.0	3.9	4.1
Singapore	2.7	0.7	1.0	1.4	1.8
Thailand	4.1	0.2	2.4	2.8	3.2
Vietnam	3.8	4.4	5.4	5.2	4.9

Source: ILOSTAT database.

except for Laos. It is likely that fiscal stimulus will continue to be used in 2017 to stimulate growth, given the continued subdued global environment and the increased probability of an increase in U.S. interest rates in 2017. However, the fiscal space to do this is highly constrained for Malaysia as it has been running a fiscal deficit since the Asian financial crisis. Although it has successfully reduced its dependence on oil revenue since the implementation of the goods and services tax in April 2015, increasing taxes further would be highly unpopular due to the dismantling of subsidies and the impact of these recent fiscal changes on the cost of living in the country.

Beyond 2017, improving the economic performance of the region will require individual economies to continue enhancing their productivity performance, since this is needed to sustain long-term growth. For 2016, six of the Southeast Asian economies are expected to see an improvement in the annual rate of growth of their labour productivity. The International Labour Organization's projections indicate continued improvement for 2017 for Brunei, Cambodia, Malaysia, the Philippines, Singapore, and Thailand.

At the country level, the different stages of development imply that different countries will face different restructuring challenges in furthering their economic development in the medium and longer term. Singapore's services sector share in GDP is similar to those of the EU, Japan, and the United States (Table 12). Future growth for Singapore continues to lie in its ability to reinvent itself to maintain its position as the services hub for Southeast Asia in key services such as finance and logistics. Upper-middle-income countries like Malaysia and Thailand have to structurally shift to a more innovation- and services-led economy, while lower-middle-income countries have to deepen manufacturing (Cambodia, the Philippines, Indonesia, and Vietnam). Laos and Myanmar, lower-middle-income countries, have to conserve their natural resources, develop their agricultural sectors, and join global value chains in manufacturing. Brunei will have to diversify from oil and gas and use the country's locational advantage in Southeast Asia to develop its manufacturing and services, but it may be limited by talent shortages.

Pursuing greater regional integration at the ASEAN level — and with its Plus partners at the RCEP level — will help each country enhance its growth prospects. ASEAN's relevance to the region will only be retained with the realization of the goals in the ASEAN Economic Community 2025 Plan.

Finally, given China's plans to develop its One Belt, One Road initiative (OBOR), the future growth of the region will also depend on how each of these countries plans to position itself in China's OBOR initiative by tapping into China's FDI and lending for their future development.

Conclusion

The slowdown in China continued to affect countries that are still dependent on exporting manufactured goods there, such as Malaysia, the Philippines, and Vietnam. This negative impact on commodity prices due to contraction in demand has been offset by other global developments in 2016. A moderate increase in palm oil prices in 2016 improved the economic climate for some countries in the region, though the price is far from its previous high level. The exodus of funds due to the increase in U.S. Federal Reserve rates at the end of 2015, Brexit, and Trump's victory in the U.S. elections contributed to the turbulence in 2016.

Internal factors were also at play, such as political uncertainties and a relatively high household debt for some of the Southeast Asian economies. Increasing fiscal deficits or decreasing surpluses were used to stimulate growth. The lower inflation rate and the rise in unemployment show that some of these economies have yet to reach their potential levels of output. This is reflected in the negative growth in producer prices for some of the economies. On the other hand, the forecast growth in labour productivity is a welcome sign, although it should not

TABLE 12
Share of Agriculture, Manufacturing, and Services in GDP

	Agriculture, value added (% of GDP)				Manufacturing, value added (% of GDP)				Services, etc., value added (% of GDP)			
	2012	2013	2014	2015	2012	2013	2014	2015	2012	2013	2014	2015
World	3.9	4.0	3.9	0.0	16.3	16.3	14.7	n.a.	67.8	68.1	68.5	0.0
China	9.5	9.4	9.2	9.0	31.0	30.1	n.a.	n.a.	45.5	46.9	48.1	50.5
European Union	1.7	1.7	1.6	1.6	15.5	15.5	15.4	15.4	73.6	73.8	74.0	74.3
Japan	1.2	1.2	1.2	n.a.	18.6	18.6	18.7	0.0	72.8	72.4	72.0	n.a.
United States	1.2	1.5	1.3	n.a.	12.5	12.4	12.3	0.0	78.2	77.9	78.0	n.a.
Brunei Darussalam	0.7	0.7	n.a.	n.a.	11.8	12.3	n.a.	n.a.	28.2	31.0	n.a.	n.a.
Cambodia	35.6	33.5	30.4	28.2	16.0	16.4	16.2	17.0	40.1	40.8	42.6	42.3
Indonesia	13.4	13.4	13.3	13.5	21.5	21.0	21.0	20.8	40.9	41.5	42.3	43.3
Laos	28.1	26.4	27.7	27.2	8.4	8.2	8.9	9.3	35.9	40.4	40.9	41.9
Malaysia	9.8	9.1	8.9	8.4	23.1	22.8	22.9	22.8	50.1	51.0	51.2	44.3
Myanmar	n.a.	n.a.	n.a.	n.a.	n.a.	n.a.	n.a.	n.a.	n.a.	n.a.	n.a.	n.a.
Philippines	11.8	11.2	11.3	10.3	20.6	20.4	20.6	20.1	56.9	57.6	57.3	58.8
Singapore	n.a.	n.a.	n.a.	n.a.	20.4	18.8	18.4	n.a	73.3	74.9	75.0	n.a.
Thailand	11.6	11.3	10.5	n.a.	28.2	27.7	27.8	n.a	51.0	51.8	52.7	n.a.
Vietnam	19.2	18.0	17.7	17.0	13.3	13.3	13.2	13.7	37.3	38.7	39.0	39.7

Note: n.a.   Not available
Source: World Development Indicators.

be taken as the panacea for recovery unless it is sustained and improved in the future. Future opportunities for the region must be exploited by completing the RCEP negotiations in 2017 in the wake of the possible demise of the TPP under the Trump administration. A stronger ASEAN will help to compensate for the external headwinds that will continue into 2017.

Appendix

TABLE A1
Top Ten ASEAN Trade Partner Countries/Regions, 2015[a]

Trade partner country/region[b]	Value (US$ billion)			% share to total ASEAN trade		
	Exports	Imports	Total trade	Exports	Imports	Total trade
ASEAN	305.57	238.1	543.6	25.9	21.9	23.9
China	133.91	211.5	345.4	11.3	19.4	15.2
Japan	113.94	124.3	238.3	9.6	11.4	10.5
United States	129.16	83.2	212.3	10.9	7.6	9.4
EU-28	127.53	100.1	227.6	10.8	9.2	10.0
Republic of Korea	45.92	76.4	122.3	3.9	7.0	5.4
Taiwan	33.27	61.2	94.5	2.8	5.6	4.2
Hong Kong	77.26	14.1	91.4	6.5	1.3	4.0
Australia	32.94	18.7	51.7	2.8	1.7	2.3
India	39.03	19.5	58.5	3.3	1.8	2.6
Total top ten trade partner countries	1,038.52	947.1	1,985.6	87.9	87.0	87.5
Others[c]	143.37	140.9	284.3	12.1	13.0	12.5
Total	1,181.89	1,088.0	2,269.9	100.0	100.0	100.0

Notes: [a] Preliminary data. Some figures may not add up to totals due to rounding errors.
[b] Identified/ranked based on share of total trade.
[c] Includes trade of all other countries and those that could not be attributed to specific countries.

Source: ASEAN Merchandise Trade Statistics Database (compiled/computed from data submission, publications, and/or websites of ASEAN member states, ASEAN Free Trade Area units, national statistics offices, customs departments/agencies, or central banks).

Tham Siew Yean and Andrew Kam Jia Yi

TABLE A2
Top Ten Sources of Foreign Direct Investment Inflows in ASEAN, 2013–15

Country/region[1]	Value			Share to total inflows		
	2013[3]	2014	2015	2013[3]	2014	2015
ASEAN	19,562.2	22,134.5	22,232.2	15.7	17.0	18.4
European Union	24,511.3	24,989.9	20,127.6	19.6	19.2	16.7
Japan	24,750.2	15,705.4	17,559.4	19.8	12.1	14.5
United States	7,157.2	14,748.5	13,646.0	5.7	11.3	11.3
China	6,426.2	6,990.1	8,256.5	5.1	5.4	6.8
Republic of Korea	4,303.3	5,750.7	5,710.4	3.4	4.4	4.7
Australia	2,587.7	6,281.5	5,246.7	2.1	4.8	4.3
Hong Kong	5,251.2	9,813.2	4,542.9	4.2	7.5	3.8
Taiwan	1,381.8	3,253.9	2,807.0	1.1	2.5	2.3
New Zealand	335.9	550.0	2,241.2	0.3	0.4	1.9
Total top ten sources	96,267.1	110,217.7	102,370.0	77.1	84.8	84.7
Others[2]	28,597.4	19,777.4	18,448.8	22.9	15.2	15.3
Total FDI inflow to ASEAN	**124,864.5**	**129,995.1**	**120,818.8**	**100.0**	**100.0**	**100.0**

Notes: Totals may not add up due to rounding.
1 Ranked according to FDI inflows in 2015; covers countries on which data is available.
2 Include inflows from all other countries, as well as total reinvested earnings and debt instruments in the Philippines.
3 Data for Laos on "by source country" for 2013 is not available. The intra-/extra-ASEAN breakdowns shown were estimated by the ASEAN Secretariat.
Source: ASEAN Foreign Direct Investment Statistics Database as of 5 October 2016 (data was compiled from the submissions of ASEAN central banks and national statistical offices through the ASEAN Working Group on International Investment Statistics).

Notes

1. Pacific Economic Cooperation Council (PECC), *State of the Region 2016–2017*, 23 November 2016 <https://www.pecc.org/publications/697-state-of-the-region-2016-2017>.

2. Based on World Bank data, there are six economies in Southeast Asia with international trade that is more than a hundred per cent of their respective GDP — Brunei, Cambodia, Malaysia, Singapore, Thailand, and Vietnam. It should be noted that there is no data on Myanmar.

3. Ralph Jennings, "Vietnam's Fast Economic Growth is Quietly Slipping, but No One Cares", Forbes, 23 November 2016 <http://www.forbes.com/sites/ralphjennings/2016/08/10/vietnams-fast-economic-growth-is-slipping-but-no-one-notices/#50404ebb78d8>.

4. International Monetary Fund (IMF), "IMF Staff Praises Myanmar's Progress in Economic Reforms", 23 November 2016 <https://www.imf.org/en/News/Articles/2016/10/28/PR16469-Myanmar-IMF-Staff-Praises-Progress-in-Economic-Reform>.

5. The World Bank, "Philippine Economic Update (October 2016): Outperforming the Region and Managing the Transition", 23 November 2016 <http://www.worldbank.org/en/news/feature/2016/10/03/philippine-economic-update-october-2016-outperforming-the-region-and-managing-the-transition>.

6. Asian Development Bank, "Myanmar's Economic Growth to Recover, Inflation to Moderate in FY2016", 23 November 2016 <https://www.adb.org/news/myanmar-s-economic-growth-recover-inflation-moderate-fy2016>.

7. Nargiza Salidjanova, Jacob Koch-Weser, and Jason Klanderman, "China's Economic Ties with ASEAN: A Country by Country Analysis", US-China Economic and Security Review Commission, Staff Report, 17 March 2015 <http://origin.www.uscc.gov/sites/default/files/Research/China's%20Economic%20Ties%20with%20ASEAN.pdf> (accessed 25 November 2016).

8. Tham, S.Y., A.J.Y. Kam, and Nor Izzatina A.A., "Moving Up the Value Chain in ICT: ASEAN Trade with China", *Journal of Contemporary Asia* 46, no. 4 (November 2016): 680–99.

9. Oxford Business Group, "Vietnam Enacts Business Reforms to Attract FDI", 18 August 2015 <http://www.oxfordbusinessgroup.com/news/vietnam-enacts-business-reforms-attract-fdi> (accessed 23 November 2016).

10. Kee Hiau Looi and Tang Heiwai, "Domestic Value Added in Exports: Theory and Firm Evidence from China", *American Economic Review* 106, no. 6 (2016): 1402–36.

11. International Monetary Fund, "World Economic Outlook: Subdued Demand: Symptoms and Realities", *World Economic Outlook October 2016* <http://www.imf.org/external/pubs/ft/weo/2016/02/> (accessed 25 November 2016).

12. V.C. Parvatha, "Crude Palm Oil Heats Up", *The Hindu Business Line*, 4 September

2016 <http://www.thehindubusinessline.com/portfolio/real-assets/crude-palm-oil-heats-up/article9072498.ece>.

13. "Oil Prices to Stay Near Current Level throughout 2016, World Bank Says", *The Guardian*, 26 January 2016 <https://www.theguardian.com/business/2016/jan/26/world-bank-oil-prices-forecast-2016>.

14. The World Bank, "World Bank Raises 2017 Oil Price Forecast", 20 October 2016 <http://www.worldbank.org/en/news/press-release/2016/10/20/world-bank-raises-2017-oil-price-forecast>.

15. Oxford Economics, "Economic Insight: Southeast Asia. Quarterly Briefing Q1 2016" <https://www.icaew.com/-/media/corporate/files/about-icaew/what-we-do/economic-insight/2016/south-east-asia/sea-q1-2016.ashx?la=en> (accessed 30 November 2016). The ASEAN-5 constitutes Indonesia, Malaysia, the Philippines, Singapore, and Thailand.

16. International Monetary Fund (IMF), "IMF Executive Board Concludes 2016 Article IV Consultation with Brunei Darussalam", 26 September 2016 <https://www.imf.org/en/News/Articles/2016/09/26/PR16427-Brunei-Darussalam-IMF-Executive-Board-Concludes-2016-Article-IV-Consultation> (accessed 9 December 2016).

17. Donald Trump announced on 21 November that the United States would signal its withdrawal from the TPP trade deal on his first day in the White House, according to "Trump Says Will Move to Withdraw from TPP 'On Day One'", *Today Online*, 21 November 2016 <http://www.todayonline.com/world/trump-says-will-move-withdraw-tpp-day-one>.

FORGING THE ASEAN ECONOMIC COMMUNITY, 2015 TO 2016 — AND BEYOND

Munir Majid

At the end of 2015, ASEAN did not any more become a community of nations than remain an association of states. Words matter for the expectations they raise. ASEAN slow marched in 2015 towards the "milestone" that it was to be proclaimed a "community" at the end of it, but in reality this remains an admitted work in progress.

The term "community" had been adopted in communion with, although not as a replication of, what existed in Europe. It seemed like a good idea, this approximation, which got more distant as Europe further integrated into a union of twenty-eight nation-states. Of course, nowadays, ASEAN may congratulate itself on its superior wisdom of not rushing into forming a community, let alone a union, seeing the strains and stresses in the European Union (EU). But the term "community" remained.

For the private sector there are clear expectations of the ASEAN Economic Community (AEC), perhaps even more so than from constituents of the political-security and sociocultural pillars, the two other legs of the community proclaimed in the Kuala Lumpur Declaration of November 2015.[1] It is in the AEC that the ASEAN Community shows the greatest promise of development. Indeed, it may very well be the AEC that will hold ASEAN together, even if it does not necessarily drive greater integration with the other two pillars. There are however challenges ahead, both internal and external to the AEC, including from geopolitical and geoeconomic forces beyond ASEAN's loose organizational control.

Tan Sri Munir Majid is Chairman, ASEAN Business Advisory Council, Malaysia, CIMB ASEAN Research Institute, Bank Muamalat Malaysia, and the Financial Services Professional Board; President, ASEAN Business Club; and Visiting Senior Fellow, LSE Centre for International Affairs, Diplomacy and Strategy.

What is the AEC to the Private Sector?

When an integrated regional market, open to the outside world, is offered with a single production base complete with the free movement of goods and services, capital and investment, and skilled labour, it is a huge attraction. If the market proposed is the third largest in the world, with a population of over 630 million people, a combined GDP in excess of US$2.4 trillion[2] — the world's seventh largest — growing at about five per cent[3] in an anaemic world economy, businesses are attracted to make decisions and plans for their future expansion there. And, with sixty per cent of the population under thirty-five years of age,[4] there is the further enticement of current investment yielding a demographic dividend not better available elsewhere.

Future prospect, however, is not current reality. Businesses understand this. When the AEC is pronounced though, businesses expect the path forward to become increasingly smooth, as in a single market without the stubborn endurance of barriers. While tariffs have been reduced to virtually zero across ASEAN, non-tariff barriers (NTBs) obstruct the free movement of goods and services, as well as of capital and skilled people. The private sector has conducted studies that have identified these barriers, quantified the economic loss they cause, and made proposals on how they might be removed. The private sector has also offered to support the process of the removal of these barriers, both through high-level harmonization and standardization and through prioritized sectoral concentration of effort.

The private sector is also concerned that the MSMEs (micro, small, and medium enterprises), which form the overwhelming part of the ASEAN economy, would be exposed in the integration process without sufficient support to enable them to compete and to bring them into the regional and global supply chains. The failure of MSMEs could cause severe socio-economic problems with serious political consequences, given the very high levels of employment they sustain. This could roll back the integration process, resulting in increasing protection instead of the original aim of the AEC to steadily open markets. The access of MSMEs to good information, management, technology, and particularly to finance has to be measurably improved.

There is thus a tension in the AEC work in progress which challenges its formation and requires a combined public–private sector effort to address.

How the Private Sector is involved in the Process of AEC Formation

The ASEAN Business Advisory Council (ASEAN-BAC) was formed in 2003. It was mandated to provide private sector feedback and guidance to ASEAN leaders in the economic integration process. One of the means of doing this is through the ASEAN Business and Investment Summit (ABIS), which coincides with the ASEAN summits.

Through the years, ASEAN-BAC — which comprises three members from each of the member states — in carrying out its mandate has been making its reports to member country leaders and interacting with ministers and officials. It has, however, mirrored the official tramline in both process and speed. Meetings are held and reports are tabled in the usual ASEAN way, with no raised voices or even gentle table-thumping. Meetings among the leaders include officials and ministers. Much-vaunted dialogue with leaders takes place without any real exchange of views. Usually conducted at a hurried pace as the foreign ministries rush the leaders to yet other meetings, it comes down to the reading of two amiable statements from one side to the other. The report is tabled. No raised voice at the next meeting when even the simplest proposals are not acted upon. ASEAN-BAC mirrors the ASEAN process even to the extent that it is ill funded, like the ASEAN Secretariat.

In 2015, when Malaysia held the chair, ASEAN-BAC achieved two things which would hopefully make it more effective in fulfilling its mandate. First, in keeping with the tradition of the outgoing chair transferring funds to the ASEAN-BAC account, the Malaysian chapter remitted the largest amount ever for activities in 2016 from funds raised during 2015, especially from the ABIS. This impetus continued under Lao leadership in 2016, with another substantial sum being passed into ASEAN-BAC coffers at the end of 2016.

Even so, these amounts are quite insufficient to sustain ASEAN-BAC activities and an efficient, professional secretariat — let alone to finance specific projects or implement meaningful efforts to reduce non-tariff barriers. There is resistance within ASEAN-BAC against a predetermined annual contribution from each of the national chapters, which is truly confounding. No organization can run effectively to a clear plan when it is not sure where the money is coming from or whether the funds will be sufficient. ASEAN-BAC's financial modus operandi of functioning hand-to-mouth and relying on uncertain ad hoc funding for particular activities is not an efficient way of running the organization. This is reflected in its less-than-stellar performance since its inauguration in 2003.

The Malaysian chapter has highlighted this point repeatedly since 2014. The matter was again discussed at the ASEAN senior officials meeting in Cebu last November, on how to ensure proper funding to achieve the effective performance of ASEAN-BAC's mandate. Various suggestions were made, but it is up to ASEAN-BAC itself — not the officials — to come up with proposals to finance itself for the objectives it has to fulfil.

The second achievement for ASEAN-BAC (and a more effective role of the private sector in the regional economic integration process) during the time

Malaysia held the chair was to ensure the continuation of ASEAN-BAC as the mandated private sector body, but based on clearer specifications of how it should go about representing business interests and offering guidance to businesses.

The Malaysian chapter worked hard to ensure explicit recognition of the important role of the private sector in ASEAN's economic integration, as well of ASEAN-BAC in the consultative process. In the ASEAN Economic Community Blueprint 2025, paragraphs 70 and 71 are clear. There will be a "more inclusive and consultative process involving the private sector", and there is a requirement for ASEAN-BAC to "take the lead in coordinating inputs from established councils and entities". The blueprint identified nine such councils and sixty-six business entities interacting with various ASEAN sectoral groups.[5]

Coordinating the viewpoints of all these bodies requires time and effort that taxes ASEAN-BAC's scant resources, not to mention its own work in the working groups on MSMEs, women, and young entrepreneurs, as well as stubborn NTB issues and new areas of interest, such as digital finance and e-commerce. So far, ASEAN-BAC has been heroically taking on this coordinating role, but resources are stretched and this cannot be sustained without a full-time, well-paid secretariat. ASEAN-BAC cannot enjoy its desired position as the "apex private sector body" (as envisioned in the blueprint) without the necessary financial resources.

In 2016 all the ASEAN+1 business councils had been working with ASEAN-BAC, with some working more closely than others. The EU-ASEAN Business Council, for instance, has been extremely supportive. The U.S.-ASEAN Business Council is watching to see how effective ASEAN-BAC will be and whether or not the interests of their members will be better served, at least in some sectors, by direct engagement with relevant ASEAN official authorities.

The fact of the matter is that every private sector representative body will seek to do what is best for its membership, including direct interface at the highest levels of ASEAN leadership. They do not need ASEAN-BAC permission to do this. Indeed, they have in the past obtained better access to ASEAN leaders and ministers than ASEAN-BAC has. For example — amazingly — ASEAN-BAC did not have any interaction with finance ministers, central bank governors, or their deputies until 2015. It is not just that the EU and U.S. councils have always had this access, but what is astounding is that the body which is supposed to provide feedback on regional economic integration has been missing out on the financial facilitation of that process.

This goes to show how the ASEAN official sector and ASEAN-BAC have been remiss in private sector engagement over a considerable number of years. There is much repair work for ASEAN-BAC to do.

It was therefore not surprising that in 2011 the ASEAN Business Club (ABC) was formed by a number of elite corporations in the region to make "ASEAN

More Open for Business". It had a particular financial sector edge to it. Given the prominence of its members, the ABC has been able to gain access to top ASEAN leaders and has organized successful business missions and visits to a number of ASEAN countries. Its major events have attracted top keynote speakers and business leaders. In 2013 and 2014 the ABC organized two major regional forums in Singapore involving the crème de la crème of international and ASEAN businesses and top global consultants. The Lift-The-Barriers Reports that emanated from the forums have become one of the major reference points in ASEAN on NTBs and what might be done to address them. The ABC has become a major regional organization in the ASEAN economic integration effort.

ASEAN-BAC became insecure following the emergence of the ABC. It felt like a poor cousin compared to the ABC with its high-profile business leaders. Indeed, most of the members appointed to ASEAN-BAC by their respective governments were from MSMEs, and there was some tension between the swashbuckling ABC and the underachieving ASEAN-BAC. Between 2014 and 2015, in my involvement with both organizations I was able to reduce ASEAN-BAC suspicion of ABC and to integrate substantive ABC work with ASEAN-BAC's efforts. This increased ASEAN-BAC's profile as the apex private sector organization — as recognized again in the 2025 Blueprint.

However, some in the ABC not entirely happy with what was felt to be a subservient relationship have gone on to form the Regional Business Council (RBC) that was launched by the World Economic Forum (WEF) in Hanoi in October 2015. This elitist regional consortium in Davos would seem to serve a number of purposes. RBC leaders gain prominence and recognition, while WEF increases its Southeast Asian regional profile in a fast-growing part of the world as membership begins to dry up in traditional catchment areas.

The openly stated objective of RBC is "to promote public–private cooperation on the most pressing issues in ASEAN" in line with the 2025 blueprint. How it will do this with and through ASEAN-BAC remains to be seen. It is to be hoped that there will not be the kind of problems and suspicions that existed between ASEAN-BAC and the ABC. On the other hand, ASEAN-BAC must up its game and not just sit on its pedestal. There are already enough politics and bureaucratic turf wars in ASEAN without the private sector adding to them.

Some Progress ... and Getting on with It

The constant bashing on the issue of NTBs has had some effect. In 2016 the ASEAN Trade Facilitation Joint Consultative Committee (JCC) — which had been more or less dormant since the trade facilitation work programme was adopted in 2008 — was revived. Its remit includes the elimination of tariffs and NTBs, customs integration through the ASEAN Single Window, and other activities consistent with the 2025 blueprint and the ATIGA (ASEAN Trade in Goods Agreement). It has drawn up the Strategic Plan for Trade Facilitation 2017–25. Its terms of reference include the objective to "achieve a more inclusive and consultative process to engage the private sector on trade facilitation issues", as well as to address specific issues proposed by private sector representatives who may be invited (including from ASEAN-BAC) to attend dedicated sessions. The committee reports to the SEOM (senior economic officials meeting), which is the highest-level committee that makes recommendations to economic ministers.

As is the case with ASEAN committees, plans and procedures are almost always in place. It is the progress they make that is the issue. The JCC, for instance, is to meet only twice a year. And it only "may" invite private sector representatives to attend "dedicated sessions". This is neither good enough in terms of the progress it will make nor in terms of private sector involvement. Having campaigned strongly on the issue of NTBs, the private sector must now knock very hard on the committee's door.

The proliferation of committees and meetings discussing issues in a general and conceptual way is not something the private sector has time for or, indeed, should encourage. In 2015 ASEAN-BAC established a Steering Committee on NTBs and NTMs (non-tariff measures). Now it is in the process of setting up a working group that will report to the steering committee. There is, however, no mention of the JCC. This shows what a maze the ASEAN process is and how the private sector, including its apex organization, can be befuddled by it. It is no exaggeration to say that the various bodies — official and private sector — often set out on a journey of a series of interminable meetings.

With respect to NTBs, there is the opportunity now to seize the moment to make meaningful progress. In 2015 the economic ministers agreed to sectoral prioritization in the elimination of NTBs — at the recommendation of the Malaysian chair — in agri-food, healthcare, retail (particularly e-commerce), and logistics. ASEAN-BAC should lead the private sector to ensure that the JCC establishes working groups in these four sectors to work in detail on NTB elimination and to meet as often as possible to achieve this, even if the consultative committee only meets twice a year. Private sector experts should be deeply involved in the working groups to make progress. It would be the start of a more meaningful effort to address the issue of NTBs in ASEAN. ASEAN-BAC of course can continue with its steering committee as well as the proposed technical working group, and should establish high-level communication with the JCC.

Another area where some headway has been made is in relation to ASEAN member states making progress towards keeping their commitments under the various economic integration agreements, especially with respect to the free movement of goods, services, capital, investment, and skilled labour. In 2015 ASEAN-BAC had discussed the issue of exposing — despite ASEAN's consensus-driven way — those who had not acted on their commitments. A consensus was actually forged in ASEAN-BAC to look into the establishment of a "name and shame" portal, so as to attack the NTB issue further. Halfway through the process, however, it was discovered that there was an ongoing project called ASSIST (ASEAN Solutions for Investment, Services and Trade), which was aimed at setting up a milder form of such a website with the assistance of the EU.

ASSIST has been operational since September 2016. Complaints can be made to the ASEAN Secretariat about NTBs placed in the way of the free movement of goods. Once verified and communicated to the ASEAN member state responsible, the complaint may be placed on the ASSIST website if no corrective action is taken within six months. The test is how many companies might be willing to expose themselves to the threat of being a marked-down entity which could jeopardize their future prospects in the offending country. It has been suggested that trade associations could complain on behalf of a particular company, but there is still a possibility that the company could be identified. Japanese companies have in the past used the leverage of their government in a particular country to serve their cause. No doubt Chinese companies would similarly benefit in the future. The free market has never been entirely free or fair. However, unless there is an objective regime of sanctions, including against victimization, the smaller and less-well-connected companies — the MSMEs — will be more exposed to the vagaries of the ASEAN NTB world. Nevertheless, it would be churlish not to admit some progress has been made with the introduction of ASSIST.

Businesses in the private sector recognize that they do not exist in a perfect world. Those better endowed and connected are better able to navigate its imperfections while seeking to eliminate or reduce their investment and trade problems, such as NTBs and choke points at customs. While private sector representation and lobbying are necessary to solve problems of doing business in ASEAN, corporations do not sit on their hands until they are resolved, nor are they blind to possible opportunities. Many operate quietly, while others are vocal about the problems they face but more reticent when they succeed.

We hear of the problems DBS, CIMB, or Air Asia face, but not as much of how they were resolved. In the case of many companies, such as Malaysia's Petronas or quite a number from Singapore, we hardly hear of their activities and penetration

of ASEAN markets. It is not possible to do justice to the many companies that
are already established in the ASEAN market. For example, Indonesian companies
such as the Lippo group are very interested in the business benefits of bringing
intra-ASEAN barriers down, even if the Indonesian government appears to be
less enthusiastic about the region's economic integration. Thai conglomerates,
particularly, prefer to operate below the radar, and have been heavily present in
ASEAN even before the AEC. Chareon Pokphand, for instance, a Thai global
conglomerate, is one of the largest private companies in the world, employing over
500,000 people, and it is by far the largest company in ASEAN's retail sector in
terms of revenue. The Central Group of Companies is another big family-based
international Thai company, with a significant presence in Malaysia, Indonesia,
and Vietnam. Siam Cement, the largest cement company in Southeast Asia, is
well positioned in the fast-growing Mekong subregion.

Whatever the shortcomings of the regional economic integration process,
the dynamism of business will, if not able to overcome them, at least circumvent
them to take advantage of opportunities of growth and expansion. The Mekong
subregion is a great example of such dynamism. Comprising Cambodia, Laos,
Myanmar, and Vietnam, plus Thailand (CLMVT), the region is expanding at well
above the average ASEAN growth rate.

Laos is being converted from a landlocked to a land-linked country (linking
it south through Thailand and the Malay Peninsula to Singapore). The proposed
Kunming–Vientiane High Speed Rail — at a cost of over half its GDP of
US$13.5 billion — will transform the country. Huge special economic zones are
being developed, with Thailand as logistical hub. Even India is in play, with a
US$1 billion line of credit earmarked for a 3,200-kilometre highway running into
Myanmar and Thailand. Most important of all, the East–West economic corridor
will take off once the 1,450-kilometre highway linking Danang in Vietnam to
Mawlamyine in Myanmar, an ADB project, is completed. This linkage from the
South China Sea to the Bay of Bengal will shorten existing sea routes by 3,000
nautical miles and generate enormous savings in freight and time.

China's Yunnan and Guangxi provinces are in the Mekong subregion mix,
making up a total population of 400 million and an economy more than half the
size of ASEAN's. Chinese tourists are pouring in. Construction materials and
equipment are coming in from Thailand to Laos. Car parts will in future flow
from Laos to assembly plants in Thailand.

The activity and business dynamism in the Mekong subregion underline
three main points. First, countries from a low economic base are coming up very
fast. Second, the integration of business activities and the pooling of resources

is leading to economic benefits. Third, there is a centrifugal pull from China, an ASEAN+ phenomenon in line with its open regionalism and the RCEP (Regional Comprehensive Economic Partnership), but this pull may move the Mekong subregion away from maritime Southeast Asia.

Businesses are agnostic. It is not a zero-sum game. But there is a trend that could lead to a bifurcated ASEAN, the antithesis of ASEAN economic centrality envisaged in the AEC. It is interesting to note how the "two-speed" ASEAN traditionally referred to could more likely develop into a "two-part" ASEAN. The AEC 2025 blueprint has not sufficiently factored in this business dynamism and the extra-ASEAN pull in the evolution of the region's economic integration. It might want to consider this even before its mid-term review is due.

Another potent enabler that has deep consequences for economic integration and activity is technology. In the context of disabling NTBs, the application of technology has massive circumventing capability. This is already happening in many fields, especially in the service industries. For example, surgeons can perform surgeries and doctors can diagnose offsite when they would not have been allowed to practise onshore. While the use and application of technology spreads and there is great excitement over artificial intelligence and the Internet of Things, the competitive battle in many economic fields is going to be decided by the balance of technological power. ASEAN has to position itself to attract giants in the field, such as technological corporations from China, Japan, and America. Just now China is the closest to ASEAN in terms of providing the power of technology.

China's giant technology companies — such as Baidu, Alibaba, Tencent, and Huawei — are huge innovative corporations involved in e-commerce, e-finance and e-payments, fintech, and communications. All these areas are ripe for takeoff and growth in ASEAN. In e-commerce alone, ASEAN Internet sales revenue is just above one per cent of total sales, when in more developed markets it is on average close to ten per cent.[6] Which ASEAN companies are well placed to charge into this lucrative growth area? As ASEAN economies integrate, as ASEAN opens up, as technology-enabled activities grow, will ASEAN companies be able to stand up to the sweeping force and challenge of technology giants?

Postscript

The world economy has not been robust in the last year, making it incumbent that growth in the ASEAN region be at least sustained if not improved through greater economic integration. The election of Donald Trump as the 45th President of the United States from 20 January 2017, with his commitment to protect the American market, will mean that there will be even greater need for regionally driven economic activity. If Trump's protectionist policies involve a trade war with China — or worse — the global environment would be eminently unsuited for export growth, which has thus far largely driven most ASEAN economies. Intraregional trade and investment — the AEC remit — would have to be the unsatisfactory substitute.

Donald Trump's promise to dump the TPP (Trans-Pacific Partnership) Agreement means that the four ASEAN states that were part of the TPP negotiations would not now be able to avail themselves of that avenue of economic growth. Vietnam, for instance, was hoping to achieve the kind of export-led growth through the TPP that powered earlier Asian tigers such as Korea, Taiwan, and, indeed, China. Malaysia, to take another example, was targeting the three sophisticated markets of the United States, Canada, and Mexico with which it had no existing bilateral FTAs. It is interesting to note that the RCEP (comprising ASEAN, China, Japan, Korea, India, Australia, and New Zealand) would accord Malaysia an income gain 41 per cent less than from the TPP.[7] This is a reflection of the diminished growth prospects of regional economies following Donald Trump's election.

The TPP would also have given its ASEAN members, qualitatively, an opportunity to attract sophisticated high technology investment from the United States, for instance, encouraged by intellectual property protection and compulsory dispute settlement provisions. Such provisions in an international agreement would promote greater confidence than if they only existed in domestic legislation involving national courts. The prospect of being a hub for higher-value products and services has diminished to a considerable extent.

With the imminent demise of the TPP, the RCEP has been popularly reported as China's alternative project that will now take centre stage in the Asia-Pacific. Strictly this is not true, because the RCEP is an ASEAN project adopted in 2012 which was in the offing even with the TPP. But now that there will be no TPP (although some countries such as Vietnam are suggesting that the remaining eleven countries could make their own compact with suitable amendments to the agreement), the RCEP will indeed become the alternative regional trade and investment project, with the FTAAP (Free Trade Area of the Asia-Pacific, comprising the twenty-one APEC economies) the longer-term objective. China is taking the lead on free trade as the United States goes protectionist. The Philippines as ASEAN chair in 2017 has expressed the desire to see the RCEP concluded during its term.

What we are seeing is the increased importance of regional free trade and investment arrangements, such as the AEC and the RCEP, which are both ASEAN projects. Regional economic leadership that ensures their fulfilment is now more critical than ever. The removal of barriers and impediments, facilitation, and enablement have never been more urgent.

Notes

1. See ASEAN, *Kuala Lumpur Declaration on ASEAN 2025: Forging Ahead Together* <http://www.ASEAN.org/storage/images/2015/November/KL-Declaration/KL%20 Declaration%20on%20ASEAN%202025%20Forging%20Ahead%20Together.pdf>.

2. Vinayek HV, Fraser Thompson, and Oliver Tonby, "Understanding ASEAN: Seven Things You Need to Know", McKinsey <http://www.mckinsey.com/industries/public-sector/our-insights/understanding-ASEAN-seven-things-you-need-to-know> (accessed December 2016).

3. FocusEconomics, *Economic Snapshot for ASEAN*, 14 December 2016 <http://www.focus-economics.com/regions/ASEAN>.

4. Sumisha Naidu, "ASEAN+ Youth Leaders Summit Aims to Inspire Youths", Channel NewsAsia, 19 November 2015 <http://www.channelnewsasia.com/news/asiapacific/asean-young-leaders/2276320.html>.

5. ASEAN, *ASEAN Economic Community Blueprint 2025*, November 2015 <http://www.asean.org/storage/images/2015/November/aec-page/AEC-Blueprint-2025-FINAL.pdf>.

6. AT Kearney, *The ASEAN Digital Revolution*, 16 December 2015 <https://www.emarketer.com/Article/Asia-Pacific-Home-Majority-of-World-Retail-Ecommerce-Market/1013352>.

7. Sangeetha Amarthalingam, "Malaysia's Potential Income Gain from RCEP 41% Less Than TPP – UOB", *The Edge Financial Daily*, 28 November 2016.

SOUTHEAST ASIA'S DEMOGRAPHIC SITUATION, REGIONAL VARIATIONS, AND NATIONAL CHALLENGES

Tey Nai Peng

This chapter provides an overview of Southeast Asia's demographic situation over the first fifteen years of this century, and highlights variations across countries. It concludes with discussions of major demographic challenges facing each country in the region. Data for this chapter are taken mainly from the United Nations' World Population Prospects — 2015 Revision database. By focusing on this period, this chapter updates and adds to the findings of an article by Gavin Jones[1] that provides a comprehensive analysis of the population situation for Southeast Asia from 1980 to 2010.

The Socio-economic Context

Demographic changes are closely interrelated with socio-economic development. Hence, a brief overview of the socio-economic conditions in the countries of Southeast Asia will be useful in understanding the variations in demographics across the region. The Human Development Report (HDR) published annually by the United Nations Development Programme provides development indicators for nearly all countries/regions of the world.[2] Some development indicators from the HDR are given in Table 1.

Since 1990 the United Nations has been using the human development index (HDI) to rank countries in terms of human development. HDI is a composite index that combines economic, health, and education indicators. In 2014, Singapore (ranked eleventh in the world) and Brunei Darussalam (at rank thirty-one) were

TEY NAI PENG is Research Fellow and Coordinator of Population Studies Unit, Faculty of Economics and Administration, University of Malaya (UM). He retired as Associate Professor of Applied Statistics, UM.

TABLE 1
Key Demographic Data, Southeast Asia, 2000–2014/15

	HDI		HDI Rank	Life Expectancy	Mean years of schooling	GNI per capita 2011 PPP$	GDP Growth (annual %)	Urbanization level	Unemployment rate
	2000	2014	2014	2014	2014	2014	2000–2013	2015	2008–13
Brunei Darussalam	0.819	0.856	31	78.8	8.8	72,570	1.4	77.1	–
Cambodia	0.419	0.555	143	68.4	4.4	2,949	8.0	20.5	0.3
Indonesia	0.606	0.684	110	68.9	7.6	9,788	5.4	53.0	6.2
Laos	0.462	0.575	141	66.2	5.0	4,680	7.2	37.6	1.4
Malaysia	0.723	0.779	62	74.7	10.0	22,762	5.1	74.8	3.0
Myanmar	0.425	0.536	148	65.9	4.1	4,608	n.a.	34.4	–
Philippines	0.623	0.668	115	68.2	8.9	7,915	5.0	49.6	5.9
Singapore	0.819	0.912	11	83.0	10.6	76,628	5.8	100.0	2.8
Thailand	0.648	0.726	93	74.4	7.3	13,323	4.1	35.2	0.8
Timor-Leste	0.468	0.595	133	68.2	4.4	5,363	7.3	29.5	3.9
Vietnam	0.575	0.666	116	75.8	7.5	5,092	6.4	33.0	2.0

Source: UNDP, *Human Development Report, 2015.*

classified as very high HDI countries, Malaysia and Thailand as high HDI countries, Myanmar as a low HDI country, and all the other Southeast Asian nations as medium HDI countries. Between 2000 and 2014, Cambodia, Timor-Leste, Myanmar, and Laos registered the most rapid rise in HDI, each with a gain of between 24 and 32 per cent.

Life expectancy at birth varied within a rather narrow range between 65.9 and 68.9 years in six Southeast Asian countries (Myanmar, Laos, Timor-Leste, the Philippines, Cambodia, and Indonesia), and between 74.4 and 78.8 years in four (Thailand, Malaysia, Vietnam, and Brunei). Singapore has one of the world's highest life expectancies at birth, at 83 years. Within each country, women live longer than men, by between 2.7 (Laos) and 9.5 years (Vietnam).[3]

In 2014 the mean number of years of schooling ranged from 4.1 to 4.4 years in Myanmar and Timor-Leste to 10.0 to 10.6 in Malaysia and Singapore.[4] Data from World Development Indicators show that, between 2000 and 2012, the tertiary enrolment ratio rose markedly for all Southeast Asian countries, except for the Philippines. Thailand registered the highest enrolment ratio of more than 50 per cent in 2011, while Myanmar had the lowest tertiary enrolment ratio, at 13.8 per cent.[5]

Income levels varied widely across Southeast Asian countries. Singapore and Brunei Darussalam are the two richest countries, followed by Malaysia and Thailand. The income level of Singapore is twenty-six times higher than that of Cambodia, the poorest country in the region, and about ten times higher than the Philippines (ranked sixth in the region). Over the period 2000–13, the low-income countries registered higher rates of GDP growth compared to the high-income countries in the region.[6]

The unemployment rate for the period 2008–13 was remarkably low in Cambodia, Thailand, and Laos (from 0.3 to 1.4 per cent), and was rather low in Vietnam, Singapore, and Malaysia (2–3 per cent). However, the Philippines and Indonesia had relatively high unemployment rates of around 6 per cent.[7]

The close link between urbanization and demographic processes and socio-economic development is well documented.[8] The wealthier countries in Southeast Asia have higher urbanization levels than the poorer ones. While the urbanization level in Southeast Asia has nearly doubled from 25 per cent in 1980 to 47.6 per cent in 2015, it is one of the less urbanized regions in the world. The urbanization level ranged from around 21 per cent in Cambodia to 100 per cent in Singapore. Apart from Singapore, Malaysia and Brunei Darussalam are two of the more urbanized countries (more than 70 per cent). About half of the populations in Indonesia and the Philippines are urban.[9] However, as noted by Gavin Jones, the low level of urbanization in Thailand is due to a rather restrictive categorization of urban areas.[10]

Population Size, Rate of Growth, and Density

The United Nations Population Division provides population estimates for the period 1950–2015 and population projections up to year 2100 for all countries, which are revised from time to time.[11] Table 2 presents the basic population facts from the UN database for the countries of Southeast Asia.

The total population of Southeast Asia increased from about 401.7 million in 1985 to 633.5 million in 2015, and is projected to reach 724.8 million by 2030. Indonesia is the fourth most populous country in the world. Brunei Darussalam, with a population of 423,000 in 2015, is one of the least populous countries in Asia.

The rate of population growth in Southeast Asia as a whole decelerated from 1.8 per cent per annum in 1985–2000 to 1.2 per cent in 2000–2015. The world population growth rate decreased from 1.55 per cent per annum to 1.21 per cent per annum over the same period. With the exception of Timor-Leste and Singapore (the latter due to the influx of migrants), all Southeast Asian countries have registered a significant decline in the rate of population growth over the period 2000–2015, falling below 1 per cent per annum in Thailand and Myanmar, and growing at only 1 per cent per annum in Vietnam. Thailand's population peaked at around 68 million in 2015, and it is projected to remain at that level for the next two decades, before declining.

A comparison of the rate of population growth and the crude rate of natural increase indicates net in-migration and out-migration. Southeast Asia as a whole has a net loss of migrants to other parts of the world. Singapore has a very low rate of natural increase, but a high rate of population growth, caused by the influx of migrants that contributed to three quarters of the population increase for the period 2000–2015.

The population density of Southeast Asia stands at 146 persons per square kilometre — this is about the same level as the average for Asia, but much higher than the world average of 57 persons per square kilometre. Population density varies widely, from 29 persons per square kilometre in Laos to 8,005 persons per square kilometre in Singapore. Within each country the population is concentrated in the more developed regions. Population density in Indonesia ranges from 9 persons per square kilometre in Papua to 1,217 in West Java; 59 per cent of the population live in provinces where population density exceeds 650 per square kilometre. Population density is very high on Java and Bali in Indonesia and in the Red River delta in Vietnam.[12]

TABLE 2
Basic Population Facts of Southeast Asia

Country	Population ('000)					Average annual rate of population growth (%)		Crude rate of natural increase (%)	Population density (per sq km)
	1985	2000	2010	2015	2030	1985–2000	2000–15	2000–15	2015
Brunei Darussalam	223	331	393	423	496	2.63	1.64	1.52	80
Cambodia	7,743	12,198	14,364	15,578	18,991	3.03	1.63	1.86	88
Indonesia	165,012	211,540	241,613	257,564	295,482	1.66	1.31	1.39	142
Laos	3,680	5,343	6,261	6,802	8,489	2.49	1.61	2.07	29
Malaysia	15,764	23,421	28,120	30,331	36,107	2.64	1.72	1.33	92
Myanmar	38,509	47,670	51,733	53,897	60,242	1.42	0.82	1.26	83
Philippines	54,324	77,932	93,039	100,699	123,575	2.41	1.71	1.98	338
Singapore	2,709	3,918	5,079	5,604	6,418	2.46	2.39	0.57	8005
Thailand	52,041	62,693	66,692	67,959	68,250	1.24	0.54	0.50	133
Timor-Leste	657	847	1,057	1,185	1,577	1.69	2.24	3.21	80
Vietnam	61,049	80,286	88,358	93,448	105,220	1.83	1.01	1.16	301
Southeast Asia	401,712	526,179	596,708	633,490	724,848	1.80	1.24	1.34	146

Source: United Nations Population Division, *World Population Prospects: 2015 Revision.*

Recent Trends in Mortality and Fertility

The changing population structures are the result of past trends in fertility, mortality, and migration. Although migration plays a role in population change, the natural increase (the excess of births over deaths) has been the primary demographic driver across the countries of Southeast Asia, with the exception of Singapore (Figure 1). Apart from Myanmar, the crude death rate in all Southeast Asian countries is below the world average. However, differences in the age structure of the population must be taken into account in comparing the crude death rate across countries, as mortality rates are invariably higher among the older population. This can be borne out by comparing the crude death rate and life expectancy figures for Thailand and Malaysia — both had about the same level of life expectancy, though the crude death rate is significantly higher for Thailand.

The infant mortality rate (IMR) is a highly sensitive measure of population health and the quality of healthcare, as well as the socio-economic status of a population. The level of IMR in Southeast Asian countries is reflective of the level of development (as measured by HDI), population health (as measured by life expectancy), and healthcare quality (as measured by number of doctors per ten thousand people). Between 2000 and 2015 the IMR declined substantially, ranging from 21 per cent in Myanmar and the Philippines to 55 per cent in Cambodia. Malaysia's IMR remained at around 7 per thousand live births over this period. Singapore's IMR of 2 per thousand live births is among the lowest in the world. Except for Laos, Myanmar, and Timor-Leste, the IMR for all the other countries of Southeast Asia are below the global average. Cambodia's IMR — which at the turn of the century was about the same level as for Laos and Timor-Leste and higher than that of Myanmar — declined by more than 50 per cent, and it is now among the lowest of the four. The sharp reduction in IMR in Cambodia is probably the result of the government's efforts in expanding healthcare services, as reflected in the higher public health expenditure as a percentage of GDP.

The crude birth rate in Southeast Asia — at 19.3 per thousand population — is close to the world average and slightly above the Asian average. It ranges widely from 9.3 and 11.2 in Singapore and Thailand to 38.7 in Timor-Leste. For the rest of Southeast Asia the rate lies between 17 (Brunei and Malaysia) and 27 (Laos) per thousand population.

The total fertility rate (TFR) in Southeast Asia — which began to decline from about 6 children per woman in the 1960s to 2.7 by 1995–2000 — continued to decline to 2.35 in 2010–15. It is slightly lower than the world average, but higher than the Asian average. Five Southeast Asian countries (Singapore, Thailand, Brunei, Vietnam, and Malaysia) have attained replacement level

FIGURE 1
Crude Birth and Death Rates, Southeast Asia, 2015

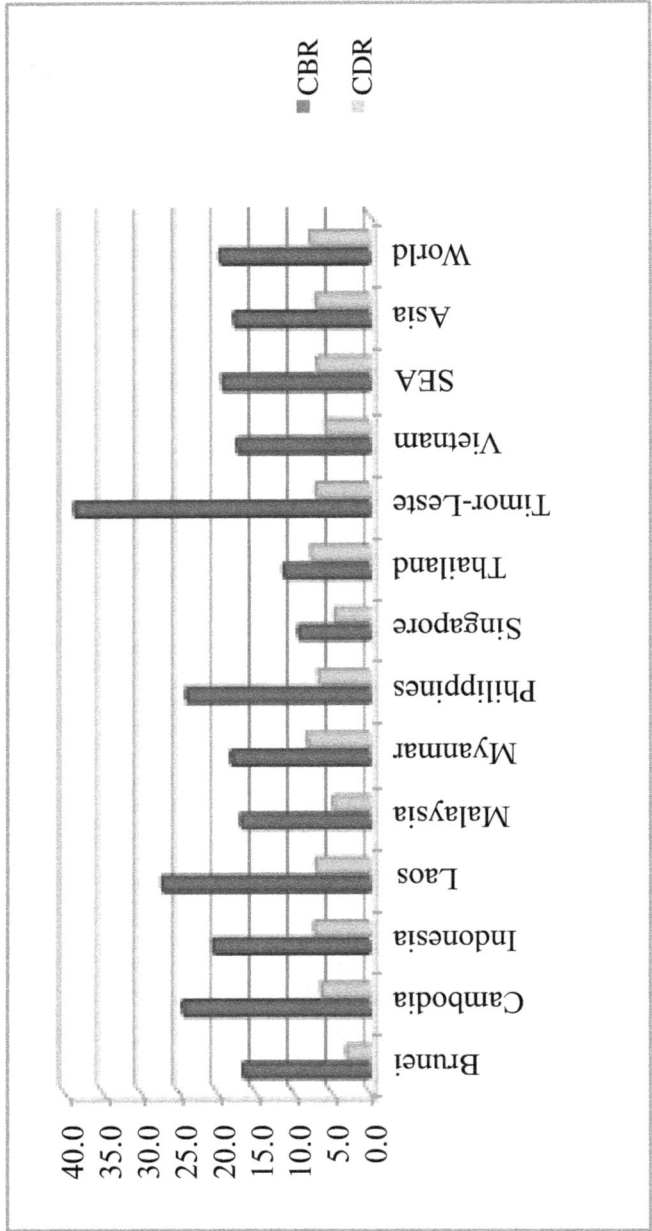

Source: United Nations Population Division, *World Population Prospects: 2015 Revision.*

TABLE 3
Key Health Indicators, Southeast Asia, 2000–15

	2000–2005 IMR	2005–10 IMR	2010–15 IMR	% change in IMR 2000–15	Physicians per 10,000 population 2001–13	Public health expenditure as % of GDP, 2013
Brunei Darussalam	8	6	4	–50.0	15.0	2.5
Cambodia	66	45	30	–54.5	2.3	7.5
Indonesia	36	30	25	–30.6	2.0	3.1
Laos	69	57	47	–31.9	1.8	2.0
Malaysia	7	7	7	0.0	12.0	4.0
Myanmar	58	52	46	–20.7	6.1	1.8
Philippines	29	26	23	–20.7	11.5	4.4
Singapore	3	2	2	–33.3	19.2	4.6
Thailand	17	13	11	–35.3	3.9	4.6
Timor-Leste	64	50	44	–31.3	0.7	1.3
Vietnam	25	22	19	–24.0	11.6	6.0
Southeast Asia	34	29	24	–29.4		

Sources: UN Population Division, *World Population Prospects: 2015 Revision*.
UNDP, *Human Development Report, 2015*.

TABLE 4
Total Fertility Rate (TFR) and Contraceptive Prevalence Rate (CPR), 2000–15

	TFR			% change in TFR 2000–15	CPR			% change in CPR 2000–15
	2000–2005	2005–10	2010–15		2000	2010	2015	
Brunei Darussalam	2.05	2	1.9	-7.3	n.a.	n.a.	n.a.	n.a.
Cambodia	3.44	3.08	2.7	-21.5	24.8	49.5	57.2	130.6
Indonesia	2.48	2.5	2.5	0.8	54.7	60.8	60.4	10.4
Laos	3.9	3.5	3.1	-20.5	31.2	48.5	54.6	75.0
Malaysia	2.45	2.07	1.97	-19.6	52.8	52.1	52.9	0.2
Myanmar	2.85	2.55	2.25	-21.1	35.6	45.4	51.2	43.8
Philippines	3.7	3.27	3.04	-17.8	48.2	50.3	54.6	13.3
Singapore	1.35	1.26	1.23	-8.9	63	65.3	66.1	4.9
Thailand	1.6	1.56	1.53	-4.4	76.5	79.3	79	3.3
Timor-Leste	6.96	6.53	5.91	-15.1	12.3	23.3	29	135.8
Vietnam	1.92	1.93	1.96	2.1	73.8	78.4	77.4	4.9
Southeast Asia	2.51	2.41	2.35	-6.4				

Sources: United Nations Population Division, *World Population Prospects: 2015 Revision.*
United Nations Population Division, *Model-based Estimates and Projections of Family Planning Indicators 2016.*

(Table 4). Replacement level fertility was attained much earlier in Singapore (in the mid-1970s) and Thailand (early 1990s), and these two countries now have ultra low fertility. Between 2000 and 2015 the TFR fell by about 20 per cent in Cambodia, Laos, Malaysia, Myanmar, and the Philippines. The slowing and stalling of fertility decline occurred in low fertility countries, namely Singapore, Brunei, and Vietnam. Indonesia is the only country where fertility stalled (at 2.5 since the late 1990s) before reaching replacement level, and this runs contrary to the demographer's dictum that once fertility has fallen by 10 per cent it is likely to fall until replacement levels are reached. The fertility level in Timor-Leste remains very high, although it has declined by 15 per cent over the last fifteen years.

The socio-economic correlates of fertility are well documented. Urbanization, rising education, female labour-force participation, the empowerment of women, rising income, and the reduction in infant mortality have been found to be associated with lower fertility.[13] Recent demographic and health surveys conducted in Indonesia (2012), the Philippines (2013), and Cambodia vindicate that fertility is strongly negatively correlated with educational level and female employment, as well as with family wealth.[14] The opportunity cost of childbearing is higher among higher-educated women, and working women are facing difficulties in combining maternal roles with career ones. In Malaysia, about two-thirds of women have cited family as the main reason for leaving the workforce, and the government is trying to encourage them to re-enter the labour market by offering tax incentives to companies that establish nurseries or allow flexible work arrangements.[15]

Fertility differentials are also evident across various social and ethnic groups within each country. For instance, in Malaysia the TFR in 2014 among the Malays (2.6) was significantly higher than that of the Chinese (1.4) or Indians (1.5),[16] although all three groups had about the same level of fertility of about 6 children per woman in the 1960s. Similar ethnic fertility differentials may also be observed for Singapore[17] and other Southeast Asian countries.

Socio-economic variables can only affect fertility through intermediate variables or proximate determinants. Analysing historical populations, it has been shown that 96 per cent of the variance in fertility level in a given society is explained by four main proximate determinants of fertility; namely, the proportion of women who are married, the prevalence of contraception, the incidence of induced abortion, and breastfeeding (postpartum amenorrhea).[18] Data on induced abortion and breastfeeding are not readily available.

Thailand and Vietnam have the highest contraceptive prevalence rate (CPR) in Southeast Asia, with close to 80 per cent of currently married women using a method. The high CPR over the last two decades has resulted in low fertility in both countries. With the exception of Timor-Leste, all other countries have a CPR of between 50 and 65 per cent.[19] In Cambodia, Laos, and Myanmar, a sharp rise in contraceptive prevalence over the period 2000–2015 following the expansion of family planning programmes launched in the 1990s has contributed to rapid fertility decline.

Besides Thailand and Vietnam, which have already achieved a high level of CPR, and Singapore which aims to raise fertility, three other Southeast Asian countries have a flat contraceptive trend; namely, Indonesia, Malaysia, and the Philippines. Despite the stalling of contraceptive prevalence since the 1980s, the fertility level in Malaysia continued its declining trend to reach the replacement level by 2012, while that of the Philippines also declined rather appreciably, although contraceptive prevalence has risen only moderately over the last fifteen years. The contraceptive prevalence rate in Malaysia might be under-reported due to the higher non-response rate among women in higher socio-economic groups. The family planning programme in Indonesia was highly successful in raising the CPR from less than 5 per cent in the late 1960s to over 50 per cent at the turn of the century; and the TFR was cut in half. However, the stagnation of contraceptive prevalence during the last decade has also resulted in the stalling of fertility. The plateau in contraceptive prevalence in Indonesia can be attributed to the de-emphasis of family planning (which witnessed the narrowing of the contraceptive method mix to temporary hormonal methods, primarily injectables), the high rate of unintended pregnancies (as evidenced by the rise in induced abortion), and the unavailability of contraceptive supplies to disadvantaged groups.[20] In the Philippines the relatively high TFR may be due to a higher rate of method failure, as close to one third of family planning acceptors rely on traditional methods[21] due to the opposition by the Catholic Church to modern contraceptive methods.[22]

Marriage at a later age and non-marriage are other important proximate determinants of fertility. The data for singulate mean age at marriage (SMAM) show that Singaporean and Malaysian women married at an older age (at 28 and 26, respectively) compared to their counterparts from Indonesia (22 years), Laos (20), and Myanmar (24).[23] In Indonesia, Laos, Myanmar, and Vietnam there was a trend towards earlier marriage during the 2000–2010 period. Marriage postponement (and probably an increase in abortion) in Malaysia has resulted in lower fertility, although the CPR is below that of Indonesia and is at about the same level as that of the Philippines.

Age Structural Shifts and Population Ageing

Demographic transition from high to low mortality and fertility resulted in significant age structural shifts of the population in Southeast Asia, with wide variations across countries. Table 5 shows the age structural shifts and population ageing in Southeast Asian countries. Between 2000 and 2015, the median age of the population rose by between four years in Indonesia, Laos, the Philippines, and Timor-Leste, and eight years in Thailand.

For all countries in the region, there has been a continuing decline in the proportion of the young and a corresponding increase of the older population and working-age population, except for Singapore, where the proportion of the working-age population declined slightly between 2000 and 2015. The changing age structure has brought about a decrease in young dependency and an increase in old-age dependency. The higher proportion of working-age population has yielded a demographic dividend as more working people are supporting relatively fewer dependents. The total dependency ratio declined by more than 20 per cent in Cambodia, Laos, Malaysia, and Vietnam for the period 2000–2015. Singapore is the only country that registered a slight increase in total dependency.

The population pyramid of Southeast Asia (Figure 2) shows a narrowing of its base and a widening at the centre, indicating a substantial increase in the proportion of the young working-age group. Owing to the continuing decline of fertility to a very low level, the population pyramid of Thailand is depicted by a barrel shape, which is typical of aged nations. While there is also a narrowing of the base of the population pyramid in the Philippines, it still has a rather broad base. With a young age structure, the population of the Philippines has tremendous potential for further growth. Malaysia's population pyramid shows that the country is heading towards becoming an aging nation, as the large proportion of middle-aged population will be aged within the next two decades.

The pace of population ageing in Southeast Asia is much faster than occurred in the developed world in the past.[24] While it took more than half a century for the elderly proportion in developed countries to double from 7.5 to 15 per cent by the 1970s, the proportion aged sixty and over in Southeast Asia is expected to double from 7.5 per cent in 2000 to 15 per cent within thirty years. With more than 15 per cent of the population aged sixty and over, Singapore and Thailand are considered to be aged nations. By 2030 the proportion of population aged sixty and over will rise to 31 per cent in Singapore, 27 per cent in Thailand, and between 13 and 17 per cent in Brunei Darussalam, Indonesia, Malaysia, Myanmar, and Vietnam.

The ageing index in Singapore has exceeded a hundred, indicating that older persons aged sixty and over outnumber those aged under fifteen. Thailand is catching up fast. By 2030 there will be two older persons to one young person in Thailand; and the ratio will be slightly higher (2.4:1) in Singapore.

TABLE 5

Changes in Age Structure and Indicators of Population Ageing in Southeast Asia, 2000, 2015, and 2030

	% below 15			% 15-59			% 60+			Median age		
	2000	2015	2030	2000	2015	2030	2000	2015	2030	2000	2015	2030
Brunei Darussalam	30.5	23.1	18.6	65.6	69.3	64.3	3.9	7.6	17.1	25.6	30.6	37.8
Cambodia	41.6	31.6	27.3	53.5	61.6	62.3	4.9	6.8	10.4	18.1	23.9	28.6
Indonesia	30.7	27.7	23.5	62.0	64.1	63.3	7.4	8.2	13.2	24.4	28.4	31.9
Laos	43.3	34.8	29.1	51.3	59.2	62.8	5.4	6.0	8.1	18.1	21.9	26.4
Malaysia	33.3	24.5	21.6	60.5	66.3	64.0	6.2	9.2	14.4	23.8	28.9	34.5
Myanmar	31.9	27.6	22.1	61.0	63.6	64.7	7.1	8.9	13.3	23.5	27.9	32.4
Philippines	38.5	31.9	28.3	56.4	60.8	61.4	5.1	7.3	10.3	20.5	24.4	27.7
Singapore	21.5	15.5	12.7	67.8	66.6	56.6	10.7	17.9	30.7	34.1	40.0	47.0
Thailand	24.0	17.7	14.0	66.1	66.5	59.1	9.9	15.8	26.9	30.2	38.0	44.9
Timor-Leste	50.0	42.4	39.7	46.0	50.4	53.4	4.0	7.2	6.8	15.0	18.5	19.2
Vietnam	31.7	23.1	20.2	59.7	66.6	62.3	8.6	10.3	17.5	24.2	30.4	37.0
Southeast Asia	31.8	26.5	22.8	60.9	64.1	62.5	7.4	9.3	14.7	24.2	28.8	33.1

	Ageing index			Young dependency burden			Old dependency burden			Total dependency burden		
	2000	2015	2030	2000	2015	2030	2000	2015	2030	2000	2015	2030
Brunei Darussalam	12.8	33.0	91.8	46.6	33.4	28.9	6.0	11.0	26.6	52.5	44.4	55.5
Cambodia	11.8	21.4	38.0	77.8	51.3	43.9	9.2	11.0	16.7	87.0	62.2	60.5
Indonesia	24.0	29.7	56.1	49.5	43.2	37.1	11.9	12.8	20.8	61.4	56.1	57.9
Laos	12.5	17.2	27.7	84.5	58.7	46.3	10.6	10.1	12.9	95.1	68.8	59.2
Malaysia	18.6	37.5	66.5	55.1	37	33.8	10.2	13.8	22.5	65.3	50.8	56.3
Myanmar	22.1	32.2	60.0	52.3	43.3	34.1	11.6	14	20.5	63.9	57.3	54.6
Philippines	13.2	22.8	36.2	68.2	52.6	46.1	9	12	16.7	77.2	64.5	62.8
Singapore	50.0	114.9	241.5	31.7	23.3	22.4	15.8	26.8	54.2	47.5	50.1	76.6
Thailand	41.3	89.2	192.5	36.3	26.6	23.6	15	23.7	45.5	51.2	50.4	69.1
Timor-Leste	8.0	17.0	17.2	108.7	84.2	74.4	8.7	14.3	12.8	117	98.4	87.2
Vietnam	27.3	44.6	86.8	53.0	34.7	32.4	14.5	15.4	28.1	67.5	50.1	60.5
Southeast Asia	23.2	35.1	64.3	52.2	41.4	36.5	12.1	14.5	23.5	64.3	55.9	60.0

Source: United Nations Population Division, *World Population Prospects: 2015 Revision.*

FIGURE 2

Population Pyramids, Southeast Asia, Thailand, Malaysia, and the Philippines, 2000, 2015

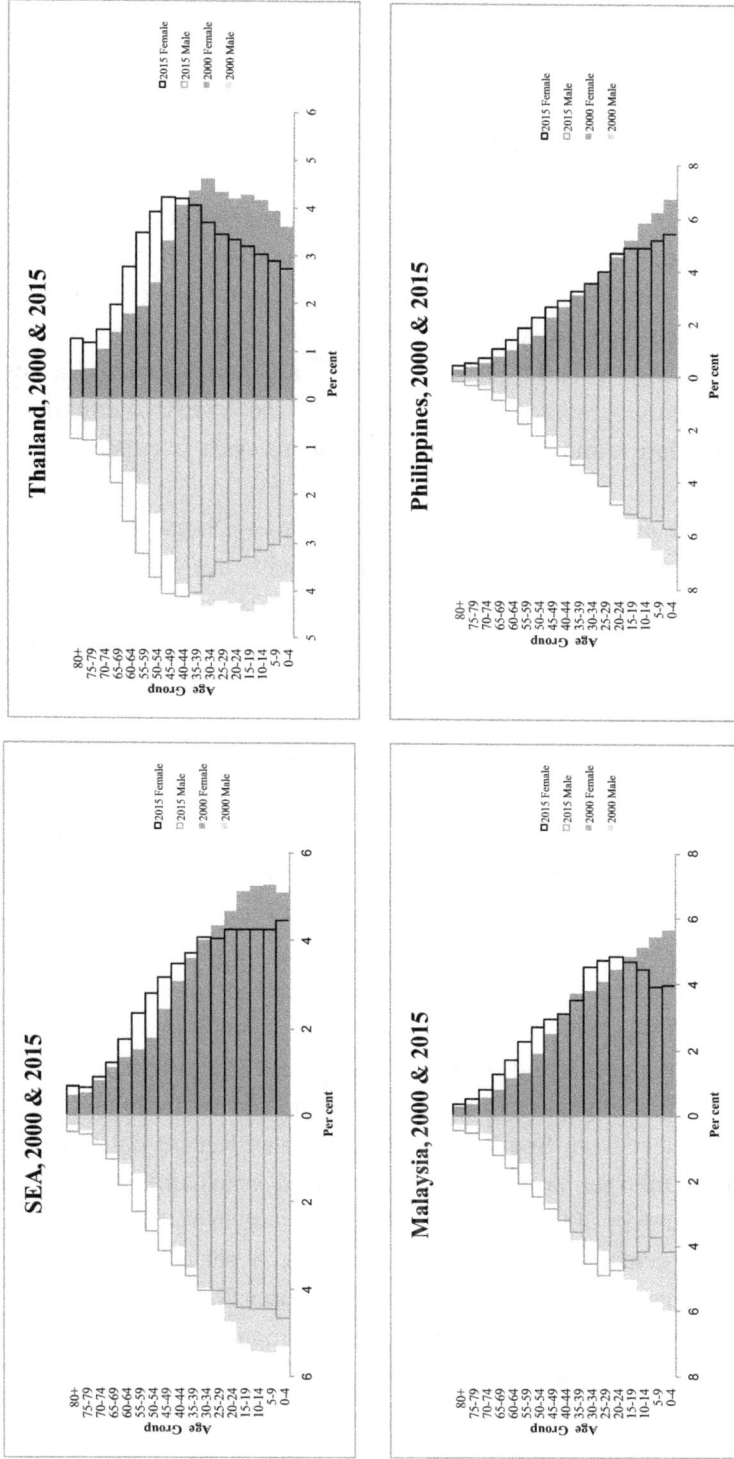

Source: Constructed based on UN Population Division, *World Population Prospect: 2015 Revision.*

International Migration

Contemporary Southeast Asia is both an increasingly important destination and an origin of international migrants. The Philippines, Myanmar, and Vietnam were among the ten countries with the highest levels of emigration in 2000–2010.[25] For the period 2000–2015, the number of migrants in Southeast Asia doubled from 4,926,833 to 9,867,722, with 70 per cent moving within the region. During the same period, the number of emigrants increased by 76 per cent — from 11.5 million to 20.3 million. And in contrast to immigration, only about 30 per cent of the emigrants had moved within the region, with 70 per cent having moved to other parts of the world. By 2015, Southeast Asia registered a net outflow of some 10.4 million persons. With the creation of the ASEAN Economic Community in 2015, population movement within Southeast Asia is expected to gain further momentum.

The more affluent countries in the region — Singapore, Malaysia, Brunei, and Thailand — are the main destinations, with net gains of labour migrants, while the rest of the countries of Southeast Asia are net exporters. Table 6 shows that, between 2000 and 2015, the number of international migrants had almost doubled in Malaysia and Singapore, and more than tripled in Thailand. The figures for Malaysia are believed to be a gross underestimate, as large numbers of undocumented migrants have entered the country illegally.[26] In 2015, Singapore, Malaysia, and Thailand together hosted up to 91 per cent of some 10 million international migrants in Southeast Asia. Almost all international migrants in Thailand were from neighbouring countries (half of them from Myanmar, about a fifth from Cambodia, and about a quarter from Laos). About half of the migrants in Singapore and 60 per cent of those in Malaysia had come from neighbouring Southeast Asian countries. In Malaysia, Indonesian workers accounted for about 43 per cent of migrants, followed by workers from Bangladesh (14.3 per cent), Myanmar (10 per cent), and Nepal (8.2 per cent). Malaysians made up the largest migrant group in Singapore (44 per cent), followed by mainland Chinese (18 per cent) and workers from South Asia (20 per cent). Recent data show that the rate of growth of migrant populations had slowed considerably in Malaysia (from above 6 per cent in 2000–2010 to just 1 per cent in 2010–15), Singapore (from 4.7 to 3.2 per cent), and Thailand (from above 8 per cent to 4 per cent).

In 2015, migrants made up a sizable proportion of the total population in four countries; by as much as 45 per cent in Singapore (up from 34.5 per cent in 2000), 25 per cent in Brunei Darussalam, 8 per cent in Malaysia, and 6 per cent in Thailand. However, the numbers of immigrants are rather small or negligible for the rest of Southeast Asia.

TABLE 6
International Migrant Stock, Southeast Asia, 2000–2015

Country	2000				2015				% change 2000–2015		
	Total	Within SEA	Outside SEA	Total	Total	SEA	Outside SEA	Total	SEA	Outside SEA	
Brunei Darussalam	96,296	78,577	17,719	102,733	83,832	18,901	6.7	6.7	6.7		
Cambodia	146,085	134,512	11,573	73,963	68,106	5,857	−49.4	−49.4	−49.4		
Indonesia	292,307	146,774	145,533	328,846	71,837	257,009	12.5	−51.1	76.6		
Laos	21,948	14,738	7,210	22,244	14,802	7,442	1.3	0.4	3.2		
Malaysia	1,277,223	928,270	348,953	2,514,243	1,539,741	974,502	96.9	65.9	179.3		
Myanmar	98,011	0	98,011	73,308	0	73,308	−25.2	0.0	−25.2		
Philippines	318,095	9,552	308,543	211,862	6,640	205,222	−33.4	−30.5	−33.5		
Singapore	1,351,691	769,659	582,032	2,543,638	1,321,552	1,222,086	88.2	71.7	110.0		
Thailand	1257,821	1,189,143	68,678	3,913,258	3,762,393	150,865	211.1	216.4	119.7		
Timor-Leste	10,602	6,572	4,030	10,834	6,716	4,118	2.2	2.2	2.2		
Vietnam	56,754	40,748	16,006	72,793	40,537	32,256	28.3	−0.5	101.5		
Southeast Asia	4,926,833	3,318,545	1,608,288	9,867,722	6,916,156	2,951,566	100.3	108.4	83.5		

Source: UN Population Division, *Trends in International Migrant Stock: The 2015 Revision* (United Nations database, POP/DB/MIG/Stock/ Rev.2015), 2015.

The sex ratio of migrant populations differs substantially across countries. In Malaysia — where labourers were brought in to work in the plantation, construction, and manufacturing sectors — male workers account for 60 per cent of migrants. There were relatively more female migrants (about 55 per cent) in Singapore, as they were brought in to work in the services sector. The gender composition of migrants in Thailand has remained balanced.

Southeast Asia is an important source of international migrants. The number of emigrants increased from 11.5 million in 2000 to 20.3 million in 2015. Of these, 26 per cent were from the Philippines, 19 per cent from Indonesia, 14.2 per cent from Myanmar, 12 per cent from Vietnam, and 9 per cent from Malaysia. Between 2000 and 2015, the number of emigrants more than doubled in Cambodia, Laos, and Myanmar. The numbers also increased by 40 per cent for Vietnam and 75 per cent for the Philippines.

Apart from the wide differential in the volume of emigration, there were substantial variations in the destination of the emigrants as well. The majority of emigrants from Malaysia (64 per cent), Cambodia (69 per cent), Laos (73 per cent), and Myanmar (77 per cent) moved within Southeast Asia. In contrast, almost all migrants from the Philippines and Vietnam (more than 95 per cent) moved to other parts of the world, as did the majority from Singapore, Indonesia, and Thailand (about two thirds to 87 per cent). Nearly half of the migrants from Indonesia had gone to the Middle East, while 46–57 per cent of migrants from the Philippines and Vietnam had gone to North America. Among the Thai migrants, almost equal proportions were in Europe and North America (about 30 per cent each). The main source of emigrants from Southeast Asia to Australia were the Philippines (291,096), Vietnam (233,691), Malaysia (173,924), and Indonesia (89,131).

Intra-ASEAN mobility is becoming very significant. Even before the establishment of the ASEAN Economic Community there was a three- to fourfold increase in the number of migrants from the three least developed countries (Cambodia, Laos, and Myanmar) to other countries within the region over the 2000–2015 period. Two migration corridors (Myanmar to Thailand and Cambodia to Thailand) had among the ten highest rates between 1990 and 2013.[27] However, there was an appreciable decrease in intraregional migration from the Philippines, and a flat trend from Thailand and Vietnam.

Cross-border migration within Southeast Asia tends to be unidirectional and limited to a few countries (Table 8). For instance, in 2015 Malaysia was host to more than a million workers from Indonesia, 250,000 from Myanmar (including close to 100,000 Rohingya refugees), and some 80,000 from Vietnam, but the reciprocal flow was negligible. On the other hand, more than a million Malaysians

Tey Nai Peng

TABLE 7
Emigrants from Southeast Asian Countries, 2000–2015

	2000			2015			% change 2000–2015		
	Total	Within SEA	Outside SEA	Total	Within SEA	Outside SEA	Total	Within SEA	Outside SEA
Brunei Darussalam	44,796	3,794	41,002	46,237	6,165	40,072	3.2	62.5	-2.3
Cambodia	454,941	173,689	281,252	1,187,142	821,659	365,483	160.9	373.1	29.9
Indonesia	2,334,652	706,902	1,627,750	3,876,739	1,257,190	2,619,549	66.1	77.8	60.9
Laos	642,221	294,425	347,796	1,345,075	976,770	368,305	109.4	231.8	5.9
Malaysia	1,202,246	759,623	442,623	1,835,252	1176,590	658,662	52.7	54.9	48.8
Myanmar	1,121,782	758,794	362,988	2,881,797	2,242,549	639,248	156.9	195.5	76.1
Philippines	3,031,119	174,498	2,856,621	5,316,320	56,680	5,259,640	75.4	-67.5	84.1
Singapore	185,921	44,317	141,604	313,884	106,355	207,529	68.8	140.0	46.6
Thailand	526,580	118,882	407,698	854,327	108,374	745,953	62.2	-8.8	83.0
Timor-Leste	148,379	143,745	4,634	37,311	22,048	15,263	-74.9	-84.7	229.4
Vietnam	1,849,385	140,176	1,709,209	2,588,678	141,776	2,446,902	40.0	1.1	43.2
Southeast Asia	11,542,022	3,318,845	8,223,177	20,282,762	6,916,156	13,366,606	75.7	108.4	62.5

Source: UN Population Division, *Trends in International Migrant Stock: The 2015 Revision* (United Nations database, POP/DB/MIG/Stock/Rev.2015), 2015

TABLE 8
Migration within Southeast Asia, 2015

Destination	Country of Origin							
	Cambodia	Indonesia	Malaysia	Myanmar	Philippines	Singapore	Thailand	Vietnam
Brunei Darussalam	0	6,165	48,285	0	13,457	1,541	14,384	0
Cambodia	–	105	172	52	152	123	30,806	36,436
Indonesia	0	–	2,201	0	3,915	21,907	21,907	0
Laos	1,231	0	0	249	0	0	1,688	11,634
Malaysia	14,127	1,070,433	–	252,292	21,732	79,519	8,283	87,272
Myanmar	0	0	0	–	0	0	0	0
Philippines	39	3,304	793	421	–	820	340	413
Singapore	0	163,237	1,123,654	0	15,392	–	19,269	0
Thailand	805,272	660	1,195	1,978,348	1,203	623	–	5,825
Timor-Leste	0	5,426	162	0	716	71	145	196
Vietnam	990	7,860	128	11,187	113	1,751	11,552	–

Source: UN Population Division, *Trends in International Migrant Stock: The 2015 Revision* (United Nations database, POP/DB/MIG/Stock/ Rev.2015)

had moved to Singapore, with a reciprocal flow of less than 80,000. Migrants to Singapore came mainly from Malaysia (85 per cent), with Indonesia a distant second (12 per cent). While Myanmar had sent out almost 2 million migrants to Thailand and 250,000 to Malaysia, it was closed to in-migration. Thailand had received almost 4 million migrants from neighbouring countries in return for less than 100,000.

Internal Migration and Urban Population Growth

Data on internal migration come from national population censuses and migration surveys. However, national data are not readily available for international comparative analysis. In most countries, especially those at low levels of urbanization, the main migration stream is from rural to urban areas. Significant urban–rural differentials in the rate of population growth can be attributed at least in part to rural–urban migration, apart from the reclassification of rural areas to urban areas. Figure 3 shows that Southeast Asia as a whole had zero population growth in the rural areas, while urban populations have been growing at an average of close to 3 per cent per annum between 2000 and 2015. Urban population growth ranged from around 2 per cent in Brunei Darussalam, Cambodia, and Myanmar; 3–4 per cent in Indonesia, Malaysia, Thailand, Timor-Leste, and Vietnam; to 5 per cent in Laos. These figures suggest substantial rural–urban migration in most Southeast Asian countries.

The urbanization level in Southeast Asia rose by 10 percentage points from 38 in 2000 to 48 by 2015 (Table 9). At the current rate, Southeast Asia is urbanizing faster than other regions, and it is projected to reach 60 per cent by 2040. Laos saw the sharpest rise in urbanization level (16 percentage points), followed by Malaysia (13 percentage points), Indonesia (11 percentage points), Vietnam (9 percentage points) and Myanmar (7 percentage points). Apart from Singapore (fully urbanized) and Brunei Darussalam (already highly urbanized in 2000), countries that had registered small increases in their urbanization level of 2–4 percentage points included the Philippines, Cambodia, and Thailand.

The less-urbanized countries have undergone more rapid urbanization. Laos registered the highest tempo of urbanization since 2000, at 3.6 per cent per annum, followed by Vietnam (2 per cent) and Myanmar (1.6 per cent). The Philippines, Cambodia, and Brunei had the lowest tempo of urbanization.

Urban populations in Southeast Asia are concentrated in capital cities. The proportion of populations of large urban centres (an agglomeration with 300,000 inhabitants) living in capital cities ranges from 4 per cent in Jakarta (Indonesia)

FIGURE 3
Rate of Population Growth in Rural and Urban Areas in Southeast Asia, 2010–15

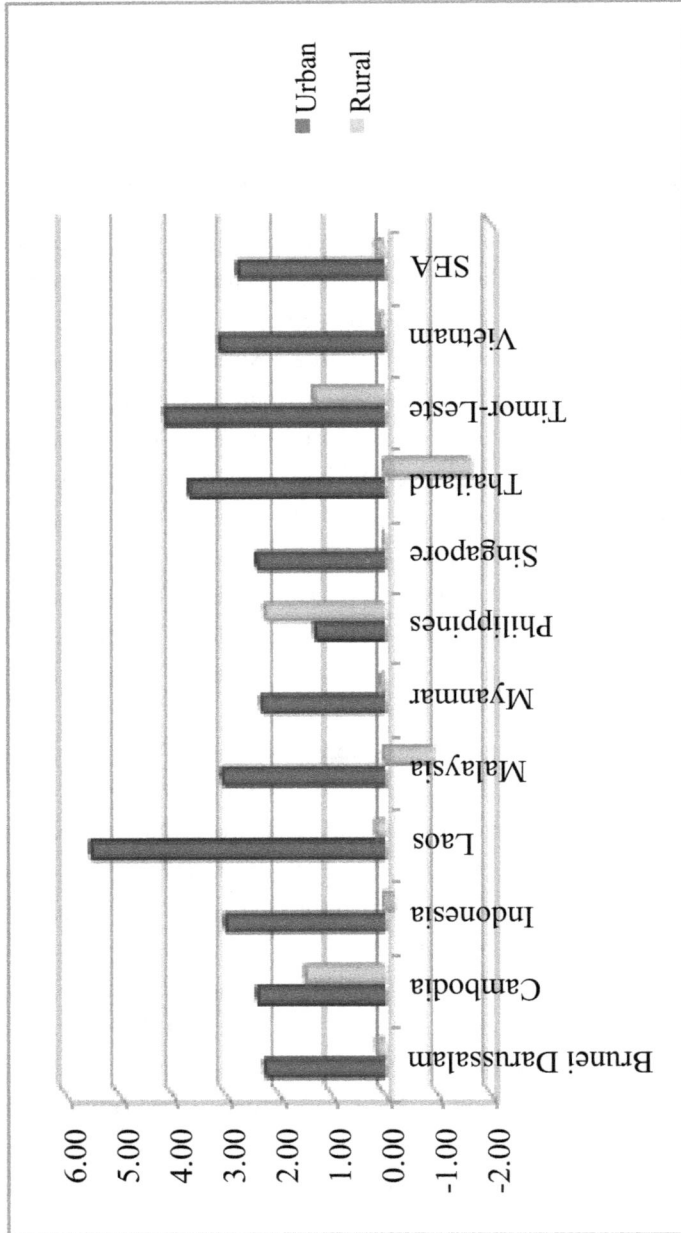

Source: UN Population Division, *World Population Prospect*, 2014.

TABLE 9
Urbanization Level and Tempo of Urbanization, Southeast Asia, 2000–2015

Country	Urbanization Level		Tempo of urbanization
	2000	2015	2000–2015
Brunei Darussalam	71	77	0.53
Cambodia	19	21	0.65
Indonesia	42	53	1.55
Laos	22	38	3.58
Malaysia	62	75	1.25
Myanmar	27	34	1.62
Philippines	48	50	0.22
Singapore	100	100	0
Thailand	31	35	0.76
Timor-Leste	24	30	1.3
Vietnam	24	33	2.02
Southeast Asia	38	48	1.48

Source: UN Population Division, *World Urbanization Prospects, 2014 Revision.*

to about 13–14 per cent in Manila (Philippines) and Bangkok (Thailand), and 18 per cent in Kuala Lumpur (Malaysia). Each of these cities is four to eight times larger than the second-largest city in each respective country. Despite efforts aimed at decentralization, city primacy has increased in Malaysia, Thailand, and Laos.[28]

Some of the world's largest cities are in Southeast Asia. These include Manila and Jakarta — with populations of 12.8 million and 10.2 million, respectively, in 2014 — and both number among the twenty-eight megacities in the world. Three cities — Bangkok (9.1 million), Kuala Lumpur (6.6 million), and Singapore (5.5 million) — are among the world's forty-three large cities (having a population of 5–10 million). For the period 2010–15, the annual rate of population growth in these cities ranged from 1.4 per cent in Jakarta to 3.3 per cent in Kuala Lumpur.[29]

National Challenges

The demographic situation varies greatly across the countries of Southeast Asia and it poses different challenges to policymakers in each country. Different policy responses are needed to deal with problems arising from the demographic changes and circumstances, such as high or low population growth, changing age structure, spatial distribution of the population, labour shortages, unemployment, international migration, and other social issues. Table 10 highlights some of the population problems that are of concern in each country.

Rapid population growth poses enormous challenges in raising standards of living and in meeting the needs for employment and basic services (health, education, housing, social pensions, transportation, and other facilities). It also results in congestion and environmental degradation. With slower population growth, more resources can be channelled for development purposes. Moreover, it will be a challenge to create jobs to cater to a fast-growing labour force, especially in countries with high unemployment rates, as in the case of the Philippines and Indonesia.

The momentum for population growth remains tremendous in several countries of Southeast Asia — namely, the Philippines, Cambodia, Laos, and Timor-Leste — due to relatively high fertility rates and young age structures. In Indonesia the challenge is to bring down the fertility rate sooner rather than later. The population projection shows that under the constant fertility assumption, the population of Indonesia will rise to 303 million by 2030, as against 283 million if the fertility

TABLE 10
Key Population Concerns and Challenges in Southeast Asia

	Fertility and population growth	Ageing a major concern	Spatial distribution – major changes desired	Immigration	Emigration
Brunei Darussalam	Too low		v		
Cambodia	Too high		v		Too low
Indonesia	Too high		v		Too low
Laos	Too high		v		Too high
Malaysia	Too high	v	v	Too high	Too high
Myanmar	Satisfactory				
Philippines	Too high		v		
Singapore	Too low	v		Too high	Too high
Thailand	Too low	v	V		Too low
Timor-Leste	Too high		V		Too low
Vietnam	Too high	v	V		Too low

Source: UN Population Division, *World Population Policy, 2013.*

rate could be brought down to replacement level. The effectiveness of efforts to revitalize family planning in Indonesia remains to be seen.

While efforts are being made to slow down the rate of population growth in the above-mentioned countries, policymakers in Singapore and Thailand — and, of late, in Malaysia — have been concerned with low fertility and low population growth, which have given rise to labour shortages and population ageing.[30] In Singapore, where fertility has fallen to a problematically low level, various efforts have been taken to raise the fertility level, including introducing housing policies that encourage early marriage, matchmaking, tax relief for children, a "baby bonus", and subsidies for childcare.[31] However, all these efforts have not produced the desired results, and fertility remains at a very low level.

The changing age structure and population ageing are of major concern in Singapore, Thailand, Malaysia, and Vietnam. Although these countries are still enjoying the demographic dividend, the window of opportunity is fast closing as the share of older persons to the total population is rising rapidly. The changing age structure affects the labour participation rate and leads to labour shortages and an increase in the elderly dependency burden. Population ageing has resulted in a rise of non-communicable or chronic diseases and disabilities that strain the healthcare system.[32] With the rapid pace of ageing, countries are ill-prepared to cater to the healthcare and social protection needs of the large number of older people. The shrinking family size and out-migration have eroded family support for the elderly. A report based on a four-country study on policy and programme responses to population ageing in Cambodia, Indonesia, Malaysia, and Thailand highlighted the weakness of coordination of different agencies in tackling issues pertaining to ageing, and the need to address the various challenges to ensure socio-economic development, sexual and reproductive health, and rights and social protection systems for the elderly, including labour participation. The report also highlighted the financial difficulties faced by older people and the inadequacy of the social protection schemes.[33]

With the exception of Singapore and Myanmar, the countries of Southeast Asia have experienced unequal regional growth, leading to population concentration. In all these countries, major changes in spatial distribution of the population are seen as desirable. Unplanned and rapid urban population growth, especially in major cities, has threatened sustainable development. In cities such as Manila, Jakarta, Bangkok, and Kuala Lumpur, inadequately managed urban expansion leads to rapid sprawl, congestion, pollution, environmental degradation, security issues, escalating housing costs, and slums and squatter settlements, together with unsustainable production and consumption patterns.[34] Kuala Lumpur is the only large city in Southeast Asia to have been able to achieve zero squatters — through the resettlement of squatters to low-cost houses and flats.

Issues and challenges of immigration are more pertinent to Singapore and Malaysia, where labour shortage has led to the continued influx of migrant workers. In Singapore the number of immigrants has escalated by 1.2 million over the 2000–2015 period, or 80,000 annually. This figure far exceeds the level of 20,000–25,000 considered to be sustainable.[35] In both countries the presence of large immigrant numbers has given rise to various social issues and challenges, such as the deterioration of public safety and conflicts between immigrants and locals as they compete for jobs.[36] Although low-skilled workers were recruited to perform the "3D" jobs shunned by locals, some have ventured into petty trade, in direct competition with locals, resulting in conflicts.

In Malaysia the number of illegal migrants has been escalating despite the many measures taken to slow illegal entry.[37] Some of these illegal migrants were found to suffer from contagious diseases such as malaria, tuberculosis, and hepatitis B, and hence their presence poses a danger to public health. Additionally, Malaysia has been accommodating asylum seekers and refugees whose number has almost doubled from 50,487 in 2000 to 98,207 in 2015. Thailand is the only other country in Southeast Asia that accommodates such a large number of refugees, estimated at more than 100,000. The refugees hail from the Middle East, Eastern Europe, South Asia, Africa, and neighbouring countries, especially Myanmar, where ethnic conflicts drove out thousands of Rohingyas.

Countries with a large population and high rates of population growth and unemployment have relied on emigration as a policy option to reduce population pressure and unemployment. The level of emigration was considered too low in Indonesia, Cambodia, Thailand, Timor-Leste, and Vietnam. In view of the growing anti-migrant sentiment and a move to restrict immigration in the main receiving countries, it will be a challenge for the major sending countries (the Philippines, Thailand, and Vietnam) to sustain their previous levels of emigration to the West. The curtailment of emigration will have significant effects on the economies of these countries, as personal remittances make up as much as 10 per cent of GDP in the Philippines and 6.4 per cent in Vietnam.[38]

On the other hand, the brain drain caused by the emigration of a large number of high-skilled professionals has been of concern to policymakers in Singapore and Malaysia. In 2010 it was estimated that a total of 258,000 tertiary-educated Malaysians were living in another country.[39] Efforts to retain and attract the emigrant diaspora through the establishment of the Talent Corporation have met with little success. As a policy option, the diaspora can be viewed in terms of its enormous potential to facilitate trade, investment, tourism, and other activities that can contribute to Malaysia's economic development, and serve as a model for other Southeast Asian countries.[40]

Concluding Remarks

Southeast Asian countries are facing various problems due to demographic changes. Some countries are still struggling to control rapid rates of population growth. On the other hand, the low fertility levels in Singapore, Thailand, and Malaysia have created a new set of problems such as rapid population ageing and labour shortages. Globalization and technological advancements will have a significant impact on demographic change. There is a need for policymakers to review the population situation regularly so that appropriate responsive policies can be adopted to ensure a harmonious balance between population and development. Individuals must also be responsive to global changes in modifying their demographic behaviour.

Notes

1. Gavin Jones, *The Population of Southeast Asia*, Asia Research Institute, Working Paper 196, 2013.
2. UN Development Programme, *Human Development Report 2014: Work for Human Development* (New York: UN Development Programme, 2014).
3. Ibid.
4. Ibid.
5. World Bank, World Development Indicators, 2013.
6. United Nations, *Human Development Report 2015: Work for Human Development* (New York: United Nations Development Programme, 2015).
7. Ibid.
8. United Nations, Department of Economic and Social Affairs, Population Division (2015). *World Urbanization Prospects: The 2014 Revision* (ST/ESA/SER.A/366).
9. Ibid.
10. Gavin Jones, "Urbanization Trends in Asia: The Conceptual and Definitional Challenges", in *New Forms of Urbanization*, edited by Tony Champion and Graeme Hugo (Hampshire: Ashgate, 2004), pp. 113–32.
11. United Nations, Department of Economic and Social Affairs, Population Division (2015). *World Population Prospects: The 2015 Revision*, DVD edition.
12. Jones, *The Population of Southeast Asia*.
13. L.W. Aarssen, "Why is Fertility Lower in Wealthier Countries? The Role of Relaxed Fertility-Selection", *Population and Development Review* 31, no. 1 (2005): 113–26; C. Hirschman, 2003, "Fertility Transition, Socioeconomic Determinants Of", in

Encyclopedia Population, vol. 1, edited by P. Demeny and G. McNicoll (New York: Macmillan Reference USA, 2003), pp. 425–31; A.R. El-Ghannam, "An Examination of Factors Affecting Fertility Rate Differentials as Compared among Women in Less and More Developed Countries", *Journal of Human Ecology* 18, no. 3 (2005): 181–92.

14. Lai Siow Li, Tey Nai Peng, and Ng Sor Tho, "Socio-Economic Status and Fertility among Currently Married Women in 3 ASEAN Countries", *Malaysian Journal of Economics Studies* (forthcoming 2017).

15. Liau Y-Sing, "Mothers Wanted Back in Workforce as Malaysia Seeks Growth", Bloomberg, 20 August 2014 <https://www.bloomberg.com/news/articles/2014-08-19/malaysia-seeks-to-draw-women-back-to-work-southeast-asia>.

16. Department of Statistics, "Vital Statistics Malaysia 2014" (Putrajaya: Malaysia, 2015).

17. Gavin Jones, "Population Policy in a Prosperous City-State: Dilemmas for Singapore", *Population and Development Review* 38, no. 2 (June 2012): 311–36.

18. J. Bongaarts, "A Framework for Analyzing the Proximate Determinants of Fertility", *Population and Development Review* 4, no. 1 (1978): 105–32; J. Bongaarts, "The Fertility-Inhibiting Effects of the Intermediate Fertility Variables", *Studies in Family Planning* 13, nos. 6–7 (1982): 179–89.

19. United Nations Department of Economic and Social Affairs, Population Division, *Estimates and Projections of the Number of Women Aged 15–49 Who Are Married or in a Union: 2016 Revision* (New York: United Nations, 2016).

20. Terence Hulland Henry Mosley, *Revitalization of Family Planning Program in Indonesia*, The Government of Indonesia and United Nations Population Fund, 2009.

21. Philippine Statistics Authority, *Philippines National Demographic and Health Survey, 2013* (Manila: Philippine Statistics Authority, 2014).

22. A.N. Herrin, "Development of the Philippines' Family Planning Program: The Early Years, 1967–80", in *The Global Family Planning Revolution: Three Decades of Population Policies and Programs*, edited by W.C. Robinson and J.A. Ross (Washington, DC: World Bank), pp. 277–98.

23. United Nations Population Division 2015, *World Marriage Data*, 2015.

24. United Nations, Department of Economic and Social Affairs, Population Division, *World Population Ageing*, 2015 (ST/ESA/SER.A/390).

25. World Bank, *World Development Indicators, 2013*; Graeme Hugo, "The Changing Dynamics of ASEAN International Migration", *Malaysian Journal of Economic Studies* 51, no. 1 (2014): 43–67.

26. Azizah Kassim, "Recent Trends in Transnational Population Inflows into Malaysia: Policy, Issues and Challenges", *Malaysian Journal of Economic Studies* 51, no. 1 (2014): 9–28.

27. Hugo, "The Changing Dynamics".

28. United Nations, Department of Economic and Social Affairs, Population Division, *World Urbanization Prospects: The 2014 Revision*, 2014. Customs data acquired via website.

29. United Nations, *Urbanization Prospects: The 2014 Revision*.

30. Yuen Meikeng, "Parliament: Malaysians Should Have More Children, Says Rohani", *The Star Online*, 25 May 2015 <http://www.thestar.com.my/news/nation/2015/05/25/parliament-malaysians-have-more-children/>; Yap Mui Teng, "Ultra-low Fertility in Singapore: Some Observations", in *Ultra-low Fertility in Pacific Asia: Trends, Cause and Policy Issues*, edited by G.W. Jones, P.T. Straughan, and A. Chan (London: Routledge, 2009).

31. Gavin Jones, "Population Policy in a Prosperous City-State: Dilemmas for Singapore", *Population and Development Review* 38, no. 2 (June 2012): 311–36.

32. World Health Organization, *Global Status Report on Noncommunicable Diseases* (Geneva: World Health Organization, 2014).

33. International Council on Management of Population Programmes (ICOMP) and International Planned Parenthood Federation (IPPF), *A Report on Consultation on Policy and Programmatic Responses to Population Ageing in Selected Asian Countries* (Kuala Lumpur: ICOMP and IPPF, ESEAOR, forthcoming).

34. United Nations, *World Urbanization Prospects: The 2014 Revision*.

35. At a forum at Nanyang Technological University in September 2011, former Prime Minister Lee Kuan Yew stated that "20,000–25,000 net migrants per year is sustainable, but certainly not the higher figure of 60,000". Cited in Li Xueying, "Population Will Shrink without Immigrants, Fewer Working Adults to Support the Old", *Straits Times*, 8 September 2011.

36. Brenda S.A. Yeoh and Lin Weiqiang, "Rapid Growth in Singapore's Immigrant Population Brings Policy Challenges", *Migration Information*, 2012; Azizah Kassim, "Recent Trends in Transnational Population Inflows into Malaysia: Policy, Issues and Challenges", *Malaysian Journal of Economic Studies* 51, no. 10 (2014): 9–28.

37. Ibid.

38. World Bank data on Personal Remittances <http://data.worldbank.org/indicator/BX.TRF.PWKR.DT.GD.ZS>.

39. World Bank, *Malaysia Economic Monitor: Brain Drain* (Bangkok: World Bank, 2011).

40. Hugo, "The Changing Dynamics".

U.S.–JAPAN–AUSTRALIA STRATEGIC COOPERATION IN THE TRUMP ERA: Moving from Aspiration to Action

Andrew Shearer

The U.S.–Japan–Australia Trilateral Strategic Dialogue (TSD) was the first formal trilateral security mechanism in the Asia-Pacific, and one of the earliest and most important nodes of what former U.S. Secretary of Defense Ashton Carter calls the "principled security network" that the United States and its partners have been constructing in the region.[1] Since it was established in 2002 the TSD has become institutionalized at the ministerial level and has met twice at the leaders' level, becoming the most developed and substantial trilateral involving the United States in the Asia-Pacific. Augmented in 2007 by a Security and Defense Cooperation Forum involving defence as well as foreign ministry officials, the TSD has developed into a useful mechanism for coordinating policy positions on regional issues such as North Korea and the South China Sea, and for driving deeper strategic cooperation between the three countries in areas including defence, security, intelligence, development assistance, capacity building, and humanitarian assistance and disaster relief (HADR). It has also helped to foster stronger defence and security ties between Japan and Australia — the weakest leg of the strategic triangle.[2]

The strategic logic of trilateral U.S.–Japan–Australia defence and security cooperation remains compelling. Threats to the United States and its allies in the Asia-Pacific are intensifying — whether from North Korea's nuclear weapons and ballistic missile programmes, China's assertiveness in the Western Pacific (increasingly backed by sophisticated area denial weapons), or the resurgence

ANDREW SHEARER is Senior Advisor on Asia-Pacific Security at the Center for Strategic & International Studies in Washington DC. He is also Director of the new CSIS project Alliances and American Leadership. Mr Shearer was previously national security adviser to Prime Ministers John Howard and Tony Abbott of Australia.

of Islamist terrorist networks in Southeast Asia. These threats will increasingly stretch the constrained resources of the United States and its allies. The only cost-effective way to remedy the ensuing capability gaps in key areas such as intelligence, surveillance, and reconnaissance (ISR), undersea warfare, missile defence, and amphibious lift is to develop greater interoperability and, ultimately, integration among U.S. and allied military forces. Japan and Australia are two of the United States' most capable and dependable allies in the region, as well as longstanding economic and diplomatic partners, who over the past decade have been steadily building their own substantial bilateral strategic relationship. Moreover, their respective strategic geographies complement each other and the United States' maritime strategy in the Indian Ocean and Asia-Pacific region. Current trilateral defence cooperation focuses heavily on combined exercises, with the three countries steadily increasing the frequency, scale, and sophistication of their three-way exercise programme.[3] Training in amphibious operations has been a particular priority, as Japan and Australia establish their own brigade-level capabilities, drawing on the unrivalled expertise of the U.S. Marine Corps.

Despite profound global and regional strategic changes over the past fifteen years, the three governments have maintained — and indeed strengthened — their commitment to trilateral defence and security cooperation. The Obama administration's Asia-Pacific Maritime Security Strategy singled out Japan and Australia as key maritime partners and noted leader-level agreement to expand maritime cooperation, trilateral exercises, and defence development.[4] Japan's most recent National Defense Program Guidelines commit Japan to further deepen its relationship with Australia and trilateral cooperation with the United States.[5] The Australian government's 2016 Defence White Paper, developed by the Abbott government and released by the Turnbull government, commits Australia to exploring opportunities for expanding cooperation with Japan in areas such as intelligence and in developing common capabilities such as the F-35 Joint Strike Fighter, air and missile defence, and maritime warfare technologies — as well as expanding trilateral defence cooperation.[6] At the most recent TSD meeting in July 2016 (the sixth held at ministerial level) the three countries reaffirmed their commitment to deepening trilateral strategic cooperation and issued a strong statement on the South China Sea. In October 2016 they concluded a trilateral information sharing treaty.

Yet, trilateral strategic cooperation among the United States, Japan, and Australia faces a number of challenges. The decision of the Turnbull government to choose France as Australia's partner to develop its fleet of new conventional submarines was presented in capability rather than strategic terms, but was an undeniable setback for the burgeoning Australia–Japan defence and security partnership. In particular, it significantly reduced the opportunity for U.S.–Japan–Australia undersea warfare cooperation to serve as a driver of closer trilateral integration at the strategic, operational, tactical, and defence industrial levels. Delays in concluding cost-sharing arrangements for the U.S. Force Posture Initiatives in Australia (agreed to only in October 2016 after a sixteen-month hiatus)[7] and a reciprocal access agreement between Japan and Australia to facilitate exercises in these two countries both point to a disappointing loss of momentum in operationalizing closer three-way defence cooperation. In Australia this occurs as senior political opposition figures, academics, and commentators call for their country to distance itself from the United States following the election of Donald Trump as president and to give more weight to China's preferences when considering its foreign, defence, and trade policies.[8]

President Trump's campaign rhetoric and seemingly entrenched views on alliances — and in particular his longstanding criticism of the U.S.–Japan alliance — have created widespread uncertainty in the Asia-Pacific region (and beyond) and sent tremors through officials in Tokyo; media reports of his testy phone call with Australian prime minister Malcolm Turnbull fed these concerns.[9] His protectionism — and particularly his opposition to the Trans-Pacific Partnership trade agreement — has deepened these misgivings. Yet, despite the risks, the advent of a new U.S. administration also presents potential upsides for the Asia-Pacific and an opportunity to reinvigorate trilateral strategic cooperation. The likelihood of increased U.S. defence funding, a larger navy, and a more robust approach to China's efforts to reshape the regional security and economic order would — if they materialize and are implemented effectively and with due regard to regional dynamics — align with Japanese and Australian interests. Moreover, if the Japanese and Australian governments are smart and make effective use of the TSD as a forum in which they can bring their combined influence to bear, they can maximize their chances of shaping the Trump administration's approach on issues that matter to both countries — including regional security and economic policies. But they will have to take the initiative. National interest has always outweighed sentiment in international relations, and the Trump administration will expect more from America's allies. Tokyo and Canberra should work together to build relationships and influence with the new administration, and need to be prepared for a more transactional and instrumental approach in Washington.

This chapter examines the prospects for U.S.–Japan–Australia trilateral strategic cooperation in the Trump era, and how Japan and Australia, two of America's most important Asia-Pacific allies, could use the TSD to influence the shape of the new administration's policies towards the region. By stepping up their own security efforts, both individually and bilaterally, they can work together to encourage President Trump to take an active interest in the Asia-Pacific and to implement a more robust strategy in response to the significant challenges confronting the region.

Rising Threats

There is little doubt that the United States and its allies in the Asia-Pacific face an increasingly daunting range of security threats.

North Korea's nuclear weapons and missile programmes are making rapid progress. The tempo quickened during 2016, with Pyongyang conducting two nuclear tests (detonated less than a year apart for the first time) and numerous short-, medium- and long-range missile tests. New United Nations sanctions negotiated with Beijing have done nothing to deflect the North Korean leadership from its pursuit of a nuclear deterrent. U.S. military bases in South Korea, Japan, and Guam are already within range of North Korean missiles, and within several years Pyongyang is likely to possess long-range ballistic missiles capable of targeting the continental United States with nuclear weapons. In his 2017 New Year message, President Kim Jong-un declared that North Korea was in the "final stage" of testing an intercontinental ballistic missile.[10] For his part, President Trump has declared that this "won't happen". North Korea is likely to pose an early foreign policy test for the Trump administration.

China's growing assertiveness in the Western Pacific poses a less acute threat, but, left unchallenged, will continue to reshape the regional security order over time in ways that run counter to U.S., Japanese, and Australian interests — with global ramifications. Despite an international tribunal ruling emphatically against many of its maritime claims in the South China Sea, China continues to militarize disputed features it controls in the Spratly Islands. Its most recent move has been to install anti-aircraft and anti-missile defence systems at several facilities.[11]

This follows the rapid construction of runways and hangars suitable for accommodating fighters and longer-range surveillance and transport aircraft and bombers — which, along with longer-range missiles, could be flown in overnight. These installations could be readily targeted by U.S. forces in any major conflict. But in a whole range of more likely scenarios, short of all-out war, their effect would be to constrain U.S. freedom of manoeuvre in a vital international waterway, complicating U.S. military planning and reducing Washington's ability to deter adversaries and reassure regional allies. During 2017, Beijing may further escalate tensions by commencing island-building at the strategically located Scarborough Shoal, deploying combat aircraft to its newly constructed facilities, or declaring a South China Sea Air Defence Identification Zone (as it did over most of the East China Sea in late 2013).

China has also stepped up its incursions into Japanese-controlled waters and airspace in the East China Sea. Despite a thaw in China–Japan diplomatic relations following a meeting between President Xi Jinping and Prime Minister Shinzo Abe in September 2016 on the margins of the Hangzhou G-20 summit, Japan filed a diplomatic protest in November after Chinese coastguard vessels entered territorial waters around the disputed Senkaku/Diaoyu Islands. In summer 2016, approximately 230 Chinese fishing trawlers, escorted by government vessels, entered disputed waters around the islands.[12]

China's more forceful posture in the South China Sea and the East China Sea has been facilitated by substantial increases in its maritime capacity and capabilities. China has by far the largest force of major combatants, submarines, and amphibious warfare ships in Asia (over 300) and easily the largest civil maritime enforcement fleet (over 200).[13] It also has 600 modern combat aircraft.[14]

By contrast, Japan — Asia's next-largest maritime power — has fewer than 70 large combatant vessels, fewer than 80 maritime law enforcement vessels, and approximately 350 combat aircraft. The leading Southeast Asian maritime nations — including claimants to disputed South China Sea territory — have smaller navies and civil maritime enforcement fleets again. The U.S. 7th Fleet has 50 to 70 vessels (including 1 aircraft carrier, 8–12 submarines, and 10–14 cruisers and destroyers) and 140 combat aircraft deployed forward in the region, while the 3rd Fleet includes 5 carrier strike groups, more than 30 submarines, and more than 400 aircraft stationed in California and Hawaii. But keeping tabs on China's burgeoning maritime presence across the region is stretching the U.S. Navy and its allied counterparts.

China's military also poses an increasing *qualitative* challenge. An aggressive and well-funded modernization programme is providing the People's Liberation Army (PLA) with weapons, sensors, and other systems to counter traditional areas of U.S. regional dominance, such as power projection by sea and air, space, and cyber capability.[15] China is also developing aircraft carriers and amphibious forces and the international logistical infrastructure needed to project power and support surface task groups operating well beyond littoral waters, including along the sea lines of communication across the Indian Ocean that connect its economy with vital energy sources in the Persian Gulf.[16] Developing genuine power projection capabilities will take time, but there is little reason to doubt Beijing's long-term intentions or resolve. Reforms to the structure, command and control, and training of the PLA will progressively strengthen China's ability to deploy effective military power in its neighbourhood and further afield.

The U.S. Department of Defense acknowledges that the PLA is "increasingly able to project power to assert regional dominance during peacetime and contest U.S. military superiority during a regional conflict".[17] Together these developments are eroding U.S. military preponderance in the Asia-Pacific, posing a growing threat to the American position in the region and to regional countries' security. Over time, China's military build-up could undermine the U.S. alliance system in Asia, because the United States' capacity to fulfil its security commitments rests on the ability to project power in the region.[18]

Aside from the state-based threats posed in the Asia-Pacific by North Korea and China, the United States and its regional allies will also be called on to respond to an increasing range of transnational challenges. The need for multilateral HADR operations along the lines of those conducted following the 2004 Boxing Day tsunami, the 2011 Fukushima earthquake disaster, and the 2013 Typhoon Haiyan in the Philippines is only likely to grow. Further regional stabilization operations such as those launched in Bougainville, East Timor, and the Solomon Islands cannot be ruled out.

Moreover, recent terrorist attacks and arrests in Australia, Bangladesh, Indonesia, Malaysia, and the Philippines show that Islamist terror networks and "lone wolf" attacks remain a significant threat, particularly in Southeast Asia. Recent coalition military successes against the self-declared Islamic State in Iraq and Syria have reduced the potency of its propaganda and denied it territory and resources. Yet, domestic conditions and the likelihood that Southeast Asian foreign fighters will return from the Middle East with training and experience in sophisticated terrorist techniques point to more capable networks and an increasing threat in Southeast Asia. Along with President Donald Trump's emphasis on terrorism, this is likely to push counterterrorism back up the security agenda for the United States and its allies in the region.

Alliance Challenges

The United States and its Asia-Pacific allies are responding to the diversity of challenges they face in the region.

Former President Barack Obama's Asia "rebalance" marked the first time a U.S. administration has explicitly identified the Asia-Pacific as its top foreign policy priority, at least rhetorically.[19] His administration was at pains to emphasize the diplomatic and economic dimensions of the rebalance and that its Asia strategy had a positive agenda of ensuring the United States engages comprehensively with the world's most dynamic region and benefits fully from the opportunities presented by its growth and prosperity — rather than just a defensive strategy to counter China's rise.[20] Yet, establishing a more robust and distributed U.S. military posture in the region in response to emerging threats was always a key element of the rebalance, and the United States has made considerable progress towards this goal.

Many of the United States' most sophisticated weapons systems are being deployed to the Asia-Pacific region, including fifth-generation F-22 and F-35 aircraft, modern submarines and surface vessels, radars, ISR platforms, and missile defence systems. Key operating facilities in South Korea, Japan, and Guam are being modernized and/or realigned, and a web of new access agreements with countries including Australia, Singapore, and the Philippines facilitates an increased U.S. military presence in Southeast Asia during peacetime and provides greater operating flexibility for a range of regional contingencies. The United States has also expanded its programme of bilateral and multilateral exercises with regional defence partners and is stepping up "minilateral" security cooperation with partners including Japan, South Korea, Australia, and India.[21]

Many of America's regional friends and allies are also stepping up their own security efforts, raising defence spending, and forging new bilateral and minilateral partnerships. Japan is increasing its defence budget, expanding the scope of its commitments under the U.S. alliance, and strengthening strategic cooperation with Australia, India, and South Korea, as well as providing capacity building assistance to Southeast Asian countries. Australia is boosting defence spending (including the biggest naval construction programme since the Second World War), hosting U.S. Marines and Air Force rotations, and intensifying its regional security engagement. Japan and South Korea — America's two northeast Asian allies, and both essential partners in most serious regional contingencies — concluded an intelligence-sharing agreement in November 2016. American forces have gained access to important naval and air facilities in the Philippines that facilitate their reach into the South China Sea. India, Singapore, and Vietnam are all looking to strengthen strategic ties with Washington.

The deteriorating regional security environment outlined above — and in particular the rising threat posed by North Korea and strategic anxiety about China's long-term intentions — has been the main driver of this strengthening of the Asia-Pacific alliance network. Yet, despite this progress, America's alliances are not keeping pace with strategic change in Asia.

This was a key conclusion of a 2016 independent assessment of the rebalance mandated by Congress and conducted by the Center for Strategic & International Studies (CSIS).[22] The CSIS review found that "the balance of military power in the region is shifting against the United States" — owing to the combined effect of rapid developments in Chinese and North Korean capabilities and the constrained pace of American capability development because of the inadequate funding levels mandated by the Budget Control Act.[23] CSIS identified critical gaps in U.S. capability, particularly systems to defend ships and bases from ballistic missiles and capabilities needed to give the United States an asymmetric, cost-imposing response to regional competitors (the Obama administration's "Third Offset Strategy").[24] It also highlighted the lack of a clearly articulated regional strategy aligned across the U.S. government and with regional allies and partners; the need for improved undersea warfare capabilities, intelligence, ISR cooperation, and theatre amphibious lift resources; and significant logistical challenges, including inadequate stockpiles of precision guided munitions. As a result CSIS concluded that the existing rebalance effort was insufficient to meet U.S. objectives in the region.

The position of the United States and its Asia-Pacific allies has further eroded since the CSIS assessment was published. Congress and the Obama administration failed to resolve the defence budget impasse — although, more encouragingly, President Trump has reaffirmed his commitment to work with Congress to increase defence funding. The election of maverick populist Rodrigo Duterte in the Philippines has reversed the momentum in U.S.–Philippines relations developed during the Aquino administration and has seen Manila tilt ostensibly away from Washington towards Beijing; some exercises and other areas of defence cooperation have been curtailed and Duterte's anti-American animus could yet jeopardize the important bilateral access agreement signed in 2014.[25] There is also concern that China is making inroads with Malaysia, a low-key but significant security partner to the United States.[26] Even Australia — long one of America's most steadfast allies — has thus far politely resisted U.S. entreaties to conduct its own freedom of navigation patrols near disputed features in the South China Sea, reportedly out of concern for Beijing's reaction.[27] Reports of sizable Chinese donations to major Australian political parties also raised eyebrows in Washington and fed concerns about China's growing influence with U.S. allies and partners across the region. Thus far the United States' alliance with South Korea has been insulated from President Park Geun-hye's fall from political grace. But with elections due in December 2017 and the prospects uncertain, American alliance managers have no cause for complacency.

It remains to be seen whether the wave of populism witnessed in the recent U.S. election result, the United Kingdom's Brexit vote, and across continental Europe will manifest in Asia. There is little doubt, however, that President Trump's campaign rhetoric questioning the value of longstanding American alliances in Asia and Europe sent tremors across the Pacific Ocean, unsettling policymakers and public opinion and casting doubt over whether the United States would continue to honour its security commitments in the region.[28] Those concerns are given added weight by the constancy and vehemence of Trump's views on NATO and the U.S. alliances with Japan and South Korea over several decades.

The early signals since the election have been more positive. Trump has spoken by telephone with the leaders of most of America's leading allies, and his first major international meeting was with Japan's Prime Minister Shinzo Abe. In subsequent meetings with Abe and other leaders, President Trump has reaffirmed America's alliance with Japan and commitment to NATO. Vice President Mike Pence, Secretary of Defense James Mattis, and Secretary of State Rex Tillerson have also worked hard on early visits to Asia and Europe to reassure allies.[28] Yet there seems little doubt that under Trump's leadership, U.S. allies in Asia should prepare themselves for a more transactional approach from Washington than they have been accustomed to.

Often much of the energy, initiative, and investment required to adapt and strengthen alliances necessarily comes from America's junior partners. This has been the case with the "special relationship" between the United States and the United Kingdom for decades. It applied during the late 1990s and early 2000s when the U.S.–Australia alliance became operationally and institutionally closer and stronger under the leadership of Prime Minister John Howard and President George W. Bush. Today it is Prime Minister Abe's political leadership and commitment that is driving a broader and deeper U.S.–Japan alliance.

The demands of the Trump administration are likely to be greater, however, and America's allies will have to work harder to demonstrate their worth and to develop and sustain high-level access and influence. This will be challenging, particularly given uncertainty about the incoming administration's priorities, Trump's relatively unknown foreign policy team, and widespread negative public perceptions of Trump (often fuelled by inaccurate or exaggerated media coverage) in allied countries. Still, it is hardly unreasonable for America to expect more of its allies given the massive benefits they have reaped over more than half a century from the liberal order established and maintained by the United States at vast cost. This is particularly the case in an era when the United States remains the world's sole superpower, with all the responsibilities that entails, but in which threats are mounting and the economic and military gap between America and peer competitors such as China is closing.[29]

Turbocharging U.S.–Japan–Australia Strategic Cooperation

Policymakers and alliance managers in Japan and Australia thus face an increasingly complex and difficult international environment. Japan, as a frontline state vis-à-vis both North Korea and China, faces particularly acute challenges, but Beijing's growing long-range missile force and increasing power-projection capabilities are reducing the strategic depth Australia has long enjoyed. There is no room for complacency in Canberra. Australia's 2016 Defence White Paper was sober about the uncertain regional security environment, but many of its threat assumptions and capability development timelines look unduly optimistic less than a year after it was published.

Alternative policies such as seeking an accommodation with China, coming to terms with a nuclear-armed North Korea, or pursuing strategic autonomy come with immense costs and risks. Any of these options would mark a seismic rupture with the Asia-Pacific order that has underpinned the region's prosperity and relative stability over the past seventy years (not to mention seriously or irreparably damaging the United States' position in Asia). Each would set in train a cascade of destabilizing realignments or other unintended consequences, including a significantly heightened prospect of nuclear proliferation in Asia.

Nor is anxious handwringing an effective policy, however. So how should policymakers in Japan and Australia respond to the challenges they face, and what role can trilateral strategic cooperation play?

Tokyo and Canberra should sustain — and wherever possible accelerate — their own defence investment programmes. The Australian government should review the planned timelines for introducing vital new capabilities such as F-35 Joint Strike Fighters, replacement submarines, surface warships, missile defence systems, and long-range strike weapons. For its part, Japan should further ramp up defence spending. The NATO standard of 2 per cent of GDP may be a bridge too far, owing to Japan's low starting point (just over 1 per cent of GDP), ingrained pacifism, and the need to manage regional reactions. But a target of 1.5 per cent over a decade is not unreasonable: the Australian government is committed to ramping up from 1.5 to 2 per cent over that interval. By modestly extending the service life of its submarines and surface combatants — say by five years — Tokyo could also rapidly expand its maritime force.[30]

Under Prime Minister Abe's leadership, Japan is stepping up its contribution to the U.S. alliance and to regional and global security more broadly. Japan is shifting to a more proactive maritime strategy, but the Japanese Maritime Self-Defense Force remains constrained in the support it can provide to American and allied forces, while the Japanese coastguard faces legal impediments in responding to coercive Chinese "gray zone" probing in the East China Sea, often by much larger and more capable vessels. Moreover, the realignment of crucial U.S. military facilities on Okinawa remains incomplete and — despite careful management by both sides — a periodic source of domestic contention and diplomatic tension. Even greater efforts are needed to remove the remaining obstacles and ensure the U.S.–Japan alliance reaches its full potential.

Australia has an unmatched record of contributing to U.S.–led coalition military operations and has itself taken the lead in numerous stabilization, peacekeeping, and HADR operations in the South Pacific and Southeast Asia. Like Tokyo, Canberra is also increasing its emphasis on maritime strategy, and it is stepping up its naval and air presence activities in the South China Sea. But it could and should do more. The energy and resource exports to Northeast Asia upon which Australia depends for much of its prosperity pass through the South China Sea. Australia should step up its maritime presence in light of the threat posed to freedom of navigation by China's activities in the region, the international tribunal's July 2016 arbitral award, and other pressures on U.S. military resources. The Australian government should overcome its reluctance to conduct freedom of navigation patrols near contested features in the South China Sea, with American naval backup nearby if necessary. It should also consider its decades old practice of keeping a surface combatant deployed to the Persian Gulf, and instead shift this commitment to the Western Pacific. Canberra should also begin rotating long-range ISR aircraft and Triton high-altitude unmanned aerial vehicles as they come on line. Canberra should also increase the tempo of surveillance flights from Malaysia's Butterworth airbase (to which it has access under the Five Power Defence Arrangements) and explore expanded access arrangements with other Southeast Asian governments such as the Philippines, Singapore, and Vietnam.

Japan and Australia should also ramp up their defence and security cooperation activities with other regional countries, particularly South Korea and India, but also cast their net wide to include Southeast Asian and South Pacific nations. Their efforts are not a substitute for sustained U.S. engagement with the region, but can complement it powerfully; in some cases Asia-Pacific countries may feel more comfortable working with Japan and/or Australia than the United States, if only because their scale is less intimidating. Notwithstanding this, as a result of history, Japan and Australia each have complicated relationships with some of their neighbours. In the case of Japan and South Korea, historical issues such as wartime "comfort women" and nationalist sentiment continue to impede diplomatic relations and vital defence cooperation. The recent signing of an information-sharing agreement between the two countries is a sign their governments understand that data-sharing and integrated missile defence capabilities are vital in the face of increasing missile threats in the region, and that Japan would play a pivotal role in any contingency on the Korean Peninsula through its hosting of U.S. forces. The January 2017 hiccup in Australia's important but historically fraught defence relationship with Indonesia is a reminder that Canberra also faces diplomatic challenges with key neighbours closer to home.[31]

Particularly in light of President Trump's campaign rhetoric, reassuring America's Asia-Pacific allies that he is committed to upholding U.S. security obligations in the region should remain a priority for the administration. His new national security team should build on the progress made over the past two decades in strengthening America's alliances with Japan and Australia. Updating coalition command and control arrangements, increasing interoperability and intelligence-sharing, and ensuring both allies have access to U.S. defence technologies are important objectives. The United States should bring Japan into its consultations with allies about the new "Third Offset" capabilities it is developing to counter anti-access/area denial strategies and give the United States areas of asymmetric advantage over potential adversaries.[32] The United States and Australia should also look for areas where they can start to bring Japan into "Five Eyes" intelligence activities.

The administration should also continue its past two predecessors' policy of encouraging both allies to strengthen their strategic cooperation. Tokyo and Canberra need to intensify their efforts to remove remaining institutional and legal impediments to closer defence and security cooperation. An enhanced Acquisition and Cross-Servicing Agreement was signed in January 2017. During Abe's visit to Australia in February the two prime ministers agreed to conclude a reciprocal access agreement — necessary to provide the legal framework for combined exercises and operations (such as HADR missions) in both countries — by the end of 2017. But progress has been slow.

Finally, the time has come for a step change in U.S.–Japan–Australia trilateral strategic cooperation. Intensifying state-based and non-state threats necessitate more urgent efforts to bolster regional deterrence and war-fighting capabilities, including enhancing interoperability in critical areas. This in turn will help to equip the United States and its Asia-Pacific allies to shape a more benign regional strategic environment — supporting their shared long-term objective of a peaceful and prosperous region underpinned by inclusive regional institutions, open economies, and adherence to the rule of law and important principles and norms such as freedom of navigation.

Achieving this shared goal will require improved trilateral coordination at the policy, strategic, and operational levels. It will demand increased interoperability in key capability areas such as ISR, undersea warfare, missile defence, amphibious operations, logistics, and sustainment. Wherever possible, the United States, Japan, and Australia should seek to employ common platforms and systems — as they are doing with the F-35 Joint Strike Fighter, the Triton high-altitude maritime surveillance drone, and the MH-60 anti-submarine warfare (ASW) helicopter. Over time, however, they should go beyond this and embrace combined capability development and three-way defence industrial collaboration.

The United States, Japan, and Australia also need to intensify trilateral exercises, personnel exchanges, cooperative deployment and — where possible — operations. They should enhance data and communications networking, particularly tactical data-sharing. Networking ISR systems and surveillance platforms can build greater shared maritime domain awareness, strengthen policy alignment, and facilitate combined responses to missile, undersea, surface, cyber, and space-based threats. The three countries should work together to develop interoperable radar capabilities, Aegis combat systems, sonar, and other undersea sensors. Undersea warfare remains an area of advantage for the United States and its advanced allies in the Asia-Pacific, including Japan and Australia. But the growing threat posed by Chinese, Russian, and North Korean submarines in the Pacific (and, in China's case, increasingly the Indian Ocean) can best be countered if the United States, Japan, and Australia — potentially joined by India, South Korea, Singapore, and other countries in due course — develop integrated theatre ASW capabilities and an agreed undersea warfare architecture for the Indo-Pacific region. This should include trilateral ASW exercises and combined development of undersea warfare systems, operating concepts, and tactics.

Trilateral undersea warfare cooperation would not only improve war-fighting capabilities but boost regional deterrence. Trilateral cooperation in amphibious operations, surface warfare, missile defence, space, and cyber would serve a similar purpose. The United States, Japan, and Australia should set the pace. Wherever possible, however, they should seek to engage India, South Korea, Singapore, and other regional partners in building interoperability and networked capabilities.

The existing TSD provides a readymade vehicle to accelerate U.S.–Japan–Australia strategic cooperation. TSD foreign ministers should meet as early as possible to identify priorities and energize their respective bureaucracies. The

Security and Defense Coordination Forum should be upgraded to deputy secretary of defence level, with standing working groups established to pursue closer cooperation in priority areas. During his first year in office, President Trump could convene a leaders-level TSD to set high-level strategy and impel greater progress.

Conclusion

Rising threats, China's growing influence, and the election of President Trump have increased uncertainty among America's Asia-Pacific allies. In this complex and challenging environment, U.S.–Japan–Australia trilateral strategic cooperation can play an important role in deterring threats, reassuring anxious allies, and influencing the Trump administration to remain closely engaged in the Asia-Pacific. Along with the three countries' strong alignment of strategic interests and values, their high-level capabilities are a source of public goods in the region, provide a strong platform for networked security approaches with other partners, and — with a necessary injection of energy and urgency — will help to shape a more peaceful and prosperous Asia-Pacific.

Notes

1. "Remarks by Secretary Carter and Q&A at the Shangri-Dialogue, Singapore", U.S. Department of Defense News Transcript, 5 June 2016 <https://www.defense.gov/News/Transcripts/Transcript-View/Article/791472/remarks-by-secretary-carter-and-qa-at-the-shangri-la-dialogue-singapore>. For a good overview of the origins of trilateral security cooperation in the region, see Michael J. Green, "Strategic Asian Triangles", in *Oxford Handbook of the International Relations of Asia*, edited by Saadia M. Pekkanen, John Ravenhill, and Rosemary Foot (New York: Oxford University Press, 2014), pp. 758–74.

2. Nick Bisley, "Enhancing America's Alliances in a Changing Asia-Pacific: The Case of Japan and Australia", *Journal of East Asian Affairs* 20 (2006): 47–73; Malcolm Cook and Thomas Wilkins, *The Quiet Achiever: Australia-Japan Security Relations* (Sydney: Lowy Institute for International Policy, January 2011); Daisuke Akimoto, "The Japan-Australia Security Alignment: Its Development and the Implications for Regional Integration of the Asia-Pacific", *Electronic Journal of Contemporary Japanese Studies* 13, no. 4 (December 2013); James L. Schoff, "The Evolution of US-Japan-Australia Security Cooperation", in *US-Japan-Australia Security Cooperation: Prospects and Challenges*, edited by Yuki Tatsumi (Washington, DC: The Stimson Center, 2015); Yusuke Ishihara, *Japan-Australia "New Special Relationship"*, NIDS Commentary, no. 44, 4 April 2015 (Tokyo: The National Institute for Defense Studies, 2015); Group Captain Lindsey (Jim) Ghee OAM, *The Australia-Japan Security*

Relationship: Valuable Partnership or Much Ado About Nothing Much? (Canberra: Australian Defence College/Centre for Defence and Strategic Studies, Indo-Pacific Strategy Papers, November 2015).

3. For details, see Andrew Shearer, *Australia-Japan-U.S. Maritime Cooperation: Creating Federated Capabilities for the Asia Pacific* (Washington, DC: Center for Strategic & International Studies, April 2016), pp. 23–24.

4. U.S. Department of Defense, *Asia-Pacific Maritime Security Strategy: Achieving U.S. National Security Objectives in a Changing Environment* (Washington, DC: U.S. Government, 2015).

5. Government of Japan, *National Defense Program Guidelines for FY 2014 and Beyond* (Tokyo: 2013), pp. 10–11.

6. Australian Department of Defence, *2016 Defence White Paper* (Canberra: Australian Government, 2016), paragraphs 5.61–5.63.

7. Phillip Coorey, "Australia, US Cost-sharing Deal on Marines", *Australia Financial Review*, 6 October 2016 <http://www.afr.com/news/politics/australia-us-strike-costsharing-deal-on-marines-20161006-grw32j>.

8. Henry Belot, "Labor Leaders Call for Careful Rethink of US Alliance", ABC News, 16 November 2016 <http://www.abc.net.au/news/2016-11-16/labor-leaders-call-for-careful-rethink-of-us-alliance/8029106>; Bob Carr, "Australia, China and the Lunacy of Trump's Talk of a Trade War", *The Guardian*, 11 November 2016 <https://www.theguardian.com/commentisfree/2016/nov/12/australia-china-and-the-lunacy-of-trumps-talk-of-a-trade-war>; Leigh Sales and Myles Wearring, "Paul Keating Says Australia Should 'Cut the Tag' with American Foreign Policy", ABC News, 11 November 2016 <http://www.abc.net.au/news/2016-11-10/keating-on-american-foreign-policy-after-trump-victory/8015028>; Hugh White, "Trump Pushes Australia toward China", *New York Times*, 9 February 2017 <https://www.nytimes.com/2017/02/09/opinion/trump-pushes-australia-toward-china.html?_r=1>.

9. Greg Miller and Philip Rucker, "This Was the Worst Call by Far: Trump Badgered, Bragged and Abruptly Ended Phone Call with Australian Leader", *Washington Post*, 2 February 2017 <https://www.washingtonpost.com/world/national-security/no-gday-mate-on-call-with-australian-pm-trump-badgers-and-brags/2017/02/01/88a3bfb0-e8bf-11e6-80c2-30e57e57e05d_story.html?utm_term=.a25758a1b125>.

10. Choe Sang-Hun, "Kim Jong-un Says North Korea is Preparing to Test Long-Range Missile", *New York Times*, 1 January 2017 <https://www.nytimes.com/2017/01/01/world/asia/north-korea-intercontinental-ballistic-missile-test-kim-jong-un.html?_r=0>.

11. CSIS, "China's New Spratly Island Defenses", *Asia Maritime Transparency Initiative*, 13 December 2016 <https://amti.csis.org/chinas-new-spratly-island-defenses/>.

12. Ankit Panda, "East China Sea: Japan Protests as Chinese Coast Guard Vessels Enter Disputed Waters", *The Diplomat*, 7 November 2016.

13. U.S. Department of Defense, *Asia-Pacific Maritime Security Strategy*, pp. 12–13.

14. Office of the Secretary of Defense, *Annual Report to Congress: Military and Security Developments Involving the People's Republic of China 2014* (Washington, DC: 2014), p. 9.

15. These include cruise and ballistic missiles designed to strike warships and bases, larger and more sophisticated surface vessels, modern submarines, advanced aircraft and air defences, advanced electronic warfare systems, and offensive systems to counter U.S. advantages in space and cyberspace. For details, see Office of the Secretary of Defense, *Annual Report to Congress*; Toshi Yoshihara and James R. Holmes, *Red Star over the Pacific: China's Rise and the Challenge to U.S. Maritime Strategy* (Annapolis, MD: Naval Institute Press, 2013); Aaron L. Friedberg, *Beyond Air-Sea Battle: The Debate over US Military Strategy in Asia* (London: IISS/Routledge, 2014); Ronald O'Rourke, *China Naval Modernization: Implications for U.S. Navy Capabilities — Background and Issues for Congress* (Washington, DC: Congressional Research Service, 21 December 2015).

16. See Peter A. Sutton and Ryan D. Martinson, *Beyond the Wall: Chinese Far Seas Operations* (Newport, RI: China Maritime Studies Institute, U.S. Naval War College, 2015).

17. Office of the Secretary of Defense, *Annual Report to Congress*, p. 43.

18. See Friedberg, *Beyond Air-Sea Battle*.

19. In reality the rebalance represents continuity with key elements of U.S. grand strategy in Asia; see Michael J. Green, *By More Than Providence: Grand Strategy and American Power in the Asia Pacific Since 1783* (New York: Columbia University Press, forthcoming March 2017).

20. For an account of the rebalance by one of its principal architects, see Kurt M. Campbell, *The Pivot: The Future of American Statecraft in Asia* (New York: Hachette, 2016).

21. For example, the establishment of U.S.–Japan–India and U.S.–Japan–South Korea trilaterals complementing the Trilateral Strategic Dialogue with Australia and Japan.

22. Michael Green, Kathleen Hicks, Mark Cancian, et al., *Asia-Pacific Rebalance 2025: Capabilities, Presence, and Partnerships: An Independent Review of U.S. Defense Strategy in the Asia-Pacific* (Washington, DC: CSIS, January 2016).

23. *Asia-Pacific Rebalance 2025*, VII.

24. See Deputy Secretary of Defense Bob Work, "The Third U.S. Offset Strategy and Its Implications for Partners and Allies", speech to the Center for a New American Security, Washington, DC, 28 January 2015.

25. Kimberly Jane Tan, "Duterte to US: Forget EDCA 'If I Stay Longer'", ABS-CBN News, 25 October 2016 <http://news.abs-cbn.com/news/10/25/16/duterte-to-us-forget-edca-if-i-stay-longer>.

26. Simon Denyer, "On Duterte's Heels, Malaysia is the Next Asian Country to Embrace China", *Washington Post*, 31 October 2016 <https://www.washingtonpost.com/world/asia_pacific/domino-theory-or-hedging-after-the-philippines-now-malaysia-embraces-

china/2016/10/31/d30984ea-9f63-11e6-b74c-603fd6bbc17f_story.html?utm_term=.
b3731ad73f96>.

27. Ellen Chambers, "Malcolm Turnbull's Reluctant Shift on the South China Sea",
CogitASIA, 7 March 2016 <https://www.cogitasia.com/malcolm-turnbulls-reluctant-
shift-on-the-south-china-sea/>.

28. For an account of Trump's views on alliances, see Thomas Wright, *The 2016
Presidential Campaign and the Crisis of US Foreign Policy* (Sydney: Lowy Institute
for International Policy, 2016).

29. Defence spending as a proportion of gross domestic product is contested as a metric
for assessing alliance contributions. But it does convey the underlying investment
asymmetry, however crudely. According to the International Institute for Strategic
Studies' 2015 Military Balance Report, Australia spent only 1.5 per cent of GDP
on defence in 2014, Japan 1 per cent, and the Philippines 0.7 per cent; by contrast
the United States spent 3.3 per cent, and this is likely to increase under the Trump
administration.

30. The author is indebted to the Congressional Research Service's Ronald O'Rourke
for this suggestion.

31. Adam Harvey, "Indonesia Backs Down on Suspension of Military Cooperation with
Australia", ABC News, 5 January 2017 <http://www.abc.net.au/news/2017-01-05/
indonesia-softens-military-suspension-with-australia/8164440>.

32. Currently the Pentagon is engaging the United Kingdom and Australia on its Third
Offset Strategy, but not Japan.

BLURRING THE DISTINCTION BETWEEN *HUAQIAO* AND *HUAREN*: China's Changing Policy towards the Chinese Overseas

Leo Suryadinata

In 2015 there were two important events regarding Beijing's policy towards the Chinese overseas. One was the World Overseas Chinese Businessmen and Industrialists Conference in Beijing and the other was the announcement of the *Huayi* Card, specially designed for foreign citizens of Chinese descent working and residing in China. These events clearly manifest Beijing's "new policy" towards the Chinese overseas. Nevertheless, when examined closely, this policy change can be seen to have taken place much earlier, as reflected in previous events.

This chapter examines both the World Overseas Chinese Businessmen and Industrialists Conference and the *Huayi* Card, and the new policy's impact on the Chinese overseas, with special reference to Southeast Asia. It also explains when and why Beijing began to change its policy towards the Chinese overseas.

Clear Distinction between *Huaqiao* and *Huaren*

Beijing's policy towards Chinese overseas has been changing. During the Deng Xiaoping period, the distinction between *huaqiao* (华侨 Chinese citizens overseas) and *huaren* (华人 foreign citizens of Chinese descent) was quite clear.

After the resurgence of Deng Xiaoping, China promulgated the first PRC Citizenship (Nationality) Law in 1980, that stipulates that China only recognizes single citizenship. Once a Chinese overseas becomes the citizen of another country

LEO SURYADINATA is Visiting Senior Fellow at the ISEAS – Yusof Ishak Institute and Professor (adj.) at the S. Rajaratnam School of International Studies, Nanyang Technological University, Singapore.

voluntarily, he or she ceases to be a citizen of the People's Republic of China. The clear distinction between Chinese nationals and foreigners resolved the historical problem of dual nationality of the Chinese overseas.

Nevertheless, with the modernization of China and globalization, there have been waves of new Chinese migrations, known as *xin yimin*. But the destinations of the new migrants have been developed countries (especially in the West) rather than the developing countries of Southeast Asia (except Singapore). These new migrants proposed that China should revive the dual nationality policy for ethnic Chinese, as such was being practised in the West. The proposal was debated by the China's People's Consultative Body, but the 1980 Chinese Nationality Law remained unamended. Apparently the Chinese government felt the present citizenship law served Beijing's national interests well.

The most striking example of the distinction between China's nationals and foreigners can be seen in Beijing's attitude towards the anti–ethnic Chinese riots that took place in Indonesia in May 1998, which affected many Chinese Indonesians. Looting, burning, and the rape of Chinese women took place, which led to protests against Jakarta by the international Chinese community. However, Beijing did not make any comment or take any action until July 1998, when it stated that it was concerned with the tragic encounters of many Chinese Indonesians and expected that the Indonesian authorities would be able to protect its nationals regardless of their ethnicity.[1]

The reasons for Beijing's inaction in the Indonesian case remain speculative. Some are of the opinion that Beijing wanted to show the world that China would not interfere in the domestic affairs of a foreign country, as those affected for the most part were not Chinese citizens. In addition, Indonesia was friendly to the People's Republic of China (PRC), and was important to Beijing for reasons of international diplomacy. Others argued that Beijing during that time was not yet ready to conduct an active foreign policy. Whatever the reasons, it is clear that China's behaviour followed strictly China's single citizenship policy.

Beijing's Changing Policy

Blurring the Distinction

Beijing's policy towards the Chinese overseas started to change after the 1998 anti–ethnic Chinese riots in Indonesia. The change began in 2001 when Beijing revitalized the Overseas Chinese Affairs Office (OCAO, also known in Chinese as *Qiaoban*) and the Federation of Returned Overseas Chinese Associations (FROCA, also known as *Qiaolian*). FROCA established the honorary positions of "Overseas Advisors" (*haiwai guwen*) and "Overseas Committee Members" (*haiwai weiyuan*) for the Chinese overseas. There were initially only 31 overseas advisors and overseas committee members.[2] But by December 2013 the federation had invited 581 such members, representing 94 countries. The majority of the advisors and committee members are *huaren*, not *huaqiao*. Legally speaking, the semi-official FROCA is for the *huaqiao* on the mainland, but *huaren* have also been included in this group, resulting in some criticism among *huaren* in Southeast Asia and scholars in China.[3]

More significant was the establishment of the Conference of World Federation of Huaqiao Huaren Associations (CWFHHA) by OCAO in the same year (2001). Soon after its establishment, the first conference was held in 2001. By 2014 there had been seven such conferences. In 2012, at the sixth conference, there were 550 participants from 109 countries and areas. By 2014, when the seventh conference was held, there were over 500 participants from 119 countries and areas.[4] At the 2014 conference President Xi Jinping made a speech referring to overseas Chinese as members of the "Zhonghua big family" (中华大家庭). When he addressed the meeting he used the term "haiwai qiaobao" (海外侨胞, overseas compatriots) rather than "haiwai huaren" (海外华人, Chinese overseas),[5] but the fact is that the occasion was the world *huaqiao* and *huaren* conference, not a *huaqiao* gathering.

The change of policy may have been closely linked with the rise of China and the large numbers of Chinese migrants. Beijing started to realize that China had industrialized and been transformed into the "World Factory". It required new markets and raw materials from all over the world. Moreover, China also had surplus capital that needed investment opportunities. Not surprisingly, China has carried out intensive economic activities overseas for the last two decades. In 2013 it proposed its "One Belt, One Road" strategy, which is one way to address its economic problems.

Significantly, overseas Chinese have also been considered as socio-political and economic capital for rising China. In the last few decades a large number of Chinese have migrated to developed countries, and they have become an important asset for China. However, Beijing also views the well-established ethnic Chinese as equally useful. Not surprisingly, China would like to mobilize Chinese overseas, regardless of their citizenship, to serve the national interests of China. The foreign policy behaviour of China since 2006 has shown its changing attitude to the Chinese overseas.

The Solomon Islands

In April 2006 an anti–ethnic Chinese riot took place that resulted in the "exodus" of ethnic Chinese from this Pacific Islands country. A few hundred Chinese, both local citizens and citizens of Taiwan, were affected. Beijing's embassy in nearby Papua New Guinea offered protection and repatriation to these ethnic Chinese, regardless of their citizenship, and more than five hundred of them were flown to Hong Kong and Guangdong to be resettled.[6] It should be noted that the Solomon Islands recognized Taiwan (ROC), and had no diplomatic ties with the PRC. The PRC's actions aimed to show that it was capable of offering protection to and assistance for overseas Chinese, whilst Taiwan had failed to do so. This intervention has been termed the "Solomon Model"[7] by mainland Chinese scholars. Such a model though is unlikely to be applied to the countries of Southeast Asia, as it would be both costly and would affect Beijing's international standing. Nevertheless, the implementation of the "Solomon model" demonstrates a deviation from Beijing's foreign policy of the past. People have begun to wonder whether protecting Chinese overseas regardless of their citizenship is now a norm rather than an exception adopted only when it suits China's national interests.

Beijing Olympics and Tibet

Including *huaren* in the category of *huaqiao* or, at least, linking *huaqiao* and *huaren* in domestic and foreign policy has become more obvious since 2006. In 2007, for instance, the then President of China, Hu Jintao, at one of the Chinese entrepreneurs gatherings, stated that although *huaqiao* and *huaren* were overseas, their "hearts are still linked to the Homeland".[8] He appealed to them to foster the unification of China and Taiwan. The following year, when Beijing hosted the Olympics, the government stressed the concept of the "Chinese Nation", and included *huaren* as part of the Chinese Nation. Beijing appealed to ethnic Chinese all over the world — regardless of their citizenship — to protect the Olympic torch relay, to become Olympic volunteers so that the Beijing Olympics would be successful, and to help "realize the great revival of [the] Chinese Nation".[9]

The success of the Beijing Olympics was crucial for China, as it symbolized the rise of China as a modern and powerful state in the world. The torch relay was part and parcel of the Olympic Games. It was unfortunate that this was linked to the Tibetan issue. In early 2008 an incident occurred that may be seen as a precursor to the troubled run up to the opening of the Beijing Olympics. Following a demonstration on 10 March (the forty-ninth anniversary of the 1959 failed Tibetan uprising) carried out by monks from the various monasteries in Lhasa, large-scale riots spread to the western part of China. This eventually culminated on 14 March 2008 in open attacks on non-ethnic Tibetans and the looting of shops owned by Han Chinese in Lhasa. The problem of Tibet thus regained international attention. This posed a challenge for the Beijing authorities — who refuse to recognize the sovereignty of Tibet.

In Beijing's view, Tibet is part of China, and any attempt to gain independence will not be tolerated. However, the Tibetans-in-exile used the "Olympics Opportunity" to put forward their demands to Beijing. Anti-Beijing demonstrations took place in many countries, especially in the West. Tibetans-in-exile and their supporters were particularly active during the Olympic torch relay from Greece to China, which passed through a number of the world's major cities. Chinese embassies organized *huaqiao* and *huaren* to protect the torch relay, and condemned those who obstructed its smooth journey. It seems that Beijing saw the success of the Olympic Games as not only linked to the prestige of China but also the territorial integrity of the PRC, as the interference came from what it saw as "splitist pro-Tibetan groups" and their supporters. Of course, the PRC also projected the Beijing Olympics as the symbol of success of the Chinese people in general, regardless of their citizenship. Indeed, many *huaren* (including those in Southeast Asia) were enthusiastic in assisting Beijing, and some even served as volunteers to help Beijing during the Olympics.

In recent years this kind of thinking, that is the lumping of *huaqiao* and *huaren* together, has become more obvious in China. The Beijing director of OCAO, Li Yinze, made a speech in April 2012 at the Chinese Chamber of Commerce in Jakarta, urging young Chinese Indonesians to learn "Hanyu" (Han Language) "in order to strengthen their identification with the Chinese Nation".[10] The Chairperson of OCAO, Qiu Yuanping, also gave a speech at the Perhimpunan INTI (Indonesians of Chinese Descent Association). She commented that "The ancestral land [of the Chinese] will never forget the major contribution of the huaqiao huaren overseas, China will always be the strong backer of the people of Chinese descent overseas."[11]

This habit of not differentiating *huaqiao* and *huaren* is worrying. At Beijing's "World Huaqiao Huaren Businessmen and Industrialists Conference", China's top leaders in their speeches referred to "*huashang*" (ethnic Chinese businessmen or foreign businessmen of Chinese descent) as "*qiaoshang*" (Chinese businessmen overseas), ignoring citizenship. They also called *haiwai huaren* (Chinese overseas) as *haiwai qiaobao* (overseas compatriots), attempting to return to past practices.

The World Overseas Chinese Businessmen and Industrialists Conference

China held its first "World Overseas Chinese [huaqiao huaren] Businessmen and Industrialists Conference" (世界华侨华人工商大会) in Beijing on 6–7 July 2015. According to the Chinese report, over three hundred overseas guests from seventy-nine countries and areas participated in the conference, and China's Prime Minister Li Keqiang met them at the People's Great Hall and delivered a speech. The official Chinese report only mentioned the name of a Thai "overseas Chinese businessman",[12] Xie Guoming (Thai name: Dhanin Chearavanont) of the Charoen Pokphand Group (better known as the CP Group), who also made a speech at the conference. No other names of Chinese entrepreneurs were mentioned in the Chinese report. However, from the CCTV video clips of Li Keqiang's speech,[13] one can see that the majority of Chinese tycoons from Southeast Asia were present at the conference.

Beijing's Huashang Conference

This conference was jointly organized by OCAO, the State Council, and China's Overseas Exchange Association. It was held after China proposed its "One Belt, One Road" programme. Wang Xiaotao, the Vice-Chairman of the State Development and Reform Committee, gave a speech entitled "To exhibit the function of *huaqiao huaren*, to assist 'One Belt, One Road' development". The Chairperson of OCAO, Qiu Yuanping, also made a speech, noting that "Overseas Chinese made major contribution to the country where they reside and to China's development; according to incomplete statistics, the capital of overseas Chinese businessmen (*qiaoshang*)[14] were about $5000 billion."[15] She went on to say that "China for huaqiao huaren is the root of the nation, the soul of the culture, and also ... the big stage for them to realize their dreams."

China's Premier Li Keqiang met all the participants and told them:

> 60 million overseas compatriots (*haiwai qiaobao*) are important members of the large Chinese Nation (*Zhonghua minzu*). Generation after generation of *huaqiao* and *huaren*, their feelings are still linked to the homeland, their hearts are tied to Zhonghua,... they have made special and important contributions to the independence and liberation of the Chinese Nation, the reform, opening and modernization of China.[16]

He expressed three expectations from *huaqiao huaren*:

> Firstly, to be the "New Effective Forces" in fostering the economic transformation and development of China, and to widely and deeply participate in the economic construction of China…. Secondly, to build a "Rainbow Bridge" for the economic cooperation between China and foreign countries, so that the "One Belt One Road" constructions will be pushed ahead…. Thirdly, to establish a "New Image" of Chinese entrepreneurs to reflect the traditional good virtue of the Chinese Nation, i.e. to live in harmony with the local population where they live, to be sincere, honest and law-abiding when doing business, and to take social responsibility.[17]

The World Chinese Entrepreneurs Convention

In 1991, international Chinese entrepreneurs, under the leadership of the Chinese Chambers of Commerce and Industry of Singapore, Bangkok, and Hong Kong, established the "World Chinese Entrepreneurs Convention" (WCEC, Shijie Huashang Dahui 世界华商大会). This huashang convention was organized under the initiative of Chinese overseas.[18] Its objective was to foster mutual understanding of international Chinese entrepreneurs, to build Chinese entrepreneurial networks, to foster ethnic Chinese to be integrated into local society (*luodi shenggen* 落地生根), and to contribute to the economy and development of the countries where they resided.[19] This convention, which is held every two years, was first held in Singapore in August 1991. About 800 representatives from 30 countries and 75 cities participated at the event. The convention was held in Chinese and English.

The WCEC convention has provided Chinese entrepreneurs with forums and networks so that they have been able to contribute to the countries where they reside. The convention has been held thirteen times, with the most recent event taking place in September 2015 in Bali, Indonesia. In the short twenty-five years of its existence, two conventions have been held in China; in 2001 in Nanking (Nanjing) and in 2013 in Chengdu. However, it appears that the WCEC convention has not satisfied the needs of a rising China; Beijing felt it necessary to run its own overseas Chinese entrepreneurs conference. The Thai Chinese tycoon Xie Guomin noted that Beijing's conference is "the Diplomacy of Big Country" (*daguo waijiao*).

Indeed, this is the "Diplomacy of Big Country" which aims to serve the interests of China rather than the Chinese overseas. Even prior to the July conference in Beijing, Zhuang Rongwen, the deputy chairman of OCAO, stated that the Beijing conference aimed to establish the organization of international Chinese entrepreneurs to lead the Chinese businessmen overseas to participate in China's development, especially the "One Belt, One Road" programme.[20] Li Keqiang openly admitted that he would like Chinese entrepreneurs to be the "New Effective Forces" (*shengli jun*) of China's economic transformation and development. In other words, it is meant to first serve the interests of China and to establish the new image of Chinese entrepreneurs; mutual wins come second, and the idea of maintaining harmonious relations with local populations comes third.

Apparently he was addressing Chinese nationals, but the majority of the entrepreneurs who participated at the conference were foreign nationals of Chinese descent. To ask foreign nationals to first serve the interests of China appears unreasonable; it would also put some participants in an awkward position. In the same year Beijing also announced a new project that would give Chinese overseas a special green card designed for them.

Huayi *Card*

On 5 December 2015, *Ming Bao*, a major Chinese language daily in Hong Kong, reported that on 27 November 2015, Guo Hong 郭洪, the director of the management committee of the Zhong Guan Cun 中关村 (known as the "Silicon Valley of China", located in Beijing), had made the unexpected announcement of a pilot project known as the *Huayi* Card (*Huayi Ka* 华裔卡) system.[21] According to the announcement, the card would be issued to any qualified person of Chinese origin so that he or she could stay in China as a permanent resident and enjoy almost all the privileges of a Chinese citizen. Possessing the card would be different from having the status of dual nationality, as the cardholder would not have the right to vote in local elections or to run for office.

According to the report the project was introduced because of China's need to recruit more professionals for high technology and economic development. The idea came from the Indian practice of issuing two types of identity cards for Indians overseas, known as Persons of Indian Origin (PIOs) cards and Overseas Citizens of India (OCI) cards.[22] According to the report, after the introduction of these two card systems, as of 2010 some four million OCIs and seven million POIs had returned to India to work.[23]

The report also said that between 1978 and 2005, US$622.4 billion worth of investments were injected into the Chinese economy, of which 67 per cent came from the Chinese overseas. Some 550,000 companies with foreign capital had been registered during the same period, of which 70 per cent were owned by ethnic Chinese. In Zhong Guan Cun there were two million entrepreneurs (*chuangye renshi* 创业人士), but foreign nationals and "returned overseas Chinese" constituted only 1.5 per cent of the total. In California's Silicon Valley, some 36 per cent of entrepreneurs are from overseas.

It was reported that, after the reform era in China, about seven million Chinese had migrated, and there were more than a million Chinese students overseas. The report noted that there were about "60 million overseas Chinese all over the world" as of 2015, of which about four million were entrepreneurs. These are the targets of the *Huayi* Card policy.

In the approximately ten years since China introduced its Green Card permanent residency system, it has issued fewer than ten thousand of them, including to people of Chinese origin. China's appears to be the hardest Green Card in the world to obtain. The *Huayi* Card system is meant to help ease the problem of obtaining some sort of status in China for the Chinese overseas. Many Chinese new migrants in the West would like to have dual nationality status, and the *Huayi* Card is a form of compromise. Some have even argued that the *Huayi* Card is the prelude to the introduction of a dual nationality law in China. The difference between the Green Card and *Huayi* Card is that the former is ethnicity-blind, while the latter is based on ethnicity.

The announcement caused a lot of confusion. Some thought that the *Huayi* Card had already been introduced, but the authorities said that this was not the case, that it would only be a pilot, and that it would be tried out in 2016. Presumably the system would be tested on a small group of foreign Chinese first, and, if the results were promising, would then be implemented on a larger scale.

It seems that Beijing has now started thinking along the lines of ethnicity. Observers may hastily conclude that China is advocating Chinese transnationalism. But the term *huayi* has not been clearly defined. Is the term used to refer to Han Chinese only, or to both Han and non-Han Chinese overseas? In any case, the *Huayi* Card system will have a tremendous impact on the Chinese overseas in Southeast Asia and beyond, as their loyalties to their host countries may come under suspicion. Owing to its sensitivity there were suggestions that the card be tried out in Canada first, where dual nationality is allowed and the issue of Chinese ethnicity is not sensitive.

The *Huayi* Card system was criticized by many observers who understand the Chinese overseas situation, especially in Southeast Asia. In China, Professor Liang Yingming of Peking University commented on its shortcomings and the risks associated with adopting the ethnic principle in issuing permanent residency rights.[24] The Chinese press in Singapore also published reports that were unflattering of the *Huayi* Card.[25] Probably due to such criticism, OCAO has had second thoughts about introducing the system for the moment. The Director of OCAO, Qiu Yuanping, announced on 8 March 2016 that the report concerning the *Huayi* Card was untrue.[26] There was later a similar report that quoted her as saying that OCAO did not have any plans to issue *Huayi* Cards. However, OCAO would amend the existing regulations to make it easier for foreigners of Chinese descent (*waiji huaren*) to obtain permanent resident status and enjoy other facilities in China.[27] In other words, the scheme has been shelved for the time being.

Concluding Remarks

Beijing's "World Huaqiao Huashang Businessmen and Industrialists Conference" cannot be separated from the rise of China. Beijing believes that the realization of "One Belt, One Road" requires the assistance and support of international Chinese entrepreneurs, hence the necessity for such a conference. Perhaps Beijing thought that because the existing "World Chinese Entrepreneurs Convention" was not initiated and controlled by China, it was unable to fulfil China's requirements, and so the country had to establish its own conference. This action creates the impression that Beijing cannot accept the "World Chinese Entrepreneurs Convention" initiated by the Chinese overseas.

More significant than this is Beijing's changing policy towards the Chinese overseas as reflected in the approach and terms used to refer to ethnic Chinese outside China. In the past, *huaqiao* and *huaren* have been widely used to distinguish China's citizens overseas and foreign citizens of Chinese descent. The 1980 Citizenship Law in fact stresses this distinction, and the law remains unamended. However, in recent practice the terms have been used together, and *haiwai huaren* (Chinese overseas) is often replaced with *haiwai qiaobao* (overseas compatriots) in the PRC leaders' speeches. This may have more significant implications for international politics and diplomacy. China should respect ethnic Chinese who have become foreign nationals. Otherwise, foreign citizens of Chinese descent would always come under suspicion by the people of their adopted country — especially in Southeast Asia — of still being loyal to China and not to their adopted country. In the long run this would be in the interests of neither China nor ethnic Chinese, as it would raise ethnic tension and destabilize Southeast Asia.

The introduction of this policy has not yet led to an official response from any Southeast Asian government, as they are currently busy with their own problems and economic development. China, as an economic power, is able to help many Southeast Asian states in temporarily solving domestic economic problems, including infrastructure development. However, when there is an economic crisis, Southeast Asians may refocus their attention on the Chinese minorities again.

Notes

1. For a brief discussion of Beijing's attitude towards the 1998 anti-Chinese violence, see Leo Suryadinata, "Postscript", *China and the ASEAN States: The Ethnic Chinese Dimension* (Singapore: Marshall Cavendish, 2005); See also Shee Poon Kim, "China Responses to the May 1998 Anti-Chinese Riots in Indonesia", *EAI Working Paper*, no. 37, 24 March 2000.
2. <http://www.guojiribao.com/shtml/gjrb/20131209/141504.shtml> (accessed 2 April 2015).
3. The most outspoken critics have been scholars from Peking University; namely, the late Professor Zhou Nanjing and Professor Liang Yingming. Both are returned overseas Chinese from Indonesia.
4. The 7th Conference for Friendship of Overseas Chinese Associations, *People's Daily*, 7 June 2014 <http://www.chinaqw.com/z/2014/sjhqhrstlydh/index.html>.
5. "Xi Jinping Meets with the Seventh World Chinese Friendship Organization" <http://pic.people.com.cn/n/2014/0607/c1016-25116878.html> (accessed 23 July 2015).
6. For a study of the event, see Grace Chew Chye Lay, "The April 2006 Riots in the Solomon Islands", *CHC Bulletin*, 7 May and 8 November 2006, pp. 11–21.
7. The term "Solomon Model" (*Suo-luo-men moshi*) was used in an article written by a PRC scholar. See Hao Mengfei, "Qiaomin liyi, lingshi baohu, guojia liyi" [Citizen's interest, consul's protection, national interest], in *Zhongguo guojia liyi yu yingxiang* [China's national interests and influence], edited by Hu Jia (Beijing: Shishi chubanshe, 2006), p. 152.
8. "Hu Jintao haozhao huaqiao huaren wei tongyi gongtong fendou [Hu Jintao urged huaqiao and huaren to jointly strive for unification]", 2 June 2007 <http://hk.crntt.com/crn-webapp/doc/docDetailCreate.jsp?coluid=7&kindid=0&docid=100392804>.
9. For a brief discussion on the Olympics and China, see Leo Suryadinata, "A New Orientation in China's Policy towards Chinese Overseas? Beijing Olympic Games Fervour as a Case Study", *CHC Bulletin*, no. 12 (November 2008): 1–4; Yong Pow Ang, "Angry China Fuels Fear", *CHC Bulletin*, no. 12 (November 2008): 5–6.
10. Beijing shi qiaoban zhuren Li Yinze fang Yinni jianghua yinqi qiaojie buan [The speech of Beijing Qiaoban director Li Yinze caused worries among the Chinese community]", *Guoji Ribao*, 21 April 2012.
11. See *Guoji Ribao*, 19 September 2014.
12. The term used is "*Qiaoshang*" (侨商), not *Huashang* (华商), indicating that he is a *huaqiao* (Chinese national residing overseas). In fact he is a *huaren* (foreign citizen of Chinese descent).

13. "Li Keqiang Will Meet with the Representatives of the Inaugural Overseas Chinese Merchant Conference [新闻联播] 李克强会见首届华侨华人工商大会全体代表], CCTV, 7 June 2015 <http://www.yangshi13.com/cctv/xinwenlianbo/2015/0706/28389.html>.

14. The original meaning of "*Qiaoshang*" is compatriot businessmen.

15. "The First Overseas Chinese Conference Opened with Overseas Chinese Capital of over USD 5 Trillion", Guancha.cn, 7 July 2015 <http://www.guancha.cn/Industry/2015_07_07_325893.shtml>.

16. "Li Keqiang Meets with All the Representatives of the First World Chinese Chamber of Commerce and Industry", *SZnews*, 7 July 2015 <http://www.sznewscom/content/2015-07/07/content_11861357.htm>.

17. Ibid.

18. The common secretariat was established in these three Chinese Chambers of Commerce in rotation. The term of the secretariat is six years.

19. Welcome address by Mr Tan Eng Joo at the first World Chinese Entrepreneurs Convention: A Global Network (首届世界华商大会专辑：环球网络), Singapore Chinese Chamber of Commerce and Industry, 10–12 August 1991, pp. 18–19.

20. "The First Overseas Chinese Business Conference will be held in Beijing in July", *Chinanews*, 29 June 2015 <http://www.chinanews.com/hr/2015/06-29/7372290.shtml>.

21. See "Zhongguo shixing huayi ka, zhenshi chengren shuangchong guoji 中国试行 "华裔卡" 真实承认双重国籍 [China's implementation of the "Green cards for those of Chinese origin" is an act of recognizing dual citizenship]", *MingPaoCanada*, 5 December 2015 <http://www.mingpaocanada.com/tor/htm/News/20151205/taa1_r.htm>. The discussion in this section is mainly based on this report.

22. For Chinese studies on PIO and OCI, see Zhang Yinglong (张应龙) and Huang Chaohui (黄朝辉), Yindu qiaomin zhengce yanjiu 印度侨民政策研究 [A study of Indian national policy], in *jingwai huaren guoji wenti taolunji* 境外华人国籍问题讨论辑, edited by Zhou Nanjing 周南京 (Hong Kong, 2005), pp. 290–311; Qiu Li Ben 丘立本, "Yindu Guoji yimin yu qiaowu gongzuo de lishi yu xianzhuang 印度国籍与侨务工作的历史与现状 [Indian citizenship and overseas Chinese affairs: Past and present], *Huaqiao huaren lishi yanjiu* 华侨华人历史研究 [Overseas Chinese historical studies], no. 1 (March 2012): 24–35. According to these studies the Indian government introduced the PIO card in March 1999 and the OCI card in January 2003. Both cards have a common feature, i.e., the cardholders do not have political rights in India. The PIO card was merged into the OCI card on 9 January 2015. See Indian Ministry of Home Affairs announcement at <http://mha1.nic.in/pdfs/Merge_PIO_OCI.pdf> (accessed 5 February 2016).

23. The *Ming Bao* report (see note 21) cited figures of forty million OCI and seventy million POI, which seem unrealistically high.

24. "Beida jiaoshou liang yingming: zhongguo yao lizhi kandai haiwai huaren lichang 北大教授梁英明：中国要理智看待海外华人立场 [PKU Professor Liang Yingming:

China should treat overseas Chinese with rational attitude]", *Lianhe Zaobao* 《联合早报》, 22 February 2016.

25. For instance, "Bendi xuezhe: mohu huaqiao huaren jiexian 本地学者：模糊华侨华人界限 [Local scholars: Blur the boundaries of overseas Chinese]", *Lianhe Zaobao*, 《联合早报》, 19 February 2016.

26. "Qiu Yuanping huiying qiaojie guanzhu redian: Huayika baodao bushushi, 裘援平回应侨界关注热点：“华裔卡”报道不属实 [Qiu Yuanping responds to overseas Chinese concern: "Chinese card" report is not true]", *Chinanews*, 10 March 2016 <http://www.chinanews.com/gn2016/03-10/7792404>.

27. "Guowuyuan qiaoban zhuren Qiu Yuanping: muqian hai wei kaolii chutai huayika 国务院侨办主任裘援平：目前还未考虑出台华裔卡 [Qiu Yuping, director of the Overseas Chinese Affairs Office of the State Council: Has not yet considered the introduction of Chinese cards], *China Daily* <http://cn.chinadaily.com.cn/.../2016/content_23844522 ht...>.

Brunei Darussalam

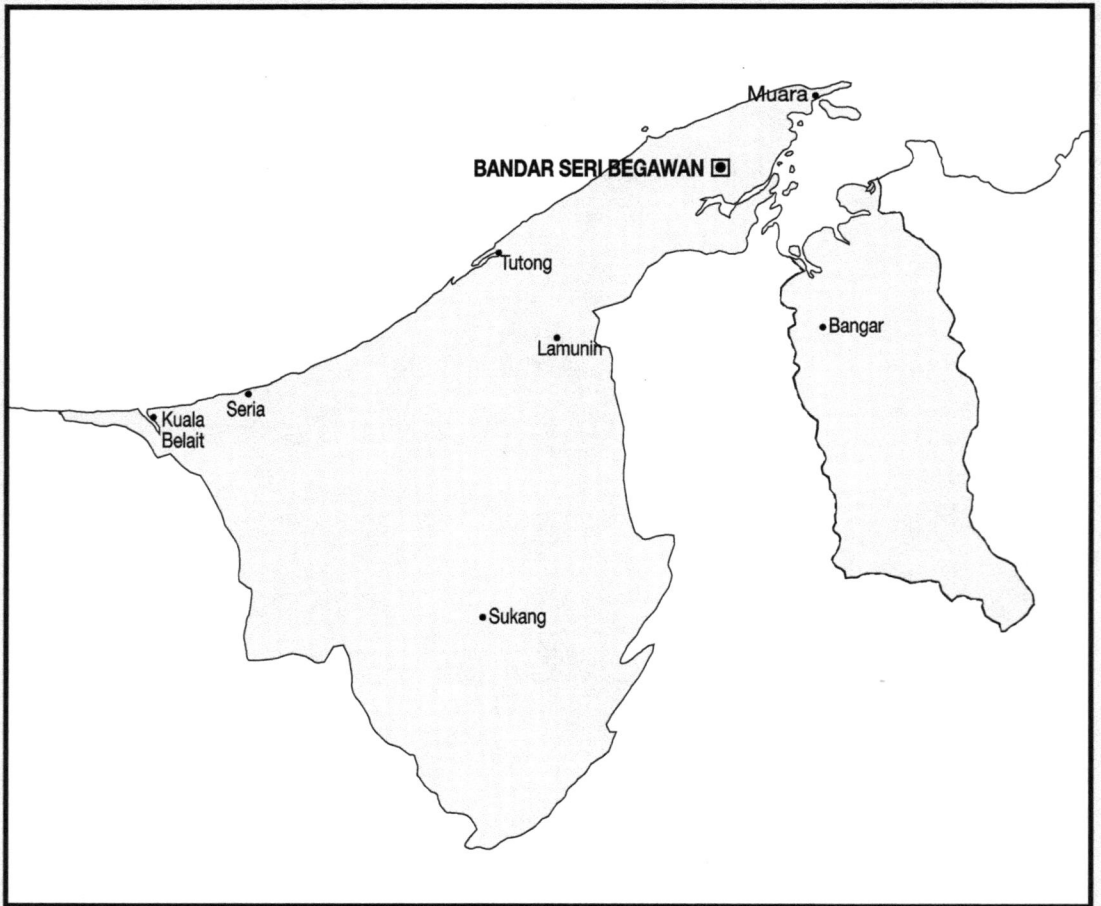

BRUNEI DARUSSALAM IN 2016:
Adjusting to Economic Challenges

Asiyah az-Zahra Ahmad Kumpoh

Following the global drop in oil prices for three consecutive years, economic developments during 2016 demonstrated the fact that Brunei was adjusting well to the challenging economic environment. Oil and gas exports traditionally account for 65 per cent of the country's gross domestic product (GDP) and for more than 90 per cent of government revenue. Due to the prolonged period of low oil prices, the country's trade deficit was about B$2 billion in 2015, and by October 2016 total national exports stood at B$545.5 million, a decrease of 12.1 per cent from the figure in the same month in 2015.[1]

However, Brunei was fortunate that the pace of contraction was moderated as production output generated a 3.6 per cent rebound in GDP,[2] mainly contributed by liquefied natural gas exports, which increased by 13.6 per cent in October 2016. However, as the non-oil and gas industrial sector's contribution to GDP decreased, Brunei's projected GDP growth for 2016 is only at 1 per cent,[3] one of the slowest growing economies in Southeast Asia.

Better Economic Climate

The government has long acknowledged the country's dependency on the energy industry, simultaneously recognizing the urgent need for fiscal and structural policy reforms to strengthen and diversify the economy. In His Majesty Sultan Haji Hassanal Bolkiah's New Year *Titah*, the monarch announced the formation of a Foreign Direct Investment and Downstream Industry Committee, which is

ASIYAH AZ-ZAHRA AHMAD KUMPOH is Lecturer in History and International Studies, Faculty of Arts and Social Sciences, Universiti Brunei Darussalam.

tasked essentially to carry out reforms to create a competitive business environment conducive for foreign investment.[4] The monarch also approved the establishment of a Small and Medium Enterprise Centre to support the development of local businesses and nurture entrepreneurs.

The monarch further made it clear that policy reforms should deliver measurable results, and for this reason he authorized the adoption of the Brunei Vision 2035 Framework to monitor and evaluate the country's progress in achieving Vision 2035's main objectives of producing an educated and highly skilled population with a good quality of life as well as a dynamic and sustainable economy. This in many ways makes economic diversification efforts imperative.

Since the cabinet reshuffle in October 2015 there have been remarkable changes in government delivery and in the country's focus on the diversification of the economy. The national budget was among the first fiscal adjustments, with a cut of 1.78 per cent from the 2015/16 budget being made for 2016/17. A figure of B$5.6 billion was allocated for the budget, and the monarch stressed that it needed to be supported by tight spending controls and aggressive efforts to transform the national economy into a diversified, dynamic, and sustainable one. The main focus areas for the financial year relevant to Brunei Vision 2035 include improvement in the country's productivity and capacity building for human capital and public welfare.[5] Similarly, infrastructure projects that will assist the government's efforts in improving the business environment received an allocation of B$523.56 million.

Enablers for Economic Growth and Diversification

In 2016, 80 per cent of the country's exports were from the oil and gas industry. Long-term supply contracts with various countries and industrial entities cushioned the aggressive fluctuations in global energy demands. In October 2016 the highest share of exports went to Japan and South Korea, with these two countries receiving 33.8 per cent and 27.2 per cent of total major exports, respectively.[6]

Despite falling oil prices, existing partners in this field continued to seek opportunities and create new mechanisms to assist the oil industry. Weatherford International, which has been offering technical support services to Brunei oil companies for thirteen years, remained committed to maintaining its presence in the country.[7] Similarly, new investors have also been incorporated in the industry. In September 2016, Korean Register Brunei was endorsed to provide third-party inspection services and certification in the oil and gas industry. The availability of these services will improve the industrial ecosystem of the country.[8]

Infrastructure Investments

In recent years there have been calls for increased infrastructure investment, primarily to support diversification efforts and deal with the challenges that the Brunei economy faces. In 2016 the government sharpened its focus on a number of major infrastructure projects. One such project is the High-Voltage Electricity Transmission Line in Kuala Belait District, which will cost B$300 million.[9] The completion of the project will not only ensure an adequate supply of electricity to the population but will also support Brunei's efforts to conserve the usage of natural resources, including natural gas. Equally important is the fact that the reliability of the electricity supply upon completion of the project will improve Brunei's ranking in key indicators that rate the business environment.

Another major push in infrastructure investment has been the construction of the 2.7-kilometre Pulau Muara Besar Bridge through a B$204 million contract awarded to China Harbour Engineering in 2015. The construction of the bridge — expected to be completed in 2018 — is critical to strengthening industrial and logistical efficiency and overall management of personnel, raw materials, utilities, and export products between the mainland and the island.[10] The completion of the bridge is even more important in view of the construction of a US$4 billion crude oil refinery and petrochemical plant in Pulau Muara Besar, initiated by the Brunei Economic Development Board with its joint-venture partner, Zhejiang Hengyi Group. The project covers 260 hectares and is expected to "produce eight million tonnes of by-products per year including aromatics, gasoline and diesel, providing enough fuel to meet local demand".[11]

The Temburong Bridge Construction Project is considered the country's most significant large-scale modernization project. The 30-kilometre bridge, costing B$1.6 billion, will connect Brunei-Muara District and Temburong District, which will not only facilitate better connectivity between the two districts but is also aimed at realizing the immense potential for tourism that the country possesses.[12]

Foreign Direct Investment

The liberalization of foreign direct investment (FDI) has been an integral part of the country's economic policy reforms. In 2016 a total FDI value of US$4.7 billion was recorded, with foreign companies operational across industries including business services, pharmaceuticals, downstream oil and gas, creative industries, and the halal industry.[13] This was a notable increase in overseas investment in the country compared to figures from the previous years.

Among the contributors to the increase in FDI are the Brunei–Guangxi Economic Corridor projects that were implemented in April 2016. Guangxi's projects in Brunei have a contractual investment value of US$8.8 million, while Brunei has invested in six projects in Guangxi with a total value of about US$11 million.[14] In July 2016 the Guangxi-based aquaculture company, Hiseaton Food, was awarded a partnership with a government-linked company to establish the joint venture Hiseaton Fisheries, which will operate an offshore aquaculture farm. The government expects the project — which will require two thousand hectares of the country's offshore aquaculture sites — to provide local employment. A memorandum of understanding (MOU) was also signed with electric vehicle manufacturer Shenglong Energy Automobile to boost bilateral trade through the development of a manufacturing and assembly plant for electric and renewable-energy vehicles.[15] Guang Zhongli Enterprise, a Quangxi-based company, would like to leverage on the Brunei halal brand and certification to produce processed oyster products. As a result, China's investments in Brunei increased ninefold to US$86 million in just the first half of 2016.[16]

Chinese companies outside the Brunei–Guangxi projects were also eyeing potential collaboration and investment opportunities in Brunei's market. Some have been very successful in their joint ventures with local companies, as demonstrated by a Guangdong-based company that has been running a joint venture with a Brunei conglomerate since 2009 under the name of Biomarine, investing in deep-sea fishing.[17] China Telecom Global Ltd, one of China's biggest telecom operators, partnered with Telekom Brunei Berhad in April 2016 specifically to provide reliable connectivity and telco services to Chinese enterprises in Brunei and Bruneian investors in China.[18]

Such collaborations have been welcomed by Brunei, as these will ensure the development and sustainability of the industries without creating too much dependence on the government. In fact, Brunei has allowed the establishment of the Chinese Enterprise Association in Brunei (CEAB), which is a new association for Chinese FDI and joint ventures. For China, the establishment of CEAB is in line with the "go-abroad" strategy of the government, whereas Brunei will gain tremendously as the CEAB will promote sustainable development in the non-energy sectors of the economy.[19]

South Korea is another important source of FDI for Brunei. During the Brunei–Korea Investment Promotion Forum, held in July 2016, South Korea pledged its support for Brunei's economic diversification initiatives. It has established contact with various economic sectors in Brunei in order to explore business and investment cooperation opportunities. South Korea has identified several key areas to develop, including ICT, cosmetics, biotechnology, and e-commerce.[20] More importantly, South Korea is extremely keen to establish public and private sector partnerships to develop financial technology (fintech) applications in the country.[21] Brunei has generally welcomed South Korean efforts, as the government is sharpening its focus on capital markets as an alternative source of financing. Fintech will improve efficiency and transparency as well as promote financial inclusion.[22]

Even the long-established foreign companies in Brunei support the country's economic diversification programmes. Mitsubishi Corporation, which has been in Brunei since the 1960s, has in the past ventured into new business opportunities in the solar and agricultural sectors. In October 2016 the first commercial biotechnology facility, run by Mc Biotech, a subsidiary of Mitsubishi Corporation, was officially launched. The government considers the facility its first step towards embracing developments in industrial biotechnology.[23]

Japan has also expressed interest in exploring potential areas of cooperation in fisheries and solar power generation. Brunei has always been seen as attractive, not only to Japanese investors but also to other overseas investors, because of its relatively low utility prices and the country's geographic accessibility to other ASEAN countries.[24]

Russia also has the potential to be a major player in Brunei's economy in the future. Brunei's trade relations with Russia have resulted in an encouraging bilateral trade volume in the energy sector of a total value of US$25 million in 2015. Russian companies have also explored opportunities to enhance economic cooperation in many sectors, including biotechnology, agriculture, tourism, infrastructure, and poultry farming. Several agreements have been signed between local and Russian companies in the areas of electronic trading and logistics.[25]

The desire to learn best practices in economic diversification also led to the signing of the Framework Cooperation Agreement and an MOU between Brunei and Costa Rica. Costa Rica might not seem an obvious choice, but Brunei appreciates the country's experience in overcoming its economic crisis and consequently transforming into a greatly diversified economy. Hence, Brunei is keen to learn from and work together with Costa Rica, particularly in the renewable energy sector, and to extend cooperation with it in other areas, including the technical, scientific, and cultural sectors.[26]

Brunei has also paid closer attention to policies that ensure inclusiveness and sustainability of economic growth. The full enactment of the 2013 Securities Markets Order and the 2015 Securities Markets Regulations in February 2016 laid the foundation for the twenty-first century capital market that offers alternative sources of finance to support business expansion and innovation. On 4 March

2016, Autoriti Monetari Brunei Darussalam (AMBD) became a full signatory to the International Organization of Securities Commissions Multilateral MOU. As a result, AMBD now has the tools for the regulatory enforcement of the securities markets and for enhancing cooperation and information sharing between signatories to the MOU. AMBD has also produced the Brunei Darussalam 10 Years Financial Sector Blueprint 2016–2025, where it has earmarked Islamic Finance as the key industry to be developed and elevated.[27]

Accordingly, Brunei's own stock exchange will be established in 2017 with the aim of boosting the financial industry and increasing its proportion of the country's GDP. Since April 2016, Brunei has issued over B$10.4 billion worth of Sukuk Al-Ijarah securities, which has put the country alongside Indonesia and Malaysia as major issuers of Islamic financial instruments.[28]

Ease of Doing Business

Brunei considered the Trans-Pacific Partnership (TPP) as one of the keys to its economic diversification efforts. As one of the original signatories of the regional trade agreement, and the fact that Brunei had indicated its intention to ratify the TPP within two years,[29] Brunei has been committed to reviewing existing legislation to ensure the compliance of national policies with international standards. Legislation dealing with institutional capacity, labour standards, environmental standards, intellectual property, and transparency laws are among those that have been revised and/or are currently under revision.[30]

Hence, 2016 saw the country exerting greater efforts to improve the business environment for all business sectors, including small and medium enterprises (SMEs) and overseas investors. In the World Bank's 2016 Doing Business report, Brunei was placed 84th out of 189 countries. The report highlighted three major barriers to business in the country: government bureaucracy, labour regulations, and access to financing. Consequently, throughout 2016 the Energy and Industry Department of the Prime Minister's Office introduced key reforms to address these major barriers. The Ease of Doing Business Initiatives, for instance, aim to reform regulations pertaining to cross-border trading, protection of minority investors, tax payment, insolvency, and starting a business.[31] Significant steps to minimize unnecessary bureaucratic procedures and improve business set-up were introduced and implemented effectively. In August 2016 Brunei's IT start-up incubation programme, iCentre, was revitalized; it has now adopted a flexible "open space" approach that allows non-IT types of businesses and aspiring entrepreneurs to seek business mentoring. Local entrepreneurs may also approach the iCentre if they need working space.[32]

Two new statutory bodies have been created to encourage economic growth beyond the oil and gas industry. These are Darussalam Enterprise (DARE), which aims to provide a platform for better facilitation of support systems, and the Foreign Direct Investment and Downstream Industry Committee, to facilitate the approval of investment processes. The Microcredit Financing Scheme was introduced in October 2016 to address the lack of access to financing. It will provide viable access to funding for micro and small enterprises.

To further improve the business environment by streamlining procedures, the Ministry of Home Affairs announced in February 2016 the exemption of the requirement for a business licence for seven business activities under the Business Licence Act. The exempted activities are eateries, lodging houses or public resorts, motor vehicle dealers, petrol stations, timber stores, furniture factories, retail stores, and workshops.[33] In May 2016 the New Companies Act was introduced to protect minority shareholders in a company[34] — it aims to facilitate prudent management to help companies achieve and sustain success.

In addition to DARE, other new agencies have been established to support policy reforms. The Foreign Direct Investment Action and Support Center was established to facilitate a clear and efficient process for FDI in Brunei.[35] A Collateral Registry System was introduced in August 2016 to centralize movable properties or assets and secure loans for them.[36] In many ways this is to ensure that SMEs will have better access to financing. In December 2016, Bank of China officially opened in the country. It is expected that the establishment of the first Chinese financial institution will facilitate and serve FDI development, particularly considering that China is one of the biggest investors in the country.[37]

By the third quarter of 2016, reform policies had started to show encouraging results. There was a significant improvement in the country's business environment indicators. In August 2016, Brunei signed an MOU with the Asian Development Bank (ADB) that paved the way for its classification as a graduated developing member country. The agreement supports the country's efforts to promote the development of the private sector, including financial services and small and medium enterprises. In line with the country's strategic development plans for Vision 2035, Brunei and the ADB will continue to cooperate in various sectors, including knowledge creation, capacity development, education, private sector development, diversification of exports, improving the investment climate, environmental protection, and regional economic cooperation.[38]

In September 2016, Brunei was ranked 58th out of 138 countries in the benchmark index that rates the competitiveness of world economies.[39] The 2016–17 Global Competitiveness Report also identified barriers to business similar to those highlighted in the 2016 Doing Business report. As government initiatives have sought to drive greater business reform and improve the country's global competitiveness, Brunei scored significant improvements in the World Bank's 2017 Doing Business report, particularly in the indicator for Getting Electricity (ranked 21st), Resolving Insolvency (57th), Getting Credit (62nd), Enforcing Contracts (93rd), and Protecting Minority Investors (102nd). Overall, the 2017 Doing Business report has ranked Brunei at 72 out of the 190 economies worldwide.[40]

For Brunei, meeting global benchmarks is crucial, as the above indicators are widely referenced by international investors. A conducive business environment in Brunei will also facilitate integration with its regional partners in the ASEAN Economic Community.

In addition, Brunei has conducted a thorough review of its intellectual property rights policy to ensure local policy is compatible with the requirements of the TPP. A fruitful outcome of the review was Brunei's decision to join the Madrid System for trademark registration and management. Starting in January 2017, foreign companies and trademark owners can submit applications to the system in order to protect their marks when introducing their products and services in the country.[41]

Domestic Politics

In 2016 there were frequent calls for the Bruneian people to maintain peace and stability, particularly in view of the challenging realities of the global economy and politics. Such calls were clearly emphasized in many of His Majesty Sultan Haji Hassanal Bolkiah's *Titahs* in 2016. In his New Year *Titah*, His Majesty cautioned the nation against " 'intellectual weaponry' in the form of corrupted ideologies and ways of thinking".[42] At the end of 2016, His Majesty repeated this message to Bruneians living overseas so that they would be more vigilant of dubious groups or gatherings that espoused principles that differed from those of the government.[43]

His Majesty also stressed that the nation should pursue the ideals of solidarity and harmony as prerequisites for peace and stability, which then in turn would be prerequisites for successfully counterbalancing economic slowdown.[44] In relation to this, potential threats to domestic stability that could emerge from the uncertain economic climate have been identified and dealt with by the government. One potential threat is youth unemployment. Reaching 25.3 per cent in 2014,[45] youth unemployment has been identified as a key cause of the rising crime rate in the country.[46] This has become an increasingly critical national issue for Brunei, as it is closely associated with the economic slowdown that has no definite end in sight.

Hence, the monarch called for youth empowerment in July 2016, strongly urging young people to become more involved in entrepreneurship.[47] The call is without doubt a two-pronged approach. Not only will it generate employment growth, as young people, particularly the unemployed, will be encouraged to go into business. But it will also eventually train them to equally shoulder the responsibilities to drive the country's economic recovery.

Capability Enhancement and Fostering Security Relationships

National security is a fundamental responsibility of the government. Since the release of the government's 2011 Defence White Paper, Brunei has become even more committed to promoting a favourable strategic regional environment and guarding the region against threats and challenges, particularly in the wake of the 9/11 attacks and the Bali bombings. As the second-highest per capita defence spender in ASEAN — with an allocation of B$564 million for the 2016/17 fiscal year, an increase of 4.7 per cent over the allocation for 2015/16 — Brunei is prepared to assume a greater role in promoting a positive strategic environment in the region and sound relations with its neighbours and strategic partners.

As outlined in the 2011 Defence White Paper, Brunei's defence policy objectives, among others, are to:

> monitor the strategic environment to ensure the early identification of both specific events and longer term trends that may impact upon the nation's security, protect national interests in adjacent maritime areas, the protection of marine and seabed resources, and fulfilling obligations to provide security for international movements, and to strengthen effective command and operational coordination arrangements with other national security agencies with particular emphasis on crisis response and management of transnational challenges.[48]

In accordance with these guidelines, in 2016 Brunei actively fostered security relationships with ASEAN members as well as its strategic partners, particularly the United States. This year marked the fortieth anniversary of Brunei–Singapore defence relations, and in August 2016 the two countries signed an MOU allowing their defence and security agencies to explore collaboration in key areas of defence technology to enhance existing security and intelligence cooperation. In October 2016, Brunei and Indonesia conducted their seventeenth joint naval exercise, codenamed Helang Laut 178.

In May 2016 the capability of the Brunei Royal Armed Forces as co-chair of the expert workshop group on maritime security was put to the test when it co-hosted the Maritime Security and Counter Terrorism Field Training Exercise with its longstanding security and defence counterpart, the Singapore Armed Forces. The multilateral training exercise is considered to be one of the largest in the region, and the first maritime security and counterterrorism exercise under the framework of the ASEAN Defence Ministers' Meeting (ADMM) and their eight dialogue partners (i.e., the ADMM-Plus).[49] With the main objectives of strengthening regional capacities and enhancing interoperability among the ADMM-Plus member countries, the training exercise involved over three thousand personnel from the eighteen participating countries.

To strengthen further operational coordination arrangements, Brunei participated in one of the world's largest international maritime warfare exercises — Rim of the Pacific Exercise (RIMPAC) — in June–July 2016. In November 2016, Brunei and the United States participated in the twenty-second annual Cooperation Afloat Readiness and Training (CARAT), a bilateral annual military exercise.

While the military exercises focus on the enhancement of interoperability in the Asia Pacific, they are also a testament to the defence cooperation between Brunei and its co-hosts and the strong cooperative relationships that exist between the participating countries, despite the complex nature of the exercises. More importantly, the success of the exercises is an illustration of Brunei's capability and preparedness to counter security and defence threats.

City of Culture, 2016-17

In August 2016, at the 7th Meeting of the ASEAN Ministers Responsible for Culture and Arts, Bandar Seri Begawan was declared ASEAN City of Culture for 2016–17. Brunei welcomed the declaration, as it will assist the promotion and protection of culture and the arts in ASEAN. From now until August 2017, Brunei will need to play a major role in showcasing the region's heritage and traditions, and in promoting cultural diversity and intercultural dialogues among the ASEAN members and dialogue partners.

Brunei also views the declaration as a sound opportunity to promote better governance in the country's tourism industry. Tourism Order 2016 was introduced in October 2016 to allow for the establishment of the Brunei Tourism Board, the licensing of travel agents and tour guides, and the registration of tourist accommodation premises.[50] The new Tourism Order was welcomed by local tour operators as they had been facing competition from unlicensed operators unfamiliar with Brunei's sites, culture, and history.[51] There was a steady growth in the number of international arrivals in 2015 — over four million — an increase of 4.5 per cent from 2014.[52] Furthermore, through the Ministry of Primary Resources and Tourism, the country has been working on initiatives and strategies to strengthen tourism security, improve public transport accessibility, and incorporate the use of ICT in marketing and promotions.

Brunei on the Right Track

The policy reforms introduced by the Brunei government in 2016 were a wake-up call for the Brunei people. As information was disseminated on the ground, the population gradually understood that the future of Brunei's economy should no longer lie completely with the traditional energy industry. As evident from the above discussion, developments in 2016 have laid a foundation for the growth of the non-energy sectors. The year 2016 also saw the government sharpen its focus on the development of small and medium-sized enterprises by creating an increasingly pro-business environment, including the provision of better access to financing. The reforms have also made Brunei a much more regulated market, which has moved the country closer to meeting the baseline in international environmental and labour standards, as required by the TPP agreement. If this gives confidence to overseas investors, Brunei would be on the right — and fast — track to establishing a dynamic, sustainable economy by 2035.

Notes

1. Department of Economic Planning and Development, Prime Minister's Office, Brunei Darussalam, "International Merchandise Trade", n.d. <http://www.depd.gov.bn/SitePages/InternationalMerchandiseTrade.aspx>.
2. Department of Economic Planning and Development, Prime Minister's Office, Brunei Darussalam, "National Statistics", n.d. <http://www.depd.gov.bn/SitePages/National%20Statistics.aspx>.
3. Asian Development Bank, *Asian Development Outlook 2016 Update* (Manila: Asian Development Bank, 2016), p. xxi.
4. Rabiatul Kamit, "HM Reveals Crucial Reforms to Diversify the Economy", *Brunei Times*, 1 January 2016.
5. "Budget Allocation for Financial Year 2016/2017", Radio Television Brunei, 22 March 2016 <http://www.rtbnews.rtb.gov.bn/index.php?option=article&id=Abudget-allocation-for-the-financial-year-20162017&Itemid=80>.
6. Department of Economic Planning and Development, Prime Minister's Office,

Brunei Darussalam, "International Merchandise Trade", n.d. <http://www.depd.gov. bn/SitePages/InternationalMerchandiseTrade.aspx>.

7. Aaron Wong, "Weatherford International to Maintain Presence in Brunei", *Brunei Times*, 4 March 2016.

8. Aaron Wong, "S Korean Technical Consultancy Firm for O&G Opens Brunei Base", *Brunei Times*, 22 September 2016.

9. Rabiatul, "HM Reveals Crucial Reforms".

10. "Construction of Pulau Muara Bridge", Radio Television Brunei, 6 May 2015 <http:// www.rtbnews.rtb.gov.bn/index.php?option=article&id=3Aconstruction-of-the-pulau-muara-besar-bridge&Itemid=106>.

11. Danial Norjidi, "US$4B Hengyi Refinery to go on Stream in '19", *Borneo Bulletin*, 27 February 2016.

12. Oxford Business Group, *The Report: Brunei Darussalam 2016*, 2016 <https://www. oxfordbusinessgroup.com/overview/distinct-advantages-focusing-key-niches-increase-tourism-receipts>.

13. Prime Minister's Office, Brunei Darussalam, "US$4.7b Worth of FDI Projects in Implementation Stage", 28 October 2016 <http://www.ei.gov.bn/Lists/ Industry%20News/NewDispForm.aspx?ID=263&ContentTypeId=0x0100585 AA17FA637114E870034FE25016A22>.

14. Brunei Ministry of Primary Resources and Tourism, "Brunei-Quangxi Economic Corridor Symposium", 1 April 2015 <http://www.mprt.gov.bn/Lists/Latest %20News/NewDisplay.aspx?ID=286&ContentTypeId=0x0100CE966CE 70C33234E8D3A6FE5411A5237>.

15. Ak Md Khairuddin Pg Harun, "Trade Agreements Open Up Chinese Market to Brunei Businesses", Asia News Network, 13 September 2016 <http://annx.asianews.network/ content/trade-agreements-open-chinese-market-brunei-businesses-27964>.

16. "Brunei Sees Ninefold Surge in China Investments", *ASEAN Affairs*, 12 July 2016 <http://www.aseanaffairs.com/brunei_news/investment/brunei_sees_ninefold_surge_ in_china_investments>.

17. Jennifer Lo, "Harvesting Sea of Potential", *China Daily Asia*, 8 November 2013 <http://www.chinadailyasia.com/focus/2013-11/08/content_15097578.html>.

18. "CTG Joined Hands with Telbru to Support Bilateral Business and Trade between Brunei and China", China Telecom, May 2016 <https://www.chinatelecomglobal.com/ data/file/2016/20160527170030375.pdf>.

19. "Brunei Sees Potential to Attract Chinese Investment: Deputy Minister", Xinhua, 18 July 2016 <http://news.xinhuanet.com/english/2016-07/18/c_135522567.htm>.

20. Leo Kasim, "Brunei Keen to Attract More FDIs to Diversify Economy", *Brunei Times*, 22 July 2016.

21. Hope William-Smith, "South Korea and Brunei Collaborate on Fintech", FST Media, 2 September 2016 <http://fst.net.au/news/south-korea-and-brunei-collaborate-fintech>.

22. "Capital Market Development Can Help in Diversification", *ASEAN Affairs*, 8 September 2016 <http://www.aseanaffairs.com/brunei_news/capital_markets/capital_markets_development_can_help_in_diversitfication>.

23. Rachel Thien, "Brunei Launches Pilot $14 million Microalgae Plant", *Asia News Network*, 27 October 2016 <http://annx.asianews.network/content/brunei-launches-pilot-14-million-microalgae-plant-31446>.

24. Ministry of Finance Brunei Darussalam, "Brunei is a Growing FDI Destination", 12 October 2016 <http://www.mof.gov.bn/index.php/news/655-brunei-is-a-growing-fdi-destination>.

25. Leo Kasim, "Russian Firms Want to Do Business in Brunei", *Brunei Times*, 26 April 2016.

26. Azaraimy HH, "Costa Rica, Brunei Ink Agreements, Strengthen Ties", *Borneo Bulletin*, 8 March 2016.

27. Autoriti Monetari Brunei Darussalam, "Policy Statement 1/2016", 29 July 2016 <http://www.ambd.gov.bn/SiteAssets/Lists/Publications/AMBD%20Policy%20Statement%201-2016%20English.pdf#search=policy%20statement>.

28. Autoriti Monetari Brunei Darussalam, "Successful Issuances of Brunei Darussalam Government Short-Term Sukuk Al-Ijarah Securities", December 2016 <http://www.ambd.gov.bn/Lists/News/Displayitem.aspx?ID=243>.

29. Quratul-Ain Bandial, "'TPP to Strengthen Brunei Economy', Says Deputy Minister", *Borneo Bulletin*, 13 February 2016.

30. Oxford Business Group, *The Report: Brunei Darussalam 2016*, 2016 <https://www.oxfordbusinessgroup.com/analysis/economic-benefits-new-trade-agreement-expected-underpin-diversification-efforts>.

31. Oxford Business Group, *The Report: Brunei Darussalam 2016*, 2016 <https://www.oxfordbusinessgroup.com/analysis/effective-measures-reforms-sultanate-saw-its-ranking-world-bank%E2%80%99s-ease-doing-business-index-rise>.

32. Darussalam Enterprise, "i-Centre", n.d. <http://www.dare.gov.bn/SitePages/iCentre.aspx>.

33. Prime Minister's Office, Brunei Darussalam, "Exempted Businesses Don't Need to Renew Licence: MOHA", 18 February 2016 <http://energy.gov.bn/Lists/LatestHeadlines/DispForm.aspx?ID=1446&ContentTypeId=0x01001197DEBBB6416A44B5571C3C02FDFBD6>.

34. Ministry of Finance, Brunei Darussalam, "Companies Act (Amendment) Order 2016", 2016 <http://www.mof.gov.bn/images/ROCBN/Companies_Act_Amendment_Order_2016.pdf>.

35. International Monetary Fund, "IMF Executive Board Concludes 2016 Article IV Consultation with Brunei Darussalam", 26 September 2016 <https://www.imf.org/en/News/Articles/2016/09/26/PR16427-Brunei-Darussalam-IMF-Executive-Board-Concludes-2016-Article-IV-Consultation>.

36. Autoriti Monetari Brunei Darussalam, "AMBD Introducing Collateral Registry System", 5 August 2016 <http://www.ambd.gov.bn/Lists/News/Displayitem.aspx?ID=217>.

37. James Kon, "Banking Milestone: BOCHK Opens 1st Branch in Brunei", *Borneo Bulletin*, 21 December 2016.

38. Asian Development Bank, "ADB to Deepen Partnership with Brunei Darussalam", 18 August 2016 <https://www.adb.org/news/adb-deepen-partnership-brunei-darussalam>.

39. Darren Chin, "Brunei Now in World's Most Competitive Economy Index", *Brunei Times*, 29 September 2016.

40. Danial Norjidi, "Whole-of-Government Approach Boosted Brunei's EODB Ranking", *Borneo Bulletin*, 14 November 2016.

41. World Intellectual Property Organization, "Brunei Darussalam Joins the Madrid System", 6 October 2016 <http://www.wipo.int/madrid/en/news/2016/news_0020.html>.

42. Wail Wardi Wasil, "Let Religion Be Our Guide in the Face of Uncertainty", *Brunei Times*, 1 January 2016.

43. "Don't Misuse Net, Avoid Dubious Groups", *Borneo Bulletin*, 24 December 2016.

44. Izzati Jalil, "Face Challenges Prudently: HM", *Brunei Times*, 23 February 2016.

45. Department of Economic Planning and Development, Labour Force Survey 2014 (Bandar Seri Begawan: Department of Economic Planning and Development), p. 2.

46. Azlan Othman, "Unemployment Shoots Up Crime", *Borneo Bulletin*, 4 August 2015.

47. Rabiatul Kamit, "HM: Empower Youth to Lead", *Brunei Times*, 31 July 2016.

48. Ministry of Defence, "Defence White Paper 2011" (Bandar Seri Begawan: Ministry of Defence, 2011), p. 11.

49. "ADMM-Plus Joint Maritime Exercise Kicks Off", *Asia Pacific Daily*, 4 May 2016 <http://en.apdnews.com/china/military/394681.html>.

50. Radio Television Brunei, "Tourism Order 2016", 2 November 2016 <http://www.rtbnews.rtb.gov.bn/index.php?option=com_content&view=article&id=39455:tourism-order-2016&catid=34>.

51. Ak Md Khairuddin Pg Harun, "Tour Operators to Benefit from New Tour Guide Policy", *Brunei Times*, 3 November 2016.

52. Julius Hong, "Brunei Sees Over 4 million Int'l Arrivals Last Year", *Brunei Times*, 23 August 2016.

Cambodia

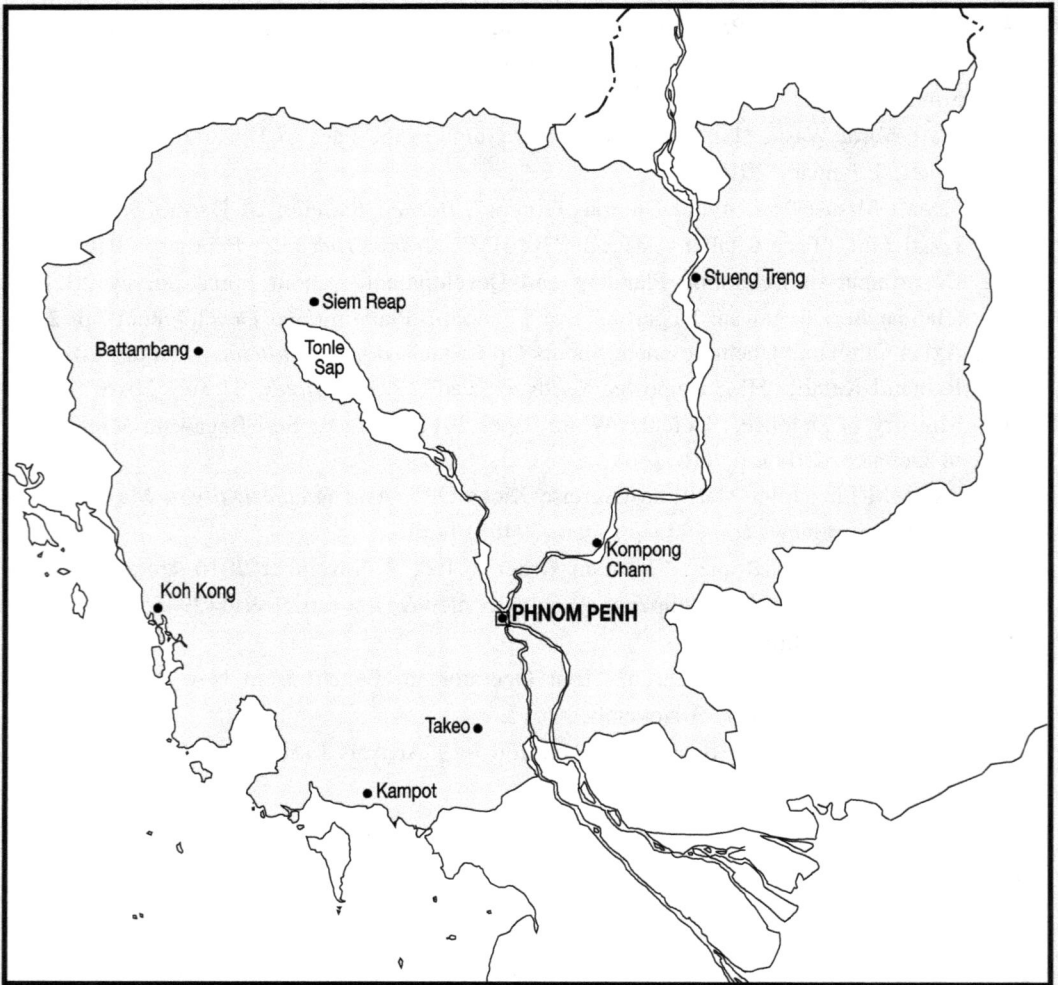

2016: A PROMISING YEAR FOR CAMBODIA?

Thearith Leng

Despite its small size and being under a dominant-party system, Cambodia has enjoyed a continuous economic growth rate of at least 7 per cent since 2011, making it one of the fastest growing economies in the world. An analysis of the Cambodian situation in 2016 will contribute to understanding how authoritarian rule may maintain its control over a country. In other words, one can ask, "What are the underlying factors that help to prolong the rule of the Cambodian People's Party (CPP)-led government?" To answer this question this chapter will present an overview of the key economic achievements of the CPP-led government and highlight some important political developments of 2016. It will also examine how this small state managed its foreign relations with important partners such as China, Vietnam, and Japan during the year.

The Economic Situation in 2016

Cambodia, as the Asian Development Bank suggests, has become a new tiger economy in the region, with an annual GDP growth rate of 7 per cent.[1] The GDP is expected to increase from US$18.5 billion in 2015 to US$20.2 billion in 2016.[2] GDP per capita is projected to rise from US$1,228 in 2015 to US$1,325 in 2016.[3] Total foreign direct investment in the second quarter of 2016 was US$15.7 billion, a slight increase from US$13.2 billion in the same period of 2015.[4]

Industry made marked progress, whereas agriculture and services appear to have slowed down in 2016. Cambodian industry still by and large relies on garment and textile exports, which account for approximately 70 per cent of total

THEARITH LENG is a PhD Candidate in Political and International Studies at the University of New South Wales at the Australian Defence Force Academy.

exports. This year the industry is projected to rise at 11.4 per cent.[5] The services sector, mainly driven by tourism growth, is projected to increase by 6.7 per cent. Tourism per se will go up by 2.2 per cent this year.

The main factor attributed to industrial growth, particularly of garments and textiles, is the shift in the export structure of the garment and textile industry. This sector has steadily shifted up the value chain, from producing low-value-added products to high-value-added ones. This is demonstrated by the increase in export value, despite the decrease in the quantity of exports. For instance, the export value increased from 10.7 per cent in 2014 to 14.5 per cent in 2015, although the export volume dropped to 13.1 per cent in 2015.[6] Similarly, despite the fact that the export volume declined by 9.3 per cent in the first six months of 2016 compared to the same period in 2015, the export value in the first half of the year still stabilized at 10.8 per cent.[7]

Notably, the number of Cambodian manufacturers, particularly the small and medium enterprises (SMEs), is on the rise. The number of SMEs increased from 29,987 in 2007 to 33,344 in 2016 (as of June).[8] In the meantime the number of large-scale manufacturers significantly surged from 98 in 2014 to 124 in 2016. This suggests that Cambodia's industry has gradually developed its exporting capacity to replace imports. For instance, the import of food, beverages, and cigarettes in the first half of 2016 slowly dropped to 21 per cent, compared to 27 per cent in the first six months of 2015.

The Cambodian economy's rapid growth has partly been spurred by its strong links with the Chinese economy in recent years. China has become the top donor and foreign investor in Cambodia. China recently assisted Cambodia in improving its internal physical infrastructure such as roads, bridges, and ports under the "One Belt, One Road" programme, which is expected to further boost the Cambodian economy. For instance, in 2016 China assisted Cambodia in speeding up the expansion of a special economic zone (SEZ) industrial park in Sihanoukville, a major port city. Once complete, this SEZ, as Chinese President Xi Jinping asserted during his visit to Cambodia in October 2016, will have approximately three hundred factories, which will generate jobs for approximately 200,000 workers.[9] The SEZ currently contains eighty-eight enterprises, which have created about 160,000 jobs.[10] Chinese investment in Cambodia in the second quarter of 2016 reached US$4.8 billion, exceeding investment from Vietnam (US$1.4 billion), South Korea (US$1.3 billion), Malaysia (US$1.1 billion), and Taiwan (US$1 billion).[11]

Cambodia's economic growth has also been driven by the ongoing preferential status granted to it by the EU and the United States. Cambodia is entitled to export its products to the EU under the "Everything-But-Arms" scheme. As for the United States, Cambodia continues to enjoy the quotas allocated for its textile exports to the United States under the 1999 Bilateral Textile Agreement. These preferential arrangements have significantly spurred the Cambodian economy in general, and the garments and textile industry in particular.

In recent years the EU and the United States have become crucial export destinations for Cambodian garment and textile goods. For example, about 40.3 per cent and 32.9 per cent of total apparel and footwear produced was exported to the EU and the United States, respectively, in 2014. The figure steadily rose to 42.5 per cent for the EU and dropped slightly to 29.4 per cent for the U.S. market in 2015.[12] In the first six months of 2016 the export growth rate of these items to the EU reached 45 per cent, compared to 41.4 per cent in the same period for 2015. Cambodia's exports to the United States, however, decreased to 24.9 per cent in the first half of 2016, compared to 31.3 per cent in the same period for 2015. Interestingly, Cambodia's exports to Japan steadily rose to 8.9 per cent in the first six months of 2016, compared to 6.8 per cent in the same period in the previous year.[13]

Despite the positive development of its industries, especially the garment and textile industry, the Cambodian economy showed signs of problems in 2016. The agricultural and services sectors appeared to slow down. The agriculture growth rate has continuously been under 4 per cent, the target rate set by the Cambodian government.[14] Specifically, the growth rate for this sector was just 0.2 per cent in 2015, and is only projected to rise to 0.5 per cent in 2016. Various factors have contributed to the slow progress in this area. Firstly, industrial development has absorbed workforce from the agricultural sector. Secondly, the lack of physical infrastructure — such as irrigation systems and roads — has accounted for rising production costs, thus reducing the sector's competitiveness. Thirdly, the government lacks technical and market support.

It is noteworthy that the government set a goal to export one million tons of rice by 2015.[15] However, the lack of proper policy to support the farmers' efforts to sell their products has resulted in a rice production surplus which culminated in a significant fall in rice prices in 2016. The significant decline of rice prices eventually triggered the recent farmers' riot in Battambang, Cambodia's main rice-producing province. The farmers spilled rice all over National Road 5 to show their anger at the sudden drop in prices.[16]

Agriculture is not the only sector facing a decline. The services sector has experienced a similar trend. This sector reached its peak of an 8.7 per cent growth rate in 2014, fell to 7.1 per cent in 2015, and is projected to fall to 6.7 per cent for 2016. Interestingly, tourism, a key service sector, is experiencing a downward trend. The growth of the number of tourists in the first six months of 2016 was just 2.6 per cent, compared to 4.6 per cent in the same period for 2015.[17] The recent decrease in services, especially in tourism, has probably been triggered by the emergence of new competitive tourist destinations, particularly Myanmar, and the slowdown of the Chinese economy.

Even a strong sector like the garment and textile industry faces potential challenges. First, the recent decline of the Chinese economy may slow down Chinese investment in this sector, which will have adverse effects on its growth (China is the top investor in garments and textiles). Second, "Brexit", the British vote to leave the EU, may pose a significant hurdle as it may lead to a fall in demand for apparel and footwear from the EU, Cambodia's biggest export destination. The EU absorbs about 45 per cent of Cambodia's total garment and textile products, followed by the United States (24.9 per cent), and Japan (8.6 per cent).[18]

Domestic Political Developments in 2016

There were two important developments in Cambodian politics in 2016. The first was the CPP's struggle to consolidate power and the second was the growing discontent of the middle class towards the CPP's style of governance. The CPP-led government has struggled to regain its popularity after a significant loss of votes to the opposition party — the Cambodian National Rescue Party (CNRP) — in the 2013 general election. The ruling party has thus adopted both soft and hard approaches in order to consolidate its power. The growing dissatisfaction of the middle class with the CPP's rule can be discerned from the number of people who attended the funeral of prominent Cambodian academic Kem Ley in early July. Kem Ley was well known for his critical comments on government policies that increasingly aroused middle-class discontent.

The Government's Soft Approach

The ruling party has implemented significant reforms with the aim of increasing government efficiency. This has contributed to satisfying Cambodian voters. For example, the heads of the agriculture and transport ministries were reshuffled in mid-March. Tram Iv Teuk and Ouk Rabun, the outgoing ministers of, respectively, transport and agriculture, had been indirectly criticized by Cambodian Prime Minister Hun Sen for demonstrating passivity in their work. Tram Iv Tuek was replaced by Sun Chanthol, who is publicly well regarded as a reform minded and meritorious figure. Upon assuming his position, Sun Chanthol implemented significant reforms within the Ministry of Public Works and Transport in order to reduce corruption. For example, instead of needing to apply for driving licences from the sole office of the Ministry of Public Works and Transport as in the past, the new minister issued a regulation, effective from June 2016, that allows individuals to lodge their licence applications with any ministry branch located in certain malls and supermarkets in Phnom Penh.[19] This is considered a remarkable achievement in eliminating government red tape that contributed to corrupt practices.

Another positive development was the appointment in April of Chea Sophara as the Minister of Land Management, Urban Planning, and Construction.[20] Chea Sophara was famous for his sound performance in resolving many pressing problems related to land and development issues in Phnom Penh, where he served as Mayor from 1998 to 2003. The CPP leaders believed his appointment as minister would help to boost the party's popularity. It is worth noting that land grabbing has become one of the key governance problems in Cambodia today, and it was used by the opposition party to undermine the ruling party's popularity in the 2013 general election.

More recently, the Hun Sen government made another important move to please the middle class. The government has become more open towards foreign companies that wish to invest in building properties at affordable prices for those in the low- and middle-income bracket in Phnom Penh.[21] As the Cambodian economy is growing quickly, the housing prices keep rising dramatically. The surge has created a significant hurdle for low- or middle-income buyers, such as teachers, public servants, and employees of NGOs/INGOs. They cannot afford houses that are increasingly in high demand, especially in Phnom Penh. The government recently allowed a joint Cambodian–Australian venture to invest in building properties in Phnom Penh's Kob Srov suburb. The prices of houses in this development are expected to be between US$20,000 and 30,000, which should be affordable for middle-income buyers.[22] Payments may be made through an instalment plan aimed at easing the financial burden.

Apart from housing, another positive reform has been made in the education sector. In order to boost its popularity with the Cambodian youth — which accounts for about 60–70 per cent of the total Cambodian population — the government nominated a clean and reform-minded individual, Hang Chuon Naron, as the Minister of Education, Youth, and Sports. Prior to Hang Chuon Naron's term in 2013, Cambodian education was mired in corrupt practices, especially during the secondary and high school national entrance exams. This had led to a loss of confidence, especially among the middle class, in the national education system. Nonetheless, the new minister has worked hard to restore public confidence by enforcing tough regulations aimed at totally eliminating corruption and bribery during examinations.

Hang Chuon Naron has recently involved the Anti-Corruption Unit in invigilating the exams. Students and invigilators who cheat or accept bribes may also face a jail term. The slogan for such rigorous enforcement is, "If You Truly Learn, You'll Truly Pass [the exams]". This reform-minded minister is likely to restore meritocracy, which has not been clearly discerned in the Cambodian education system for decades. His actions have helped to reduce middle-class dissatisfaction towards the ruling regime.

The Government's Hard Approach

In addition to the government's soft approaches, the ruling party has simultaneously adopted hard approaches to consolidate its power. These have been mainly aimed at weakening the CNRP, both inside and outside Cambodia. On the domestic front the CPP has sought ways to persecute the CNRP's leaders — Sam Rainsy and Kem Sokha. Sam Rainsy, the president of the CNRP, has been forced to stay in exile in France, while Kem Sokha, the CNRP vice-president, has been hiding in his party headquarters after receiving arrest threats by a court allegedly influenced by the government.[23]

Sam Rainsy has been in exile in France since October 2016. He was charged with defamation and incitement after he accused Prime Minister Hun Sen of involvement in the murder of high-profile socio-political analyst Kem Ley in July. Kem Sokha, in the meantime, faces a charge of having had an extramarital affair (with a hairdresser) — which is against the Cambodian marriage law. To avoid being detained he has hidden himself inside the CNRP headquarters since 26 May 2016. Since then he only made his first appearance in public in October to register to vote.[24]

On the overseas front the government has adopted the so-called "divide-and-rule" tactic to weaken an important economic backbone of the CNRP. It has assigned its officials who work as diplomats in Cambodian embassies to be responsible for the CPP's affairs in the United States, Australia, and New Zealand — which are CNRP strongholds. It is believed that the Cambodian diaspora in these countries has provided significant economic resources to the CNRP. Cambodian ambassadors in these countries, besides playing their official government roles, also assume party duties. They have steadily created structures inside these territories to promote the CPP's reputation and undermine that of the opposition. For instance, the new Cambodian Ambassador Koy Kuong is in charge of the CPP's affairs in Australia and New Zealand. CPP youth groups have been created in important Australian cities — such as Canberra, Sydney, and Melbourne — to carry out party propaganda and attract new party members. The youth groups have even at times been responsible for disseminating critical and damaging news about the opposition party among Cambodian Australians.

The adoption of hard approaches by the government has been aimed at crippling the opposition party, whose popularity has been dramatically on the rise in recent years, challenging the paramount control of the CPP. While the soft approaches appear to have yielded some positive results for the CPP, it is hard to assess the effects of the hard approaches adopted against the CNRP. These actions seem to have had a mixed affect on the CPP's popularity. One positive aspect for the CPP is that the CNRP has had fewer opportunities to criticize or highlight the CPP's weaknesses, which will enable the CPP to rectify its mistakes ahead of the 2018 national election. On the negative side, the hard measures of the CPP are likely to make the Cambodian middle class perceive the government as unable to resolve pressing issues such as salary increases for public servants, deforestation, and land grabbing. This perceived inability may have compelled the CPP to find ways to undermine the CNRP.

Growing Discontent of the Middle Class towards the Government

Cambodia's rapid economic growth has resulted in a continually expanding middle class, which has increasingly demanded greater government efficiency and respect for individual rights and freedoms. Such discontent was reflected in the participation of large numbers of people at the funeral of the high-profile socio-political analyst Kem Ley in July. Kem Ley was well known among Cambodians, particularly the middle class, owing to his fearless and unbiased analysis of socio-political issues. He frequently pointed out the government's weaknesses, basing his analysis on sound research and evidence, and he made his ideas well known to the public through media interviews.

Following his assassination, the huge participation by Cambodians at his funeral was seen as an indication of the growing discontent of the middle class towards the government. Approximately two million people participated in the funeral procession in Phnom Penh.[25] This outnumbered any funeral procession of famous Cambodian personalities, except that of the late King Norodom Sihanouk.

Middle-class discontent is clearly on the rise, although its members have not thus far openly defied or directly challenged the government.

Cambodia's Foreign Relations in 2016

Cambodia's management of its relations with China and Vietnam is one of the outstanding themes of its foreign relations in 2016. In recent years, China and Vietnam have been locked in a heated dispute over the South China Sea. At times this has nearly led to armed clashes between the two. Despite this worrisome situation, Cambodia has been able to diplomatically manoeuvre itself well between the two competitors, which are both important partners for the country. Cambodia's ties with Japan, another major power, is also worth discussing. Relations with Japan have been generally stable, albeit with some friction.

Cambodia has long considered China to be one of its closest allies. Bandwagoning is a common form of diplomatic behaviour for Cambodia in relation to China. Phnom Penh clearly echoed Beijing's position over the South China Sea by rejecting efforts by some ASEAN members to call on China to respect the Arbitral Tribunal's ruling issued on 12 July 2016.[26] It is noteworthy that the South China Sea dispute has in recent years rocked ASEAN–China relations. ASEAN claimant states have been concerned about China's expansionist policy in the South China Sea, eventually pushing the Philippines, under President Benigno Aquino, to file a legal case against Beijing at the Arbitral Tribunal in The Hague on 22 January 2013.[27]

Before the court's ruling was announced, Cambodia openly declared that it would reject the Arbitral Tribunal's jurisdiction over the South China Sea, a position in line with that of Beijing's, but contradicting that of ASEAN claimant states. It is worth noting that Laos and Myanmar, which had frequently aligned their policies with China, did not adopt a similar position to Cambodia, for doing so might have upset the other ASEAN members. Cambodia's position was explicitly laid out in Prime Minister Hun Sen's remarks on the occasion of the CPP's sixty-fifth founding anniversary in Phnom Penh:

> The CPP does not support, and more so is against, any possible declaration by ASEAN to support [the] decision of the Permanent Court of Arbitration in relation to the South China Sea disputes, which some countries outside the region have wire-pulled and pressured ASEAN members even before the court reaches a decision.... The CPP foresees this issue, and views it as the worst political collusion in the framework of international politics,

the result of which would lead to division among ASEAN members themselves and between ASEAN and China.[28]

This bandwagoning behaviour has yielded positive outcomes for Cambodia. China has rewarded Cambodia with enormous economic aid and cooperation. During Chinese President Xi Jinping's visit to Cambodia in October 2016, China committed to provide US$600 million in aid to Cambodia over three years.[29] Thirty-one cooperation agreements were also concluded between the two countries. In the meantime, China acceded to Cambodia's request to increase the quota for Cambodian rice exports to China from 100,000 to 200,000 tons, starting from 2016.[30] This can be regarded as a generous offer by the Chinese, since Cambodia faces a problem of surplus rice production, which resulted in the September riot in Battambang province.

While trying to please Beijing, Phnom Penh has simultaneously attempted to accommodate Hanoi, which has been disappointed with the former's position over the South China Sea dispute. Prime Minister Hun Sen has tried to stabilize relations with Vietnam by taking a hard stance on the CNRP, which used the anti-Vietnamese nationalism card to undermine the popularity of the ruling party at home. Prime Minister Hun Sen threatened to arrest those who had accused the Cambodian government of using "a fake map" in the Cambodia–Vietnam border demarcation, which favoured Vietnam. The opposition suggested that the current government did not use the maps submitted by the late King Norodom Sihanouk to the United Nations in 1964. The CNRP considered the 1964 maps to be the correct versions that would ensure Cambodia's territorial sovereignty. Nonetheless, after the Hun Sen government made a request in early July to the UN for the so-called correct maps, it was found that the versions held by the UN were similar to the ones used by the Cambodian government in the border demarcation agreement with Vietnam.

CNRP lawmaker Um Sam An was arrested by the authorities in April. He had accused the government of using fake maps in the border demarcation agreement with Vietnam.[31] In October 2016, Um Sam An was convicted and sentenced to two and a half years in prison. His charges were "incitement to commit a felony" and "incitement to cause discrimination". He had made accusations against the government with regards to the Cambodia–Vietnam border problems, including that the use of incorrect maps in the border demarcation resulted in Cambodia ceding territory to Vietnam.

The government's move was partly driven by its need to stabilize ties with its larger neighbour — Vietnam. For Hun Sen, making peace with neighbouring countries is crucial to the stability and development of the country. While thus appeasing Vietnam, Hun Sen does not want to see Cambodia — which has been ravaged by civil wars for more than three decades — totally losing its independence to Vietnam, either. This is one of the reasons why he has forged close ties with China, which has been at odds with Vietnam over the South China Sea. Hun Sen, for example, expressed his feelings on his Facebook page in August 2016 that Vietnam was not his boss.[32]

Cambodia's ties with Japan are also worth mentioning. Japan remains one of Cambodia's largest aid donors. The two countries have deepened their cooperation in multifaceted areas, especially security and trade. Japan has been engaged with the Cambodian peace-building process since the 1990s, making it one of Cambodia's closest friends. More recently, Tokyo supported Cambodia's electoral reform efforts, which are crucial for peace-building. Phnom Penh, in turn, supports Tokyo in its efforts to push for the denuclearization of the Korean peninsula. These bilateral efforts were manifest in Cambodian Prime Minister Hun Sen's meeting with Japanese Prime Minister Shinzo Abe at the Cambodia–Japan Summit Meeting in July.[33]

The Cambodia–Japan bilateral relationship, however, came under some pressure in 2016. Cambodia's policy of bandwagoning with China over the South China Sea in recent years has upset Japan. While Tokyo wants Beijing to obey the Arbitral Tribunal ruling, Phnom Penh is unwilling to support Japan's stance, given its own political commitment to Beijing. To a certain extent this has disappointed the Japanese, causing Tokyo to be less friendly with Phnom Penh. At the Asia-Europe Meeting in July, Japanese Prime Minister Shinzo Abe's dissatisfaction with the Cambodian position over the South China Sea was reported by the media.[34] More interestingly, Tokyo took a bolder stance in expressing its disappointment by sending its ambassador to the funeral of Kem Ley.[35] Ambassador Kumamaru Yuji's presence at the funeral of the high-profile academic and critic of the government alerted CPP leaders to Japan's displeasure.

Japanese Foreign Minister Fumio Kishida's visit to Southeast Asian countries in July 2016 is another indicator of Tokyo's dissatisfaction with Phnom Penh. Although the two countries have been strategic partners since 2013, the Japanese Foreign Minister decided to skip a visit to Cambodia while paying official visits to other Southeast Asian states such as Thailand, Myanmar, Laos, and Vietnam. During his visit the minister pledged US$7 billion to the Mekong river countries, of which Cambodia is included.[36] Leaving Cambodia out of his Southeast Asian travel itinerary may be further evidence of Tokyo's dissatisfaction with the fact that Phnom Penh has become increasingly beholden to Beijing.

Conclusion

In 2016 the CPP government generally performed well in the areas of economics, politics, and foreign relations, despite certain setbacks. The government succeeded in achieving continuous economic growth, especially in the industrial sector. Chinese foreign direct investment, as well as the continuous preferential treatment granted by the EU and the United States to Cambodian garment and textile exports, has significantly contributed to growth. In spite of this positive trend the economy appears to have slowed down in sectors such as agriculture and services. The industrial sector is also likely to experience problems in the near future, given the slowdown of the Chinese economy and the vote for Brexit.

In relation to domestic politics, the government's efforts to consolidate power and the rising discontent of the middle class were the outstanding themes of 2016. The ruling party adopted both soft and hard approaches to consolidate its power. The soft approaches can be discerned in the government's efforts to implement significant reforms across a wide range of sectors in order to regain the people's trust. The adoption of hard approaches was evident in their persecution of the opposition, the CNRP. Within Cambodia the opposition party has been crippled and its leaders have not been able to highlight the government's problems as they used to do. They have faced legal charges that have crippled their ability to increase their popularity ahead of the 2018 national election. In the contest outside Cambodia, the CNRP has also met another challenge as a result of the CPP's divide-and-rule tactic — the Cambodian diaspora that previously provided significant resources for the opposition has gradually become divided as the CPP has attacked their overseas economic bases. Simply put, the CNRP is losing strength to challenge the ruling government. However, the hard approaches taken by the government may also have adverse effects. The middle class in Cambodia may begin to believe that the ruling government is losing its ability to resolve the pressing problems that the country faces.

In foreign relations, Cambodia seems to have taken advantage of the rocky Sino–Vietnamese relationship over the South China Sea dispute. It has steadily tilted more towards China in its position on the South China Sea, whilst trying to maintain cordial relations with its closer large neighbour, Vietnam. Such diplomatic manoeuvring has enabled Cambodia to continue enjoying Chinese investment and aid, whilst maintaining peace with Vietnam. Phnom Penh's relations with Tokyo, another regional competitor of China, has been stable, in spite of some problems.

Overall, the CPP is likely to maintain its grip on the country in the medium term given its sound economic performance, its flexibility to achieve reforms, and its ability to stabilize the country's key relations with other nations such as China, Japan, and Vietnam. As long as the CPP-led government can maintain strong economic growth and carry out internal reforms that satisfy the middle class, it is unlikely that the rival CNRP will take power in the near future. The ability to stabilize Cambodia's relations with important powers such as China, Vietnam, and Japan adds to the ruling party's resilience, as it will avert dangerous interference by those countries in Cambodia's domestic politics. Further, strong ties with those countries will help boost the Cambodian economy. In short, one can say that 2016 was the year in which the government had several opportunities to mitigate the rising discontent of the middle class. In the long run, the CPP may face a credible challenge to its rule as the size of the middle class keeps growing. Demands have begun to be made for good governance and efficient governmental institutions rather than just reshuffling the positions of government officials.

Notes

1. ADB, "Here Comes Cambodia: Asia's New Tiger Economy" (2016).
2. Ibid.; Cambodian Ministry of Economics and Finance, "Foreign Direct Investment, 2016" (Phnom Penh: Ministry of Economics and Finance, 2016).
3. Ibid.
4. Ibid.; "Progress Report of Cambodian Macroeconomic Development, the First Half of 2016" (Phnom Penh: Ministry of Economics and Finance, 2016).
5. Cambodian Ministry of Economics and Finance, "Budget in Brief: Fiscal Year 2016" (Phnom Penh: Ministry of Economics and Finance, 2016), p. 9.
6. Ibid., p. 39.
7. Ibid.
8. Ibid., p. 10.
9. Phina Ros, "Special Economic Zone in Sihanouk Ville Will Become the Second Shenzhen City of Cambodia", *Kohsantepheap*, 24 October 2016.
10. Ibid.
11. Cambodian Ministry of Economics and Finance, "Foreign Direct Investment, 2016".
12. Cambodian Ministry of Economics and Finance, "Budget in Brief", p. 39.
13. Ibid.
14. Ibid., p. 4.
15. Theara Khuon, "Rice Production Increases as Country Moves toward 2015 Export Goal", Voice of America, 6 September 2012.
16. Sothear Kang, "Farmers Block Road amid Rice Price Crisis", *Cambodia Daily*, 19 September 2016.
17. Cambodian Ministry of Economics and Finance, "Budget in Brief".

18. Ibid., p. 39.

19. Ministry of Public Works and Transport, "Places to Issue Driving Licenses Are Expanded to Aeon Mall from 15 June 2016" <http://www.mpwt.gov.kh/4352.html?lang=en>.

20. Naren Kuch, "Government Reveal Ministers in Cabinet Reshuffle", *Cambodia Daily*, 18 March 2016.

21. Manet Sum, "Cambodia-Australia Affordable Houses Venture", *Khmer Times*, 3 November 2016.

22. Ibid.

23. Kem Sokha received a royal pardon in early December 2016. The pardon was apparently driven by the ruling party's intent to break the unity of the CNRP. Once Kem Sokha is free and Sam Rainsy is still considered guilty, the CPP will likely be able to manipulate factions within the CNRP.

24. Vida Taing and Sokha Cheang, "Kem Sokha Now a Wanted Man", *Khmer Times*, 26 May 2016.

25. RFA's Khmer Service, "Millions of Cambodians Join Kem Ley's Funeral Procession", Radio Free Asia, 24 July 2016.

26. Alex Willemyns, "Cambodia Blocks Asean Statement on South China Sea", *Cambodia Daily*, 25 July 2016.

27. Paterno Esmaquel, "Aquino: The President Who Brought China to Court", *Rappler*, 29 June 2016.

28. Tien Shaohui, "Cambodia's Ruling Party Not to Support Arbitration Court's Decision over South China Sea: PM", Xinhua, 28 June 2016.

29. Chanthul Prak, "Chinese President Xi Jinping Visits Loyal Friend Cambodia", Reuters, 13 October 2016.

30. Sokunthea Hang, "Cambodian Commercial Centers to Open in China", *Cambodia Daily*, 17 October 2016.

31. Sokunthea Vann, "Story of the Border Maps: Hun Sen to Threaten to Handcuff Anyone Who Accuses His Government of Using Fake Maps", Radio France Internationale Khmer Service, 13 April 2016.

32. Rathavong Ven, "Prime Minister in Facebook Fight", *Khmer Times*, 2 August 2016.

33. Ministry of Foreign Affairs of Japan, "Japan-Cambodia Summit Meeting", news release, 16 July 2016 <http://www.mofa.go.jp/s_sa/sea1/kh/page3e_000513.html>.

34. Julia Wallace, "Cambodia Prime Minister Takes Issue over Japan Rebuke Allegation", *Anadolu*, 22 July 2016.

35. LICADHO, "Dr. Kem Ley's Funeral Procession" <http://stream.licadho-cambodia.org/kem_ley_funeral_procession/>.

36. Alex Willemyns, "On Regional Tour, Japanese Minister Skips Cambodia", *Cambodia Daily*, 3 May 2016.

Indonesia

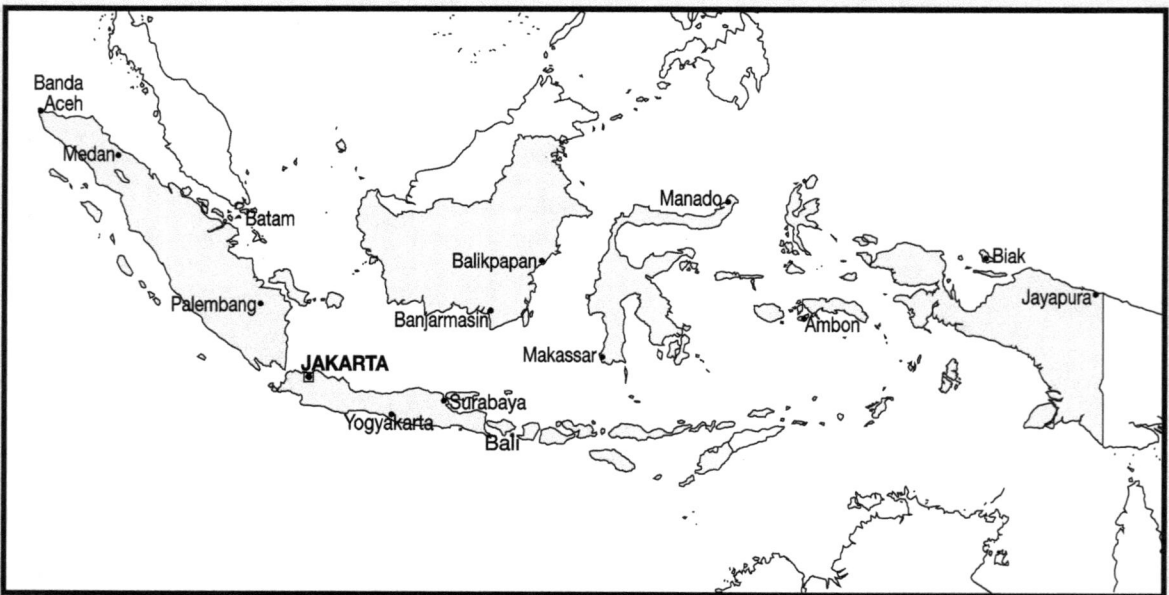

Banda Aceh
Medan
Batam
Palembang
JAKARTA
Yogyakarta
Surabaya
Bali
Banjarmasin
Balikpapan
Makassar
Manado
Ambon
Biak
Jayapura

INDONESIA IN 2016:
Jokowi Consolidates Power

Dirk Tomsa

After a difficult first year in office, President Joko Widodo (Jokowi) showed in 2016 that he has grown increasingly adept at manoeuvring through the maze of political and economic interests in Jakarta. For most of the year he continuously consolidated his power through a range of political manoeuvres that included the broadening of his governing coalition, a cabinet reshuffle, and the appointment of his preferred choice for police chief. Towards the end of the year, however, a new challenge emerged for Jokowi when his political opponents joined forces with Islamist hardliners to mobilize hundreds of thousands of protestors to demonstrate against Jakarta governor Basuki Tjahaja Purnama (Ahok), an ally of Jokowi, who faced politically motivated blasphemy charges. In terms of policy, the President and his reshuffled team focused much of their attention on economic matters, in particular the development of Indonesia's ailing infrastructure and the implementation of a tax amnesty law. Internationally, the need to attract more foreign investment and the rising tensions in the South China Sea prompted Jokowi to pay more attention to foreign policy than in his inaugural year.

All in all, the President tightened his grip on power in 2016, but challenges remain, not least because there is still a lack of coherence and clear direction in Jokowi's policymaking and personnel decisions. This chapter will highlight these seemingly contradictory features of Jokowi's second year in office through an analysis of some of the most significant events in Indonesian politics in 2016. First, it will provide an overview of domestic politics, which were dominated by Jokowi's quest to strengthen his governing coalition on the one hand and an ongoing

DIRK TOMSA is Senior Lecturer at the Department of Politics and Philosophy at La Trobe University, Melbourne. He was Visiting Senior Fellow at the ISEAS – Yusof Ishak Institute in 2016.

slide towards religious and political conservatism on the other. Second, it will outline key trends in the Indonesian economy, emphasizing that Indonesia's GDP growth remained relatively flat compared to 2015 despite a number of ambitious economic reform initiatives aimed at stimulating investment and improving fiscal space. Third, the discussion will shift to foreign policy, where Indonesia attempted to be more assertive in its pursuit of tangible benefits yet remained constrained by its lack of military capabilities and effective diplomatic resources.

Domestic Political Developments

By the time President Jokowi completed his second year in office in October, many observers regarded 2016 as the year when Jokowi matured as a President and started to impose his will on key stakeholders in parties and parliament. Not only did he cement his grip on power by expanding his governing coalition, but he also increasingly emancipated himself from Megawati Sukarnoputri, the powerful leader of the Indonesian Democratic Party-Struggle (PDIP), which had nominated him for president back in 2014. At the same time though, political developments this year also showed that Jokowi still lacks a compelling political narrative for Indonesia that would go beyond his vaguely formulated developmentalist ideas.[1] Even more troubling for many of his original supporters was Jokowi's ongoing indifference towards corruption and human rights. At the end of the year this indifference towards a reformist agenda came back to haunt him when his political opponents used a huge Islamist protest rally against incumbent Jakarta governor Basuki Tjahaja Purnama (Ahok), who was accused of blasphemy, as a pretext for trying to undermine the president's authority. As the fallout from the blasphemy case against Ahok continued into the New Year, Jokowi's tightened grip on power faced its first serious challenge, with consequences that will only become clearer in the coming months.

Consolidating Power

The first indication of Jokowi's increasingly assertive presidential posture was the expansion of his governing coalition and the concomitant weakening of parliamentary opposition. By mid-2016 no less than three political parties (Golkar, PPP, and PAN) had abandoned the opposition coalition led by Prabowo Subianto's Gerindra Party and pledged allegiance to Jokowi's government. As a result, the President's support in parliament surged from a meagre 37 per cent at the beginning of his term to a two-thirds majority of 69 per cent. Such broad support is of course reminiscent of the rainbow coalitions Jokowi's predecessors had assembled, yet there was a significant difference in the way Jokowi forged his new rainbow coalition. While PAN's defection from the Prabowo camp was relatively straightforward after an orderly change of leadership, Golkar and PPP only came on board after the Jokowi administration actively intervened in bitter factional disputes that had paralysed these two parties for more than a year.[2] By threatening to withhold legal recognition for a party leadership that refused to support the government, Jokowi practically coerced both Golkar and PPP into electing new leaders who were amenable to his government.

In July, the changing power constellation was reflected in a cabinet reshuffle that promoted members of the new coalition parties into cabinet. But in another indication that Jokowi was clearly calling the shots in this unequal relationship, Golkar and PAN both received only one relatively unimportant ministry each, while PPP was denied another ministerial post apart from the Ministry of Religious Affairs, which PPP stalwart Lukman Hakim Saifuddin has held since mid-2014. Thus, it became apparent that Jokowi had succeeded in enlarging his coalition without making extraordinary concessions to the new members.

There were other signs that the cabinet reshuffle constituted an important moment of power consolidation for Jokowi. First, the reshuffle demonstrated that Jokowi was becoming increasingly emancipated from Megawati, as he obviously defied pressure from PDIP to dismiss certain ministers deemed unacceptable by Megawati and her party. In particular, the retention of Rini Soemarno as Minister for State-Owned Enterprises was seen as a rebuff for Megawati, as it was well known that PDIP wanted Rini to be removed from the cabinet.[3] Second, Jokowi demonstrated that even close allies should know their place in the pecking order. For example, the demotion of Luhut Pandjaitan, one of Jokowi's closest political confidants and a key figure in the government's intervention in Golkar — from Coordinating Minister for Political, Legal and Security Affairs to Coordinating Minister for Maritime Affairs — was a subtle but clear rebuke for Luhut, indicating that the Minister's prominent public profile had apparently become an irritant for Jokowi.

Third, the appointment of former General Wiranto as Luhut's replacement showed that Jokowi does not shy away from controversial appointments, even if these are not required as part of party political calculations. In the case of Wiranto, who was chairman of the Hanura Party at the time of his appointment, there appeared to be no obvious need to grant this ministry to Hanura, and yet Jokowi obviously wanted the former commander-in-chief of the armed forces to occupy that position. Like previous appointments in the security sector, this was another painful slap in the face for human rights activists, many of whom had supported Jokowi in the hope that he would usher in a new era of democratic reform.

Whither Human Rights and Diversity?

Indonesia made little progress in improving its human rights record in 2016, as the country continued a fundamental turn towards political and religious conservatism. As in the previous year, the government once again executed a number of convicted drug smugglers, the military expanded its influence over civilian affairs, and members of religious and sexual minorities faced intimidation and harassment.

Compared to previous years though, when Christians, Ahmadis, and Shi'i had been prime targets of religious hardliners, 2016 initially saw the focus shift towards the lesbian, gay, bisexual, and transgender (LGBT) community. Following comments by cabinet Minister Muhammad Nasir at the beginning of the year that LGBT Indonesians should be banned from universities in the country,[4] a wave of discrimination and intimidation began, culminating in efforts to make all sex outside marriage, and hence all gay sex, illegal.

By the end of the year, anti-Christian and anti-Chinese sentiments were also on the rise again. Trigger was the re-election bid of incumbent Jakarta governor Ahok, which was vehemently opposed by Islamist groups like the Islamic Defenders Front (FPI) because of Ahok's religion and ethnicity. Having mobilized against Ahok for some time without much public response, the FPI was handed a welcome opportunity to raise the stakes when the governor made provocative comments about a Quranic verse and religious scholars during a speech to city officials. The remarks gave the FPI and other hardliners a pretext to join forces with Ahok's political opponents and stir up racist attitudes at two large demonstrations in Jakarta on 4 November and 2 December. Bowing to public pressure, the police swiftly declared Ahok a suspect and indicted him for blasphemy. When the trial began on 12 December, it damaged not only Ahok's electoral prospects but also Indonesia's already fading reputation as a moderate Muslim democracy.[5]

The demonstrations and Ahok's blasphemy trial were alarming manifestations of the FPI's growing political clout. Perhaps even more concerning, however, was that the mass mobilization was reportedly sponsored by powerful political interests who sought to use the protests as a means to weaken President Jokowi. Among those "Machiavellian old elites"[6] rumoured to have supported the demonstrations was former President Susilo Bambang Yudhoyono, whose son Agus is one of two candidates challenging Ahok in the 2017 gubernatorial election. While Yudhoyono himself was not seen at the rallies, some members of parliament eagerly joined the protests, and deputy House speaker Fadli Zon even appeared on the same vehicle as FPI leader Habib Rizieq Shihab.[7] Thus, less than twenty years after the deadly anti-Chinese riots of 1998, Islamist vigilante groups and mainstream politicians were jointly fanning the flames of racism again, raising the spectre of renewed anti-Chinese violence should Ahok be re-elected in 2017.

Another setback for human rights in Indonesia was the government's apparent withdrawal from earlier initiatives to promote reconciliation and rehabilitation for the victims of the anti-communist mass killings of 1965. In April 2016, the Jokowi government had won cautious praise from human rights activists when it took the unprecedented step of endorsing the organization of a public symposium about the violence that killed an estimated 500,000 people. The event brought together representatives of the government and military on the one hand and activists, academics, and survivors of the atrocities on the other.[8] Luhut Pandjaitan, a key confidante of President Jokowi, spoke at the event, and even though he maintained the government's official stance that there is no need for a public apology, Luhut's very appearance was interpreted by many as an important first step towards reconciliation. More generally, observers praised the open and candid atmosphere at the symposium, but also urged the government to follow up on this important initiative.[9]

This follow-up, however, is yet to materialize. Instead, Jokowi has strengthened archconservative elements in the military who are vehemently opposed to reconciliation. As a consequence, the armed forces not only continued their intrusion into civilian affairs, such as agricultural development, but also commenced their controversial "Bela Negara" (Defend the Country) programme, which combines nationalist indoctrination with military training for civilians in order to "inspire a love for the homeland and protect it from 'extreme ideologies' and 'influences', such as communism, radicalism and homosexuality".[10] Arguably, these developments do not bode well for the future of human rights in Indonesia.

The Economy: Desperately Seeking Revenue

President Jokowi's gradual consolidation of power was also evident in economic policy and personnel decisions, for example in the choice of ministers appointed to economic portfolios in the mid-year cabinet reshuffle, the renewed push for infrastructure development, and in the deliberations about the tax amnesty which was passed into law in June and commenced in July. The government also announced yet another series of economic reform packages intended to improve Indonesia's global competitiveness and the ease of doing business. Observers cautiously welcomed the initiatives, but also pointed out that they were somewhat incoherent and overly ambitious.[11] Overall, many macro-economic indicators remained weak, and efforts to liberalize selected economic sectors continued to be undermined by entrenched protectionism.

New Reform Packages and a New Team of Economic Ministers

While the economy failed to gain significant momentum, GDP growth in 2016 was at least slightly higher than in 2015, reaching 4.9 per cent in the first quarter, 5.2 per cent in the second quarter, and 5.0 per cent in the third. In order to improve these figures in the coming years, the Jokowi administration announced another series of economic reform packages (it had already announced eight packages in 2015), targeting a broad range of issues, from beef prices to foreign investment regulations to e-commerce. Taken together, these initiatives signalled that Jokowi was determined to boost market confidence in his administration after GDP growth in 2015 had fallen to a six-year low. But implementation of these reforms will take time and require good coordination between different ministries, as well as between the central and local governments. Perhaps more importantly, the reforms seem to lack a clear direction. According to Hamilton-Hart and Schulze, "they are of extremely varying importance and reach; neither are clear priorities visible, nor is a staging of reform steps in a broader reform agenda existent. Reforms, sensible as they may be, are rather ad hoc."[12] It is therefore doubtful whether the reform packages will achieve their intended outcomes.

Apart from the reform packages, Jokowi also sought to provide a new impetus for the economy by appointing a new team of economic ministers in his July cabinet reshuffle. Dissatisfied with the slow progress of his economic agenda up to this point, the President made changes to several key economic portfolios, including the Ministry of Finance, the Ministry of Energy and Mineral Resources, the Ministry of Trade, and the Ministry of Industry. In addition, Jokowi's close confidante Luhut Pandjaitan took charge of the Coordinating Ministry for Maritime Affairs, whose responsibilities include the development of Indonesia's ailing maritime infrastructure. Apart from improving the government's economic score card, these changes were also aimed at instilling a better sense of cabinet unity, as some of the ousted ministers had a tendency to squabble publicly about government policies.

The undisputed star in the new economic team is Finance Minister Sri Mulyani Indrawati, a highly respected economist who returned to Indonesia after six years at the World Bank. Between 2005 and 2010 she had already served as Finance Minister under President Yudhoyono. Given her impeccable track record, her return to cabinet was almost universally welcomed by international observers. But even though the rupiah and the Indonesian stock exchange rallied in the months after her appointment,[13] Sri Mulyani and the rest of the team will have their work cut out in the coming years as the Indonesian economy faces some significant challenges. Among the most urgent of these challenges are the need to lure more foreign investment, improve sluggish productivity, and increase government revenue.

China's Growing Presence

In 2016, economic growth in Indonesia was, among other factors, hampered by stagnant foreign direct investment, which in turn was caused by protectionist policies, entrenched corruption, and enduring problems with infrastructure and land acquisition. Therefore, one might argue that the most significant development in foreign direct investment in 2016 was not the trajectory of the overall volume, but the rank order of states investing in Indonesia. Compared to the first half of 2015, China had climbed from tenth to fourth spot by mid-2016, raising its investment in Indonesia fivefold, from US$0.2 billion to US$1 billion.[14] And even though China's realization of FDI in Indonesia remained relatively low compared to other large investors such as Japan, the Indonesian Investment Coordinating Board (BKPM) reported that China's realization of FDI grew by a staggering 291 per cent from January to September compared to the same period in 2015.[15]

This increase in Chinese activities is closely linked to Indonesia's ambitious infrastructure development programme, which has attracted considerable Chinese interest. However, many signature projects are still running behind schedule, including the much publicized high-speed rail connection between Jakarta and Bandung, a project funded as a joint venture between Chinese and Indonesian companies. Since construction commenced in January 2016, the project has made little progress due to a series of problems related to land acquisition and obtaining permits and funds.[16] There was better news for Jokowi from some other construction sites further afield. For example, three small airports in Sulawesi were completed in 2016, giving the President welcome opportunities to attend festive opening ceremonies.[17] Looking ahead, Jokowi's infrastructure agenda received another boost when Indonesia became one of the first recipients of loans from the new China-led Asian Infrastructure Investment Bank (AIIB). In June the AIIB announced that it would contribute US$216.6 million for a large-scale urban infrastructure project co-financed with the World Bank.[18]

But to keep the momentum for the infrastructure development programme alive, the government will also need to raise more domestic revenue. In 2016, government spending on infrastructure increased significantly, reaching an estimated Rp313.5 trillion (15 per cent of the total state budget).[19] But other priority policy areas such as health have also required large expenditures, so that the budget deficit was set to reach 2.4 per cent of GDP. Indonesia has now recorded consecutive budget deficits since the end of the commodity boom in 2011. Though not an immediate cause for concern, it does reflect an inability to find adequate policy responses to the losses from diminishing commodity exports.[20] Manufacturing, in particular, remains woefully underdeveloped. For 2017, the government has projected a similar deficit as spending on infrastructure is estimated to further increase by 11 per cent, reaching Rp347 trillion (17 per cent of total state budget, or 3 per cent of GDP).[21] Well aware of the ongoing budgetary constraints, the Jokowi administration launched a tax amnesty programme in 2016 in the hope of repatriating overseas funds, broadening the tax base, and increasing much-needed revenue.

A Tax Amnesty as Silver Bullet?

Widely seen as the economic flagship programme in 2016, the tax amnesty was designed to offer Indonesian citizens who had failed to file tax declarations in the past, preferential tax rates ranging from 2 to 10 per cent, depending on when they declared and whether they would repatriate the funds they have kept overseas. The programme was divided into three phases, two of which were completed in 2016. The first phase, which ran from 1 July to 30 September 2016, offered the lowest tax tariffs and was therefore the most eagerly anticipated. After a slow start it eventually elicited the desired response, with thousands of new taxpayers registering for the programme and prominent businesspeople like James Riady, Anthoni Salim, Franky Oesman Widjaja, and Sandiaga Uno all reporting their assets. At the end of the first phase the total amount of declared assets had reached Rp3,603.6 trillion (approx. US$277 billion), or 90.1 per cent of the government's target of Rp4,000 trillion. The programme also yielded Rp97.2 trillion (approx. US$7.5 billion) in additional tax revenue by the end of September, which was equivalent to 58.9 per cent of the full nine-month target of Rp165 trillion.[22]

But while more than expected assets were declared, fewer than expected were repatriated. By 30 September the government could only announce repatriated offshore funds worth Rp136.5 trillion (approx. US$10.5 billion), or 13.6 per cent of the full target of Rp1,000 trillion. The reluctance to repatriate more funds exposed Indonesia's ongoing difficulties in creating a more conducive business environment, as many business people preferred to keep their assets in tax havens abroad. Furthermore, the looming spectre of ethnic or religious tensions that emerged at the end of the year in the wake of the anti-Ahok demonstrations also added to fears about uncertainty and volatility, contributing to the slow start of the second phase (1 October to 31 December 2016). Ultimately, however, whether the tax amnesty will be deemed a success or not, it is not a silver bullet to solve Indonesia's revenue problems. While it has temporarily boosted the government's budget space, far more comprehensive long-term measures will be needed to simplify the tax regime and improve trust in the tax administration.

Foreign Policy: Balancing Economic Diplomacy and Security Concerns

The need to improve key economic parameters also influenced Indonesian foreign policy in 2016, as President Jokowi dedicated much of his overseas travels to trying to attract more foreign direct investment. This intensified economic diplomacy was in line with Jokowi's declared goal of shifting Indonesia's foreign policy priorities from good global citizenship to more narrowly defined national interests, especially economic development. At the same time, though, Indonesia was also confronted with the limits of its own diplomatic capabilities as it faced an ever more assertive China, which in 2016 repeatedly challenged Indonesia's sovereignty over its territorial waters around the resource-rich Natuna Islands. China's activities in the Natunas and other parts of the South China Sea raised questions about Indonesia's long-practised hedging strategy in the region and its preferred role as an "honest broker" in the various territorial disputes in the South China Sea. Arguably, these questions will become even more pertinent in 2017 as the United States looks set for a foreign policy shift after the election of Donald Trump as the new President in November 2016.

Economic Diplomacy

Under Jokowi, Indonesian diplomats have been asked to become salesmen for Indonesia and its products. Two years into his presidency, however, there are few signs that diplomats excel at this role. This is hardly surprising, because economic expertise in the Ministry for Foreign Affairs remains underdeveloped and the ministry's organizational structure, which is still largely focused on traditional diplomacy and negotiations, does not match Jokowi's foreign policy ambitions in this regard. The President has therefore intensified his own efforts at boosting Indonesian exports and selling Indonesia as an attractive market by visiting some key trading partners in 2016, including Germany, the United Kingdom, Belgium, and the Netherlands (all in April), as well as South Korea and Russia in May. At the end of the year, Jokowi also visited India and Iran. These visits followed a widely debated state visit to the United States in October 2015, which Jokowi himself had described as a "business trip".[23]

The five-day tour of Europe in April 2016 was particularly timely, not only because Indonesian exports to Europe have decreased significantly over the last five years,[24] but also because talks about a Comprehensive Economic Partnership Agreement (CEPA) between Indonesia and the European Union (EU) have long stalled. Despite Jokowi's best intentions, however, the visit yielded relatively few tangible results, apart from some noteworthy business agreements. With regards to CEPA, a general scoping paper was completed but there was no indication when formal negotiations on this trade agreement would commence. Reflecting on Jokowi's final stop in the Netherlands, one observer noted wryly that "there had been no disturbances and that in itself was perhaps the biggest success of the whole visit".[25]

Preventing disturbances could also be said to be the main aim of Indonesia's current diplomacy with China, Indonesia's biggest trading partner. In 2016, economic ties between the two countries deepened significantly as Chinese investment in Indonesia grew rapidly, Chinese billionaire Jack Ma was invited to become an advisor to Indonesia's e-commerce committee,[26] and the countries' two presidents, Jokowi and Xi Jinping, came together for a fifth meeting in less than two years. But their meeting at the sidelines of the G20 Summit in Hangzhou in September was, despite the familiar strong focus on economic cooperation, not just another business trip. Conducted in the aftermath of some subtle but noticeable diplomatic tensions between the two countries over Chinese fishing activities off the Natuna Islands and China's response to a ruling by the Arbitral Tribunal initiated by the Philippines under UNCLOS in July, Jokowi's meeting with the Chinese President demonstrated instead that it may become increasingly difficult for Indonesia to continue its policy of isolating its economic interests from growing strategic concerns about China's assertive manoeuvres in the South China Sea.

Rising Tensions around the Natunas

Indeed, Indonesia's relations with China mirror broader developments in the Indo-Pacific region, where, as Laksmana put it, "economic ties are thriving while strategic trust is floundering among the resident powers".[27] The main reason for the growing diplomatic tensions between Indonesia and China is the increasing frequency of illegal Chinese fishing activities in Indonesian waters. In three separate incidents throughout 2016, Indonesian navy ships confronted Chinese fishing vessels that had entered Indonesian waters around the Natuna Islands.[28] The small island chain is part of Indonesian territory, but parts of the surrounding waters are claimed by China as part of its "nine-dash line" policy. Accordingly, Chinese authorities strongly protested the actions by the Indonesian navy, prompting President Jokowi to take a number of highly symbolic steps to signal to China that he was serious about defending Indonesian sovereignty. First, in June 2016 he held a cabinet meeting on board a warship at the Natuna Islands. Then, in October 2016 the Indonesian military sent another strong message of intent when it staged a large-scale exercise at the Natuna Islands that involved around seventy warplanes dropping bombs on targets off the coast.[29] Moreover, Jokowi has also made several public statements in which he insisted that he would defend "every inch" of Indonesian territory and that there would be no compromise on Indonesian sovereignty.[30]

The growing tensions around the Natunas have exposed a number of dilemmas in Indonesian foreign policy. First and foremost, they threaten to undermine Indonesia's long-established policy of neutrality in the South China Sea. According to Laksmana, this "hollow neutrality" is resting on increasingly untenable assumptions; for example, that China is actually interested in maintaining the status quo, or that territorial disputes in the region can be resolved by adhering to an established code of conduct.[31] Indeed, China's recent activities indicate that the parameters of diplomatic engagement in the region may be shifting. For Indonesia to ensure that neither its bilateral relations with China nor its preferred broader regional role as a non-claimant state and honest broker in the South China Sea will be put at risk, it will need to tread carefully when confronting the next Chinese fishing vessel.

So far, Indonesian officials have been adamant that the various incidents in the Natunas should only be treated as disputes over fishing rights, not over sovereignty.[32] But, and here is the second dilemma, the Natuna incidents also exposed, not for the first time, a distinct lack of coherence in the Indonesian government's articulation of foreign policy across different ministries. In responding to the Chinese incursions into Indonesian waters, Foreign Minister Retno Marsudi and Fisheries Minister Susi Pudjiastuti appeared to express somewhat contradictory views about the incidents.[33] While the Foreign Minister reiterated Indonesia's traditional position that, unlike its neighbours, Indonesia has no territorial disputes with China, the Fisheries Minister took a decidedly more confrontational stance.

This poor coordination between ministries is indicative of a lack of direction and a lingering uncertainty about the future direction of Indonesia's China policy.

Conclusion and Outlook

One year ago, Robin Bush wrote in the 2016 edition of this publication that "President Jokowi has spent the first year of his presidency finding his feet".[34] Twelve months on, it is fair to say that Jokowi has now found his feet in the cauldron of Jakarta power politics, but he is still struggling to endow his presidency with a clear policy direction or even a grand vision for the remainder of his first term. While he showed remarkable shrewdness and ruthlessness in his tactical manoeuvres to enlarge his coalition, his policy and personnel decisions at times appeared arbitrary, incoherent, and lacking in preparation. Both the cabinet reshuffle in July as well as the various economic reform packages illustrate this vividly. The cabinet reshuffle, for example, included not only the widely discussed selections of Sri Mulyani and Wiranto, but also the farcical appointment and subsequent removal from cabinet of Archanda Tahar, who was found to possess U.S. citizenship not long after he had been appointed as Minister for Energy and Mineral Resources. The 2016 reform packages for the economy, meanwhile, appeared incoherent and, in parts, overly ambitious, as they contained several measures aimed at liberalizing the economy, yet at the same time rarely challenged key protectionist tenets of Indonesia's political economy.

So far, however, this apparent lack of direction has not damaged Jokowi's approval ratings. On the contrary, public opinion surveys conducted in 2016 showed a clear upward trend in public satisfaction with the President's performance.[35] The improved ratings are primarily a result of policies with a direct and immediate impact on people's lives, such as reforms to the health and education systems, as well as some of the already completed infrastructure projects. Here, Jokowi's "technocratic populism"[36] is already paying dividends, and, with many more infrastructure projects still in the pipeline, Jokowi is clearly laying the groundwork for his re-election campaign in 2019. Jakarta's established elite has taken note of these developments. Remarkably, former opposition parties like Golkar have already begun to position themselves as potential partners for Jokowi in the next presidential election.

Until that election, several challenges await Indonesia and its President. As 2016 drew to a close, the country was facing an aggressive resurgence of anti-Chinese sentiment and religious discrimination, which, if allowed to spread, has the potential to unravel many of the achievements of Indonesian democratization. Political instability, or even riots, will be the last thing Jokowi wants now that he has finally consolidated his grip on power, so several political observers have already speculated that Jokowi will seek retaliation against those political operators believed to be behind the large demonstrations in Jakarta in late 2016. Only if Jokowi succeeds in stymying these latest opposition manoeuvres will he be able to focus his attention on other imminent tasks, such as translating his enhanced power in parliament into tangible policy achievements, developing a sustainable blueprint for stimulating economic growth, or formulating a coherent foreign policy agenda.

Notes

1. Eve Warburton, "Political Update", presentation at the Indonesia Update conference in Canberra, 16–17 September 2016.
2. Marcus Mietzner, "Coercing Loyalty: Coalitional Presidentialism and Party Politics in Jokowi's Indonesia", *Contemporary Southeast Asia* 38, no. 2 (2016): 209–32.
3. Tom Power, "Cashing In", *New Mandala*, 8 August 2016.
4. Hendri Yulius, "LGBT Indonesians on Campus: Too Hot to Handle", *Indonesia at Melbourne*, 26 January 2016.
5. Charlotte Setijadi, "Religious Freedom on Trial in Indonesia", *East Asia Forum*, 5 January 2017.
6. Philips Vermonte, "National Politics: The Year of Calm and Storm", *Jakarta Post Outlook 2017*, p. 33.
7. "Amien Rais, Fadli Zon, Fahri Hamzah, dan Rizieq Shihab berada dalam satu mobil komando" [Amien Rais, Fadli Zon, Fahri Hamzah and Rizieq Shihab in one command car], *Kompas*, 4 November 2016.
8. Vannessa Hearman, "1965 Symposium: A Glimmer of Hope?", *New Mandala*, 9 May 2016.
9. Katharine McGregor and Jemma Purdey, "Indonesia Takes a Small but Critical Step Towards Reconciliation", *Indonesia at Melbourne*, 26 April 2016.
10. Bhatara Ibnu Reza, "Bela Negara: Thinly Veiled Militarisation of the Civilian Population", *Indonesia at Melbourne*, 12 July 2016.
11. Natasha Hamilton-Hart and Günther G. Schulze, "Taxing Times: The Challenge of Restoring Competitiveness and the Search for Fiscal Space", presented by Schulze at the Indonesia Update conference in Canberra, 16–17 September 2016.
12. Ibid., p. 25.
13. Patrick McDowell, Ben Otto, and Anita Rachman, "Indonesia President Navigates Cautious Course in Tense South China Sea", *Wall Street Journal*, 18 October 2016.
14. Ibid.
15. Farida Susanty, "China Strengthens Grip on Indonesia", *Jakarta Post*, 24 November 2016.

16. "Jakarta-Bandung High-Speed Rail Project Stalls", *Nikkei Asian Review*, 28 July 2016.

17. "Ke Pulau Miangas, Jokowi resmikan tiga bandara" [Going to Miangas Island, Jokowi officiates three airports], *Kompas*, 19 October 2016.

18. Prashanth Parameswaran, "Indonesia and China's AIIB", *The Diplomat*, 26 July 2016.

19. Siwage Dharma Negara, "Indonesia's 2017 Budget Seeks Cautious Economic Expansion", *ISEAS Perspective* 2016, no. 51, 15 September 2016, p. 6.

20. Hamilton-Hart and Schulze, "Taxing Times".

21. Negara, "Indonesia's 2017 Budget".

22. "Update Indonesia's Tax Amnesty Program: 1st Phase Ended Successfully", *Indonesia Investments*, 1 October 2016.

23. Robin Bush, "Indonesia in 2015", in *Southeast Asian Affairs 2016*, edited by Malcolm Cook and Daljit Singh (Singapore: ISEAS – Yusof Ishak Institute), pp. 131–44.

24. Anton Hermansyah, "Indonesian Exports to Europe in Decline", *Jakarta Post*, 19 April 2016.

25. Henk Schulte Nordholt, "After Jokowi's Visit: Indonesia and the Netherlands Back on Track", KITLV blog, 25 April 2016 <http://www.kitlv.nl/blog-jokowis-visit-indonesia-netherlands-back-track/> (accessed 25 November 2016).

26. Resty Woro Yuniar, "Alibaba's Jack Ma to Give Indonesia Tech Support", *Wall Street Journal*, 9 September 2016.

27. Evan Laksmana, "A Post-Non-Claimant South China Sea Policy", *Jakarta Post*, 20 June 2016.

28. Amelia Long, "Something's Gotta Give: Indonesia's Policy Options in the Natunas", *ASPI Strategist*, 24 June 2016.

29. "Amid South China Sea Uncertainty, Indonesia Stages a Show of Force", Reuters, 6 October 2016.

30. Catherine Wong, "Indonesian Leader Widodo's Emphasis on Development Boosts China Ties", *South China Morning Post*, 25 August 2016.

31. Laksmana, "A Post-Non-Claimant South China Sea Policy".

32. Rizal Sukma, "Indonesia and China Need to Combat the IUU Problem", *Jakarta Post*, 31 March 2016.

33. Donald E. Weatherbee, "Re-assessing Indonesia's Role in the South China Sea", *ISEAS Perspective* 2016, no. 18, 21 April 2016.

34. Bush, "Indonesia in 2015", p. 140.

35. "Survei CSIS: 66.5 persen responden puas dengan kinerja pemerintah" [66.5 per cent of respondents are satisfied with the government's work], *Kompas*, 13 September 2016.

36. Marcus Mietzner, *Reinventing Asian Populism: Jokowi's Rise, Democracy, and Political Contestation in Indonesia*, Policy Studies 72 (Honolulu: East-West Center, 2015).

INDONESIA'S FOREIGN POLICY IN 2016:
Garuda Hovering

Donald E. Weatherbee

The Garuda — the man-bird — in Indian mythology is the vehicle of Vishnu. Perhaps the best known image of the Garuda in ancient Javanese art has it transporting historical eleventh-century East Javanese king Airlangga. The Garuda has been adopted as the symbol of the modern Indonesian state. The author has used the Garuda as a metaphor for Indonesian foreign policy and has likened it to the Phoenix, the fabulous bird of Greek mythology that arises from the ashes of the fire that consumed its previous incarnation, to fly again.[1] Sukarno's Garuda was left in ashes in 1965. Under Soeharto, it rose to fly again, towards Indonesia's leadership in ASEAN and the so-called "South". It was immolated in the economic meltdown and political turmoil of the collapse of the regime in 1998. The ashes of the Garuda were barely stirred by the short presidencies of B.J. Habibie and Abdurrahman Wahid (Gus Dur); the former engulfed in the disastrous separation of East Timor from Indonesia and the latter by the leader's erratic eccentricity. It was not until President Megawati Sukarnoputri's term of office that the Garuda began to struggle out of the ashes of its predecessor. It was a wounded Garuda, bleeding from the internal war in Aceh, but able to stretch its wings at the 2003 Bali ASEAN Summit (Bali II), where it sought to reclaim ASEAN leadership. Only in the presidency of Susilo Bambang Yudhoyono (SBY) did the Garuda take full flight again. SBY's high-profile global foreign policy outreach was viewed as a tool to advance Indonesia's place in the world as an emerging middle power actively engaged in international affairs.

DONALD E. WEATHERBEE is the Donald S. Russell Distinguished Professor Emeritus at the University of South Carolina. He was ISEAS Visiting Professorial Fellow, February–April 2016.

In President Joko "Jokowi" Widodo's first two years in office, the Garuda has been hovering, circling a more self-restricted flight zone while casting about for direction, still unsettled on a course. Jokowi seems uninterested in foreign policy, or at least only in how it connects to his domestic agenda. During the 2014 election campaign, both Jokowi and his opponent, Prabowo Subianto, trashed the globalist internationalism of outgoing President SBY. The fact that SBY's high-level international visibility showcased Indonesia as a rising middle power was dismissed as having no direct domestic payoff. SBY showed the Indonesian flag to the world; Jokowi has furled it. In 2016, for the second year in a row, the Indonesian President passed up the opportunity to address the opening of the United Nations General Assembly annual session. Also, for the second year in a row, Jokowi did not attend the APEC Leaders Meeting, although it was important enough to bring Barack Obama, Xi Jinping, and Vladimir Putin to the twenty-one-country gathering. Of the seven ASEAN countries that are APEC members, besides Indonesia, only Thailand was not represented by its head of government. That was because of the death of the Thai king. Jokowi did make the 2014 APEC meeting when China's Xi Jinping hosted it. Jokowi also attended the 2016 G20 meeting, likewise hosted by Xi Jinping. This may say more about Jokowi's interest in Indonesia's bilateral relationship with China than his interest in high-level multilateral diplomacy. Vice President Jusuf Kalla is increasingly fronting for Indonesia internationally.

Jokowi's Distancing from Foreign Policy Process

There are foreign policy consequences for a diminished visibility on the world stage. SBY and his aides presented Indonesia to the world as a modernizing Muslim democracy sharing with other democracies commitments to political and human rights. No matter how flawed that image might have been, it was far more positive than that which is emerging under Jokowi. The new picture of Indonesia is one of religious intolerance, Islamic radicalism, church burnings, legislative attacks on the LGBT community, group executions, and other indicators of a retreat from democracy. Rather than defending democracy, the President has acquiesced in the spread of the military-backed ultranationalist Bela Negara ("Defend the Country") indoctrination programme, with its anti-Western-culture bias.

Jokowi's distancing from the foreign policy process has meant that there has been no captain; no single voice speaking authoritatively from Jakarta to the world, nor giving foreign policy leadership across the ministerial spectrum. The question is, "Who's in charge?" For example, at the height of the 10 March 2016

Indonesia–China fisheries face-off in Indonesia's Natuna Islands' EEZ (discussed below), there were uncoordinated responses from five ministers, but none from Jokowi. Foreign Minister Retno L.P. Marsudi does not seem to play an important role in policymaking. Her appointment — from her post as Indonesian Ambassador to the Netherlands — seems a result of the blessing of Jokowi's political backer Megawati for another woman in the cabinet, and Jokowi's indifference. Not having served as chief of a major mission such as the UN or EU, she did not bring the same professional standing or diplomatic grooming to the job at the Ministry of Foreign Affairs (Kemlu – Kementerian Luar Negeri) as her two predecessors in SBY's cabinet: Hassan Wirajuda and Marty Natalegawa.

For major foreign policy issues, Jokowi has depended on advisors outside of the Kemlu culture. Through the first two years of Jokowi's term in office, retired General Luhut Pandjaitan seemed to be the go-to person for foreign policy; first as the President's Chief of Staff, then as Coordinating Minister for Political, Legal, and Security Affairs, who has oversight of Kemlu in his brief. The close personal and political bond between Luhut and the President goes back to Jokowi's days as mayor of Surakarta. Luhut has had the most prominent official profile in dealings with China. A foreign policy wild card was dealt in the July 2016 cabinet reshuffle which saw Luhut moved to Coordinating Minister for Maritime Affairs. He was replaced at Political, Legal, and Security Affairs by former General Wiranto, whose appointment sent shockwaves through the global human rights community. He has been accused of crimes against humanity as Indonesia's military commander during the vengeful military-backed rampage after the 1999 East Timor vote for independence. As Amnesty International put it, Jokowi's appointment of Wiranto "showed contempt for human rights".[2] The U.S. State Department acknowledged that it was aware of the human rights allegations against Wiranto.

From his post as Indonesia's Ambassador to the United Kingdom and Ireland, Rizal Sukma — Jokowi's foreign policy intellectual guru — maintains his line to the presidential palace. He and Luhut had major input into the foreign-policy platform in Jokowi's election manifesto.[3] Rizal was a major contributor to establishing the conceptual underpinning for Jokowi's vision of Indonesia as a Global Maritime Axis.[4] One of the explanations for Luhut's shift to Coordinating Minister for Maritime Affairs was to energize the maritime master plan, which, in Jokowi's vision, held the future of Indonesia's economic growth. Luhut replaced Rizal Ramli, who at times had been at odds with the President and ministerial colleagues.[5]

Rizal Sukma has described the long-standing Indonesian strategy for navigating between the U.S. and China reefs as one of "hedging" against the uncertainties for Indonesia's national interest in its bilateral relations with both great powers as their interests clash.[6] Indonesia's goal is to further its bilateral interests with both great powers without compromising its relationship with either one. He has also described Jokowi's foreign policy as maintaining "equal relations" with China and the United States.[7] There is no question that the formal architecture of the two bilateral relationships is the same. As a nonaligned country, Indonesia does not have a military alliance with either. Indonesia has a Comprehensive Strategic Partnership with both countries, a diplomatic umbrella under which it engages in a wide variety of functional activities, including security cooperation. After two years of Jokowi's administration, it may be asked whether Indonesia is showing a "tilt" towards China. By "tilt", I mean a depth of engagement with China which limits Indonesia's policy autonomy in its hedging strategy.

A "Tilt" towards China?

If there is a "tilt" towards China, it is most obvious in the deepening of the Indonesia–China economic relationship. In the two-year course of his presidency, Jokowi has had an unprecedented five one-on-one encounters with Xi Jinping. This can be compared to the two bilateral meetings he had with U.S. President Obama. Jokowi's latest meeting with his Chinese counterpart was on 2 September 2016, when the two leaders reaffirmed their economic relationship.[8] China is Indonesia's single-largest trading partner, at more than 15 per cent of Indonesia's total trade.[9] In 2015, two-way trade was US$44.4 billion; just less than double that of the U.S.–Indonesia figure of $23.8 billion. As the growth in Sino–Indonesian trade continued in 2016, so too has the Indonesian trade deficit. Standing at US$14.4 billion in 2015, it will exceed US$16 billion for 2016 if the trend for the first three quarters continues. At the September meeting, Xi promised to ease the importing of Indonesian fruits, an important Indonesian export. The two sides also renewed their bilateral currency swap (BCS) agreement, worth about US$1.5 billion, for another three years. This is in addition to a 2015 loan to Indonesian state banks worth about US$3 billion, linked to the BCS swap agreement, as Indonesia shifts its trade payments from the U.S. dollar to the yuan.

While trade is important, Jokowi's focus is on access to Chinese loans and investment. Since he became President, Chinese investment in Indonesia has doubled, taking it from the ninth- to third-largest Indonesian FDI source, after Singapore and Japan.[10] It remains to be seen whether the promised Chinese FDI will actually be realized. The past record is not promising. Between 2005 and 2014, only 7 per cent of Chinese investment had been realized. This is far short of that of other major investing countries.

More critical for Jokowi's domestic programme is China's financing of his grand plans for infrastructure development, including billions of dollars in mega-projects. The estimated 2015–19 cost of Jokowi's infrastructure development programmes is $450 billion, and this is at the heart of his goal of achieving a GDP growth rate of 7 per cent by 2019.[11] Only 30 per cent of the amount is planned to come from Indonesia's state budget, leaving the balance to come from state-owned enterprises — most of which are deeply in the red — and foreign borrowings. Beijing's initial response to Jokowi's appeal for assistance was the 23 April 2015 China–Indonesia MOU in which Beijing pledged $50 billion in loans from the China Development Bank and the Industrial and Commercial Bank of China.

In 2016, attention centred on one particular Chinese-funded infrastructure project: the controversial $5.5 billion Jakarta–Bandung high-speed railway. The contract was awarded to China in September 2015, with the railway scheduled for operation in 2019. According to Rini Soemarno, Minister of State-Owned Businesses, the railway loan was the first instalment of the $50 billion package.[12] The project was greatly criticized on economic, technical, and political grounds, but strongly pressed forward by China. President Jokowi officially broke ground for construction on 21 January 2016. This was premature. To the chagrin of all concerned, actual construction has been stalled. Land acquisition had not been completed. Necessary permits had not been issued. Technical problems had not been resolved. Track design was under revision. The China Development Bank, which is financing 75 per cent of the project, was unwilling to disburse until all of the issues were settled. It now seems that it will be 2017 before actual construction begins, with the 2019 completion date unrealistic. Jokowi has been politically embarrassed, since success in his domestic programmes will be key to his re-election in 2019.

The question has been raised as to why Jokowi forced the decision to go forward with a project that had so many domestic opponents and practical question marks. One interpretation is that it signalled that Indonesia is serious in partnering with China in its development plans for the Global Maritime Axis. The high-speed railway would be a lure or precondition to unlock future Chinese loans and investment.[13] Among other elements of the Global Maritime Axis blueprint are upgrading Indonesia's six international ports, building twenty-four new container ports, and improving over a thousand non-commercial ports.[14] The cost of the new ports has been put at US$6–7 billion. The port projects are only one part of a "maritime highway" vision estimated by the National Planning Board (Bappenas) to cost US$55 billion by 2019.[15] Jokowi's maritime ambitions coincide with

China's efforts to build its Maritime Silk Road as part of its "One Belt, One Road" (OBOR) strategic plan. In a March 2015 Jokowi–Xi meeting, the two Presidents stated that the Global Maritime Axis and the Maritime Silk Road were "highly complementary".[16] In Jokowi's September 2016 meeting with Xi, they agreed to strengthen consultation and activity "to connect the 21st-century Maritime Silk Road initiative with the Global Maritime Axis vision".[17] For Indonesia, the most important activity in the connection will be Chinese financing. Outwardly, Jakarta seems unconcerned by the longer-range geostrategic implications of China's maritime expansionism for its own regional maritime ambitions.

The Natunas and China

The smooth surface of the Indonesia–China bilateral relationship was ruffled in 2016 by maritime confrontation in the troubled waters north of Indonesia's Natuna Islands, where China's nine-dash line delimiting its claims in the South China Sea overlaps Indonesia's EEZ. The encroachments of Chinese Coast Guard–protected fishing fleets into Indonesia's EEZ was the most critical issue facing the Jakarta decision makers during the year. It forced them to grapple with balancing the totality of Indonesia's relations with China with a response to China's challenge to Indonesia's sovereign rights. For Indonesia, there is no overlap of Chinese jurisdiction in Indonesia's EEZ. For Jakarta, the nine-dash line has no legal basis. Indonesia has taken care to separate the bilateral question of Chinese intrusions into Indonesian waters from the South China Sea territorial disputes in the Spratlys, where Indonesia has no claims. Jakarta still — nominally at least — clings to the illusion that as a non-claimant it can be an "honest broker". Moreover, it is still in the fruitless pursuit of a binding Code of Conduct in the South China Sea, which, if after the July 2016 ASEAN Foreign Ministers Meeting is not already dead, is at a dead end.

Since 2015, China's claim to fishing rights in Indonesia's waters has become entangled in Indonesia's aggressive campaign against illegal fishing in its maritime space. Spearheaded by Minister of Marine Affairs and Fisheries Susi Pudjiastuti, by September 2016 the count of destroyed and sunk vessels had reached 220, the majority Thai and Vietnamese, leading to a quip that "Susi is blowing up her opposition", a reference to her business interests in Indonesia's fishing industry. Susi has categorically stated that "all boats caught fishing illegally in the country will be treated the same".[18] In large measure, impounded Chinese vessels have been exempted. When one Chinese boat was destroyed in May 2015, Beijing expressed its "strong concern", advising Indonesia to adopt a constructive attitude towards fishery cooperation.[19] According to Susi, the deterrent effect of the hard line is working, with Indonesian catch rising from an annual low of 2.5 million tons to 6.6 million tons, and the potential to normalize at 9.9 million tons in two or three years.[20]

The first Indonesian encounter in 2016 with the Chinese Coast Guard occurred on 19 March, when a Chinese Coast Guard vessel forcibly intervened to prevent an Indonesian fishery enforcement vessel from seizing a Chinese fishing boat in Natuna waters. Confusion among Indonesian officials was evident when Foreign Minister Retno insisted that China and Indonesia did not have a border problem and Cabinet Secretary Pramono said that Indonesia wanted to settle border problems with China peacefully. Without details, Pramono explained that the issue had been a "misunderstanding" that had been resolved.[21] On 17 May, the Indonesian navy impounded a Chinese fishing boat, bringing a stern Chinese protest. On 27 June, an Indonesian navy corvette used live ammunition to halt and seize a Chinese fishing vessel and arrest its crew members. The Chinese Coast Guard arrived on the scene to rescue the vessel. In all three cases, China claimed that their ships were in traditional Chinese waters and fishing grounds. The language of China's protest over the June confrontation was particularly strong. Beijing accused Indonesia of abusive force in harassing a Chinese fishing vessel operating in Chinese fishing grounds. Indonesia was urged to "stop taking actions that complicate, exaggerate and undermine peace and stability, and handle the fishery issue at sea in a constructive way".[22]

Indonesia has reacted to the boldness of the Chinese assertion of its claims in Indonesia's EEZ with a crash programme of building up its military defence and surveillance capabilities in the Natunas. Its seriousness of purpose was demonstrated by President Jokowi's three trips to Natuna during the year, including showing of the flag in an assertion of sovereignty on a cruise through the disputed waters on board the same corvette involved in the June incident.[23] It seems unlikely, however, that China will be deterred by an Indonesian show of force. Even more unlikely is that Indonesia is prepared to use force against the Chinese Coast Guard or other official fishery protection vessels. Jakarta knows from the Philippines' experience that the economic cost of defying China is high.

The PCA Ruling and Indonesia's Response

A legal page was turned in the Indonesia–China maritime dispute when the Arbitral Tribunal housed at the Permanent Court of Arbitration in The Hague handed down its decision in the Philippines' application for a ruling on the legality of

China's claims in the Philippines' EEZ. When Manila originated the case in 2013, Indonesia's Foreign Minister Marty Natalegawa scorned it as unhelpful to the ASEAN effort to negotiate the Code of Conduct with China. Of course, the issues raised by the Philippines with respect to China's claims in the Philippines' EEZ were relevant to Indonesia's China problem. This was recognized by Coordinating Minister Luhut, who is quoted as saying, "We would like to see a solution on this in the near future although we could bring it to the International Criminal Court." He misspoke, meaning the PCA.[24] Even as Indonesia was dealing with the domestic and international fallout from the June clash with the Chinese Coast Guard, the Arbitral Tribunal ruling came down on 12 July. It declared that the nine-dash line had no legal basis and that claims to traditional fisheries were extinguished by UNCLOS 1982 (United Nations Convention on the Law of the Sea). In anticipation of the judgment, President Jokowi had instructed his ministers to formulate a common position on Indonesia's response so that they could be on the same page when answering questions about it. Rather than welcome the Arbitral Tribunal's sweeping judgment, Jakarta was silent about the implications of the ruling for its own EEZ problem. Kemlu issued a four-point bromidic statement calling on all parties to "exercise self-restraint and to refrain from any actions that could escalate tensions".[25] It called on the parties to respect international law and UNCLOS and to continue to uphold their shared commitment to regional peace. Chinese commentators found this statement unsatisfactory, claiming it was not objective or impartial.[26]

From Jakarta's perspective, while the Arbitral Tribunal ruling supported Jakarta's legal position, it hardened China's position that UNCLOS did not apply to its South China Sea domain. China cracked the whip through its political surrogates at the July ASEAN Foreign Ministers' Meeting to ensure that the Arbitral Tribunal ruling did not become part of the official record, proving again that ASEAN is incapable of taking any action that contradicts Chinese policies. Nor was a draft ASEAN communiqué implicitly criticizing China's militarization of the South China Sea allowed to be adopted. Malaysia, Vietnam, and the Philippines separately released the rejected draft communiqué. Indonesia did not, with Kemlu saying its release was a "mistake". Again in 2016, Kemlu's conceit that Indonesia can give ASEAN leadership was proved groundless.

President Jokowi remains adamant that there will be "no compromise" of Indonesian sovereignty in the Natunas.[27] This does not rule out compromise on Chinese access to the fisheries. This possibility seems implicit in Rizal Sukma's advice. After the March incident he argued that "the problem between Indonesia and China lies with fishing rights, not territorial disputes".[28] He warned that a fisheries dispute should not be allowed to develop into a political feud. "It is inconceivable", he wrote, "that the two nations cannot find an amicable solution to the problem." Such a solution, it would seem, would require China's acknowledgement of Indonesian sovereignty and Indonesia's willingness to normalize Chinese fishing in the disputed waters. This was hinted at by Luhut, who travelled to China in April. Before leaving Jakarta he vowed not to sell the country short on the Natunas.[29] On his return, however, he said his visit to China had been aimed at easing tensions that had escalated over illegal fishing. Indonesia, he said, wants to come to a mutual understanding on fishing, "some sort of win–win solution".[30] This would seem to conform to what for Beijing would be a "constructive way" to handle the dispute. A model for Indonesia may be evolving in the Philippines' dealing with China over Scarborough Shoal. Any possible "sharing" scheme raises new questions. If the nine-dash line becomes the basis for sharing fishery resources, will China want to extend it to the oil and gas reserves beneath the Natuna Sea? If China and Indonesia go the joint-development route, will accommodations be made for fishing by Indonesia's ASEAN partners?

Relations with Australia

Although relations with China dominated Indonesian foreign policy in 2016, to its south, the often-troubled relationship with Australia markedly improved. Relations were at a near nadir at the end of SBY's presidency, over issues of beef, boat people, and espionage. The already fraught relationship was jolted again by the Jokowi government's inclusion of two Australians in the April 2015 group execution of convicted drug mules. The reset of the relationship began in August 2015, with a productive meeting in Jakarta between Australian Foreign Minister Julie Bishop and Foreign Minister Retno. It gained momentum with the September 2015 change of government in Canberra, which saw Tony Abbott replaced as Prime Minister by Malcolm Turnbull. Bishop remained at her foreign ministry post. Jakarta was delighted when Turnbull made Indonesia the first stop on his first foreign trip as PM. Seeking to leave the inflammatory issues of the past behind — although they bubble under the surface — the two leaders focused on growing their economies with expanded trade and investment opportunities.

Foreign Minister Bishop was back in Jakarta in March 2016 to open a gleaming new Australian embassy building. She claimed that Australian–Indonesian relations "have never been closer, never been stronger".[31] Bishop again was in Jakarta in October, meeting with Jokowi looking towards his scheduled 4–6 November Australian visit. This was cancelled because of violent demonstrations in Jakarta against the governor of Jakarta's alleged blasphemy. Put on hold was the signing of five bilateral MOUs.

Sulu Sea Patrol Initiative

In the field of maritime security, Indonesia, Malaysia, and the Philippines negotiated a trilateral agreement for cooperation among them to meet the escalating acts of piracy and kidnapping in the Sulu and Sulawesi seas. On 5 May, in Yogyakarta, Foreign Minister Retno met with the Malaysian and Philippines' Foreign Ministers and the military chiefs of the three countries to establish a framework to strengthen their cooperation and collaboration in handling security threats in the region. They agreed "to carry out coordinated patrols in waters that are our common concern".[32] Although some media outlets reported this as an agreement on "joint" patrols, the communiqué said "coordinated" patrols, leaving the details of operating procedures open. These were worked out by the Defence Ministers over the course of three meetings in May, July, and the final meeting on 1–2 August in Bali, where the framework agreement for what is called the Sulu Sea Patrol Initiative (SSPI) was signed. The model is the Malacca Straits Patrol (MSP) initiated in 2004 and including Indonesia, Malaysia, Singapore, and Thailand. The coordinated patrols in the Sulu Sea restrict the parties to their own waters, with the question of "hot pursuit" not yet fully resolved.

Indian Ocean Rim Association

The one multilateral forum in which Indonesia can actually claim leadership — at least for two years — is the Indian Ocean Rim Association (IORA). Established in Mauritius in 1997, the IORA is an organization of twenty-one countries bordering the Indian Ocean loosely linked to promote and support economic and investment facilities, maritime safety and security, tourism and cultural exchange, and science and technology in the Indian Ocean area. President Jokowi has singled out Indonesia's role in the IORA as an important element in Indonesia's attention to the Indian Ocean as part of the Global Maritime Axis doctrine and Indonesia's position as the crucial link in the Indo-Pacific region. Therefore, it became a "golden opportunity" for Indonesia when, in the rotation of the IORA chairmanship, it became Indonesia's turn in 2015–17. Foreign Minister Retno, assuming the chair of the IORA Council, said she would "shape the IORA to Indonesia's interest".[33] Her emphasis on security and stability was captured in Indonesia's theme for its two-year tenure: "Strengthen Cooperation in a Peaceful and Stable Indian Ocean".

During 2016, Indonesia's attention to the IORA has been focused on preparing for the first-ever IORA Summit in Jakarta, scheduled for 7 March 2017. During that summit the leaders will sign an "IORA Concord" designed to strengthen economic and strategic cooperation. The draft of the "concord" was approved at the IORA's 16th Council of Ministers meeting in Bali on 27 October. As with similar documents, the IORA Concord will be a statement of good intentions, with follow-through up to the member states. Indonesia's ambitious goal of refocusing on the IORA and enhancing its lasting influence in the Indian Ocean region is likely to be fleeting, as the chairmanship rotates to South Africa in 2017.

Middle East and Islamic Factor in Foreign Policy

In a surprising, perhaps quixotic, foray into Middle East politics, in January 2016 Indonesia offered itself as a possible mediator in the Saudi Arabia–Iran conflict. This is an area where Indonesia has no close historical, political, or direct strategic interest. Indonesia's primary concern in the Arabian region is protection of the thousands of Indonesian labourers in the Middle East. Jokowi dispatched Foreign Minister Retno with a personal message from him to the Saudi King and the Iranian Prime Minister calling for peace. She also visited the United Arab Emirates and Doha to urge the Gulf Cooperation Council (GCC) to be proactive in trying to reduce tensions. She finished her week-long excursion in Jeddah at an Organization of Islamic Cooperation (OIC) meeting on the worsening relations between Saudi Arabia and Iran. In the absence of any previous engagement in the affair, it is doubtful that Indonesia had any real leverage to use on any of the parties. What was important for Jokowi is that it played well at home, showing his concern for the peace, stability, and welfare of the *Ummah*, the global Islamic "community". To follow up, Jokowi named Alwi Shihab, an Islamic scholar and President Abdurrahman Wahid's Foreign Minister, as a special envoy to the Middle East. Indonesian governments have always been a strong supporter of Palestine, and Jokowi's is no different. In March 2016, Jakarta hosted the 5th Extraordinary OIC Summit on Palestine and Al-Quds Al-Sharif (Jerusalem), originally scheduled for Morocco. Jokowi also gave symbolic special notice to Palestine by credentialing an Indonesian Honorary Consul in Ramallah, Palestine's West Bank capital. To show how important this was, Foreign Minister Retno was to personally make the appointment. Because Israel would not allow her to go to Ramallah, the inauguration took place in Amman, Jordan.

Unlike their immediate predecessors, Jokowi and Retno have not shown, publically at least, concern for the fate of Islamic minorities in Southeast Asia. Even though Indonesia has been long engaged with the peacemaking process for the Moro insurgency in the Philippines as a designated representative of the OIC, the Jokowi government does not seem to have taken notice of the breakdown in the peace process. SBY's government had been poised to assist in peacemaking in Southern Thailand, but now, as the Muslim insurgency gains steam in resisting Thailand's military dictatorship, Jakarta looks away. The worldwide clamour over the brutalization of Myanmar's Rohingya Muslim minority has not been heard in Jakarta, even though the previous Indonesian government broke new ASEAN ground in openly challenging Naypyidaw's policies. Jokowi has ceded leadership on the Rohingya to Malaysian Prime Minister Najib.

U.S.–Indonesia Relations after Obama

It is too soon to comprehend the full implications of the results of the American Presidential election on Indonesia–U.S. relations. What gave the relationship a special boost, of course, was the Obama personal connection. Other than that, there is no natural American–Indonesian affinity. The political pragmatism of the relationship is to be found in Indonesia's "hedging" strategy. For Jakarta, this depended on two foundations of Obama's approach to Asia: the "pivot" and the Trans-Pacific Partnership (TPP). It was the constancy of the U.S. regional presence that allowed Indonesia to "hedge". TPP is dead and the incoming Trump administration is sending mixed signals about America's role in the Asia-Pacific. The current trajectory of Indonesian domestic politics suggests growing and deeper divergences from SBY's model of a "moderate Muslim democracy" that was important in building American domestic political support for a U.S.–Indonesia partnership. As Indonesia's ASEAN partners begin to "bandwagon" towards China, Indonesia may not be able to resist the attraction.

Notes

1. Donald E. Weatherbee, "Indonesian Foreign Policy: A Wounded Phoenix", in *Southeast Asian Affairs 2005*, edited by Kin Wah and Daljit Singh (Singapore: Institute of Southeast Asian Studies, 2006), pp. 159–70.
2. Amnesty International, "Indonesia: Gen. Wiranto's Appointment Shows Contempt for Human Rights", 27 July 2016 <http://www.amnesty.org/en/news/latest/2016/07/gen-wiranto-is-a-threat-to-human-rights>.
3. *Jalan Perubahan untuk Indonesia Yang Berdaulatan: Visi, Misi, dan Program Aksi* <http://www.kpu.go.id/koleksigambar/Visi_Misi_Jokowi-JK.pdf>.
4. Rizal Sukma, "Gagasan Poros Maritim", *Kompas*, 21 August 2014.
5. "I've Done My Best: Rizal Ramli", *Jakarta Post*, 27 July 2016.
6. Rizal Sukma, "Indonesia and the Emerging Sino–US Rivalry in Southeast Asia", in *The New Geopolitics of Southeast Asia*, edited by Nicholas Kitchen (London: LSE IDEAS Report SRO 15, 2012), pp. 42–46 <http://www.lse.ac.uk/IDEAS/publications/report/SRO15.aspx>.

7. Rizal Sukma, "Insight: Is Indonesia Tilting to China?" *Jakarta Post*, 11 December 2015.

8. "Jokowi Has Fifth Meeting with China's Xi", *Jakarta Post*, 3 September 2016.

9. Trade data is that of the Indonesian Ministry of Trade <http://www.kemendag.go.id/en/economic-profile/indonesia-import-export-balance-of-trade-with-trade-partners-country?/negara=116>.

10. "China Strengthens Ties with Indonesia as Investment Doubles", *Bloomberg News*, 31 October 2016 <http://www.bloombergnews.com/news/articles/china-deepens-economic-ties-with-indonesia-as-investment-doubles>.

11. "Infrastructure Development in Indonesia: $450 Billion Required", *Indonesia-Investments*, 19 May 2016 <http://www.indonesia-investments.com/news-columns/infrastructure-development-in-indonesia-450-billion-required/item6829?>.

12. As cited in "Desperate for Investment, Indonesia Plays China vs Japan", *Bloomberg News*, 19 May 2015 <http://www.bloombergnews.com/news/articles/2015-05-19/desperate-for-investment-indonesia-plays-china-vs-japan>.

13. Wilmar Salim and Siwage Dharma Negara, "Why is the High-Speed Rail Project So Important to Indonesia?" *ISEAS Perspective* 2016, no. 16, 17 April 2016.

14. Pandu Pradhana, "Marine Highway Program in Supporting Indonesia as the World's Maritime Pivot", in *Sustaining Partnership Marine Transportation Edition 2015* <http://pkps.bappenas.go.id/attachments/article/1320/Majalah%20PS%20Edisi%20Transportasi%20Laut(Eng%Version).pdf>.

15. "Government ADB Team Up to Evaluate Maritime Highway", *Jakarta Post*, 29 January 2016.

16. Ministry of Foreign Affairs of the People's Republic of China, "Joint Statement on Strengthening Comprehensive Strategic Partnership between the People's Republic of China and the Republic of Indonesia", 27 March 2015 <http://www.fmprc.gov.cn/mfa_eng/wjdt_6653852/2648_665393/t124920.shtml>.

17. Ministry of Foreign Affairs of the People's Republic of China, "Xi Jinping Meets with President of Indonesia" <http://www.fmprc.gov.cn/mfa_en/topic_665678/XJCPXBZCESGJTLDRSYCFHJCXYGHD/11395033.shtml>.

18. Embassy of Republic of Indonesia (Washington DC), "All Illegal Fishing Boats to be Treated Equally: Minister Susi", 6 April 2016 <http://www.embassyofindonesia.org/ ?press=6448>.

19. See Chinese Foreign Ministry Spokesperson Remarks, Ministry of Foreign Affairs of the People's Republic of China, 21 May 2015 <http://www.fmprc.gov.cn/mfa_eng/xwfw665399/s2510_665401/2511_665403/t1265874.shtml>.

20. "Blowing Up Boats Sets Indonesia's Scarce Fish Swimming Again", *Bloomberg News*, 18 September 2016 <http://www.bloomberg.com/news/article/2016-09-18/blowing-up-boats-sets-indonesia-s-scarce-fish-swimming-again>.

21. "Indonesia, China Dispute in Natuna Waters Settled: State Palace", *Tempo*, 19 April 2016.

22. "Foreign Ministry Spokesperson Hua Chunying Remarks on Indonesian Navy Vessel Harassing and Shooting Chinese Fishing Boats and Fishermen", 19 June 2016 <http://www.fmprc.gov.cn/mfa_english/xwfw_665399/s2510_665410/2535_665405/t13734021.shtml>.

23. "Indonesian President Joko Widodo Trip to South China Sea Islands a Message to Beijing, Says Minister", *Straits Times*, 23 June 2016.

24. "Indonesia Says Could Take China to Court over South China Sea", Reuters, 11 November 2013 <www.reuters.com/article/us-southchinasea-china-indonesia-idUSKCNOTOOVC20015111>.

25. Indonesia Ministry of Foreign Affairs, "Indonesia Calls on All Parties to Respect International Law Including UNCLOS 1982" <http://www.kemlu.go.id/ berita/Pages/indonesia-calls-on-all-parties-to-respect-international-law-including-unclos-1982>.

26. "Indonesia's Statement on South China Sea Dissatisfying: Chinese Experts", *Jakarta Post*, 14 July 2016.

27. "Indonesia's Widodo Tells China No Compromise on Sovereignty", *Bloomberg News*, 4 November 2016 <http://www.bloomberg.com/new/articles/2016-11-04/indonesia-tells-china--no-compromise-on-sea-sovereignty>.

28. Rizal Sukma. "Fishing Rights the Crux of the Issue," *Jakarta Post*, as reprinted in the *Straits Times*, 2 April 2016.

29. "Indonesia to Settle Score with China on Natuna Feud", *Jakarta Post*, 22 April 2016.

30. "Luhut: Indonesia, China to Step Up Strategic Security Partnership", *Tempo*, 22 April 2016.

31. Foreign Minister Julie Bishop Speech, 21 March 2016 <http://foreignminister.gov.au/speeches/Pages/2016/jb_sp_160321aspx?w=tb1CaCpkPX%2FISOK%2Bg9ZKEg%3D%3D>.

32. Indonesia Ministry of Foreign Affairs, "Indonesia-Malaysia-Philippines Trilateral Meeting Discusses Common Challenges" <http://www.kemlu.go.id/en/berita/Page/meeting-challenges.aspx>.

33. "Indonesia's Maritime Axis to Pivot Westwards through IORA", *Jakarta Post*, 26 February 2015.

Laos

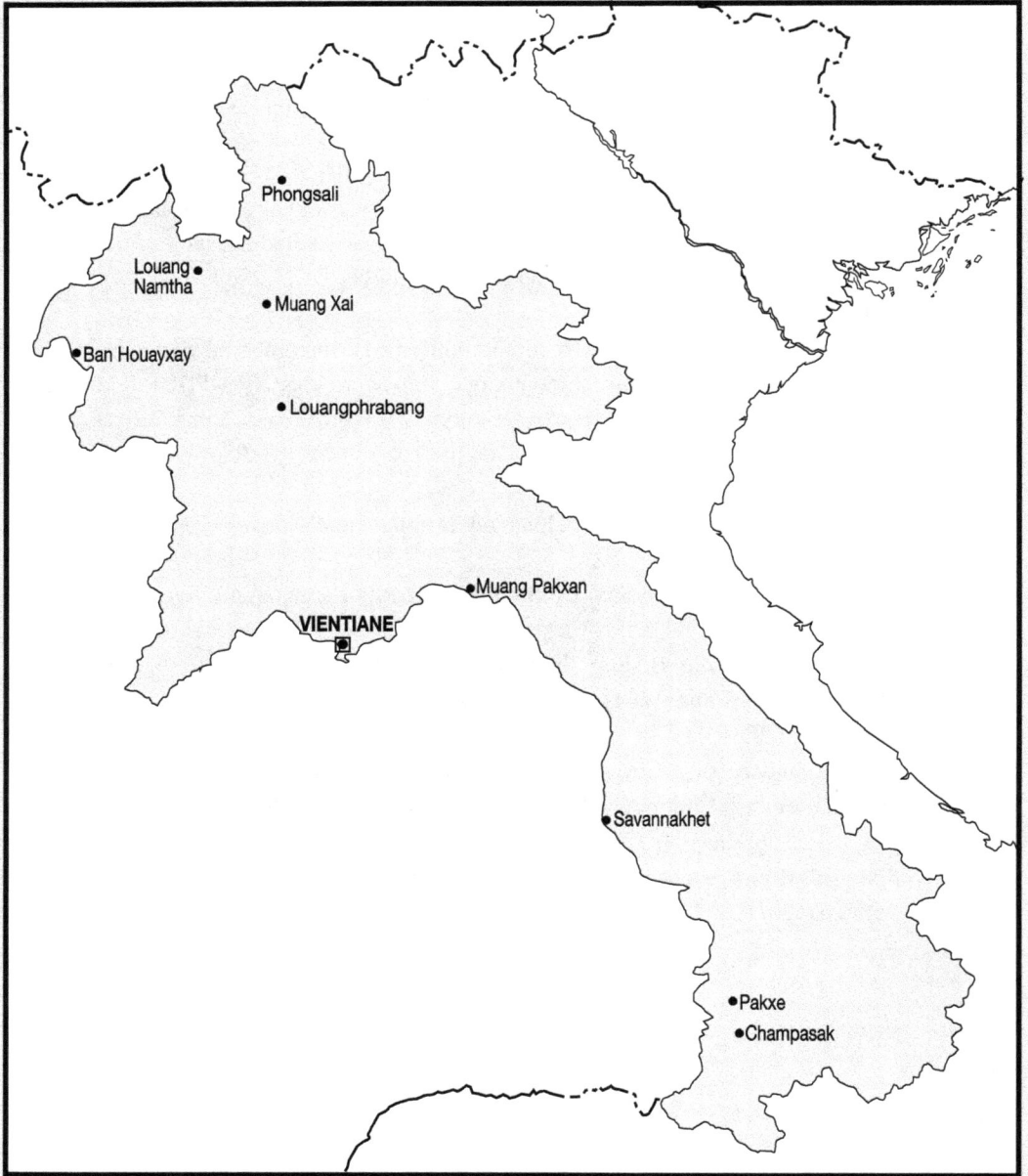

Phongsali

Louang
Namtha

Muang Xai

Ban Houayxay

Louangphrabang

Muang Pakxan

VIENTIANE

Savannakhet

Pakxe
Champasak

REGIME RENEWAL IN LAOS:
The Tenth Congress of the
Lao People's Revolutionary Party

Soulatha Sayalath and Simon Creak

The year 2016 was a crucial one in Laos. According to an established five-yearly cycle, the year was punctuated by a series of key political events, foremost among them the Tenth Congress of the ruling Lao People's Revolutionary Party (LPRP). As on past occasions, the Tenth Party Congress took stock of the country's political and economic performance over the previous five years and adopted the country's next five-year National Socio-Economic Development Plan. Most importantly, it also elected the new Party Central Committee (PCC), the party's main decision-making body, together with the Politburo, PCC Secretariat, and Secretary-General. The congress was followed in March by elections for the National Assembly, which then approved party nominations for the President and Prime Minister, who in turn appointed a new cabinet. Throughout this process, Laos occupied the chair of ASEAN, just its second time in the role, and in September played host to U.S. President Barack Obama, the first sitting U.S. President to visit the country, for the East Asia Summit.

While all these events were important, most consequential was the process of party renewal that culminated with the congress. Given the LPRP's grip on political power and the control its leaders exercise over Laos' rich reserves of natural resources — the main source of the country's rapid economic growth since the early 2000s — LPRP congresses represent critical moments of leadership renewal and

SOULATHA SAYALATH is a Postdoctoral Researcher in the Global Career Design Center, Hiroshima University.

SIMON CREAK is Lecturer in Southeast Asian History in the School of Historical and Philosophical Studies, the University of Melbourne.

transition. Even by these standards, the 2016 congress was particularly significant given the expectation that around half the positions in the eleven-member Politburo would change hands. With old age finally catching up with the revolutionary generation, most anticipated changes were due to retirement. At the top of the list was party Secretary-General and State President, Choummaly Sayasone, and several of his ageing Politburo colleagues who seemed likely to follow.

The stakes were raised further by a plane crash in May 2014, which had taken the lives of another four high-ranking members of the PCC. These were Lieutenant General Douangchai Phichit, the party number six who was Defence Minister, Deputy Prime Minister, and mooted as a possible Secretary-General of the future; Thongbane Sengapone, the Public Security Minister, PCC number twelve, and member of the PCC Secretariat; and two more members of the PCC Secretariat — Soukhanh Mahalath (PCC number fourteen), the Mayor of Vientiane Capital, and Cheuang Sombounkhanh (PCC number sixteen), Chief of the party Propaganda and Training Commission — who were likely promotions to the Politburo in 2016. All together, at least half of the party's top-sixteen-ranked cadres from 2011 seemed likely to be replaced just at the time when generational change was threatening to strip the party of prestige associated with the revolutionary generation's personal involvement in the "30-year struggle" (1945–75).[1]

It would be a mistake, however, to focus solely on the high-profile elections to the eleven-member Politburo or even the sixty-nine-member Party Central Committee. While international news reports naturally focused on the most senior appointments, these ballots represented the final two phases of a four-stage process of renewal, which regenerated the party from the district level to the Politburo. As such, this chapter adopts a holistic perspective, considering intra-party elections at the district and province/ministry level before moving to the PCC and Politburo elections. It then considers how this process delivered a new leadership exhibiting much continuity with the past, despite the high level of turnover, and lessons that could be derived in the fields of international relations and economics.

The opaque nature of party activities means that analysis of this process remains tentative. Nevertheless, publicly available data reveals a tension between official principles of democratic centralism, according to which elections at lower levels feed delegates up the chain, and the party's institutionalized politics of patron–client relations, according to which party committees and leaders identify, nurture, and promote talent to higher levels. While it is common to suggest that, in practice, democratic centralism works from upper levels down to enforce PCC decisions and maintain party discipline, this analysis suggests lower-level elections remained an important part of renewing the party. The balance between party electoral processes and patron–client relations functioned as a key aspect of the party's culture of regeneration and renewal.

Intra-party Elections

The first two stages of intra-party elections took place over a period of two years. The first phase involved meetings of all 146 district party committees across the country, occurred throughout 2014.[2] The district party meetings had two main functions: to approve the political reports of the district party committees and adopt their respective socio-economic plans for the next five years (2016–21); and, more importantly, to choose delegates to attend the upper-level meetings. In these elections, according to party statutes, members of district party cells were permitted to choose candidates freely according to the principles of democratic centralism.[3] In practice, members were made aware of which candidates — known as "targets for building" (pao-mai sang) — had been anointed heirs to the local leadership.[4] In this way, local party patrons ensured that their preferred clients were promoted at the district level, while still allowing party members to play a role in the process. By the year's end, Secretary-General Choummaly Sayasone, speaking at the ninth plenum of the PCC, issued an instruction directing that all district party elections must be completed by the end of January 2015.[5]

Once the leadership transition in the district party committees had been completed, the second phase of elections took place in fifty-four meetings of party committees representing the provinces, Vientiane Capital, ministries, and ministry-level organs of the state and party. These meetings took place throughout 2015.[6] Regulated by party statutes, the most important duties of these meetings were to select party committees through internal ballots and to nominate delegates to attend the Tenth Party Congress in 2016.[7] Once again, while these ballots were officially open, they rewarded existing leaders and those members identified as heirs to the leadership. Significantly, they took place against the backdrop of a major cabinet reshuffle in July 2015, which, coming a year after the previous year's plane crash, the leadership used to pave the way to the congress. Unlike the 2014 district-level elections, which went largely unreported, province- and ministry-level elections received widespread press coverage. This second phase of elections ended with the public nomination of 685 delegates to represent party members across the country at the Tenth Party Congress in January 2016.

This preparation in the two years leading up to the congress served to regenerate leadership and consolidate party authority across the country. On the one hand, the meetings renewed the leadership from the bottom up by reshuffling cadres identified as future leaders into various party committees. These committees would in turn provide political authority for the implementation of local five-year socio-economic development plans. On the other hand, the same meetings concluded with the selection of delegates to higher-level meetings, including the Tenth Party Congress. To ensure the leadership reshuffle took place in a satisfactory manner, the meetings were closely regulated and supervised. At the ninth plenum of the PCC in late 2014, Secretary General Choummaly Sayasone restated that the elections were to be correctly organized under the designated principle of party building.[8] In practice this would mean the PCC Secretariat sending senior cadres such as a Politburo member or a member of the inspection commission to attend provincial and ministerial congresses. However, direct supervision by the Secretary General is now uncommon.

The Election of Party Secretaries

The importance of intra-party elections was revealed by the elevation of province and ministry party secretaries to the PCC at the congress in 2016. This was not a matter of chance but a reflection of the statutory "duty" of each province and ministry committee, restated at the congress, to foster and put forward at least two leadership heirs from which to choose.[9] Table 1 shows seventeen of the sixty-nine cadres elected to the PCC, who had previously in 2015 been elected provincial or ministerial secretaries. The table includes the institution from which each secretary was elected, his/her executive role in that institution (according to the rule that party secretaries also hold equivalent executive or state positions), and his/her ranking in the PCC elected in 2016. This list is not comprehensive, being based on comparison between available press reports published during intra-party elections in 2015 and the PCC elected in 2016. But it is sufficient to reveal that much of the leadership reshuffle in the PCC was anticipated well in advance of the congress.

Examples from three of the most influential ministries are worth highlighting. In the Ministry of National Defence, Lieutenant General Sengnoune Xayalath, who replaced Lieutenant General Douangchay Phichit as Minister (initially acting) after the plane crash in 2014, was elected as Secretary of the ministry in June 2015, and then number twelve in the PCC in 2016. Likewise, Major General Somkeo Silavong, who replaced the civilian Minister of Public Security, Thongbane Sengapone, after the same incident, was elected Party Secretary in August 2015 before being elected to the PCC (number fourteen). Finally, in anticipation of his elevation to Prime Minister, Foreign Minister Thongloun Sisoulith handed

TABLE 1
Comparison of Results from 2015 Intra-party Elections and 2016 PCC Elections

Name of party secretary elected or re-elected in 2015	Secretary's institution in 2015	Position	PCC rank in 2016
Lt. Gen. Sengnoune Xayalath	Ministry of National Defence*	Minister	12
Maj. Gen. Somkeo Silavong	Ministry of Public Security	Minister	14
Khamjane Vongphosy	Phongsaly province	Governor	34
Khampheuy Bouddavieng	Sekong province	Governor	37
Khammany Inthirath	Ministry of Energy and Mines	Minister	41
Oday Soudaphone	Khammoune province	Governor	42
Khongkeo Xaysongkham	Borlikhamxay province	Governor	43
Khemmani Pholsena (Ms.)	Ministry of Industry and Commerce	Minister	46
Saleumxay Kommasith	Ministry of Foreign Affairs	Vice Minister	50
Somphao Faisith	Bank of Lao PDR	Governor	53
Bounchan Sinthavong	Ministry of Transport and Public Works	Minister	56
Sisouvan Vongchomsy	Saravan province	Governor	57
Phet Phomphiphak	Ministry of Agriculture and Forestry*	Minister	58
Phongsavanh Sithavong	Xayaboury province	Governor	59
Khamphan Pheuyavong	Bokeo province	Governor	60
Vidong Sayasone	Vientiane province	Governor	62
Souphan Keomixay	Savannakhet province	Governor	66

Note: * Sengouane and Phet lost their posts in 2016.
Source: Data compiled from Lao News Agency (KPL), *Pasason, Vientiane Mai,* and *Vientiane Times* from January 2015 to January 2016.

his position as Party Secretary of the Ministry of Foreign Affairs to his deputy, Saleumxay Kommasith, who went on to be elected number fifty in the PCC (and appointed Foreign Minister in April).[10]

Nevertheless, there were exceptions. For instance, the Minister of Justice, Bounkert Sangsomsak, a former deputy foreign minister, failed to be elected to the PCC in 2016, despite being chosen the previous year as the ministry's party secretary, though he was later appointed Minister for the Prime Minister's Office.[11] On one level, the exception might be explained as the result of a democratic vote at the congress, suggesting that the election of a nominated heir apparent was not guaranteed. However, this is unlikely and it is more likely that his election was overturned with the intervention of the Central Party Organization Commission, a key organ of the Central Party Office responsible for personnel.

The party also seems to have intervened in Xaysomboun, a province northeast of Vientiane. This province remains sensitive due to an ethnic-Hmong insurgency during the Vietnam War, in which insurgents were recruited and trained by the U.S. Central Intelligence Agency to undertake secret operations in Laos during the Vietnam War. While this insurgency is most likely defunct, anti-government forces remain active. In 2015 the intra-party election in Xaysomboun ended with no new secretary being appointed, with the previous secretary, Sombat Yialaoher (who is ethnic-Hmong), overlooked.[12] In 2016, however, two weeks after the Tenth Party Congress, Major General Thongloy Silivong, the former director of the Kaysone Phomvihane Military Academy, who had been elevated to number forty in the new PCC, was named the new Governor of the province. The replacement of an ethnic-Hmong civilian with a military cadre could be explained by the resurfacing of armed violence in the area, apparently targeting Chinese workers.[13]

Patronage Networks and the Rise of the Princelings

Intersecting with intra-party elections, another major factor that shaped pre-congress preparations was the rise of the "princelings", the children, nephews/nieces, and grandchildren of former revolutionary leaders. As Martin Stuart-Fox wrote on these pages a decade ago, the five-yearly cycle of Party Congresses is aimed at protecting the political interests of powerful figures within the ruling regime: "These interests have to do with how political power is concentrated and applied, which in Lao political culture is through patronage networks that take in not just extended families (through birth and marriage), but also close friends, business partners, and regional representatives."[14] In this respect, it is commonly known that one cannot be elected to the PCC merely by being a loyal and competent party member — you need to have a backer. Like the rise of party secretaries, discussed above, the elevation of well-connected cadres was foreshadowed over the year preceding the 2016 congress, particularly in the cabinet reshuffle of July 2015. According to one estimate, 25 per cent of the 2016 PCC was connected through birth or marriage to the families of famous revolutionaries.[15] While the most prominent of these was probably Xaysomphone Phomvihane, the eldest son of former Prime Minister Kaysone Phomvihane (1920–92), who was elevated to seven in the Politburo, the families of two of Kaysone's successors benefited in greater numbers.

Most revealing was the network of the still powerful former party Secretary-General and State President, Khamtay Siphandone. Having been elevated to the PCC at the Ninth Congress in 2011, Khamtay's son-in-law, Khampheng Saysompheng, was in 2015 transferred from his position of Governor of Luang Prabang province to Minister of Labour and Social Welfare.[16] As expected, he was then re-elected to the 2016 PCC, lifting his rank from forty-nine to thirty-one. Not long before Khampheng took up his new position, his wife and a former Deputy Finance Minister, Viengthong Siphandone, was promoted to President of the State Audit Organization, a precursor to her election (number forty-eight) to the PCC. Most notably, in an earlier reshuffle, her brother, Sonxay Siphandone, was promoted from Governor of Champasak province to Minister for the Government Office.[17] At the congress he was elevated from thirty-four in the PCC to number eleven in the Politburo, positioning him strongly to rise further in subsequent congresses.

The other revealing network was that of the retiring party Secretary-General, Choummaly Sayasone. Like his predecessor, Choummaly built his political power through a long career in the military.[18] In recent years the concentration of power in Choummaly's hands helped several family members gain promotions. In the cabinet reshuffle of mid-2015, the President's brother-in-law, Khammeung Phongthady, elected to the PCC in 2011, was reassigned from Governor of Vientiane province to Minister and cabinet chief of the President's Office.[19] This opened the way for his deputy and Choummaly's eldest son, Vidong Sayasone, to be elected as Provincial Secretary in September.[20] As expected, Vidong was later elected to the PCC (number sixty-two). As if to balance his family's promotions with those of the Siphandone clan, the President's other two sons were also elevated. Phoxay Sayasone secured leadership of Kaysone Phomvihane district in Savannaket province before being elected the seventh-ranked alternate member of the PCC.[21] The last of Choummaly's sons, Phokham Sayasone, was elected party chief of Sisatthanak district in Vientiane Capital. Like those made from within the Siphandone family, these elevations provide interesting watch points for the next congress, expected in 2021, when the princelings can be expected to gain further promotions.

The Tenth Party Congress and Leadership Transition

The Tenth Congress of the LPRP took place from 18 to 22 January 2016, earlier in the year than has been customary, and was attended by the 685 party delegates and 400 "honourable guests".[22] According to the statutes of the LPRP, the five-day meeting had five formal duties: to adopt the party's political report and the party-endorsed NSEDP (2016–20); accept a report on the performance of the outgoing PCC of the Ninth Congress; amend the party statutes; elect the new PCC, from which the new Politburo and Secretary General would also be elected; and, finally, to adopt resolutions of the congress.[23] As usual, these duties were carefully choreographed to ensure the maximum appearance of stability.

The election of a new PCC and Politburo took place on the final two days of the congress. First, the 685 delegates, chosen by and on behalf of almost 253,000 party members countrywide, elected 69 full members of the new PCC (from 77 nominated delegates), as well as 8 alternate or substitute members (from 11 candidates).[24] As we have seen, the preceding intra-party elections, patronage networks, and interventions of the party leadership meant these elections were largely ceremonial, formalizing decisions that had already been taken. The small gap between the number of candidates and the number of positions confirmed that, in general, only those assured of election were nominated.

On the final day of the congress, the new PCC held its first plenum to elect a new eleven-member Politburo, including the Secretary General. In the event, there were four resignations, bringing to five (with Douangchay's death) the number of Politburo members that did not re-contest. Secretary General Choummaly stepped down according to the statutory requirement that the party leader cannot retain the position for more than two consecutive terms.[25] Despite there being no age restriction in the statutes, three other senior members of the Politburo resigned: Prime Minister and party number two, Thongsing Thammavong; number six, Asang Laoly, who served as Public Security Minister before becoming Deputy Prime Minister in charge of public administration; and another Deputy Prime Minister, Somsavath Lengsavad, widely associated with a number of agreements between Laos and China, including the US$6 billion 427-kilometre railway project connecting the southwestern Chinese city of Kunming to Vientiane, and the US$256 million Chinese-made communication satellite, Lao Sat-1, launched in November 2015.[26]

Of the remaining six members of the ninth Politburo, five moved up the hierarchy. As expected, Bounnyang Vorachit was elected Secretary General. Thongloun Sisoulith (number two), a long-serving Deputy Prime Minister, Foreign Minister and prime ministerial heir apparent, leapfrogged the relatively weak ethnic-Hmong President of the National Assembly Madame Pany Yathorthou (three), presumably to align his party rank and expected executive role. Next came Bounthong Chitmany (four), former Governor of Udomxai province, stalwart and current chief of the influential Central Party Inspection Commission, and Phankham Viphavanh (five), Deputy Prime Minister, Minister of Education and Sport, and former Governor of Houaphan.[27]

Having been elevated to the Politburo in 2011, both Bounthong and Phankham emerged in much enhanced positions: the former as second-ranked member (behind Bounnyang) of the PCC Secretariat, as well as continuing as chief of the Central Party Inspection Commission; the latter as standing member of the PCC Secretariat, a role previously occupied by Bounnyang. On the other hand, the rising star of Bounpone Bouttanavong, a third up-and-comer elevated to the Politburo in 2011, dimmed. Bounpone, the cabinet chief of the Party Central Office, had, with Phankham, been promoted to Deputy Prime Minister in 2014, leading to speculation of a future role as Prime Minister or even Secretary-General. Instead, he dropped out of the Politburo to PCC number sixteen, providing the main surprise among the ranks of the existing Politburo.

Bounpone's demotion brought the number of new faces in the Politburo to six. First among these was Chansy Phosikham, a member of the PCC Secretariat and head of the influential Central Party Organization Commission, who rose to number six. Then came Xaysomphone Phomvihane (seven), a vice president of the National Assembly, though his appointment as chief of the relatively marginal Lao Front for National Construction suggested his climb up the ranks may have peaked. Unexpectedly, perhaps due to internal military dynamics, Lieutenant-General Chansamone Chanyalath assumed the eighth-ranked position in the Politburo, leapfrogging his minister and PCC Secretariat member, Lieutenant-General Sengnoune Xayalath (PCC number twelve).

The final positions in the eleven-member Politburo reflected the meteoric rise of three cadres previously positioned between thirty-one and thirty-four in the PCC. Khamphan Phommathath, the former Party Secretary of Attapeu province, was elevated to number nine as well as being appointed to the PCC Secretariat; Sinlavong Khoutphaythoune, promoted to Mayor of Vientiane Capital after the 2014 plane crash that killed his predecessor, was made number ten; and Sonxay Siphandone, the best positioned of the princelings — assuming Xaysomphone

Phomvihane is unlikely to advance much further — was promoted to number eleven. Combined with the elevation of Bounthong and Chansy, Khamphan's appointment to replace Bounpone as cabinet chief of the PCC Central Office securely ensconced the heads of the major party commissions in the Politburo.

National Assembly Elections and the New Government

The next stage in the leadership renewal took place in March, with new elections for the National Assembly. Populated almost entirely by party members, the National Assembly is typically dismissed as a "rubber-stamp" parliament. There are many reasons, however, why authoritarian regimes conduct elections, and the National Assembly has become an important component of the LPRP's pursuit of legitimacy.[28] As one of the only institutions in which concerns over development projects and other controversies can formally be raised, the parliament has played an increasingly prominent oversight function, even if this does not extend to the role of the party itself. Likewise, as the legislative arm of the government, it occupies an important symbolic role as the party and state continue to talk about, and enact legislation in support of, making Laos a "rule of law state".[29] For the first time, moreover, ballots to elect Provincial and Vientiane Capital People's Councils accompanied the National Assembly election.

In the event, 211 candidates stood for election to 149 seats in the National Assembly, up from 132. Of these, a surprisingly small proportion — just under a quarter (48) — were standing for re-election; a similar number (50) were female. With little campaigning permitted, voters based their choice on candidates' published curricula vitae and stated issues of interest. With overt political matters strictly curtailed, local, economic, and development issues dominated. Results followed a similar pattern to past elections: the overwhelming majority of elected deputies (144 of 149) belonged to the LPRP, the remaining five being independents; 41 (27 per cent) were female, up slightly from 2011; and 30 (about 20 per cent) were said to be from non-Lao-Tai ethnic groups. Official statistics suggested a barely credible 97.9 per cent of 3.73 million eligible voters cast their ballots.[30]

In the final stage of party-state renewal, the new National Assembly was charged with selecting a new President and Vice President, before the President then nominated a Prime Minister and Deputy Prime Ministers for the legislature's approval. The Prime Minister would then finally select his cabinet. In reality, executive appointments were carefully aligned with party posts and ranks determined in January's congress. Thus, as in the previous five-year period, the new party Secretary-General, Bounnyang Vorachit, was made State President while his number two, Thongloun Sisoulith, took over as Prime Minister. Among other Politburo members, Pany (ranked three) remained President of the National Assembly; Phankham's (five) rise was confirmed in his election as State Vice President; and Bounthong (four) and Sonxay (eleven) were made Deputy Prime Ministers. The next generation of leaders looks likely to come from these men and perhaps the princelings. Lieutenant General Chansamone (eight) took over as Defence Minister, reflecting his elevation above Sengnouane, who became the Vice President of the National Assembly (Table 2).

Continuity at the Top

Despite the significant turnover in personnel, the new leadership reflected efforts to preserve the status quo. Despite being just one year younger than Choummaly, seventy-eight-year-old Bounnyang Vorachit was the highest ranked among non-retiring members of the Politburo and satisfied a number of traditional criteria for party leaders. Like all previous secretaries general, he hailed from the south of the country and boasted a military career. He also possessed long experience of leadership, having been elected to the PCC in 1982, the Politburo in 1996, and having previously served as a governor of Savannakhet, Mayor of Vientiane, and Prime Minister. Just as importantly, he was well integrated into the patronage networks of his two predecessors, fellow southerners Choummaly and party elder Khamtay Siphandone. Having profited handsomely from the unbridled expansion of the timber industry in the 1980s and 1990s, Bounnyang was also known to have close links with business groups, giving him little cause to upset neo-patrimonial ties between the party and business community.[31] With Bounnyang's age suggesting he will be a stopgap leader, his election represented continuity with the old guard while the post-revolutionary generation takes final shape.

Slightly younger than Bounnyang, seventy-year-old Thongloun Sisoulith, the new Politburo number two, also represented a safe bet. Having been Foreign Minister and a Deputy Prime Minister since 2006, Thongloun was a polished performer on the international stage and the preferred choice to replace Thongsing as Prime Minister during Laos' year in the chair of ASEAN. Making the presumptive Prime Minister number two in the party retained the alignment between party and executive roles. In addition, Thongloun possessed impeccable connections of his own, being a protégé of Khamtay and son-in-law of another party founder, the late Phoumi Vongvichit.

Among the next tier of leaders, Phankham was a former governor of Houaphan, the seat of the revolution, and a close ally of the previous Prime Minister, Thongsing Thammavong, who hailed from the same province. Likewise, Bounthong and

TABLE 2

Party and State Positions of Members of the Tenth Politburo and Party Central Committee (Selected) of the Lao People's Revolutionary Party (2016–21)

Rank, 2016	Name	Party position, 2016	Government position, 2016	Rank, 2011
1	Bounnyang Vorachit	Secretary-General; Politburo; Secretariat	President	3
2	Thongloun Sisoulith	Politburo	Prime Minister	4
3	Madame Pany Yathorthou	Politburo	President, National Assembly	5
4	Bounthong Chitmany	Politburo; Secretariat, Chief of Central Party Inspection Commission	Deputy PM; Chief of the State Audit Commission	9
5	Phankham Viphavanh	Politburo; Standing Member of Secretariat	Vice President	11
6	Chansy Phosikham	Politburo; Secretariat; Chief of Central Party Organization Commission		13
7	Xaysomphone Phomvihane	Politburo; President, Lao Front for National Construction		17
8	Lt. Gen. Chansamone Chanyalath	Politburo	Minister of Defence	27
9	Khamphan Phommathat	Politburo; Secretariat; Cabinet Chief of Party Central Office		32
10	Sinlavong Khoutphaythoune	Politburo	Mayor of Vientiane Capital	31
11	Sonxay Siphandone	Politburo	Deputy Prime Minister	34
12	Lt. Gen. Sengnouan Xayalath	Secretariat	Vice President, National Assembly	15
13	Kikeo Khaykhamphithoun	Secretariat, Chief of Central Party Propaganda and Training Commission		39
14	Maj. Gen. Somkeo Silavong	Secretariat	Minister of Public Security	53

Note: The top 11 ranks constitute the Politburo.

Chansy followed well-worn paths to seniority as, respectively, chiefs of the Party's Inspection and Organization Commissions, which oversee internal party affairs in the areas of discipline and personnel. The military also retained influence despite the deaths of Defence Minister Douangchay in 2014 and his deputy, Sanyahak Phomvihane (another of Kaysone's sons), from a treatable disease the previous year.[32] Although the influence of the armed forces had started to wane over the past decade, as veterans of the 1945–75 war were replaced by a new generation of civilian technocrats, four serving officers (all ranked in the top fifteen of the party) were made members of the Politburo or PCC Secretariat.[33]

In a final indication of continuity, the four retiring Politburo members — Choummaly, Thongsing, Asang, and Somsavath — were elected advisors to the PCC. Although several retired leaders have obtained this largely ceremonial title in the past, the most recent appointee, Khamtay Siphandone, has remained highly influential. It remains to be seen whether the election of the four most recent advisors represents a face-saving gesture or will offer similar access to continued influence. Either way, these appointments add further evidence that the old guard does not intend to relax its oversight of the party's direction. On the other hand, Somsavath was apparently disappointed at the outcome, suggesting the decision not to stand for re-election was not his own.[34] This was significant given his close association with Chinese investment and development projects, which have generated increasing levels of anti-Chinese sentiment in Laos. As a result of Somsavath's exit, some pundits speculated that the new leadership would engage more cautiously with China.[35]

International Relations and Party-to-party Aid

In fact, speculation about the orientation of Laos' leadership — towards Vietnam or China — is a simplistic and often misguided exercise. While China has continued to grow in importance in Laos since relations were normalized in the late 1980s, the LPRP has long understood the importance of maintaining close relations with all of its neighbours, particularly the two communist nations with which it shares borders.[36]

This strategy was exemplified by the carefully crafted communiqué of the ASEAN Minister's Meeting in July, drafted under the chairmanship of the new Foreign Minister, Saleumxay Kommasith. Contrary to expectations — and in sharp contrast to 2012 in Phnom Penh, when no such statement could be settled on — the communiqué addressed tensions in the South China Sea in a manner that was acceptable to claimant countries (including Vietnam); non-claimant nations that enjoy strong trading ties with China (including Laos); and China itself.[37] While Laos' small size and economy means it will never compete with ASEAN's major countries for regional influence, this episode left a positive impression of how the country balances relations with much more powerful neighbours. As a *Nikkei Asian Review* reporter noted, Laos' adroit diplomatic skills could be observed in Vientiane's infrastructure: airports built by Japan; an international conference hall built by China; and the Mekong riverbank redeveloped by Korea.[38]

Less commonly observed, the contest for influence in Laos is also waged through party links with the "fraternal" communist parties of China and Vietnam. This competition was illuminated in the lead-up to the Tenth Party Congress, when the LPRP received multi-million-dollar support from both communist parties. In August 2013, at the request of the party, the Chinese Communist Party (CCP) approved grant aid of 400 million yuan (nearly US$61 million) to build new facilities for the party.[39] The fruits of this aid — a grand new three-storey building at the party's Vientiane headquarters (Kilometre 6), including a thousand-person capacity grand hall, two smaller conference rooms, and offices — were unveiled last year. Overseen by a Chinese company, the eighteen-month, 295-million-yuan (US$45 million) construction project was reported to be the CCP's gift to commemorate the sixtieth anniversary of the LPRP (1955–2015) and the fortieth year since the foundation of the Lao PDR (1975–2015). Most notably, the handover ceremony, attended by the Chinese Vice Minister of Commerce, Zheng Xiangchen, and the Lao Deputy Prime Minister, Phankham Viphavan, took place on 21 March to coincide with the fifty-fifth anniversary of diplomatic relations (1961–2016) between the two states.[40] The CCP aid also funded twenty-five smaller facilities for the party.[41]

Material aid is one of several ways in which the CCP has striven to promote a "comprehensive strategic cooperative partnership" between the two parties. Another example is a bilateral agreement resulting in exchanges to discuss theoretical issues arising from the two countries' efforts to "build socialism". A joint seminar in September 2015, titled "New Creativity in Development and Social Administration", in Kunming, Yunnan province, was the fourth such meeting since these contacts were initiated in the early 2000s.[42] In a further indication of the CCP's efforts, a special envoy arrived in Vientiane four days after the 2016 congress to convey Secretary General Xi Jinping's congratulations to his newly elected counterpart, Bounyang Vorachit, and his wish to continue to enhance the "comprehensive strategic cooperative partnership" between the two parties.[43]

In keeping with its oft-cited "special relationship" with the LPRP, the Vietnamese Communist Party (VCP) seeks to maintain balance with the CCP's influence. In recent years, for example, the Central Committee of the VCP provided the Party Central Office with capacity-building grant aid — to fund information technology infrastructure for the six commissions of the party — valued at US$3.5 million. According to reports, this aid was aimed at strengthening the capacity of the six bodies in research and administration and linking party committees in the capital, provinces, and ministries.[44] The VCP also funded several buildings in the party's Kilometre 6 compound, including a new complex for the Lao Academy of Social Sciences.

If these dollar amounts are lower than CCP largesse, LPRP–VCP relations are also affirmed through rhetoric and ritual. For instance, during a visit to Laos in December 2015, the Vietnamese Deputy Prime Minister and Minister of Foreign Affairs, Pham Binh Minh, awarded a number of medals — the Order of Independence (Class 2 and 3), Order of Labour (Class 3), and Order of Friendship — to senior cadres of his counterpart ministry for their "outstanding performance" in enhancing the special relationship and comprehensive strategic cooperative partnership between the two countries.[45] Such ceremonies are seen rarely, if ever, between the CCP and LPRP, and come on top of long-term relations forged through intermarriage, the presence in Laos of overseas Vietnamese, and the bonds of war.

The primacy of Vietnam's relationship can also be discerned from the observance of protocols after the LPRP congress. Whereas the CCP's special envoy arrived four days after the congress, the special envoy of the Secretary General of the VCP — the chief of the VCP's external commission — called on the newly elected chief of the Lao party, Bounnyang Vorachit, at the conference venue immediately after the congress concluded. That evening the envoy called on the outgoing Secretary General, Choummaly Sayasone, at the Presidential Palace, typifying the warmth and familiarity that defines relations between the two parties.[46] Likewise, after being elected President in March, Bounnyang dutifully undertook separate trips to Vietnam and China, in late April and early May, respectively, to affirm his party's and government's relations with the VCP and CCP — in that order.[47]

Against this background, Barack Obama's high profile visit for the East Asia Summit represented little more than a sideshow, though one that was not without symbolic importance. For those with knowledge of U.S. support for the Royal Lao Government (1949–1975), the symbolism of Obama in Luang Prabang, dressed in shirtsleeves and aviator glasses, sipping languidly from a coconut, was powerful. But for the vast majority of the population, which was born more recently and tends to steer clear of history, Obama's celebrity power represented the biggest drawcard. Obama's main policy announcement, the trebling of aid (to US$90 million over three years) for the clearance of unexploded ordinance — the legacy of U.S. bombing during the war — also had symbolic value, but will make little more than a dent in this vast and ongoing scourge. Although Obama and Bounnyang also inaugurated a broader "Comprehensive Partnership", part of the United States' so-called pivot to Asia, the election of Donald Trump in November suggested little would come of this. For the foreseeable future, Laos' most important relationships will remain with countries closer to home, whose political and economic engagement in the country dwarfs that of the United States.

Economics and Governance

Besides electing the new leadership, the other major task of the Tenth People's Congress was to take stock of the country's economic performance. Here it was necessary to distinguish between the party's political message and deeper analysis of Laos' ongoing economic transition, buried in the 8th Five-Year National Socio-Economic Development Plan (NSEDP) adopted by the congress.

As in the past, the outgoing Secretary General Choummaly Sayasone's political report firmly restated the aim of the party — despite rapid capitalist growth — to build towards socialism for the welfare of the people. By "creating favourable conditions for people to earn a living, as well as facilitate trade, investment and tourism", he stated, the party had progressed over the past five years towards its mantra-like goal of lifting the nation above least-developed country (LDC) status by 2020.[48] With the economy growing at an average rate of 7.9 per cent per annum — among the highest in the Asia-Pacific region — average per capita income had increased from US$1,217 in 2010/11 to US$1,970 in 2014/15, exceeding the targets of the five- and ten-year NSEDPs.[49] According to Choummaly, this fulfilled the party's pledge to create a strong, wealthy country; prosperous people; and a harmonious, democratic, just, and civilized society — the official definition of the imagined socialist society.[50]

As Choummaly's political report made clear, the LPRP's main claim to legitimacy is rapid economic growth, driven primarily through the expansion of the extractive resource industries of mining, hydropower, and commercial agriculture. In this respect Prime Minister Thongsing Thammavong's delivery of the 8th Five-Year National Socio-Economic Development Plan (2016–20) foreshadowed more of the same. Although projected growth would drop slightly to 7.5 per cent per annum over the period of the 8th NSEDP, per capita income was forecast to increase to US$3,190 by 2020.[51]

Underlying these headline rates, however, was the persistent challenge of distribution. While poverty fell from 33.5 to 23.1 per cent of the population in the decade to 2012/13 (the most recent data available) — helping Laos to meet its Millennium Development Goal target of halving extreme poverty by 2015 — this translated into the East Asia and Pacific region's second-smallest reduction in poverty relative to economic growth (0.47 per cent for every 1 per cent increase in GDP per capita). According to the World Bank, the reason for this sluggish return is the reliance on growth in the natural resources sectors, which are capital intensive but create relatively few jobs, thus resulting in small increases in employment and household consumption. Such inequity is not inevitable, however. The World Bank noted also that Laos compared unfavourably with resource-rich developing countries that employ effective redistribution policies.[52]

The 8th NSEDP recognized these challenges as a barrier to achieving the party-state's much-cherished goal of "graduating" from LDC status by 2020. As in past years, high levels of foreign direct investment, particularly in the natural resources sector, were forecast to drive the growth necessary to reach the threshold level of gross national income. However, the NSEDP stressed, "government policies to diversify the economy beyond the extractive, natural resource-based industries are of critical importance" for achieving threshold levels in one of the other two criteria — human asset index and vulnerability to external shocks — as required for graduation.[53] Thongsing addressed this challenge in his speech to the Tenth Party Congress, noting the party's ambitious target of reducing the poverty rate to 10 per cent by 2020.[54] Achieving this target will be another matter, however, given the party's addiction to FDI-funded projects and the rent-seeking opportunities they present.

If the party's economic plans went to script, less expected was the party's effort at the Tenth Party Congress to highlight a "wide-ranging" campaign against corruption. According to the vision of "building a transparent and strong party", Bounthong Chitmany's Central Party Inspection Commission was reported to have disciplined 567 party members in 2015, with 306 having had their memberships revoked due to corruption.[55] In a further report in September, the State Inspection Commission and Anti-Corruption Agency (also under Bounthong), announced that one (unnamed) provincial party committee had been warned, seven district party committees criticized, three party units warned, and three party units dissolved due to corruption. The party's leadership role had been diminished by disclosure of embezzlement of timber totalling almost US$600 million and illegal logging of 300 million cubic metres.[56] Like the emphasis on distributing the fruits of economic growth, this unprecedented focus was aimed at increasing the party's legitimacy in the eyes of "the people", who have become increasingly jaded by corruption at all levels of Lao society. But, again, it will be more challenging to act. Despite the ramped up rhetoric, only one senior official (a former Minister of Finance and member of the PCC) appeared to be among those targeted despite the common knowledge that membership of the highest party organs provides unrivalled opportunities for rent-seeking and other corrupt activities.[57]

Conclusion

As age finally overtakes the last of the revolutionary generation in Laos, the long-forecast transition to a new generation of leaders is nearing completion. The process of regime renewal that culminated in the Tenth Party Congress demonstrates not only the degree to which the party's structures and processes have been designed to maintain party power and stability, but also to ensure elite prerogatives are not unduly challenged. Beginning in 2014, this renewal was completed and formalized in 2016, regenerating the party leadership from the level of the district right through to the Politburo. As we have argued in this chapter, this procedure captured the tension between internal democratic processes, on the one hand, and patron–client relations, on the other. These patron–client relations extend from local party committees, identifying and putting forward their own "targets for building", to the most powerful families of the party leadership, including a new generation of princelings that are now strongly positioned to move further up the ranks. But as the four stages of party elections show, patron–client relations are also filtered through a party system that involves widespread participation of party members and committees across the country. This system divides power and its spoils between different patronage networks, families, levels of government, and regional interests. Despite the recognition that corruption and a widening gap between rich and poor undermine the party's legitimacy, nothing that happened in 2016 suggested this system and the processes that ensure its renewal are likely to change in the foreseeable future.

Notes

1. Tamaki Kyozuka, "Laos Prepares for a Changing of the Guard", *Nikkei Asian Review*, 28 January 2016 <http://asia.nikkei.com/magazine/20160128-SHATTERED-HOPES/Politics-Economy/Laos-prepares-for-a-changing-of-the-guard>.
2. "Samlet kongpasum khop khanabolihanngan sunkangphak kang thi kao samai thi kao" [The ninth session of the ninth plenary meeting of Party Central Committee completed], *Pasason*, 24 November 2014 <http://pasaxon.org.la/Index/24-11-14/Content1.html>.

3. See Articles 22 and 25 of Lao People's Revolutionary Party, *Kotlabiap khong phak pasason pativat lao: samai thi IX* [Statutes of the Lao People's Revolutionary Party] (Vientiane: Lao Youth Printing Service, 2011), pp. 53–54, 57.

4. "Sang phak hai podsai kemkaeng" [To build a transparent and strong party], *Pasason*, 20 January 2016 <http://www.pasaxon.org.la/index/20-01-16/content3.html>.

5. *Pasason*, 24 November 2015.

6. *Pasason*, 20 January 2016.

7. See Articles 18 and 19, Statutes of the Lao People's Revolutionary Party (2011), pp. 46–47, 70–71.

8. *Pasason*, 24 November 2014.

9. This regulation was read at the congress by the Deputy Head of the Central Party Organization Commission. See *Pasason*, 20 January 2016.

10. Vientiane Mai, "Mop-hap nathi lekha khanabolihangnarnphak kasuang kantang pathet" [Hand-over Foreign Ministry's Party Secretary position], 31 August 2015 <http://www.vientianemai.net/teen/khao/1/14690>.

11. Pasason, "Samlet kongpasum nyai samasik phak ongkanaphak kasuang nyutitham" [Ministry of Justice Party committee meeting completed], *Pasason*, 28 October 2015 <http://pasaxon.org.la/index/28-10-15/content2.html>.

12. Pasason, "Samlet kongpasum tua thaen samasikphak tua kwaeng xaysomboun" [Xaysomboun Party committee's meeting completed], *Pasason*, 5 October 2015 <http://www.pasaxon.org.la/index/05-10-15/content3.html>.

13. "Lao Authorities Arrest 30 Suspects in Bus Shootings", Radio Free Asia, 21 April 2016 <http://www.rfa.org/english/news/laos/lao-authorities-arrest-30-suspects-in-bus-shootings-04212016165419.html>.

14. Martin Stuart-Fox, "Laos: Politics in a Single-party State", *Southeast Asian Affairs 2006*, edited by Daljit Singh and Lorraine C. Salazar (Singapore: Institute of Southeast Asian Studies, 2007), p. 162.

15. For this estimate, see Richard Taylor, "Reasons Business Should Be Optimistic About the Lao 10th Party Congress", LinkedIn, 29 February 2016 <https://www.linkedin.com/pulse/reasons-business-should-optimistic-lao-10th-party-congress-taylor>.

16. "NA Approves Cabinet Reshuffle", *Vientiane Times*, 9 July 2015.

17. Vientiane Mai, "Sapha huphong ao kansapson bukkalakon kongchaklatthaban" [National Assembly approves proposed government reshuffle], 9 July 2014 <https://www.vientianemai.net/khao/12180.html>.

18. Stuart-Fox, "Laos: Politics in a Single-party State".

19. *Vientiane Times*, 9 July 2015.

20. K. Siluanglath, "kongpasum nyai phuthaen ongkhanaphak kwaeng viangchan khang thi sip at longduay phonsamlet an chopngarn" [Tenth Vientiane province party congress successfully completed], *Pasason*, 28 September 2015 <http://www.pasaxon.org.la/index/28-09-15/content5.html>.

21. Lao News Agency, "Kongpasum nyai khang thi sip khong phak leuak tang kao

khanabolihanngarn sunkangphak sutmai" [The 10th Party Congress elects new Party Central Committee], Lao News Agency, 21 January 2016 <http://kpl.gov.la/detail. aspx?id=9891>.

22. "10th Party Congress Opened Today", Lao News Agency, 18 January 2016 <http:// kpl.gov.la/En/Detail.aspx?id=9749>.

23. See Article 14 of Statutes of the Lao People's Revolutionary Party (2011), pp. 36–37.

24. Pasason, "kongpasumyai khang thi sip kongpak leuktang ao kana boliharn ngarn sudmai" [The 10th congress selects new Party Central Committee], *Pasason*, 22 January 2016 <http://www.pasaxon.org.la/index/22-01-16/content1.html>.

25. See Article 17 of the Statutes of the Lao People's Revolutionary Party (2011), p. 42.

26. Nirmal Ghosh, "China's Dream of Rail Link to S-E Asia Coming True", *Straits Times*, 21 January 2016 <http://www.straitstimes.com/asia/east-asia/chinas-dream-of-rail-link-to-s-e-asia-coming-true>.

27. "The 10th Central Committee of the Lao People's Revolutionary Party", Lao News Agency, n.d. <http://kpl.gov.la/En/Page/Politic/partyx.aspx>.

28. Lee Morganbesser argues that elections allow authoritarian regimes to collect information, pursue legitimacy, manage political elites, and sustain patrimonial domination. Lee Morganbesser, *Behind the Façade: Elections under Authoritarianism in Southeast Asia* (Albany: State University of New York Press, 2016).

29. The rhetorical features of the "rule-of-law state" in Laos are discussed in Simon Creak, "Laos in 2013: International Controversies, Economic Concerns and the Post-Socialist Rhetoric of Rule", *Southeast Asian Affairs 2014*, edited by Daljit Singh (Singapore: Institute of Southeast Asian Studies, 2015), pp. 149–71.

30. Phetsamone, "Women Share Almost 30 per cent of the New National Assembly", Lao News Agency, 28 March 2016 <http://kpl.gov.la/En/Detail.aspx?id=11769>; Inter-Parliamentary Union, Lao People's Democratic Republic: Sapha Heng Xat (National Assembly), Last Elections <http://www.ipu.org/parline-e/reports/2175_E. htm> (accessed 21 December 2016).

31. Martin Rathie, "Histoire et evolution du Parti révolutionnaire populaire lao" [History and evolution of the Lao People's Revolutionary Party], in *Laos: Sociétés et pouvoirs*, edited by Vanina Bouté and Vatthana Pholsena, pp. 17–44 (Bangkok: Irasec, 2012), p. 38. Along with Thongsing, the outgoing Prime Minister and Party number two, Bounnyang also enjoyed a close association with the late Nouhak Phoumsavanh (1910–2008), another party elder from the south. Martin Stuart-Fox, "Family Problems", *Inside Story*, 19 January 2011 <http://insidestory.org.au/family-problems>.

32. "Major General Sannhahak Phomvihane Dies", *Vientiane Times*, 19 July 2013. Anonymous, "Mystery Surrounds Death of Key Laos Officials", Crikey, 10 June 2014.

33. Martin Rathie, "The History and Evolution of the Lao People's Revolutionary Party",

in *Changing Lives in Laos: New Perspectives on Society, Politics, and Culture in a Post-Socialist State*, edited by Vanina Bouté and Vatthana Pholsena (Singapore: NUS Press, forthcoming).

34. Kyozuka, "Laos Prepares for a Changing of the Guard".

35. "Selection of New National Leaders in Laos Indicates Tilt to Vietnam", Radio Free Asia, 22 January 2016 <http://www.rfa.org/english/news/laos/Laos-elect-01222016112729. html>; Luke Hunt, "Leadership Change in Laos: A Shift away from China?", *The Diplomat*, 25 January 2016 <http://thediplomat.com/2016/01/leadership-change-in-laos-a-shift-away-from-china/>.

36. Stuart-Fox, "Laos: Politics in a Single-party State".

37. The relevant phrase was as follows: "We further reaffirmed the need to ... pursue peaceful resolution of disputes in accordance with international law, including the 1982 United Nations Convention on the Law of the Sea (UNCLOS)". Joint Communiqué of the 49th ASEAN Foreign Ministers' Meeting, Vientiane, 24 July 2016, p. 24 <https://www.asean2016.gov.la/kcfinder/upload/files/Joint%20Communique%20of%20 the%2049th%20AMM%20(ADOPTED).pdf>.

38. For praise, see Yusho Cho, "Laos Showing Off Some Diplomatic Skills", *Nikkei Asian Review*, 14 August 2016 <http://asia.nikkei.com/Politics-Economy/International-Relations/Laos-showing-off-some-diplomatic-skills>; for another recent example, see foreign support for the Southeast Asian Games conducted in Laos in 2009. Simon Creak, *Embodied Nation: Sport, Masculinity, and the Making of Modern Laos* (Honolulu: University of Hawai'i Press, 2015); Simon Creak, "Laos: Celebrations and Development Debates", *Southeast Asian Affairs*, edited by Daljit Singh (Singapore: Institute of Southeast Asian Affairs, 2011), pp. 107–28.

39. Vientiane Mai, "Vang sila leuk khongkan kosang samnakgnan sunkangphak" [Stone-laying ceremony for construction of Party Central Office], 16 February 2015 <https:// www.vientianemai.net/khao/13683.html>.

40. Ibid.; Phouviengkham, "Mop-hap khongkan korsang samnakngan sunkangphak pasason pativat lao [Handover of central office of Lao People's Revolutionary Party construction project]", *Pasason*, 22 March 2016 <http://www.pasaxon.org.la/index/22-03-16/ content3.html>.

41. *Vientiane Mai*, 16 February 2015.

42. "Samana kanpaditsangmai nai kanphattana lae khumkhong sangkhom [Seminar on new creativity in development and social administration]", *Pasason*, 23 September 2015 <http://www.pasaxon.org.la/index/23-09-15/content2.html>.

43. "Khana phuthaen phak kommunit chin doenthangma somsoei phonsamlet kongpasumnyai khangthi sip khong phak [Chinese Communist Party's delegates come to congratulate the achievements of the 10th Party Congress]", *Pasason*, 27 January 2016 <http://www.pasaxon.org.la/index/27-01-16/content4.html>.

44. "Mop-hap khongkan suainun ongkan sunkangphak [Hand-over supporting project for

Party Central Office]", *Vientiane Mai*, 29 May 2014 <https://www.vientianemai.net/khao/11909.html>.

45. "Laos, Vietnam Confirm Continuous Friendship and Cooperation", *Vientiane Times*, 5 December 2014.

46. "Sahai lekhathikan nyai lae pathan pathet tonhap phutangnaphiset khong sahai lekatikan nyai phak kommunit viatnam" [Secretary general and state president receives special envoy of Vietnam Communist Party secretary general], *Pasason*, 25 January 2016 <http://www.pasaxon.org.la/index/25-01-16/content3.html>.

47. "President Bounnhang Visits Vietnam", Lao News Agency, 25 April 2016 <http://kpl.gov.la/En/Detail.aspx?id=12424>; "Secretary General Begins Goodwill Visit to China", Lao News Agency, 3 May 2016 <http://kpl.gov.la/En/Detail.aspx?id=12644>.

48. "Party Leader Proud of Accomplishments", *Vientiane Times*, 19 January 2016.

49. "Laos's GDP Constantly Grows at 7.9 per cent", Lao News Agency, 18 January 2016 <http://kpl.gov.la/En/Detail.aspx?id=16854>. For the comparison, see Ministry of Planning and Investment, 8th Five-Year National Socio-Economic Development Plan (2016–20) (Officially approved at the Eighth National Assembly's Inaugural Session, 20–23 April 2016), Vientiane, June 2016, p. 4.

50. Lao People's Revolutionary Party, "Ekkasan kongpasum nyai khang thi kao phak pasason pativat lao 2011 [Documents of the Ninth Congress of the Lao People's Revolutionary Party 2011]", (Vientiane: State Printing House, 2011), p. 57.

51. Singkham, "Continued, Steady and Sustainable Growth Highlighted at the 10th Party Congress", Lao News Agency, 18 January 2016 <http://kpl.gov.la/En/Detail.aspx?id=9776>.

52. World Bank Group, *Lao Economic Monitor: Challenges in Promoting More Inclusive Growth and Shared Prosperity*, May 2016, p. 38.

53. 8th Five-Year NSEDP (2016–20), p. 85.

54. Singkham, "Continued, Steady and Sustainable Growth Highlighted at the 10th Party Congress".

55. "Sang phak hai podsai kemkaeng [To build a transparent and strong party]", *Pasason*, 20 January 2016 <http://www.pasaxon.org.la/index/20-01-16/content3.html>.

56. The report mentions embezzlement in various currencies (4,145.86 billion Lao kip; US$70.77 million; 381.68 million Thai baht, and 539,515 Chinese yuan). "Kankuatka lat-tankan solatbangluang phop 700 kua paomai [State inspection-anti-corruption identifies more than 700 targets]", 29 September 2016 <http://www.vientianemai.net/khao/16882.html>.

57. "Former Lao Finance Minister Named in Corruption Probe", Radio Free Asia, 8 January 2016 <http://www.rfa.org/english/news/laos/corruption-01082016142933.html>.

Malaysia

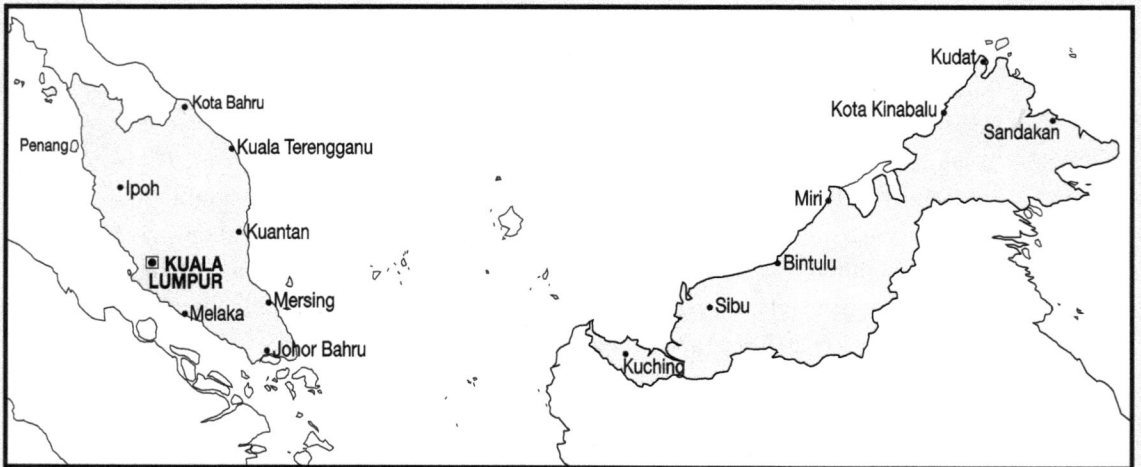

MALAYSIA IN 2016:
Persistent Crises, Rapid Response, and Resilience

Helena Varkkey

Malaysia entered 2016 with the baggage of many unresolved political, economic, social, and foreign policy issues from 2015. Especially notable has been the 1Malaysia Development Berhad (1MDB) political saga that spilled over to economic, social, and foreign policy domains. In response, Malaysian civil society continues to build momentum and confidence, despite various crackdown efforts. All this amidst continued economic slowdown and a sustained currency slide, made worse by the post-U.S. General Election "Trump Tantrum". Quite drastic foreign policy adjustments were employed, especially towards the end of the year, to attempt to counter these negative developments. Despite the sustained challenges, Malaysia has displayed surprising resilience through it all.

Political Distractions and Divisions

The 1MDB debacle that consumed much of Malaysia's political attention and energies in the previous year continued to do so well into 2016. 1MDB is a strategic development company owned by the government of Malaysia which aims to promote foreign direct investment and establish strategic global partnerships to drive the country's long-term economic development. The company was thrust into the limelight in 2015 when *Sarawak Report*, an investigative news portal, started releasing information on the misappropriation of 1MDB funds by prominent members of the ruling government.

HELENA VARKKEY is Senior Lecturer at the Department of International and Strategic Studies of the University of Malaya.

Early in the year, Malaysia's new Attorney General (AG), Mohamed Apandi Ali, who abruptly took over from the previous AG in mid-2015, announced that $681 million of funds transferred into Malaysian Prime Minister Najib Razak's personal account was a donation from the Saudi royal family, and was not linked to 1MDB. It was further announced that $620 million of that sum was returned to the royal family because it was unutilized. With this, the AG closed Malaysian Anti-Corruption Commission (MACC) investigations into 1MDB and cleared Najib of corruption, as "no crime was committed".[1] Najib also set about removing members of his party — the United Malays National Organisation (UMNO) — who had expressed dissent over official explanations on 1MDB. This included former Deputy Prime Minister Muhyiddin Yassin (who was dropped from the DPM position during a surprise cabinet reshuffle in 2015) and Mukhriz Mahathir, the son of Malaysia's former Prime Minister and Najib's adversary Mahathir Mohamed.[2] This strategy of removing dissenting individuals seemed to have successfully stemmed much of the criticism over the issue from within the party.

To contain public dissent over 1MDB, the government has focused on consolidating its authority over public space. This has included the increased use of existing laws like the Sedition Act, the Communications and Multimedia Act 1998 (CMA), and the draconian Security Offences (Special Measures) Act 2012 (SOSMA), together with the introduction of a new National Security Act (NSA). A suspension under the CMA for "causing confusion" over the 1MDB scandal ultimately led to the closure of online news portal *The Malaysian Insider*, while both the CMA and the Sedition Act were used to detain local artists Fahmi Reza (for depicting Najib as a clown[3]) and Zunar (for criticizing the government).[4]

Despite the government promising not to use the SOSMA for "political reasons", it was used to detain Bersih chairperson Maria Chin Abdullah for alleged involvement in activities detrimental to parliamentary democracy on the eve of the Bersih 5 rally in November.[5] She was held for ten days. The new NSA (which allows the Prime Minister to suspend civil liberties in designated security areas) was launched in August, despite not obtaining royal assent. While the law was expected to act as a deterrent for protesters,[6] this did not prevent around 25,000 Malaysian citizens from participating in the Bersih 5 rally on 19 November. Bersih, or the Coalition for Clean and Fair Elections, has been active since 2006. It seeks to reform the current Malaysian electoral system, and has formally called for Najib's resignation.

While the government continued to work hard to quell dissent at the national level, a statement released by the United States Department of Justice (DOJ) in July 2016 was a major blow to these efforts. The statement announced that the

DOJ was filing for the forfeiture and recovery of more than $1 billion in assets associated with "an international conspiracy to launder funds misappropriated from" 1MDB. Najib's stepson, Riza Aziz, was among those identified in the lawsuit, including one "Malaysian Official 1" (MO1). Arising from this, speculation ran rife as to the identity of MO1. Minister in the Prime Minister's Department Abdul Rahman Dahlan finally confirmed that MO1 was Najib, but qualified this by saying that the fact that the DOJ did not explicitly name him proves that the Prime Minister is "not part of the investigation".[7]

The MACC, which played a supporting role in the 1MDB drama (it experienced major leadership changes while investigating the case), has found renewed momentum under new Chief Commissioner Dzulkifli Ahmad. The commission has successfully nabbed several high-ranking officials and dignitaries for corruption this year. Notably in October, the MACC arrested several Sabah Water Department officials for allegedly receiving lavish kickbacks from awarding projects worth some RM3.3 billion under the department to their cronies. This led to the biggest ever seizure from individuals by any Malaysian enforcement agency, as the MACC confiscated cash, luxury jewellery, watches, handbags, cars, and land grants related to the case.[8] This was held up as a signal that despite what transpired during its 1MDB investigations, the MACC was not afraid to go after "big fish".

Despite such cracks within UMNO and its coalition — the Barisan Nasional (BN) — and seemingly increasing public dissent, the ruling coalition still managed to secure wins in two major rounds of elections during the year. The East Malaysia state of Sarawak, a long-time BN stronghold, held its state elections in May 2016, where BN component parties won a comfortable 87.8 per cent of the seats contested. Twin by-elections held in June 2016 in Selangor and Perak on the Peninsula also saw convincing wins for both BN candidates. These results were held up as proof of the Malaysian public's continued confidence in Najib's leadership. Analysts predict that a snap general election may be called early in 2017 to take advantage of Najib's still-high popularity.

An early general election may also be able to take advantage of the continued disarray among the opposition parties. In 2015, following a string of internal disagreements, the country's strongest opposition coalition, Pakatan Rakyat, split apart into its component parties of Parti Keadilan Rakyat (PKR), Democratic Action Party (DAP), and Parti Islam Se-Malaysia (PAS). Soon after, PKR, DAP, and the new progressive spinoff of PAS, Parti Amanah Rakyat (Amanah), formed a new coalition named Pakatan Harapan. The more traditional Islamist PAS has since teamed up with Parti Ikatan, a three-year-old multiracial party, to form its own coalition called Gagasan Sejahtera.

The possible implementation of the strict Islamic *hudud* penal code, which served as a flashpoint between the former members of the now-defunct Pakatan Rakyat, continues to have the potential to tear the various opposition coalitions apart. While Amanah has not declared its official stance on *hudud*, it has agreed to consult with coalition partners on all *hudud* matters, something which PAS purportedly did not do. The PAS–Ikatan coalition, however, remains a wild card, following an announcement from a senior Ikatan leader that he will quit the party if PAS continues to push for *hudud*. Indeed, PAS did table a bill in Parliament for the implementation of the Islamic penal code in Kelantan in November; however, debate on the bill has been deferred to next year due to strong protests.[9] Non-Muslims and progressive Muslims on both sides of the political divide remain staunchly against the implementation of *hudud* for fear of how it will change their way of life, especially in terms of freedom of dressing and of socializing.

Mahathir, who was one of the leading critical voices against Najib from within UMNO, quit the party on his own accord in February 2016. He then founded his own new opposition party, Parti Pribumi Bersatu Malaysia (PPBM). PPBM is chaired by Mahathir, with the recently ousted Muhyiddin and Mukhriz becoming the party's President and Vice-President, respectively. As it stands, PPBM does not have any formal ties with Pakatan Harapan; however, a recent handshake between former arch-enemies Mahathir and PKR founder Anwar Ibrahim sparked rumours that inclusion of PPBM into the new coalition may be imminent.[10]

Despite this disarray, the opposition parties appear to have a unified strategy; to ensure that the 1MDB scandal remains top-of-mind among the voting public. While PKR's lawsuit against Najib over purported illegalities related to 1MDB was struck down by the High Court early this year,[11] Mahathir followed this up in March by filing his own lawsuit against Najib for obstructing investigations into the 1MDB issue. Mahathir also made headlines in October when he met the Yang di-Pertuan Agong (King) to hand over a citizen's declaration bearing 1.4 million signatures voicing concerns about the country's current leadership.[12] In addition, ironically, the November sentencing by the Sessions Court of Rafizi Ramli, PKR's Secretary-General, to eighteen months prison for unauthorized possession and dissemination of a page from a 1MDB audit report[13] also played into the opposition's 1MDB top-of-mind strategy.

At the same time, minor scandals among opposition leaders have diverted some attention from 1MDB. An example is the ongoing infighting within PKR. PKR's President and Anwar's wife, Wan Azizah, is seen to be aligned with Rafizi against the party's Vice-President and Selangor state Chief Minister, Azmin Ali. Matters came to a head when Rafizi filed a report with the MACC in May over claims that money and women were sought in certain negotiations with the

Selangor government.[14] Investigations are still ongoing. Furthermore, various UMNO members have raised questions regarding several properties owned by opposition personalities. Firstly, DAP Secretary-General Lim Guan Eng was arrested by the MACC in July over his bungalow that was allegedly bought below market value. However, DAP organized a public donation drive that managed to collect the RM1 million needed to release Lim Guan Eng on bail.[15] Secondly, PKR Youth leader Adam Rosly's luxurious "Disneyland castle" home was brought to the public's attention; however, he maintains that it was purchased with hard-earned cash.[16] It is clear that both the ruling coalition and the opposition parties are locked in a continuing battle to win the hearts and minds of the Malaysian public.

A Strategic Budget for a Challenging Economy

The global economic slowdown has continued into 2016, fuelled primarily by the uncertainties surrounding the mid-year Brexit and the slower-than-expected growth of the U.S. economy. Entering the third quarter of 2016, the IMF World Economic Outlook projected a modest 3.1 per cent world growth rate for the year. As a major trading nation, Malaysia's economy continues to be negatively affected by the slowdown of its important trading partners. This has translated into weak demand for crude oil (of which Malaysia is a major exporter) and lower export prices for the country's manufactured products.

The Malaysian Ringgit also did not fare well amid international pressures. A weaker Chinese Yuan and an expected hike in the U.S. Federal Reserve rate have had a negative effect on regional currencies, including Malaysia's. After a hopeful recovery in early 2016, the ringgit reverted to a steady decline and reached its lowest level in over a decade as the worst performing currency worldwide amid the "Trump Tantrum" following the surprising result of the U.S. presidential election.[17] However, even as foreign players might benefit from the weak local currency, foreign investment in Malaysia is suffering as confidence continues to decline, not least because of the international reach of the 1MDB saga.[18] Despite the Ministry for International Trade and Industry insisting that 1MDB will not have a long-term impact on investments, between April and October foreign investors divested about RM4.47 billion worth of stocks from the Malaysian stock exchange.[19]

Due to these external factors, Malaysia is continuing to rely on domestic demand to maintain economic growth. In a bid to encourage private spending, Malaysia's central bank, Bank Negara, has employed an expansionary policy to lower interest rates and bring inflation under control. However, continued rising household debt has stemmed consumer spending growth; to a forecasted 4 per cent compared to 6 per cent last year.[20] As a result, Malaysia's forecasted growth for

2016 stands at a moderate 4.2 per cent; lower than the 5 per cent achieved in 2015. If this projection holds up, the Malaysian economy would have failed to achieve the newly launched 11th Malaysia Plan's goal of yearly growth of 5–6 per cent.

International conditions are also affecting government revenue collection. Petronas, the state oil company, directly provides dividends to the government on a yearly basis. However, lower world oil prices in 2015 severely affected the revenues of Petronas, which dropped 25 per cent at the end of 2015 compared to the previous year. Besides having to conduct an unprecedented retrenchment exercise to cull all non-critical staff (a trend among many Malaysian companies), this has also meant that Petronas could only contribute RM16 billion to the government in 2016 (making up 14.6 per cent of government revenue), compared to RM26 billion the previous year.[21] This drop in dividends was flagged by the Prime Minister in his 2015 year-end speech, where he said that every U.S. dollar off the price per barrel means a 300 million ringgit drop in government revenue.

This shortfall in government revenue was not significantly stemmed by Goods and Services Tax (GST) collection. GST was introduced in 2015 to make up for such projected shortfalls. However, reduced consumer spending resulted in underwhelming collection, which fell slightly below RM30 billion in the first nine and a half months of 2016, compared to more than RM30 billion achieved in just nine months in 2015.[22] This has led to speculation by opposition parties that the government is being intentionally over-optimistic with its projected 2016 revenue of RM219.7 billion announced at the 2017 Budget briefing,[23] slightly higher than the 2015 revenue of RM216 million. However, much to the relief of the Malaysian public, the 2017 Budget did not announce an increase of the GST rate to make up for continued shortfalls.

The 2017 Budget was presented on 21 October 2016, around the theme of "ensuring unity and economic growth, inclusive prudent spending, wellbeing of the *rakyat* [people]". While this sentiment was reflected in the unchanged GST rate, drastic subsidy cuts seems to be the government's newest strategy to make up for revenue shortfall. Subsidies have been cut from RM26.1 billion in 2016 to only RM10 billion for 2017.[24] The remaining 10 billion in subsidies have been redeployed to strategically benefit BN's crucial demographics, especially low-income earners, the youth, and those in rural areas. Accordingly, the benefits of the *Bantuan Rakyat 1 Malaysia* (1 Malaysia's People Assistance programme, or BR1M), long criticized as a "handout" tool to buy votes, have increased for every category. This year, seven million low-income Malaysians will qualify to receive assistance under the programme.[25] Other areas that have suffered notable cuts are education (with public universities suffering combined cuts of more than

19 per cent) and healthcare (a cut of RM600 million for supplies to government hospitals and clinics). General dissatisfaction with the announced budget, as well as over the Prime Minister admonishing an opposition leader during his budget speech, led opposition Members of Parliament to stage an unprecedented walkout.[26]

Several notable economic events that occurred during 2016 are worth mentioning. The first was the foreign worker ban in February, followed by a partial lifting of the ban in May for workers in four critical sectors; namely, manufacturing, construction, plantation, and furniture making.[27] The ban came on the back of allegations in late 2015 that the brother of Deputy Prime Minister Zahid Hamidi, through an online management system for foreign workers, was set to benefit from a memorandum of understanding (MOU) between Malaysia and Bangladesh to receive 1.5 million workers in stages over the next three years.[28] Local groups argued that Malaysians should be given priority for these jobs instead. However, foreign workers have long been the workhorses of the Malaysian economy, especially in terms of jobs considered dirty, difficult, or dangerous (3D). Unsurprisingly, unwilling Malaysians resulted in major labour shortages, and this motivated the government to partially lift the ban in these four 3D sectors. It is estimated that there are around 2.1 million registered foreign workers in Malaysia, along with another 1.7 million who are in the country illegally. With the partial lifting of the ban, this trend is set to continue in the years to come.

Two major railway projects were also announced this year. The first was the highly anticipated KL–Singapore High-Speed Rail project, that was confirmed as a result of an MOU in July 2016. While this opens up exciting prospects of quick (ninety minutes) and easy travel, which is hoped to encourage economic linkages between the two major Southeast Asian cities, the line is only due to be operational in 2026. The other major project is the East Coast Rail Line Project, which was formally announced in the 2017 Budget speech. This line connects Klang Valley to major East Coast cities such as Kuantan, Kuala Terengganu, and Kota Bharu. Najib visited China in November to finalize arrangements for the project, which is to be built and financed by China (under the China Communications Construction Company, or CCCC) to the tune of RM55 billion. However, the plans for it are not free from controversy, as there have been allegations that the cost of the project has been inflated to plug holes in 1MDB accounts.[29]

High and Low Society

An item in the 2017 Budget was notable for addressing the long-running feud between taxi drivers and ride-sharing services in the country. Malaysian taxi drivers are notorious for being thuggish and dishonest. When Uber entered the Malaysian public transport market in 2014, taxi drivers vehemently, and often violently, objected to the new competition. Giving in to pressure from this important demographic group, the government temporarily banned all ride-sharing services in 2015. However, the 2017 Budget formalized an about-turn on the government's stance by announcing that BR1M recipients could use their allocation as a down payment for a Proton Iriz for ride-sharing purposes, together with an additional RM4,000 rebate.[30] This was meant to solve several social problems. Low-income earners were projected to earn an extra RM1,500 per month as part-time drivers. Taxi drivers are encouraged to switch to ride sharing and leave the thuggish taxi culture behind. Additionally, this would also help boost sales of the ailing national car.

Another long-running societal feud is the one between two major civil society groups, the yellow-clad Bersih and the pro-government *Baju Merah* (Red Shirts). The Red Shirts, known as UMNO's unofficial "muscle", have consistently gone head-on with peaceful Bersih protesters. In October, viral footage of a small Bersih rally in Sabak Bernam, Selangor showed a group of Red Shirts violently attacking a Bersih supporter who had fallen off his motorbike. The increasingly brazen displays of violence by the Red Shirts have steadily worsened the group's reputation. Some UMNO members — such as UMNO Youth Chief and Minister for Youth and Sports, Khairy Jamaluddin — have also criticized the group's actions.[31] Khairy, however, has flip-flopped on his stance. The Red Shirts also took to the streets during Bersih 5. Their leader, Jamal Yunos, was among those remanded during the rally. He was, however, held to assist investigations for an earlier incident.[32] Unlike Maria Chin Abdullah, the Bersih chairperson, Jamal was not held under SOSMA, and was only held for four days.

In addition to politics, religious concerns continue to hold sway over the Malaysian public, as Islamic values continue to seep into Malaysian mainstream public awareness. This is evident in the rising popularity of *"hijabista"* (hijab+fashionista) clothing. Malaysia hosted several major *hijabista* events in 2016, including the Kuala Lumpur International Hijab Fair in May and Kuala Lumpur Modest Fashion Week in December. Additionally, *halal* (permissible) issues are increasingly, sometimes unreasonably, receiving much public attention. Most recently, popular snack chain Auntie Anne's Pretzels came under fire for not having *halal* certification. This led to a minor boycott of the chain among conservative Muslims. It was later revealed that part of the requirements for certification was for them to change the name of a menu item, the "pretzel dog" (Muslims consider dogs unclean, along with pigs), to a more Muslim-friendly name.[33] However, demand for more Muslim-friendly products was unable to sustain

Malaysia's first Sharia-compliant airline, Rayani Air, which was launched with much fanfare in December 2015. The airline folded in April 2016, after several embarrassing incidents, including handwritten boarding passes. Separately, non-Muslims managed a small victory when the police barred the controversial preacher Zakir Naik from delivering his talk entitled "Similarities between Hinduism and Islam" at Universiti Teknikal Malaysia after receiving complaints from the Hindu community. Naik was later allowed to deliver the talk after agreeing to change its theme.[34]

While haze, the almost-annual mainstay of Malaysian environmental issues was relatively mild this year, several other green issues have captured the Malaysian public's attention. In September 2016 the government announced plans to develop a 26.7-hectare park just outside the Kuala Lumpur City Centre, styled after New York's Central Park. In response, many argued that instead of spending RM650 million to develop a *new* "green lung", the government should instead focus on conserving the few intact green areas. Most notable of these is the existing Bukit Kiara Park, a popular 188.93-hectare recreation spot in Klang Valley, which has slowly been chipped away for development. Friends of Bukit Kiara, a civil society movement, conducted its fourth Walk to Save Bukit Kiara in January to pressure the government to gazette the area as a forest reserve.[35] Furthermore, questionable logging practices once again became a topic of focus as newspapers in October 2016 reported a dramatic standoff between *orang asli* (indigenous peoples) and loggers attempting to transport logs out of the Balah Permanent Forest Reserve in Kelantan. The Kelantan government is facing considerable pressure from the *orang asli*, civil society groups, and some political parties for having allowed logging to occur in this forest reserve, but stands firm by arguing that timber is an important source of state revenue.[36]

Despite these divisive issues, the Malaysian public came together in a heartening display of patriotism during the Olympic and Paralympic season this year. Malaysian society was united as Lee Chong Wei battled for Olympic gold for the second time, this time against China's Chen Long. Chong Wei lost the match, but he was received back home as a hero. While the gold remains elusive for the country's Olympians, the Malaysian Paralympic team performed above and beyond expectations. Mohamad Ridzuan Mohamad Puzi made history when he won Malaysia's first ever Paralympic gold medal for the hundred-metre T36 (cerebral palsy) event. This was followed up by two other golds and one bronze. Khairy, who had recently announced equal rewards for para- and able-bodied athletes, was praised for his foresight.[37] The Paralympic gold-medal winners will receive RM1 million and lifetime pensions of RM5,000 per month. Sports continue to have the special ability to unite Malaysians beyond race, politics, or religion.

This is further attested by the fact that one of the highest-grossing local films this year was Ola Bola, a film inspired by the 1980 Malaysian football team that managed to qualify for the Olympics.

Malaysia ends the year with a new Agong to be installed in December. Sultan Muhammad V of Kelantan will take over from the current King, the Sultan of Kedah, Tuanku Abdul Halim Mu'adzam Shah. The highly popular and politically outspoken Sultan of Johor, Sultan Ibrahim Sultan Iskandar, was reported to have politely declined the offer to be the next King. The election of the new Agong received above-normal attention from the public, as the usually apolitical Malaysian royal institution is now seen by some as the final bastion against the government (exemplified by the outgoing Agong's refusal to give royal assent to the NSA).

Rapid Adjustment of Foreign Policy

In the foreign policy sphere, the spectre of 1MDB continues to hold sway. This has been particularly obvious in Malaysia's relations with the two major superpowers: the United States and China. Malaysia has always tried to maintain balanced relations between the two superpowers; however, in the years prior to the U.S. DOJ announcement, relations between President Obama and Najib had become increasingly cordial. This cordiality was threatened with the DOJ announcement, which was followed one day later by a statement from the White House urging Malaysia to demonstrate good governance and a transparent business climate.[38] Seemingly unfazed, the Malaysian government was quick to insist that its relations with the United States would not be affected by the probe.

However, a close reading of the Prime Minister's statements revealed his anger towards the United States. During a speech at the World Islamic Economic Forum soon after the DOJ announcement, Najib stated that "we have seen the devastating results of foreign intervention in the Muslim world, often based on incomplete, wrong or partisan information. We must make clear that we reject it."[39] This sentiment continued in his National Day speech, where he stated that "at this point, what we have before us is not just an external enemy, but a new form of colonialism, which permeates and poisons the minds of the people". More recently, during his six-day official visit to China, Najib openly complained about foreign (Western) meddling and of being treated unfairly by "larger countries" and former colonial powers. Daniel Russel, the U.S. Assistant Secretary of State for East Asia, chided Najib for these comments, saying that they were more akin to Mahathir's anti-West rhetoric.[40]

Indeed, Malaysia is still formally on board with two current major United States' projects — the economic Trans-Pacific Partnership (TPP) Agreement and the anti-terrorism Global Coalition to Counter ISIL (GCCI). However, Malaysia now seems to be subtly backpedalling from these commitments. Malaysia has announced a "wait and see approach"[41] to the TPP in the face of the installation of Donald Trump as the new U.S. President, as Trump has indicated that he is against the TPP. Furthermore, a Malaysia-based U.S.–Malaysia collaboration under the GCCI that was announced in late 2015, the Regional Digital Counter-Messaging Communication Center (RDC3), continues to face delays. The RDC3 was meant to boost Malaysia's contribution to the U.S.-led war against the Islamic State.[42] Despite a Facebook posting in September 2016 where Najib said he had a "pleasant chat" with his former golf buddy Obama in Laos, these two examples may be early indications of cooling Malaysia–U.S. relations.

These developments are especially stark when contrasted with Malaysia's flurry of engagements with China over recent months. In September, Malaysian Transport Minister Liow Tiong Lai reaffirmed Malaysia's support for China's One Belt, One Road (OBOR) strategy. In relation to this, Malaysia signed a "port alliance" with China, linking six of Malaysia's ports to eleven of China's. And Malaysia announced in October its participation in the China-initiated Asian Infrastructure Investment Bank,[43] which has been described as an alternative to the TPP. Furthermore, the Prime Minister signed a reported RM143.36 billion worth of deals with China during his visit there in November. This included the East Coast Rail Line Project mentioned above and Malaysia's first significant defence deal with China, where Malaysia has agreed to buy four Chinese naval vessels.[44] These developments come close on the heels of the Filipino President Duterte's official "decoupling" from his country's traditional ally (the United States) and his statement that the Philippines would cooperate with China over the South China Sea dispute. Malaysia has followed suit in announcing a more cooperative position towards China over the disputed waters.[45] This could be a blow to the U.S. strategy of using regional alliances to preserve its position of dominance in the Pacific, and in fact to the United States' pivot to Asia in general.

During Malaysia's chairmanship of ASEAN in 2015, Malaysia was unable to broker a unified position over the South China Sea dispute. It remains to be seen whether these new developments can bring the ASEAN region closer to a unified position in 2017. Malaysia handed over the chairmanship to the Philippines this year; however, Malaysia still maintains ASEAN as a cornerstone of its foreign policy. Malaysia's relations with its fellow ASEAN members have continued to be cordial, barring some mild exceptions. Following the highly publicized cross-border issues involving human trafficking between Malaysia and Thailand at the end of 2015, Malaysia and Thailand have been avidly discussing strategies to collaboratively handle the problem, the most recent being the proposal to build a border wall to combat transnational crime and smuggling. Relations between Malaysia and the Philippines have also been growing positively after recent developments in China, with Duterte conducting an official visit to Malaysia almost immediately after his China visit. And healthy Malaysia–Singapore relations are set to continue well into the future with the long-term KL–Singapore High-Speed Rail project.

Malaysia–Indonesia relations were not marred this year by haze; however, an MOU that was discussed between Malaysia and Sumatra in 2015 on haze cooperation has been put on hold as requested by Indonesia in May.[46] Indonesia has also announced that it will stop allowing its people to be sent to Malaysia to work as domestic maids from 2017 onwards. This follows Malaysia's partial ban of foreign workers to the country earlier this year. Even though the ban did not include domestic maids, further limits on maids by Indonesia will be a great blow to the Malaysian economy and society, especially working households that are heavily reliant on such maids. Indonesians currently are the largest group of both legal and illegal foreign workers in Malaysia. In addition to those in land-based employment, six thousand Indonesians are working legally on Malaysian fishing vessels in the waters of Sabah.[47] The recent kidnappings of several Indonesians working as sailors here raised diplomatic concerns that Malaysia may be lax in its responsibility to protect Indonesian citizens working in its jurisdiction. As part of a trilateral agreement between Indonesia, Malaysia, and the Philippines, Malaysia is supposed to conduct coordinated naval patrols in the Sulu Sea to boost security and prevent kidnappings by pirates in the area.

Notwithstanding such tensions, Malaysia and Indonesia are still actively cooperating over counterterrorism. Particularly, as a result of an International Meeting on Counter-Terrorism in August, Malaysia and Indonesia, together with Singapore, agreed on two priority areas to further enhance cooperation: (1) the sharing of biometric information of known fighters and those convicted of terrorism offences, and (2) the sharing of best practices in deradicalization and countering violent extremism. This urgently follows what was reported to be the Islamic State's first successful attack on Malaysian soil, at a nightclub in Puchong in July. More recently, in November it was announced that Duterte and Najib, together with Jokowi in Indonesia, will be discussing joint military and police operations to combat the Abu Sayyaf group in the region.[48] Malaysia continues to be the ASEAN focal point for counterterrorism, with its Southeast Asian Regional Centre for Counter Terrorism, and such regional collaborations are especially important in consideration of Malaysia's recent military deal with China, which may disrupt some of the long-running Malaysia–U.S. joint military and counterterrorism exercises.

Malaysia has been on the receiving end of criticism of its refugee policy. Malaysia is not a signatory of the 1951 UN Refugee Convention or its 1967 Protocol to recognize the status of refugees. This provided the setting in 2015 for when Malaysia at first turned away boatloads of Rohingya refugees then later grudgingly allowing some of them to enter the country on transit. However, early this year Malaysia surprised both local and international civil society when it welcomed about a hundred Syrian refugees. To add to the irony, the Prime Minister attended a local rally for solidarity with the Rohingyas in December, where he condemned Aung San Suu Kyi's government for their treatment of this ethnic group but made no mention of Malaysia's own unwelcoming stance towards them. This led to accusations that Malaysia practices a "two-tier" refugee system; accepting "first-class" refugees but not "low-class" ones like the Rohingyas.[49] In any case, this was a positive development for the United Nations High Commission for Refugees (UNHCR) as it continues to try to get the Malaysian government to soften its policy that prohibits some 150,000 refugees in Malaysia from securing jobs and obtaining proper education for their children.

Malaysia's concern for the plight of Syrian refugees prevails at the international level, where solidarity with other Muslim nations continued to shape Malaysia's focus in its second year as a non-permanent member of the United Nations Security Council (UNSC). Malaysia continued to push for a quick and permanent solution for the conflict in Syria, and the delegation expressed concern over the failure of U.S.–Russia talks in reaching an amicable solution there. Malaysia has consistently pushed for a just and fair resolution to the Palestine question, and it has notably equally criticized violence by Palestinian non-state actors and by the Israeli armed forces. When Malaysia took its turn for the rotating UNSC presidency, it highlighted the issue of children in armed conflicts, and conducted an unofficial interactive dialogue to promote peace.[50] Malaysia's fourth outing as a UNSC non-permanent member has been described as "constructive" by the Malaysian permanent representative to the UN.

Conclusion

Overall, it remains to be seen whether the ruling coalition can successfully steer the country's politics forward beyond 1MDB. However, while the 1MDB debacle has significantly affected the Malaysian public's confidence in Najib and his government, tumultuous internal politics within the country's major opposition parties may remain as the major stumbling block for a change of leadership in the country. It is a race against the clock as to whether the opposition parties can organize themselves to stand as a united front before the next general election, whenever it is called (the next general election has to be held on or before 24 August 2018). BN remains the only ruling coalition that the country has ever known, and it continues to garner considerable support among the public, not necessarily because of its strengths, but rather because of the opposition parties' weaknesses.

While the political situation in Malaysia and the volatile global economy has put considerable pressure on the Malaysian economy, it seems to be proving more resilient than expected. While growth is below target, it is only slightly below. And Malaysia has still been able to maintain "stable" ratings from most of the reputable credit rating agencies: A− from Fitch and A3 from Moody's. However, the price for Brent crude oil continues to decline, indicating that the government will not be able to rely on steady revenues from Petronas in the future to make up for any budget shortfall. In line with its *Wawasan* 2020 (Vision 2020), Malaysia remains committed to achieving the status of a "high-income" nation by 2020. This goal includes a RM55,695 annual per capita income target. The current per capita income is at RM44,284. To achieve this target, for the coming three years the country must overcome the current economic challenges to achieve higher-than-projected growth rates, or risk burying a vision that was first sown during Mahathir's leadership in 1991.

In terms of society, 2017 looks set to continue in much the same vein as the past year, with social attention continuing to be dictated by race, politics, and religion. And at the international level, even as Malaysia steps back from the UNSC next year, it is expected to continue to focus on Muslim solidarity at international forums. At the ASEAN level, counterterrorism, people smuggling, and maritime piracy should remain priority areas for Malaysian border areas. The full extent of the effects of Malaysia's elevated cordiality with China may only be revealed next year, especially on two fronts: the South China Sea situation, and Malaysia–U.S. relations.

Notes

1. Oliver Holmes, "Malaysian Prime Minister Cleared of Corruption over $681m Saudi 'Gift' ", *The Guardian*, 26 January 2016.
2. Trinna Leong, "Umno Sacks Party Rebels Muhyiddin and Mukhriz", *Straits Times*, 25 June 2016.
3. Malaysian Progressives United Kingdom (MPUK), "The Fine Line between Hate Speech and Freedom of Speech", *Malaysiakini*, 10 March 2016.
4. "Malaysian Political Cartoonist Zunar Arrested under Sedition Law", Channel NewsAsia, 26 November 2016.

5. Nurbaiti Hamdan, "Nazri Hits Back at Dr M over Maria's Arrest under Sosma", *The Star*, 24 November 2016.

6. A. Ananthalakshmi, "Malaysia's Najib Gets New Powers amid Planned Protests over Fund Scandal", Reuters, 27 July 2016.

7. Shannon Teoh, " 'Malaysian Official 1' is Najib, Says Minister", *Straits Times*, 2 September 2016.

8. Stephanie Lee and Muguntan Vanar, "MACC Seizes RM52mil Cash in Sabah Water Dept Probe", *The Star*, 5 October 2016.

9. "PAS Chief Tables Hudud Bill for Third Time; Proposes Stiffer Penalties", *Today*, 25 November 2016.

10. Tasnim Lokman and Adrian Lai, "PPBM Seeking Anwar's Blessing", *New Straits Times*, 12 September 2016.

11. "High Court Strikes Out PKR's Civil Suit against Malaysia's PM Najib", *Jakarta Post*, 21 January 2016.

12. Trinna Leong, "Sultan of Kelantan Named New Malaysian King", *Straits Times*, 14 October 2016.

13. M. Mageswary, "Rafizi Sentenced to 18 Months' Jail", *The Star*, 14 November 2016.

14. Fazleena Aziz, "Rafizi Lodges MACC Report over Selangor Govt 'Money and Women' Claims", *New Straits Times*, 30 May 2016.

15. Opalyn Mok, "DAP Hits RM1m Target, Ends Donation Drive for Guan Eng's Bail", *Malay Mail*, 1 July 2016.

16. Joceline Tan, "A 'Disneyland Castle' in Ampang", *The Star*, 20 November 2016.

17. Leslie Shaffer, "Malaysia's Ringgit May Keep Tumbling amid the Market's Trump Tantrum", CNBC, 21 November 2016.

18. "1MDB Scandal Taking Toll on Malaysia Stock Market as Foreigners Sell", Bloomberg, 31 May 2016.

19. Surin Murugiah, "Foreigners Offloaded RM396.8 Million Last Week, Says MIDF Research", *The Edge Markets*, 31 October 2016.

20. Ee Ann Nee, "Consumer Spending Seen Continuing to Drive Malaysia's Economic Growth", *Sun Daily*, 13 July 2016.

21. "Petronas Committed to Paying RM16b Dividend to Gov't in 2016", Bernama, 1 March 2016.

22. "No GST Hike in Budget 2017", *Malay Mail*, 21 October 2016.

23. "Pua: Putrajaya 'Overly Optimistic' in Predicting Revenue for Budget 2017", *Malay Mail*, 21 October 2016.

24. Iris Lee, "Everything You Need to Know about Budget 2017", iMoney.my, 21 October 2016.

25. "FULL TEXT: PM Najib Razak's 2017 Budget speech", *New Straits Times*, 21 October 2016.

26. Dina Murad, "Budget 2017: Opposition MPs Stage Walkout Midway through PM's Speech", *The Star*, 21 October 2016.

27. Noel Foo, "Four Sectors Allowed to Hire Foreign Workers", *The Star*, 12 May 2016.

28. Aidila Razak, "Zahid's Kin Eyes System for 1.5m Bangladeshis", *Malaysiakini*, 11 August 2015.

29. Ben Butler, "China Communications Construction Company Denies 1MDB Claim", *The Australian*, 1 August 2016.

30. "Govt's Move to Assist Taxi and Uber Drivers Hailed by All", *The Star*, 22 October 2016.

31. "Khairy Condemns Red Shirt Supporters' Violence in Sabak Bernam", *Astro Awani*, 9 October 2016.

32. Farhana Syed Nokman, "Red Shirts' Jamal Yunos Remanded Four Days", *New Straits Times*, 19 November 2016.

33. Sumisha Naidu, "'Pretzel Dog' Holds up Halal Certification for Auntie Anne's in Malaysia", Channel NewsAsia, 18 October 2016.

34. "Zakir Naik Back in Malaysia", *The Star*, 24 October 2016.

35. Wong Pek Meil, "Experts Have Their Say on Taman Tugu", *The Star*, 26 September 2016.

36. "Kelantan Highly Dependent on Forest-derived Revenue", *The Star*, 28 October 2016.

37. "Khairy: 100pc Pride in Paralympians, So 100pc Reward", *Malay Mail*, 11 September 2016.

38. "White House Calls for Malaysian Transparency in Wake of Fund Scandal", Reuters, 21 July 2016.

39. "At WIEF, Najib Warns Muslim Nations of Foreign Intervention", *Malay Mail*, 2 August 2016.

40. David Brunnstrom, "U.S. Envoy Chides Malaysia's Najib, Says Rhetoric Sounded Like Mahathir", Reuters, 3 November 2016.

41. "Malaysia to 'Wait and See' over Fate of TPPA after US Presidential Election", *The Star*, 11 October 2016.

42. Prashanth Parameswaran, "When Will Malaysia Launch its New Center to Counter Islamic State Messaging?", *The Diplomat*, 31 October 2016.

43. Johan Saravanamuttu and David Han, "Malaysia-China Relations: A New Turn?", *RSIS Commentary*, no. 274, 4 November 2016.

44. Lokman Mansor, "RM143.64bil Worth of Deals Signed with China: PM Najib", *New Straits Times*, 1 November 2016.

45. Christopher Bodeen, "Recent Developments surrounding the South China Sea", *Washington Post*, 31 October 2016.

46. Bernard Cheah, "Haze MoU Discontinued, Says Minister", *The Sun*, 11 May 2016.

47. Siafulbahri Ismail, "Indonesia Expresses Deep Concern to Malaysia over Latest Kidnapping Incident", Channel NewsAsia, 7 November 2016.

48. Edith Regalado, "Philippines, Malaysia, Indonesia to Join Forces vs Abus", *Philippine Star*, 4 November 2016.

49. Boo Su-Lyn, "Why Jobs, Education Only for Syrian Refugees? Rights Groups Ask Putrajaya", *Malay Mail*, 7 January 2016.

50. "Malaysia Plays 'Constructive Role' as Security Council Member", *Astro Awani*, 24 May 2016.

REALIGNMENT OF STATE–CENTRE RELATIONS: The Adenan Factor in Sarawak

Neilson Ilan Mersat

> *The Chief Minister has said time and again that Sarawak will never secede from Malaysia but that doesn't mean the State cannot fight for its rights as enshrined in the Federal Constitution, The Malaysia Agreement 1963, The Malaysia Act, The Inter-Government Committee Reports and Recommendations and the Cobbold Commission Reports.* (Press Statement from Chief Minister's Office, 7 November 2016)

The statement above issued by the Chief Minister's office partly explains why Sarawak's politics took a slightly different trajectory after Adenan Satem took over as the new Chief Minister for Sarawak from Taib Mahmud on 28 February 2014. He argues in his speeches that Sarawak had been left behind and needs to catch up with other states in the Federation of Malaysia. In Sarawak's local dialect, Adenan Satem used the word "*ngepong*", referring to catching up with other states. His catching-up strategies are central to the current centre–state relations in Sarawak. This chapter discusses centre–state relations between Putra Jaya and Kuching, specifically after Adenan Satem took over from Taib Mahmud. Responses from the centre to this political realignment are also discussed.

Federalism in Malaysia

A federal system divides power between the national government and the smaller local governments. The advantage of a federal government is that it helps to

NEILSON ILAN MERSAT is Dean of the Faculty of Social Sciences, Universiti Malaysia Sarawak.

address the needs of a geographically large country. The needs at the local level of each state differ, and they should have different local governments to address those needs. In theory, federalism assumes that there exist diverse and separate communities who want to unite but which are at the same time eager to maintain a separate existence.[1] More often than not, centre–state relations in a federation are quite fluid. However, they should be stable if local leaders support the concentration of power at the centre as a means to safeguard the integrity of the country. In cases where states are controlled by a different political party, relations between the centre and state might be quite fluid.

The Federation of Malaysia was established in 1963 by an agreement between the governments of Malaya, the United Kingdom, and the leaders of the people of Sarawak, Sabah (North Borneo), and Singapore, through the 1963 Malaysian Agreement signed on 8 July 1963. Sarawak has a population of almost 2.5 million, made up of some twenty-six ethnic groups. The non-Muslim indigenous groups, collectively called Dayak, account for about 40 per cent of Sarawak's inhabitants. The Chinese, at around 30 per cent, make up the second-largest ethnic group. The number of Malays has increased to about 25 per cent of Sarawak's population. The size of Sarawak is about 124,449 square kilometres. It is bounded by Brunei to the north, Sabah to the northeast, Indonesia to the east and south, and the South China Sea to the west.

The Sarawak Corridor of Renewable Energy (SCORE) was created by dint of national planning in 2009 as one of the five regional development corridors being developed throughout Malaysia. SCORE's ambition is to develop the Central Region and transform Sarawak into a developed state by the year 2020. It aims to accelerate the state's economic growth and development, as well as improve the quality of life for the people of Sarawak. The corridor is located within the Central Region of Sarawak, stretching 320 kilometres along the coast from Tanjung Manis to Samalaju and extending into the surrounding areas and hinterland. SCORE covers an area of approximately 70,000 kilometres, with a population of 607,800 people. The major urban centres within the corridor are Sibu, Bintulu, Mukah, and Kapit.[2]

Centre–State Relations

Centre–state relations are shaped by various factors. More often than not, states that are unwilling to operate within the parameters of national priorities are bound to be discriminated against through insufficient financial support from the central government. Of course, from the federal government's point of view, such actions are considered important in order to force recalcitrant state leaders to support national initiatives.[3] But such actions clearly deviate from a basic principle of federalism, where any one state should be treated the same as other states, irrespective of the political party it supports.[4] In the case of Malaysia, one-party dominance by the United Malays National Organisation (UMNO) and the Barisan Nasional (BN) coalition it leads, at both the centre and state levels, has done much to shape centre–state relations.[5]

The lowest point in relations between Sarawak and the federal government was in 1966, when the Federal Parliament used emergency powers to alter Sarawak's constitution. Early incidences of friction occurred over the appointment of the Governor of Sarawak, the expatriate issue, and the use of the Malay language, particularly in education. Governor Ningkan was removed and replaced by Tawi Sli in September 1966, a leader who was more acceptable to the central government.[6] In the Sarawak cabinet led by Tawi Sli — a Muslim Melanau intelligentsia from the Bumiputera Parti — Taib Mahmud dominated most of the decision-making.

Abdul Rahman Yakub was installed by Prime Minister Tunku Abdul Rahman as the Malayan Government's first proxy in Sarawak, becoming Chief Minister in 1970. In return for his undivided loyalty to his political masters in Kuala Lumpur, Abdul Rahman Yakub had licence to do as he pleased in Sarawak.[7] The federal attitude towards politics in Sarawak under Taib Mahmud, Yakub's cousin who took over as Chief Minister in 1981, has been described by scholars as "hands off" as long as BN reigned supreme. Under Taib Mahmud's leadership, Sarawak consistently delivered the federal BN more than ninety per cent of Sarawak's parliamentary seats. State–centre relations during Taib Mahmud's reign were good, and on many occasions Prime Minister Mahathir in particular lent his support to Taib Mahmud's leadership; for example, in 1987 in order to tame Dayakism sentiments among the non-Muslim natives of Sarawak, and during the 1999 parliamentary elections when a group of Malay politicians in Sarawak attempted to bring UMNO to Sarawak and threaten Taib's Pesaka Bumiputera Bersatu party.

Centre–State relations began to change after the 2008 general elections when the BN lost in five states and failed to secure a two-thirds majority in parliament. Due to declining support for the BN in Peninsular Malaysia, BN leaders started to depend on votes from Sarawak and Sabah to remain in power. Both states are seen as "fixed deposits" for the BN, and for the opposition Pakatan Rakyat coalition they are potential kingmakers. In the words of opposition leader Anwar Ibrahim, the electorates in Sabah and Sarawak hold the key to Putra Jaya. Both states flexed their electoral muscles by asking for more representatives in the federal cabinet and for a greater budget allocation from the federal government.

In the case of Sarawak, the new state leadership under Adenan Satem seized the opportunity to do the "catching up" work for Sarawak.

Prime Minister Najib Razak has referred to the bloc of seats from Sarawak as one of the "fixed deposits" that would help to maintain his grip on power. It is not difficult to fathom why Sabah and Sarawak are seen as such for the ruling party. For the past two elections, in 2008 and 2013, both states contributed a significant number of seats for the ruling BN. In 2013 a total of 47 out of 133 seats won by the BN came from the two states. Had the two states decided to withdraw their votes from the BN, then Pakatan Rakyat would have formed a new government. At that time, Pakatan Rakyat needed 33 seats to form a simple majority government.

The Adenan Factor

When Adenan Satem took over from Taib Mahmud as the new Chief Minister in early 2014, centre–state relations changed and business as usual ended. Since assuming power as Chief Minister he has continued to surprise Sarawakians in his desire to change the way things are done and by trying to do the right thing.[8] Most important of all, he is trying to return dignity to Sarawak. A case in point being the fact that, after more than fifty years of independence, Sarawak is still one of the poorest states in Malaysia. Now that the ruling coalition is desperate for support from Sarawak, it is time for Adenan to highlight Sarawak's case to Putra Jaya. Adenan has also claimed that God has given him a new lease of life to "do what I have to do" after his close shave with death due to a heart ailment three years ago. "When God gives me a new lease of life, he must be trying to drop a message to give me a hint of what I have to do."[9]

Adenan argues that Sarawak has been "short changed" by the federal government since independence in 1963, and that some of its promises have remained unfulfilled. In a strong statement, he said: "We have been colonized by London [the British] before the formation of Malaysia, and I certainly don't want to be colonized by Kuala Lumpur after we formed the country. Sarawakians would not accept it if we free ourselves from one colonialist only to be colonized by another."[10]

The power of autonomy in certain areas is required for Sarawak. According to the Chief Minister, Sarawak needs to reclaim some powers, as "there has been constant erosion of power given to us over the last 50 over years".[11] These powers are needed to improve the basic needs of the people. For example, even after more than fifty years of independence, there are schools that fall into the river, schools without electricity, schools without water supplies, and unfinished roads and public utilities. Adenan once said, "If it is 20 or 30 years we don't mind but if it is more [than] 50 years we cannot tolerate anymore and therefore we have asked the federal government to be more sympathetic to us and we question their right over our resources because these are our resources."[12]

Sarawak has asked for greater autonomy and empowerment in the following areas:

- In recognition of self-government on 22 July 1963, the state declared 22 July as a public holiday.
- The state government is committed to continue negotiations with the federal government on an increase in oil royalties, from five per cent to twenty per cent.
- Sarawak will insist on greater autonomy as enshrined in the Federal Constitution, Malaysia Agreement 1963, Inter Governmental Committee (IGC) Report, and the Cobbold Commission Report.

The first of three phases of negotiations took place in January 2016. This phase secured a thirteen-point agreement with the federal government on the delegation of administrative powers to state authorities.[13] The second ongoing phase of negotiations now focuses on laws that impinge on Sarawak's rights under the Federal Constitution. The third phase of negotiations on the devolution of powers will involve matters of financial provisions.

Strategies of Winning Hearts

Adenan's unique approach since becoming Chief Minister has surprised and won over many. His first strategy was to win the support of Sarawakians by claiming that he is the Chief Minister for all and not for any particular group. He then extended an olive branch to opposition leaders. He said he was willing to work with the opposition parties for the interests of Sarawak. Later, various initiatives aimed at improving living standards in the state were announced. His administration introduced fifty-three principles and initiatives for the benefit of all races.[14]

Adenan Satem has managed to attract attention to several issues, some of which are deemed sensitive by federal leaders, and which previous chief ministers have not dared to discuss openly.

More Teachers from Sarawak for Sarawak

One proposal put to the federal government is that at least ninety per cent of teachers in Sarawak should be from Sarawak. One reason for this is many teachers from Peninsular Malaysia preferred to return to their home states after serving a few months in Sarawak. Adenan's reaction to this was: "If they want to go back home, then let them. So that's why we have to increase the intake of Sarawakians as teachers. If there are not enough trained teachers from Sarawak to teach here, then more Sarawakians should be trained and be posted in the state here as they know the local issues well and are more sensitive to local needs."[15]

The Ministry of Education later approved the applications of 1,164 teachers to return to Peninsula Malaysia, and the Sarawak Education Department has been tasked to reach a posting ratio of nine local teachers to one from outside the state, under Initiative 90:10, by 2018. In September 2016 the ratio in primary schools of locals to teachers from outside the state was 78:20:2 (20,369 locals, 5,211 from Peninsular Malaysia, and 517 from Sabah and Labuan). For secondary schools the ratio was 73:25:2 (10,628 locals, 3,687 West Malaysians, and 229 from Sabah and Labuan).[16]

To his critics, this proposal is a form of regionalism. Adenan was accused of perpetuating regionalist sentiments by stirring emotions and building walls around Sarawak in the name of protecting the state. Regionalism would add another layer of division, and Sarawakians should not be deprived of good teachers from Peninsular Malaysia. His critics also questioned whether police and army personnel from Peninsular Malaysia would be the next to be sent back.[17] His concern with education also prompted the Chief Minister to suggest that education should come under the state's control so that the needs of rural schools could be better looked after. He asked for some degree of autonomy in education and funding to improve rural schools.[18]

Petronas and Oil Royalties

A contentious issue with regards to federal–state relations concerns the "oil royalties". This is an evergreen issue frequently used by all political parties in elections in Sarawak. Adenan's administration promised not to stop, and to repeat the state's request for greater oil and gas royalties. He was reported saying,

> I keep on reminding Petronas, if it's gas or oil from Terengganu or Kelantan, whatever, I do not care. But if it is from Sarawak, then I do care. Not successful yet, our talks on oil royalty, but I will not stop. We

> won't do it altogether. We'll do it step by step. And we want the royalty
> to be increased from 5 per cent to more than 5 per cent.[19]

He promised he would not desist from asking for the royalty increment, and put his promise in the form of a pantun (traditional Malay poetic form) that he has cited frequently in his speeches: *Nyiur gading puncak mahligai, Sayang ketupat berisi inti, Hancur daging tulang berkecai, Belum dapat belum berhenti* (Even with broken bones and shattered flesh, No stopping unless success achieved).[20] The higher royalty is needed due to the rich–poor gap between Peninsular Malaysia and the state and the need for more money for development.

While negotiations for the devolution of powers were ongoing, Adenan Satem shocked the country by suspending work permits for Petronas jobs in the state. The moratorium imposed by the state government was part of the overall push to ultimately raise Sarawak's share of revenue collected from its oil and gas wells. Adenan insisted that Sarawakians be given priority. He had urged Petronas to give more vacancies in the company to Sarawakians, as there are people from the state who have the qualifications to hold senior posts within Petronas. He threatened to cancel the work permits already given and replace them with Sarawakians. Of course, that decision did not go down well with Petronas. It prompted the company to issue a statement that retrenchment could not be avoided.[21]

English Language and United Examination Certificate (UEC)

Another decision made by Adenan's administration was to treat English as an important language, even though Malay is the official language. Interdepartmental correspondence in English is allowed in Sarawak.[22] Apparently this decision may not go down well among the Malay language activists who argue that the Malay Language, not English, should be given emphasis. His critics argue that this decision is against the national policy on language.

Adenan criticized the federal government for its "stupid" policy of refusing to endorse the globally recognized UEC awarded to graduates of local Chinese independent schools. Even though the federal government may not recognize the UEC, the Sarawak government and state institutions will recognize it. This is possible because the state civil service is strictly a state matter. Declaring that Sarawak recognizes the UEC, he accused Putrajaya's policy of contributing to the country's brain drain problem, as UEC graduates would continue working abroad after pursuing their studies there.[23]

2016 Sarawak State Election

The 2016 Sarawak state election was a litmus test for Adenan Satem and his team. Prior to the election, Adenan Satem's appeal to Sarawakian voters was loud and clear: "I am relying on your wisdom on this. I need a strong mandate for me to face Kuala Lumpur."[24] "If I have a big and strong mandate, I can stand up to Kuala Lumpur and say 'listen to me, I represent the whole of Sarawak'.... If I have a very weak mandate, they won't even bother to listen to me."[25] A strong mandate would allow him to demand greater attention from the federal government to implement efforts to develop the state and to push for greater autonomy for it.

He argued that he needed five more years as Chief Minister as there is so much catching up to do. He argued that "In the last two years, we have made about 50 decisions — lowered electricity tariffs, abolished tolls, reduced ferry charges, [built] infrastructure[,] including the Trans-Borneo highway. If we can do this in two years, why not five more years to finish the work? That is my plea. If after five years I am no good, kick me out. I would be happy to retire."[26]

From Prime Minister Najib's point of view, a strong mandate to form a state government would guarantee political stability and enable the Sarawak government to be able to negotiate with the federal government for any development needed in the state: "The strong mandate is the voice of the people of Sarawak and we [the federal government] must respect the mandate given."[27]

I Am Not Taib Mahmud

One of the reasons for the withdrawal of Chinese support for the BN in the previous elections was as a protest against Taib Mahmud's leadership in Sarawak. The Chinese business people claimed that Taib's family involvement in business had deprived them of opportunities in the state. Taib's family is involved in various enterprises through the diversified conglomerate Cahaya Mata Sarawak — the majority shareholders of which are his family members. Adenan Satem openly declared that he had his own team to manage the state. He allayed fears, especially among the Chinese, that the former Chief Minister Taib Mahmud still has a strong influence on him. He described his relations with Taib Mahmud as good, but that he would be managing the state in his own way. He summarized his relations with Taib Mahmud as follows:

> Ini Adenan bukan White Hair [this is Adenan, not White Hair (Taib Mahmud)]. I have my own gang. I have [a] good relationship with White Hair. Now he is the Governor and above politics. He doesn't tell

> me what to do. He told me you are now the Chief Minister of Sarawak. "Whatever you do, you are responsible for it. If you want some advice, I will give [it], I will not tell you what to do, what you ought to do and so on, but I will not interfere in your job as Chief Minister, unlike some people I know."

This strategy of "distancing" himself from Taib Mahmud while at the same time maintaining a good working relationship with him seemed to work in the last state election. Adenan and his team managed to win back a significant proportion of Chinese votes from the opposition, particularly in Democratic Action Party strongholds.

Outcome of the Election

It was a big victory for the Barisan Nasional, winning 72 out of 82 seats. Apparently it was not only Adenan but also Najib who needed a resounding BN victory in Sarawak. Najib's critics had positioned the Sarawak election as a test of public support for the Prime Minister and the ruling coalition, after months of political turmoil over scandals embroiling federal investment fund 1Malaysia Development Berhad (1MDB). The test was passed.

But from another perspective, Najib has no reason to be happy. According to former Prime Minister Mahathir Mohamad, what BN Sarawak achieved was to weaken the authority of the federal government. Najib is now going to be even more dependent on the support of Sarawak than previously. According to Mahathir, Najib had unwisely given in to all of Sarawak's demands. Mahathir professed that "there must be a balance in terms of power between the centre and the state to ensure interdependence between the two".[28] Adenan retaliated by claiming that Mahathir failed to do enough for his state in the twenty-two years he served as Prime Minister. The first-term Chief Minister recounted the number of visits Mahathir made to Sarawak during his rule, which he claimed could be counted on the fingers on both hands, whereas Najib has visited Sarawak forty-seven times since he became Prime Minister in 2009.[29]

Responses from the Centre

At the federal level, the BN leaders are preoccupied with various issues. Najib's leadership is haunted by the ongoing 1MDB scandal. The resignation of his deputy Tan Sri Mahyudin Yassin, who later teamed up with Mahathir, has worsened the political situation in the country. A high profile corruption case in Sabah in early October 2016 has further tarnished the country's image internationally. The economic slowdown driven by low prices of raw materials such as petroleum has bruised the economy. Apparently, the federal leadership is busy putting their house in order. From Sarawakians' point of view, this is the best time for the state to demand the opportunities lost over the past fifty years. The voices from Sarawak, and even Sabah, are getting louder by the day.

Najib has responded quite positively to demands from Sarawak. Putra Jaya needs Sarawak's cooperation to face the global challenges that are adversely affecting Malaysia's oil revenue. "Sarawak must be at par with Peninsula Malaysia. Malaysia will succeed if Sarawak succeeds, as Sarawak is a key economic contributor and major oil and gas producer."[30]

The federal government responded by appointing a committee — co-chaired by Nancy Shukri (from Sarawak) and Anifah Aman (from Sabah) — to pursue the devolution of state rights for Sarawak and Sabah under the federal constitution. Nancy Shukri and Anifah Aman co-chaired the first high-level meeting on 13 June 2016, which was attended by the Attorney-General and representatives from the Sarawak and Sabah federal governments.[31] Sarawak has requested for the relevant historical documents to be considered in granting administrative and constitutional empowerment to the state.

Several opposition leaders in West Malaysia, such as Mohamad Sabu and Azmin Ali, argued that Najib could not check Adenan for fear of losing support among the Sarawak parliamentarians. They argued that, should Sarawak BN parliamentarians decide to no longer support the Prime Minister, his government would collapse. This is partly true, because Sarawak BN contributes a substantial number of seats for the federal BN.

The Malay language activists have criticized Sarawak's adoption of English as an official language alongside Bahasa Malaysia, but post-election the Chief Minister holds firm to the decision he first announced on State Civil Service Day. Social and Cultural Affairs Advisor Rais Yatim said that the state government's move to use English could sow seeds of discord among the people. But Adenan is adamant on his decision to use English in Sarawak:

> Whether they agree with me in the Semenanjung [peninsula] or not, I don't care. I made English the second language in Sarawak. Of course, Bahasa Malaysia is still the main language. We agree and have no issue with that. But what is wrong with us also being proficient in English? It's the language of science, learning, literature, technology, business, research, communication and international relations.[32]

No Separation

Adenan is also riding on the sentiment of Sarawak for Sarawakians as promoted by a few local pressure groups. While agreeing with the slogan of "Sarawak for Sarawakians", Adenan made it very clear that there will be no separation of Sarawak from the Federation of Malaysia. "If you advocate cessation our answer is no. Our position is no cessation — Malaysia before, Malaysia now and Malaysia forever in the future. To be part of the Federation of Malaysia was one of the wisest decisions made by Sarawak 53 years ago."[33]

Conclusion

The discussion in this chapter has been an attempt to explain why there has been a political realignment in centre–state relations under the new Chief Minister of Sarawak. Central to this realignment is none other than Adenan himself. Since becoming Chief Minister he has been vocal on the issues he feels are important to Sarawak. His main contention is that Sarawak has been left behind compared to other states in Malaysia, despite having plenty of natural resources such as oil. To catch up, Sarawak needs more development funds and power. Therefore, the devolution of power is essential. He is asking for what is due for Sarawak based on the 1963 Malaysian Agreement, signed prior to the formation of the country, and he has ruled out secession from the federation. Since his team was given a stronger mandate in the last state election, the people of Sarawak expect that the voice of the state will grow louder in Malaysia.

Notes

1. A.V. Dicey, *An Introduction to the Study of the Law of the Constitution* (Basingstoke: Macmillan Education, 1959), p. 140.
2. See "The Sarawak Corridor of Renewable Energy", Sarawak Energy <http://www.sarawakenergy.com.my> (accessed 11 November 2016).
3. Mohammad Agus Yusoff, *Malaysian Federalism: Conflict or Consensus* (Universiti Kebangsaan Malaysia: Bangi, 2006), p. 339.
4. K.C. Wheare, *Federal Government* (New York: Oxford University Press, 1946), pp. 34–37.
5. Agus Yusoff, *Malaysian Federalism*, p. 325.
6. R.S. Milne and Diane K. Mauzy, *Politics and Government in Malaysia* (Singapore: Federal Publications, 1978), pp. 113–15.
7. Ibid.
8. Joceline Tan, "A Dream for Sarawak", *The Star Online*, 20 December 2015 <http://

www.thestar.com.my/news/nation/2015/12/20/a-dream-for-sarawak-it-has-not-been-business-as-usual-since-tan-sri-adenan-satem-took-over-as-the-ch/>.

9. "Adenan: God Gave Me a New Lease of Life to Do What I Have To", *The Star Online*, 16 March 2016 <http://www.thestar.com.my/news/nation/2016/03/16/adenan-god-gave-me-a-new-lease-of-life-to-do-what-i-have-to/>.

10. "Sarawak Does Not Want to be Colonised by KL, Says Adenan", *Free Malaysia Today Online*, 20 February 2016.

11. Lim How Pim, "We'll Keep Fighting, Remind Putrajaya of Sarawak's Rights", *Borneo Post Online*, 22 July 2016.

12. "Support Us in Asking for Devolution of Powers, Says Adenan", *Free Malaysia Today*, 22 July 2016.

13. Adib Povera, "Federal Govt Grants 13 Items to S'wak under First Phase of Devolution of Powers", *New Straits Times Online*, 21 January 2016.

14. "BN Working Hard to Transform Sarawak: Adenan", *The Sun Daily Online*, 26 April 2016.

15. Peter Sibon, Lian Cheng, and Karen Bong, "Recruit More Locals as Teachers", *Borneo Post Online*, 26 February 2015 <http://www.theborneopost.com/2015/02/26/recruit-more-locals-as-teachers/>.

16. Lian Cheng, "90 PCT Local Teachers by Year 2018", *Borneo Post Online*, 8 October 2015 <http://www.theborneopost.com/2015/10/08/90-pct-local-teachers-by-year-2018/>.

17. Robin Augustin, " 'Sarawak for Sarawakians' Not Healthy for Nation-Building", *Free Malaysia Today Online*, 3 May 2016 <http://www.freemalaysiatoday.com/category/nation/2016/05/03/sarawak-for-sarawakians-not-healthy-for-nation-building/>.

18. Sharon Ling, "Sarawak Seeks Own Education Policy", *The Star Online*, 18 August 2015 <http://www.thestar.com.my/news/nation/2015/08/18/sarawak-seeks-own-education-policy/>.

19. <http://www.thestar.com.my/news/nation/2015/06/16/cm-repeats-oil-and-gas-royalty-request/>.

20. Richard T.W., "Adenan: We'll Scrap Permits If Petronas Doesn't Cooperate", *Free Malaysia Today Online*, 12 August 2016 <http://www.freemalaysiatoday.com/category/nation/2016/08/12/adenan-well-scrap-permits-if-petronas-doesnt-cooperate/>; "Support Adenan in Fight for More Oil Royalty — Minos", *Borneo Post Online*, 23 March 2015 <http://www.theborneopost.com/2015/03/23/support-adenan-in-fight-for-more-oil-royalty-minos/>.

21. Stephen Then, "Najib: Putrajaya Needs Sarawak's Cooperation", *The Star Online*, 16 September 2016 <http://www.thestar.com.my/news/nation/2016/09/16/najib-putrajaya-sarawak/>.

22. "Sarawak to Allow Official State Correspondence in English", *The Star Online*, 18 November 2015 <http://www.thestar.com.my/news/nation/2015/11/18/english-official-sarawak-admin/>.

23. CM: Sarawak Will Keep Recognizing UEC, Doesn't Matter What Putrajaya Decides", *Malay Mail Online*, 21 March 2016 <http://www.themalaymailonline.com/malaysia/article/cm-sarawak-will-keep-recognising-uec-doesnt-matter-what-putrajaya-decides>.

24. Adenan to Sarawak: Give Me Bigger, Stronger Mandate to Face KL", *New Straits Times*, 16 January 2016.

25. "CM: Sarawak Will Keep Recognizing UEC".

26. *The Star Online*, 20 December 2015.

27. "Give Strong Mandate to CM Adenan Satem", *Astro Awani*, 28 February 2016 <http://english.astroawani.com/malaysia-news/give-strong-mandate-cm->.

28. William Mangor, "Mahathir: Adenan's Victory 'Weakens' Najib's Gov't", *Free Malaysia Today Online*, 9 May 2016 <http://www.freemalaysiatoday.com/category/nation/2016/05/09/mahathir-adenans-victory-weakens-najibs-govt/>.

29. Sulok Tawie, "Najib Trumps Dr M in Number of Visits to Sarawak, Adenan Says", *Malay Mail Online*, 12 March 2016 <http://www.themalaymailonline.com/malaysia/article/najib-trumps-dr-m-in-number-of-visits-to-sarawak-adenan-says>.

30. Then, "Najib: Putrajaya Needs Sarawak's Cooperation".

31. "Adenan Welcomes Government Response", *The Star Online*, 28 June 2016 <http://www.thestar.com.my/news/nation/2016/06/28/adenan-welcomes-govt-response-negotiations-to-begin-but-process-will-be-complex-and-drawn-out/>.

32. Yu Ji, "Adenan Stands Firm on English", *The Star Online*, 23 December 2015 <http://www.thestar.com.my/news/nation/2015/12/23/adenan-stands-firm-on-english-sarawak-cm-its-an-important-language-and-criticism-wont-deter-me/>.

33. Lim How Pim, "Content No Longer — CM", *Borneo Post*, 22 July 2016.

Myanmar

MYANMAR'S NEW ERA:
A Break from the Past, or
Too Much of the Same?

Ardeth M. Thawnghmung and Gwen Robinson

The resounding victory of Aung San Suu Kyi and her National League for Democracy (NLD) in the national elections in November 2015 ushered in what many hailed as a new era for Myanmar, after more than a half-century of military and semi-military rule. While the NLD's ascension has generated overwhelming optimism, a more open environment, a surge of foreign aid, and — after a four-month hiatus — investment, the fledgling government's performance in addressing Myanmar's age-old challenges has received mixed reviews. We examine how the rise of the NLD government and its de facto leader, Aung San Suu Kyi, has transformed the political landscape, and highlight key opportunities and challenges confronting the party and Myanmar's overall transition to democracy.

The Aftermath of the NLD Elections

Immediately after taking power on 1 April, the NLD government dropped charges against and/or released approximately 235 political prisoners; filled top-level positions, including the first all-civilian contingent of chief ministers for the 14 states and regions; slashed the number of government ministries from 36 to an

ARDETH MAUNG THAWNGHMUNG is Chair and Professor of Political Science at the University of Massachusetts Lowell.

GWEN ROBINSON is Senior Fellow at the Institute of Security and International Studies at Chulalongkorn University in Bangkok and Chief Editor of the *Nikkei Asian Review*, an English-language website and journal of Asian affairs published by Japanese media group Nikkei Inc.

initial 21; and vowed to cut bureaucratic red tape.[1] In a clear push for "quick wins", the new government also broadened anti-corruption rules for officials and lawmakers; stepped up agricultural loans to farmers; accelerated the previous government's move to return confiscated land to individuals; and reached out to migrant Burmese workers, particularly in neighbouring Thailand.

After creating a new role for herself of State Counsellor, equivalent to prime minister in a semi-presidential system, Aung San Suu Kyi — who also took the post of Foreign Minister — set up a series of committees and commissions to address priority areas, from land disputes to environmental and economic reforms, and announced general policies to address an array of economic and political problems.[2] Some initiatives, such as the release of political prisoners and loans to farmers, had immediate and positive impacts; but others — including sweeping promises to create more jobs, reform state enterprises, and return seized land — highlighted the complexity of problems that will require carefully structured, multi-faceted solutions. With this in mind, we first examine how the NLD's accession to power has affected the nature and composition of government and the dynamics within major political parties and institutions.

Composition of New Government and Dynamics among Major Political Parties and Institutions

The NLD's rise to government has transformed its relationships with the military and the former ruling party, the Union Solidarity and Development Party, from one of confrontation to a more workable dynamic entailing compromises by all three component elements. While still tense — or, at best, awkward — on some levels, both military and USDP lawmakers have rarely openly opposed NLD-sponsored initiatives in the national parliament. At most, they have abstained from voting or, on at least two occasions in 2016, stood silently in the NLD-dominated parliament to register protest over certain bills — notably, the 6 April passage of a bill to create the State Counsellor position subsequently taken by Aung San Suu Kyi.[3]

In public, at least, the leadership of the Tatmadaw — or armed forces — and the NLD have avoided criticizing or opposing each other, particularly on key issues such as the military's escalation of attacks on ethnic armed groups in northern Shan and Kachin states in late 2016 and, on the NLD's side, moves to delay deals or abandon initiatives set in train under the previous military-backed USDP administration of Thein Sein.[4] Suu Kyi even went as far during an early December visit to Singapore to justify the widely criticized military crackdown on the majority Muslim population of northern Rakhine state as an understandable response to attacks by Muslim militants on police posts along Myanmar's border with Bangladesh on 9 October.[5] Overall, the NLD administration has signalled unexpected pragmatism, including through its moves to incorporate some officials from the previous administration (see details below).[6]

Top-level government positions are now filled predominantly by civilians (mostly NLD supporters and sympathizers), although the military continues to exercise strong influence with its constitutionally mandated allocation of twenty-five per cent of all legislative seats in both national and regional parliaments, and control over the nomination/appointment of one of the two vice presidents, as well as the three security-related cabinet positions: defence, border affairs, and home affairs. Overall, the military controls six out of eleven positions in the National Defence and Security Council (NDSC), a once-powerful body that meets on an ad hoc basis on urgent security issues at the request of the President. The military's commander in chief, Senior General Min Aung Hlaing, meanwhile, has repeatedly emphasized that the armed forces would adhere to its constitutional role of safeguarding the charter; defined as preserving national unity and sovereignty, including the non-disintegration of the union, and perpetuation of sovereignty and the role of the military in politics.[7]

Nevertheless, the military stood by in early 2016 as a civilian — for the first time since General Ne Win seized power in 1962 and established military rule — assumed the presidency. The role was denied to Aung San Suu Kyi due to constitutional restrictions against those whose direct family members hold foreign citizenship (her two sons by her late husband, British academic Michael Aris, held British citizenship). Instead, she chose her childhood friend and senior aide Htin Kyaw — who studied at the Yangon Institute of Economics and the University of London — to be her "proxy", declaring that she would be "above the President".[8] The two vice presidential positions were filled in a parliamentary vote in March through what was widely seen as a direct bargain. One post went to Henry Van Thio, a little-known ethnic Chin lawmaker and NLD member with a military background. The military-nominated candidate, Myint Swe, the former Chief Minister of Yangon and a known hardliner, may have been grudgingly accepted by the NLD in return for the military's acceptance of NLD leadership in government. All three were initially nominated for the presidency, with the two who received fewer votes automatically gaining the two Vice Presidential posts.

Some days later, the NLD in a surprise move presented a "state counsellor bill" to parliament. The bill easily passed the two NLD-dominated houses, despite strong criticism from military lawmakers, who boycotted the vote, and outright opposition from a handful of USDP lawmakers. In effect it gave Suu Kyi the status of a particularly powerful Prime Minister, and dodged the constitutional restrictions on the presidency.[9] Suu Kyi had already expanded her power by assuming the position of Minister of Foreign Affairs, a post that carries with it membership of the National Defence and Security Council. Although the NLD administration had not activated the military-dominated council by December, under one interpretation of the loosely worded constitution, it has the authority to determine issues relating to defence and security.

Overall, the leadership of the bicameral parliament, or Pyidaungsu Hluttaw, has become more diverse with the rise of the NLD — despite growing criticism among some NLD lawmakers that the administration was reducing their autonomy and therefore the importance of parliament; for example, by ordering lawmakers to toe the party line and avoid asking ministers awkward questions.[10] Under the previous Thein Sein administration, the chairs and deputy chairmen of both lower and upper houses were USDP members (chairs Shwe Mann and Nanda Kyaw Swa, and vice-chairs Khin Aung Myint and Mya Nyein). Under the NLD government, only two of the four chairs and deputies belonged to the winning party, while one represented the USDP (Khun Mya), and the other the ethnic minority Arakan National Party (Aye Thar Aung).

Having trumped the military and USDP via parliamentary processes to consolidate her hold on power, Suu Kyi made a few conciliatory gestures by incorporating some who were associated with the previous administration into the new NLD government — either as ministers or informal advisors. Apart from the move to appoint previous presidential spokesman Zaw Htay to the new President's Office, notable appointments included the Minister of Religious Affairs and Culture, Aung Ko; Minister of Labour, Immigration and Population, Thein Swe; and Minister of the State Counsellor's Office, Kyaw Tint Shwe, Myanmar's former Ambassador to the United Nations. Police Brig.-Gen. Win Naing Tun, who used to be in charge of monitoring Aung San Suu Kyi when she was an opposition leader, was appointed her head of personal security. Aung Kyi, a former Labour Minister under Thein Sein and the main liaison under Than Swe's junta with Suu Kyi during her house arrest, was appointed to head a research unit set up to support the government's peace negotiation team with armed ethnic groups, while some military officers, including former army Lt.-Gen. Khin Zaw Oo, were given proactive roles in the new peace negotiating team under Suu Kyi's trusted friend and former physician, Dr Tin Myo Win.[11]

Suu Kyi's most significant new appointment — albeit in symbolism more than substance — was to appoint Shwe Mann, former Speaker of Parliament and leading member of Than Shwe's junta, to head the Commission for the Assessment of Legal Affairs and Special Issues, an advisory body to both the government and legislature on legislative reform. Despite his ouster in early 2015 as acting head of the USDP and his failure to win a seat in the November national election, that appointment showed the close relationship between Suu Kyi and the formerly powerful figure. The two built a close working relationship after Suu Kyi entered parliament as an elected member in 2012, a factor widely seen as the key reason for the rapid deterioration of his standing with the military and other USDP leaders.[12] Several sources close to the government noted that some appointees to the new administration and related commissions or committees were close associates of Shwe Mann's, and that Suu Kyi often consulted the former speaker, who was widely seen as a key member of her inner circle.[13]

Within the ministries, top appointments also featured greater diversity in terms of background — except in gender balance, which ironically took a big step back from the previous administration of Thein Sein. The former USDP government did not include any NLD members in the cabinet (out of 36), but the NLD government includes 4 USDP members (in addition to the constitutionally mandated posts for the military in the ministries for Defence, Border Affairs, and Home Affairs). While more than two-thirds of the 36 ministers in the previous administration came from military backgrounds, 14 of 21 NLD cabinet ministers (or 15 out of 22 cabinet ministries, counting Suu Kyi herself) are civilians, with no previous significant military involvement.[14] The cabinet was slashed by more than one third in efforts to save costs and streamline the bureaucracy. The cuts, which initially entailed the elimination of all deputy ministers, were later revised to restore some deputy minister positions and fine-tune the scope of the ministries. In a move that riled some lawmakers, the new administration also cut the salary of parliamentarians, slashing their pay by 25 per cent, while state lawmakers saw a 10 per cent cut to their monthly salaries.[15]

Human rights activists and media in particular were disappointed that the Ministry of Information, once seen as the key weapon of the earlier junta against the media, was not among the ministries to be eliminated. Concerns about freedom of expression grew throughout 2016, particularly following the arrests and imprisonment of two top members of the Eleven Media Group, including the chief executive, Than Htut Aung — for violating a section of the 2013 Telecommunications Law. The charges were brought by the Yangon Regional Government for an article published in the 6 November issue of *Daily Eleven* that accused the Chief Minister of Yangon of "rosy relations with corrupt officials" — an accusation that was denied, but which remained in the news into December.[16]

In the states and regions, a marked shift came in the form of the 14 newly appointed regional chief ministers and state ministers. All came from the NLD, and some were long-time political prisoners under the military government.[17] This compares to the Thein Sein government, where chief ministers were nearly all from military backgrounds. The gender balance in the new government, as noted above, is less impressive. Although a total of 150 women were elected to the national and state assemblies (out of 1,171 seats) in 2015, compared to only 53 in the previous assemblies, women account for only a tiny segment of top positions in the new administration.[18] There are no female cabinet members, apart from Suu Kyi, who accounts for 2 positions — Foreign Minister and State Counsellor — while only 2 of 14 state/regional chief ministers are women. While the previous administration lacked any women chief ministers, it did feature several women ministers and deputy ministers.[19]

Military Relations

One of the most significant events in terms of government–military relations and accountability of the armed forces came in September 2016, when a military court tried and convicted seven Myanmar soldiers — four of them officers — for killing five villagers while interrogating them in Shan state. The seven, who were given five-year prison terms with hard labour, confessed to the killings in June after the men's bodies were found with knife wounds in a shallow grave. As widely noted by observers and international and domestic media, it is extremely rare to see Myanmar's army acknowledge its own brutality, let alone prosecute those responsible.[20]

The conviction came shortly after news that military chief Min Aung Hlaing had promoted younger officers in an annual military reshuffle in late August — including his intelligence chief Lt. Gen. Myat Tun Oo and other officers who are regarded as more reform-minded than their seniors. Myat Tun Oo was promoted in the reshuffle to the post of Joint Chief of Staff of the army, navy, and air force, the third-top position in the armed forces and widely seen as the springboard to becoming military chief.[21] The reshuffle came shortly after the Commander-in-Chief decided to extend his term beyond his scheduled retirement in July 2016 by five years. The decision, permissible under military rules, added to earlier indications from the senior general that he was eying a possible run for the presidency after Suu Kyi's term ends in 2021.[22] If so, there is every reason for the military's top brass to appear more cooperative with the civilian government — and for the military chief in particular to aim to win hearts and minds in the coming years.

The crushing electoral defeat of the former ruling party, the USDP, in the November 2015 poll handed the military another (albeit unforeseen) role, making the military-appointed Members of Parliament a de facto opposition party. The dynamics under the NLD administration suggest an informal compact between the two sides, with the military retreating from overt intervention in the daily affairs of government, to allow the administration to tackle myriad economic, social, and political issues. In another sign of what some describe as an "uneasy coexistence", economic planning officials confirmed privately in October that there would be no moves to slash the official military budget. Roughly 15 per cent of the national budget is reserved for the military. But with increased spending on military modernization over the past three years — featuring a push to diversify sources of procurement amid high-level military visits to countries including Israel, Pakistan, Russia, and Belarus — and the rising costs of retirement benefits for retirees, the military is anxious about sustaining itself.[23] Aung San Suu Kyi and the NLD have not publicly raised the issue of cutting the military's budget.[24]

However, while the perception over the first six months of the new administration was of unprecedented momentum towards a civilian-dominated process, the final part of the year saw the reassertion of military authority — largely due to the escalation of fighting between the military and ethnic armed groups in Shan and Kachin states and the Tatmadaw's ferocious response in Rakhine state to a series of attacks on police units from 9 October by suspected Muslim militants. The attacks, which killed nine police, led to a brutal crackdown in northern Rakhine that triggered international outcry amongst human rights groups and international organizations, with hundreds of Muslim men detained as "suspects" and reports of rights abuses by military interrogators and soldiers in the field.[25] Suu Kyi's administration became the target of unprecedented criticism from regional neighbours — in particular Muslim Indonesia and Malaysia — which called into question ASEAN's long-held principle of non-interference in each other's affairs.

Overall, the hybrid nature of the new administration — with its large parliamentary majority and an NLD-dominated executive offset by the military's hold on cabinet positions and 25 per cent of all parliamentary seats — has prompted some critics to coin phrases such as "democratic dictatorship".[26] Underlying such criticisms is the widespread concern that Suu Kyi's administration could become more autocratic — not only because of her overwhelming dominance in key policymaking areas, but also due to her unwillingness to delegate responsibilities and her well-known stubbornness. She not only occupies the dual positions of State Counsellor and Foreign Minister, but she also heads a burgeoning culture of "rule by committee", facilitated through the steady formation of high-level committees and commissions on a range of critical issues since her administration took office. With special status, and membership confined largely to ministers and her "inner circle" of advisors, these committees bypass bureaucracy and parliament to varying degrees. This parallel — and, in some respects, elitist — structure was seen as necessary by some of Suu Kyi's advisors to streamline decision-making processes alongside a bureaucracy long run by officials loyal to the previous military regime, and to offset the yawning lack of capacity in the general bureaucracy and the fledgling administration.[27]

Relations with Minority Ethnic Nationalities

The 135 or so ethnic minority groups of Myanmar are represented by a wide variety of competing or overlapping organizations, ranging from civil society and political parties to armed ethnic groups. Thein Sein's administration collaborated with the United Nations Population Fund to carry out in early 2015 the first national census in more than three decades, and released all data (on population count, religious affiliation, socioeconomic situation, etc.) except for information on ethnic identity. The data on ethnic identity — expected to be released in 2017 — are seen as sensitive due to the contested nature of 135 officially recognized categories for ethnicity and the implications for negotiations with ethnic groups over demands for autonomy, particularly in the context of the peace process.[28] The data will also figure in determining which groups are eligible for self-administered zones, or the number of ethnic affairs ministers they will be represented by.

Minority ethnic groups constitute between 30 and 40 per cent of the entire population and represent over half the political parties that contested elections in 2010 and 2015. Many ethnicity-based political parties were resoundingly defeated by the NLD in the 2015 elections. The total proportion of national and regional legislative seats held by ethnic-based parties shrank from approximately 16 per cent to 12 per cent of all seats over this period. Many ethnicity-based political parties (both elected and non-elected) harbour suspicions about the Burman-dominated NLD. Among the most problematic of these for Suu Kyi and her NLD-dominated administration are the Arakan National Party (ANP), based in Rakhine state, and the Shan National League for Democracy (SNLD). The ruling party's relations with these parties — the two best-performing ethnicity-based parties, which won more seats than did the NLD in their respective state legislatures — deteriorated after the NLD rejected their request to consider their members in the appointment of state chief ministers. The NLD instead chose two of its elected members as Rakhine and Shan chief ministers, which triggered a local backlash and further deepened tensions within the ANP over its policy towards the NLD.[29]

The ANP was formed in January 2014 expressly to contest elections through the merger of the Rakhine Nationalities Development Party (RNDP) and the Arakan League for Democracy (ALD), an NLD ally which boycotted the 2010 elections. The hybrid party won 23 of the 35 available seats in the Rakhine State Parliament. But a rift within this fragile coalition opened up when Aye Thar Aung, founding chairman of the ALD, accepted his appointment by the NLD government as deputy speaker of the upper house of the national parliament in February, against the wishes of former RNDP members. Deepening the internal turmoil, the ANP's leadership expelled six prominent members — all former ALD members — who refused to follow the ANP's policy of opposing the NLD. In the aftermath, many predicted that the days of the ANP as a single political party were numbered.

Overall, the NLD has given some key positions to ethnic minorities. For instance, Henry Van Thio, an ethnic Chin, became one of two Vice Presidents. While one chair and two deputy chairs from the national legislature come from minority ethnic nationalities; respectively, T Khun Myat, Manh Win Khaing Than, and Aye Thar Aung. At least six of the fourteen chief ministers are of ethnic origin (under the previous administration of Thein Sein, four chief ministers represented minority ethnic nationalities). Shortly after taking power the NLD administration implemented the Protection of National Races law (passed by the national parliament in 2015 under the previous administration) by creating the Ministry of Ethnic Affairs, and appointed Naing Thet Lwin of the Mon National Party — an NLD ally — as Minister of Ethnic Affairs. Despite criticism among ethnic parties about the administration's handling of the peace process and a lack of consultation on state and local issues — including taxes and land use — the creation of the Ministry of Ethnic Affairs has been interpreted by some as a sign of Suu Kyi's support for Myanmar's minority ethnic groups, particularly given the stringent cost-cutting measures that prompted the NLD government to slash many ministries shortly after it came to power.

While Suu Kyi enjoyed more instant legitimacy and trust as leader than the former President, Thein Sein, she eventually retained most of his administration's policies in dealings with ethnic armed organizations and the overall peace process. Despite her concerted push to broaden and accelerate the government's peace initiative, fighting intensified in late 2016 between the armed forces and the four main armed groups that have waged campaigns since 2011: the Kachin Independence Army (Kachin state), Ta'ang National Liberation Army (northern

Shan state), Myanmar National Democratic Alliance Army (northern Myanmar, Chinese border region), and Arakan Army (Kachin, Chin, and Rakhine states). The escalation of fighting added to more than half a million civilians already displaced by conflict and it formed an awkward backdrop to the government's efforts to engage all ethnic armed groups in the peace process.[30] More significantly, the fresh conflict and widespread reports of human rights abuses by the military fuelled questions about Suu Kyi's apparent lack of control over the army — or worse, criticism that she was indifferent to the conduct of the campaign. In late November, after coordinated attacks by the KIA, AA, TNLA, and MNDAA in northern Shan state, the military launched heavy artillery bombardments, further intensifying the civil war.[31]

Some months after coming to power the NLD announced it would honour the Nationwide Ceasefire Agreement (NCA) that had been negotiated by the Thein Sein administration, the army, and an alliance of ethnic groups. Seventeen ethnic groups had initially been involved in the discussions, but only eight of these signed the NCA on 15 October 2015, after the final rounds of negotiations broke down amid accusations of a lack of inclusivity. One reason for the breakdown was the government's refusal to allow three groups that had not separately negotiated bilateral ceasefire agreements with the government — the Arakan Army, TNLA Ta'ang National Liberation Army, and MNDAA — to come to the negotiating table.[32]

The NLD, however, announced its intention to make the process more inclusive by renaming the Union Peace Conference as the 21st Century Panlong conference — after the town where Suu Kyi's father, late independence hero Gen. Aung San, staged the original Panglong peace conference in 1947. The NLD administration then invited all non-NCA signatories to attend the new peace talks (although they had been excluded from the Union Peace Conference that had been hastily arranged by the Thein Sein government from 12 to 16 January 2016 in order to convince the NLD to adopt the existing NCA framework). The inaugural 21st Century Panglong conference was meant to be symbolic, with presentations but no negotiations or decisions, and attended by nearly all armed ethnic groups (except for the three previously excluded groups, which refused to agree to the army's demands to disarm as a precondition for attending), elected political parties, government, military, experts, and civil society organizations.

The NLD, however, maintained the previous government's position to allow only NCA signatories to participate in future political dialogue. The "Panglong-21" conference was held in Naypyitaw from 31 August to 3 September and was attended by some 850 participants. Logistical flaws and poor event management resulted in numerous hitches, including the walk-out of the United Wa State Party delegation after the first day over what it claimed was discrimination in conference accreditation. Even so, the completion of the first conference and the announced scheduling of further Panglong-21 conferences every six months were regarded as concrete signs of the NLD's commitment to agreements that were negotiated under Thein Sein's government. However, the subsequent intensification of fighting in late 2016 and the collapse of scheduled talks in Kunming, China in December led critics to note that the process was unravelling.[33]

To head its peace effort the NLD, nonetheless, replaced most key participants, including chief peace negotiator, Aung Min, a former general and a leading member of Thein Sein's inner circle. It retained and promoted two prominent members of the previous line-up — businessman Hla Maung Shwe and security expert Min Zaw Oo — in its negotiation team, and renamed the Myanmar Peace Centre (the secretariat to the peace process under Thein Sein) the National Reconciliation and Peace Center. This is now headed by Suu Kyi's close advisor and former physician, Dr Tin Myo Win.[34]

However, Suu Kyi's stated intention to exclude non-elected political parties from participating in the conference and her failure to delegate and give a clear mandate to the NRPC team have raised grave concerns among ethnic leaders about the nature of the NLD's claim to inclusivity. This has been a missed opportunity to build confidence by addressing easier issues.[35]

Rakhine Tensions

Long-simmering sectarian tensions in Rakhine boiled over in late 2016 with a series of attacks by suspected Muslim militants that led to harsh military reprisals. In the initial attacks, on 9 October, at least 350 Rohingya militants — armed mainly with knives, sticks, and swords — coordinated raids on several police posts along Rakhine's border with Bangladesh. But the escalation of violence and the military crackdown in northern Rakhine — which saw more than 600 self-identified Rohingya men rounded up and detained, villages burned, aid suspended for at least forty days, and reports of military abuses — complicated the situation further. Allegations by state officials of overseas terrorist connections — possibly to Pakistan and Saudi Arabia — have changed the tone of the conflict in Rakhine. Indeed, Rakhine state officials have been at pains to show visitors videos and photographs, some posted on the Internet, that purport to show Rohingya men in northern Rakhine vowing to create their own state in the country and declaring jihad. Similar videos were posted by the group on YouTube.[36]

After the NLD came to power, Suu Kyi adopted a more neutral tone to refer to Muslims from Rakhine state, rather than the traditional derogatory term of "Bengalis" — which reinforces the belief among most Bamar Buddhists that they are interlopers from Bangladesh. In August (well ahead of the October attacks by Muslim militants) she formed an advisory commission chaired by former United Nations Secretary General Kofi Annan. The stated aim of his committee was to provide "rigorously impartial" assessments and recommendations to the government on solutions to the state's problems. The nine-member commission was created with three foreign members: Annan; Ghassan Salamé, a former Lebanese Minister for Culture; and Laetitia van den Assum, a former UN special advisor to the Secretary General. Annan himself had made just two visits to Rakhine by December to meet with key figures and travel to affected areas. Many Rakhine Buddhists, especially those representing the ANP, have opposed the inclusion of foreigners in the commission, and have refused to collaborate.[37]

Underpinning the recent violence in Rakhine were the earlier mass attacks on Muslims that erupted in 2012 and spread to other parts of the country. These occurred amid the rise of Ma Ba Tha (the ultra-conservative Association of Race and Religion Protection) led by extremist Buddhist monks. Ma Ba Tha was a key force in lobbying for four "race and religion" laws — some with anti-Islamic provisions — that were passed in 2015.[38] However, in the aftermath of the NLD's electoral victory, Ma Ba Tha's anti-NLD campaign not only demonstrated the limited popularity of the extremist group but also marked a new era which could radically transform the government's relationships with Buddhist extremists. This began with a statement made by Yangon Chief Minister Pyo Min Thein, who, during a meeting with the Burmese community in Singapore on 6 July, said that Ma Ba Tha was "unnecessary", since there was already a government agency tasked to oversee the activities of Buddhism in the country.[39]

His statement generated opposition from Buddhist extremists, but was soon endorsed by high profile organizations and individuals, including the Sangha Maha Nayaka (Ma Ha Na), the state Buddhist authority, as well as armed forces chief Senior General Min Aung Hlaing, who urged citizens — during an official visit to Sittwe, the capital of Rakhine state, in July — to avoid religious extremism.[40] On 21 July the government released long-awaited data on religious affiliation from Myanmar's 2014 census, after a delay attributed to official concerns over maintaining peace and stability during the election period. According to the figures (which also include an estimate of the non-enumerated population of approximately 1.2 million, mostly in Rakhine state), of Myanmar's total population of 51.4 million, Buddhists constitute 87.9 per cent, Christians 6.2 per cent, Muslims 4.3 per cent, animists 0.8 per cent, and Hindus 0.5 per cent. The 2014 figures revealed a slight decrease in the percentage of Buddhists and a small increase in the percentage of Christians and Muslims, which were recorded as 89.4 per cent, 4.9 per cent, and 3.9 per cent, respectively, in the 1983 census.[41] The lower than predicted number of Muslims may have averted some fears about a rapid growth of the Muslim population and, possibly, prevented potential violence.

The Economy

Myanmar has experienced significant upswings in economic growth and foreign investment, averaging 6.5 per cent annual growth over the five years since the reformist administration of Thein Sein came to power in early 2011. By the time Suu Kyi's administration took office on 1 April, the country had notched up 8 per cent annual growth and was predicted to reach 8.4 in 2016 and 8.3 in 2017.[42] In recent years, according to the Myanmar Investment Commission, the country had also achieved a record amount of foreign direct investment, amounting to $8 billion of investment approvals in 2015.

Much of this has been due to economic reforms enacted under the previous administration of Thein Sein and, significantly, the easing of Western sanctions from 2012 onward. The NLD's electoral victory in late 2015 generated a further sense of economic optimism among ordinary Burmese, as well as growing interest from private investors — both foreign and domestic. The new mood was further reinforced by the steady return of skilled and educated expatriate Burmese, many of whom expressed hope that the new government would bring substantial changes and job opportunities.[43]

Adding further momentum was the move by U.S. President Barack Obama in September to lift all remaining sanctions on Myanmar, including ending the so-called Specially Designated Nationals "blacklist" of sanctioned individuals and entities.[44] The end of sanctions had an immediate effect on U.S. business in the country, which had loudly complained through lobby groups that it was competing with "one hand tied behind its back" against Japan and countries of Southeast Asia and the European Union for investment opportunities in Myanmar.

These positive developments, however, have not been substantial enough to transform the country, which continues to rank among the poorest in the world, with more than a quarter of its estimated 53.4 million population living in extreme poverty. Nearly all business groups acknowledge that it will take a long time for Myanmar to develop the framework to attract investors. The country still suffers from poor infrastructure (about a third of the population has access to electricity;

and the country has the worst road, rail, and port networks in Southeast Asia), corruption, underdeveloped human resources, inadequate access to capital, outdated revenue collection and banking systems, a low income tax revenue base, a high rate of tax evasion, poorly enforced property rights, and laws that impede foreign investment. Another economic hit came from extreme weather in 2015 and 2016. Monsoon rains and flooding in July and August 2016 disrupted the lives of nearly 500,000 people and damaged crops, including rice production, in the Ayeyarwady Delta. A cyclone in 2015 destroyed a million acres of farmland and affected a million people.[45]

There has been another, unforeseen, price of the NLD's sweep to power; with some economists blaming the recent economic paralysis — including a marked slowdown in foreign investment and economic growth — on the lack of economic competence, inadequate capacity, and slow processes of the new administration. The NLD government has sought advice from foreign academic and long-time Myanmar-watcher, Sean Turnell. But its appointment of two high-profile NLD supporters to economic cabinet posts resulted in an embarrassing controversy when it was reported that the doctorate degrees of Kyaw Win, Minister of Planning and Finance, and Than Myint, Minister of Commerce, were either from fake or unaccredited institutions.[46] The CVs they posted were described as an oversight, and both officials continued in their jobs.

All foreign investment applications were put on hold in the first months of the administration as the government reviewed staffing of the Myanmar Investment Commission, the key investment approval body that was dissolved in March, just before the new government took power. The revamped MIC did not swing into action until June. As a result, investment approvals by the new government in the first six months, from 1 April to 30 September, plunged to about $1.3 billion in total, a slide of sixty per cent from a year earlier. By the end of December the figure had risen to about $3.5 billion — nearly one third below the figure of a year earlier.[47]

In late July, Suu Kyi presented the government's twelve-point five-year economic policy to a group of business people, government officials, foreign diplomats, and donors. The document provided few concrete details about policy goals or implementation plans, stressing, among other things, the importance of developing a market-oriented system "in all sectors" of the economy; a fair distribution of natural resources between states and divisions to promote national reconciliation and the building of a federal state; addressing infrastructure shortcomings; and reviving agriculture and boosting agricultural exports.[48]

The "start" came nearly seven months after the government took power, when Suu Kyi and her key economic ministers called about 150 business leaders (both foreign and local), diplomats, international organizations, and others to Naypyitaw on 22 October to provide more details. She talked about the importance of vocational training, the rule of law, and the equitable distribution of income. But there were still no numerical goals or any blueprint that investors and aid organizations had been hoping for. Instead, her Planning and Finance Minister, Kyaw Win, urged investment in smaller municipalities and sectors such as healthcare to offset shortfalls in the national budget. Key business people present signalled deep disappointment, saying they had expected to hear about concrete policies and not that the onus was on the business sector to help government budget priorities.[49]

Ultimately, though, in the eyes of many investors, the signs are good. Particularly for sectors such as telecommunications and banking, where Myanmar is already reaping the benefits of "leapfrogging", by learning from other countries' mistakes or by simply forging ahead with the newest technology. One revealing example is that, as the country is getting hooked up to telecommunications networks, many people are going straight to mobile and Internet communications, shunning the need for landlines. On banking, Myanmar has gone from a backward system with no ATMs and a vastly under-banked population, to building networks of ATMs, introducing credit cards, and giving a total of thirteen foreign banks wholesale licence to focus on corporate business. Foreign insurers are likely to be licensed in the first half of 2017, and plans are afoot to boost the country's bond market and break up and privatize some of the more attractive state-owned enterprises, including the military-owned Union of Myanmar Economic Holdings, which operates more than fifty businesses, ranging from tourism to beer and tobacco.

Foreign Affairs

Shortly after her administration came to power, Suu Kyi embarked on a carefully managed series of foreign tours (including to Laos, Thailand, China, the United Kingdom, the United States, India, Japan, and Singapore) as Foreign Minister and State Counsellor to improve and repair relationships and enhance prospects for economic and political collaboration and investment and, in the case of the EU and United States, the flow of aid and assistance. The NLD government has retained the general principles of Myanmar's foreign policy, which are based on independence, non-alignment, peaceful coexistence, and international collaboration, to maintain peace and stability. The government appointed new ambassadors loyal to the NLD to several countries, including the United States, Canada, and India.

Suu Kyi particularly focused on improving relations with China, a major trade partner and investor in Myanmar throughout the period of economic sanctions imposed by the West. Thein Sein's policy to reduce the country's dependence on China and improve its relations with the West was seen as a key factor in the previous military regime's decision to open up the country and launch a "roadmap" of democratic reform. But the distancing from China ruptured bilateral relations.

Under Suu Kyi, the two sides are seeking to revitalize their friendship, after trade between the two nations dropped in 2015. Whilst it remains one of the top three investors in Myanmar by various counts, China's investment ranking went down and relations suffered during the five-year transition from a military junta. China was concerned about protecting its economic interests under the new government, given its view of Myanmar's long shoreline on the Indian Ocean as a vital shortcut for oil imports from the Middle East, a welcome source of natural gas, and its rich mineral deposits as strategic assets. China is particularly anxious to resume its $3.6 billion Myitsone mega hydroelectricity dam project in Kachin state, suspended by Thein Sein in 2011.[50] In a style that has already become her hallmark, Suu Kyi set up a committee to review the environmental and other aspects of all planned dam projects, reassuring the Chinese that some compromise could be reached. As the twenty-member commission reviews the suspension decision and China's other planned dam projects, negotiations are already under way for Myanmar to recompense China (possibly an estimated fee of $800 million, according to government sources) in the event that the dam is not built, or to use the money for other projects, such as a series of smaller hydro projects that will have less of an impact on the environment and might draw less local resistance.[51]

In addition, China is preparing to finalize its bid to build on its existing facilities in Rakhine state, which features oil and gas pipelines running from the port of Kyaukphyu on the Bay of Bengal into southern China. Politically, the NLD government has attempted to improve its relationship with China — which is reported to have provided arms to ethnic armed groups in northern Myanmar near the Chinese border — and has invited China to help mediate the peace talks in northern Myanmar.

Other countries to figure in Suu Kyi's unofficial "non-aligned" foreign policy include India and Japan. Despite her earlier criticism of India for its engagement with Myanmar's former military government (which kept her under house arrest for fifteen of the past twenty-two years), the State Counsellor had a productive visit to India and established good relations with Prime Minister Narendra Modi. India has been particularly concerned about separatist movements in Northeast India that have been using staging areas inside the Myanmar border. Also of interest is the potential for importing oil and gas from Myanmar. India has offered to assist the new government to transform the country's old system of government and to collaborate in a campaign against militants with alleged terrorist links along the Myanmar–Bangladesh border.[52]

But it is Japan that has carved out the most striking role in Myanmar relations, providing vast amounts of aid, debt forgiveness, and investment, all while taking a back seat politically. Tokyo had sank low in Suu Kyi's priorities in her days under house arrest, due to its refusal to impose trade or financial sanctions against Myanmar's military government. Today, Japan has made Myanmar a key priority for business, investment, aid, and trade, and has a significant presence, with more than three hundred Japanese companies currently operating in the country. A significant development is the construction of the Japan-led Thilawa Special Economic Zone industrial project on the outskirts of Yangon.[53]

Japan has also played an active role in Myanmar's peace process, by supporting the talks over some years and providing humanitarian assistance in conflict areas. It also promised to assist with Myanmar's extensive infrastructure and development needs. It has pledged to provide Myanmar with public- and private-sector assistance totalling at least 800 billion yen ($7.76 billion) over the next five years.[54]

In the United States, the Obama administration began to ease financial and investment sanctions following political reforms in 2012–13. But it retained more targeted restrictions on military-owned companies and dozens of officials of the former ruling junta. These remaining sanctions were lifted after Suu Kyi met with Obama in late 2016. The Myanmar government congratulated Donald Trump on his election victory in November, but it remains unclear how Trump's accession to power will reshape long-term U.S. policy towards Myanmar. Outstanding issues over the status of the Rohingya, concern about deteriorating human rights in Rakhine state, and areas of fighting between ethnic groups and the military in Kachin and Shan states remain unresolved.

Conclusion

It may be premature to evaluate the performance of a popularly elected government after only nine months in power; particularly given the limitations imposed by the country's military-drafted constitution, which vests considerable power in the military and renders the ruling party's leader ineligible for the post of President. However, there is no doubt that the NLD will continue to face daunting — and possibly insurmountable — challenges as a fledgling government, particularly in dealing with Myanmar's long-running security problems and conflict areas.

The NLD's accession to government, however, has had several immediate and positive consequences. Along with fresh inflows of aid, investment, and goodwill, the political environment has become freer in the eyes of domestic media and ordinary people. No doubt there have been problems, with some focus on perceived backsliding, particularly over human rights and media freedoms. Some commentators have put this down to an inability to control the military, and a certain naivety on the part of the NLD administration in punishing media outlets that dare to criticize. Other factors include the NLD's innate mistrust of the old military-controlled bureaucracy, and Suu Kyi's natural inclination towards a top-down decision-making process.

The structure and composition of the government has become relatively more diverse in terms of ethnic, professional, and occupational backgrounds. There seems to be improved relations between the NLD and the military, with growing signs that all sides are exercising self-constraint and making compromises. The spoilers have increasingly been marginalized, and extremists side-lined.

The government announced laudable goals to create greater transparency and accountability, as well as broad policies to address the root problems of the country's struggling economy. However, it remains to be seen whether the NLD government can continue to build its capacity and develop effective strategies to implement economic policies, advance the peace process, negotiate with the armed groups that are still fighting, improve its relations with minority religious and ethnic groups, and deal with the brutal actions against Rohingya in northern Rakhine state. By the end of 2016 it had become clear that the NLD was emerging as a hybrid administration — partly captive to, and partly in concert with, an entrenched military — in what some critics refer to as a "democratic dictatorship". It is the result, perhaps, of Suu Kyi's ambitions to be too many things to too many people — an aspect that will have to be adjusted over time if the administration is to drive Myanmar into a progressive new era.

Notes

1. Ei Ei Toe Lwin and Htoo Thant, "NLD Reduces Government Ministries", *Myanmar Times*, 18 March 2016.
2. The Assistance Association for Political Prisoners (Burma), however, reported that, as of 18 November 2016, there were 206 political prisoners in Myanmar: 98 currently serving prison sentences, 24 awaiting trial inside prison, and 84 awaiting trial outside prison.
3. "State Counsellor Approved", *Global New Light of Myanmar*, 7 April 2016, p. 1.

4. "Cranes Stand Idle as Myanmar Businesses Bemoan Economic Policy Drift", Reuters, 25 July 2016.

5. Lin Xueling, "Focus on Resolving Difficulties in Rakhine Rather than Exaggerating Them, Says Suu Kyi", Channel NewsAsia, 2 December 2016.

6. Ei Ei Toe Lwin, "NLD Defends 'Experimental' Cabinet as Pressure Builds", *Myanmar Times*, 22 April 2016.

7. "Myanmar's Military Leader Says the Military Will Remain Political Force", *Mizzima*, 27 March 2016.

8. "Suu Kyi 'Will be above President' if NLD Wins Myanmar Election", BBC, 5 November 2015; "Military Chief Mentions State of Emergency Provisions amid Ongoing Clashes", *The Irrawaddy*, 28 November 2016.

9. Timothy Mclaughlin, "Suu Kyi's State Counselor Bill Passes Vote Despite Military Protest", Reuters, 5 April 2016.

10. Ei Ei Toe-Lwin, "Don't Ask Tough Questions: Checks on Power out the Window as NLD Asserts Its Majority", *Myanmar Times*, 7 October 2016.

11. Kyaw Kha, "Aung Kyi to Head Govt-Linked Peace Think Tank", *The Irrawaddy*, 15 July 2016.

12. International Crisis Group, "Myanmar's New Government: Finding its Feet?", ICG Report No. 282, July 2016, pp. 10–11; Ei Ei Toe Lwin, "Don't Ask Tough Questions".

13. Based on extensive conversations and interviews conducted by the authors with senior government and NLD members during 2016.

14. "Meet Burma's Next Cabinet", *The Irrawaddy*, 24 March 2016. See also Myanmar's President Office's website <http://www.president-office.gov.mm/en/?q=cabinet/ministries>.

15. Kyaw Phyo Tha, "NLD Lawmakers to Forfeit Bonus, Take Pay Cut for Party", *The Irrawaddy*, 2 February 2016; Authors' interview with NLD member, Yangon, 15 June 2016.

16. Aung Theinkha Thiri Min Zin, "Myanmar Court Denies Bail for Detained Eleven Media CEO and Editor", Radio Free Asia, 30 November 2016.

17. "Meet Your Chief Ministers", *Myanmar Times*, 4 April 2016.

18. Burma Partnership, "2015 Elections Highlight Longstanding Gender Imbalance", 2015; Thida, "Will Myanmar's Election Narrow the Gender Gap in Politics?", *New Mandala*, 29 October 2015.

19. The two women ministers in U Thein Sein's government were Khin San Yee, Minister of Education, and Myat Myat Ohn Khin, Minister of Social Welfare, Relief, and Resettlement.

20. Jonah Fisher, "Myanmar Soldiers Jailed for Village Murders in Rare Case", BBC, 16 September 2016.

21. Shwe Yee Saw Myint, "Myanmar Army Chief Reshuffles Officers, Promotes Intelligence Chief", Reuters, 26 August 2016.

22. Jonah Fisher, "Myanmar's Strongman Gives Rare BBC Interview", BBC, 20 July 2015.

23. Saw Yang Naing, "In Israel and Elsewhere, Burma Army Sees Fruits of Reform", *The Irrawaddy*, 22 September 2015.

24. Kyaw Sein and Nicholas Farrelly, "Myanmar's Evolving Relations: The NLD in Government", Institute for Security & Development Policy, Asia Paper, October 2016, p. 30.

25. Human Rights Watch, "Burma: Allow Access to Investigate Abuses in Rakhine State", 17 November 2016.

26. Tony Cartalucci, "Myanmar's New 'Democratic Dictator': Aung San Suu Kyi", Global Research, 21 November 2016.

27. Interviews by second author with NLD advisors and officials in July, September, and November 2016.

28. Transnational Institute, "Ethnicity without Meaning, Data without Context: The 2014 Census, Identity and Citizenship in Burma/Myanmar", Burma Policy Briefing, no. 13; Jane Ferguson, "Who's Counting? Ethnicity, Belonging, and the National Census in Burma/Myanmar", *Journal of Humanities and Social Sciences of Southeast Asia* 171, no. 1 (2015): 1–28.

29. Kyaw Phone Kyaw, "NLD Goes it Alone, Raising Ethnic Party Ire", *Frontier*, 2 May 2016.

30. Figures of displaced populations vary, but the Internal Displacement Monitoring Center estimates there were up to 662,400 IDPs as a result of conflict and violence in Myanmar as of March 2015.

31. Lawi Weng, "Muse 105th Mile Trade Zone Abandoned", *The Irrawaddy*, 25 November 2016.

32. "International Crisis Group, "Myanmar's Peace Process: A Nationwide Ceasefire Remains Elusive", 16 September 2015.

33. Htet Naing Zaw and Nyein Nyein, "UWSA Walks out of Panglong, Decrying Inequality", *The Irrawaddy*, 1 September 2016.

34. International Crisis Group, "Myanmar's Peace Process: A Nationwide Ceasefire Remains Elusive".

35. Authors' interviews with civil society organizations and ethnic political parties, Myanmar, June 2016.

36. Carlos Sardina Galache, "In Democratic Myanmar, War Wracks Rakhine State", *Nikkei Asian Review*, 23 November 2016.

37. "Myanmar Buddhists Protest against Advisory Commission on Troubled Rakhine State", Radio Free Asia, 6 September 2016.

38. Human Rights Watch, "Burma: Discriminatory Laws Could Stoke Communal Tensions", 23 August 2016.

39. Mong Palatino, "Myanmar's Radical Buddhist Group Gets Rebuked", *The Diplomat*, 20 July 2016.

40. Ye Mon, "Military Chief Condemns Religious Extremism", *Myanmar Times*, 14 July 2016.

41. San Yamin Aung, "Govt Publishes Data on Populations of Religious Groups", *The Irrawaddy*, 21 July 2016.

42. Asian Development Bank, "Asian Development Outlook Update, Myanmar Economy", September 2016.

43. Lam Shushan, "For Myanmar Migrant Workers, Election Results Bring Hope of Returning to a Better Country", Channel NewsAsia, 21 November 2015.

44. "U.S. Lifts Economic Sanctions against Myanmar", *NPR*, 7 October 2016.

45. Aung Hla Tun and Wa Lone, "Myanmar Monsoon Floods Kill Eight, Disrupt Lives of 400,000", Reuters, 15 August 2016.

46. Richard Cockett, "Can Aung San Suu Kyi Save Burma's Economy?", *Foreign Policy*, 12 April, 2016.

47. Directorate of Investment and Company Administration, Myanmar, "Information on the Myanmar Investment Commission (MIC)" <http://www.dica.gov.mm/en/information-myanmar-investment-commission-mic>.

48. "Myanmar's Economy: Miles to Go", *The Economist*, 6 August 2016.

49. Motokazu Matsui and Thurein Hla Htway, "The Buck Stops with Suu Kyi — But is That for the Best?", *Nikkei Asian Review*, 2 November 2016.

50. Jane Perlez and Wai Moe, "Visiting Beijing, Myanmar's Aung San Suu Kyi Seeks to Mend Relations", *New York Times*, 17 August 2016.

51. Ibid.

52. "Daw Aung San Suu Kyi Goes to India", *The Irrawaddy*, 17 October 2016.

53. Minami Funakoshi and Elaine Lies, "Myanmar's Suu Kyi Visits Japan, Seeking Investment, as Crisis Builds at Home", Reuters, 1 November 2016.

54. "Daw Aung San Suu Kyi Arrives in Japan", Agence France Presse, 2 November 2016.

EMERGING PATTERN OF CIVIL–MILITARY RELATIONS

Maung Aung Myoe

With the promulgation of a new constitution in 2008 and subsequent elections in 2010 and 2015, Myanmar has undergone a process of political transition which could lead eventually to full-scale democratization. One important aspect of the political transition is the changing pattern of civil–military relations, which started with the Union Solidarity and Development Party (USDP) coming to power in 2011, ending more than two decades of direct military rule by the Tatmadaw (Myanmar Armed Forces). This process of structural adjustment in civil–military relations, from domination to influence, was expected to enter into a new phase when the National League for Democracy (NLD), led by Nobel laureate Daw Aung San Suu Kyi, came to power in March 2016, as there were high expectations for further steps towards democratization and democratic consolidation.

What should be an ideal model of civil–military relations in a democratic setting? In conventional literature, the most desirable form of civil–military relations in a democracy is what Samuel Huntington called "objective civilian control" over the military. Huntington's model emphasizes the separation of civilian and military institutions, non-involvement of the military in domestic politics, and the subordination of the military to the civilian authorities. According to Huntington, "objective civilian control" can be achieved by maximizing military professionalism, which involves the recognition of an independent military sphere within government and a clear distribution of power and responsibilities between the military and civilians. The other form of civil–military relations, according to Huntington, is "subjective civilian control", which is maintained through "maximizing the power of the civilian groups in relation to the military". Historically, subjective civilian control has been identified with maximizing the power of particular governmental

MAUNG AUNG MYOE teaches Foreign Policy Analysis and Southeast Asian International Relations at the International University of Japan (IUJ).

institutions, social classes, or constitutional forms. Subjective civilian control is possible in the absence of a professional officer corps and a lack of democratic principles in governance.[1] In a recent study on civil–military relations, Zoltan Barany claimed that, "democracy cannot be consolidated without military elites who are committed to democratic rule and obedient to a democratically elected political elite".[2]

On the other side of the equation is the military's supremacy over civilians, where the military holds the monopoly of power to make political decisions. This pattern of civil–military relations is not democratic in nature. Rebecca Schiff has put forward an alternative model of civil–military relations, known as "concordance theory". According to this model, though it may not necessarily be democratic, it is the concordance or agreement among the military, political elites, and citizenry over the role of the armed forces and the social composition of the officer corps, political decision-making process, recruitment method, and military style that prevents domestic military intervention. The theory embraces cultural aspects of a given society in determining the pattern of civil–military relations.[3] Unlike the separation theory, the concordance theory is a partnership or integration model.[4] In fact, civil–military relations is not simply about relations between the military leadership and elected civilian politicians, but also about relations between the military as an institution and other non-military apparatus of the state, as well as civil society.

This chapter argues that there is little indication to suggest that Myanmar has democratic civil–military relations, and it is by no means anywhere close to what could be described as democratic objective civilian control with parliamentary oversight over the Tatmadaw. In spite of this lack of major progress in "democratizing" civil–military relations, it is safe to argue that, at least since 2011, the Tatmadaw's leading national political role has subtly shifted from one of direct participation in state administration to one of consultation in policy processes, and from dominance to influence. The Tatmadaw is not yet prepared to tolerate any structural changes that would undermine its national political role. Moreover, the NLD's attempts to alter the current pattern of civil–military relations through constitutional amendments appears to be suspended for the time being, yet the NLD minimizes the Tatmadaw's influence by circumventing the latter's involvement in policy processes. Now both sides of the civil–military relations dichotomy are prepared to live with each other. The primary focus of this chapter is on the relations between the military (and its leadership) and civilian politicians, and it will pay close attention to recent developments in civil–military relations under the NLD administration.

Civil–military Relations under the Constitution

The Tatmadaw enjoys enormous privileges and exercises substantial influence in Myanmar's politics through constitutional provisions. There is no mechanism for meaningful civilian oversight of the Tatmadaw. One of the basic principles of the Constitution is for the "Defence Services to be able to participate in the National political leadership role of the State".[5] In addition, the Tatmadaw is entrusted with the task of safeguarding the Constitution. The Commander-in-Chief (C-in-C) of Defence Services even has the constitutional right to take over state power if he deems it necessary. Article 40(c) of the Constitution says:

> If there arises a state of emergency that could cause disintegration of the Union, disintegration of national solidarity and loss of sovereign power or attempts therefore by wrongful forcible means such as insurgency or violence, the Commander-in-Chief of the Defence Services has the right to take over and exercise State sovereign power in accord with the provisions of this Constitution.

The Constitution essentially gives the C-in-C and the Tatmadaw the role of guardian of the state, not simply the guard, and they hold keys to important aspects of government and legislature.

Under the 2008 Constitution, the C-in-C is perhaps the single-most important power holder in Myanmar politics. Although the C-in-C's position is equivalent to that of the Vice-President, he can easily undermine the authority of the President. It is the C-in-C who has complete control over the most important aspects of national defence and security. The C-in-C and not the President is the supreme commander of all armed forces, including the police, paramilitary organizations, and even the civil defence forces. Since the Tatmadaw "has the right to administer for participation of the entire people in Union security and defence" under the Constitution,[6] the C-in-C is the person who in practical terms can mobilize the entire manpower of the nation for national defence.

At the institutional level, the Tatmadaw is an autonomous institution within the state, with little or no civilian oversight. According to the Constitution it has the right to administer and adjudicate all affairs of the armed forces independently; and even in matters before military tribunals, the decision of the C-in-C is final and conclusive. Civilian or non-military apparatuses of the state are not in a position to comment on the Tatmadaw's command structure or its financial allocations and procurement, nor are they at liberty to scrutinize military businesses. Also, in the area of national defence policymaking and implementation, the Tatmadaw enjoys the exclusive right to set its own agenda. Furthermore, the government is not permitted to interfere in the appointment and promotion of military personnel.

In both houses of the Pyidaungsu Hluttaw (Union Assembly), the Tatmadaw occupies 25 per cent of the seats; 110 for the Pyithu Hluttaw (House of Representatives; lower house) and 56 for the Amyotha Hluttaw (House of Nationalities; upper house). Therefore, a total of 166 military officers sit in both houses. Comprising one-third of the total number of region/state Hluttaw representatives elected under the Constitution, they are nominated by the C-in-C in each and every state and regional legislature. At present, there are also 222 Tatmadaw representatives in fourteen states or regions. What is important is that the Tatmadaw representatives hold the veto to any structural change in Myanmar's politics, as constitutional amendments can be carried out only with "the prior approval of more than 75 per cent of all the representatives of the *Pyidaungsu Hluttaw*".[7] In fact, Aung San Suu Kyi once implied that Article 436 places the Tatmadaw above the Hluttaw; hence it is necessary to amend it.[8]

The Tatmadaw also controls three ministerial portfolios — Defence, Home Affairs, and Border Area Affairs. The President does not have the authority to appoint his own choices, but needs to obtain a list of suitable Defence Services personnel nominated by the C-in-C for the above-mentioned ministries. While these ministers and their ministries in theory answer to the President, they are supervised by the Tatmadaw leadership. At the state and regional level, the Tatmadaw nominates Ministers of State for Security and Border Affairs; there are fourteen colonels in state/regional governments in this role. Moreover, the Tatmadaw can indirectly exercise its influence on local administration, since the head of the General Administration Department (GAD) — under the Ministry of Home Affairs — in each state or region is the ex-officio Secretary of the regional or state government.[9]

The other avenue through which the Tatmadaw can exercise its influence is the National Defence and Security Council (NDSC), where the C-in-C controls at least six out of eleven members and commands a majority.[10] In the event of any major political and security issue, and in any state of emergency, the President needs to consult with and seek approval from the NDSC. Before declaring a state of emergency, if not all the members of the NDSC are able to attend the meeting, the President needs to at least consult with the C-in-C, the Deputy C-in-C, and the Ministers for Defence and Home Affairs before any announcement can be made. If the state of emergency finally leads to a declaration of military administration, then the C-in-C will take over the state and exercise executive and judicial power.

The Tatmadaw and Civilian Legislators

The pattern of civil–military relations outlined in the Constitution provides the military considerable leverage over civilians, although the Tatmadaw is no longer directly involved in the day-to-day running of the state. During the USDP administration, relations between the Tatmadaw and the government were smooth, and the former supported the latter; however, relations between the Tatmadaw and elected members of the Hluttaw, most of whom were from the USDP, were problematic. In fact there were several sources of friction, and some of them were related to the military's interests at both institutional and individual levels. After its electoral victory in November 2015, the NLD controlled both houses of the Pyidaungsu Hluttaw, with 255 out of 440 seats in the lower house and 135 out of 224 seats in the upper house.

During the tenure of the First Hluttaw (2011–15), there were three major cases where the civilian legislators and the military clashed. First, in July 2012, the Pyidaungsu Hluttaw proposed forming a commission to investigate land confiscations. The Deputy Minister for Agriculture and Irrigation came to the Hluttaw and explained the government position and said that land acquisitions in the previous governments were carried out in conformity with the laws then in place, so it was not possible to change them. At the same time he promised that the USDP government would handle any land confiscation in the future fairly, while urging the Hluttaw not to approve the motion to form a commission to investigate land confiscations of the past. However, 395 voted for the proposal and 176 against, with 24 abstentions. The opposition to the proposal came mostly from the Tatmadaw representatives. When asked, they explained that the Tatmadaw's position was not to create difficulties for the incumbent government for the "past" that it had inherited, and, more importantly, the motion was unconstitutional. However, in reality the Tatmadaw had confiscated large areas of land for its use and it was in its interest to oppose the investigation.

The second case concerned the Constitutional Tribunal. In March 2012, a constitutional crisis emerged as the Hluttaw challenged the decision undertaken by the Constitutional Tribunal which stated that "parliament-formed committees, commissions and organizations are not the union (central) level organizations under the constitution". Then, on 27 August, the Pyidaungsu Hluttaw overwhelmingly approved instituting impeachment proceedings against the Constitutional Tribunal, with 447 votes against 168 and 4 abstentions. The military delegates voted against the impeachment proceeding. However, on 6 September 2012, all members of the tribunal voluntarily resigned en masse. The Hluttaw then took another step and submitted a bill to amend the "Constitutional Tribunal Law", which included four major changes.[11] All four amendments were approved by a majority of votes, yet with substantial opposition: 368 to 200 votes with 26 abstentions; 332 to 236 votes with 28 abstentions; 360 to 210 votes with 25 abstentions; and 387 to 186 votes with 37 abstentions. In each of these the Tatmadaw representatives (166) voted against the amendments, viewing them as unconstitutional.[12]

The third case involved a constitutional amendment. In June 2015, after several rounds of discussion, voting took place for proposed constitutional amendments drafted by the USDP members of the Hluttaw. There were six proposed changes to articles of the Constitution. On the day of voting, 583 members of the Hluttaw were present, including 166 Tatmadaw representatives. Out of six proposed changes, five were defeated with the backing of the military representatives; the amendments required 75 per cent support of the vote cast. The only amendment approved (556 for and 27 against; 95.37 per cent) was a minor technical change to Article 59(d), replacing the words "military outlook" with "defence outlook" in relation to qualifications for presidential candidates.[13] The proposed change to Article 59(f), to remove the phrase "one of the legitimate children of their spouses" in relation to their enjoying the rights and privileges of a foreign government or being a citizen of a foreign county, which bars a candidate from holding the office of the President or Vice-President, was rejected (371 for and 212 against; 55.06 per cent). This is the clause that barred Aung San Suu Kyi from becoming President, because her two sons are foreign citizens. The proposed change to Article 60(c) that required vice-presidential and presidential candidates to be members of the Hluttaw was defeated, yet it drew considerable support (386 for and 197 against; 66.21 per cent). The USDP's attempt to change Article 60(c) was politically motivated, as it would require service personnel to retire in order to campaign and run in elections, thus hurting senior military officers interested in entering into the highest political offices in the country. The amendment to Article 418(b), which tried to make the C-in-C's authority conditional in relation to a state of emergency, was rejected by the same vote count (386 for and 197 against; 66.21 per cent).[14] Finally, amendments to Articles 436(a) and 436(b), to lower the threshold for amending the constitution from 75 to 70 per cent of votes in the Hluttaw, in other words to remove the military's veto of constitutional amendments, were rejected by the same number of votes (388 for and 195 against; 66.55 per cent).

Friction in civil–military relations appears to have become more frequent since the start of the tenure of the second, NLD-controlled, Hluttaw in February 2016. So far, up until the end of 2016, there have been five sources of friction.

The first source of friction came when the Hluttaw nominated the vice-presidential candidates. On 10 March 2016, the NLD, which dominated and controlled both houses of the Pyidaungsu Hluttaw, nominated two vice-presidential candidates. While the Pyithu Hluttaw's nominee, U Htin Kyaw, who is not a member of the Hluttaw, did not encounter any major problem, some issues arose with regard to the Amyotha Hluttaw's nominee and member, U Henry Van Thio. During the screening process by the seven-member committee for eligibility, the Tatmadaw representative, Major General Than Soe, although neutral, suggested that U Htin Kyaw's background should be reviewed thoroughly in accordance with the law. However, he opposed the nomination of Henry Van Thio, as the nominee had lived in a foreign county for six years, and it was necessary to refer the case to Constitutional Tribunal to define what was meant by "the state's permission" as prescribed in the Constitution. This was because the Constitution requires a (vice-)presidential candidate to stay in the country for an unbroken period of twenty years, except when he or she is staying overseas with the permission of the state. In both cases the other six members of the committee voted in favour of the nominees, and their candidacies were approved. On 15 March 2016, 360 out of 652 members of the Pyidaungsu Hluttaw voted for Htin Kyaw as President and Ex-General Myint Swe and Henry Van Thio as Vice-Presidents. Although the latter's case could have been brought to the Constitutional Tribunal, the military delegates did not pursue it.

Second, when the issue of appointing members of the Constitutional Tribunal came up on 29 March 2016, Tatmadaw representatives were against the appointment of two individuals, Daw Khin Htay Kywe and U Twar Kyin Paung, nominated, respectively, by the speakers of the Pyithu Hluttaw and Amyotha Hluttaw. Their grounds were "insufficient information on the profiles" to ascertain their eligibility for the posts, and they asked the nominees to resubmit fuller CVs. They did however say they would support them if they met the criteria after reviewing the full CVs. The Speaker of the Pyithu Hluttaw strongly intervened in this case, and the military's proposals to discuss whether the nominees were eligible for the posts were voted down (195 for, 435 against, and 4 abstentions for Daw Khin Htay Kywe; 196 for, 432 against, and 5 abstentions for U Twar Kyin Paung).

A week later another major issue stirred up civil–military relations in both houses of the Pyidaungsu Hluttaw. On 30 March 2016, the draft of the "State Counsellor Bill" was circulated among Hluttaw members for parliamentary debate and approval. On 1 April the bill was debated in the Amyotha Hluttaw, where three Tatmadaw representatives along with four other members of the house strongly argued against it and asked for revisions. Nevertheless, the bill was immediately approved in the NLD-dominated house (135 for, 70 against, 2 abstentions).[15] Then, on 5 April 2016, in the Pyithu Hluttaw, three Tatmadaw representatives and one member from the USDP proposed thirteen amendments to the bill; all were rejected by vote. Brigadier General Maung Maung proposed that the title of the bill and the position itself should be changed from "state counsellor" to "presidential counsellor", because the use of the term "state" is the embodiment of all three branches of power, and the Constitution encouraged the separation of power as much as possible. He also said that the term "democratic federal union" in the preamble of the bill was contrary to a basic principle of the Constitution that holds that "the Union practises genuine, disciplined multi-party democratic system"; therefore, it should be changed accordingly. In addition, he proposed that the holder of the office should answer only to the President, and not to the Hluttaw as stated in the bill. He then told the house that the bill violated constitutional provisions, and if the house pushed it through without revision, the military representatives would boycott the vote. Despite the boycott by the military delegates — who stood up in protest — the bill was approved by the house by 262 votes in favour, with 22 against and 9 abstentions, out of a total of 406 eligible voters. Brigadier-General Maung Maung told reporters after the bill was passed that its passage constituted "democratic bullying by the majority", or the "tyranny of majority".

Next, when a motion was submitted by a member of the Pyithu Hluttaw from Rakhine state to reorganize the "Rakhine State Advisory Commission" — headed by Kofi Annan and staffed by two other foreign citizens — so that it comprised only local experts, the Tatmadaw representatives supported it. Colonel Khin Maung Tun told the house that the Rakhine issue was a domestic one, and an investigation commission with local experts had thoroughly studied and submitted a report on the issue. If another commission was necessary, it should be formed in consultation with the Pyidaungsu Hluttaw, "As seeking opinions and advice from a foreigner-led commission for a domestic affair or nationalities affair, because of international pressure or for better international image, is inappropriate and could undermine the interests of the local people; thus it is necessary to reconsider the formation of an advisory commission", the colonel said. Despite the support from the military delegates, the motion was defeated, as it secured only 148 votes, with 250 against and 1 abstention.

The last source of friction of the year was the voting on an emergency motion "urging the Hluttaw to express concern over sovereignty, stability and [the] peace process due to attacks of four armed groups in Shan State that led to the losses of lives and property", proposed by an USDP Pyithu Hluttaw member on 2 December 2016, and which was supported by the military delegates. The Minister for Defence explained the situation from a broad historical and political perspective, and urged the Pyithu Hluttaw to brand these armed groups as terrorist organizations. A military delegate supported the Defence Minister's suggestion. When voting took place, the motion received only 141 votes in support, with 244 against, and 7 abstentions, and so it was not approved; it was just put on record.[16]

Tatmadaw and the NLD Administration

When the NLD and its leaders realized that they were going to form a government in the aftermath of the November 2015 elections, they tried to reach out to the Tatmadaw leadership. Before the transfer of power from the USDP to the NLD, Aung San Suu Kyi met the C-in-C three times. After their first encounter on 2 December 2015, the C-in-C said that the meeting had produced "good results". The office of the C-in-C issued a statement saying, "in line with the desires of the people, they agreed to cooperate on peace, the rule of law, reconciliation and the development of the country".[17] However, little was reported on their second and third meetings on 25 January and 17 February 2016, respectively. There was speculation that the matters discussed centred on power-sharing, presidential nominations — including the possible amendment or suspension of the constitutional provision that barred the NLD leader from the presidency — and the appointment of chief ministers in states such as Kachin, Shan, and Rakhine.[18] The meetings appeared to draw a line in the area of cooperation and mutual interest.

In the meantime, in February 2016, the Tatmadaw published its very first Defence White Paper. The timing appeared to suggest that amidst the country's unprecedented transition from decades-long, military-backed rule to an administration run by the NLD, the Tatmadaw wanted to signal that it remained the institution controlling security policy. At that time, its release could be a signal to the incoming NLD-led government that the Tatmadaw intended to remain at the heart of the country's political and security life — and that it was willing to and capable of playing a leading role in governing the country. Not only that, the paper sent a strong message that it was the Tatmadaw that defined the security of the nation and that was responsible for its defence.

In the midst of friction between the NLD's Hluttaw representatives and the military's delegates, on the seventy-first anniversary of Armed Forces Day, 27 March 2016, the C-in-C reminded the country of the constitutionally guaranteed leading political role of the Tatmadaw, and outlined broadly the position of the Tatmadaw in the emerging political context. He said:

> The two main hindrances in democratization are lack of abiding by the
> rule of law, regulations and the presence of insurgencies. These could
> lead to chaotic democracy. If we want multi-party democracy to take root
> in our country, there must be proper discipline and adherence to the law.
> We will have to work with our maximum capacity both physically and
> mentally with unity and loyalty to the country if we love our motherland
> and want to witness its development. The Tatmadaw will cooperate to
> serve the interests of the country and the people. Shouldering the national
> political duty by the Tatmadaw is only to safeguard and act in the national
> interest, the interest of the people and the state. Not of party politics.[19]

The Tatmadaw's position was clear; it would safeguard the Constitution and protect
the interest of the state and the people.

At the same time, the Tatmadaw leadership has been watching the NLD's
policies and activity on political transition and democratization very closely. In
fact, in the event of political instability at the time of transition or any challenge
to the existing pattern of civil–military relations, the Tatmadaw had prepared to
maintain leadership continuity to cope with the situation. During his meeting with
the Myanmar Press Council on 21 September 2015, without explicitly referring
to War Office Council Instruction (WOCI) 18/73, the C-in-C said that he could
serve in the Tatmadaw beyond the retirement age of 60.[20] On 20 July 2016,
Lt. General Mya Tun Oo explained that War Office Council Order (WOCO) 4/2014,
issued in 2014, allowed the C-in-C and Deputy C-in-C to serve until the age of
65. Therefore, Senior General Min Aung Hlaing will remain in the C-in-C position
until 2021 and Vice Senior General Soe Win as Deputy C-in-C (possibly later as
C-in-C) for a much longer period. Meanwhile, for better career management, the
Tatmadaw introduced an "Up-or-Out" policy, and capped the service terms for
senior military commanders through WOCI 1/2016 in January 2016.[21]

The NLD's attempt to reshape the pattern of civil–military relations could be
seen in its signature campaign for constitutional amendments in 2014, which ran
from 27 May to 19 July. The target of the campaign was to end the military's
veto on constitutional amendments by changing Article 436 to lower the threshold
for approval for amendment as a starting point for other structural changes in the
Constitution. The NLD managed to gather about five million signatures.[22] The
issue of constitutional amendment was a policy platform upon which the NLD
and its leaders campaigned during the 2015 elections. Yet, once the NLD came
to power, the issue of constitutional amendment was somehow shelved, although
the party leadership is still morally committed to it. In fact the NLD itself found

the Constitution useful for advancing the party's interests. For example, thanks to the 2008 Constitution the NLD appointed chief ministers from among its ranks in Shan and Rakhine states, where the local assemblies were controlled by non-NLD members. Finally, during a press conference on 10 June 2016, the Speaker of the Pyithu Hluttaw, U Win Myint, said that the constitutional amendment would not be carried out until the peace process was completed.[23] In other words, the NLD is, for the time being, prepared to accept the current pattern of civil–military relations enshrined in the Constitution.

If a constitutional amendment is not the avenue to adjust civil–military relations in Myanmar, then the alternative could be legislation that constrains the Tatmadaw's political role and minimizes its influence. In this case, the enactment of a National Defence and Security Council (NDSC) law is one possibility. On 21 December 2015, the Speaker of the Amyotha Hluttaw, U Khin Aung Myint (from USDP), informally distributed a nine-page draft of an NDSC bill, presumably drafted in 2012, in the chamber for study; yet, up to the end of the tenure of the first Hluttaw in February 2016, no discussion of the bill had taken place.[24] The draft included nineteen articles under six chapters. While the proposed functions of the NDSC were generally in accordance with the Constitution, the procedural aspect of the bill was controversial, as the President could cast his vote only in the event of a hung decision, and the meeting of the NDSC must be held if thirty per cent of its eleven members called for it. Critics pointed out that the bill would further empower the Tatmadaw leadership. One MP commented that "the power entrusted to the NDSC prescribed in the constitution should be limited to some degree and authority should not be exercised more than required as the council is not the highest organization".[25] Whether the NLD-dominated Hluttaw will draft a similar bill to deal with the NDSC and to minimize the power of the Tatmadaw is not publicly known. Nevertheless, in order to downplay the role of the Tatmadaw, the NLD government has so far avoided calling a NDSC meeting. The meeting held on 14 October 2016 to discuss the security situation in border areas was not an NDSC meeting. (Two Vice Presidents, two Speakers of the Hluttaw, and the Minister for Border Affairs were absent, while the Minister for State Counsellor's Office was present.)

Although the NLD's plan to alter the current pattern of civil–military relations through constitutional amendment will not be a possibility for the foreseeable future, there are ongoing discussions among public intellectuals and political activists on civil–military relations. Much of the debate on the subject in Myanmar reflects normative reference to "objective civilian control".[26] To what extent the NLD is prepared to listen to these opinions is difficult to ascertain.

Meanwhile, the Tatmadaw is paying greater attention to its public image. Public relations exercises are being carried out. Recent examples include disaster-relief operations, mobile medical teams for local people, and disciplinary action against military personnel for violations of ethical codes and humanitarian laws. At the same time, the Myanmar polity has begun to witness shrinking democratic space, illiberal democratic practices, and the weakening of checks and balances and parliamentary oversight over the government.[27]

Conclusion

In conventional literature the most desirable form of civil–military relations, especially in a democracy, is "objective civilian control", "parliamentary oversight" over the military, and a separation of the military from politics. Purely from this conventional normative perspective, there is little indication that Myanmar has democratic civil–military relations, and it is not anywhere close to having democratic objective civilian control with parliamentary oversight over the Tatmadaw. In spite of this lack of any major progress in civil–military relations, it is safe to argue that the Tatmadaw's leading national political role has subtly shifted from one of direct participation in state administration to that of consultation in the policy process — from a role of dominance to one of influence.

The classic model of "objective civilian control" of a professional military insulated from politics has never been realistic for the Tatmadaw, which from its origins has had a proud tradition of being a national political force, and which has been socialized through indoctrination. Moreover, application of this classic model is also problematic in the current political and security setting of the country, as instability and armed conflicts are prevalent. The model of objective civilian control requires the civilian leadership to make policy decisions while the military plays only an advisory role in the security domain and implements the government's decisions.

The 2008 Constitution, drafted primarily by the military, is essentially designed to provide a limited democratic space for a ruling partner for the Tatmadaw, with the latter remaining very much in control. The Tatmadaw obviously continues to hold an influential position. It is not yet prepared to tolerate any structural change that would undermine its national political role, the basic principles it has laid down for national unity, or its institutional autonomy. Yet there is room for cooperation and for making the current pattern of civil–military relations work for their mutual benefit. While the military's view of civil–military relations reflects an attitude of "integration and partnership" in national politics, the NLD's focus has been on "separation and subordination". However, the NLD seems for the time being to have suspended its attempts to alter the current pattern of civil–military relations through constitutional amendment. Instead, the NLD minimizes the Tatmadaw's influence by circumventing the latter's involvement in the policy process. At the same time, it appears that the NLD understands that it is in the interest of the NLD administration not to undermine the Tatmadaw's political role, as it needs its cooperation in dealing with several important issues, the most important of which is the peace process. They are now learning to live with each other.

Notes

1. Samuel Huntington, *The Soldier and The State* (Cambridge: Harvard University Press, 1957), pp. 80–85.
2. Zoltan Barany, *The Soldier and the Changing State: Building Democratic Armies in Africa, Asia, Europe, and the Americas* (Princeton: Princeton University Press, 2012), p. 3.
3. Rebecca L. Schiff, *The Military and Domestic Politics: A Concordance Theory of Civil-Military Relations* (New York: Routledge, 2009), pp. 3–15.
4. Ibid., pp. 6, 11.
5. Article 6(f) of the 2008 Constitution of Myanmar.
6. Article 20(d) of the 2008 Constitution of Myanmar.
7. Article 436 of the 2008 Constitution of Myanmar.
8. For an interview with Daw Aung San Suu Kyi on 30 May 2014, see *Street View Journal* 3, no. 20 (2 June 2014): 3, 9.
9. Article 260 of the 2008 Constitution of Myanmar. For instance, police colonels and GAD directors are now required to study at the National Defence College for one year, together with Tatmadaw officers.
10. The eleven-member NDSC consists of the President, two Vice-Presidents, two Speakers from the lower and upper houses of the parliament, the incumbent C-in-C and deputy C-in-C, and Ministers for Defence, Foreign Affairs, Home Affairs, and Border Affairs. Among the eleven, at least six are from the Tatmadaw: the President or the Vice-President (nominated by the C-in-C), the C-in-C himself, the Deputy C-in-C, and the Ministers for Defence, Home Affairs, and Border Area Affairs (nominated by the C-in-C). Therefore, the C-in-C commands the majority in the NDSC, and his decisions will prevail.
11. For instance, according to the 2008 Constitution, "The President shall submit the candidature list of total nine persons, three members chosen by him, three members chosen by the Speaker of the Pyithu Hluttaw and three members chosen by the Speaker of the Amyotha Hluttaw, and one member from among nine members to be assigned as the Chairperson of the Constitutional Tribunal of the Union to the

Pyidaungsu Hluttaw for its approval." However, in the bill, the Hluttaw proposed that the President must "consult" with the Speakers of the Pyithu Hluttaw and Amyotha Hluttaw for the appointment of the chairperson prior to the submission of the list. Another proposed change introduced ambiguity as to whether the decision of the Constitutional Tribunal was final, contrary to Article 324 of the Constitution. Commenting on the bill, the President pointed out that the proposed changes were against the Constitution and would undermine the independence of the judiciary and that the Hluttaw should amend the Constitution in accordance with the prescribed procedure. However, the Pyidaungsu Hluttaw ignored this advice.

12. Based on the above development, a blogger by the name of "Dr Seik Phwar" published an article online entitled "Is Hluttaw above the Law?" The author was critical of the way Hluttaw representatives performed their duties. The author pointed out that the Hluttaw and its members were acting like they were above the law and accused them of knowingly violating the Constitution. The author commented: "they should amend the Constitution by inserting a clause that says that whatever the Constitution says the decisions through voting by the speakers of the houses and their cohorts are final". The article so infuriated the majority of members that the Hluttaw voted (347 for, 157 against, 42 abstentions) on 17 January 2013 to form a commission to seek to determine the identity of Dr Seik Phwar and to take action against the individual. Again, the Tatmadaw representatives voted against the motion, believing it would be a waste of resources.

13. Aye Min Soe, "Pyidaungsu Hluttaw Votes Down 5 of 6 Changes to Constitution", *Global New Light of Myanmar*, 26 June 2015.

14. In the original article, "notwithstanding anything contained in the Constitution", all parliamentary appointments (except for the President and the Vice Presidents) should be terminated once the state of emergency commences and the C-in-C takes control of the state. The amendment was to replace "notwithstanding anything contained in the Constitution" with "by making exception to the Constitution as in order to resolve [an] extraordinary situation", meaning there is a "condition" for the termination of duty.

15. *Kyemon*, 2 April 2016.

16. *Kyemon*, 3 December 2016; *Global New Light of Myanmar*, 3 December 2016; *Democracy Today*, 3 December 2016.

17. Thomas Fuller, "Aung San Suu Kyi and Myanmar General Meet, Taking Steps toward Sharing Power", *New York Times*, 2 December 2015 <http://www.nytimes.com/2015/12/03/world/asia/myanmar-aung-san-suu-kyi-meets-president-army.html?mwrsm=Facebook&_r=1>.

18. Ei Ei Toe Lwin, "General and NLD Leader Talk Transition", *Myanmar Times*, 26 January 2016 <http://www.mmtimes.com/index.php/national-news/18648-general-and-nld-leader-talk-transition.html>; Ei Ei Toe Lwin and Htoo Thant, "Military Chief,

NLD Leader Begin Third Meeting", *Myanmar Times*, 17 February 2016 <http://www.mmtimes.com/index.php/national-news/19038-military-chief-nld-leader-begin-third-meeting.html>.

19. "Senior General Maha Thray Sithu Min Aung Hlaing Address 71st Anniversary Armed Forces Parade", *Myawady Daily*, 28 March 2016.

20. *Tomorrow*, 29 September 2015, p. 5.

21. *Myawady*, 21 July 2016. According to WOCI 1/2016, a brigadier general is to retire after serving in his position for 7 years, a major general after 6 years, a lieutenant general after 5 years, and a general after 4 years, with the possibility of an extension for 2 more years.

22. Htoo Thant, "NLD leader Hails Constitution Petition's Five Million Signatures", *Myanmar Times*, 9 August 2014 <http://www.mmtimes.com/index.php/national-news/11278-nld-leader-hails-petition-result-as-unprecedented-in-myanmar.html>.

23. *Kyemon*, 11 June 2016. In his words: "constitutional amendment could be successfully made only after the prevalence of the rule of law, national reconciliation and internal peace. Only after the success of national reconciliation and attainment of internal peace, could the constitutional amendment be successfully done on the basis of mutual understanding, trust and respect."

24. *7Day Daily*, 30 December 2015, pp. 1, 34–35; *The Voice*, 6 January 2016, pp. 1, 12; *Daily Eleven*, 29 December 2015, p. 3.

25. "MPs Unhappy at Being Forced to Rush Security Bill into Law", Eleven Media, 25 December 2015 <http://elevenmyanmar.com/politics/mps-unhappy-being-forced-rush-security-bill-law>.

26. Examples are: Kyaw Saw Han (Myanmar-born Goulka), "From Good Civil-Military Relations to Civilian Control", *The Voice*, 5–11 October 2015, pp. 20, 37; Pe Myint, "Let There Be Smooth Civil-Military Relations", *Pyithu Ayae* 2, no. 70 (26 January 2016): 3.

27. For example, members of the Hluttaw were told not to raise questions in the houses that would be difficult for the government to answer. The NLD party leadership has been accused of authoritarian practices in decision-making. Media freedom has also been significantly restricted.

Philippines

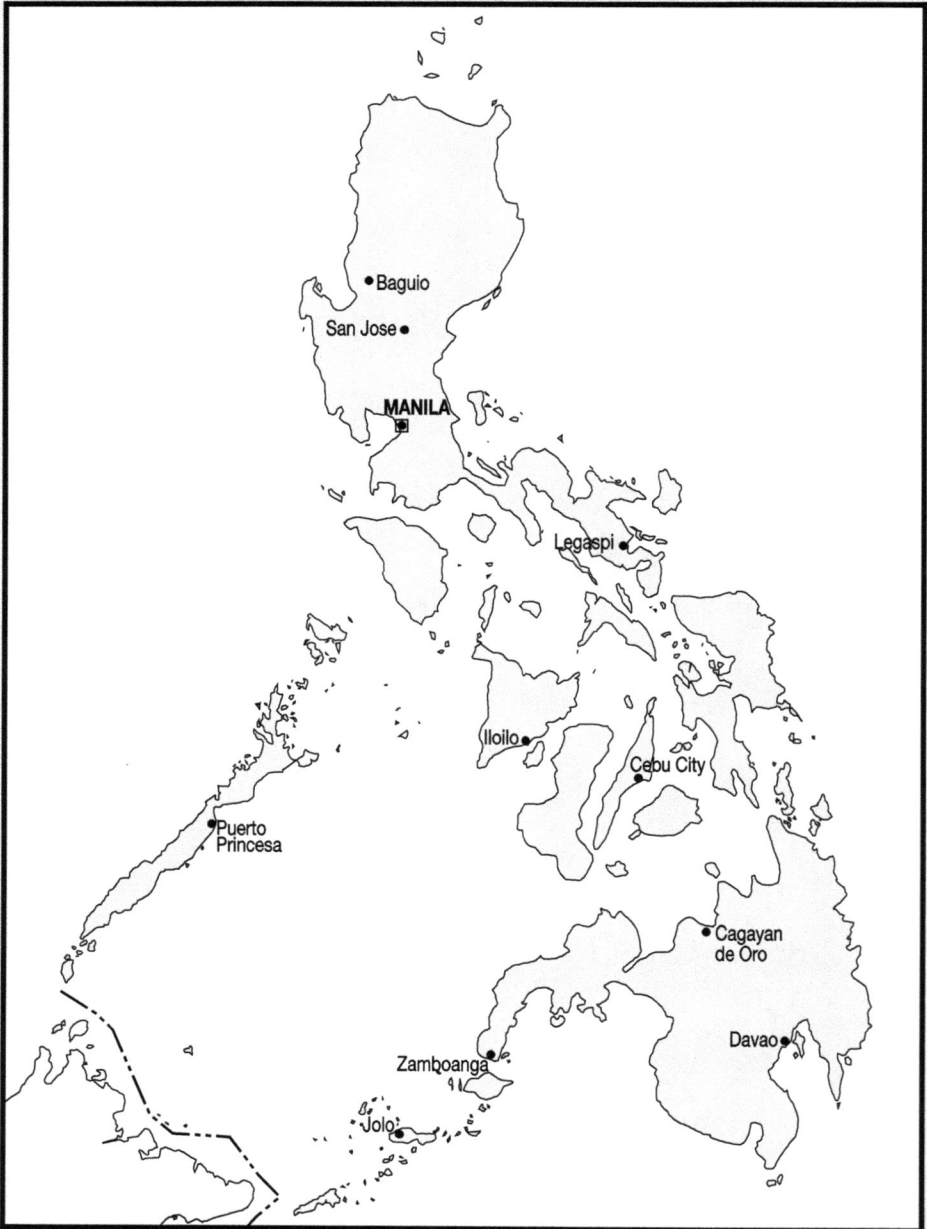

THE PHILIPPINES IN 2016:
The Electoral Earthquake and its Aftershocks

Aries A. Arugay

Anyone familiar with Philippine politics knows that the hundred-million strong nation is very passionate about holding elections. As an election year, 2016 proved that elections remain important and complicated political events in the country.[1] But rather than just another exercise of peacefully transferring power from one faction of the Filipino elite to another, the main outcome of the 2016 elections resembled a powerful earthquake that shifted the tectonic plates of Philippine politics. On 9 May 2016, more than 55 million voters cast their ballots in what many described as one of the most electrifying, fiercely contested, and politically significant electoral contests since the restoration of democracy in 1986. At stake were national posts for the presidency and vice-presidency, seats in the bicameral legislature, and local government positions. Expectedly, political dynasties and members of the country's elite once again dominated the polls of Asia's oldest democracy — with one glaring exception. Less than a day after voting officially ended, maverick city mayor and political firebrand Rodrigo Duterte secured an overwhelming victory in the presidential elections with almost forty per cent of the popular vote.

Electoral politics in the Philippines is a game mastered by the Filipino political class. This level of comfort was seen when outgoing Philippine President Benigno Simeon Aquino delivered his State of the Nation address to Congress in July 2015. With the members of the political establishment in attendance, and

ARIES A. ARUGAY is Associate Professor of Political Science at the University of the Philippines in Diliman.

watched by millions of Filipinos, Aquino confidently declared that the coming elections would be a referendum on his "Daang Matuwid" (Straight Path) legacy of accountable governance. The television screen then split into three showing his likely successors — Vice-President Jejomar Binay, Senator Grace Poe, and Interior Secretary Manuel Roxas III. Not invited to the all-elite affair, Davao City Mayor Rodrigo Duterte was sitting on a plastic stool watching the event hundreds of kilometres south of Manila. The 2016 elections proved that even masters of the political game can be prone to miscalculation, especially during times when they think the odds are overwhelmingly in their favour.

Coming from Mindanao, Duterte's unprecedented triumph is an important rebuke of the elites who have dominated politics for decades. Under their watch, Philippine democracy has neither matured nor collapsed. Instead, it has become trapped in a grey zone where weak political institutions coexist with widespread economic disparities, governance deficits, and lingering internal conflicts. Duterte's electoral mandate was a result of the collective rage of numerous Filipinos against the status quo, and their belief that as a catalyst for change, he can provide decisive leadership to solve their everyday problems.[2]

Duterte's inauguration as the republic's sixteenth President is the landmark that neatly divides 2016 into two parts. The first concerned Aquino's remaining months in office and his attempt to leave a lasting legacy within the context of one of the most acrimonious and closely fought national elections in recent history. The second half focused on the array of Duterte's new policies that included a hard-line war against drugs, which has been criticized for undermining human rights. The second half of the year also included Duterte's controversial push for an independent Philippine foreign policy in the midst of a favourable arbitral ruling given to the country regarding its territorial claims in the South China Sea (SCS), together with a turbulent Asia-Pacific security environment defined by the intense strategic rivalry between the United States and China.

Duterte's electoral victory was the political earthquake that is causing aftershocks and ripples throughout the country and beyond. With change naturally comes uncertainty, disturbance, and displacement. What are the likely trajectories and repercussions of Duterte's attempt to singlehandedly reshape the country's democracy? While it is too early to tell, it is expected that the more the unpredictable chief executive embarks on radical changes that entail undermining the entrenched interests of oligarchic elites, the more the nation's future will be defined by political instability and social polarization.

Aquino's Legacy: Selective Accountability without Leadership

In 2016, Aquino remained widely popular as he steered the country into the remaining months of his presidency. His improved approval ratings were the highest of any outgoing Filipino President in the post-dictatorship era, given that his immediate predecessors were disgraced, if not incarcerated, after their terms. With the help of a savvy public relations campaign, his set of "Daang Matuwid" reforms improved the country's international credit ratings and generated high economic growth rates.

Though Aquino's performance impressed foreign audiences, there were significant shortcomings in his brand of leadership. His accountability campaign was selective: it severely punished his party's enemies, while his political allies remained unscathed. Given their loyalty, he refused to fire grossly incompetent cabinet members and executive appointees. While the economy was doing well, its benefits were monopolized by the top one per cent of the population, with many Filipinos still unemployed and mired in deep poverty.[3]

Aquino became President as a result of the public's contempt for corruption. However, the deep-seated problems of the country cannot be solely addressed by accountable governance. "Daang Matuwid" was insufficient in responding to other pressing problems, like the country's decrepit public infrastructure, deficient social services, and rampant criminality. The Aquino administration thought that it could satisfy the populace so long as it continued to blame past administrations, prosecute select politicians, and deny the existence of problems.

To a large extent, the outgoing President governed in safe mode, refusing to embark on building democratic institutions, promoting greater transparency through a freedom of information law, and curbing political dynasties. Such measures would negatively impact ruling elites supportive of Aquino, but could improve democratic practices through more inclusion, participation, and responsiveness. It should be pointed out that democratic quality was not better under Aquino, as the Philippines was only given a "partly free" status in terms of political rights and civil liberties throughout his tenure.[4] Not even the lavish celebrations of the 1986 People Power uprising's thirtieth anniversary could hide the stagnation of the democratic regime — one that was defective, exclusionary, and institutionally hollow.

In the end, the Aquino administration's refusal to recognize its limitations — especially its inability to mind what one political scientist referred to as "the gap between democracy and governance" — jeopardized its legacy in Philippine politics.[5] The democratic regime that Aquino promised to protect failed to deliver public goods such as law and order, infrastructure, and security. What seemed to be trivial concerns like heavy traffic, illegal drugs, and crime became major electoral issues that his government continued to rebuff. After years of negotiation, the door tragically closed on the prospects of a lasting peace settlement with the Moro Islamic Liberation Front (MILF) when Aquino's legislative majority in Congress failed to pass the Bangsamoro Basic Law (BBL). Peace once again proved elusive for Mindanao, a conflict-ridden and economically poor region which has been marginalized in Philippine politics. In the end, Aquino left a legacy subject to questions by Filipinos in search of a different kind of leadership.

A Mean, Costly, and Divisive Campaign: The 2016 Elections[6]

Unlike in 2010, when there was a clear frontrunner, the degree of competitiveness of the 2016 presidential polls had not been seen in decades. The stakes were high, since the fate of notable politicians would be subsequently decided by the election's winners. As Philippine politics has been defined by exacting personal vendettas, an election is also an opportunity for victors to promote their standing, protect their interests, and retaliate against their political enemies. Given that elections in the Philippines operate on a "winner takes all" logic, candidates cannot help but be embroiled in a bitter and mean campaign that brings out the worst not only of themselves but the entire political process. This was displayed in the first ever series of presidential debates, curiously watched by millions of Filipinos, where the primary candidates engaged less in substantial policy discussions but more in mutual mudslinging and ad hominem attacks.[7]

The pre-election polls showed the uncertainty that influenced the presidential campaigns of the five leading candidates. Of all of them, Roxas represented the quintessential Filipino elite politician. Heir to a powerful family, he was Aquino's anointed successor, with the huge responsibility of carrying forward the legacy of "Daang Matuwid" and maintaining the Liberal Party's grip on the government. Roxas had every conceivable electoral advantage imaginable: an impeccable pedigree (a grandson of a former president), an Ivy League education, substantial political experience, a strong party machinery, economic wealth, local networks, and access to the state apparatus. He had the biggest campaign war chest and his advertisements bombarded the television and radio airwaves. If the Philippines was perhaps a mature democracy with the necessary social requisites, Roxas would have easily clinched the Presidency.

Despite these favourable factors and a significant head start over his opponents, Roxas never topped a pre-election survey (See Figure 1). His electability proved challenging to even the most savvy campaign strategists. He stumbled in handling strategic cabinet portfolios like the Interior and Transportation. Traffic, particularly in Manila, worsened under his watch. Roxas failed to capitalize on an opportunity to prove his mettle as a future chief executive. His inability to make swift and effective decisions was diagnosed by one of his opponents as "analysis paralysis".[8]

Roxas's decision to embrace "Daang Matuwid" hook, line, and sinker proved to be the bane of his presidential bid. The administration party expected that Aquino's popularity would benefit him. But during the campaign, Roxas had no choice but to defend Aquino's mixed governance record. The debacle over the government's response to Typhoon Haiyan, the Mamasapano Massacre of elite police officers, the violent dispersal of peasant protests in Mindanao, and the pork barrel scandal took a toll on the Roxas campaign. The more he championed Aquino's legacy the more unpopular he became, since his message of continuity was very insensitive to the prevailing realities.[9] In the end the candidate who appeared to have a presidential birthright failed to connect with ordinary Filipinos and their daily struggles against poverty, inequality, corruption, lack of order, and criminality.

Incumbent Vice-President Binay was Roxas's initial challenger. Known for his long stint as the Mayor of the premier financial hub, Makati City, Binay was an unapologetic populist. This strategy worked effectively, given the prevalence of poverty in the city. His rags-to-riches story also appealed to Filipino voters, with his humble origins a stark contrast to Roxas's *cacique* (feudal elite) background. A known political veteran, Binay's performance in the electoral surveys nosedived once he was linked to more corruption scandals. Investigations initiated by administration party stalwarts accused him of possessing ill-gotten wealth. Deserted by his allies, Binay failed to use his campaign to directly confront these allegations. While he maintained core support from low-income Filipino voters, it was not enough to secure a victory in the polls.[10]

The lack of viable candidates compelled seasoned legislator and cerebral politician Miriam Defensor-Santiago to join the presidential race. Known as being feisty, reform-oriented, and intelligent, the incumbent senator was idolized by students, the youth, and educated Filipinos.[11] But the absence of political networks, inconsistent political stances, and issues of poor health prevented Santiago from being a competitive presidential candidate. While she made televised presidential debates interesting, it was not enough for her to garner votes.

Until a few weeks before election day, incumbent Senator Poe, a daughter of a fallen presidential candidate in the 2004 elections, was the clear poll frontrunner.

FIGURE 1
Voting Preferences for President

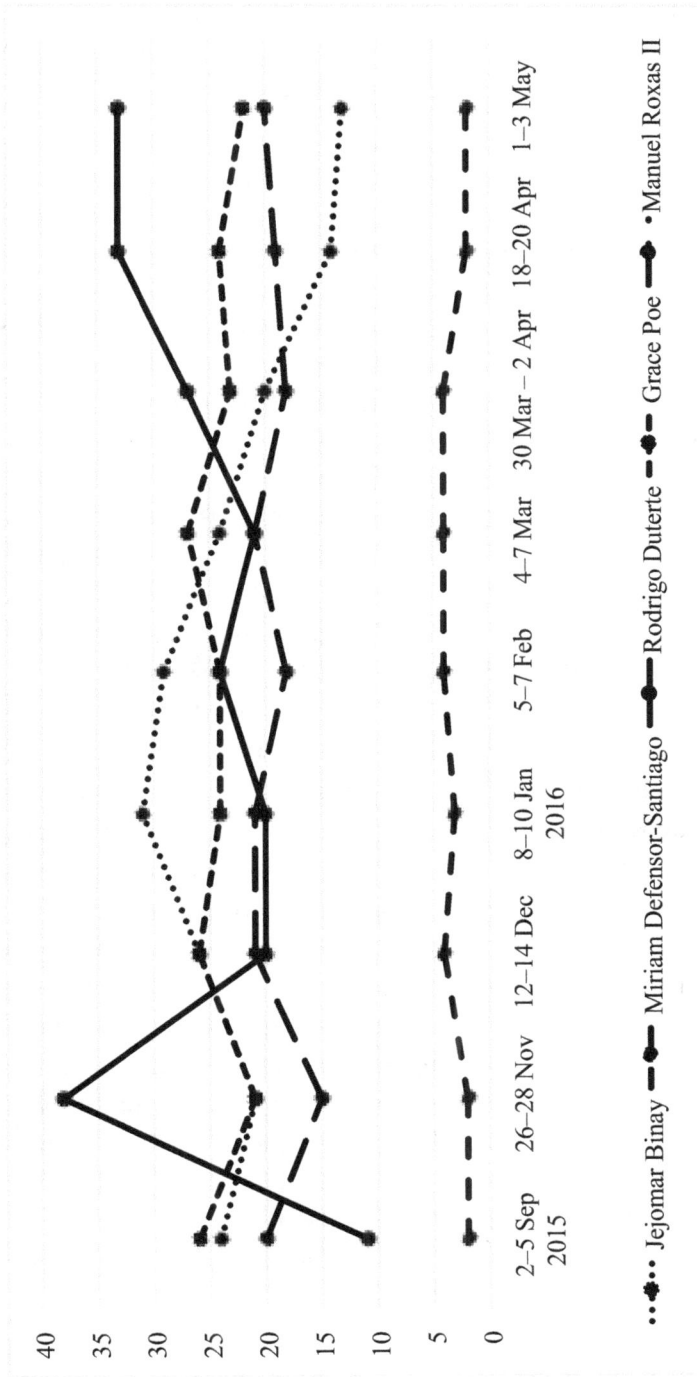

Source: Social Weather Stations and *Businessworld.*

Poe had little political experience but had popular appeal among a Filipino electorate hungry for an inspirational leader. Leading the election surveys she refused the offer to be the administration party's vice-presidential candidate. With the backing of a more experienced running mate, Poe embarked on a "government with a heart" campaign that resonated with the youth as well as middle-class Filipinos. While she is linked with the Aquino government, she explicitly drew attention to its mistakes. The Poe campaign capitalized on her squeaky clean image and her moderate policy positions. Her momentum was stalled after a gruelling legal battle on issues concerning her legal citizenship. It was only two months before the elections that the Supreme Court ruled with finality that Poe could be a viable presidential candidate. Six weeks before the elections, her lack of political machinery and campaign funds weakened her standing as she lost the top spot in the polls to Duterte.[12]

Duterte entered the electoral fray as a substitute candidate two months after the deadline for filing as a presidential candidate. He formally threw his hat into the ring after being discontented with the existing crop of presidential contenders, but also after he had secured adequate financial and human resources. To a large extent he represented the antithesis of cacique politicians like Aquino and Roxas. He is by all appearances humble, tough talking, inarticulate, not well born, foul-mouthed, and allergic to the politics in imperial Manila. The Catholic Church, the country's moral compass, does not view him as an epitome of morality. His alleged involvement in extra-judicial killings in Davao and his intimate connections with the Marcos family generated apprehension among human rights defenders.[13] Aquino warned that Duterte constituted a serious threat to Philippine democracy.[14]

To educated Filipinos the former public prosecutor seemed simple-minded and inarticulate, and therefore was deemed unfit to be head of state; he cursed the Pope, cracked jokes about rape, and made acerbic remarks against foreign envoys. Analysts found themselves scrambling to fit the firebrand candidate into contradictory political labels — populist, socialist, demagogue, fascist, strongman.[15] But Duterte's polemics dictated the campaign, with his opponents passively reacting to his next outrageous move. A few days before the elections, Aquino desperately tried to broker an alliance between Roxas and Poe against Duterte. The plan was for either of them to withdraw and instruct their supporters to transfer their support to the remaining candidate. It was an utter failure, since both believed they could still individually beat Duterte.[16]

For the first time in election history, the vice-presidential race had more candidates than the presidential contest, given the country's electoral system of separate elections for the two posts. Just like his running mate Grace Poe, early frontrunner Francis Escudero lost the lead to the other main candidates, Leni Robredo and Ferdinand Marcos Jr. Robredo's strong performance was due to her credible reputation, good track record, and, most importantly, the administration party's powerful machinery. For its part, the Marcos candidacy symbolized the lingering national support for the dictator and his family. In the end, Robredo narrowly clinched the Vice-Presidency against Marcos, who then filed an election protest that will be heard by an electoral tribunal composed of the Supreme Court.

Duterte's Victory: The Road Less Travelled

Despite the odds, the Filipino electorate awarded Duterte a significant plurality. With 82 per cent voter turnout, the highest recorded rate since 1987, Duterte scored an overwhelming victory, with an estimated 16.6 million of the 44 million votes cast.[17] What are the factors behind his surprising come-from-behind Presidential victory?

Duterte was the underdog in this four-cornered fight, with Roxas, Binay, and Poe possessing significant advantages. He was carried by a defunct party, the Partido ng Demokratikong Pilipino-Laban ng Bayan (Filipino Democratic Party-Struggle of the People), together with a loose coalition of Mindanao-based politicians. His apparent core financiers were Davao's small economic elite and a few tycoons. Though the Duterte campaign lacked political machinery, it implemented a clever strategy that directly appealed to the common Filipino. Duterte's slogan of Courage and Concern ("Tapang at Malasakit") was simple but highly effective, since it connected with the populace's daily battles against poverty, corruption, and crime.[18]

For voters, this message was credible given Duterte's track record of transforming Davao City from a relatively conflict-ridden backwater town into a sprawling urban metropolis. Duterte pounced on his opponents over their lack of concern with basic, visceral issues that affected all Filipinos. He promised to violently crack down on crime and illegal drugs, but at the same time to offer a hand of peace to communists and Muslim rebels. As a candidate from the margins of society mocked by the Manila-based elite, he wanted to develop the outer regions of the Philippines by shifting to a federal system of government. Duterte did not provide the important details of these grand plans; his political will seemed sufficient for Filipinos desperate for leadership with a vision.

The surprise of the 2016 elections was the emergence of a loose citizens' movement that championed Duterte's presidential bid through countless uncoordinated acts of campaign support. This cross-class coalition of conservative

FIGURE 2
Official Results of the 2016 Presidential Elections

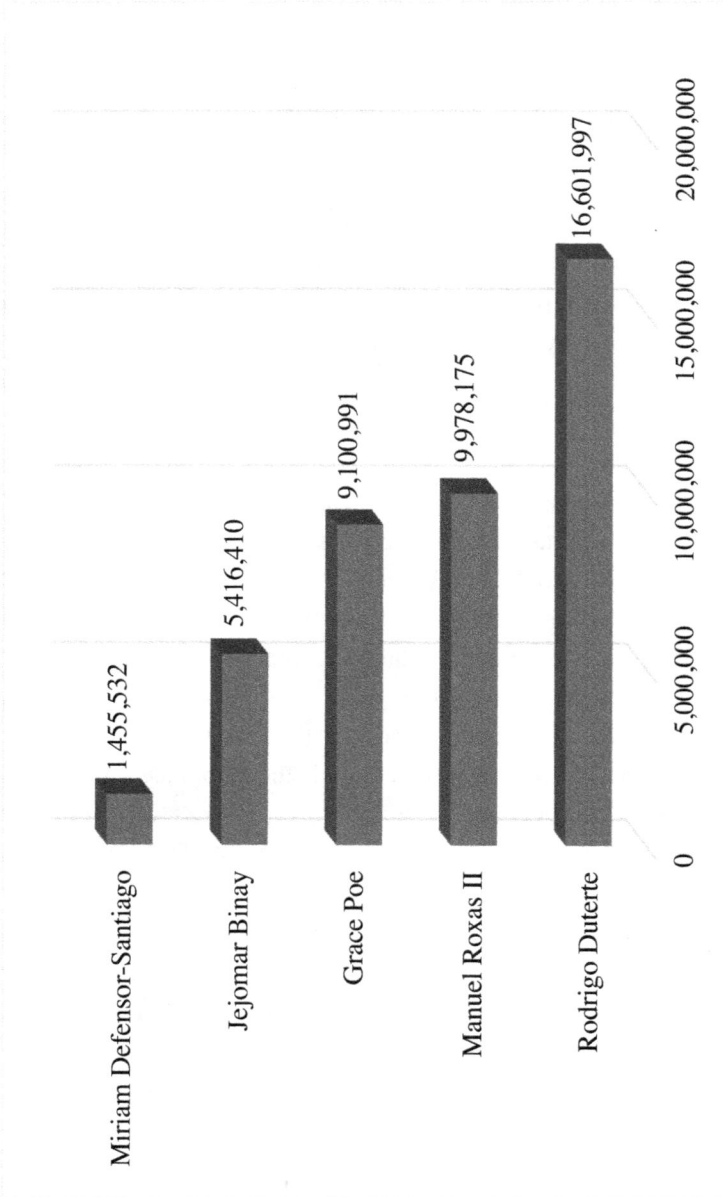

Source: *Philippine Daily Inquirer.*

Filipinos, overseas labour migrants, the educated middle class, the urban poor, and informal workers constituted a grass-roots "army of true believers". Ridiculed as "Duter-tards", they voluntarily lent their time, money, and energy to campaign for their candidate, even without orders from the campaign's central command.[19] Their activity on social media proved effective in a country where Internet usage has beaten global records.[20] Duterte's campaign events across the country were highly attended, and images of vast crowds and packed parades were diffused throughout the Internet, shared by members of this army. The 2016 elections showed new dimensions to political campaigning, where the pressing of palms is as critical as the sharing of tweets and Facebook posts.

Duterte's victory was unprecedented, since he received support from across the socio-economic spectrum and from major geographic regions in the country. According to an exit poll, he garnered the highest percentages in the ABC (46 per cent), C (39.6 per cent) and E (35.3 per cent) classes. Never has Mindanao delivered a big chunk of its votes to one presidential candidate. But Duterte received the bulk of votes in Metro Manila and some islands in the Visayas.[21]

Duterte's Crusade: A Bloody War on Drugs

The new President went immediately to work, even before he formally assumed office, by articulating some of his new policies. Duterte had his work cut out for him, given the problems left by his predecessor with regard to public infrastructure, criminality, and corruption. Given the country's weak bureaucracy and party system, Duterte had difficulty finding suitable cabinet officials and appointees with proven competence and integrity. A self-confessed leftist, Duterte immediately asked exiled members of the Communist Party of the Philippines to recommend cabinet officials. In the end, his cabinet was a diverse mix of appointees from previous administrations, retired military generals, and progressives endorsed by the communists, all who share very little in common with each other.[22]

During his first State of the Nation Address, Duterte reminded the members of Congress that he owed them no political debt. In a speech that laid out his plans for the country, punctuated by spontaneous remarks, he relayed his simple message to the Filipino people — he intended to fulfil his campaign promises, be they bureaucratic reform, social justice programmes, an unwavering pursuit of peace, or the relentless campaign against corruption, crime, and illegal drugs.[23]

Typically, politicians in the Philippines do not have a sense of urgency when they assume office. Many Filipinos were caught by surprise with the swiftness of Duterte's action, particularly in launching his war on drugs. Less than a hundred days into his term, Duterte's war on drugs had resulted in more than three thousand casualties, and this number increases by the day. These deaths resulted either from police operations where suspects resisted arrest or from summary executions by unknown perpetrators. Tens of thousands of drug pushers and users have voluntarily turned themselves in to the police, exacting a toll on the country's already decrepit jail system. There were also not enough drug rehabilitation centres to absorb many of them.[24]

Foreign media, human rights groups, the United Nations, and the United States have condemned this crackdown. Duterte quickly retaliated against this criticism by exposing their hypocrisy. Fulfilling a campaign promise, the firebrand leader is showing no sign of retreating from what he has described as a "bloody war" to prevent the Philippines from becoming a narco-state.[25]

Critics have raised the alarm on the increase in extrajudicial killings, as poorer members of Filipino society have been the ones mainly hit.[26] International non-governmental organizations, such as Human Rights Watch, have encouraged Western nations to suspend foreign aid to the Philippines, while political opponents have used the issue to discredit the highly popular President very early into his term.[27] One of the latter is a sitting senator who previously served as Justice Secretary under the Aquino Administration, and who did little to address the proliferation of illegal drugs in the country.

Duterte's scorched-earth policy on illegal drugs has put the human rights and security debate front and centre in the Philippines. Liberal-minded Filipinos see the President as a serious threat to the rule of law and civil liberties. A public opinion poll, however, revealed that almost 84 per cent of respondents approved of Duterte's drug war.[28] Many supporters had direct personal experience with how drugs had destroyed their families and communities. By striking fear into the hearts of members of drug cartels, the government has generally improved peace and order in many parts of the country. The socio-political context that undergirds human rights in the Philippines points to the fact that the idea remains a lofty concept that most ordinary Filipinos appreciate less than their desire to overcome poverty and insecurity. The lack of rule of law and unequal access to justice has made civil rights a privilege enjoyed only by the affluent and politically powerful. While it is wrong to totally dismiss human rights, it is also insensitive to nonchalantly demand them without recognizing the underlying problems of an elitist and unresponsive democracy.

So far there has been neither a serious nor credible attempt to investigate the extrajudicial killings in Duterte's drug war, though the President has extended an invitation to a special rapporteur from the United Nations to conduct a probe.[29]

While the government vowed to respect human rights, criticism that ranges from complacency to complicity have yet to be fully addressed by the government. The President's negative reactions in the face of criticism only bolstered the as yet unfounded insinuations of state-sponsored executions. There is also a need to improve the professionalism and accountability of the police forces involved in anti-drug operations. As seen from the experiences of Colombia, Mexico, and Thailand, drug wars without other kinds of policy interventions lead to further violence and insecurity.

There is hope that the Duterte administration will focus its anti-drugs efforts on the rehabilitation and reintegration into society of those with drug dependencies. The success of this campaign cannot be measured in terms of the number of dead bodies it has left. It is a multidimensional and transnational problem requiring comprehensive solutions from the lenses of public health, economics, and transnational security. While the government has vowed to go after the drug lords and the government officials to have coddled them, the victims of this bloodshed so far have largely been ordinary Filipinos — those that Duterte had promised to serve and protect.

The Economy: Robust but Still Not Inclusive

It was anticipated that the economy would perform well given the aggressive election spending in 2016. However, this exceeded expectations when the country posted a 7.1 per cent growth rate for the third quarter, making it the region's strongest performer. The annual economic growth rate will be between 6.4 and 7 per cent.[30] This was also fuelled by overseas remittances, sound macroeconomic policies, household consumption, and improvements in the industrial and services sectors. The agricultural sector suffered due to the effects of massive droughts and lack of government support.

Duterte's deadly war on drugs and his threats of cutting ties with major allies did not cause any major economic panic, though there was a decline in stock investments and some investor flight. However, large-scale infrastructure projects and commitment towards more public spending dispelled economic fears. The government's push to reduce bureaucratic red tape, ease the conduct of business, open several strategic sectors like telecommunications to foreign competition, and improve the country's security situation are all contributing to positive prospects for 2017.[31]

Apart from improving infrastructure and services, the critical challenge for the new administration is to address economic inequality. A reform of the country's highly regressive tax system is one of the President's main economic thrusts. He has reinstated his predecessor's conditional cash transfer programme, but he has also adopted a long-term plan to wipe out poverty in twenty-five years.[32] All of these schemes are contained in the government's as-yet-unreleased development plan.[33]

Duterte's Pivot: Toward an Independent Foreign Policy

Few expected the new President to cause a political shockwave in the country's once predictable foreign policy, especially since Duterte refused to see himself as a statesman. But prior to his controversial foreign policy stances, the Arbitral Tribunal handed its unanimous award on 12 July 2016 in the case filed by the Philippines against China concerning maritime rights disputes in the South China Sea (SCS). Though the Tribunal's decision did not include aspects related to sovereignty or boundary delimitation between the parties, it rendered final and binding judgments in favour of the Philippines on a host of critical issues. It ruled that there is "no legal basis for China to claim historic rights to resources within the sea areas falling within the 'nine-dash line' ". Second, it stated that certain sea areas in the SCS fall within the exclusive economic zone (EEZ) of the Philippines, and none of the features in the Spratly Islands could generate its own EEZ. Third, it observed that China has caused serious damage to the marine environment through its "large-scale land reclamation and construction of artificial islands" and "violated its obligation to preserve and protect fragile ecosystems".[34]

The arbitral case was Aquino's major foreign policy thrust, with significant U.S. prodding but without serious regional consultation with other SCS claimants and members of ASEAN. Instead of immediately conducting the necessary groundwork for its enforcement, the Duterte administration chose to put the ruling aside. The President described the ruling as one that "fell on his lap", but he swore that he would deal with the ruling in due time.[35] For the time being, his government has expressed a desire to smoothen bilateral relations with China.

As the country's chief diplomat, Duterte wanted to implement a truly independent foreign policy divorced from the influence of any major power. He articulated this, often in the form of spontaneous outbursts, during his first participation in the ASEAN Summit, with regional and global leaders in Vientiane, Laos. Apart from his insults to Pope Francis and UN Secretary General Ban Ki-Moon, the President also cursed U.S. President Barack Obama over U.S. criticism of his war on drugs.[36] This led Obama to skip a planned bilateral meeting with the Philippine President. Duterte shrugged off the snub and went on a tirade about U.S. colonial atrocities in Mindanao and its consistent hypocrisy in dealing with small states like the Philippines. Many observers were caught by surprise, while other governments became worried, given the fact that the Philippines will be ASEAN's Chair on the occasion of its fiftieth anniversary in 2017.

The anti-U.S. remarks shook the Philippine foreign policy and security community to the core, given the intimate relations between the two countries. Duterte's stance is a combination of his knowledge about America's colonial sins, a bad experience dealing with the U.S. government, and the criticism by the United States on his war on drugs. Duterte felt the U.S. rebuke was both a personal attack and a sign of disrespect of Philippine sovereignty, something he thinks he has the burden to uphold. In his off-the-cuff and inflammatory statements, he threatened to abrogate a long-standing military alliance, invalidate the Enhanced Defence Cooperation Agreement (EDCA), and sever diplomatic ties. As his cabinet attempted to creatively interpret them without success, the provocative tirades of the nation's chief architect of foreign policy grabbed worldwide attention.

Duterte officially visited Indonesia, Brunei, and Vietnam before proceeding to a critical visit to China in 2016. Chinese President Xi Jinping described Duterte's visit as springtime after years of mutual discontent. Both leaders pledged to continue stalled cooperative ventures and embark on new ones, ranging from intelligence sharing to combating illegal drugs to the development of public infrastructure, agriculture, and people-to-people exchanges.[37] The Philippine President left China with reportedly US$24 billion worth of deals, loans, and aid.[38]

As expected, Duterte's fiery rhetoric trumped the economic outcomes of the trip. He praised China's generosity, identified with its ideological slant, and promised to pursue a joint alliance with other countries. In that same vein, however, he announced his economic and military "separation" from the United States. Some feared that the President would abandon the Scarborough Shoal in exchange for economic deals or reinstated fishing rights for Filipinos.[39] After the trip, it was reported that China's coastguard granted Filipino fishermen access to the disputed shoal. During the Asia-Pacific Economic Cooperation meeting in Lima, Peru, the Philippine government announced that the internal lagoon within the shoal has been classified as a no-fishing zone in order to preserve marine life in the area. China did not seriously reject the idea of a marine sanctuary, and has even hinted at the possibility of a fishing deal with the Philippines.[40]

The President's pivot to China did not mean an abandonment of U.S. relations. Duterte was among the first leaders to congratulate President-elect Donald Trump after the U.S. elections, and has even appointed Trump's Filipino business partner as a U.S. trade envoy.[41] Military exercises between the Philippines and the United States will continue in 2017, but are now limited to capacity-building in humanitarian action and disaster response. The United States however withdrew its pledge of development aid over concerns with the deterioration of the rule of law programme in the country.[42]

Duterte's singlehanded approach to re-crafting foreign policy is risky, and could have a toll on the ability of the Philippines to make credible commitments abroad. Foreign policy requires a level of consistency that reduces significant risks and follows a shared strategic playbook influenced by expertise and long-term planning. Duterte's policy approach implies a careful distinction between impulsive pronouncements and actual implementation, with a keen eye on the latter. However, his future antics on foreign policy might not be given the same amount of patience by the elites and masses alike, especially if it threatens the country's national interests. Politics in the Philippines rarely stops at the water's edge.[43]

Conclusion: Duterte's Grand Design and the Coming Polarization

It was proved in 2016 that actual change can occur within the span of a single year. The Philippines witnessed a hotly contested election that produced an outcome that not even the most astute political observers predicted. The political earthquake was in the form of a new leader who vowed to change the ways things are done in the country. Widespread discontent with the state of affairs propelled a relative unknown, peripheral, and unpolished politician to the presidency. Duterte's victory caused a considerable displacement of the elites who thought they had the country in their perpetual grip.

When Duterte's campaign promised that "Change is coming!", many dismissed it as pure rhetoric. But the first few months of his presidency showed the many aftershocks that his leadership instigated. The change was welcomed by most Filipinos but despised by those who thought the new President undermined their values and lifestyles. Critics wasted no time in highlighting Duterte's flaws: from his use of foul language and his violations of human rights to his intimate relations with disgraced Presidents. His decision to allow the burial of the late dictator Ferdinand Marcos in the Heroes Cemetery was met with public resistance from the opposition and the youth. While the protest did not seriously affect Duterte's popularity, it might lay the seeds for future political conflict. One political consequence of this is the resignation of Vice-President Robredo in Duterte's cabinet. This premature political divorce made her the default head of the opposition, but it is too early to tell whether she can provide leadership to discontented political groups against a hugely popular president.[44]

Duterte intends to use his tremendous political capital to embark on the elements of his grand design. He recognizes the importance of settling internal conflicts with Muslim separatists and communist rebels. Having personally lived in a conflict zone, Duterte knows that development cannot be attained without inclusive peace with all disgruntled parties. If mutual good faith can be maintained, it is expected that the peace process will proceed at an accelerated pace with renewed confidence from both negotiating parties.[45]

The new President also envisions a new constitution that will make the Philippines a federal republic. Duterte is convinced that rewriting the rules and redesigning the country's institutions are critical to achieving meaningful change for all Filipinos. The vision is to further empower the regions in order to address economic inequality and curb corruption. This has the potential to be another polarizing issue, since many Filipinos are anxious about attempts to tinker with the 1987 Constitution. As the public awaits the details of the proposed amendments, the President must ensure that this process will improve rather than undermine democracy.[46] Failure to do so could galvanize his political enemies and force the Philippines into a downward spiral of political instability and polarization. The more that Duterte harnesses the collective power that catapulted him to the presidency and orients it towards deepening democracy and institution building, the more he will truly become the catalyst for meaningful and lasting change in the Philippines.

Notes

1. S. Rood, "Elections as Complicated and Important Events in the Philippines", in *How Asia Votes*, edited by J.F. Hsieh and D. Newman (New York: Chatham House, 2002), pp. 147–65.

2. Aries A. Arugay, "Duterte's Plan to Revive Philippine Democracy", *New Mandala*, 28 October 2016 <http://www.newmandala.org/dutertes-plan-revive-philippine-democracy/>.

3. Bea Orante, "Despite High Economic Growth, PH Poverty on the Rise", *Rappler*, 24 September 2015 <http://www.rappler.com/move-ph/106966-economic-growth-ph-poverty>.

4. The Philippines under the Arroyo administration (2001–9) did better by achieving a "free" status from 2001 to 2005. See Freedom House, *Freedom in the World 2016, Anxious Dictators, Wavering Democracies: Global Freedom under Pressure* (Washington, DC: Freedom House, 2016).

5. D.K. Emmerson, "Minding the Gap between Democracy and Governance", *Journal of democracy* 23, no. 2 (2012): 62–73.
6. A major portion of this section was taken from Aries A. Arugay, "The 2016 Philippine Elections: Democracy's Discontents and Aspirations", *Canada-Asia Agenda*, 24 June 2016 <https://www.asiapacific.ca/canada-asia-agenda/2016-philippine-elections-democracys-discontents-and>.
7. "Analysts: Candidates Fell Short in Final Debate", ABS-CBN News, 26 April 2016 <http://news.abs-cbn.com/halalan2016/focus/04/25/16/analysts-candidates-fell-short-in-final-debate>.
8. "VP Binay Claims Mar Roxas Has Links to Corruption", GMA News Online, 20 March 2016 <http://www.gmanetwork.com/news/story/559820/news/nation/vp-binay-claims-mar-roxas-has-links-to-corruption>.
9. Bea Cupin, "Can 'Daang Matuwid' Win a Philippine Election?", *Rappler*, 17 February 2016 <http://www.rappler.com/newsbreak/in-depth/122662-daang-matuwid-philippine-elections>.
10. Mara Cepeda, "Jejomar Binay's Impossible Dream", *Rappler*, 22 May 2016 <http://www.rappler.com/nation/politics/elections/2016/133814-jejomar-binay-what-went-wrong-campaign>.
11. Patty Pasion, "Does Miriam Santiago Own the Youth Vote?", *Rappler*, 24 March 2016 <http://www.rappler.com/newsbreak/in-depth/126920-miriam-santiago-youth-vote>.
12. Camille Elemia, "Grace Poe and the Lost Presidency", *Rappler*, 20 May 2016 <http://www.rappler.com/nation/politics/elections/2016/133522-grace-poe-what-went-wrong-campaign>.
13. Rosette Adel, "Duterte on Amnesty International Report: I Killed 1,700", *Philippine Star*, 9 December 2015 <http://www.philstar.com/headlines/2015/12/09/1530823/duterte-amnesty-international-report-i-killed-1700>.
14. "President Aquino Calls for United Front against Duterte", CNN Philippines, 7 May 2016 <http://cnnphilippines.com/news/2016/05/06/president-aquino-roxas-poe-binay-santiago-alliance-against-duterte.html>.
15. Randy David, "Dutertismo", *Philippine Daily Inquirer*, 1 May 2016 <http://opinion.inquirer.net/94530/dutertismo>.
16. Nikko Dizon, "President Asks Roxas, Poe to Join Forces vs Duterte", *Philippine Daily Inquirer*, 7 May 2016 <http://newsinfo.inquirer.net/783763/president-asks-roxas-poe-to-join-forces-vs-duterte>.
17. "The Philippines 2016 General Election: Election Automation in the Philippines — Get the Facts", Smartamatic <http://www.smartmatic.com/case-studies/article/the-philippines-2016-general-election-election-automation-in-the-philippines-get-the-facts/>.
18. Pia Ranada, "Why Duterte's Message of 'Care and Power' Attracts", *Rappler*, 26 April 2016 <http://www.rappler.com/newsbreak/in-depth/130827-rodrigo-duterte-message-care-power-supporters>.

19. "Duterte Rape Remark Won't Faze True Believers: Analyst", *ABS-CBN News*, 18 April 2016 <http://news.abs-cbn.com/halalan2016/focus/04/18/16/duterte-rape-remark-wont-faze-true-believers-analyst>.

20. Aim Sinpeng, "How Duterte Won the Election on Facebook", *New Mandala*, 12 May 2016 <http://www.newmandala.org/how-duterte-won-the-election-on-facebook/>.

21. Mahar Mangahas, "Revelations of the TV5-SWS Exit Poll", *Philippine Daily Inquirer*, 14 May 2016 <http://opinion.inquirer.net/94736/revelations-of-the-tv5-sws-exit-poll>.

22. RG Cruz, "Analysts: Where Are the Women, Youth in Duterte's Cabinet?", *ABS-CBN News*, 23 May 2016 <http://news.abs-cbn.com/focus/05/22/16/analysts-where-are-the-women-youth-in-dutertes-cabinet>.

23. "SONA 2016: What Are Duterte's Priorities?", *CNN Philippines*, 26 July 2016 <http://cnnphilippines.com/news/2016/07/25/sona-2016-duterte-priorities.html>.

24. Janjira Sombatpoonsiri and Aries Arugay, "Duterte's War on Drugs: Bitter Lessons from Thailand's Failed Campaign", *The Conversation*, 29 September 2016 <https://theconversation.com/dutertes-war-on-drugs-bitter-lessons-from-thailands-failed-campaign-66096>.

25. Jason Silverstein, "Philippine President Rodrigo Duterte Extends Bloody War on Drugs", *New York Daily News*, 18 September 2016 <http://www.nydailynews.com/news/world/philippine-president-rodrigo-duterte-extends-bloody-war-drugs-article-1.2796876>.

26. Megha, Mohan, "The Philippines: No Country for Poor Men", *BBC News*, 3 December 2016 <http://www.bbc.com/news/world-asia-38144237>.

27. "Duterte Enjoys Record 91% Trust Rating — Pulse", *Manila Times*, 20 July 2016 <http://www.manilatimes.net/duterte-enjoys-record-91-trust-rating-pulse/274995/>.

28. Though another poll stated that 7 out of 10 Filipinos want drug suspects to be kept alive. Nestor Corrales, "SWS: Duterte's War on Drugs Earns 'Excellent' Rating", *Philippine Daily Inquirer*, 7 October 2016 <http://newsinfo.inquirer.net/822906/sws-dutertes-war-on-drugs-earns-excellent-rating>; Rayan F. Javil, "Killings Worry Filipinos – Survey", *Businessworld*, 19 December 2016 <http://www.bworldonline.com/content.php?section=TopStory&title=killings-worry-filipinos----survey&id=137926>.

29. Nestor Corrales, "UN Rapporteur Welcomes PH Invitation to Probe Killings", *Philippine Daily Inquirer*, 12 October 2016 <http://newsinfo.inquirer.net/824685/un-rapporteur-welcomes-ph-invitation-to-probe-killings>.

30. Danica Uy, "ESCAP Raises Philippine Economic Growth Forecast for 2016", *Businessworld Online*, 2 December 2016 <http://www.bworldonline.com/content.php?section=TopStory&title=escap-raises-philippine-economic-growth-forecast-for-2016&id=137206>.

31. Siegfired Alegado and Cecilia Yap, "Philippines Posts Strongest Economic Growth in Asia at 7.1%", Bloomberg 16 November 2016 <https://www.bloomberg.com/news/articles/2016-11-17/philippine-growth-quickens-to-7-1-on-duterte-s-spending-spree>.

32. "Duterte Signs EO Adopting 25-yr. Plan to Wipe Out Poverty", *GMA News Online*,

14 October 2016 <http://www.gmanetwork.com/news/story/585081/money/economy/duterte-signs-eo-adopting-25-yr-plan-to-wipe-out-poverty>.

33. Alexis Romero, "Duterte Orders NEDA to Craft New Philippine Development Plan", *Philippine Star*, 28 October 2016 <http://www.philstar.com:8080/business/2016/10/28/1637928/duterte-orders-neda-craft-new-philippine-development-plan>.

34. "PCA Press Release: The South China Sea Arbitration (The Republic of the Philippines v. The People's Republic of China)" <https://pca-cpa.org/en/news/pca-press-release-the-south-china-sea-arbitration-the-republic-of-the-philippines-v-the-peoples-republic-of-china/>.

35. Patricia Lourdes Viray, "Duterte Wants to Set Aside Arbitral Ruling – for Now", *Philippine Star*, 29 August 2016 <http://www.philstar.com/headlines/2016/08/29/1618421/duterte-wants-set-aside-arbitral-ruling-now>.

36. Duterte later apologized for the remarks and expressed that they were not intended as a personal attack. In Elise Hu, "Philippine President Expresses 'Regret' for Cursing Obama", NPR, 6 September 2016 <http://www.npr.org/sections/thetwo-way/2016/09/06/492778889/philippines-president-expresses-regret-for-cursing-obama>.

37. Ben Blanchard, "Duterte Aligns Philippines with China, Says U.S. Has Lost", Reuters, 20 October 2016 <http://www.reuters.com/article/us-china-philippines-idUSKCN12K0AS>.

38. Andreo Calonzo and Cecilia Yap, "China Visit Helps Duterte Reap Funding Deals Worth $24 Billion", Bloomberg, 21 October 2016 <https://www.bloomberg.com/news/articles/2016-10-21/china-visit-helps-duterte-reap-funding-deals-worth-24-billion>.

39. Emily Rauhala, "Duterte Renounces U.S., Declares Philippines Will Embrace China", *Washington Post*, 20 October 2016 <https://www.washingtonpost.com/world/philippines-duterte-saysgoodbye-washington-and-helloto-beijing/2016/10/20/865f3cd0-9571-11e6-9cae-2a3574e296a6_story.html>.

40. Mike Ives, "Philippines to Declare Marine Sanctuary in South China Sea", *New York Times*, 21 November 2016 <http://www.nytimes.com/2016/11/22/world/asia/philippines-rodrigo-duterte-scarborough-shoal-china.html>.

41. Aries A. Arugay, "Engagements and Disengagements", *ASEAN Focus*, no. 7 (October–November 2016): 6.

42. Felipe Villamor, "US Halts Aid Package to Philippines amid Drug Crackdown", *New York Times*, 15 December 2016 <https://www.nytimes.com/2016/12/15/world/asia/philippines-us.html?_r=0>.

43. Aries A. Arugay, "Duterte's Pivot to China, *Australian Outlook*, 27 October 2016 <http://www.internationalaffairs.org.au/australian_outlook/dutertes-pivot-to-china/>.

44. Camille Elemia, "Leni Robredo: The New 'Default' Face of the Opposition", *Rappler*, 6 December 2016 <http://www.rappler.com/newsbreak/in-depth/154629-leni-robredo-new-face-opposition>.

45. Aries A. Arugay, "Duterte's Crusade for Peace in the Philippines", *Australian Outlook*, 24 September 2016 <http://www.internationalaffairs.org.au/australian_outlook/dutertes-crusade-to-win-peace-in-the-philippines/>.

46. Arugay, "Duterte's Plan to Revive Philippine Democracy".

UNCERTAINTY IN DUTERTE'S MUSLIM MINDANAO

Joseph Franco

President Rodrigo Duterte's ascent to Malacañang has been hailed as the best chance to resolve the challenges of secessionism and terrorism in Mindanao. Hailing from Davao City, Duterte has emphasized his Mindanao roots. Coupled with the curated image of an everyman, the new Philippine President has promised a definitive end to the Mindanao conflict. Lofty promises aside, it would appear that Duterte has yet to craft a coherent and consistent policy to steer Mindanao out of conflict.

Instead, contradicting policies reflecting volatility and continuity appear to be the Duterte model for peace. For extremist groups such as the Abu Sayyaf Group (ASG) and the Maute Group, Duterte appears to take a hard-line combat and intelligence-driven approach — for now. However, volatility has also characterized Duterte's stance against these fringe extremist groups, from casting them as "desperate" poverty-stricken individuals to criminals "slaughtering people as if they were chickens".[1] In contrast, continuity appears to be the direction his administration has taken as it deals with the Moro Islamic Liberation Front (MILF), as seen in the reconstitution of the Bangsamoro Transition Commission (BTC).

It is uncertain whether Duterte's ambivalent policy towards Mindanao peace will suffice to address the complexity of conflict in the southern Philippines. Duterte can ill afford missteps, considering the growing salience of external factors that impinge on Mindanao; namely, the spectre of violence inspired by the Islamic State of Iraq and Syria (ISIS) and the outcome of peace negotiations with the National Democratic Front (NDF). A cohesive policy to address the

JOSEPH FRANCO is Research Fellow with the Centre of Excellence for National Security at the S. Rajaratnam School of International Studies, Nanyang Technological University, Singapore.

socio-economic roots of conflict would be more effective than gallivanting from continuity to volatility and back.

The Current State of Play in Mindanao

On 26 November 2016 the Maute Group occupied the abandoned portions of Butig municipality in Lanao del Sur province. Nearly ninety per cent of the town's population were displaced, as another round of clearing operations by the Philippine Army (PA) was under way. After a five-day campaign the military declared that eighty per cent of Butig had been retaken, with the Maute Group on the run.[2] Just a few months ago, in June 2016, the military declared that the final Maute stronghold, Camp Darul Imam, had been captured and the group defeated — the supposed culmination of months of sporadic skirmishes in Lanao del Sur that began in February.

But rather than being an exceptional occurrence, this resurgence of the Maute Group is just symptomatic of the cyclical nature of conflict in Mindanao. Military operations — whether small-unit special operations or large-scale conventional campaigns — will never resolve the political and socio-economic drivers of conflict.

It is often referred to in jest that Mindanao has always been "under control" — by various armed factions, both state and anti-state.[3] A map of Mindanao's main landmass and outlying islands can be overlaid with the different flags, banners, patches, and camouflage uniforms of various armed units. The Armed Forces of the Philippines (AFP) has historically deployed a significant portion, around sixty per cent, of its military capacity in Mindanao. To date, Mindanao plays host to four PA Infantry Divisions, most of the assets of the PA's lone Mechanised Infantry Division, and several Philippine Marine Corps' (PMC) Battalion Landing Teams. In addition to these conventional forces are contingents from the PA Special Operations Command (SOCOM) and their counterparts from the Navy and Air Force.

This formidable line-up of military units is arrayed against a diverse range of threat groups in Muslim Mindanao — more formally known as the Autonomous Region in Muslim Mindanao (ARMM) — which is comprised of five provinces (Basilan, Lanao del Sur, Maguindanao, Sulu, and Tawi-tawi) and two chartered cities (Lamitan and Marawi). The Mindanao threat groups described below have pledged allegiance to ISIS, although not all have been recognized by the latter's leadership.

The armed group currently most active is the ASG, which is estimated to have around four hundred members operating in the island provinces of Basilan and

Sulu.[4] The ASG began as a jihadist organization founded by Abdurajak Abubakar Janjalani, after joining anti-Soviet mujahidin fighters in Afghanistan in the late eighties. Janjalani was killed in 1998 by police operatives and was succeeded by his younger brother, Khadaffy Janjalani. Khadaffy, however, did not have the same charisma as his elder brother, leading to the ASG's fragmentation and devolution into a kidnap-for-ransom and extortion group. When Khadaffy was killed in a PMC raid in 2006, the ASG's dream to build a cohesive militant organization devoted to establishing a caliphate in Mindanao died with him.

At present the ASG is fragmented into multiple factions as its core leaders have been either killed or arrested. Factions based in Sulu province, specifically Jolo Island, are prolific kidnappers and extortionists. The Sawadjaan faction is notorious for the kidnapping of Westerners and was responsible for the execution of two Canadian hostages — John Ridsdel and Robert Hall — in 2016.[5] More recently, an ASG faction in Sulu kidnapped German national Juegen Kantner from a yacht in the waters off the coast of western Mindanao.[6]

Of greater concern for the Duterte administration is the Basilan-based faction of the ASG, which pledged allegiance to ISIS.[7] The faction is led by Isnilon Hapilon, a contemporary of the elder Janjalani and long-time leader of the ASG in Basilan province. Unlike the preference of the Sulu factions for attention-grabbing kidnappings of foreign hostages, Hapilon's group prefers more low-key extortion activities to sustain their presence, coupled with playing up alleged linkages with the Islamic State. Hapilon's self-proclaimed "IS Basilan" has been recognized by the official ISIS leadership, but the latter stopped short of declaring an official ISIS *wilayah*, or province, in the Philippines. Hapilon has basked in being recognized as the *emir* of ISIS supporters in Mindanao, but remains keen on formally being named *wali*, or governor, of a *wilayah*.

The aforementioned Maute Group became known when it occupied the town of Butig in February 2016. Prior to the February clashes, the group operated as an extortion gang, targeting sawmill operators and bombing electrical transmission towers belonging to the state-owned firm TRANSCO. Leadership was exercised by the Maute brothers, Omar and Abdullah, until the latter was reported killed in the February skirmishes that dislodged the group from the town. While the group is known colloquially by residents of Lanao del Sur as "*grupong ISIS*",[8] or the ISIS group, there is little evidence of actual affinity with ISIS central. The resilience of the Maute Group is rooted in their kinship ties with local politicians in the province on the one hand, and their ties to a faction of the MILF on the other. Alleged Maute Group involvement in the 2 September 2016 bombing of a Davao City night market appears more as an exception to their extortion-heavy modus operandi. Three suspects were arrested in Cotabato City for their involvement in the blast.

Aside from the more notorious ASG and Maute Group, two other terrorist groups are known to have pledged to ISIS. The Bangsamoro Islamic Freedom Fighters (BIFF)[9] in Maguindanao is split between the pro-ISIS faction of Esmael Abubakar (aka Commander Bungos) and the mainstream faction headed by Imam Minimbang (aka Commander Karialan).[10] The BIFF is known for its very insular orientation and it is not known to operate outside the handful of towns it influences in Maguindanao province. Among all the groups who have pledged allegiance to ISIS, the BIFF appears to be least concerned with the pan-Islamic narrative, and is more preoccupied with using the ISIS brand to increase its stature among other private, non-sectarian militias operated by Mindanao politicians as "private armies".[11]

Operating on the fringes of central Mindanao, in the provinces of Sarangani and Sultan Kudarat, is the Ansar al-Khilafah Philippines (AKP). Founded by Mohammad Jafar Maguid, aka Commander Tokboy, the group broke away from the BIFF. Most recently, several followers of Tokboy were killed by police commandos in a small skirmish.[12] The limited capabilities of the AKP are manifest in the type of firearms they possess. The most credible threat Tokboy's group poses is the ability to emplace improvised explosive devices; using knowledge allegedly learned from the late Zulkifli bin Hir, aka Marwan, a Malaysian bomb-making expert.

Volatile Policies against Extremist Groups?

It is clear that the Duterte administration will pursue a security-centric approach to defeat extremist groups. The AFP has recently unveiled Development Support and Security Plan (DSSP) Kapayapaan, which prescribes the use of intelligence-driven combat operations to destroy terrorist groups.[13] While *Bayanihan* preceded the Maute Group, AKP, and the pro-ISIS BIFF, it is clear that the AFP intends to use the same template it has used against the ASG.

At the tactical level, combat operations take precedence over negotiations, yet there is ambivalence at the strategic-level, specifically concerning the way Duterte views groups like the ASG. Unlike the Aquino administration, which has cast groups like the Abu Sayyaf as an organized crime group, Malacañang at present has rambled along. Duterte's references to the ASG have ranged from desperate men driven by poverty to barbarians the President intends to literally eat raw, with vinegar and salt on the side.[14] It is unclear how far the whims of

Duterte have affected the planning of operations in Mindanao. The ambivalence of Duterte will probably not affect the day-to-day conduct of combat missions.

Conflicting messages from Duterte may harm efforts of constructing a narrative against extremist groups. The "benevolent Duterte" view — that groups like the ASG are driven by desperation — legitimizes the latter's extortion and kidnapping activities. It has been established that in Mindanao, common crimes far outnumber incidents of violent conflict associated with extremism and secessionism.[15] The benevolent characterization of the ASG and other similar groups would only reinforce the Robin Hood–esque persona of leaders like Hapilon and the Maute brothers. A benevolent outlook will also reinforce the erstwhile recruitment pitch of terrorist leaders, who present membership in these groups as a vocation. It is no secret that the prevalence of kidnappings in Mindanao is akin to a cottage industry that is both sustained and reliant on a network of illicit actors.[16]

On the other hand, Duterte has shown an aggressive stance which better corresponds to the hyper-masculinized persona he and his inner circle promotes. "Aggressive Duterte" has pledged previously to destroy the Abu Sayyaf and has subsequently ordered the deployment of additional PA infantry battalions in Sulu and Basilan provinces. In total, nearly nine thousand troops are in place in ASG-influenced areas.[17] Unfortunately, such troop movements are no different to the cyclical pattern of deployment and redeployment that took place whenever there was a perceived spike in ASG activity in western Mindanao under the previous Arroyo and Aquino administrations. The lack of deviation from the tactical precedent set by the previous administrations suggests that Duterte's stated aggression may be nothing more than posturing. Duterte's threat to suspend the writ of habeas corpus as a result of a "rebellion being waged" in Mindanao appears consistent with his usual hyperbolic statements.[18]

But the President's statements can have far-reaching implications and second-order effects. The brash and aggressive pledge to destroy threat groups like the Abu Sayyaf may inspire local government executives in the ARMM (i.e., the mayors and governors) to resort to extrajudicial measures in the name of maintaining the trappings of peace and order. Worse, political and family feuds in Muslim Mindanao may escalate as local executives use the discourse of counterterrorism — specifically, defeating the purported ISIS presence in Mindanao — to settle old scores and take revenge. "Us versus them" narratives would only serve to further inflame existing *ridos* — clan conflicts — that are prevalent in Mindanao.[19]

It is curious that Philippine military intelligence appears to be cautious in attributing actual links between extremist groups in Mindanao and ISIS in the

Middle East,[20] while the President and his personal circle have brashly made unsubstantiated statements regarding alleged foreign terrorist presence.[21] Maintaining a level-headed assessment of the terrorist threat in Mindanao would prove to be more complicated, as the usual hyperbolic Duterte recently provided the first high-level admission of ISIS links on 29 November 2016.[22] Only time will tell whether this pronouncement will be followed by the presentation of verifiable information, or whether it would just form part of Duterte's penchant for exaggerated claims.

Taking Duterte's statements as license to conduct extrajudicial activities is not limited solely to pro-government actors. For example, some MILF commanders had taken the discourse of Duterte's anti-drug campaign to conduct armed raids and unlawful arrests.[23] MILF involvement to counter the narcotics trade in Mindanao is limited only to advocacy drives and information campaigns on the perils of drug use. Abdullah Macapaar, aka Commander Bravo, is a MILF commander active in Lanao del Sur, who had a history of being a "spoiler" prior to the signing of the Comprehensive Agreement on the Bangsamoro (CAB) between the MILF and the Government of the Philippines in early 2014.[24] Misappropriation of Duterte's drug crusade by MILF commanders is a worrying development, as it may lead to spiralling conflict where purported anti-drug operations degenerate into full-scale conflict between the MILF and other armed groups in Mindanao. There are already worrying indications that Duterte's vacillating stance on MILF involvement in anti-drug operations may lead to future clashes with Bravo.[25]

Continuity with the Bangsamoro Peace Process: Keeping Peace with the MILF

Fortunately, the Duterte approach to the mainstream MILF appears to be a continuation of the Aquino peace paradigm. The MILF appears to be adhering to mechanisms such as the Ad Hoc Joint Action Group, which is intended to prevent unintended clashes with the AFP when the latter pursues extremist groups in MILF-influenced territories. For example, the MILF is working in coordination with the military to assist residents of Butig displaced by operations against the Maute Group.[26]

It augurs well for peace in Mindanao that the MILF appears committed to keeping with the CAB signed with the Aquino administration, in spite of the long delay to pass the Bangsamoro Basic Law (BBL) promised by the CAB. The BBL is intended to provide the legal framework to operationalize the demand of the MILF for meaningful political autonomy in Mindanao, specifically the establishment of a subnational Bangsamoro government. BBL legislation was derailed in the aftermath of the 2015 Mamasapano Massacre, where forty-four police commandos were killed in an unintended encounter involving MILF units in Maguindanao province. Public outcry over the desecration of the fallen commandos by alleged Muslim gunmen scuttled legislation of the BBL.[27]

With political capital to push for the BBL all but expended by the Aquino administration, it was tacitly accepted that meaningful strides to achieve peace with the MILF would only come after the May 2016 presidential elections. As Duterte steadily gained in the polls and subsequently clinched the presidency, hopes were raised that the first president from Mindanao would be best poised to bring peace to the region. His first step to reinvigorate the stalled BBL was to sign an executive order on 7 November 2016 to reconstitute the BTC. From fifteen members, Duterte's executive order expanded the BTC to a group twenty-one strong which would be tasked with crafting the draft BBL for concurrence by the Philippine Congress. The expansion of membership is supposed to bring in more voices and make the process more inclusive.

In short, Duterte appears to have taken on board the hard-won knowledge of the Aquino administration in dealing with the MILF — the need for greater transparency. Philippine history has seen how opaque negotiations such as those that led to the defunct Memorandum of Agreement for Ancestral Domain under the Arroyo administration can lead to the resurgence of conflict.[28]

The Misuari Wildcard

The only point of concern with the Duterte administration's thrust to transparency is how he has brought in Nur Misuari, founder of the Moro National Liberation Front (MNLF). On the surface, the inclusion of Misuari and his MNLF faction in the future of the Bangsamoro government appears to follow Duterte's inclusive approach to dealing with the MILF.

Misuari was the pioneer of the Muslim Filipino secessionist movement, which was triggered by the 1968 Jabidah Massacre.[29] After decades of fighting, Misuari and his MNLF signed a Final Peace Agreement (FPA) with the Ramos administration. This led to an expansion of the MNLF, with Misuari getting the helm of the new regional government. Unfortunately, Misuari's revolutionary streak did not translate to proper governance. As Misuari fell out of favour due to corruption charges and incompetence, the MNLF fragmented into a mainstream faction based in the Mindanao mainland city of Cotabato.

Disgruntled at being sidestepped by the mainstream MNLF and the ascendance of the MILF, Misuari waged two insurrections, apparently to persuade Manila that he is still a force to be reckoned with. Without a credible programme to disarm, demobilize, and reintegrate the MNLF's armed wing, Misuari was able to lay siege to Zamboanga City in 2001[30] and 2013. The latter siege was considered the largest urban warfare scenario for the AFP, which razed ten thousand homes and left nearly two hundred of Misuari's armed followers dead.[31] In the aftermath of the 2013 Zamboanga City Siege, Misuari was charged with rebellion and crimes against humanity.

Up until the end of the Aquino administration, Misuari had used his time on the run to criticize how the signing of the CAB with the MILF excluded the MNLF. It was an invalid claim dismissed by the Aquino administration, considering that the mainstream MNLF — the faction holding true to the 1996 FPA — continued its political participation and governance of the ARMM.

Immediately after Duterte assumed the presidency, moves were made to suspend multiple warrants of arrest targeting Misuari. This culminated in Misuari travelling from Mindanao straight to Malacañang. On 3 November 2016, Misuari spoke on the presidential podium, pledging support to the renewed drive to bring about a Bangsamoro government that would encompass the aspirations of both the MILF and the MNLF. To date, Misuari has yet to take concrete action to bring his promise to reality. But it also uncertain whether Duterte's personalized overture to Misuari will alienate the mainstream MNLF — those who patiently worked within the government bureaucracy and spared the country from additional violence.

On the Fringes: The New People's Army and the NDF

Any discussion of Muslim Mindanao's security during the Duterte administration and beyond would have to consider the externalities and impact posed by the ongoing peace negotiations between Manila and the NDF. While central and western Mindanao are the stomping grounds of jihadist and secessionist groups, eastern Mindanao is arguably the largest source of illicit financing for the communist insurgency.

Duterte is no stranger to the New People's Army (NPA), the NDF's armed wing, which he confronted in his more than two decades as Davao City Mayor. To manage the threat of the NPA, Duterte employed a "displacement strategy", turning Davao into an open city for communist cadres and political activities for as long as the downtown district was spared from skirmishes.[32]

As President, Duterte immediately set out to talk peace with the NDF, with the Norwegian government acting as a third-party facilitator. One of the first demands of the NDF was the release of all detained communist cadres and fighters — referred to as "political prisoners" in NDF propaganda. At least twenty high-ranking detainees — including former Communist Party of the Philippines Chairman Benito Tiamzon and Secretary-General Wilma Tiamzon — were allowed bail to join the Oslo talks as "peace consultants".[33] By 26 August 2016, six major "agenda points" had been agreed to by the two sides; including the future release of all political prisoners, a subsequent amnesty proclamation by President Duterte, and an interim ceasefire.[34]

With the prospect of diminished fighting with the NPA, the Duterte administration was able to redeploy forces from communist-influenced areas to the ARMM. But after the initial gains by the NDF in having their top leaders released from detention, there are indications that the communist movement is back to their hard-line stance that bedevilled previous attempts by the Arroyo and Aquino administrations to talk peace. Duterte's goodwill and the expectation of his cabinet for a bilateral ceasefire by 10 December 2016 had been met with denials by the NDF.[35] Non-combat operations conducted by the AFP, such as medical and dental outreach missions, have been unduly miscast by the NDF as ruses for intelligence gathering and surveillance.[36] At the same time, the NPA leadership has started to revert to its propaganda campaign, which was conspicuously absent during the start of the Oslo talks.

At the tactical level, there are already indications that NPA extortion activities have resumed after the short détente in preparation for a renewed round of fighting once the negotiations collapse. Whether the looming collapse of talks with the NDF is due to irreconcilable differences or a deliberate power play by the communist movement, it is another uncertainty that Duterte's Muslim Mindanao will have to face. Having more troops in Muslim Mindanao is the linchpin of the AFP's strategy to defeat extremist groups. But having the troops stay is contingent on the willingness of the NDF and the NPA to keep on the path to peace.

Other Challenges to Duterte's Ambivalent Policies on Muslim Mindanao

Assessing the challenges to Duterte's Mindanao also entails looking beyond the groups and personalities able to wage violence to wider trends. First, Duterte's fixation with historical revisionism could prove problematic. Duterte has repeatedly argued that the roots of Moro secessionism lie with American colonial rule at the turn of the twentieth century. Specifically, the massacre of several hundred Muslim inhabitants of the now-defunct Sulu Sultanate is frequently mentioned.[37] Duterte's anti-American stance appears to have transitioned from retorts against

U.S. criticism of his "war on drugs" to completely glossing over the invaluable support the U.S. military has provided in the fight against Mindanao extremists. Since 2002, under *Oplan Balikatan* (Shoulder-to-Shoulder), American special operations forces have been providing intelligence, training, and medical support for AFP units in western Mindanao.

What is further unsettling to some observers is the complete silence of Duterte on the atrocities committed by the Ferdinand Marcos dictatorship during Martial Law against the Filipino Muslims, such as the aforementioned Jabidah massacre. Duterte also seems to have forgotten how Jolo on Sulu was razed in 1974 by Philippine military forces on the orders of Marcos. In short, Duterte's simplistic narrative of the historical roots of the Mindanao conflict misses the complexity of problems that need to be resolved.

Second, even if Duterte manages to craft a coherent and unifying narrative as a clarion call to attain peace in Mindanao, the complexity of violence can hamper the attainment of meaningful peace. The conflict milieu in Mindanao has become intractable, as violence has been the norm for decades. Even if armed ideological conflict between state actors and armed groups — "vertical conflict" — were to cease immediately, violence is unlikely to abate in Mindanao in the short term. The absence of rule of law and effective governance in parts of Muslim Mindanao would mean that instances of "horizontal conflict", or violence associated with common crimes, would continue.[38] It does not help that Duterte is outspoken in his endorsement of shortcuts to law enforcement and extrajudicial measures against suspected criminals.

Third, Duterte's conception of Mindanao must go beyond the parochial and city-bound mindset he constructed for himself as Davao City Mayor. Mindanao is no longer just the backyard of his city. Rather, Mindanao is increasingly being drawn into international developments — namely, the prevalence of the ISIS narrative. Mindanao has been repeatedly mentioned by ISIS propagandists as one of its potential *wilayahs*.[39]

Closer to home, some Indonesian and Malaysian jihadists have stated their intent to wage jihad in Mindanao instead of travelling to Syria and Iraq. A *hijrah*, or migration, to Mindanao to wage their notion of violent jihad is premised on two points: avoiding detection by various state security forces, and the relative affordability of travelling to the Philippines instead of the Middle East. Those two factors that explain the appeal of Mindanao as a new jihadist battleground are themselves premised on the continued lack of governance and the porosity of Philippine borders. In short, the longer the Mindanao conflict persists, the louder the clarion call for foreign fighters displaced from ISIS territory in Syria and Iraq will ring.

Conclusion

Duterte should transition from his opening salvo of shock and awe to a more nuanced and quiet approach to the Mindanao conflict. By limiting his pronouncements to actionable pledges and not grandiose promises, Duterte can more effectively use the political capital he has built up. Peace with reliable partners such the MILF must be pursued. On the other hand, tempestuous alliances with personalities with dubious claims to mass support like Misuari's MNLF faction should be avoided. For extremist groups like the Abu Sayyaf and Maute Groups, treating them as the organized crime gangs they truly are would deny them the legitimacy they crave as purported allies of ISIS.

Mindanao post-Aquino remains an extremely complex milieu that requires nuanced policies. Duterte's penchant for candour (or at times bluster) appears to be the much-needed stimulus to break the ossified nature of the Mindanao conflict. Supporters may claim that the ambivalent stance of Duterte regarding Mindanao may be a deliberate attempt to achieve strategic ambiguity and keep adversaries off balance. But this assumes that there is a well-thought-out strategy at play behind the scenes. In reality, the continuing volatility of Duterte's policy pronouncements and official acts belie the existence of a master plan in place. Duterte has an unprecedented opportunity to bring lasting peace to Mindanao. But with it comes the necessity of mitigating if not mastering uncertainty. Whether the self-styled strongman can unlearn his decades of iron-fisted rule in the City of Davao to become a rallying point for the Republic of the Philippines remains to be seen.

Notes

1. "Duterte Says ASG Not Criminals; Gunmen Were 'Driven to Desperation' ", GMA News Online, 9 July 2016 <http://www.gmanetwork.com/news/story/572986/news/nation/duterte-says-asg-not-criminals-gunmen-were-driven-to-desperation>; Germelina Lacorte, "Duterte Says Abu Sayyaf Lost His Trust When Killings Began", *Inquirer Mindanao*, 26 August 2016 <http://newsinfo.inquirer.net/810194/duterte-says-abu-sayyaf-lost-his-trust-when-killings-began>.
2. Frances Mangosing, "Gov't Troops Retake 80 percent of Butig from Maute Group", *Philippines Daily Inquirer*, 30 November 2016 <http://newsinfo.inquirer.net/849366/govt-troops-retake-80-percent-of-butig-from-maute-group>.

3. A phrase often mentioned in jest by seasoned veterans of the Mindanao conflict, in personal conversations with the author during the latter's stint with the AFP from 2007 to 2011.

4. Jamela Alindogan, "Inside the Abu Sayyaf: Blood, Drugs and Conspiracies", Al Jazeera, 24 July 2016 <http://www.aljazeera.com/news/2016/07/abu-sayyaf-blood-drugs-conspiracies-160724090604857.html>.

5. Floyd Whaley and Ian Austen, "Philippines Confirms Killing of Robert Hall, Canadian Hostage, by Abu Sayyaf", *New York Times*, 15 June 2016, p. A3; Brian Murphy, "Islamist Militants Behead Canadian Man in Southern Philippines", *Washington Post*, 25 April 2016 <https://www.washingtonpost.com/world/asia_pacific/islamist-militants-behead-canadian-man-in-southern-philippines/2016/04/25/c4d94a60-0b14-11e6-bfa1-4efa856caf2a_story.html>.

6. "Abu Sayyaf Militants Say They've Kidnapped a German Tourist and Killed Another", *TIME*, 7 November 2016 <http://time.com/4560251/abu-sayaf-kidnap-kill-german-tourists/>.

7. Caleb Weiss, "Philippines-based Jihadist Groups Pledge Allegiance to the Islamic State", *Long War Journal*, 14 February 2016 <http://www.longwarjournal.org/archives/2016/02/philippines-based-jihadist-groups-pledge-allegiance-to-the-islamic-state.php>.

8. This is the self-ascribed moniker that Maute supporters use, regardless of any actual ideological knowledge or commitment. From social media and chat app conversations with PA infantry officer assigned to the 49th Infantry Battalion in Butig, Lanao del Sur. The sporadic conversations occurred from July to September 2016.

9. The BIFF is itself a splinter group of the secessionist MILF. The split occurred in November 2011, nearly three years before the signing of the Comprehensive Agreement on the Bangsamoro (CAB) on 27 March 2014.

10. "Military Bares Leadership Split in BIFF", GMA News Online, 25 July 2016 <http://www.gmanetwork.com/news/story/575019/news/regions/military-bares-leadership-split-in-biff>.

11. A common phrase used to refer to illicit groups of goons and/or armed thugs maintained by politicians to intimidate rivals. See Alfred McCoy, *An Anarchy of Families: State and Family in the Philippines* (Madison: University of Wisconsin Press, 2009).

12. "Military Launches Hunt for ISIS Man", *Manila Times*, 6 January 2016 <http://www.manilatimes.net/military-launcheshunt-for-isis-man/238101/>; "SAF Men Kill 3 Alleged ISIS Supporters in Sarangani", GMA News Online, 20 August 2016 <http://www.gmanetwork.com/news/story/578375/news/regions/saf-men-kill-3-alleged-isis-supporters-in-sarangani>.

13. Lui Claudio, "Kapayapaan: AFP New Campaign Intends to Destroy Terrorist Groups", *DWDD*, 9 January 2017 <http://dwdd.com.ph/2017/01/09/kapayapaan-afp-new-campaign-intends-to-destroy-terror-groups/>.

14. Marlon Ramos, "Duterte Warns Abu Sayyaf: I Will Eat You Alive...", *Inquirer*, 6 September 2016 <http://newsinfo.inquirer.net/813248/duterte-warns-abu-sayyaf-i-will-eat-you-alive-literally>.

15. International Alert Philippines, "Violence in the Bangsamoro and Southern Mindanao: Emerging Actors and New Sites of Conflict", *Conflict Alert 2016*, October 2016.

16. Gabriel Dominguez, "Abu Sayyaf 'Seeking Global Attention' with Hostage Kill Threat", Deutsche Welle, 25 September 2014 <http://www.dw.com/en/abu-sayyaf-seeking-global-attention-with-hostage-kill-threat/a-17954921>; See also Michael Miklaucic and Jacqueline Brewer, eds. *Convergence: Illicit Networks and National Security in the Age of Globalization* (Washington, DC: National Defense University Press, 2013).

17. Frances Mangosing, "AFP Sends More Troops to Sulu, Basilan to Fight Abu Sayyaf", *Philippines Daily Inquirer*, 25 August 2016 <http://newsinfo.inquirer.net/809734/afp-sends-more-troops-to-sulu-basilan-to-fight-abu-sayyaf>.

18. Christina Mendez, "Duterte May Suspend Writ of Habeas Corpus", *Philippine Star*, 13 November 2016 <http://www.philstar.com/headlines/2016/11/13/1643272/duterte-may-suspend-writ-habeas-corpus>.

19. For a discussion on rido, see Wilfredo Magno Torres III, ed., *Rido: Clan Feuding and Conflict Management in Mindanao* (Makati: Asia Foundation, 2007).

20. Alexis Romero, "Duterte: ISIS 'Has Connected' with Maute Group", *Philippine Star*, 29 November 2016 <http://www.philstar.com/headlines/2016/11/29/1648620/duterte-isis-has-connected-maute-group>.

21. "PNP Chief: Drug Lords Teaming up with ISIS, BIFF to Kill Me", GMA News Online, 9 August 2016 <http://www.gmanetwork.com/news/story/576883/news/nation/pnp-chief-drug-lords-teaming-up-with-isis-biff-to-kill-me-duterte>.

22. Carmela Fonbuena, "Duterte Confirms Maute Terror Group's ISIS Links", *Rappler*, 29 November 2016 <http://www.rappler.com/nation/153905-duterte-confirmation-maute-isis-links>.

23. Richel Umel, "Hundreds Flee from MILF Anti-Drug Ops", *Philippines Daily Inquirer*, 13 November 2016 <http://newsinfo.inquirer.net/843881/hundreds-flee-from-milf-anti-drug-ops-in-lanao-sur>.

24. Joseph Franco, "Violence and Peace Spoilers in the Southern Philippines", Middle East Institute Essay Series, 15 July 2014 <http://www.mei.edu/content/map/violence-and-peace-spoilers-southern-philippines>.

25. Genalyn Kabiling, "Duterte Mulls Offensive vs. MILF's 'Commander Bravo'", *Manila Bulletin*, 27 November 2016 <http://news.mb.com.ph/2016/11/27/duterte-mulls-offensive-vs-milfs-commander-bravo/>.

26. "Dureza: Duterte Taking Bold Steps to Deal with Maute Group", GMA News Online, 27 November 2016 <http://www.gmanetwork.com/news/story/590396/news/nation/dureza-duterte-taking-bold-steps-to-deal-with-maute-group>.

27. For a timeline on the Mamasapano massacre, see Bea Cupin, "Mamasapano Clash: What Did Aquino Know?" *Rappler*, 22 January 2016 <http://www.rappler.com/nation/119709-aquino-timeline-mamasapano-probe-reopening>.

28. Joseph Franco, "Malaysia Unsung Hero of the Philippine Peace Process", *Asian Security* 9, no. 3 (2013): 211–30; Joseph Franco, "The Moro Islamic Liberation Front — A Pragmatic Power Structure", in *Impunity: Countering Illicit Power in War and Transition*, edited by Michelle Hughes and Michael Miklaucic (Washington, DC: National Defense University Press, 2016), pp. 170–89.

29. The Jabidah Massacre saw the murder of dozens of Filipino Muslim military recruits. The recruits were being trained in preparation for a covert operation named *Oplan Merdeka*. Merdeka was an irredentist plot by Philippine President Ferdinand Marcos to reclaim Malaysian-occupied North Borneo. See T.J.S. George, *Revolt in Mindanao: The Rise of Islam in Philippine Politics* (Kuala Lumpur: Oxford University Press, 1980).

30. Leila Vicente, "MNLF Leader in Nov 2001 Hostage Crisis in Zambo Dies", ABS-CBN News, 9 June 2008 <http://news.abs-cbn.com/nation/regions/06/09/08/mnlf-leader-nov-2001-hostage-crisis-zambo-dies>.

31. Carmela Fonbuena, "Zamboanga Siege: Tales from the Combat Zone", *Rappler*, 13 September 2014 <http://www.rappler.com/newsbreak/68885-zamboanga-siege-light-reaction-battalion>.

32. Joseph Franco, "Duterte's Displacement Strategy", Policy Forum, 18 July 2016 <http://www.policyforum.net/dutertes-displacement-strategy/>.

33. Jodesz Gavilan, "Who's Who: Political Prisoners Released for Oslo Peace Talks", *Rappler*, 22 August 2016 <http://www.rappler.com/newsbreak/iq/143498-political-prisoners-ndf-consultants-peace-talks>.

34. H. Marcos Mordeno, "GPH, NDF Peace Panels Agree on 6 Major Agenda in Oslo Talks", *MindaNews*, 26 August 2016 <http://www.mindanews.com/peace-process/2016/08/gph-ndf-peace-panels-agree-on-6-major-agenda-in-oslo-talks/>.

35. John Paolo Bencito and Sara Susanne Fabunan, "Reds Deny Bello Yarn on Dec. 10 Peace Deal", *Manila Standard*, 25 November 2016 <http://thestandard.com.ph/news/-main-stories/top-stories/222438/reds-deny-bello-yarn-on-dec-10-peace-deal.html>.

36. Earl Condenza, "NDF Slams Gov't 'Disinformation' on Ceasefire Agreement", *Davao Today*, 16 November 2016 <http://davaotoday.com/main/politics/ndf-slams-govt-disinformation-on-ceasefire-agreement/>.

37. ABS-CBN News, "After Bud Dajo, Duterte Brings up Balangiga Massacre", ABS-CBN News, 13 September 2016 <http://news.abs-cbn.com/focus/09/13/16/after-bud-dajo-duterte-brings-up-balangiga-massacre>.

38. For a discussion on the definition of horizontal and vertical conflicts, see International Alert, "Rebellion, Political Violence and Shadow Crimes in the Bangamoro: The Bangsamoro Conflict Monitoring System (BCMS), 2011–2013", International

Alert Report, August 2014 <http://bcms-philippines.info/vers1/sites/default/files/ BCMS%20General%20Paper.pdf>; and International Alert Philippines, "Violence in the Bangsamoro and Southern Mindanao".

39. "ISIS to Followers in SE Asia: 'Go to the Philippines'", *Rappler*, 25 June 2016 <http://www.rappler.com/nation/137573-isis-fight-southeast-asia-philippines>.

Singapore

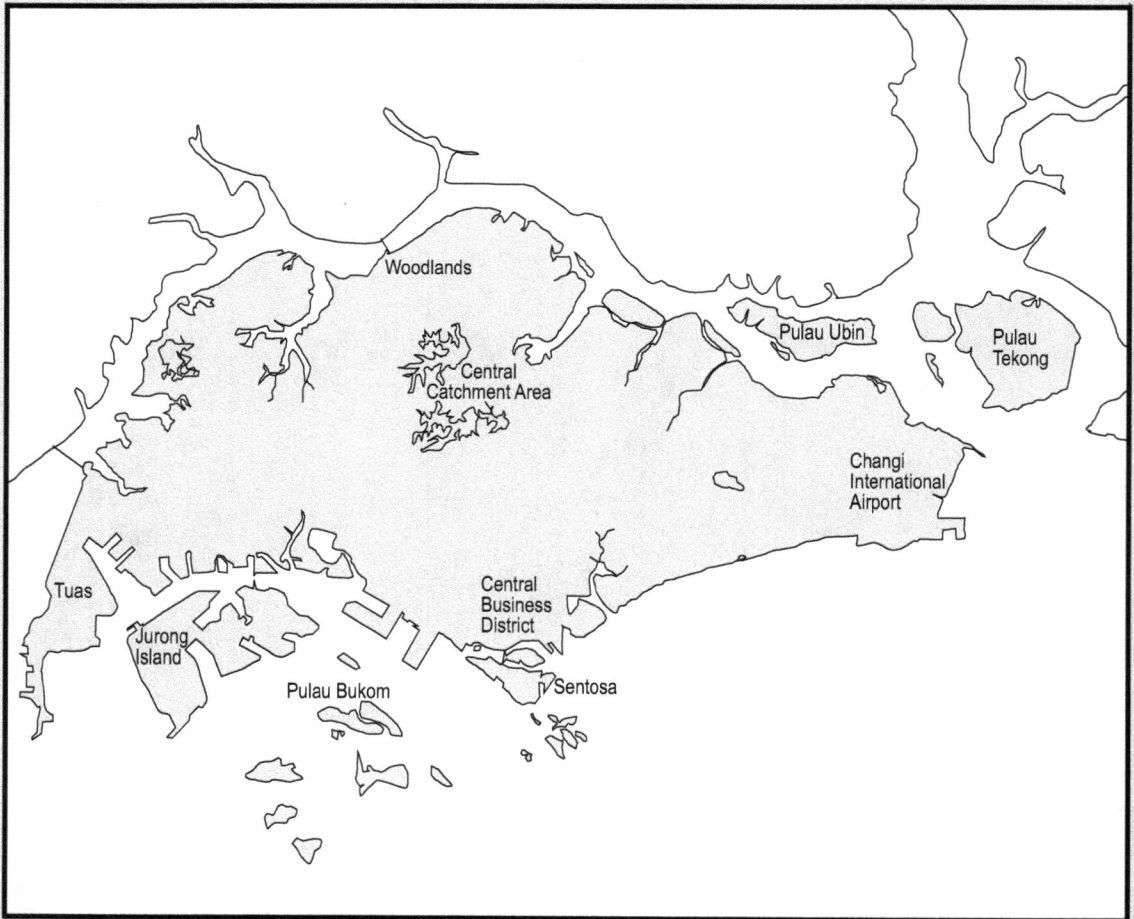

Woodlands

Central
Catchment Area

Pulau Ubin

Pulau
Tekong

Changi
International
Airport

Tuas

Jurong
Island

Central
Business
District

Pulau Bukom

Sentosa

SINGAPORE IN 2016:
Life after Lee Kuan Yew

Kenneth Paul Tan and Augustin Boey

For Singapore, 2015 was an extraordinary year. Proud of their country's numerous accomplishments, Singaporeans celebrated their fiftieth year of independence and participated in a year-long series of events and projects that were branded SG50. They mourned the death of their founding Prime Minister Lee Kuan Yew and wondered what the future would bring in his towering absence. Would there be an SG100 for Singapore and, if so, what would it be like? Also in 2015, the ruling People's Action Party (PAP) surprised many observers by winning 69.9 per cent of votes, and 83 out of 89 seats, in a general election in which all seats were, for the first time, contested. This suggested that opposition parties, which had been making strong inroads since the general election of 2006, were not after all going to have an easy time strengthening their presence in Singapore's government and politics. Liberal democratization was not going to be a straightforward linear process in Singapore.

In the afterglow of its convincing electoral victory, a more confident PAP government concentrated on consolidating its power and protecting Singapore's interests in a post–Lee Kuan Yew world. In his National Day message, Prime Minister Lee Hsien Loong focused on the theme of political, economic, and social stability in Singapore amidst an increasingly uncertain global and regional environment.[1]

KENNETH PAUL TAN is Associate Professor and Vice Dean for Academic Affairs at the National University of Singapore's Lee Kuan Yew School of Public Policy.

AUGUSTIN BOEY is Research Associate at the National University of Singapore's Lee Kuan Yew School of Public Policy.

Leadership Succession and Renewal

In August 2016, midway through his National Day Rally speech, an annual address to the nation that can typically go on for more than three hours, PM Lee almost collapsed. Officially explained as a brief loss of consciousness caused by fatigue and dehydration, Lee's highly televised fainting spell was reported widely in both local and foreign news outlets.[2] Earlier in May, Finance Minister Heng Swee Keat had suffered a stroke due to an aneurysm during a cabinet meeting and was only discharged from hospital in late June.[3] These two events, still broadly in the shadow of Lee Kuan Yew's passing, brought focus once again to the longstanding question of top leadership succession and renewal in Singapore.[4]

In a press conference immediately following the 2015 general election, PM Lee stated that one of the goals of his new cabinet was to prepare the next generation of political leadership. Even earlier, during a parliamentary debate in 2007 when Lee argued for higher civil service salaries to facilitate recruiting highly talented individuals for top government leadership positions,[5] he announced his intention to have a successor ready to take over his position by 2017. The then 55-year-old PM pointed out that his two predecessors — Goh Chok Tong and Lee Kuan Yew — had stepped down when they were 63 and 67 years old, respectively.

During the 2011 general election, the PAP asserted that the next Prime Minister would very likely emerge out of the slate of new candidates fielded by the party. Four of these new parliamentarians were later identified as likely successors to PM Lee. The four — Chan Chun Sing, Heng Swee Keat, Tan Chuan Jin, and Lawrence Wong — were later joined by two parliamentarians newly elected in 2015: Ong Ye Kung and Ng Chee Meng.[6] All six of these Members of Parliament (MPs), three of whom were high-ranking military officers, have since been promoted to full ministerial positions, clearly intended as part of the government's leadership renewal strategy.[7]

However, a clear successor for the premiership has still to be identified amongst these six likely candidates.[8] Lee has repeatedly stated his plans to step down after the next general election, which has to be held by April 2021.[9] Both Lee and former Prime Minister Goh had been identified and groomed for the top government job at least half a decade prior to assuming the position. With less than five years left before 2021 and no clear successor named yet, Singapore's future appears somewhat less predictable. The conventional wisdom in Singapore holds up predictability and the political stability that results from it as features that have kept Singapore attractive to foreign investors and businesses.[10]

Constitutional Amendments to the Elected Presidency

On 22 August 2016, former President S.R. Nathan died at the age of 92. He had suffered a stroke in July and had been in a critical condition since then. Well respected by both political elites and ordinary Singaporeans, Nathan had served two six-year terms as Singapore's longest-serving head of state, from 1999 to 2011. Part of Singapore's first generation of civil servants, he was eulogized by his former colleagues and friends as a highly dedicated and influential member of the nation's pioneering leadership.[11] As a local political commentator noted, his presidency solidified the office's roles and responsibilities in relation to the rest of the government, following a somewhat more difficult relationship between the government and Nathan's predecessor.[12] Nathan was also Singapore's second popularly elected President after constitutional amendments in the early 1990s transformed the office that had originally been a mostly ceremonial appointment by parliament into a directly elected one with limited powers. He was succeeded by Tony Tan Keng Yam, the current President, who narrowly won in the presidential election of 2011. The next presidential election is expected to take place in 2017.

The elected presidency (EP) was first publicly mooted by then Prime Minister Lee Kuan Yew in 1984 as an institutional check against the executive powers of Singapore's Westminster-modelled parliament.[13] The office was initially conceived as primarily fiduciary in nature, justified as a safeguard for Singapore's substantial budgetary reserves from the profligacy of a possible populist government. Additional provisions in four other areas included veto powers over restraints under the Maintenance of Religious Harmony Act and the appointment of key public service officials.[14] The institution has continued to evolve incrementally as further constitutional amendments since 1991 altered the elected President's fiscal powers.[15]

However, in 2016 the EP was subjected to a major constitutional review. In parliament's first sitting after the 2015 general election, PM Lee spoke of the need to amend the EP for three reasons: to improve its ability to represent minorities, to update the qualifying criteria for EP candidates, and to strengthen the Council of Presidential Advisors.[16] A White Paper published by the government in mid-September described significant amendments to the institution, which included substantially raising the qualifying threshold for presidential candidates, increasing the size and powers of the Council of Presidential Advisors, and reserving the elections for a racial group if it had not been represented for five terms.[17]

These proposed changes provoked disagreement from some quarters. Objections were raised by two unsuccessful candidates from the last presidential election held in 2011. These former presidential hopefuls publicly speculated that the tightening of candidature eligibility requirements were deliberately crafted to exclude them from standing for office in 2017.[18] Law Minister K. Shanmugam repudiated these claims, stating that the amendments were designed to improve the EP for the long-term and were not intended to prevent specific individuals from qualifying.[19] The Worker's Party (WP) vociferously objected to the amendments and proposed calling for a national referendum.[20] The WP is Singapore's most successful opposition party to date, and it is also the only opposition party in the current parliament. Describing the amendments as regressive, the WP's position was consistent with longstanding opposition rejection of the EP as an anti-opposition measure. These objections were, in turn, thoroughly dismissed by PAP MPs.[21]

In a parliamentary statement, PM Lee announced that the presidential election in 2017 would be reserved for Malay candidates. He reiterated the need for an EP as a fiduciary safeguard, but argued that new minority candidate provisions were needed to ensure the EP's role as a unifying symbol for multiracial Singapore.[22] In early November, a bill to institute the proposed EP amendments was passed with an overwhelming majority in parliament, with only the six opposition MPs from the WP voting against it.[23] The next presidential election will be held in September 2017 if more than one candidate stands for the position.[24]

Contempt of Court Laws

In August 2016, parliament passed the Administration of Justice (Protection) Bill, after a lengthy debate between PAP and WP MPs.[25] The bill was designed to codify Singapore's existing case law on contempt of court into statute. It clarifies what constitutes contempt of court and covers three main areas of conduct: disobeying court orders, publishing material that prejudice ongoing court matters, and scandalizing the court by making allegations of bias against judges. Minister Shanmugam explained in a July interview that the idea of proposing such a bill was mentioned in 2010 by the then Chief Justice, but was only put forward in 2016 as other more pressing changes to the law had to be dealt with first.[26]

The WP MPs argued against the bill as they believed it would, in effect, "protect the ruling elites at the expense of ordinary citizens" by making it easier for the government to charge people for scandalizing the court, while also stultifying discussion on "pending court cases", preventing them from discussing "current affairs" in "good faith".[27] The WP also criticized what they perceived as a lack of adequate public consultation and poor justificatory grounds for introducing the bill, given existing case law. Some observers believed that the contempt of court bill would more firmly establish self-censorship.[28] In response, the PAP rejected the allegation that the new law would stifle free speech and pointed out that the law was only legislated six years after it was proposed.

One of the more prominent critical responses to the new law came rather surprisingly from PM Lee's sister, Lee Wei Ling, who said in a Facebook post that the bill would "gag debate on issues that are important to Singaporeans".[29] While she later retracted her post and apologized for some of the points she had made in it, she also reiterated her view that the law represents "an attempt to muzzle public opinion".[30] Lee Wei Ling had also made the news earlier in the year when she wrote about how her opinion piece had been censored by the local broadsheet. In that piece she expressed disapproval of how the public seemed to be commemorating her late father, the former PM, Lee Kuan Yew, in excessive ways that he would not have approved of when he was alive.[31]

Leadership Renewal in the Worker's Party

Leadership succession was also an important theme for opposition party politics in 2016. Most notably, the leadership of the WP was put up to the vote during the party's biennial Central Executive Committee (CEC) election in May. The CEC elections were held to fill thirteen posts within the WP's top decision-making body. However, the position of Secretary-General, held unchallenged by party chief Low Thia Khiang since 2001, was unexpectedly contested by fellow MP and former WP treasurer Chen Show Mao. Chen was a former high-flying corporate lawyer who was fielded by the WP as its star recruit in the 2011 general election.[32]

While Low maintained his post, with 61 votes against Chen's 45, the surprise challenge publicly suggested, for the first time, intraparty disparities in confidence in Low's leadership style after the party's poorer electoral showing in the 2015 general election compared to the previous one in 2011.[33] Following the party elections, Low dismissed the possibility of a split within the WP, asserting instead that the unexpected contest strengthened the WP, as it demonstrated to the polity the party's acceptance of "open competition" and a "diversity of views".[34]

Political commentators were generally sanguine about the WP's prospects following the May CEC election, noting in particular the significance of a younger profile of CEC members. A local academic, for instance, suggested that the WP's political dynamism will be renewed through the strong competition for key leadership positions that these newly elected younger CEC members will likely engage in.[35] Low himself stated that the election of these younger members to the CEC indicated that the WP's leadership succession plans were proceeding as planned.[36] Another observer noted that the election clearly signalled to performance-oriented Singaporean voters the WP's organizational stability and its ability to muster younger and highly capable individuals for key positions in the party.[37]

In the aftermath, Chen stepped down from his post as WP treasurer at a CEC meeting in September, while still holding a seat in the CEC. While neither Chen nor the WP were initially forthcoming on explaining this decision, Chen later reaffirmed his commitment to his role as an MP, clarifying that he stepped down in accordance with the terms of his appointment in the May CEC meeting.[38] Anonymous WP insiders were reported to have said that Chen's relinquishment of the treasurer post was unrelated to his unsuccessful leadership contest, revealing that Chen only agreed to a short-term reappointment as party treasurer after the May election at the CEC's behest to facilitate a smooth transition to his successor.[39]

A More Inclusive Society

In August 2016, Joseph Schooling, a Eurasian Singaporean competitive swimmer, took first place in the hundred metres men's butterfly event at the Rio 2016 Olympics, becoming Singapore's first-ever Olympic gold medallist.[40] Schooling was also awarded a million Singapore dollars under Singapore's official Multi-Million Dollar Award Programme for medalling athletes. Widely feted across the country, Schooling's outstanding performance inspired an outpouring of national pride and provided an occasion for prominent commentators to reaffirm Singapore's continued ability to punch above its weight.[41]

Although the success of Singapore's development experience has often been described as underpinned by its unremittingly competitive meritocratic system,[42] public attitudes have been evolving to take into greater account a regard for equity and fairness, and a healthier approach to competition. In this light, the Olympic win also prompted many to argue that Singapore's para-athletes, who had secured two gold medals at the Rio 2016 Paralympics, should also receive the same amount of prize money as Schooling did, in the name of fairness and building a more inclusive society.[43] Similar calls for a more equitable and less individualistic society have also been made this year with regard to other issues, such as the rights of the physically disabled, gender equality, workplace discrimination against older workers, LGBT rights, and multiracial relations.[44] These calls were part of a growing social and political momentum behind the notion of tempering the highly stressful nature of Singapore's system towards a more socially cohesive and holistically oriented "compassionate meritocracy".[45] This has also been seen in public discussions surrounding the education system.

Changes to the Education System

According to Deputy Prime Minister (DPM) Tharman Shanmugaratnam, the government has been actively attempting to find "new solutions" to address the disparities in education levels and relative access to the benefits of globalization. He identified both of these amongst the main factors worsening Singapore's inequality gap.[46] Speaking at a local conference in May, Tharman described a vision of transforming Singapore into a more innovative and inclusive society.[47] Echoing his previous statements on the topic, he identified the ongoing changes to the education system to reduce its current emphasis on academic results as a key aspect of this transformation. Instead, Singapore's education system will be given a more skills-development focus, greater flexibility, and an increasing orientation towards recognizing and developing a diversity of thinking and interests. Some observers have suggested that the unprecedented appointment of two concurrent Ministers for Education, one focusing on schools and the other on higher education and skills development, reflects the government's continuing commitment to education-based reform at both the lower and higher levels.[48]

These amendments to both the school system and adult education are part of the government's more recent attempts to put in place the institutional changes and resources necessary to encourage and support a culture of continuing education and lifelong learning.[49] As DPM Tharman explained in a 2014 speech, the goals of developing a "lifelong meritocracy" are simultaneously economic and social: to help ensure that Singaporeans will remain competent and well-equipped to thrive in the more rapidly evolving, technologically involved, and less predictable job markets of the future; while also building a more inclusive society by giving more opportunities for all Singaporeans to develop their fullest potential throughout life.[50]

Accordingly, the SkillsFuture movement was implemented in January to enable working Singaporeans of all ages and education attainment to continually upgrade themselves and adapt better to Singapore's ongoing economic restructuring. The initiative has thus far enjoyed a high uptake, and has also been expanded to include more courses and programmes.[51] In November, Minister for Education (Higher Education and Skills) Ong Ye Kung announced a five-year transformation plan to upgrade the country's training and adult education sector to complement the national SkillsFuture movement.[52]

In July 2016, the government announced some changes to the Primary School Leaving Examination (PSLE) system, an examination that all students take at the end of their formal primary schooling.[53] The PSLE scoring system, which scored students based on their relative performance to their peers, will be revamped so that it is based only on individual performance. Thus, from 2021 onwards, pupils taking the PSLE will be assigned a score from 4 to 32 based on the sum of their own level of achievement attained for each of the four PSLE subjects, replacing the current system which gives an aggregate score based on normalized performance in each PSLE subject from a maximum of 300. As officially explained by the Ministry of Education, the phasing out of the current relative scoring system is designed to make competition over the PSLE less intense and to reduce the narrow emphasis on "book smarts" by encouraging students to focus on their own learning.[54]

These changes were in line with the previous Minister for Education Heng Swee Keat's statement in 2015 that bold transformations were needed in Singapore's education system to create more holistic pathways to success beyond its current narrow focus on academic qualifications.[55] Nevertheless, some parents and observers considered the upcoming changes to be insufficient to reduce the emphasis on competing for high test scores and encourage students to focus on non-academic skills and activities, pointing out that parents, teachers, and employers will also need to do away with their competitive mindsets over grades.[56]

Singapore's Economy in Transition

These changes to the education system have also been part of the government's efforts to prepare Singapore for the growing economic challenges from globalization and the advancement of disruptive technologies.[57] The Council for Skills, Innovation, and Productivity (CSIP) was officially launched in May to guide the structural transformation of Singapore's economy.[58] Chaired by DPM Tharman, the CSIP's responsibilities include advancing SkillsFuture and driving industrial transformation and internationalization efforts towards skills-, innovation-, and productivity-based growth. These initiatives to transform Singapore's national economic strategy have been implemented against the background of a slowing economy.

While Singapore continued to be ranked highly in international measures of national competitiveness, the city-state also showed several indications this year of an ongoing reduction in economic growth.[59] Singapore's total employment shrunk in its third financial quarter due to a slowing economy and softening labour market.[60] Temasek Holdings, the nation's sovereign wealth fund, suffered its first annual loss since 2009, losing nine per cent, or S$24 billion, of its net portfolio value globally.[61] This gloomy economic situation also contributed to a fall in both commercial and residential property prices and rental values.[62] Mall vacancies were at their highest level in a decade.[63] In November, Manpower Minister Lim Swee Say noted in parliament that the ongoing economic restructuring and slowing growth will likely lead to higher retrenchments in 2016 compared to the previous year.[64] Singapore's central bank, the Monetary Authority of Singapore, reported in October that the national economy was in a cyclical downturn and gave a sluggish GDP growth outlook for the rest of the year and 2017.[65]

A national broadsheet explained these economic developments as a convergence between short-term cyclical and longer-term structural factors.[66] Four of these factors were described in that article: (1) slow global economic growth, (2) a prolonged fall in oil prices, (3) shifts in international trade flows, and (4) a mismatch between current workforce skills and new jobs being created by disruptive technologies. Nonetheless, PM Lee gave reassurances in a November dialogue that Singapore was not currently in an economic crisis and noted that the weak external demand driving Singapore's economic slump will likely reverse.[67] He emphasized the importance of the long-term restructuring strategy initiated by the government to transform the city-state's economy towards productivity-driven growth.

Singapore has continued to grow its existing economic strengths, for instance by solidifying its role as a regional energy hub by joining the influential International Energy Agency as an association country this year.[68] However, such initiatives came amidst a growing consensus amongst both private and public sector leaders that Singapore must build the requisite capacity to deal with the looming challenges posed by disruptive digital technologies.[69]

Accordingly, the theme of economic restructuring was emphasized in the Singapore Budget 2016, particularly through the continued upgrading of the SkillsFuture movement and the Industry Transformation Programme, which has thus far been initiated to aid the transformation efforts of businesses in three sectors, with twenty more such sector-based programmes to be implemented.[70] The budget also introduced several measures to help the labour force adapt to the evolving economy, including an upgrading of the Workfare Income Supplement scheme for lower-income workers, the creation of a new training and job placement hub focused on the ICT sector, and an expansion of wage support and reskilling schemes for retrenched workers.[71]

The Singapore government has been proactive in significantly increasing the role of ICT in urban development. As part of its "Smart Nation" initiative, launched in 2014, the government aims to deploy an island-wide network of sensors and other embedded digital infrastructure as a platform to facilitate more innovations and seek new opportunities.[72] A sign of this increasing turn towards ICT is the growing popularity of computer programming classes and workshops designed for children.[73] Investing in and trialling emerging technologies such as machine learning, virtual reality, cleantech, fintech, driverless cars, and advanced robotics, as well as allocating substantial budgetary resources to expanding ICT capacity, these policies are to come under the aegis of two new government agencies, the Government Technology Agency (GovTech) and the Info-communication Media Development Authority (IMDA).[74]

Another notable shift in Singapore's urban development trajectory is the ongoing reversal of the privatization of the public transportation system. The government's Land Transport Authority has taken over the billion dollars worth of operating assets from the two train operators, SMRT and SBS Transit, that make up the public rail network.[75] This was to enable the two firms to focus solely on the operations and maintenance of the train system. In September, SMRT shareholders approved a proposed Temasek Holdings buyout of the 46 per cent of the company's shares it did not own.[76] This was justified as a means of enabling SMRT to focus on "its primary role of delivering safe and high-quality rail service[s], without short-term pressures of being a listed company".[77] These moves to boost the reliability of the rail network came after a series of large-scale train disruptions and allegations of train defects that have occurred over the past few years. The resulting public discontent also provided grist for the opposition parties' past election campaigns.[78]

The Threat of Terrorism

Singapore has been part of the multinational coalition fighting against ISIS (Islamic State of Iraq and Syria) since 2014. The nation-state had also deployed servicemen from the Singapore Armed Forces to Afghanistan from 2007 to 2013.[79] In March this year, Minister Shanmugam noted that a terrorist attack in highly globalized Singapore was a matter of "when", rather than "if".[80] Less than five months later, six suspected terrorists were arrested for plotting to launch rockets aimed at Singapore from the nearby Indonesian island of Batam. The arrests were conducted by the Indonesian authorities in coordination with their counterparts in Singapore's security agencies.[81] The ringleader was reported to be an active ISIS supporter who had also helped Indonesian militants travel to Syria.[82] DPM Teo Chee Hean responded to the foiled attack in a Facebook post, saying that it demonstrated the seriousness of the terrorist threat facing Singapore. On the domestic front, Singapore has strengthened several security measures and launched a national initiative this year, the SG Secure movement, to better prepare Singapore for the growing terror threat.[83]

In July Singapore was identified as the safest country in the world to do business — in an index that included terrorism threats — by Pinkerton, a leading global provider of corporate risk management services.[84] Nevertheless, Singapore's risk of being targeted by terrorists has risen due to the emergence of ISIS in Southeast Asia.[85] In June ISIS launched its first Malay language newspaper in the Philippines, which was regionally distributed, including to Singapore.[86] The newspaper was quickly banned by Singapore's Ministry of Communications and Information, which called it a tool to spread ISIS propaganda with a "clear intention to radicalize and recruit Southeast Asians to join them".[87] As Defence Minister Ng Eng Hen said in an interview in October, the threat from extremist groups to the region is steadily increasing as they become more organized and focused over time.[88] In response, Singapore has reaffirmed its continuing strategic partnership with the United States with respect to counterterrorism security and defence cooperation during meetings between PM Lee and the U.S. President in August.[89] Within the region, Singapore has also signed a joint declaration between ASEAN member states to combat terrorism.[90]

Singapore–China Bilateral Relations and the South China Sea

China has been embroiled in a long-running and acrimonious territorial dispute with Taiwan and four ASEAN countries (Brunei, Malaysia, the Philippines, and Vietnam) over China's claims to large portions of the South China Sea. In July this year an international tribunal at the Permanent Court of Arbitration (PCA) at The Hague ruled in favour of the Philippines in a case brought by the Philippines against China under the United Nations Convention on the Law of the Sea.[91] In making its ruling the tribunal rejected China's claims to historic and other sovereign rights over the disputed territories. China did not participate in the tribunal's proceedings and refused to "accept or recognize" the ruling.

Public opinion in China has been turning against Singapore. Singapore has been acting as the country coordinator for ASEAN–China Dialogue Relations.[92] In this regard, China's Foreign Ministry has called for Singapore to "respect" its rejection of the South China Sea ruling.[93] This request was made amidst a growing critical attitude in China towards Singapore, provoked by a belief that Singapore should have been more supportive of China in the South China Sea territorial disputes. Articles published in some Chinese media outlets have also alleged that Singapore has instead deliberately attempted to raise support for the Philippines and made unproven claims that Singapore has been attempting to get China to abide by the PCA ruling.[94] An influential Chinese policy advisor, who is also a general in the People's Liberation Army, called for sanctions to be imposed upon Singapore for its role in "seriously damaging China's interests". A written rebuttal from Singapore's Ambassador to China was issued denying these claims as wholly fabricated.[95] However, this did little to stem continued allegations that Singapore had failed to reciprocate China's "brotherly affections" for the city-state and had instead chosen to support U.S. interests in the Asia-Pacific.[96] These criticisms have also provoked hostility amongst Chinese social media users, many of whom have come out in support of their country and strongly castigated Singapore for what they perceive as the latter's bad faith towards China on this issue.

Singapore's response to these tensions has been both consistently conciliatory and insistent upon maintaining the city-state's objectivity on the matter.[97] In this year's National Day Rally speech, PM Lee said that Singapore cannot afford to be partisan on the South China Sea issue, and must instead support a "rules-based international order" for the sake of the country's survival.[98] Mentioning that both China and the United States are amongst Singapore's closest friends, Lee also pointed out that the city-state's close relations with China are "much broader than the South China Sea", and there will thus be "many more opportunities to strengthen our friendship and cooperation with each other". These statements were reiterated by the PM in September during a speech in Tokyo.[99] In an opinion piece, Singapore's Ambassador-at-Large Tommy Koh argued that China has often had "unreasonable expectations" of Singapore, built upon a misconception that the city-state, being populated by a Chinese ethnic majority, was a "Chinese nation" that would act accordingly to support Chinese policies.[100] Highlighting that Singapore was in fact a multiracial and culturally distinct country that may thus have interests and commitments that "are not always similar to those of China", the Ambassador expressed his desire that Singapore and China "try to avoid misunderstanding each other" and instead continue to build upon their long history of friendly bilateral relations.

At the end of November, a shipment of Singapore armoured vehicles was seized by Hong Kong customs.[101] The vehicles were en route to Singapore on a commercial shipping carrier after they had been deployed in a military exercise in Taiwan. The vehicles were returned to Singapore in late January 2017 after being detained for two months.[102] While the shipment was apparently detained because the commercial carrier did not provide appropriate permits, some commentators speculated that these military vehicles were impounded partly to penalize Singapore for its position on the South China Sea territorial disputes and its longstanding military cooperation with Taiwan.[103] A spokesman for China's Foreign Ministry explained that the detention was due to Singapore's failure to abide by the "one China" policy by having official relations with Taiwan, which Beijing sees as a renegade province. Singapore's Foreign Affairs Minister Vivian Balakrishnan responded by stating that Singapore has continued to respect the "one China" policy ever since the two countries first established diplomatic relations.[104]

Conclusion

For Singapore, life after Lee Kuan Yew will continue to pose several challenges. While the PAP government attempted to consolidate its power after a convincing electoral win in 2015, it has been uncharacteristically slow to identify and groom PM Lee's successor. Constitutional changes, including amendments to the elected presidency in order to ensure ethnic minority representation at the highest level, met with some controversy, a reflection of a much more politically sophisticated citizenry that was sceptical of the anachronistically racialized view of Singapore held by the elite. Meanwhile, opposition politics — disenchanted by the results of the 2015 general election — continued to evolve with some uncertainty.

As Singapore society moved towards becoming more broadly inclusive, the education system has also evolved to take into account a broader set of talents and interests, while attempting to minimize the uglier aspects of competitiveness. The education system also started to move away from being simply an intensive front-loaded affair, as policies and programmes were launched to get Singaporeans to embrace continuous learning and opportunities for upgrading their skills. Partly, this was aimed at equipping members of the Singapore workforce with the resources and means to keep themselves relevant and productive in the face of disruptive technologies that are transforming the nature of work. Partly also, this was a way of moving from a meritocracy of exams to a more compassionate and continuous meritocracy where people who do well can find opportunities for self-betterment throughout the course of their lives.

Without the benefit of Lee Kuan Yew's international stature, Singapore will have to find its way through a more dangerous world where superpower China's friendliness to Singapore can no longer be taken for granted and where terrorism becomes much more than a possible and sometimes distant threat.

Notes

1. Chew Hui Min, "National Day Rally 2016: 7 Things You Need to Know from PM Lee's Speech", *Straits Times*, 21 August 2016.
2. Agence France-Presse, "Singaporean Prime Minister Lee Hsien Loong Faints during

Televised Speech", *The Guardian*, 22 August 2016 <https://www.theguardian.com/world/2016/aug/22/singaporean-prime-minister-lee-hsien-loong-faints-during-televised-speech>.

3. Channel NewsAsia, "Heng Swee Keat Discharged from Hospital: Prime Minister's Office", 25 June 2016.

4. Stephan Ortmann, "Singapore's Succession Struggles", East Asia Forum, 24 September 2016 <http://www.eastasiaforum.org/2016/09/24/singapores-succession-struggles/>.

5. Speech by Lee Hsien Loong, 11 April 2007 <http://www.nas.gov.sg/archivesonline/speeches/view-html?filename=20070411980.htm>.

6. Charissa Yong, "The Next Prime Minister: 6 Men to Watch", *Straits Times*, 4 September 2016.

7. AsiaOne, "Ong Ye Kung and Ng Chee Meng Promoted to Full Ministers of Education", 28 October 2016.

8. Charrisa Yong, "Countdown to Next PM Picks Up Speed", *Straits Times*, 4 September 2016.

9. Rachel Au-Yong, "Expect More Changes Ahead, Say Observers", *Straits Times*, 29 October 2016.

10. Marius Zaharia, "PM Lee's Health Scare Exposes Singapore's Leadership Uncertainty", Reuters, 23 August 2016.

11. Han Fook Kwang, "A Last Meeting with S R Nathan", *Straits Times*, 23 August 2016.

12. Yahoo Singapore, "S R Nathan Leaves Lasting Legacy in Singapore: Colleagues, Analysts", 23 August 2016 <https://sg.news.yahoo.com/s-r-nathan-leaves-lasting-legacy-in-singapore-174215005.html>.

13. Hussin Mutalib, "Constitutional-Electoral Reforms and Politics in Singapore", *Legislative Studies Quarterly* 27, no. 4 (2002): 659–72.

14. Kenneth Paul Tan, "Singapore in 2011", *Asian Survey* 52, no. 1 (2012): 220–26.

15. Yvonne Lee, "Under Lock and Key: The Evolving Role of the Elected President as a Fiscal Guardian", *Singapore Journal of Legal Studies* (Dec 2007): 290–322.

16. Pearl Lee, "Panel Submits Report on Elected Presidency", *Straits Times*, 18 August 2016.

17. Royston Sim, "White Paper Spells Out Significant Changes to be Made to Elected Presidency Scheme", *Straits Times*, 16 September 2016.

18. See, for example, *The New Paper*, "Tan Jee Say: Wrong to Raise the Bar and Rule Me Out", 9 September 2016; Lim Yan Liang, "Changes to EP Meant to Improve System: Shanmugam", *Straits Times*, 19 September 2016.

19. Ibid.

20. Danson Cheong, "WP Calls for National Referendum on Presidency", *My Paper*, 9 November 2016.

21. Channel NewsAsia, "WP's Senate Proposal 'Not Well Thought Through': DPM Teo", 9 November 2016.

22. Charissa Yong, "Singapore's Next President Set to be Malay", *Straits Times*, 9 November 2016.

23. Channel NewsAsia, "Elected Presidency: Amendments to Constitution Passed in Parliament", 9 November 2016.

24. Siau Min En, "Presidential Elections to be Held in September", *Today*, 6 February 2017.

25. Lianne Chia, "Bill on What Constitutes Contempt of Court Passed in Parliament", Channel NewsAsia, 15 August 2016.

26. Chong Zi Liang, "Codifying Contempt of Court Laws to Make Dos and Don'ts", *Straits Times*, 12 July 2016.

27. Speech by Sylvia Lim, 15 August 2016 <http://www.wp.sg/administration-of-justice-protection-bill-speech-by-sylvia-lim/>.

28. Kirsten Han, "COMMENT: Contempt of Court Bill Will Entrench Self-Censorship", Yahoo News, 31 July 2016 <https://sg.news.yahoo.com/comment-contempt-of-court-bill-will-entrench-075605480.html>.

29. *Straits Times*, "Lee Wei Ling Apologises for Remarks on Contempt of Court Bill", 15 August 2016.

30. Channel NewsAsia, "Lee Wei Ling Apologises for Attacking Bill on Contempt of Court", 14 August 2016.

31. *Straits Times*, "How the Saga Unfolded", 11 April 2016.

32. Rachel Au-Yong, "Low Thia Khiang Beats Chen Show Mao in Workers' Party Polls to Retain Secretary-General Post", *Straits Times*, 30 May 2016.

33. Rachel Au-Yong, "What Challenge to Low Thia Khiang Means", *Straits Times*, 31 May 2016.

34. Lim Yan Liang, "Low Thia Khiang Dismisses Talk of Split, Says WP Stronger after Party Election", *Straits Times*, 2 June 2016.

35. Rachel Au-Yong, "Leadership Succession Plans in Place: Low", *Straits Times*, 30 May 2016.

36. Ibid.

37. Chong Zi Liang and Rachel Au-Yong, "Workers' Party to Elect New Exec Council on Sunday", *Straits Times*, 27 May 2016.

38. *Today*, "End of WP Treasurer Tenure in Accordance with Terms of My Appointment: Chen Show Mao", 12 September 2016.

39. Chong Zi Liang, "Chen Show Mao Quits as Workers' Party's Treasurer; Still in Exco", *Straits Times*, 12 July 2016.

40. May Chen, "Olympics: Joseph Schooling's Coronation Complete as He Wins Singapore's First Gold", *Straits Times*, 13 August 2016.

41. Tommy Koh, "Small and Successful Nations Climb to Top of the League", *Straits Times*, 16 October 2016.

42. Kenneth Paul Tan, "Meritocracy and Elitism in a Global City: Ideological Shifts in Singapore", *International Political Science Review* 29, no. 1 (2008): 7–27.

43. Chua Siang Yee, "Para-athletes Get Standing Ovation from the House", *Straits Times*, 13 August 2016.

44. For examples, see *My Paper*, "1st Primary School to Accept Deaf Pupils to Be Revealed", 21 September 2016; William Wan, "Should We be Wary of a Heightened Sense of Entitlement?", *Straits Times*, 13 August 2016; Olivia Ho and Clement Yong, "WSQ Course on Effective Communication Gets F Mark", *Straits Times*, 14 June 2016; Chua Siang Yee, "Ageism Complaints Down but More Can be Done: Experts", *Straits Times*, 13 August 2016; *Straits Times*, "Foreign Views and Speakers' Corner: MHA Replies", 20 June 2016; AsiaOne, "Most Singaporeans Try to Live out Multiracial Ideals but Racism Still a Problem: CNA-IPS survey", 19 August 2016.

45. Amir Hussain, "Singaporeans Want 'Compassionate Meritocracy' ", *Today*, 26 August 2016.

46. Robin Chan, "Rich-Poor Gap Not Caused by Recent Growth Strategies: DPM Tharman", *Straits Times*, 24 August 2013.

47. Yuen Sin, "S'pore in 2035: Inclusive and Innovative", *Straits Times*, 31 May 2016.

48. Amelia Teng, "MOE to Get Two New Acting Ministers", *Straits Times*, 29 September 2016.

49. Speech by Tharman Shanmugaratnam, 17 September 2014 <http://www.mof.gov.sg/news-reader/articleid/1426/parentId/59/year/2014?category=Speeches>.

50. Siau Ming En, "Adopt 'Meritocracy Through Life', Tharman Urges S'pore", *Today*, 18 September 2014.

51. Ministry of Finance, "Singapore Budget 2016", 2016 <http://www.singaporebudget.gov.sg/budget_2016/>.

52. Calvin Yang, "5-year Plan to Revamp Adult Education Sector", *My Paper*, 4 November 2016.

53. Nicholas Yong, "PSLE Scoring System to Undergo Major Revamp in 2021", Yahoo news, 13 July 2016.

54. Sandra Davie, "New PSLE Grading Aims to Reduce Rivalry", *My Paper*, 14 July 2016.

55. Ng Jing Yng, "Heng: Bold Changes Needed in Education", *Today*, 7 March 2015.

56. Sandra Davie, "Tweaking Scoring System Unlikely to Have Much Impact Unless Mindsets Change Too", *Straits Times*, 14 July 2016.

57. Linette Lim, "Singaporean Workers and Firms Face Challenges from Globalisation and Technological Disruptions: PM Lee", Channel NewsAsia, 26 October 2015.

58. Linette Lai, "New Tripartite Council to Steer Skills Drive", *Straits Times*, 24 May 2013.

59. Yasmine Yahya, "Singapore Retains No. 2 Competitiveness Spot", *Straits Times*, 29 September 2016.

60. Joanna Seow, "Employment Shrinks in Q3, Axe Falls Mainly on Foreigners", *My Paper*, 28 October 2016.

61. Kenneth Lim, "Temasek Portfolio Shrinks 9% in 2016; First Negative Return Since 2009", *Business Times*, 7 July 2016.

62. Lynette Khoo, "Negative News on Economy Raises Concerns, Hurting Buying Sentiment", *Business Times*, 30 October 2016.

63. "It's Official: Singapore Malls Are Dead, as Occupancy Reaches its Lowest Level in 10 Years", *Vulcan Post*, 2 November 2016.

64. Chuang Peck Ming, "Retrenchments Likely to Go Up This Year: Lim Swee Say", *Business Times*, 8 November 2016.

65. Tang See Kit, "No Significant Pick-up in Singapore's GDP Growth in Near Term: MAS", Channel NewsAsia, 25 October 2016.

66. Chia Yan Min, "What Ails Singapore's Economy?", *Straits Times*, 30 October 2016.

67. Neo Chai Chin, "No Economic Crisis, Long-Term Plan to Fix S'pore Economy Set in Motion: PM Lee", *Today*, 1 November 2016.

68. Leslie Shaffer, "Singapore Underlines Energy Hub Status by Joining Key Oil Group", CNBC, 24 October 2016.

69. Jacquelyn Cheok, "Firms Need to Forge Customised Swords to Tackle Disruption", *Business Times*, 2 June 2016.

70. Lim, "Singaporean Workers and Firms Face Challenges from Globalisation".

71. Chew Hui Min, "Singapore Budget 2016: 6 Schemes to Help Workers Adapt to Changing Economy", *Straits Times*, 24 March 2016.

72. SPRING Singapore, "Setting the Standard Worldwide: Intelligent City, Smart Nation", 3 August 2015 <https://www.spring.gov.sg/Inspiring-Success/Enterprise-Stories/Pages/Setting-the-standard-worldwide-intelligent-city-Smart-Nation.aspx>.

73. Lester Hio, "Coding Classes for Kids in High Demand", *Straits Times*, 9 March 2016.

74. See, for example, Lester Hio, "Singapore Eyes a Slice of the Artificial Intelligence Pie", *Straits Times*, 21 April 2016; Amit Roy Choudhury, "Singapore to Call Projected $2.82b of Infocomm Technology Tenders", *Business Times*, 24 May 2016; Yasmine Yahya, "Fintech 'Crucial to Singapore's Status as Asian Finance Hub'", *Straits Times*, 19 August 2016; Irene Tham, "Govt Looks to Push E-citizen Services on Mobile Devices", *Straits Times*, 29 April 2016.

75. AsiaOne, "LTA to Take Over All Operating Assets from SMRT from Oct 1", 15 July 2016.

76. Reuters, "Temasek Holdings Set for Deal to Buy Out SMRT: Sources", 18 July 2016.

77. Yasmine Yahya, "What SMRT's Likely Privatisation Means", *Straits Times*, 22 July 2016.

78. See, for example, Adrian Lim, "Train Defects Did Not Pose Safety Risks, Says Khaw", *My Paper*, 13 July 2016; Christopher Tan, "Mysterious Signal Fault Hits Circle Line Again", *Straits Times*, 3 November 2016; Christopher Tan, "East-West Line Worst Performer in First Half of the Year", *My Paper*, 10 November 2016;

"SMRT's 'Long Overdue' Financing Plan Fixes 'Policy Mistake': Workers' Party", Yahoo Singapore, 21 July 2016.

79. Pearl Lee and Lim Yan Liang, "Singapore Was Aware of Terror Cell: Shanmugam", *Straits Times*, 6 August 2016.

80. *Today*, "Attack on Singapore a Matter of When, Not If, says Shanmugam", 23 March 2016.

81. AsiaOne, "6 Arrested in Batam for Plotting to Launch Rockets Aimed at Marina Bay", 5 August 2016.

82. Arlina Arshad, "Ringleader of Little-known Cell GR", *Straits Times*, 6 August 2016.

83. Faris Mokhtar, "SG Secure Can Help Singaporeans Remain Vigilant: Experts", *Straits Times*, 5 May 2016.

84. "Singapore is Safest Country to Do Business In, Says New Pinkerton Index", Reuters, 12 July 2016.

85. Jalelah Abu Baker, "ISIS Threat to Region 'Far Worse' than Earlier Groups", *Straits Times*, 13 July 2016.

86. *Straits Times*, "ISIS Launches First Malay Language Newspaper in South-east Asia; Distribution Includes Singapore: Report", 13 July 2016.

87. AsiaOne, "Singapore Bans ISIS Newspaper Al Fatihin; Gazetted It as Prohibited Publication", 22 July 2016.

88. Reuters, "Threat from Extremist Groups to Southeast Asia Growing: Ng Eng Hen", 1 October 2016.

89. Channel NewsAsia, "Singapore, US Enhance Strategic Partnership", 3 August 2016.

90. Channel NewsAsia, "ASEAN Defence Ministers Sign Joint Declaration on Combating Terrorism", 25 May 2016.

91. Jane Perlez, "Tribunal Rejects Beijing's Claims in South China Sea", *New York Times*, 12 July 2016.

92. "Chinese Social Media Users Lash Out at Singapore Over S China Sea Dispute", *Today*, 23 August 2016.

93. Chong Koh Ping, "China Asks Singapore to 'Respect' its Position on South China Sea Ruling", *Straits Times*, 6 August 2016.

94. "Singapore Embroiled in South China Sea Dispute", *The Middle Ground*, 2 October 2016.

95. "Singapore Accuses Chinese Paper of Fabricating South China Sea Story", Reuters, 27 September 2016.

96. "China Should Make Singapore Pay over South China Sea Dispute, Says PLA Adviser", *Straits Times*, 1 October 2016.

97. Transcript of Minister for Foreign Affairs K Shanmugam's Reply to the Parliamentary Questions, 13 August 2012 <https://www.mfa.gov.sg/content/mfa/overseasmission/phnom_penh/press_statements_speeches/embassy_news_press_releases/2012/201208/Press_13082012.html/>.

98. "NDR 2016: Singapore Must Choose its Own Place to Stand on South China Sea issue, Says PM Lee", Channel NewsAsia, 21 August 2016.

99. Lin Yanqin, "S China Sea dispute: Republic 'Does Not Take Sides but Has Key Interests' to Protect", *Today*, 29 September 2016.

100. Tommy Koh, "China's Perception of Singapore: 4 Areas of Misunderstanding", *Today*, 21 October 2016.

101. Ben Bland, "Mystery Over Seized Singapore Army Vehicles in Hong Kong", *Financial Times*, 25 November 2016.

102. Channel NewsAsia, "SAF Terrex Vehicles Arrive in Singapore after Being Detained in Hong Kong", 30 January 2017.

103. Minnie Chan, "How Singapore's Military Vehicles Became Beijing's Diplomatic Weapon", *South China Morning Post*, 3 December 2016.

104. Seow Bei Yi, "Seized SAF Vehicles: APL Meets HK Customs Again", *Straits Times*, 2 December 2016.

THE THREAT OF TERRORISM AND EXTREMISM: "A Matter of 'When', and Not 'If'"

Kumar Ramakrishna

The Rising ISIS Threat: Physical and Ideological Dimensions

The counterterrorism front proved a busy one for Singapore in 2016. By far the biggest story of the year involved the so-called Batam rocket plot. In August, media reports emerged of a plan by a cell of Indonesian militants associated with the Islamic State of Iraq and Syria (ISIS) to fire a rocket from Batam island — south of Singapore — at the iconic Marina Bay Sands (MBS) complex on Singapore island itself. The five-man cell was colourfully called Katibah Gonggong Rebus (KGR), meaning "Boiled Snails Cell" in Bahasa Indonesia. It appeared to be influenced by the incarcerated extremist cleric Aman Abdurrahman, but operationally directed by a Syria-based Indonesian ISIS militant called Bahrun Naim, also an associate of Aman's, and had intended to launch the projectile from a point on Batam island called Habibie Hill, about seventeen kilometres from Singapore's shoreline and eighteen kilometres from MBS. Investigations revealed that the Batam cell leader, Gigih Rahmat Dewa, had coordinated the planned strike with Bahrun Naim via social media. Planning for the attack reportedly began in October 2015, and in addition to Singapore the cell had intended to attack Indonesian targets such as an international seaport in Batam, shopping malls, and other places in the archipelago using suicide bombers. A month later, Indonesian police reported the arrest of one Leonardus Hutajulu, also linked to the KGR cell, who had apparently planned to seek employment on Sentosa Island, a tourist attraction in Singapore, though it was unclear whether this was linked to the MBS plot. It further emerged that

KUMAR RAMAKRISHNA is Associate Professor, Head of Policy Studies and Coordinator of the National Security Studies Programme in the Office of the Executive Deputy Chairman, S. Rajaratnam School of International Studies, Nanyang Technological University.

Nur Rohman, a suicide attacker who had targeted a police station in July in Solo, Central Java, was also linked to the KGR cell. Some reports suggested that the KGR cell members did possess some technical skills that could have enabled them to build a rocket capable of striking Singapore's MBS from Batam; in any case, the cell may also have relied on expertise brought in from outside Batam by Bahrun Naim. One of Bahrun Naim's protégés, Dodi Suridi, had been able — based on information gleaned from YouTube — to build and successfully test-fire a makeshift rocket launcher employing a plastic tube, potassium nitrate extracted from fertilizer, and other substances. Most analysts, however, expressed scepticism that the KGR cell would have been able to build or easily acquire the military-grade rocket system necessary to be able to hit MBS from Batam, such as the Russian-built Katyusha or Grad, or Chinese-type WS-1E rockets. Still, some observers conceded that a home-made rocket could also have been launched from a boat nearer to the Singapore coastline.[1]

The ISIS threat in 2016 manifested itself not merely in the physical sphere, but ideologically as well. This was driven home on several occasions throughout the year. First, on 20 January, Singaporeans were alerted to the arrests under the Internal Security Act (ISA) of twenty-seven radicalized Bangladeshi foreign workers employed in the local construction sector. They had been arrested between 6 November and 1 December 2015 for being involved in a "closed religious study group" that "subscribed to extremist beliefs and teachings of radical ideologues like" the late al-Qaeda ideologue Anwar al-Awlaki, as well as the extremist ideological output of ISIS — exemplified by its members' support of the Sunni terror group's drive to kill members of the Shia minority sect of Islam. The group had viewed video footage of children being trained in "terrorist military camps" and had in its possession literature graphically demonstrating various methods of "silent killings". While some of the radicalized Bangladeshis had plans to join ISIS in the Middle East, a number also contemplated returning to Bangladesh itself to wage war against the government and had sent donations to domestic extremist groups in that country. While twenty-six of the group's members were repatriated, one was jailed for attempting to flee Singapore illegally on learning of the arrests of other group members.[2]

That was not all. Four months later, in early May, it was reported that another six Bangladeshi workers, purportedly belonging to a group called Islamic State of Bangladesh (ISB) had been detained under the ISA in April. The ISB cell had initially sought to join up with ISIS in the Middle East, but due to the difficulty of travelling there its members had switched plans, now seeking to return to Bangladesh "to topple their government through violence, set up an Islamic State there, and bring it under the self-declared caliphate" of ISIS. The ISB cell leader, Rahman Mizanur, apart from documents on weapons and making explosives, apparently possessed "a significant amount of ISIS and Al-Qaeda radical material that he used to recruit ISB members in Singapore", and had identified specific targets in Bangladesh for liquidation, including "disbelievers", "media peoples", as well as Bangladeshi government and military figures. Significantly, Singapore government leaders noted that while the city-state itself had not figured in ISB targeting plans, Mizanur had expressly indicated that "he would carry out an attack anywhere if he was instructed by ISIS to do so" — and ISIS certainly identified Singapore as a target in several social media posts in 2015.[3]

The worryingly adroit exploitation by ISIS of social media platforms such as Facebook, Twitter, and YouTube to propagate its extremist ideology was evinced just two months later in July, when reports emerged of the arrest of Singaporean ISIS supporter Zulfikar Mohamad Shariff for glorifying the terrorist group online. Zulfikar had been known to be a hardline social activist since the Jemaah Islamiyah (JI) arrests in Singapore of 2001 and 2002. He was founder of the short-lived but controversial website *fateha.com*, and had asserted that the government's geopolitical alignment with the United States and Israel was partly to blame for the JI members' behaviour. Zulfikar had also agitated on behalf of a few Muslim parents for their daughters to be allowed to wear the *tudung*, or headscarf, to school in violation of the common uniform policy, despite the fact that this was not a widely supported position within the Muslim community in Singapore. When his hosting of politicians from the Parti Islam SeMalaysia (PAS) to discuss the *tudung* issue and his own speaking engagements on the same topic across the Causeway instigated police investigations, he decamped to Australia with his family. He was arrested in 2016 for his Facebook postings in support of ISIS beheadings, which also urged fellow Muslims to take up arms in overseas conflict zones as a religious duty. Worryingly, he even planned to start his own training programmes to socialize young Singaporeans into his extremist agenda of replacing Singapore's secular, democratic system with an Islamic state, violently if necessary. He had also started a Facebook page called Al Makhazin Singapore to propagate his ISIS-influenced interpretation of local Muslim issues in Singapore and criticize fellow Muslims who had more sober views. In the process he had built up a Facebook following of a few thousand and was said to have radicalized two Singaporeans into the ultraviolent ISIS worldview, prompting the authorities to act.[4]

The ISIS Threat in Global and Regional Perspective

These developments on the home front very much reflected general trends globally. Throughout 2016, ISIS has been on the strategic defensive in both Iraq and Syria, and its so-called Caliphate, centred in Mosul in Iraq and Raqqa in Syria, has been subjected to tremendous military pressure by an international coalition of military forces led by the United States and Russia and which includes Iraqi and Syrian government troops and pro-government militias. By October 2016, by some estimates, ISIS had lost almost twenty-eight per cent of "strategically significant" territory in both Iraq and Syria since January 2015, six months after it inaugurated the Caliphate at the end of June 2014.[5] This has prompted its leadership to seek other relatively poorly governed and restive zones to establish some sort of *"wilayat"*, or province, to act as alternate fallback positions should the current territorial infrastructure within Iraq and Syria collapse. While some analysts have pointed to areas, particularly within Libya, but also, inter alia, Yemen, Egypt, West Africa, Pakistan and Afghanistan as potential *wilayat*,[6] others have suggested that Southeast Asia, which straddles important sea lines of communication and, importantly, is home to a quarter of the world's Muslim population, could also be another area ISIS planners would logically consider — all the more so as Southeast Asian fighters currently fighting with ISIS may return to the region if ISIS loses critical territorial mass in the Middle East.

In particular, reports suggested that in April 2016 an ISIS *wilayat* was declared in Mindanao in the southern Philippines, the arena of a decades-long insurgency by Muslim separatists agitating for independence from a central Christian government in Manila. Furthermore, some of these separatist entities — such as the Abu Sayyaf Group (ASG) — have had links with transnational terrorist networks such as al-Qaeda and JI in the not too distant past. One reason the southern Philippines appears to have become "the fulcrum of IS activity" in the region is that Santoso, the leader of the East Indonesian Mujahidin network operating in Poso, Central Sulawesi, who had pledged allegiance to ISIS, was killed in July. Hence the titular leader of the ISIS groups in the southern Philippines and, by implication, potentially the region, may well be Isnilon Hapilon, a senior ASG leader who himself has pledged allegiance to ISIS. There have been reports that Arabs, Uighurs from Xinjiang in China, and even Caucasians have begun arriving in Mindanao,[7] while Indonesian militants who have been thwarted in their plans to travel to Syria to fight have also turned eastwards towards Mindanao instead, joining up with their Philippine counterparts and triggering concerns about "cross-border violence".[8] Apart from the ASG there have been a number of other violent

Islamist groups that have sprung up in Mindanao that have declared support for ISIS, including Ansar Khalifah Sarangani, Khilafa Islamiyah Mindanao, the so-called Maute group, and Ansar al Khilafah — the latter two prompting particular concern amongst Philippine security officials.[9]

Little wonder that IHS Jane's Terrorism and Insurgency Center went so far as to declare that "it is only a matter of time before ISIS controls swathes of southern Philippines with its base on Mindanao, the country's second-largest island with a population of 20 million".[10] The residual vulnerability of the southern Philippines — taken together with ISIS-orchestrated strikes on the Jakarta business district in January 2016 in which eight people, including four militants, were killed;[11] as well as on a nightclub in Puchong, near Kuala Lumpur in late June, injuring eight people; and a raft of other smaller-scale incidents in both countries over the course of the year — have not been lost on the Singapore authorities.[12] In March, Home Affairs and Law Minister K. Shanmugam, responding to the ISIS-orchestrated attacks on the Brussels international airport and nearby subway that killed more than thirty-one people, argued that this incident showed just how difficult it was to protect cities from terrorist attacks, as Brussels had been attacked despite having been on the highest state of alert. Hence, he assessed that realistically speaking an attack on Singapore "was a matter of 'when' and not 'if' ".[13] Shanmugam subsequently pointed to three groups that could pose a threat to Singapore: "battle-hardened" returning fighters from Iraq and Syria; "those freed from detention but who still harbour radical inclinations"; and those radicalized online by "ISIS propaganda".[14]

A Comprehensive Response: SGSecure

Following a review of the situation, in September the Singapore government announced a comprehensive strategy to cope with the intensifying ISIS threat: SGSecure. Launched by Prime Minister Lee Hsien Loong on 24 September, SGSecure is described on its official website in the following manner:

> It is a national movement to sensitize, train and mobilize the community to play a part to prevent and deal with a terrorist attack. It is a call to action for everyone to unite and safeguard our way of life. The intent of terrorists is to inject fear and weaken the psychological resilience and social fabric of our society. *This is why the cornerstone of our counter-terrorism strategy must be the strengthening of community vigilance, cohesion and resilience.* We can all do our part to keep Singapore safe and secure. [emphasis mine][15]

SGSecure — which builds upon the existing Community Engagement Programme (CEP) inaugurated in 2005, that sought to strengthen inter-communal bonds ahead of crises[16] — is spearheaded by the Ministry of Home Affairs (or Home Team) but with the support of other agencies, including the Singapore Armed Forces (SAF). The SGSecure movement is built on the three pillars of "vigilance, cohesion and resilience". These three pillars are in turn encapsulated in the corresponding slogans: "Stay Alert", "Stay United", and "Stay Strong".[17]

SGSecure and the Physical Dimension

SGSecure deals with the physical threat of ISIS terrorism by, first and foremost, significantly ramping up security force counterterrorist capabilities. What seems clear is that the ISIS-orchestrated attacks in Paris on 13 November 2015 that killed 130 people, involving urban swarming tactics by small, fast-moving teams of suicide attackers, has shaped the threat perception of local security agencies.[18] The Home Team, for instance, by June 2016 had retrained elements of the Singapore Police Force (SPF) in enhanced security response capabilities and deployed them in Emergency Response Teams (ERTs). These units are "specially trained in counter-assault skills and equipped with weapons to deal with armed threats quickly to minimise the number of casualties", and engage in "high-visibility patrols at locations with heavy human traffic, such as retail malls and their vicinities", so as to serve as "deterrence against would-be attackers and criminals". ERTs would, in a terrorist assault, "be the first to respond to the situation".[19]

Like the Home Team, the SAF has also responded to the intensified ISIS threat by fine-tuning its counterterrorist capabilities. A month after the Home Team unveiled its ERTs, the Ministry of Defence announced the creation of a new Army Deployment Force (ADF) to support Home Team units who would be the first to respond to a terrorist attack, although there may be scenarios where both the SAF and Home Team units may have to respond simultaneously in multiple locales — as happened in Paris. The ADF is a "battalion-sized unit comprising highly-trained regulars with niche capabilities, able to respond to terrorist threats in an urban setting", and coordinating its operations with "other SAF task forces such as the Special Operations Task Force (SOTF) and the Island Defence Task Force (IDTF)".[20] The general concept is that of "three rings": Within the first, innermost ring, "special forces" — such as the ERTs and the SOTF — will respond to "direct-shooter threats". In the outer second ring, the ADF will form a cordon to contain the terrorists, while in the outermost third ring, the day after the attack, full-time national servicemen and NSmen will be deployed in "confidence patrols in Singapore for all the soft targets [and] to restore the confidence of the public".[21] These concepts were integrated and operationalized in Singapore's biggest-ever counterterrorism exercise, in October, involving 3,200 personnel from the Home Team and the SAF. During the exercise, joint teams of police and soldiers were sent to more than 360 locations, such as "public transport hubs, shopping malls, residential areas and immigration checkpoints" in response to reports of an "imminent threat" to Singapore following "bomb attacks" in the region.[22] Under the SGSecure framework, counterterrorism coordination between Home Team and SAF units will be further enhanced technologically, as the Defence Science and Technology Agency will set up a National Security Centre for this purpose.[23]

It has not been forgotten moreover that kinetic measures are only part of the SGSecure response to the physical ISIS threat. As discussed, community vigilance and resilience are also part of the mix. In this connection, Prime Minister Lee, in inaugurating the SGSecure movement in September, observed that the ideal is that Singaporeans would — through more extensive participation in various emergency preparedness and crisis response initiatives organized by the Singapore Civil Defence Force and the People's Association — understand and embrace their threefold roles in a terrorist situation and its immediate aftermath:

> So, I think we all have a part, either to be a *Prepared Citizen*, you know what to do for yourself, for your family. Or an *Active Responder*, you know how to help others if there's a crisis. Or to be a *Mobiliser*, to spread the message, to get people to understand that this is important, to work with people to bring them together at a time when there will be a lot of stress and people will be pulled apart.[24]

As of September, 2,700 residents and volunteers had been trained in emergency response skills in case of a terrorist incident; the aim is to ensure residents in all of Singapore's constituencies are similarly trained by 2018.[25]

SGSecure and the Counter-Ideological Dimension

As noted, amongst the pillars of SGSecure is community cohesion. Prime Minister Lee observed in his September speech that racial and religious harmony remained central to globalized, multicultural Singapore's security and success, and that this was something the likes of ISIS would likely target:

> Our problem will continue. Terrorism threats are not going to disappear for quite a long time and we must expect the terrorists to continue to

attack and to plan to attack Singapore. *They are targeting not just our physical safety, but the fabric of our society.* When we are confronted with something like this, we can respond in two ways. Either with fear, cowed, hankered down, pretend nothing is happening, pretend that the threats do not exist, and hope that the troubles will pass us by. Or we can stand up, look the problem straight in the face, understand the dangers we face, know what we can do, do what we can, now and continuing into the future, and make sure that if something does happen, we are ready. [emphasis mine]

In this respect it is clear that one of the initiatives of SGSecure is to strengthen the social fabric against the ideologically virulent extremists online, or, for that matter, the real-world appeal of ISIS ideologues. At one level, Muslim religious leaders and the community have been periodically reminded "to stand up strongly against extremist views that could undermine the peace of the country" and to alert "the authorities to any extremist idea or information".[26] Furthermore, in a significant bid to prevent Singaporeans being radicalized by extremist religious preachers — whether local or foreign — it was announced in August that the Asatizah Recognition Scheme (ARS),[27] first introduced in 2005, will be made compulsory for all teachers of Islam from January 2017. Currently 80 per cent of all Islamic religious teachers in Singapore are registered, but local Muslim leaders "had proposed ways to make the scheme stricter, amid reports of Singaporeans radicalized by extremist ideology". To this end the Islamic Religious Council of Singapore (MUIS) will work with the Asatizah Recognition Board and the Singapore Islamic Scholars and Religious Teachers Association to make the ARS mandatory, although private freelance teachers not currently registered — some of whom have apparently been teaching the faith for decades — would be given a year's grace to obtain "at least a diploma in Islamic studies from a recognised institution".[28]

In a parallel and not altogether unrelated development, a month earlier Yaacob Ibrahim, Minister-in-charge of Muslim Affairs, had asked MUIS to explore the possibility of setting up an Islamic college in Singapore to offer tertiary-level training for religious leaders. Yaacob, while conceding that "the various Islamic universities in the Middle East and the region have served us well", nevertheless maintained that Singapore's needs were such that "there is a need for home-grown religious leaders anchored in our local multi-racial, multi-religious context and attuned to the concerns of our community in the ever changing global environment".[29] This is especially so, as some foreign religious teachers and institutions had been found to have promoted a rather parochial interpretation of the faith that did not take into account Singapore's "multiracial context". Instead, such teachings promoted "separation between believers and non-believers", whilst condemning those who practised other faiths, and sometimes even those who practised the same faith but in a different style. In short, as Prime Minister Lee pointed out in August, the "practices and customs" advocated by such narrow religious interpretations would quite simply "cause grave harm in Singapore".[30] This highlights the underappreciated dangers of what some analysts call "non-violent" extremism — identifying, understanding, and coping with which may well prove to be a key challenge for Singapore in the year — and possibly even years — ahead, as we shall see below.

Two Key Challenges

Generating Greater Situational Awareness

Going forward it is envisaged that with the impending decline of the ISIS strategic presence in the Middle East and the looming threat of returning Southeast Asian fighters to the region, likely centred in the incipient *wilayat* in the southern Philippines, Singapore would likely face two challenges on the terrorism and extremism front. First, as far as dealing with the physical threat of ISIS and its regional affiliates is concerned, one challenge the national SGSecure movement is likely to have to confront is that of generating greater levels of situational awareness amongst a public that has not experienced a terrorist attack in decades. After the MacDonald House bombing by Indonesian saboteurs that killed three people at the height of *Konfrontasi* with Indonesia in March 1965, the most significant terrorist incidents that have occurred in Singapore were in the early 1970s, involving small-scale bombings by splinter factions of the Communist Party of Malaya, whose peak of terrorist activity had been in the 1950s; the Laju ferry hijack episode of 1974 involving Palestinian and Japanese left-wing revolutionary militants; and the hijacking of Singapore Airlines flight SQ117 in 1991 by Pakistani militants. Since then, while there was the close shave of the foiled JI plot of December 2001, the Singaporean authorities have thus far kept the country safe from attacks.[31] This has created what some commentators have described as the "paradox of success", because "the Government has been doing such a good job of preventing attacks since then that Singaporeans are inured to the threat". Professor David Chan alluded to the worrying results of this paradox: Drawing on his own recent experience in 2016, he recalled noticing an "unattended bag left near an escalator at the Harbourfront Ferry Terminal", and although "there was a considerable crowd, no one had reported it". He explained that research had shown that when there are more people around, "the impetus to take responsibility and do something is reduced", because, in his words, "The responsibility is diffused and you begin to wonder: Is it my job?"[32] Social psychologists refer to this as the "bystander effect".[33] Chan's advice to the public is to be aware of and to consciously make the effort to overcome the bystander effect, because if they do they may be able to "prevent something", if the need arises.[34]

Countering Non-Violent Extremism

However, it is on the counter-ideological front that a more profound challenge presents itself: detecting and countering what some have called non-violent extremism. The British counter-extremism think tank, the Quilliam Foundation, for instance, has long argued that certain groups motivated by a political — if not necessarily violent — understanding of Islam, such as Hizb-ut-Tahrir, Jamaat-e-Islami, and the Muslim Brotherhood, can be problematic for societal cohesion. This is because despite their formal non-violent agendas, the uncompromising, adversarial us-versus-them theme embedded in their public messages can nevertheless "create a 'mood music' conducive to acts of terrorism"; hence, Qulliam recommended that the "harmful aspects of their work and ideology should correspondingly be identified, challenged and tackled".[35] The Quilliam stance appears to have relevance for Singapore. As early as 19 January 2016, Minister Shanmugam noted that "Singaporeans as a whole are becoming more religious" and that influences from the "Middle East have had an impact on our Muslim population as well". More precisely, he worried that some "younger Muslims feel that we should not wish Christians Merry Christmas or Hindus Happy Deepavali", while some "groups preach that it is wrong for Muslims to recite the National Pledge, sing the National Anthem and serve National Service", as such practices "would contradict the Muslim faith". In short, he observed that the Muslim community was growing "somewhat distant" from the rest of the society.[36]

Such anxieties appeared to crystallize in the Radio Hang affair seven months later. On 19 August two Singaporeans were detained under the ISA because it was found that they had become radicalized after listening to Radio Hang, a Batam-based radio station devoted to religious programming, and whose coverage included southern Malaysia, the Riau islands, and Singapore. While it had been in existence for a long time, some Singaporean Muslim scholars observed that the owner of the station had apparently become "influenced by the ideas of a puritanical Indonesian scholar Abdul Hakim Abdat in the mid-90s and decided to start airing" his lectures. The station had since then become known for "promoting religious scholars from a puritanical sect of Islam".[37] In particular it transpired that while Radio Hang's "teachings may not directly encourage violence, they ask believers to stay apart from non-Muslims and Muslims who don't share their views, and this is a slippery slope". Even Batam-based Muslim listeners had criticized the station "for divisive leanings" that, inter alia, "say Muslims should isolate themselves to maintain their purity".[38] Hence the concern was that in the context of a multireligious society like Singapore, the "exclusivist preachings" put out by Radio Hang, "even if they don't preach violence overtly", could nevertheless influence people to be "less tolerant and more receptive of violent preachings".[39] In like vein, certain foreign Muslim preachers with a wide following globally — such as the Indian national Zakir Naik — have also been viewed with concern. Naik, whose teachings include assertions that it is wrong for Muslims to wish Christians "Merry Christmas", because doing so "means that such Muslims agree with Christians that Jesus was the only begotten son of God", have also been regarded by local Muslim observers as possessing dubious relevance for the Singaporean context. Local Muslim scholar Syed Farid Alatas, for instance, has in this respect also echoed the Quilliam line of a "slippery slope" between "non-violent extremism" and "terrorism", citing the apparent influence of Naik on two of the Bangladeshi militants who attacked the Holey Artisan Bakery in Dhaka in July.[40]

The challenge, however, is that not everyone agrees on what "non-violent extremism" means. Radio Hang, for example, is seen by some avid local Muslim listeners as a respectable radio station merely promoting religious faith, and they have expressed concern online that a link has been made between the station's messaging and ISIS.[41] More fundamentally, there appears to be an ongoing contemporary contest for the hearts and minds of Singapore's Muslim community as to what being a Muslim in Singapore means. The key question appears to be: Is an Islam that is contextualized to Singapore's multicultural context acceptable, or is an Islam that is stripped of contextual nuance and theologically synchronized with the Middle Eastern version the only true, authentic faith? If the latter position trumps the former, then social distancing between the Muslim community and non-Muslim communities in Singapore would not only be regarded as not "extremist" but would actually represent a religious obligation. Moreover, the theological homilies of the likes of Zakir Naik and Radio Hang would in fact typify the "true" mainstream interpretation. If such a view takes greater hold, then such local community initiatives as the ARS, the Singapore Muslim Identity project,[42] and plans for an Islamic college customized to Singapore's needs would ironically be seen as deviant from the "norm". Worse, such a narrow theological narrative would readily complement the more violent ideological pronouncements of ISIS and its affiliates, as several commentators have pointed out, referencing the evolving situation in neighbouring Malaysia and Indonesia.[43] Exacerbating matters would be emergent Islamophobia among the small number of non-Muslim Singaporeans with the tendency to lump genuinely soul-searching and ordinary devout Singaporean Muslims with ISIS, and behaving reprehensibly in response. Minister Shanmugam decried the fact that some non-Muslims had scribbled "Islam murderers" at a Bukit Panjang bus stop and on a toilet seat in Jurong Point mall.[44]

Conclusion

Going into 2017, beyond dealing with the physical ISIS threat, effectively engaging with the non-violent ideologues and not just the violent extremists of ISIS — whilst discouraging Islamophobic sentiments amongst non-Muslims — would appear to be the crucial counter-ideological tasks that the designers of SGSecure and related community initiatives should not ignore. In any case, the centre of gravity of the current counterterrorism struggle against ISIS — winning the hearts and minds of the Singapore Muslim community — is not beyond influence. In essence it involves fully mining the rich history of Islamic civilization with a view to extracting counter-narrative themes that are digestible for a largely younger, social media-savvy public. The central counter-message should be simple: A major reason that Islam is the world's fastest growing religion at this point in time[45] is precisely that down the centuries it has been what Khaled Abou El Fadl calls a vital, hugely adaptable *lived* Islam, rather than the *imagined*, decontextualized, monochrome version promulgated by the non-violent extremist ideologues and their violent cousins.[46] As another observer argues, "the very reason that Islam took wings and spread so rapidly is because it could adapt itself to different cultures", and that the worldwide "multiplicity of expressions" of this dynamic faith, from Europe to Asia, evinces "the strength and beauty of Islam".[47] Hence the aforementioned community initiatives — from a compulsory ARS to a local Islamic college — promoting a modern, progressive faith that meshes well with a globalized, multicultural Singapore, makes total sense. However, this is an argument that must not be confined to dry theological arenas, but rather brought into the mainstream and pushed out across all channels as vigorously as possible. Countering extremism and terrorism in Singapore in 2017 and beyond, therefore, will essentially be about winning this war of ideas. To be sure, this will prove a task that will likely last a generation. This is one fight, nevertheless, that right-thinking Singaporeans of all persuasions dare not lose.

Notes

1. Francis Chan and Wahyudi Soeriaatmadja, "Plotter's Plan: Strike Singapore from Batam Hill", *Straits Times*, 28 September 2016 <http://www.straitstimes.com/asia/se-asia/plotters-plan-strike-spore-from-batam-hill>; Francis Chan, "Suspect in Foiled Marina Bay Rocket Attack Planned to Get Job on Sentosa", *Straits Times*, 6 September 2016 <http://www.straitstimes.com/asia/se-asia/suspect-planned-to-get-job-on-sentosa>; Arlina Arshad and Lee Seok Hwai, "Indonesian Police Foil Rocket Attack Plot on Marina Bay; Singapore Steps Up Security", *Straits Times*, 10 August 2016 <http://www.straitstimes.com/asia/se-asia/indonesian-police-arrest-six-batam-militants>; Arlina Arshad, "IT Guy Who Plotted Terror from Batam", *Straits Times*, 14 August 2016 <http://www.straitstimes.com/singapore/terror-in-batam-it-guy-who-plotted-terror-from-batam>; Jeremy Koh, "'Military-Grade Rocket Needed' to Hit S'pore from Batam", *Straits Times*, 6 August 2016 <http://www.straitstimes.com/singapore/military-grade-rocket-needed-to-hit-spore-from-batam>; V. Arianti, "Gigih Rahmat Dewa: The IT Jihadist in Batam", *Counter-Terrorist Trends and Analysis* 8, no. 11 (November 2016): 11–14.
2. Lee Min Kok, "27 Radicalised Bangladeshis Arrested in Singapore under Internal Security Act: MHA", *Straits Times*, 20 January 2016 <http://www.straitstimes.com/singapore/courts-crime/27-radicalised-bangladeshis-arrested-in-singapore-under-internal-security-act>.
3. Zakir Hussain, "Bangladeshis Plotting Terror Attacks Held under ISA", *Straits Times*, 4 May 2016 <http://www.straitstimes.com/singapore/bangladeshis-plotting-terror-attacks-held-under-isa>.
4. "Singaporean Man Detained under Internal Security Act", Channel NewsAsia, 29 July 2016 <http://www.channelnewsasia.com/news/singapore/singaporean-man-detained/2996896.html>; Kumar Ramakrishna, "From Radicalism to Extremism: The Case of Zulfikar Mohamad Shariff", Channel NewsAsia, 1 August 2016 <http://www.channelnewsasia.com/news/singapore/from-radicalism-to/3002318.html>.
5. Jenny Awford, "New Setback for ISIS as it is Revealed They Have Lost a QUARTER of the Territory They Seized since 2015", *Daily Mail*, 9 October 2016 <http://www.dailymail.co.uk/news/article-3829345/ISIS-lost-quarter-territory.html>.
6. Brian L. Steed, *ISIS: An Introduction and Guide to the Islamic State* (Santa Barbara: ABC-CLIO, 2016), pp. 145–46.
7. Bilveer Singh and Kumar Ramakrishna, "Islamic State's Wilayah Philippines: Implications for Southeast Asia", *RSIS Commentary*, CO1687, 21 July 2016 <https://www.rsis.edu.sg/rsis-publication/rsis/co16187-islamic-states-wilayah-philippines-

implications-for-southeast-asia/#.WEJkbUtVpPo>; Francis Chan, "Indonesia Terror Cell Was Planning Dec Holiday Strike", *Straits Times*, 1 December 2016, p. A8.

8. Kanupriya Kapoor and Augustinus Beo Da Costa, "Some Indonesians 'Joining pro-Islamic State Groups in Philippines'", Reuters, 25 October 2016 <http://news.abs-cbn.com/news/10/25/16/some-indonesians-joining-pro-islamic-state-groups-in-philippines>.

9. Thomas Koruth Samuel, *Radicalisation in Southeast Asia: A Selected Case Study of Daesh in Indonesia, Malaysia and the Philippines* (Kuala Lumpur: Southeast Asia Regional Centre for Counter-Terrorism, 2016), pp. 100–103; "Philippine Troops Shell ISIS-Linked Militants", *Straits Times*, 28 November 2016, p. A11; Raul Dancel, "Manila Put on Highest Terror Alert in 16 Years", *Straits Times*, 2 December 2016, p. A6.

10. David Harris, "ISIS Sets Eyes on Creating 'New State'", *The Clarion Project*, 1 December 2016 <http://www.clarionproject.org/analysis/isis-sets-eyes-creating-new-'state'>.

11. Saifulbahri Ismail, "Indonesia Jails Bomb Maker Linked to Jakarta Attacks", Channel NewsAsia, 20 October 2016 <http://www.channelnewsasia.com/news/asiapacific/indonesia-jails-bomb-maker-linked-to-jakarta-attacks/3221424.html>.

12. Akil Yunus, "Local IS Fighter Claims Movida Bombing is 'First Attack on Malaysian Soil'", *The Star*, 4 July 2016 <http://www.thestar.com.my/news/nation/2016/07/04/local-is-fighter-claims-movida-bombing-is-first-attack-on-malaysian-soil/>.

13. "Attack on Singapore a Matter of When, Not If, Says Shanmugam", *Today*, 24 March 2016 <http://www.todayonline.com/singapore/unless-we-turn-city-prison-not-possible-counter-every-terror-attack-shanmugam>.

14. Chong Zi Liang, "ISIS Terror Threat Greater Now, Says Shanmugam", *Straits Times*, 3 December 2016, p. A6.

15. For an overview of SGSecure, please see Ministry of Home Affairs, "SGSecure: Overview" <https://www.sgsecure.sg/Pages/overview.aspx>.

16. Faris Mokhtar, "SG Secure Can Help Singaporeans Remain Vigilant: Experts", Channel NewsAsia, 5 May 2016 <http://www.channelnewsasia.com/news/singapore/sg-secure-can-help/2756276.html>.

17. See ibid. for more information.

18. Kumar Ramakrishna, "The Paris Attacks: Ramping Up of ISIS 'Indirect Strategy'?", *RSIS Commentary*, CO 15248, 17 November 2015 <https://www.rsis.edu.sg/rsis-publication/rsis/co15248-the-paris-attacks-ramping-up-of-isis-indirect-strategy/#.WEvo-UtVpPo>.

19. Mabelle Yeo, "Emergency Response Teams Set to Battle Terror Threat with Quick, Direct Response", Home Team News, 22 July 2016 <https://www.hometeam.sg/article.aspx?news_sid=20160722oiQcLevKo8Xv>.

20. Faris Mokhtar, "New SAF Unit to Boost Singapore's Response to Terror Attacks", Channel NewsAsia, 30 June 2016 <http://www.channelnewsasia.com/news/singapore/new-saf-unit-to-boost/2917980.html>.

21. Ibid.; Ng Jun Sen, "Army Chief: How SAF Will Deal with Counter-Terrorism", *New Paper*, 2 July 2016 <http://www.tnp.sg/news/singapore-news/army-chief-how-saf-will-deal-counter-terrorism>.

22. Ng Huiwen, "3,200 Personnel Mobilised in Islandwide Anti-Terror Drill", *Straits Times*, 18 October 2016, p. A6.

23. Mokhtar, "New SAF Unit".

24. Prime Minister's Office, "PM Lee Hsien Loong at Official Launch of SGSecure", 24 September 2016 <http://www.pmo.gov.sg/mediacentre/pm-lee-hsien-loong-official-launch-sgsecure>.

25. Ibid.

26. Ng Huiwen, "Muslim Religious Leaders, Worshippers Have to Stand Up against Extremist Views: Yaacob", *Straits Times*, 12 September 2016 <http://www.straitstimes.com/singapore/religious-leaders-worshippers-have-to-stand-up-against-extremist-views-yaacob>.

27. The Asatizah Recognition Scheme (ARS) was set up to enhance the standing of Singapore's Islamic teachers and to serve as a reliable resource for the Muslim community.

28. Pearl Lee and Nur Asyiqin Mohamad Salleh, "Islamic Teachers Must Be Registered from Jan 1", *Straits Times*, 22 August 2016 <http://www.straitstimes.com/singapore/islamic-teachers-must-be-registered-from-jan-1>.

29. Rachelle Lee, "Yaacob Asks MUIS to Study Feasibility of Setting up Islamic College in Singapore", Channel NewsAsia, 15 July 2016 <http://www.channelnewsasia.com/news/singapore/yaacob-asks-muis-to-study/2960744.html>.

30. Lee and Salleh, "Islamic Teachers Must be Registered".

31. *Why the ISA?* (Singapore: Ministry of Home Affairs, 2002), pp. 7–10.

32. Danson Cheong, "How Prepared is Singapore for an Attack?", *Sunday Times*, 20 November 2016, p. B2.

33. Melissa Burkley, "Why Don't We Help? Less is More, at Least When it Comes to Bystanders", *Psychology Today*, 4 November 2009 <https://www.psychologytoday.com/blog/the-social-thinker/200911/why-don-t-we-help-less-is-more-least-when-it-comes-bystanders>.

34. Cheong, "How Prepared is Singapore".

35. The Quilliam Foundation, "Quilliam Welcomes New UK Direction on Extremism", 5 February 2011 <http://www.quilliamfoundation.org/press/quilliam-welcomes-new-uk-direction-on-extremism/>.

36. Kumar Ramakrishna, "Religious Fundamentalism and Social Distancing: A Cause for Concern?" *RSIS Commentary*, CO023, 1 February 2016 <https://www.rsis.edu.sg/rsis-publication/rsis/co023-religious-fundamentalism-and-social-distancing-cause-for-concern/#.WEt7mUtVpPo>.

37. Amanda Lee, "Extremist Ideology a Staple Item on Batam's Radio Hang", *Today*, 20 August 2016 <http://www.todayonline.com/singapore/radio-0>.

38. Lim Yan Liang, "Exclusivist Teachings Could Prime Listeners to ISIS Propaganda", *Straits Times*, 20 August 2016 <http://www.straitstimes.com/singapore/exclusivist-teachings-could-prime-listeners-to-isis-propaganda>.

39. Ibid.

40. Syed Farid Alatas, "The Perils of Non-Violent Extremism", *Malay Mail*, 3 August 2016 <http://www.themalaymailonline.com/what-you-think/article/the-perils-of-non-violent-extremism-syed-farid-alatas>.

41. For a sampling of online opinion, see the "Comments" section of Amanda Lee's *Today* report, "Extremist Ideology a Staple Item on Batam's Radio Hang".

42. Started in 2005, the Singapore Muslim Identity (SMI) project is an attempt to foster a Singaporean Muslim community that is deeply rooted in the precepts of the faith as well as effectively integrated into the wider Singaporean multicultural milieu. Since its inception though there have been concerns raised in some conservative circles that the "SMI is packaged with touches of the 'establishment' views and preferences or that it was a self-correcting effort to align the community with mainstream secular thinking in the larger society". Yusof Sulaiman, "Reflections on the Singapore Muslim Identity", *Karyawan: Professionals for the Community* 9, no. 2 (January 2009): 2–4.

43. Adri Wanto and Abdul Mateen Qadri, "Islamic State: Understanding the Threat in Indonesia and Malaysia", *RSIS Commentary*, CO 15231, 29 October 2015 <https://www.rsis.edu.sg/rsis-publication/rsis/co15231-islamic-state-understanding-the-threat-in-indonesia-and-malaysia/#.WEuXCEtVpPo>.

44. Ramakrishna, "Religious Fundamentalism and Social Distancing".

45. "The Future of World Religions: Population Growth Projections, 2010–2050", Pew Research Center, 2 April 2015 <http://www.pewforum.org/2015/04/02/religious-projections-2010-2050/>.

46. Khaled Abou El Fadl, *The Great Theft: Wrestling Islam from the Extremists* (New York: Harper San Francisco, 2005), pp. 278–79.

47. D. Latifa, interview in Jonas Yunus Atlas, *Halal Monk: A Christian on a Journey through Islam* (Brussels: J. Staats, 2015).

Thailand

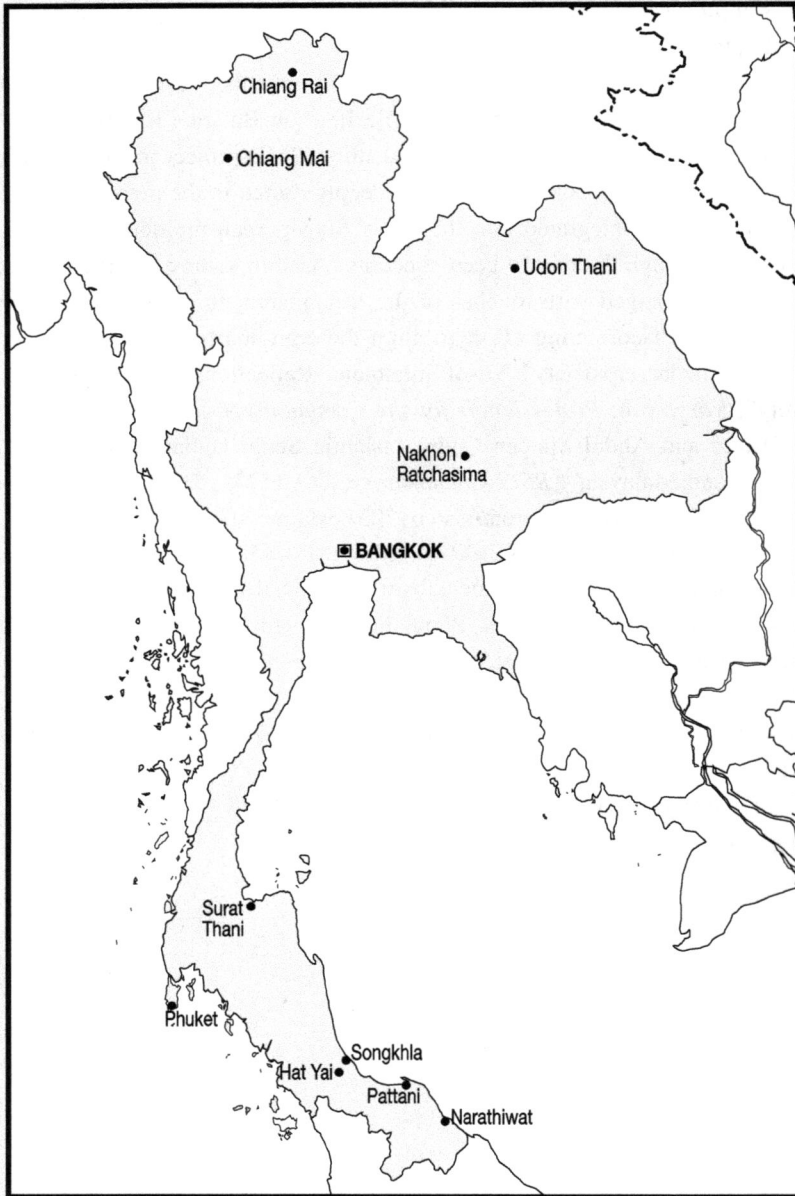

THAILAND:
The Historical and Indefinite Transitions

Chookiat Panaspornprasit

The year 2016 was arguably one of shock and unpredictability for Thailand. No other major event in 2016 was as historically significant as the passing away of His Majesty King Bhumibol Adulyadej (1927–2016) on 13 October 2016 at the age of eighty-nine. He was the beloved King of all Thai people,[1] and the world's longest-serving monarch, reigning for seventy years. His frail health since 2014 had been closely monitored by Thailand's leading medical professionals. The Royal Household Bureau's various announcements on the condition of his health time and again caused concern nationwide and led to many religious ceremonies to wish him a speedy recovery. Once the official announcement of his passing became public knowledge, the whole nation seemed to come to a standstill. Most commuters travelling home that evening shed tears publically without embarrassment while checking the news on social media. Every sector of Thai society agreed that the King's passing was a major historical transition. Once they overcame this sense of great loss, the other prevailing question was what would happen in terms of the royal succession.

Aside from the King's passing, the political landscape in Thailand in 2016 was more pessimistic. Thai society continued to be characterized by polarized contention and other negative political features. The full blossom of democratization was still far from reality, though the draft charter was completed and approved by a nationwide referendum in August 2016. Some argued that Thailand was still in an indefinite transition, while others labelled it a great leap backward. For those with a pessimistic view, the acronym COSTUP would describe the state of affairs

CHOOKIAT PANASPORNPRASIT is Associate Professor in the Department of International Relations, Faculty of Political Science, Chulalongkorn University, Bangkok, Thailand.

in the country in 2016, standing for Corruption, Oppression, Social injustice, Tyranny, Unequal rights or unemployment, and Poverty — representing the rise in political, economic, and social costs confronting the military-led regime, and Thailand in general, in 2016.

The King's Passing: His Enduring Legacy and a Historical Transition

To most Thai people the passing of the revered monarch in October 2016 was so overwhelming that nationwide bereavement and grief ran very high. The "all-in-black" practice was adopted nationwide, governed by different timeframes according to the sector of the country; i.e., the general public, regardless of gender or age, donned black outfits as a sign of mourning for at least thirty days, while the government has decreed that its officials will wear black for a full year. Black fabric was suddenly in short supply due to the unexpected high demand. Some fabric retailers had no idea what to do with all the yellow outfits stocked up in preparation for the annual celebration of the late King's birthday, which falls on 5 December — known as National Father Day.

All government agencies nationwide were expected to fly the national flag at half-mast for thirty days. A total ban has been imposed on daily entertainment activities, both in the hospitality sector and media outlets. Most Thai and foreign language newspapers, websites, and TV stations switched to black and white and toned down their colourful content. Regular television programmes were replaced by repeated national broadcasts, especially of a programme on the history of the monarch and his various contributions to the nation during his reign. The Prayut administration sought Thai society's cooperation in toning down the *Loy Krathong* (the Thai tradition of floating *krathong* on waterways, a tradition believed to dispel bad luck), Christmas, and New Year celebrations.[2] There is no denying that His Majesty King Bhumibol Adulyadej was a multitalented monarch — ruler, developer, philosopher, thinker, musician, environmentalist, composer, sportsman, photographer, to name some of his talents.

His development philosophy, the so-called self-sufficiency economy, has been praised to varying degrees at both the national and international levels. Since his passing, the influx of Thai people into Bangkok from various parts of the country to pay their final respects at the Grand Palace has become a daily phenomenon. At the time of writing, scores of Thai people continued to assemble at an unabated rate at the Grand Palace to pay their respects. The Ministry of Social Development and Human Security, under its campaign called "999 hearts to pay respects to the King", has sponsored the round-trip for a total of 999 hill tribe people from nine different hill tribes in the northern highlands of Thailand to pay their final respects to the late King.[3]

Crown Prince Vajiralongkorn initially informed the military government that he himself would like to join Thai society in mourning for one year; hence, the next King's royal coronation will be postponed to after the royal cremation of the late King.[4] In effect, Privy Council President Prem Tinsulanonda automatically assumed the role of *regent pro tempore* until the proclamation of the new King. On 29 November the President of the National Legislative Assembly (NLA) officially convened an NLA special session in order to invite the Crown Prince to ascend to the throne. He will be formally crowned after the royal coronation, which will be held at a later stage.[5] In early December the Crown Prince ascended to the throne as His Majesty King Maha Vajiralongkorn Bodindradebayavarangkun, or King Rama X of the Chakri Dynasty. So General Prem Tinsulanonda ceased being *regent pro tempore* and was reappointed as the President of the Privy Council.

At the international level, condolences poured in from various leaders around the world.[6] Many Asian leaders came personally to pay their respects at the Grand Palace, including Singapore's Prime Minister Lee Hsien Loong and his wife,[7] Malaysian Prime Minister Najib Razak, Indonesian President Joko Widodo, Myanmar's first civilian President Htin Kyaw, and Philippine President Rodrigo Duterte.

To most Thai people, the month of October is one of remembrance because of the fact that many historic figures passed away in this month; i.e., King Rama IV, King Rama V, the 19th Supreme Patriarch, His Majesty King Bhumibol's mother, and now King Bhumibol himself. It has been widely speculated that the Prayut government will honour the late King with the royal title of "The Great King", the same given to King Rama V. The Culture Ministry has been preparing to publish a volume of about five hundred condolence poems composed by various national artists for nationwide distribution,[8] and other activities have been organized both by state agencies and the private sector in remembrance of the late King. On 22 November, General Prayut Chan-o-cha led the Thai nation in pledging an oath of loyalty to all Kings of the Chakri dynasty.[9]

Referendum on the New Draft Charter: An Indefinite Transition to Democracy?

Democratization and democratic values in Thailand are still under siege. The draft constitution drafted by the Constitution Drafting Committee (CDC) under the leadership of Bowornsak Uwanno was rejected in September 2015 by the now-defunct National Reform Council,[10] raising questions of who Prime Minister Prayut Chan-o-cha, the leader of the National Council for Peace and Order (NCPO), would pick to lead the new CDC. Once it became more or less certain that Meechai Ruchupan would be the "knight on the white horse", criticism — even social uproar — immediately emerged among liberals and reformists. Meechai is well known as an ultra-right conservative constitutional law expert who has served many military junta governments in the past. Once he was officially confirmed as the leader of the new CDC commissioned to draft the new charter for the national referendum scheduled for 7 August 2016, there was speculation over the contents of the new draft.

One of the major contentious issues was Prime Minister Prayut Chan-o-cha's proposal to press ahead with the appointed senate plan, with all members of the NCPO appointed as senators as well.[11] Deputy Prime Minister Wissanu Krea-ngam, who is widely believed to be loyal to the NCPO and was the architect of the 2014 interim charter, defended the proposal.[12] Abhisit Vejjajiva, the Democrat Party leader, together with politicians of other political parties, voiced his opposition to the NCPO's sixteen-point demands, especially the provision dealing with the 220-member appointed Senate.[13] Quite unexpectedly, the military-appointed NLA later proposed increasing the total number of appointed senators to 250, who would be appointed solely by the NCPO.[14] The draft charter also paved the way for the senators to have a role in "selecting the prime minister" in a situation where the elected House of Parliament is unable to agree on a choice of prime minister, which can happen under the German-style mixed-member proportional representation system. This system is meant to prevent the domination of parliament by any one party, and can lead to the formation of a coalition government comprising many weak political parties, making the selection of a prime minister more difficult. Hence, the so-called "outsider prime minister" scenario cannot be ruled out under the draft charter, with the likelihood that General Prayut could be appointed as the outsider prime minister. He has expressed no objection to this special provision.[15] This is why former Prime Minister Chuan Leekpai has severely criticized the draft charter, calling it a backward charter.[16]

The so-called influential five-river political polity — the NCPO, the military regime's cabinet, the NLA, the National Reform Steering Assembly (NRSA), and the CDC — wielded authoritarian power to propose and endorse two more contested initiatives; namely, the regime's twenty-year national strategy plan and the crisis panel. The former is the long-term blueprint for national reform on various fronts, to which subsequent elected civilian governments, regardless of political party, are expected to adhere. Liberal reformists, economists, and political pundits have cast serious doubts on the validity of the logic behind this blueprint. Reform issues in the long term, for instance, are unlikely to remain the same in the future. In other words, this national strategy blueprint may be easily rendered outdated or outpaced by unforeseen issues in the future. The crisis panel — where, again, members are appointed by the NCPO — is a mechanism intended to resolve future political or constitutional crises. The idea is totally unacceptable to democratic and liberal political circles in Thai society. On referendum day, voters were expected to cast their ballots on whether they approved the new draft charter and whether the senate would have a joint role in selecting the next prime minister, an unprecedented proposal to increase the senate's role in choosing the leader of the executive branch.

The controversial contents of the draft charter aside, the process of preparing the referendum and the atmosphere it was conducted in were highly biased. For example, most households nationwide did not receive even a summary of the draft charter, let alone the full text.[17] Negative criticism of the draft charter was forbidden. The military regime banned any movement — for example, the New Democracy Movement — opposed to the controversial draft charter. Still, a group called Civilians Reserving the Right to Reject Results of the Unfair and Not Free Referendum launched a last-minute campaign against it.[18] On the other hand, some pre-recorded orientation programmes, approved by the regime and orchestrated by members of the CDC or the Election Commission, were broadcast on TV to explain the draft charter.[19] Social critics dismissed such programmes as "one-way communication" forcing Thai society to wed the mysterious charter bride.[20] No public or free forum discussion of the draft charter was allowed, out of fear that such forums would sway voters.[21] Prime Minister Prayut himself, however, publicly expressed his total support for the "yes" camp.[22] This tightly controlled referendum process provoked the ire of domestic and international poll watchdogs. The Asian Network for Free Elections (Anfrel) and the Open Forum for Democracy Foundation both complained that the political environment was not conducive for them to conduct referendum monitoring, leading to their decision to withdraw from their mission.[23]

The reaction to the 7 August 2016 referendum was a mixture of anxiety and complacency on the one hand and hopelessness and desperation on the other. The result of the vote turned out to be sixty-one per cent in favour of the draft charter, much to the delight of the NCPO.[24] Shortly after the referendum it was officially announced that the military regime had pledged that the return to democracy would be pursued according to the road map after the relevant laws are complete. However, the political horizon has been clouded by uncertainty after recent conflicting remarks by leading members of the NCPO and the Prime Minister himself.[25]

Section 44 and Other Controversial Issues

Implemented since the May 2014 coup, Section 44 of the interim charter — authorizing the junta leader unlimited power to issue any order he deems appropriate to maintain order and stability — still poses a "clear and present danger" to the democratization process in Thailand. It has given the Prime Minister overwhelming legislative, administrative, and judicial power, regardless of the existence of the NLA, cabinet, and judicial system. Prime Minister Prayut Chan-o-cha has vowed to exercise this section if deemed necessary.[26] What is worrisome to liberals and reformists is that most Thai people are indifferent about the implementation of Section 44.[27] Worse still, government officials at various ministries have considered evoking Section 44 to advance the government's agenda. For example, there was a rumour that a high-ranking official at the Ministry of Commerce had considered resorting to this section as a shortcut measure — to allow Thailand to join the Trans-Pacific Partnership without any prior deliberation at the NLA. In another case, it is widely known that the Ministry of National Resources and Environment is seriously planning to use Section 44 to approve the construction of a controversial coal-powered plant in the South of Thailand, despite the opposition of local residents and the findings of an Environmental and Health Impact Assessment report. Prime Minister Prayut Chan-o-cha has also exercised his special power through Section 44 by sacking the previous Bangkok Metropolitan Administration's Governor — who was directly elected by Bangkok residents — and appointing a new one, who is expected to report directly to the Prime Minister.[28] Above all, it is estimated that the Prime Minister has resorted to using Section 44 as many as 104 times since the putsch in May 2014, an average of almost once a week.[29]

There are other controversial issues. On the role of the media in Thai society, six leading media watchdogs are adamantly opposed to the proposal to establish a central media council, out of fear that the new council would result in both media interference and biased news reporting.[30] Although the military government has put much effort and focus into curbing corrupt practices in Thai society, Thailand is still placed 76 out of 168 countries in Transparency International's Corruption Perceptions Index Report.[31] This ranking is on par with Burkina Faso, Tunisia, and Zambia. A proposal made by one of the NRSA members to increase the salaries of the Prime Minister, Members of Parliament, Senators, and Cabinet Members[32] to the same level as the private sector in order to curb corruption did not appear to find favour with the general public.[33] Beneath all this, the yellow-shirt versus red-shirt polarization still remains. Freedom of speech and expression continue to be suppressed for the sake of "national reconciliation and unity".

The Thai Economy[34]

The economic skies in 2016 were grey and the prospects uncertain. Economist Intelligence Unit (EIU) data showed that in the first three quarters of 2016, Thailand's real GDP growth averaged 3.3 per cent year-on-year.[35] Private consumption and public investment were the key drivers of growth in 2016, with the recovery of consumer sentiment and the implementation of large public infrastructure projects such as the dual rail track and rail upgrading projects. Tourism growth remained strong in 2016, with the number of tourist arrivals — mostly from China — increasing by 13.1 per cent in the third quarter.[36] In the last quarter of the year, tourist arrivals appeared to slow down during the period of mourning for His Majesty King Bhumibol Adulyadej, but it was offset in part by holiday tax breaks on shopping and domestic tourism at the end of the year. EIU analysis predicted that the negative impact of the King's death on domestic demand, particularly private consumption, would be short-lived, and that economic activity would recover relatively quickly in 2017.[37]

However, exports grew by only 0.3 per cent in 2016 due to the sluggish global economy. Household debt ran high, leading to a decline in household consumption, with inflation still on the rise.[38] According to data from the Thai Commerce Ministry, in the first eleven months of 2016 exports had eased 0.05 per cent from the same period in 2015 due to higher global oil prices, which helped lift the prices of Thai commodities and oil-related goods.[39] In more promising news, agriculture rebounded and showed positive growth at 0.9 per cent after recovering from a long and severe drought.[40] Foreign direct investment (FDI) and portfolio flows into Thai assets also continued in the third quarter of 2016, as Thai direct investment abroad expanded.

The Prayut government introduced two important economic measures in 2016. First, as a short-term measure, it approved fresh cash handouts worth thirteen billion baht in order to assist low-income people.[41] Critics doubted that this measure would be efficient or effective. Second, as a longer-term measure, the government launched an ambitious plan to boost the economy to the digital-based 4.0 economy through the so-called fourth industrial revolution. Ten digital-based industries, mainly through the free flow of innovation and information, are involved. In line with these plans, the Prayut government finally replaced the now-defunct Ministry of Information, Communication and Technology with the Ministry of Digital Economy and Society (DE) in September 2016.[42] Dissatisfied with the long-overdue implementation of the ambitious nationwide low-cost broadband Internet, the Prime Minister has removed DE's former permanent secretary as a punitive measure for her inefficient performance.[43] However, this ambitious plan is not without flaws. One main question that needs to be asked is whether Thailand is ready for it.[44] It has also been argued that Thailand still lacks the necessary qualitative and quantitative workforce and infrastructure for digital implementation. Most government agencies at the local level do not have the necessary infrastructure to provide efficient e-government public services. In terms of digital structural reform, the Asia-Pacific manager for the Internet Society has encouraged the military regime to open up Internet communications in order to serve and drive the digital economy,[45] especially in light of the army's recent decision to launch a cyber centre.[46]

The EIU projected a moderate recovery in external demand for Thailand in 2017, supported by rising demand from other ASEAN countries.[47] However, the World Bank highlighted two risks confronting the Thai economy in 2017. The first is the deterioration in global economic prospects following Brexit and the U.S. elections, particularly in the eurozone, which accounts for almost 10 per cent of total Thai exports and 12 per cent of its FDI. The second risk is a rise in Thailand's political uncertainty if ongoing political reforms are postponed or fail to satisfy broad segments of society, which could delay public spending, ongoing economic reforms, and undermine consumer and investor confidence.[48]

Foreign Relations: Dire Efforts to Break the "Isolation"

Thailand's foreign relations were in limbo in 2016 at both the bilateral and multilateral levels. For instance, Thailand's official reaction to the Hague Arbitral Tribunal on the South China Sea dispute was one of sitting on the fence.[49] Thailand clearly cannot afford to damage its close ties with China nor alienate ASEAN. The country's foreign policy orientation was broadly outlined in the keynote address of Thai Prime Minister Prayut Chan-o-cha to the Shangri-La Dialogue on 3 June 2016. In the speech Prayut stated that Asia must build a "new strategic balance" in view of the uncertainty of the post–Cold War multipolar order and the rise of new global challenges such as tensions in the South China Sea and on the Korean Peninsula.[50] In particular he emphasized the need for the international community to help Thailand achieve its own "balance and strength", as that would in turn help to maintain balance within ASEAN and create a new balance in the Asia-Pacific.[51]

As this was Prayut's first major foreign policy speech abroad, the viewpoints expressed in it were dubbed "Thailand's Post-Coup Foreign Policy", a reference to the May 2014 military coup.[52] Under the Yingluck administration, Thailand had maintained its traditional focus on "concentric circles of foreign relations", placing its immediate neighbours as its top priority, followed by the major powers and the broader regional context.[53] Judging by Prayut's rhetoric and the actions taken by his administration, it appears that Thailand has undergone a shift in foreign policy in favour of strengthening bilateral relations with China, instead of its traditional ally, the United States.[54] This is demonstrated by growing Sino–Thai economic ties and military cooperation. Besides conducting joint military exercises, it was also reported that both sides were in talks about building military production facilities in Thailand.[55]

Some political analysts attribute this shift to the U.S. reaction to the military coup, which included the freezing of security and defence aid to Thailand, as well as the scaling back of annual military exercises.[56] However, others point out that following Thailand's national referendum on the new constitution in August 2016, Washington had softened its overall policy towards the Kingdom.[57] Another view holds that Bangkok is not tilting towards China, but rather trying to chart a more omni-directional course by building closer ties with all major powers, including Russia, India, and Japan.[58] The last view seems to echo Prayut Chan-o-cha's rhetoric on "new strategic balance".

A number of initiatives were taken during the year. First and foremost, Thailand kicked off the mega-project called the Asian Cooperation Dialogue (ACD), initially launched during the Thaksin government in 2002. The Thai government hosted the fourteenth ministerial meeting in Bangkok, which focused on the ACD as the hub for medical cooperation.[59] This meeting was the precursor to the second ACD Summit held in Bangkok in early October 2016.[60] A few observations should be noted. One is that the fundamental objectives of this second ACD Summit deviated from its original focus. Instead of the originally planned agenda, the emphasis of the two-day summit was placed on regional connectivity, financial links, and the growth of small to medium-sized enterprises. The areas of cooperation previously decided upon had included energy security, poverty alleviation, biotechnology, e-commerce, and human resources development.[61] Another is that the ACD gathering was arguably overshadowed by the passing away of His Majesty King Bhumibol Adulyadej. Any concrete implementation of plans from this ACD remains to be seen.[62] Also, only a few Asian leaders attended the ACD summit in person, diminishing the stature of the event.

Second, Thailand had to push very hard in its global campaign for a non-permanent member seat on the United Nations Security Council during 2017–18. While the total budget for this international campaign is still unconfirmed and controversial,[63] Thailand lost to Kazakhstan, securing only 55 votes against Kazakhstan's 138 votes in the second round of voting.[64] Although Thailand has claimed to be the president of Group 77, a loose and low-profile association of developing countries, it still could not secure enough support from the seventy-seven countries. In addition, China and Russia, with whom Thailand has sought closer ties, supported the candidacy of Kazakhstan.

Third, a closer Thai–Russian relationship could be discerned by the arrival of the first two Sukhoi Superjet 100LR aircrafts from Russia.[65] In February 2016, Deputy Prime Ministers Prawit Wongsuwan and Somkid Jatusripitak paid an official visit to Moscow to seek an enhanced relationship in security and investment cooperation.[66] One indicator that the military regime wanted to depend less on the West was its readiness to negotiate a free trade area with Eurasian Economic Union states, which include Russia, Kazakhstan, Belarus, Armenia, and Kyrgyzstan.[67] In a similar vein, the main driving force behind General Prayut's official visit to India was to ink some deals — both security and commercial — with the Indian government.[68] Thailand also seeks to conclude a free trade agreement with Pakistan.

Donald Trump's election victory in 2016 has thrown President Obama's "pivot" towards Asia into jeopardy, with an uncertain impact on U.S.–Thai relations. In response to Trump's shock victory, Prime Minister Prayut Chan-o-cha, in his congratulatory message, said that "no matter who the next U.S. president is, we will continue to cherish the U.S.–Thai relationship that's lasted more than 180 years. We have to be prepared and adjust ourselves to change ... we will always adopt a proactive and balanced foreign policy".[69] Many international relations experts considered the remarks both controversial and ambiguous. The main question is what he meant by "a proactive and balanced foreign policy" under the current circumstances, given the fact that the annual 2017 Cobra Gold joint military exercise is expected to go ahead as scheduled, though on a smaller scale.[70] Furthermore, although Washington had been urging Bangkok to hold a high-level security and strategic dialogue with the United States before Trump's inauguration in January 2017, Thailand had not responded positively, preferring to adopt a "wait and see" attitude.[71]

The passing of King Bhumibol Adulyadej also led to questions about the future of Thailand's domestic politics and foreign policy. The year 2016 also saw the loss of a well-known and world-class Thai diplomat, Thanat Khoman. Khoman, a former distinguished Foreign Minister, passed away in March 2016 at the age of 102.[72] A former Thai ambassador praised him as a "visionary diplomat, a statesman and an authoritative scholar on diplomacy, international law and Thailand-US relations". The U.S. Ambassador to Thailand, Glyn Davies, hailed his past contributions to the betterment of Thai–U.S. relations during the peak of the Cold War in his capacity first as Thailand's Ambassador to the United States and later as Foreign Minister.[73]

Conclusion

For 2017 it looks very likely that the military-led regime under General Prayut Chan-o-cha will remain in power until the cremation of the late King takes place by the end of the year. Should the Thai populace be fortunate enough to see a general election at the end of 2017, as speculated, there is likely to be a new coalition, but a weak civilian government, faced with rising political, economic, and social costs due to the military regime's long-term intention to control democratically elected governments. In other words, the military establishment in Thailand is still poised to hold on to power through undemocratic means beyond 2017. Democratization in Thailand is therefore still in indefinite transition, with no guarantee it will soon return to being a role model of full democratization in Southeast Asia.

Notes

1. "End of an Era", *Bangkok Post*, 14 October 2016, p. 1.
2. "Loy Krathong Sets Muted Tone For Year", *Bangkok Post*, 15 November 2016, p. 1.
3. "Nine Tribes Honour HM the Late King", *Bangkok Post*, 10 November 2016, p. 2.
4. "Prince Wants to Wait for Coronation", *Bangkok Post*, 16 October 2016, p. 1.
5. "HRH Invited to be Next King", *Bangkok Post*, 30 November 2016, p. 1.
6. "Condolences Pour in from World Leaders", *Bangkok Post*, 19 October 2016, p. 2.
7. "Asian Leaders Pay Respect", *Bangkok Post*, 23 October 2016, p. 1.
8. "King's Literary Work to Get New Airing", *Bangkok Post*, 18 November 2016, p. 2.
9. "PM Leads Nation in Loyalty Pledge to King", *Bangkok Post*, 23 November 2016, p. 1.
10. This body has now been replaced by the National Reform Steering Assembly, again handpicked by the NCPO.

11. "PM to Push for Appointed Senate Plan", *Bangkok Post*, 16 March 2016, p. 1.

12. "Wissanu Defends Appointed Senate", *Bangkok Post*, 19 March 2016, p. 3.

13. "Abhisit Says No to Top Brass in Upper House", *Bangkok Post*, 18 March 2016, p. 3.

14. "NCPO to Have Final Say on Senate Picks", *Bangkok Post*, 25 March 2016, p. 1; "NLA Seeks Total Senators to 250", *Bangkok Post*, 27 August 2016, p. 3.

15. "Prayut Ready to be Outside PM", *Bangkok Post*, 18 August 2016, p. 1.

16. "Draft a Step Back, Says Chuan", *Bangkok Post*, 4 April 2016, p. 1.

17. "Draft Charter Not Widely Distributed", *Bangkok Post*, 6 August 2016, p. 8.

18. "Poll Critics Urge New Draft Vote", *Bangkok Post*, 5 August 2016, p. 5.

19. "TV Debates to be Held on Charter", *Bangkok Post*, 19 July 2016, p. 1.

20. "Forced to Wed Mysterious Charter Bride", *Bangkok Post*, 14 July 2016, p. 9.

21. "Voters in the Dark about Reform Changes", *Bangkok Post*, 6 August 2016, p. 9.

22. "Prayut Throws Weight behind 'Yes' Camp", *Bangkok Post*, 6 August 2016, p. 1.

23. "Anfrel Pulls Out of Poll Monitoring Role", *Bangkok Post*, 29 July 2016, p. 3.

24. "Yes 61%", *Bangkok Post*, 8 August 2016, p. 1.

25. "Wissanu Hints at Delay to Next Govt", *Bangkok Post*, 24 November 2016, p. 1; "Prawit Vague on Plans for Next Election", *Bangkok Post*, 25 November 2016, p. 3; "Prayut Says Govt Firm on Roadmap", *Bangkok Post*, 26 November 2016, p. 1.

26. "Prayut Insists on Retaining Section 44", *Bangkok Post*, 11 August 2016, p. 1.

27. "Polls Show Support for Section 44", *Bangkok Post*, 28 August 2016, p. 3.

28. "Prayut Wields S44 Appoints New City Boss", *Bangkok Post*, 19 October 2016, p. 1.

29. "Caught in a Messy Web of S44 Orders", *Bangkok Post*, 30 September 2016, p. 9.

30. "Leading Media Watchdogs Say No to Council", *Bangkok Post*, 13 September 2016, p. 3.

31. "Thailand Places a Low 76th in TI Corruption Rankings", *Bangkok Post*, 28 January 2016, p. 1.

32. "NRSA Wants Government Pay Rise", *Bangkok Post*, 7 November 2016, p. 1.

33. "Pay Rise is Uncalled For", *Bangkok Post*, 9 November 2016, p. 8.

34. The author would like to thank Gao Jiankang from the ISEAS – Yusof Ishak Institute for his research support on the sections on foreign policy and the economy.

35. Economist Intelligence Unit (EIU), *Thailand Country Report*, 2016 <http://bit.ly/2ia0zbn> (accessed 29 December 2016).

36. World Bank, *Thailand Economic Monitor: Services as a New Driver of Growth*, 19 December 2016 <http://bit.ly/2isrkW6> (accessed 29 December 2016).

37. EIU, *Thailand Country Report*, 2016.

38. "Inflation Continues to Rise", *Bangkok Post*, 2 November 2016, p. B1.

39. "Thailand's Main Exports, Markets in November", Reuters, 26 December 2016 <http://www.reuters.com/article/thailand-economy-trade-idUSL4N1E12YK>.

40. World Bank, *Thailand Economic Monitor: Services as a New Driver of Growth*.

41. "Govt to Give Poor B10bn New Year Gift", *Bangkok Post*, 22 November 2016, p. 3; "Fresh Stimulus in the Pipeline", *Bangkok Post*, 23 November 2016, p. B1.

42. "PM Outlines Tasks for New DE Ministry", *Bangkok Post*, 17 September 2016, p. B1.

43. "Reshuffle over Broadband Delay", *Bangkok Post*, 6 November 2016, p. 3.

44. "Industry 4.0: Is Thailand Ready for It?", *Bangkok Post*, 9 November 2016, p. 9.

45. "ISOC Urges Open Internet to Drive Digital Economy", *Bangkok Post*, 17 November 2016, p. B3.

46. "Army Launches Cyber Centre", *Bangkok Post*, 2 November 2016, p. 2; "Cyber Centres Fighting on All Fronts", *Bangkok Post*, 7 November 2016, p. 3.

47. EIU, *Thailand Country Report*, 2016.

48. World Bank, *Thailand Economic Monitor: Services as a New Driver of Growth*.

49. Department of Information, Ministry of Foreign Affairs, Thailand, press release No. 290/2016, 12 July 2016.

50. The full transcript of Prayut Chan-o-cha's keynote address to the Shangri-La Dialogue is published on the website of the International Institute for Strategic Studies (IISS), 3 June 2016 <http://bit.ly/288gIQO> (accessed 4 January 2017).

51. Ibid.

52. Shawn W. Crispin, "Thailand's Post-Coup Foreign Policy: Omnidirectional or Directionless?", *The Diplomat*, 10 June 2016.

53. Thitinan Pongsudhirak, "Thailand's Foreign Policy in a Regional Great Game", in *The New Geopolitics of Southeast Asia*, edited by Nicholar Kitchen (London: LSE IDEAS, 2012), p. 74.

54. Pavin Chachavalponpun, "Thailand Playing a Risky Game with China, Russia", *Japan Times*, 6 June 2016.

55. Thanarith Satrusayang, "Thailand Seeks to Develop Military Production Facilities with China", Reuters, 21 December 2016.

56. Pavin, "Thailand Playing a Risky Game".

57. Kavi Chongkittavorn, "Thailand Awaits Trump's Foreign Policy Team", *The Nation*, 12 December 2016.

58. Ron Corben, "Thailand Expanding Relations with China amid Pivot to Other Nations", Voice of America, 27 December 2016.

59. "ACD Lauds Medical Tourism", *Bangkok Post*, 8 March 2016, p. 4.

60. "Prayut Steers Investment Drive", *Bangkok Post*, 10 September 2016, p. 1.

61. See the official documents drafted by the Policy and Planning Office, the Ministry of Foreign Affairs, Thailand, 20 May 2003.

62. "Critics Say ACD 'All Talk, No Substance'", *Bangkok Post*, 7 October 2016, p. 4.

63. "Pheu Thai Says B600m Spent on UN Bid", *Bangkok Post*, 30 June 2016, p. 3.
64. "Lessons in Foreign Affairs", *Bangkok Post*, 1 July 2016, p. 6.
65. "First Two Russian-made Superjets Arrive", *Bangkok Post*, 1 September 2016, p. 1.
66. "Somkid to Visit Russia", *Bangkok Post*, 22 February 2016, p. 2.
67. "Regime Seeks Russia's Backing", *Bangkok Post*, 27 February 2016, p. 1.
68. "Prawit Concludes Security Deal", *Bangkok Post*, 19 March 2016, p. 3.
69. "Prayut Sends Congratulations", *Bangkok Post*, 10 November 2016, p. 1.
70. "Cobra Gold Takes Shape", *Bangkok Post*, 2 August 2016, p. 3.
71. Kavi, "Thailand Awaits".
72. "Ex-Democrat Boss Dies at Age 102", *Bangkok Post*, 4 March 2016, p. 1.
73. "Regional Bloc 'Is Thanat's Main Legacy' ", *Bangkok Post*, 5 March 2016, p. 1.

THAILAND'S NORTHEAST "PROBLEM" IN HISTORICAL PERSPECTIVE

Porphant Ouyyanont

The turbulent events of the last fifteen years have brought to the fore a number of critical issues in Thailand's political and social structure.

One of these issues concerns the unparalleled attention given to regions in the nation's political make-up, especially the role of the northeast region. It is with this region that the present chapter will be concerned. In the present circumstances of the recent passing of King Bhumibol, it is more important than ever to understand the roots of the regional and political divisions in Thailand.

I will first summarize a few salient points about the northeast, also termed Isan, and sometimes termed the Khorat Plateau. As far as terminology is concerned, I will use the three terms interchangeably, and will generally refer to Siam, rather than Thailand, for events prior to 1939 (when the name Thailand was adopted). It should be noted, though, that the term "Isan", supposedly meaning "northeast", is of rather recent origin, used for an administrative unit called a *monthon* only since 1900.

Most scholars would agree that the vast majority of those living in the northeast are of Lao descent, perhaps eighty per cent. It is beyond the scope of this chapter to enter into the complex issue of ethnic identity, but this question has been discussed informatively by a number of writers.[1]

The northeast region consists of 20 of the country's 77 provinces. Many of these Isan provinces are among the poorest in the nation. The northeast is a significant region in a number of respects, in terms of land area, production, population, and also in terms of the political landscape. The twenty provinces account for approximately a third of the nation's land area and roughly a third

---

PORPHANT OUYYANONT is Associate Professor at the School of Economics, Sukhothai Thammathirat Open University, Thailand.

of the population. These ratios have remained fairly constant since the beginning of the twentieth century, when Thailand's present-day boundaries were settled and the first population census was taken. In 2014, Thailand's population was estimated at just over 67.9 million, of which 18.9 million lived in the northeast. Although the proportion of the northeast's to Thailand's total population has been falling in recent years, the northeast remains easily the most populous of the major regions. Thus, in 2014 the Central region had 3.1 million people, the Eastern region 5.3 million, the South 8.9 million, the North 11.6 million, and Bangkok and surrounding provinces 15.0 million.

Since many northeasterners live and work in other provinces, especially in Bangkok, the census, and estimates based on the census, may exaggerate the weight of the northeast in relation to the total population. On the other hand, eligibility to vote is based on registration, which is usually based on place of birth. Thus, in political terms, the high count for the northeast population is of immense significance. A system based on one man, one vote gives a clear major weighting to the northeast region.

A broad picture of the various regions of Thailand might conclude that the northeast is, in some respects, the most homogenous. In turn this would cement a sense of identity, common values, and shared aspirations. The northern region, for example, has a long history of separate kingdoms and cultural diversity, with Chiang Mai, Lampang, Lampoon, Phrae, and Nan all having ancient traditions and divergent local histories. The South has obvious sharp contrasts and diversity, stemming from the former Malay sultanates and the strong Islamic influences in the provinces bordering the Malay regions, as well as the old centre of Nakhon Sri Thammarat, and the numerous coastal regions. Similar local diversity and old traditions mark much of the central and southeastern provinces, the latter influenced by its seaports and trading traditions. By contrast, the entire northeastern region is landlocked, without significant mountain ranges, without any ancient urban centres such as Chiang Mai, Ayutthaya, Nakhon Sri Thammarat, or Phitsanulok, and with a village culture based for much of its history — until relatively recent times — on rural self sufficiency.

It is common knowledge that the northeast is the poorest of Thailand's regions. Many factors account for this, including geography and climate, and the relative neglect of communications and social infrastructure by the Bangkok-based government. Whatever the causes, a great variety of social statistics — such as the levels of poverty and the provision of education and health services — all attest to the relative deprivation of the northeast. Wide differences remain in the northeast at present, despite the relatively fast growth recently. It is not necessary here to give detailed examples of this relative deprivation. A striking indication, however, is provided by GPP (gross provincial product) per head. In 2006, the year of the coup against Thaksin, out of the then 76 provinces, the 12 with the lowest GPP were all in the northeast, as were 14 of the lowest 15 (the exception being Mae Hong Song in the north, near the border with Burma). On this measure, the poorest province was Nong Bua Lamphu, with a GPP of 17,271 baht per capita. This may be contrasted with Rayong, a province with large industrial centres within the orbit of Bangkok, which had a per capita GPP of 850,253 baht. Bangkok Metropolis had a GPP of 298,043 baht per head, and provinces immediately adjacent to Bangkok had a GPP three to four times that of Bangkok Metropolis itself. The wealthiest Isan province in 2006 was Khon Kaen, which was over half way down the list, at number 39, having a per capita product of 58,977 baht. Indeed, 12 southern provinces ranked above Khon Kaen.

There is no doubt that the forces unleashed in Thailand after the turn of the present century caught the country's leaders, the elites, and the media unawares. The success of Thaksin Shinawatra's Thai Rak Thai Party in the 2001 election was a surprise. Thaksin became the first prime minister in Thai history to see out his full term of office, and in the 2005 election Thaksin achieved such a huge majority that some opponents feared his power would become permanent. In that election Thai Rak Thai won 375 seats out of a possible 500. The second-placed party, the Democrats, won 96 seats. The point should be made, though, that all regions, with the exception of the South (overwhelmingly Democrat), produced a clear majority for Thaksin. Thus, in the North Thai Rak Thai gained 70 out of 76 seats, in the northeast 126 out of 136, in Bangkok 32 out of 37, and in the Central region 79 out of 97. To this extent, the concentration in the northeast as the heartland of pro-Thaksin support requires some explanation.

Thaksin's success was generally explained by his opponents as a combination of opportunistic "populist" policies, vote buying, and other forms of corruption. Less emphasized was the personal charisma of Thaksin himself, or the striking economic advances made by the country as a whole as it recovered from the depths of the financial crisis of 1997.

Given the nationwide support for Thaksin (except in the South), it is worth asking why the Thaksin and pro-Thaksin political parties (that is, the pro-Thaksin parties formed after the overthrow of Thaksin and the abolition of the Thai Rak Thai Party) should be so firmly associated with the northeast. Three reasons may be suggested. First, in terms of sheer numbers the northeast could control more parliamentary seats than any other region due to the size of its electorate. Second, the most obvious examples of vote buying and vote rigging often came from the northeast. Third, when the red-shirt movement developed after the anti-Thaksin coup of 2006, the leadership, many of the demonstrators, and the speeches and entertainment provided by the red-shirt media were dominated by northeasterners.

Faced with the success of Thaksin and pro-Thaksin parties after 2006, large sections of Thai society, especially the Bangkok-centred elite, had difficulty coming to terms with the divisions that appeared during these years. In particular, the regional element in this division — crystallized, as we have noted, in the "red-shirt" movement — lay outside the mainstream narrative of "Thainess", which emphasized a cohesive nation united under the guidance of a benevolent monarchy and based on Buddhist values.

The problem, as seen from the perspective of those opposed to the red shirts, and especially the pro-monarchy, pro-elite "yellow shirts", was that the essential cohesiveness of the Thai state and the unity this implied was under threat. This understanding, in turn, was rooted in a very long tradition that elevated the Thai nation-state, and emphasized the essential unity of "Thainess" as a single "family" of ethnic Thais, under the banner of "King, Religion, Nation". In this view of the country, division — and especially regional division — was intolerable.

There is extensive literature on the evolution of the Thai nation-state and Thai nationalism.[2] Important elements in this evolution include the formation of a country with settled geographic boundaries, a "geo-body", as Tongchai Winichakul has termed it, that had appeared by the first decade of the twentieth century.[3] The emergence of Thailand within its present boundaries (with only a few minor exceptions) had resulted in part from the pressures wrought by colonial expansion outside the country. As a result of the short 1893 war with France and subsequent treaties with France in 1893, 1904, and 1907, territories traditionally claimed by Siam in Laos and Cambodia were lost; other treaties with Britain defined boundaries between Thailand and the Malay States in the South, and between Thailand and British Burma. For the Khorat Plateau, the new boundaries with French-controlled Laos had important consequences, which will be touched upon later.

Another element in the development of a sense of nation-state and the essential unity of the country came from the strengthened absolute monarchy under King Chulalongkorn (1868–1910), and administrative centralization of the country under the reforms of the King's brother, Prince Damrong, who was Minister of the Interior between 1892 and 1915. Murashima has noted that already in the 1880s the concept of a "nation-state" was apparent in the country, spurred not only by the threat of Western colonial expansion but also by notions of Western political thought that encompassed the concept of a nation-state.[4] Under Chulalongkorn's successor, King Vajiravudh (1910–25), Thai nationalism was given greater emphasis, and the association of monarchy, Buddhism, and the nation became entrenched. The spread of primary education, improved communications, and the growth of the media all tended to promote the dominance of a single Thai identity and a single — central Thai — dialect of the Tai language.[5] At the same time, the official Thai view of its own history focused on wise kings, heroic victories, and a seamless thread of national development from the first Sukhothai kingdom in the thirteenth century, followed by Ayutthaya until 1767, and then the Thonburi and Bangkok periods. We may quote a Thai scholar who recently expressed it thus: "The master narrative of Thai history that emerged in the 1910s tells a long history of how great monarchs have saved the country's independence time after time since the birth of the nation in the 12th or 13th c. until the modern time and led it to its current prosperity."[6] The history of the country thus became largely the history of the central Siamese and their expansion. The "official state ideology", to use Murashima's term, "was formulated by the ruling elite as a device to integrate the Thai people in the name of Nation and national traditions at a time when Siam faced a most dangerous threat from Western colonialism".[7] We should emphasize Murashima's use of the word "integrate".

The different elements that have combined to develop the concept of a nation-state and national unity have varied over time. Particularly important in recent decades has been the renewed elevation and reverence for the King and the monarchy that occurred under the prime ministership of Sarit Thanarat between 1957 and 1963. The King became to an ever-increasing extent the symbol of Thai unity and cohesion.

Given, then, the long period over which a Siam-centred sense of unity has evolved, despite a series of military coups since the overthrow of the absolute monarchy in 1932, the shock caused by the divisions and factionalism that occurred after the election of 2005 can readily be understood. Earlier decades of Thai history and political philosophy had no answer to the events that occurred in the first decade of the present century. As a result, a rather simplistic view emerged among the anti-Thaksin forces that emphasized the ignorance and stupidity of the northeasterners in particular. They were duped by the populist policies of Thaksin — and later, pro-Thaksin parties — and they succumbed to blatant vote-buying and corruption. As a result they were unprepared for true democracy, and this justified the anti-Thaksin coup of 2006 as well as the military takeover in 2014. The English-language newspaper, *The Nation*, reflecting on Thaksin's decision to hold a snap election early in 2006, spoke of "a major fallacy of the concept [of democracy], particularly in a less-developed democracy like ours, in which the impoverished, poorly informed masses are easily manipulated by people of his ilk. And Thaksin's manipulation has been well documented."[8] The central Thai characterization of northeasterners as an ignorant and rather stupid peasantry had long been entrenched in Thai perceptions. Thai films and television soap operas frequently portrayed northeasterners in this light, and a popular song of the 1990s, sung to northeastern traditional music, has a northeasterner arriving in Bangkok and asking "Where Are the Buffaloes?" The transition from this sort of derogatory attitude to the characterization of pro-Thaksin support in the northeast as deriving from ignorance and cupidity was an easy one.

The argument of the present chapter is that the political role of the northeast in recent times must be seen in a much longer historical perspective. The integration of the northeast — Isan — into the Thai polity is of relatively recent origin. In particular, we should focus on several elements in this integration:

1. Until the thirteenth century, the dominant ethnic population of the Khorat Plateau had been Khmer, and for several hundred years it had been part of the great Khmer Angkor Empire. There are numerous traces of Khmer influence in the northeast, mostly dating from after the tenth century, including the famous Phimai temple complex at Nakhon Ratchasima, and Prasat Phanom Rung, in Buriram province.

2. Ethnic Lao people, speaking a distinct dialect of the Tai language, moved gradually and unevenly on to the Khorat plateau, probably only from the fourteenth century. In time they replaced the formerly dominant Khmer on most of the Plateau.

3. Importantly, the Sukhothai and Ayutthaya kingdoms exercised little effective rule or influence over the Khorat Plateau, though they claimed authority over much of the region. The first, and for a long time the only effective, move on to the Plateau came in the reign of King Narai in the late seventeenth century. This was a fortified post at Nakhon Ratchasima (Khorat), on the southwestern edge of the Plateau.

4. At the same time, the Lao kingdoms to the east of the Mekong also had little direct influence on the Plateau, with the exception of certain provinces on the west bank of the Mekong near Vientiane.

5. Thus, virtually the entire Khorat Plateau seems to have been largely politically autonomous until the fall of Ayutthaya in the late eighteenth century. Over a lengthy period before this time, ethnic Lao populations came to predominate at the expense of the Khmer over most of the northeast. The prevailing social structure and economy of a region that remained sparsely populated was based largely on self-sufficient rice-growing villages.

Isan and History

During the mid-fourteenth century, three important developments occurred that would shape the character and political alignments of the northeast. First, there was a decline in power of the Khmer Angkor Empire. The decline had been in evidence from the late thirteenth century and continued during the fourteenth. The collapse seems to have occurred quite suddenly after 1431, when Ayutthaya armies sacked Angkor. The growing weakness of Angkor left a vacuum which allowed the rise of two Tai-speaking kingdoms: Ayutthaya in central Siam, and Lan Sang in Laos. These two kingdoms rose at nearly identical times, Ayutthaya being traditionally dated from 1351 and Lan Sang from 1349.[9]

Lan Sang arose from a notable Lao king, Fa Ngum, who united a number of Lao principalities from his capital at Luang Prabang, and created the first unified Lao kingdom. Under this king, Lan Chang brought virtually the whole of the Khorat Plateau under unified control in the 1350s, with the exception of the Khmer outpost around Khorat.

The significant point, from the perspective of this discussion, is that the rise of Lan Sang led to a long period of movement of ethnic Lao people to the Khorat Peninsula. According to Keyes, the first record of significant migration came with an order by Fa Ngum to relocate some twenty thousand Lao families from around Vientiane to the northern Khorat Plateau during the 1350s.[10] From this point various small-scale movements continued, and the Plateau became increasingly ethnically Lao. Neither Lan Sang nor Ayutthaya exercised much direct control over the Khorat Plateau, although Martin Stuart-Fox says rather bluntly that "The traditional kingdom of Lan Xang lasted from 1345 to 1707 and included territory on both banks of the Mekong, notably the entire Khorat Plateau, now comprising northeastern Thailand."[11] It seems, though, that from the 1560s the interest of Lan Sang in the region was mostly confined to areas on the right bank of the Mekong around present-day Nong Kai, Nakhon Phanom, and Loei. Lao migrations continued in the latter decades of the sixteenth century, and it is recorded that large numbers from around Vientiane migrated to a wide area on the Plateau, extending from Roi Et to Champasak, as a result of political disturbances.[12]

At the end of the seventeenth and beginning of the eighteenth century, the kingdom of Lan Sang fragmented, and this ushered in a long period of upheaval which led to further Lao inroads on to the Khorat Plateau. The last king of a unified Lan Chang, King Surayawongsa, died in the 1690s, and Lan Sang broke into three separate kingdoms in 1707: Luang Prabang, Vientiane, and Champasak. While

Vientiane remained a dominant force in the central Mekong provinces inherited from Lan Chang, Champasak, on the right bank of the Mekong, was important in areas of the northeast watered by the Chi and Mun rivers, notably including Roi Et and Ubon. The disintegration of Lan Sang gave considerable impetus to the movement of ethnic Lao on to the Khorat Plateau. From this time, according to Grabowsky, the break-up "helped foster the migration of the Lao southwards along the Mekong"; the foundation of the kingdom of Champasak in particular "gave the Lao movement to the South a new, decisive, impetus".[13] Communities of Lao migrants from the Mekong basin, we are told, became "large and important *muang* in an area that is now the northeastern region of Thailand, for e.g. Ubon Ratchatani, Roi Et, Sakhon Nakhon, Yasothon, and others".[14] There was also a significant migration to Kalasin in the late eighteenth century, and a number of Lao came to Roi Et and Ubon from Champasak in the early eighteenth century.

There seems agreement among scholars that the migrations of Lao to the northeast were precipitated and encouraged by political factors. Dispossessed Lao came often as a result of political upheaval, both during the flourishing of Lan Sang and, more especially, thereafter. A number of Lao local rulers (*nai*) moved with their followers (*phrai*) to establish new centres on the Khorat Plateau. The pattern seems to have been the formation of villages and *muang* under traditional ruling elites and their followers who moved into sparsely inhabited regions in the northeast. In this way, Lao customs, organization, allegiances, and traditions were brought to wide areas of the northeast.

There appears to be no evidence of economic migration in search of more productive land or better opportunities, or of movements forced by population pressures. Since the Khorat Plateau was then, as now, a region without major rivers (except the Mekong) to provide annual inundations and hence bring greater productivity to wide areas, the Plateau was dependent on rainfall for rice cultivation. But rainfall was uncertain, and there were long periods of drought, and sometimes damaging floods. It would seem, therefore, that by comparison with the central Chaophraya basin, the characteristics of a poor and unproductive northeast were already marked by the eighteenth century.

By the time the Lan Sang kingdom dissolved at the beginning of the eighteenth century, the Khorat Plateau had become largely ethnically Lao — except for some provinces bordering present-day Cambodia — while Lao migrants adopted various Khmer traditions and culture from the inhabitants they replaced. At this stage, Ayutthaya had impinged little on the region. The only exception — though it was a significant one — was a fortified outpost established through the conquest of a Khmer stronghold at Khorat in 1657, during the reign of King Narai (1656–88).

Khorat is situated at the southwest edge of the Khorat Plateau, and was termed, significantly, the "gateway to enter the northeast".[15]

To sum up briefly: At the beginning of the eighteenth century we can reflect that the northeast was little touched politically by either Lan Sang or Ayutthaya. Only a few provinces on the right bank of the Mekong were integrated into Lan Sang, including Nong Kai, Loei, and Nakhon Phanom, and none at all into Ayutthaya.

This leads to a further reflection. No important political centre comparable to Chiang Mai or other Lan Na kingdoms or Nakhon Sri Thammarat ever emerged on the Khorat Plateau. Thus, the northeast had a legacy of autonomy, independence, and even a form of egalitarianism.

Steps Towards Integration

In retrospect, the destruction of Ayutthaya by Burma in 1767, and the subsequent rebuilding and strengthening of Siam thereafter, marks an important turning point in the integration of the Khorat Plateau under Siam. An overarching circumstance was the emergence of Siam as the major regional power, able to retain its independence while other states fell under colonial rule. Thus, by the mid-nineteenth century, Burma was in the process of being colonized by the British, and Indochina, including Vietnam and Cambodia, was falling under the sway of France. Siam, in the meantime, had strengthened its position in the old Lan Na kingdom, centred on Chiang Mai, and also brought Isan under its permanent sway.

There were two significant steps after 1767 in the gradual integration of the Lao regions on the Khorat Plateau into Siam prior to the mid-nineteenth century. First, during the reign of King Taksin (1767–82) — a strong king who established his capital at Thonburi, opposite Bangkok on the Chaophraya River — the previously autonomous Lao kingdoms of Luang Prabang, Vientiane, and Champasak lost their independence and became vassals of the Siamese kingdom. As a result of military defeat, the Lao kingdoms were reduced in status and forced to recognize the suzerainty of Siam in 1778. A gradual process of political control by Siam then evolved.

In this way the regions of the northeast, hitherto mostly subservient to Vientiane and Champasak, came under Siamese influence and control. This control increased in intensity and reach during the reign of the first Bangkok king (Rama I; 1782–1809), and thereafter during the succeeding two reigns before 1851. Khorat was a significant centre of Siam's influence, and various local principalities pledged allegiance to Khorat, and hence Bangkok, rather than to the former Lao kingdoms.

The second important step in the integration of the northeast into Siam came as a result of a major war between the revitalized Lao state of Vientiane and Siam in 1827–28. The crushing of Vientiane meant the final and irrevocable absorption by Siam of all the northeast provinces.

It should be emphasized that the administrative changes brought by Siam to the northeast did not initially cut deep into existing social structures, customs, or traditions. Until the 1880s the northeast was characterized by local rule through local elites, under the authority of Bangkok, and with the local rulers yielding taxes to Bangkok in various forms, and sometimes providing corvée labour.

This process of administrative control came through the application to the northeast of the central Siam "*hua muang* system", itself emanating from old Ayutthaya. The system was a form of semi-feudal indirect rule used for Siam's "outer provinces". Following King Taksin's incursions into the northeast, and the reduction in the status of the earlier Lao kingdoms, numbers of *hua muang* were formed. Keyes has explained the process, which involved the grouping of villages into small principalities, termed *hua muang*.[16] The villages were subject to indigenous elites, and the elites were subject to the Siamese king. Starting with Khorat, the number of *hua muang* in Isan rose from 13 to 35 between 1778 and 1826, and Grabowsky notes that for interior development (that is, to the west of the Mekong), the foundation of Kalasin in 1793 and of Khon Kaen in 1797 were particularly important.[17] By 1840 there were some 56 *muang* on the Plateau. This rose to 70 in 1860 and to over 100 by 1882, when the system was ended.[18] Growing numbers of *muang* reflect not only increasing Siamese influence and control but also a growing population. Major *hua muang* were under the direct authority of Bangkok, while lesser *hua muang* were under the major *hua muang*. In 1882 there were 27 major *hua muang* on the Khorat Plateau, and through this system of indirect rule Bangkok was able to control the "outer provinces" in the northeast by ensuring that the local elites were loyal to Bangkok. The major *hua muang* were headed by a local lord (*Chao*) and other high officials, but they had to be appointed (in practice confirmed) by Bangkok. The *hua muang* had considerable autonomy, and the *Chaos* were often de facto hereditary rulers.

The War of 1827–28

The war between Siam and Laos (although Thais like to refer to this conflict as a "rebellion") marks an important step in the integration of Isan into Siam.[19] As Grabowsky has noted: "Few scholars would disagree that the war between Bangkok and Vientiane in 1827–28 marked a major watershed in Thai–Lao relations in general, and in the history of Isan in particular."[20]

The rather complex origins of the conflict need not concern us here, but for various (and disputed) reasons, the king of the vassal Lao state of Vientiane, Chao Anu, attempted to restore Vientiane's independence and, perhaps, recreate the former kingdom of Lan Chang. Chao Anu, hitherto a trusted ally of Siam, attacked Siamese forces, and was joined by a number of allies, including Champasak (Chao Anu's son, Chao Yo, had become King of Champasak in 1821). In Siam, a new monarch, Rama III (1824–51) had recently come to the throne, and it appears that he was intent on intensifying his control over certain outer provinces, including the northeast. One measure was to brand the inhabitants by tattooing, carried out by officials sent from Khorat. Such a measure implied Bangkok control of the local population rather than control by the traditional rulers.[21]

In any event, Chao Anu was defeated towards the end of 1827, and Vientiane was destroyed and depopulated in 1828 and the following years. For the northeast the consequences were considerable. Both Vientiane and Champasak were reduced to the status of "outer provinces", and the *hua muang* system was applied with greater intensity throughout the Khorat Plateau. Especially after 1840, increasing numbers of *muang* were established in the central and western parts of the Plateau, whereas many of the first *muang* had been in the areas around the Mekong. Although traditional elites were largely left in place, Bangkok's influence intensified. There was a "massive resettlement of Lao populations across the Mekong to the Khorat Plateau, and even to the fringes of the Central Plain (e.g., Lopburi, Suphanburi, Chachoengsao, Prachinburi)",[22] a resettlement that continued until the early 1850s.

For more than a decade, starting in 1834, the Siamese made sustained efforts to move all of the Lao population on the left side of the Mekong to the Northeast Plateau and parts of central Siam. The purpose was to create a buffer zone between Siamese territories and Vietnam during the Siam–Vietnamese war of 1834–47. It is estimated that some eighty thousand Lao were initially removed from Vientiane in 1827, and the total resettlement numbers might have been several hundred thousand.[23]

Deportations were, of course, part and parcel of traditional warfare in Southeast Asia. Sparse populations meant a continual search for additional manpower, for slaves, and in order to reduce the resources of the enemy. However, the deportations carried out by the Siamese after 1828 seem to have been carried through with unusual thoroughness and brutality. Dr Puangthong has recently stressed the importance of Lao deportations and resettlement to make up for the manpower deficiencies of the Siamese during the Thonburi and early Bangkok periods (from 1782 to 1851). She writes: "Although the Siamese had successfully put down the Chao Anu revolt in early 1828, a series of depopulation campaigns along the left bank continued until the 1840s with the purpose of removing as many people as possible to resettle in the area under effective Siamese control on the right bank. The successive mass exoduses during this period contributed to the creation of forty new provinces in northeast Siam."[24]

The aftermath of the 1827 conflict was momentous for the northeast. The population expanded rapidly through forced settlements and natural increase, including, doubtlessly, voluntary migration from the east of the Mekong. By the second half of the nineteenth century, two broad ratios had emerged, largely the result of forced resettlement after 1828, that are still defining patterns at the present time. First, the vast majority of ethnic Lao people live outside the territory that came to be independent Laos. Roughly four times as many ethnic Lao live in the northeast regions as in the territory of Laos. Second, as the population in the northeast expanded, the proportion of that population living in Siam (and later Thailand) grew. By the end of the nineteenth century, about a third of the population of the kingdom lived in the northeast, and that proportion has remained fairly constant.

Administrative Reforms in the Late Nineteenth Century

As a result of military conquest, resettlement of populations, the spread of the *hua muang* system, and the disappearance of threats from Burma and Laos, Siam had been able to achieve firm hegemony over the entire Khorat Plateau by the second half of the nineteenth century. At this stage, though, the impact of Siamese administration on the northeast was limited and indirect. Local rulers held sway, and as far as villages were concerned, local customs and traditions prevailed as they had done for several centuries.

During the last two decades of the nineteenth century, however, major steps were taken by the Siamese government to centralize provincial administration under Bangkok, and so bring greater control over outlying areas.[25] All major regions beyond the inner provinces were affected, including the South and the North as well as the northeast.

The administrative reforms are associated with the work of Prince Damrong, who became head of the new Ministry of the Interior in 1892. The essence of the reforms was to centralize authority of the whole country under Bangkok, and therefore lessen or remove local autonomy.

There were various reasons for the reform measures. Some were domestic, such as the need to increase tax revenues and ensure that taxes reached Bangkok directly rather than be collected locally. Bangkok saw a need to rein in the power of local rulers, especially where there was a latent threat of a push for independence. At the same time, there were significant external factors. Western colonial expansion on Siam's borders threatened the territories traditionally claimed by Siam. The greatest threat came from France in Laos and Cambodia. As a result of a treaty with France in 1893, following a short war, Siam lost its Lao provinces on the left bank of the Mekong, and some in Bangkok feared that France might then claim the entire Khorat Plateau on the pretext that it was "Lao". Beyond the need to enhance control of the region, both militarily and administratively, there was a general impulsion towards modernization and "civilization" that might stave off Western encroachment. Thus, centralization and modernization were intertwined.

These fundamental steps in the strengthening of Siam in the last two decades of the nineteenth century were linked also to the growing absolutism of the Siamese monarchy under King Chulalongkorn. The King's relatives, often brothers and half-brothers, were put in charge of various ministries, and former elites (including provincial elites) were often replaced or downgraded.[26] Such measures would enable central control and help unify the country at a time when Western colonial expansion, especially French, was threatening the integrity of Siam along its Lao and Cambodian territories. At the same time, centralization would enhance Bangkok's control over tax revenues and enforce Bangkok legislation. The reforms did not happen suddenly, but took place gradually, and were implemented in different places at different times.

The means by which centralization was achieved was through Bangkok's appointment of Royal Commissioners, who would thus bypass the traditional authority of local elites. The status of the *muang* thus became secondary rather than primary. In the late 1880s, Royal Commissioners were appointed in the important centres of Chiang Mai in the North and Phuket in the South, and were also appointed at Luang Prabang (still under Siamese authority) and Nong Khai and Ubon Ratchatani on the right bank of the Mekong. However, the most significant developments took place following Prince Damrong's appointment as Minister of the Interior in 1892.[27] Building upon earlier measures, and determined to centralize and modernize the country in response to both internal and external threats, he introduced a new form of administration, which he called the *thesaphiban* system. The system commenced in Nakhon Ratchasima in 1893 and was extended steadily to other regions of the country. It involved the grouping of a number of provinces into a new administrative unit, the *monthon* (circle), and Wyatt termed it a "dramatic and rapid centralization".[28]

In implementing these reforms, it is notable that Damrong treated the northeast very differently from other regions of the country. In other parts of the country the former elites were allowed some form of face-saving status, even if it was only titular, and in some provinces, such as Pattani and Phuket, local dynasties retained very real power. But in the northeast the former elites were mostly swept away under Damrong's reforms. In the North and South a form of indirect rule was maintained. Thus, Monthon Payap was composed of the old vassal states in the North, with the traditional title of Nakhon being retained for Chiang Mai, Lampang, Lampoon, Nan, and Phrae. These also retained their old ruling families, and in each Nakhon there were hereditary rulers and two Royal Commissioners. Hereditary rulers remained (though with little authority) for a long time, except in Phrae.[29]

Michael Vickery has traced the effects of the reforms on the regional elites.[30] Prior to these reforms, a complex hierarchy of vassal states and various classes of provinces existed under the overarching hegemony of the Siamese centre. Vickery notes that various "small states" in the northeast were governed until well into the nineteenth century by what were effectively hereditary ruling families (*Chao*).[31] Some of the families dated well before the Bangkok era, and some were of trans-Mekong origin. Thus, for over two hundred years Roi Et and Suvannaphum had the families of Phra Khatiyavong and Phra Ratanavong as hereditary *Chao Muang*. Both Buriram and Ubon also had ruling families established in the reign of Taksin. In Buriram the local ruling family continued until 1898, when an official from Bangkok was sent as governor, though in Roi Et the local ruler was replaced by a Royal Commissioner as early as 1886.[32] An example of a local elite with a trans-Mekong origin was Kalasin, where the population of the province apparently derived from Vientiane in 1778. At the time of Damrong's reforms, when local rulers were replaced by central Siamese officials, there were eleven provinces or districts in the northeast with local ruling families going back to the eighteenth or the beginning of the nineteenth century. Thus, several provinces of the northeast had a tradition of local elites at least as old as the Chakri dynasty, and in some cases they hailed from the left bank of the Mekong rather than from central Siam.[33] Vickery writes that, "In contrast to the relative success of other local families in achieving integration into the new bureaucracy, the elites of the northeast are conspicuous by their almost total exclusion from high office under the reformed system."[34] None were appointed Royal Commissioners of *monthons*, and many were demoted. Vickery suggests some reasons for the different treatment, in particular stressing Prince Damrong's "prejudice against any kind of regionalism in the northeast". Damrong claimed the Isan people "were Thai (Siamese), not Lao", and he forbade the use of the word "Lao" in census reports.[35] Vickery also speculates that there was perhaps residual resentment against Chao Anu's rebellion, while the perceived danger from French ambitions in the Plateau also demanded strong control of the region. In any event, "the northeastern provinces were integrated into the standard *monthon* system as developed in the inner provinces without any preparatory stage to mitigate the effects of the change, and their hereditary governors were within a few years replaced by central government appointees".[36]

The impact of Damrong's administrative reforms on the sense of identity and sense of grievance in the northeast is difficult to establish. However, both Keyes and Ishii link the significant *phu mee bun* (Holy Men) revolts that occurred in many parts of the northeast in 1902 to the loss of autonomy and independence occasioned by the reforms.[37] And the northeast remains a troubled political region. McCargo and Hongladorom noted that,

> Isan has been a site of frequent rebellion and resistance, a challenge to the power of the Thai state. The history of Isan in the 20th century was a long time of resistance towards domination from Bangkok, demonstrated in the millenarian movements of the early 20th century (especially the Holy Men revolt of 1902), the dissenting voices of independent-minded leftist Isan MPs from the 1930s, the emergence of Isan as the main base of the Communist Party of Thailand in the 1960s and 1970s, and the Isan focus of much non-government organization, people's organization and protest activity from the 1980s onwards.[38]

Conclusion

This chapter began with a discussion of recent divisions in Thai society and noted the regionalism associated with the pro-Thaksin "red-shirt" movement. In light of the subsequent discussion we can make a few concluding remarks.

From what we may call the Bangkok "yellow-shirt" perspective, the notion of regional division was contrary to a lengthy process of nation-state formation that stressed the cohesion and essential unity of Thai society. Focusing on the northeast (though most other regions showed as much support for Thaksin in the elections of 2001 and 2005 as did the northeast), the elites highlighted the ignorance of northeasterners, born into poverty and lacking education, to account for pro-Thaksin support.

From the northeast perspective, the absorption of the Isan region into Thailand was a relatively recent and gradual process. Through historical tradition, local rulers, and religious practice, the northeast population often looked east, across the Mekong, rather than west towards Bangkok, at least until the 1920s. This, combined with the obvious sense of superiority towards northeasterners shown by central Thais until the present day, can only have cemented feelings of separateness and regional identity within the Isan region.

We have emphasized two strands that can help in our understanding of the complex position of the northeast in Thailand's political landscape. On the one hand, many of the characteristics that seem to distinguish the northeast, such as economic backwardness, social disadvantage, and a feeling of separation from the mainstream of Thai society (both from the perspective of many in other Thai regions as well as of northeasterners themselves) have been long-standing. On the other hand, regional separation and diversity runs counter to the prevailing narrative of "Thainess", with its stress on cohesion and cultural uniformity, and with the Bangkok-centred monarchy at its core. To fit the northeast into the narrative of a lengthy linear history, rooted in ancient Siamese kingship, is as problematical for the northeast as it is for Thailand's southern provinces. For the northeast, integration and uniformity are to be understood as part of a long, and uneasy, process.

Acknowledgements

The author is grateful to Professor Emeritus Malcolm Falkus, University of New England, who helped with the presentation of the paper, the discussants, and the other participants at the Thailand Forum 2015, "Society in Transition", held at the ISEAS – Yusof Ishak Institute, 27–28 July 2015 for their helpful comments.

Notes

1. B.J. Terwiel, "The Development of Consensus Nationalism in Thailand", in Sri Kuhnt-Saptodewo et al., *Nationalism and Cultural Revival in Southeast Asia: Perspectives from the Centre and the Region* (Wiesbaden: Harrassowitz, 1997), pp. 135–43; Duncan McCargo and Krisadawan Hongladorom, "Contesting Isan-ness: Discourses of Politics and Identity in Northeast Thailand", *Asian Ethnicity* 5 no. 2 (2004) and works cited there.

2. See, for example, Terwiel, "The Development of Consensus Nationalism"; McCargo and Hongladorom, "Contesting Isan-ness"; Eiji Murashima, "The Origin of Official State Ideology in Thailand", *Journal of Southeast Asian Studies* 19, no. 1 (1988): 80–95.

3. Thongchai Winichakul, *Siam Mapped: A History of the Geo-Body of A Nation* (Chiangmai: Silkworm, 1994).

4. Murashima, "The Origin of Official State Ideology", p. 83.

5. The word "Tai" is used here to refer to the group of languages related to Tai, including Lao.

6. Thongchai Winichakul, "A Short History of the Long Memory of the Thai Nation", 2004 <http://web.uvic.ca/~anp/Public/abstrcts01/Winichakul.html>.

7. Murashima, "The Origin of Official State Ideology", pp. 88–89.

8. "Democracy Put to the Ultimate Test", *The Nation*, 21 March 2006.

9. Variously transliterated as Lan Sang, Lan Chang, and Lan Xang.

10. C.F. Keyes, *Finding Their Voice: Northeastern Villagers and the Thai State* (Chiangmai: Silkworm, 2014), p. 20.

11. Martin Stuart-Fox, "The French in Laos, 1887–1945", *Modern Asian Studies* 29, no. 1 (1995): 111.

12. Keyes, *Finding Their Voice*, pp. 21–22.

13. Volker Grabowsky, "Lao and Khmer Perceptions of National Survival: The Legacy of the Early Nineteenth Century", in *Nationalism and Cultural Survival in Southeast Asia: Perspectives from the Centre and the Region*, edited by Sri Kuhnt-Saptodewo, Volker Grabowsky, and Martin Grossheim (Weisbaden: Harrassowitz, 1997), p. 147.

14. Ibid.

15. Ibid.

16. Keyes, *Finding Their Voice*, p. 29.

17. Grabowsky, "Lao and Khmer Perceptions", p. 148; and Volker Grabowsky, "The Isan up to its Integration into the Siamese State", in Volker Grabowsky, ed., *Regions and National Integration in Thailand, 1882–1992* (Wiesbaden: Harrassowitz, 1995), pp. 115–16.

18. Figures for the numbers of *hua muang* are from Keyes, *Finding Their Voice*, p. 29, and Grabowsky, "The Isan up to its Integration", p. 121.

19. A major study, written from the Lao perspective, is Mayoury Ngaosyvathn and Pheuiphanh Ngaosyvathn, *Paths to Conflagration: Fifty Years of Diplomacy and Warfare in Laos, Thailand, and Vietnam, 1778–1828* (Cornell University Southeast Asia Program, 1998).

20. Grabowsky, "Lao and Khmer Perceptions", p. 148.

21. See the discussion in Mayoury Ngaosyvathn and Pheuiphanh Ngaosyvathn, *Paths to Conflagration*, pp. 145–48; also Puangthong R. Pawakapan, "Warfare and Depopulation of the Trans-Mekong Basin and the Revival of Siam's Economy", *Southeast Asia Research Centre Working Paper Series*, no. 15 (August 2014): 8–9 <http://www6.cityu.edu.hk/searc/Resources/Paper/156%20-%20WP%20-%20Dr%20Puangthong.pdf>.

22. Grabowsky, "Lao and Khmer Perceptions", p. 150.

23. Kennon Breazeale, "Historical Population Movements in the Interior of Mainland Southeast Asia", 1994, quoted in James Gustafson, "Northeast Thailand: The

development of a Marginalized Periphery" <http://www.thaicov.org/resources/documents/underdevelop.html>; Kennon Breazeale, "Historical Population Movements in North and Northeast Thailand", *Journal of Population and Social Studies* 20, no. 2 (January 2012): 135.

24. Puangthong, "Warfare and Depopulation", pp 14–15.
25. For a discussion of Damrong's reforms, see Tej Bunnag, *The Provincial Administration of Siam, 1892–1915* (Kuala Lumpur: Oxford University Press, 1977); see also Neil A. Englehart, *Culture and Power in Traditional Siamese Government* (New York: Cornell Southeast Asia Publications, 2001), pp. 98–103.
26. Terwiel, "The Development of Consensus Nationalism", p. 207.
27. Prince Damrong took over the former Kalahom in 1892. The Kalahom was then transformed into the Ministry of the Interior in 1894, with authority throughout the kingdom.
28. David Wyatt, *Thailand: A Short History* (New Haven: Yale University Press, 1982), p. 20.
29. Michael Vickery, "Thai Regional Elites and the Reforms of King Chulalongkorn", *Journal of Asian Studies* 19 no. 4 (1970): 876–77.
30. Ibid.
31. Ibid., p. 868.
32. Ibid.
33. Ibid., pp. 868–70.
34. Ibid., p. 878.
35. Ibid., p. 879.
36. Ibid., p. 880.
37. Keyes, *Finding Their Voice*, chap. 3; and Yoneo Ishii, "A Note on Buddhistic Millenarian Revolts in Northeastern Siam", *Journal of Southeast Asian Studies* 6, no. 2 (1975): 121–26.
38. McCargo and Hongladorom, "Contesting Isan-ness", pp. 221–22.

Timor-Leste

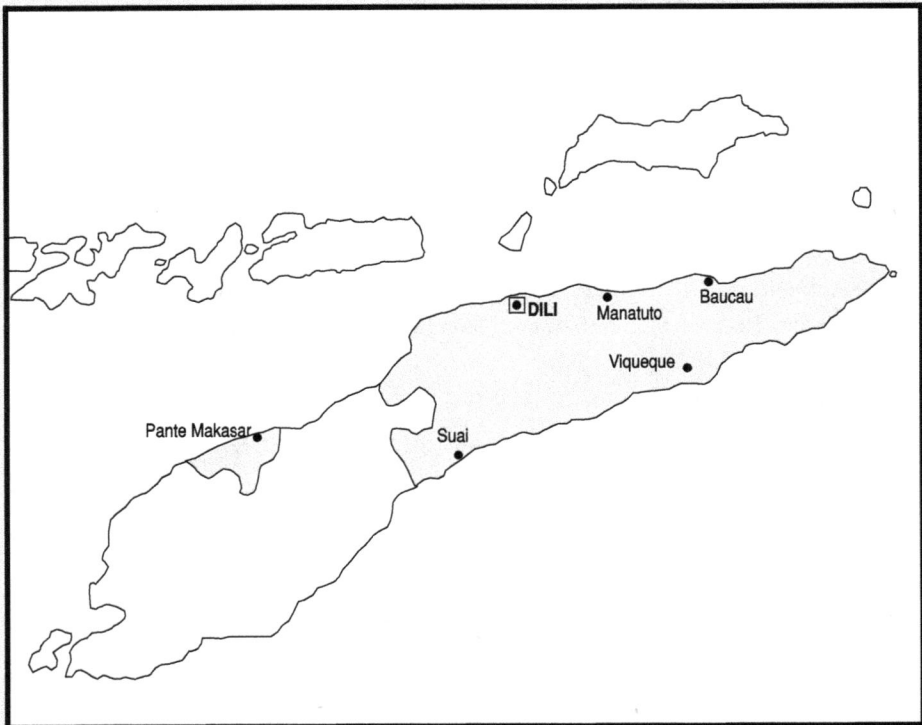

TIMOR-LESTE IN 2016:
Redefining Democracy

Dennis Shoesmith

In the lead-up to presidential and parliamentary elections in 2017, Timor-Leste in 2016 occupied a seriously ambivalent political space. The ambivalence arose from what appears to be the aspiration for national unity and the actuality of what appears to be the end of opposition politics in Timor-Leste, and therefore a possible diminution of democratic representation. The creation of a Government of National Unity (GNU) in February 2015 set up what Arend Lijphart has termed a "consociational democracy" in Timor-Leste, an arrangement where the opposition, in effect, surrenders that role and possibly the opportunity to replace the government at the next national elections in return for a share in government. It is an arrangement between previously rival leaders and their parties, where national elites agree to share power.[1] This is a type of "controlled democracy" intended to replace political conflict with political cooperation. What it actually may entail is a loss of accountability and transparency and a consequent tendency towards political collusion, or worse.

The Redefinition of East Timorese Democracy

To understand the operation of national politics in Timor-Leste in 2016 it is necessary to consider again the major changes to the political system that occurred in 2015. These have been reviewed by Maj Nygaard-Christensen in *Southeast Asian Affairs 2016*,[2] but they will be further discussed here in order to explain the transition that the country is undergoing between the formation of the GNU in February 2015 and the expected presidential and parliamentary elections in 2017.

DENNIS SHOESMITH is University Professorial Fellow at Charles Darwin University in the Northern Territory, Australia. He served in the United Nations Transitional Administration in East Timor in 2000–2001 and since then has maintained regular contact there.

In its second year of operation, the Sixth Constitutional Government continued to redefine democracy in Timor-Leste. This redefinition began on 6 February 2015 when Xanana Gusmão resigned as Prime Minister. He appointed as his successor Dr Rui Maria de Araújo, who on 16 February was sworn in to lead a Government of National Unity. Araújo is a senior member of FRETILIN, the party that formed the government upon independence but lost power in the 2007 election to the CNRT. The CNRT was created in that year by then President Gusmão as his vehicle to win the Prime Ministership and replace the FRETILIN government with his own.[3] In February 2015 he also brought two senior members of FRETILIN into the Council of Ministers: Estanislao da Silva, a former FRETILIN interim prime minister (2007), was appointed Minister of State, Coordinator of Economic Affairs, and the Minister of Agriculture and Fisheries; Hernâni Coelho, a former ambassador to Australia in the previous FRETILIN government, was appointed to the key position of Minister of Foreign Affairs and Cooperation.[4] FRETILIN's Aleixo Maria da Silva was also made one of the two Ministers of State and Coordinating Minister of the Economy.

The formation of the Sixth Constitutional Government of Timor-Leste in 2015 was the final step in Xanana Gusmão's plan, in what he sees as his role as the "Father of National Unity", to establish a system of national reconciliation that in effect turns Timor-Leste for the time being into almost a *non-competitive* democracy. Whether this becomes a permanent situation and survives the 2017 elections is to be seen.

Xanana Gusmão's Pivotal Role in the Transition

As Maj Nygaard-Christensen noted in the review of Timor-Leste in 2015, Timorese politics is rarely predictable.[5] What has made East Timorese politics particularly unpredictable since 2007 is Gusmão himself. He has personally dominated the national political scene. A common observation is that "Timorese politics remain far more personality driven than ideologically driven".[6] Parties tend to revolve around their leader. This is very much the case with Gusmão. He, and not his party or his Council of Ministers, ran his governments between 2007 and 2015 as the charismatic leader. It is his ambitious strategic development plan that has created massive infrastructure projects in the south and in the enclave of Oecussi. He still exercises considerable personal influence over national affairs as the Senior Mentor in the cabinet and as Minister of Planning and Strategic Investment, a position that provides him with continued access to the country's Petroleum Fund.

Gusmão's political history underlies current developments. He was a founding member of FRETILIN, and in time became the leader of FALINTIL, the military wing of the party.[7] By the early 1980s he had become increasingly opposed to the ideological extremists in the party's Central Committee, to the point that he left FRETILIN, taking FALINTIL with him. From then until their startling reconciliation in 2013, Gusmão was a sworn political enemy of Marí Bim Mude Alkatiri, the Secretary-General and leader of FRETILIN.[8] As President, Gusmão opposed the Alkatiri government and was instrumental in Alkatiri's forced resignation as Prime Minister in the crisis of 2006.

In 2013, however, Gusmão took the first step to realize a programme of national unity he has pursued more or less consistently since 1986 when he formed the CNRM, a broad coalition intended to bring together all East Timorese groups in national unity, later succeeded by his National Council for Timorese Resistance in 1998.[9]

In January 2013 Gusmão called on Mari Alkatiri at his home to offer him a major position in his government. Alkatiri was initially appointed to oversee the creation of the Special Social Market Economy Zone (*Zona Especial de Economia Social de Mercado*; ZEESM) in Oecusse, the East Timorese enclave in West Timor. He was then appointed by the Council of Ministers as the head of the Oecusse Special Administrative Region with a wide range of executive powers and "an unprecedented degree of independence". The non-government organization La'o Hamutuk observed that "Perhaps it shows the real purpose of this project — bringing opposition leader and former Prime Minister Mari Alkatiri under the tent of current Prime Minister Xanana Gusmão." It warned that this action undermined FRETILIN's role as the opposition and therefore weakened East Timor's democracy.[10] This reconciliation with Alkatiri prepared the way for the Prime Minister to remake the party system and bring FRETILIN into a government of national unity.

Dr Araújo expressed the aspiration, following his inauguration, that the formation of the GNU represented "a selfless decision to put the interests of The People above all else".[11] The associated benefit, he explained in one of his first interviews after becoming Prime Minister, was that "given the limited pool of talent we have in the country, we should bring all the available talent to work together in the government. We are too small to be divided when it comes to governance."[12]

Positive and Negative Consequences of National Unity

The overarching political objective of the GNU is stability. In the longer term, the lesson of the crisis of 2006 for that small group of leading political actors from the generation of 1975 then competing for power in advance of the 2007 election was that polarized political conflict could threaten the very survival of the state.[13] It is in this broader context that a national unity government can be understood by those players as a guarantor of stability.

The claim is also made that the GNU is better positioned to offer strong and effective government. Lydia Beuman has identified some practical benefits that can flow from the GNU arrangement. The national unity government is likely to speed up and streamline decision-making and potentially improve the government's economic and policy performance. With its new stake in the government's success, FRETILIN would no longer be tempted to destabilize it. It would now stand united with the CNRT against dissident groups such as the so-called martial arts groups, the MAGs, and against hostile veteran's movements such as CPD-RDTL and the KRM which had previously clashed with security forces.[14] The record of the Sixth Constitutional Government in 2016 is reviewed below.

Is There an Opposition?

There has been widespread concern expressed that the arrangement set in place in February 2015 means that Timor-Leste no longer has an opposition. The downside to the form of consociational democracy now in place is that a political system without competition and opposition calls into question the opportunity for *alternancia*, the possibility of an alternation of leaders and parties in government which is a necessary condition for representative democracy.

It may be that the 2017 elections will revive FRETILIN's ambition to seek government in its own right. Prime Minister Araújo has insisted that FRETILIN remains "technically" in opposition. FRETILIN is not part of the government: "I have to clarify that FRETILIN as a party is not in government, although three senior members of the party have joined the government in an individual capacity."[15] Three senior FRETILIN officials I interviewed in December 2015 also stressed that the FRETILIN members of the government are there "as individuals". They offered the curious distinction that Dr Araújo had accepted the Prime Ministership with FRETILIN's approval but he was Prime Minister as an individual and not as a representative of his party. FRETILIN would contest the 2017 election as a real alternative government, offering the electorate a real choice.[16]

In practice, since February 2015 and even as early as 2013, the FRETILIN members of the ministry have increasingly acted in concert with the CNRT. FRETILIN supported the national budget in 2013, 2014, and unanimously again in 2015 and 2016. In the national parliament, FRETILIN has not opposed legislation, such as the controversial new Media Law, which previously it would have been expected to denounce.[17] Adriano do Nasimento, a Democratic Party

(PD) member of the parliament pointed out in an interview with me that Prime Minister Rui Araújo and Minister Estanislao da Silva are both leading members in the FRETILIN Central Committee: FRETILIN is no longer an opposition, "they are *all* in government".[18] Effectively, FRETILIN pulled back from its role as a critical opposition as early as January 2013, when Gusmão appointed Alkatiri to be in charge of the Oecussi Special Administrative Region.

Beuman has pointed out that the absence of an opposition may increase the likelihood of political issues arising, such as corruption, which is already a serious problem in Timor-Leste. The GNU "is, arguably, incompatible with inherent elements of democracy such as competitiveness, the independence of political identities and the freedom of choice among ideological and political alternatives".[19] The loss of an active opposition has conceivably further weakened an already under-institutionalized party system and undermined the already limited capacity of the National Parliament to keep the political executive accountable. It sets aside the principle of majority rule. The constituencies who voted for the two major parties in the 2012 elections, the CNRT or FRETILIN, are now, without their consent, represented by a CNRT government with a FRETILIN Prime Minister and FRETILIN representation in the Council of Ministers.

In so far as consociational democracy "violates the principle of majority rule",[20] a government of national unity conceivably may not accord with the intention of Section 7.2 of the Constitution:

> The state shall value the contribution of political parties for the organised expression of the popular will and for the democratic participation of the citizen in the governance of the country. (Section 7.2)

It may also not accord with Law No. 3/2004, which defines the role of political parties as to "critically appraise the actions of government and the public administration" (Section 2.c and Section 16.e). The role of critical appraisal translates into the responsibility of the legislature to exercise scrutiny of the political executive; that is, the Prime Minister and the Council of Ministers. The responsibility of the parliament to critically review the policies of government is clearly weakened by the absence of an autonomous opposition.

A Weakened Party System? Assessing Party Institutionalization

The Government of National Unity may further undermine a party system that is under-institutionalized and composed of generally institutionally weak individual political parties. Randal and Svåsand (2002) point out that to the extent that individual parties and the party system as a whole are well institutionalized, the rules and processes of competitive politics result in real, competitive, representative politics:

> In a competitive party system that is institutionalized one can expect continuity among party alternatives, enhancing prospects of electoral accountability. This is the structural component. The attitudinal component is that the parties accept each other as legitimate competitors, essential to the notion of political opposition.[21]

Randal and Svåsand propose a four-cell matrix with which to assess the institutionalization of political parties: two structural dimensions, "systemness" and "decisional autonomy", and two attitudinal dimensions, "value infusion" and "reification". Systemness and value infusion are internal dimensions of party institutionalization. Systemness concerns the "increasing scope, density and regularity of the interactions that constitute the party as a structure". This involves routine application of accepted conventions guiding the party's operations. Value-infusion refers to "the extent to which party actors and supporters ... acquire an identification with and commitment to the party which transcend mere instrumental or self-interested incentives for involvement". It is an important aspect of party cohesion. Reification refers to the extent to which the party's existence is established in the public imagination.

Timor-Leste's party system and the parties that constitute it are institutionally underdeveloped. With the partial exception of FRETILIN, parties are not organizationally robust. They tend to revolve around an individual leader. In terms of the two attitudinal dimensions of the institutionalized matrix, FRETILIN and CNRT may have enjoyed in the past a clearer identity in the electorate's mind. The question raised by the inclusion of the government party and the former opposition in a unified government is whether FRETILIN and CNRT lose their "value infusion" and "reification". CNRT faces the further problem that voters have identified with Xanana Gusmão, the leader, rather than with the party that, in the 2017 elections, he will not lead as Prime Minister.

Party Leadership

The workings of the party system and the parties in that system are singularly decided by the role of party leaders in Timor-Leste. During both the FRETILIN and the CNRT periods in government, the leader largely defined the relationship between political parties operating in the parliament with the political executive, to the detriment of parliament. The limited organizational capacity of most parties in Timor-Leste encourages personalist politics. Personalist politics operate within networks of patronage and reward political collusion rather than representative accountability.

The personalization of politics weakens party institutionalization. Particularly in the case of FRETILIN, Alkatiri's reconciliation with Gusmão since 2013 could bring into doubt his personal authority as Secretary-General with his own Central Committee, as well as with rank and file supporters. What role will he play in the 2017 elections? In the case of the CNRT, the party's Secretary-General conceded in an interview with me in 2010 that Prime Minister Gusmão preferred to operate independently of his party machine.[22] His appointment of Dr Araújo without consulting his party is the most recent and startling example of his practice of independent action.

The creation of a government of national unity has potentially weakened FRETILIN more than the CNRT. Until recently the party projected a clear separate identity as the party of the independence struggle and as a party ideologically defined by its past. Voters in its core support base — the three eastern districts of Baucau, Viqueque, and Lautem — could be confused over what FRETILIN now represents. The government's reconciliation with FRETILIN leaves the scrutiny and critique of government almost entirely up to Timorese civil society.[23] The party maintains its active engagement with the electorate through its district and sub-district organizations and claims it will campaign vigorously in 2017. But it may struggle to explain what alternative it offers to a government of which it is a part.

The unity government may also have weakened the CNRT. Gusmão's unexpected move to appoint Dr Araújo disconcerted if not dismayed some CNRT senior party members, who naturally assumed that the incoming Prime Minister would be chosen from among them.[24] At its national conference in 2013, the CNRT had agreed that the Prime Minister could decide who would hold each position in the ministry and that he could seek a resolution of political divisions in national politics. His decisions in February 2015 went beyond this brief. He may have seen himself as acting as the Father of National Unity by including FRETILIN in the project of nation-building and state-formation, but this had some negative consequences for his own party.[25] Two senior CNRT representatives indicated when I interviewed them in December 2015 that this had unsettled the CNRT party leadership and also would have an unsettling impact at the grass-roots level.[26] Gusmão maintains an active and possibly still decisive role in the Council of Ministers as Minister of Planning and Strategic Investment and as national mentor. Nevertheless, he will not lead the CNRT into the 2017 election as Prime Minister. The party system in the 2017 election will be operating in new territory.

The Electoral System

The electoral system rather rigidly confines political choice. As in 2012, in 2017 voters will not have a choice of individual candidates or of candidates representing specific electoral districts. The electoral system constitutes Timor-Leste into a single electorate. There are no individual electorates. Candidates for parliamentary office appear ranked on a single party list.[27] Each voting citizen is entitled to a single vote for a list. Lists of candidates must include names of women at a ratio of at least one in three. Party list systems have some advantages: They can result in a parliament that represents the electorate through a greater number of parties. They can ensure, as Timor-Leste's electoral system does, representation of women candidates for parliamentary office. The disadvantages include the removal of the direct link between parliamentary representatives and local constituents. The top-down electoral system denies voters the opportunity to choose individual, local members of parliament and, therefore, substantially diminishes the workings of representative democracy.

Party leaders can decide who appears on their party list and in what ranking. Parties become heavily centralized, as aspiring MPs are dependent upon the party leadership for any hope of election. In terms of Gusmão's influence over the CNRT beyond the 2017 election, he will need to decide (or at least to influence) the order of the CNRT party list (as he has done in the past). Again, if Alkatiri can retain his influence over the FRETILIN party list, he could project his choice of favoured candidates into the next parliament.

President versus Government: Elements of a Constitutional Crisis

A further new and unsettling element in East Timorese politics and government that threatened a constitutional crisis in 2016 was the assertive and critical role undertaken against the Government of National Unity by President Taur Matan Ruak. President Ruak — a former FALINTIL resistance commander and, after independence, the Major-General in command of the Defence Forces (F-FDTL) before his election to the Presidency in 2012 — has emerged as a determined opponent of the government and of Xanana Gusmão and Mari Alkatiri personally.

In October 2015 he refused a proposal from the government to renew the mandate of the General Chief of Staff of the F-FDTL, Major-General Lere Anan Timur whose term as Chief of Staff ended in that month. His argument was that General Lere had passed the F-FDTL retirement age. The President rejected two further proposals from the government for Lere's term to be renewed for a further four years. The President then decided to unilaterally nominate the Vice Chief of Staff, Brigadier Filomeno Paixão de Jesus, to replace General Lere.

On 24 February 2016 the Council of Ministers adopted a resolution to interpose an appeal for the annulment of the President's decision to dismiss the Chief of Staff and his decision to appoint the Vice-Chief of Staff in his place. The National Parliament also rejected the President's action, saying he did not have the power under the Constitution to appoint the Chief of Staff of the Defence Forces. Members of parliament and at least one CNRT Minister raised the possibility of impeachment.[28] Article 86(m) of the Constitution states that "it is incumbent on the President of the Republic with regard to other organs to appoint and dismiss, following proposal by the Government, the General Chief of Staff of the Defence Force".[29] The key here is the condition "following proposal by the Government". In 2012 the President had then opposed the appointment of Prime Minister Gusmão's choice for the Ministry of Defence. As Commander-in-Chief, the President has acted as if he has an overarching authority over such appointments as the Chief of Staff and even the Minister of Defence.

President Taur Matan Ruak for the first time used the presidential power to summon a special session of parliament on 25 February 2016. In his unscripted address to parliament he compared Xanana Gusmão and Mari Alkatiri to the former Indonesian dictator Soeharto, saying that there was "widespread discontent" among the public that Gusmão and Alkatiri's families were benefitting from lucrative government contracts.[30] He claimed that the government was using the Lere debate "to get to the President of the Republic". He said that

> The President of the Republic had received complaints concerning privileges granted to our brothers Xanana's and Mari's family members and friends within regarding contracts signed with the State.... There is widespread discontent over the granting of privileges.

The Government of National Unity should have brought political stability and economic prosperity. Instead, Alkatiri and Gusmão "do not use unanimity, mutual understanding to solve political and economic issues but use it for purposes of power and privilege".[31] The standoff between the President and the government over Major-General Lere's position continued unresolved in 2016 with the Major-General continuing in the position of Chief of the F-FDTL.

The President exercised his right under the Constitution to veto the 2016 General State Budget (GSB) passed by the National Parliament on 18 December 2015. The President finally, reluctantly, approved the budget on 14 January 2016, aware that under the Constitution, as the parliament had voted on the budget a second time on 8 January and returned it to the President, he was required to approve it. In a message to parliament the President reminded parliamentarians that he had warned that the current investment cannot be made at the expense of future development, "especially taking into account the amount of budgetary appropriations mobilized for this year, the amounts withdrawn from the Petroleum Fund above the Estimated Sustainable Income (ESI) limit and the priorities established in the GSB".[32] He disapproved of the large increased budgets for the ZEESM Special Economic Zone in Oecussi (up 63 per cent to US$218 million) and the Tasi Mane development project on the south coast at the expense of cuts to the public service, health, education, and other sectors.[33]

President Ruak has supported the formation of a new political party, the PLP (*Partai Libertasaun Popular*; People's Liberation Party), and there is speculation that he will run as this party's candidate for Prime Minister.[34] The PLP leader, Aderito Soares, is said to be close to the President. Members of parliament and at least one CNRT Cabinet Minister called for the President to resign, arguing that his association with the new party was unconstitutional.[35] The PLP campaigned in 2016 in the districts, claiming to be the new opposition party and that it was attracting support from both former CNRT and FRETILIN voters. Clearly, Taur Matan Ruak, if he were to win the Prime Ministership, would represent a new force that would overturn the established pattern of inter-party cooperation between FRETILIN and the CNRT. He would be no ally of Xanana Gusmão.

The Government Record in 2016

Given the extent of its challenges, the Sixth Constitutional Government appears to be working. An Australian diplomat I interviewed in Dili in November 2016 said the Araújo government was functioning reasonably well. The government announced its National Priorities for 2017 in July 2016. These were "agriculture (combating hunger and malnutrition); health; education; water and sanitation; basic infrastructure and the elections next year". These priorities addressed the broader planning framework of Timor-Leste's Strategic Development Plan 2011–30 and the Program of the Sixth Constitutional Government 2015–17. The Prime

Minister said his government was deeply committed to achieving the new United Nations Sustainable Development Goals (SDGs), which would be integrated into all government planning and budgeting for 2017. The focus would be on SDG number 2 (nutrition and food security), number 4 (education) and number 9 (infrastructure), while paying attention to human development goals such as health (SDG 3), gender equality (SGD 5), and water and sanitation (SDG 6).[36] Strategic Development Goal 2 must be a first priority in a country that has been identified by the International Food Policy Research Institute in its Global Hunger Index as the second-hungriest country in Asia. Seventy per cent of Timor-Leste's citizens are subsistence farmers, who faced a particularly severe dry season in 2016.[37] Unemployment and underemployment were a growing social problem in 2016. Included among the unemployed were a rising number of jobless graduates; a potentially serious source of social unrest. The private sector generates very limited employment opportunities, and an increasing number of East Timorese seek work overseas.[38]

In his speech to the national parliament on the state of the nation, President Taur Matan Ruak noted government achievements in 2016, including progress on strategic development plans, steps taken towards economic decentralization, that ninety per cent of the population now had access to electricity, that more than two hundred kilometres of roads were built, new schools opened, the healthcare network extended, and new administrative duties assigned to the municipalities to bring public services closer to the people. But he also expressed his "great sadness" that, after fourteen years of independence, "the assistance provided to vulnerable groups is often below the real needs and poverty continues to afflict many sons and daughters of Timor-Leste".[39] In fact, the country has made some progress in poverty reduction and in improved healthcare. In September 2016 the government launched a report that confirmed that Timor-Leste had made significant progress in poverty reduction since 2007.[40] Among other legislation, a draft law on Preventing and Combating Human Trafficking was approved in parliament in October.

The Economy in 2016

Timor-Leste recorded steady growth with real GDP growth of around five per cent in 2016. There was some increase in foreign direct investment and some growth in the private sector in an economy that remains very underdeveloped outside state spending in the public sector through large withdrawals from the Petroleum Fund. Oil revenues were just under US$1 billion in 2015, down by a third of their level in 2013. The decline of the petroleum sector has meant that the government budget has moved rapidly from an overall budget surplus of 40 per cent in 2013 to a 10 per cent deficit in 2015.[41]

The World Bank's *East Asia Pacific Economic Update October 2016: Reducing Vulnerabilities* noted that Timor-Leste

> is facing an outlook starkly different to its recent past. Previously one of the most oil-dependent countries in the world, it could become a post-oil country in as little as five years' time.

Government has invested heavily in domestic infrastructure drawing on the oil receipts, and economic reform efforts are beginning to show some results. It still needs to implement key reforms to support a more diversified economy.[42] The *Update* warned that the government's expansionary spending programme driven by an ambition to boost long-term growth is subject to "limited capacity to implement the program with execution rates for the infrastructure budget low and increasingly high prices demanded for construction works". There are important questions concerning the quality and prioritization of the investment programme. Timor-Leste "still ranks as having one of the least conducive regulatory environments for business in the world".[43]

The 2017 General State Budget of US$1.386.8 billion was significantly less than the US$1.562 billion 2016 budget. As in 2016, the 2017 budget was passed unanimously, supported by all parties in the parliament. The eight Democratic Party MPs have supported the past three budgets despite the party's serious reservations regarding what it saw as the undemocratic budget process introduced in 2015, whereby the process was taken over by a Special Budget Committee in which PD only had one representative. In an interview, the PD representative, Adriano do Nascimento, insisted that PD wanted the extended plenary process before 2015 to continue rather than the process being handled by the Special Budget Committee, which only required a relatively brief plenary discussion to approve the budget. He also complained that parliamentary oversight of separate budgets such as the Autonomous Fund (previously the Infrastructure Fund) was no longer practised, and these substantial funds were deployed at the discretion of the executive.[44]

Security

At the same time, problems of unemployment, poverty, corruption, and organized violence continue unabated. Transparency International ranks Timor-Leste as 123rd out of 168 countries on its Corruption Perceptions Index, a very poor result. There are a number of cases of alleged corruption by high officials and politicians before the courts, but cases are moving very slowly.[45] The issue of corruption at high levels of government has been taken up by veterans groups to confront the government and clash with security forces. The OECD's "States of Fragility 2016: Understanding Violence" report identified Timor-Leste as one of the three most fragile states in the region; more fragile than some Middle-Eastern states that had recently endured coup attempts.[46]

Veterans groups have posed a serious threat to the government in the past, provoking in 2015 a four-month security operation against former FALINTIL commander, Mauk Moruk, who called for a revolution to wipe out corruption, nepotism, and collusion. His group launched a series of attacks against security forces. He was killed in August 2015. Veterans groups such as CPD-RDTL and the KRM continued to be a security problem in 2016. Conflict between martial arts groups (MAGs) remains a serious public concern, with a rising number of assaults, fatalities, and destruction of property. There are claims that some political parties have used MAGs to intimidate opponents. A significant number of police officers belong to MAGs. The government has responded with Law 10/2008 and the Council of Ministers Resolutions 35/2011, 24/2012, and 16/2013, without containing the problem.[47] Fundasaun Mahein, an independent NGO, issued a report in August that claimed police "vigilantism" and the use of violence were becoming worse, with incidents of police using unnecessary force against civilians, including a local journalist.[48] There were further issues of censorship and the Prime Minister taking out criminal defamation charges against journalists in 2016.[49]

International Relations

The major national issue for Timor-Leste in 2016, more pressing than the long process to gain entry into ASEAN, was the assertion of Timor-Leste's rights over the maritime resources of the Timor Sea. The government vigorously pursued negotiations with Australia throughout 2016 over the disputed maritime boundary Timor-Leste and Australia share in the Timor Sea. On 10 February 2016, the Timorese government officially welcomed the decision by the Australian Labor Party at its National Conference held in Melbourne on 26 July 2015 that if elected to government it would renegotiate the settlement of maritime boundaries between the two countries. A Labor government would uphold a commitment to a rules-based international system, including a review of Australia's reservations concerning the United Nations Convention on the Law of the Sea (UNCLOS) and a preparedness platform for maritime boundary disputes to be settled through the International Court of Justice (ICJ) and the International Tribunal of the Law of the Sea.[50]

In April 2016, Timor-Leste launched United Nations Compulsory Conciliation Proceedings on Maritime Boundaries with Australia under UNCLOS. It noted that while there are "temporary" resource-sharing arrangements, there are no permanent maritime boundaries between the two countries. Australia had excluded cases of maritime boundary delimitation from its participation in the ICJ and strictly limited its participation in compulsory arbitration under UNCLOS in 2002, two months before Timor-Leste's independence, limiting Timor-Leste's means to enforce its rights under international law.[51]

Australia appointed its two conciliators to the five-member UN Conciliation Commission in May. The commission was established on 29 June. Hearings were held at the Permanent Court of Arbitration premises in The Hague in late August and they continued through September. When the commission published its Decision on Competence, Australia indicated its intention to contest the competence of the commission to rule on the dispute. Australia lost its claim that the international commission had no jurisdiction to hear the complaint by Timor-Leste. Australia must renegotiate the agreement forced on Timor-Leste in 2002. Prime Minister Malcolm Turnbull earlier in 2016 had rejected the call for fresh negotiations on the maritime boundary, but the decision released on 26 September from the Permanent Court of Arbitration at The Hague opened the way for formal talks between the two countries in 2017.[52]

On 10 January 2017 the Timor-Leste government formally notified Australia of the termination of the 2006 Treaty on Certain Maritime Arrangements (CMATS), the agreement of the division of revenues between Timor-Leste and Australia from the Greater Sunrise oil and gas fields. The termination would come into effect on 10 April 2017. Both governments agreed that the Timor Sea Treaty signed in 2002 would remain in force in its original form before the 2006 treaty.[53]

Conclusion

Timor-Leste in 2016 experienced its second year under a government of national unity with possible negative consequences for the development of a competitive, representative democratic system. In terms of its performance, the GNU system has provided some benefits in terms of new cooperation between CNRT and FRETILIN on national security. It achieved unanimous agreement on the national budget which expedites the government agenda. The problem here is that the priorities of the national budget constitute the core of the government's programme and objectives. It deserves critical scrutiny and the consideration of alternative strategies. This was the argument put by the President when he vetoed the 2016 budget. FRETILIN once provided this critical scrutiny. Now the budget debate is not subjected to the scrutiny of a robust opposition.

It has been argued here that while the Sixth Constitutional Government has operated reasonably well, particularly considering the range of challenges facing a government in Timor-Leste, the continuation of a unity government represents significant new limitations on the operation of a representative, competitive democratic system. It has probably weakened a party system that was already underdeveloped. It has also further limited the autonomous capacity of parliament to hold the political executive to account. It could encourage a loss of transparency and therefore enhance opportunities for leaders and political elites to negotiate deals that serve private rather than the public interest. The fuel that runs the economy and the government's highly ambitious — and expensive — infrastructure and development programmes is the petro-dollars from the Petroleum Fund. Petro-dollars may also fund the distribution of state resources through systems of patronage and cronyism. The need for a strong, accountable, and transparent democratic system is all the more critical if the negative consequences of major developments like the Tasi Mane Infrastructure project in the south and the ZEESM project in Oecussi are to be managed and contained.

Notes

1. Arend Lijphart, *Thinking about Democracy: Power-Sharing and Majority Rule in Theory and Practice* (Routledge, 2007), p. 30. Lijphart first explained the term in the article "Consociational Democracy", *World Politics* 21, no. 2 (January 1960): 207–25.
2. Maj Nygaard-Christensen, "Timor-Leste in 2015: Petro-Politics or Sustainable Growth?", *Southeast Asian Affairs 2016*, edited by Malcolm Cook and Daljit Singh (Singapore: ISEAS – Yusof Ishak Institute, 2016), pp. 347–59.
3. FRETILIN (*Frente Revolucionária de Timor-Leste Independente*; Revolutionary Front for an Independent East Timor). CNRT (*Conselho Nacional de Reconstrução de Timor*; National Congress for Timorese Reconstruction).
4. Nygaard-Christensen, "Timor-Leste in 2015", p. 350.
5. Ibid., p. 348.
6. International Crisis Group, 2012, quoted in Rui Graça Feijó, *Dynamics of Democracy in Timor-Leste, The Birth of a Democratic Nation, 1999–2012* (Amsterdam: Amsterdam University Press, 2016), p. 197.

7. FALINTIL; Armed Forces for the National Liberation of East Timor.

8. Dennis Shoesmith, "Timor-Leste: Divided Leadership in a Semi-Presidential System", *Asian Survey* 43, no. 2 (March/April 2003): 240. See Sarah Niner, ed. *To Resist is To Win! The Autobiography of Xanana Gusmão with selected letters and speeches* (Melbourne: Aurora/David Lovell, 2000).

9. CNRM (*Conselho Nacional de Resistência Maubere*; National Council of Maubere Resistance). CNRT (*Conselho Nacional de Resistência Timorense*; Natonal Council of Timorese Resistance). The party formed in 2007 deliberately used the same acronym to identify with the earlier council.

10. La'o Hamutuk, "Special Economic Zone in Oecussi", 31 July 2014 <http://www.laohamutuk.org/econ/Oecussi/ZEESMIndex.htm>.

11. Rui Mariade Araújo, "Speech by His Excellency the Prime Minister Dr Rui Maria de Araújo on the Occasion of the Swearing-in of the Sixth Constitutional Government", Lahane Palace, Dili, 16 February 2015 <http://timor-leste.gov.tl/?cat=27&lang=en&page=4> (accessed 12 October 2016).

12. Quoted in S. Roughneen, "In the Footsteps of Gusmao", *Nikkei Asian Review*, 10 March 2015. See the discussion on this in Lydia M. Beuman, *Political Institutions in East Timor, Semi-Presidentialism and Democratisation* (London: Routledge, 2016), p. 201.

13. Although FRETILIN denied the legitimacy of Gusmão's AMP coalition government installed by President Ramos-Horta in 2007, in practice it acted as the parliamentary opposition between 2007 and 2012 and accepted the need for some degree of stable government. Author's interview with Adriano do Nascimento, Democratic Party MP, Parliament House, 17 December 2015.

14. Beuman, *Political Institutions in East Timor*, p. 207.

15. Quoted in Roughneen, "In the Footsteps of Gusmao".

16. Interview with three FRETILIN party leaders, FRETILIN Headquarters, Comoro, Dili, 18 December 2015.

17. Beuman, *Political Institutions in East Timor*, p. 207; See also Graça R. Feijó, "Timor-Leste: The Two Sides of Success", in *Southeast Asian Affairs 2015*, edited by Daljit Singh (Singapore: Institute of Southeast Asian Studies, 2015), pp. 369–83.

18. Interview with Adriano do Nascimento, MP, Parliament House, Dili, 17 December, 2015.

19. Beuman, *Political Institutions in East Timor*, p. 207.

20. Lijphart, *Thinking about Democracy*, p. 30.

21. Vicky Randall and Lars Svåsand, "Party Institutionalisation in New Democracies", *Party Politics* 8, no. 5 (2002): 7.

22. Dionisio Babo Soares, Interview with Secretary-General of CNRT, Dili, 24 August 2010.

23. Nygaard-Christensen, "Timor-Leste in 2015", p. 350.

24. Dionisio Babo Soares, Interview with Minister of State and Secretary-General of the CNRT Dili, 17 December 2015.

25. Ibid.

26. Author Interviews, Dili, December 2015.

27. The electoral rules are encoded in Law No. 6/2006, the Law on the Election of the National Parliament, which establishes that "[t]here shall be only one single constituency in the election of the National Parliament corresponding to the entire national territory, headquartered in Dili" (Article 9).

28. Presidential Power, "Timor-Leste — Mr President, How Does Democracy Work in Timor if There is No Opposition?", 13 April 2016 <http://presidential-power.com/?tag=president-ruak> (accessed 21 December 2016).

29. "Exoneration of Chief of Staff of the F-FDTL Major-General Lere: Confusion over the Constitutionality of This Move", *East Timor Law and Justice Bulletin*, 2 March 2016.

30. Speech by His Excellency the President of the Republic, Taur Matan Ruak, to National Parliament on the Dismissal of Major-General Lere Anan Timur, Dili on 25 February 2016; See also Tom Allard, "Discontent about Xanana Gusmao, Mari Alktiri Families: East Timor", *Sydney Morning Herald*, 27 February 2016.

31. Presidential Power, "Timor-Leste — Mr President".

32. "His Excellency the President of the Republic, Taur Matan Ruak, Enacts the 2016 Amending General State Budget", press release, Nicolau Lobato Palace, 8 August 2016.

33. For a critical analysis of the 2016 budget, see La'o Hamutuk, "2016 Budget Proposal Puts Fantasies before People's Needs", 8 November 2015 <http://laohamutuk.blogspot.com/2015/11/2016-budget-proposal-puts-fantasies.html>.

34. Ted McDonnell, "Timor-Leste President Taur Matan Ruak Urged to Resign", *The Australian*, 18 November 2015.

35. Ibid.

36. Government of Timor-Leste, "Government Announces National Priorities for 2017", 5 July 2016 <http://timor-leste.gov.tl/?p=15755&lang=en>.

37. Wendy Levy, "In Timor-Leste, 'Hunger Season' Will Be Worse after El Niño", 12 October 2016 <https://www.irinnews.org/news/2016/10/12/timor-leste-%E2%80%9Chunger-season%E2%80%9D-will-be-worse-after-el-ni%C3%B1O>.

38. "Unemployment Rate in Timor-Leste reaches 11 per cent", *Dili Weekly*, 8 July 2016. Thousands of East Timorese work in Britain, often on Portuguese passports. After BREXIT their future employment in Britain will be at risk. Father Pat Smythe, "After Brexit Timorese Workers Are Worried about Their Future in the UK", 5 July 2016.

39. Speech by His Excellency President Taur Matan Ruak to the National Parliament on the State of the Nation, Dili, National Parliament, 20 September 2016.

40. World Food Program, Timor-Leste Country Brief, August 2016 <http://reliefweb.

int/report/timor-leste/wfp-timor-leste-country-brief-august-2016>; "Poverty Declining in Timor-Leste", *Timor-Leste Survey of Living Standards*, 28 September 2016; "Government Launches Report on Poverty", ETAN, 30 September 2016 <http://timor-leste.gov.tl/?p=16277&lang=en>; Ministry of Finance, Government of Timor-Leste, "Poverty Declining in Timor Leste" <https://www.mof.gov.tl/poverty-declining-in-timor-leste/?lang=en> (accessed 20 December 2016); and "Timor-Leste Announced World's 'Most Improved' in the Health-Rated Index", Dili, 26 September 2016.

41. World Bank, *East Asia Pacific Economic Update, October 2016: Reducing Vulnerabilities*, 4 October 2016, p. 154.

42. Ibid.

43. Ibid., p. 155.

44. Interview with Adriano do Nascimento, Parliament House, 17 December 2015.

45. Bureau of Economics and Business Affairs, *Investment Climate Statement for 2016*, 29 September 2016 <http://www.state.gov/e/eb/rls/othr/ics/2016/eap/254321.htm>.

46. IOECD, "States of Fragility 2016: Understanding Violence", 2 December 2016 <http://www.sbs.com.au/news/article/2016/12/02/fragile-ratings-australias-near-neoighbours>.

47. Abel Amaral, Outreach Officer, Fundasaun Mahein, Dili, 1 December 2016.

48. "Police 'Vigilantism' and the Use of Violence are Increasing", Fundasaun Mahein, 15 August 2016 <http://www.fundasaunmahein.org/2016/08/08/polisia-main-hakim-sendiri-no-brutalismu-ironiku-aumenta-makaas-liu-tan/>.

49. ETAN, "East Timor Journalists Face Defamation Trial after Story on Prime Minister Rui de Araujo", ABC News, 6 October 2016 <http://www.abc.net.au/news/2016-10-06/east-timor-journalists-face defamation-trial/7910892>; "Journalists call on Timor-Leste PM to Drop Defamation Complaint against Reporters", Globalvoices, 18 October 2016 <https://globalvoices.org/2016/10/18/journalists-call-on-timor-leste-pm-to-drop-defeamtion-complaint-against-reporters/>. The Prime Minister took defamation action against two journalists, Raimundos Oki and Lourenço Martins, who alleged in an article in the *Timor Post*, 10 November 2015, that Araujo had been involved, when a senior advisor in the Finance Ministry in 2014, in the corrupt award of a government contract for information technology. The story misidentified the company that actually won the contract. The trial was due to be heard in December 2016.

50. Government of Timor-Leste Media Release, Dili, 10 February 2016 on the Resolution of the Australian Labor Party on Timor-Leste, 26 July 2015.

51. Government of Timor-Leste, "Timor Launches United Nations Compulsory Conciliation Proceedings on Maritime Boundaries with Australia", Dili, 11 April 2016.

52. Daniel Flitton, "Australia Loses Attempt to Knock out East Timor's Maritime Boundary Dispute", *Sydney Morning Herald*, 26 September 2016.

53. Grant Wyeth, "Timor-Leste Seeks a Better Maritime Border with Australia", *The Diplomat*, 11 January 2017 <http://thediplomat.com/2017/timor-leste-seeks-a-better-maritime-border-with-australia/> (accessed 16 February 2017).

Vietnam

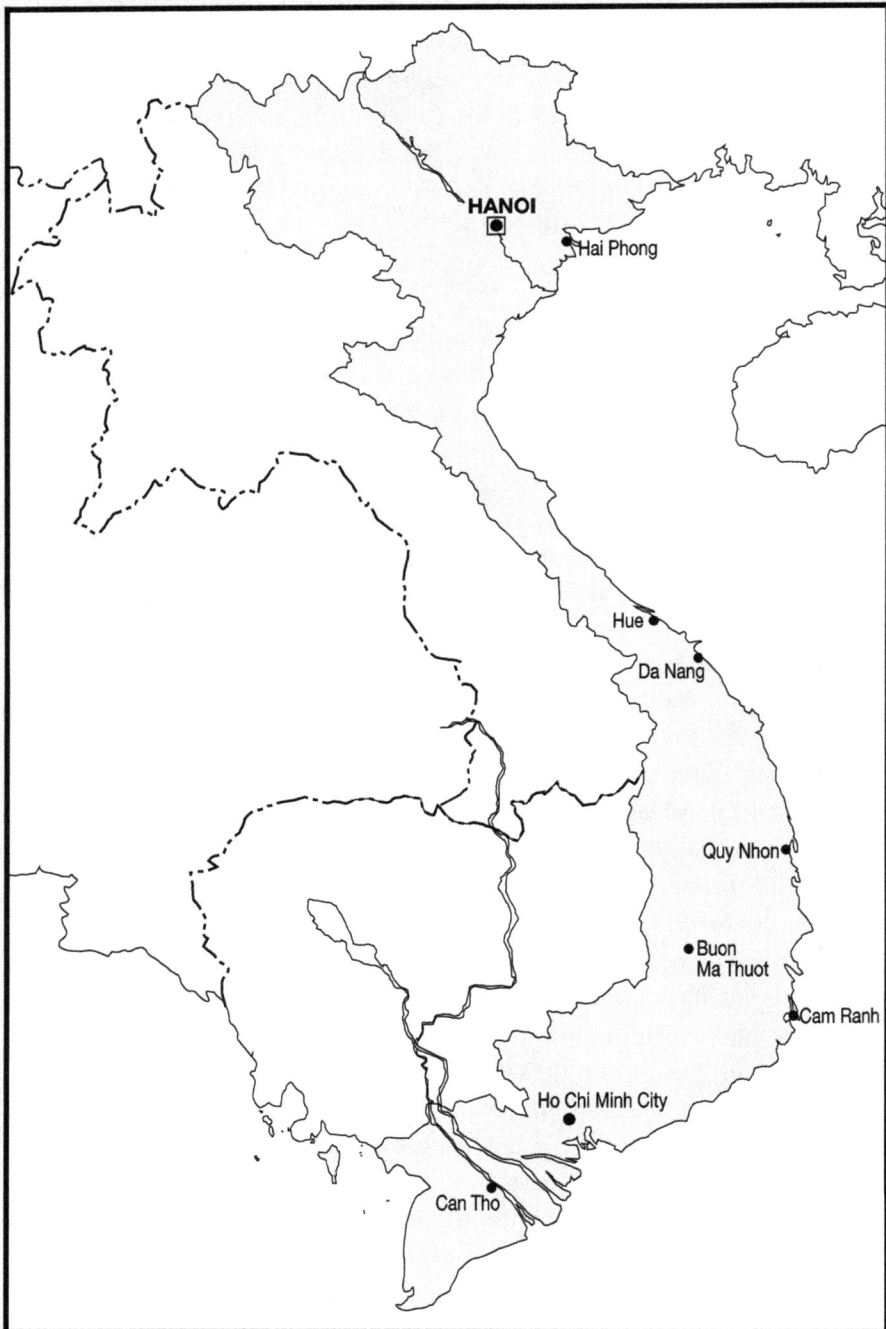

VIETNAM IN 2016:
Searching for a New Ethos

Phuong Nguyen

Vietnam in 2016 went through a crucial leadership transition at the 12th Congress of the ruling Vietnamese Communist Party in January. Its economy stands at a crossroads, after thirty years of *doi moi*, or renovation, turned Vietnam into a lower-middle-income country with a thriving manufacturing-based, export-led economy, but which still leaves much to be desired. Vietnam still occupies the lower end of the global supply chain, and remains bridled with a largely inefficient state-owned sector and a weak financial sector. The government, however, aspires to achieve "modernity, industrialization, and a higher quality of life" by the year 2035, when Vietnam will have been reunified for sixty years.[1]

On the international front, Vietnam has forged a wide range of partnerships with foreign countries — including with both neighbouring countries and larger powers — and has managed to redefine its relations with the West, in particular the United States. Yet it faces ever more complex foreign policy challenges, which emanate primarily from an increasingly aggressive posture by China in the South China Sea — where Vietnam is an active claimant in the maritime territorial disputes — and an evolving regional order. The leadership and populace alike seem to be looking for a game changer that can help address the host of geostrategic and socio-economic challenges facing Vietnam. If the past thirty years were foundational in Vietnam's charting of its post-war history and the terms of its relations with the outside world, the period from 2016 onward is slated to usher in a new, more dynamic era in this country of nearly a hundred million.

PHUONG NGUYEN is a non-resident WSD-Handa Fellow with Pacific Forum and based in Washington, DC.

Leadership Transition and Contest

After a decade of freewheeling politics under the controversial former Prime Minister, Nguyen Tan Dung, large parts of Vietnam's leadership preferred to return to an equilibrium in domestic politics where collective leadership, the unwritten rule of Vietnamese politics, was the norm. Political infighting has always existed among the elite, and competition to varying degrees between the country's top four posts — Party Chief, President, Prime Minister, and Head of the National Assembly — is not a new phenomenon. But during his rule, Dung's relentless pursuit of power and personal wealth, as well as his outspokenness and brash rhetoric that defy the parameters of Vietnamese politics, alienated many within the party leadership and bureaucracy.

This dynamic tended to make it difficult for the leadership to reach consensus or compromise at important junctures. Although Dung managed, through his vast patronage network, to set the agenda for a number of economic portfolios and amass significant power for his office — charged in principle with implementing party policy — he also made sworn enemies of many within the historically powerful party apparatus. To make matters worse, the former premier made no secret of his ambition to be propelled to the post of party chief, the highest-ranking position in Vietnam's political system, in the months leading up to the Party Congress. Some in Hanoi were concerned that a scenario in which Dung would lead the party would sooner or later spell trouble for the sustainability of the party-state apparatus.

What happened at the five-yearly Party Congress in January can be summed up as follows. A so-called "anybody but Dung" coalition led by then party chief Nguyen Phu Trong had emerged to squash Dung's ambition by attacking his party bona fide, management track record, and fitness to lead.[2] The strategy worked, and Dung ended up with neither a formal nomination by the Politburo — a prerequisite for candidates standing for the top leadership positions — nor the necessary popular support among the delegates to upend the balance of power. Trong, meanwhile, was voted to stay on as party chief, given his uncontroversial record and commitment to protecting the party's pre-eminence in internal politics.

Trong's reappointment was a crucial development that set the tone for Vietnam's politics and direction in the wake of the congress. His mission is an overarching one: reasserting party authority in all decision-making, tempering the rampant corruption and rent-seeking that was allowed to mushroom under Dung, and giving a sense of direction to the next phase of Vietnam's *doi moi* efforts. To round out the top leadership, Nguyen Xuan Phuc, a former Deputy Prime Minister and economist by training, was put in place as Prime Minister; former internal security czar Tran Dai Quang as President; and former Vice Chair of the National Assembly Nguyen Thi Kim Ngan as Chairwoman of the legislature, making her the first woman to ever hold that post. Phuc and his cabinet, in particular, shouldered the enormous task of developing the broad economic restructuring agenda for the 2016–20 period that was approved at the Party Congress.

The leadership transition resulted in a realignment in internal dynamics. The nineteen-member Politburo, seven of whom were retained from the previous term, reflects a variety of views and backgrounds and includes several new faces that had been promoted under Dung — a conscious effort to maintain continuity and party unity. Yet, under the current government, elements seen as moderate and conservative have unmistakably risen to play a large role in economic policymaking, reclaiming the mantle previously occupied by Dung's supporters, who could be characterized broadly as a mix of opportunistic rent-seekers and reformists.

Deputy Prime Minister Vuong Dinh Hue, a former head of the party central economic committee, embodies the new coalition led by Trong. Within the cabinet, his portfolio as deputy premier includes helping the Prime Minister in areas of international integration and the reform of state-owned enterprises (SOEs); and monitoring economic ministries, financial regulatory agencies, and the central bank. Hue has further been tapped to lead the National Council for Financial and Monetary Policy Consultation, a thirty-nine-member body established in June to advise the Prime Minister on comprehensive financial sector reforms. In this capacity, Hue is to play a crucial role in the development of a plan that is under way to restructure credit institutions and bad debt management for the 2016–20 period.

Another powerful figure to have emerged under Trong is Dinh The Huynh, who was previously the party's propaganda chief. As the Executive Secretary of the party secretariat, Huynh plays a crucial role in Trong's party-building efforts, including by preventing and rooting out elements seen as ideologically deviant or too corrupt. In particular, Trong has devoted significant energy to a campaign launched in October to detect and combat what in Hanoi is termed "self-evolution", the process by which elements in the leadership — unwittingly or otherwise — come to adhere to the ideology of Western liberal democracy and begin to advocate change from within.[3] Observers have suggested that Huynh would be a likely candidate to succeed the seventy-two-year-old Trong if and when he decides to step down.

Shortly after resuming office, Trong stepped up his rhetoric on combatting corruption in the government. For Trong's faction, the anti-corruption drive and stamping out remaining elements within Dung's patronage network are two sides of the same coin. They understand fundamentally that economic reforms cannot be advanced as long as a network of opportunists and rent seekers still controls important levers of power. Above all, Trong, a party ideologist, firmly believes that chronic corruption and cronyism at the highest levels of government, if unchecked, will ultimately threaten the legitimacy of the regime.

As a result, investigations into management practices and past appointments at several large SOEs have been launched, with the targets often being current and former officials with links to Dung. Most notably, the leadership in late 2016 decided, at the suggestion of the party secretariat, to "discipline" a former senior official under Dung, Vu Huy Hoang, for the mismanagement of state assets and a number of personnel appointments during his time as Trade Minister.[4] The legislature's standing committee in early 2017 issued a resolution to strip the retired minister of all his past titles, erasing any and all official recognition and benefits that came with them.[5] The decision to punish a retired official — unprecedented in Vietnamese politics — was a warning signal to currently serving officials that the days of "politics as usual", when leaders who enriched themselves could still have a safe landing after retirement, may well be a thing of the past. Government ministries are said to be working on new legislation that would allow for the "fair and strict punishment" of state officials retroactively.[6] During the early years of *doi moi*, those in the leadership who favoured change also painstakingly pushed through a campaign of "purification" designed to rid the bureaucracy of elements deemed incompetent or fervently resistant to reforms. It is still too early to judge the effectiveness of the ongoing anti-corruption campaign — interwoven as it remains with lingering battles among competing elite factions at times — and whether it will ultimately lead to a mindset change among current policymakers in Hanoi.[7]

The past five years also witnessed Vietnam's expanding regional profile, the rise of an informed and affluent urban middle class, rapprochement with the West — most notably the United States — and the emergence of different views among the ruling elite and intellectual class over the country's long-term direction, politically, socio-economically, and strategically. These trends, which were set in motion either by Vietnam's economic opening or external forces beyond Hanoi's control, can be easily reversed. An essential question facing the leadership over the next five years, therefore, will be how to push forward comprehensive economic reforms, as it has set out to do, and harness the potential of a more vibrant society, all the while retaining the party's iron grip.

Searching for a New Growth Model

Vietnam is in need of a new growth strategy. Thirty years of market-oriented reforms have transformed the once war-torn country into a lower-middle-class society, a thriving regional manufacturing hub for garments and electronics, and an increasingly attractive destination for foreign investment. At the same time, its economy remains only loosely integrated with the global supply chain, depends primarily on foreign investment to fuel its export-led growth, and suffers from a large and inefficient state-owed sector and an underdeveloped domestic private sector. At the same time that steadily rising labour costs are putting Vietnam's garment manufacturing sector at a disadvantage compared to competitors such as Bangladesh and Myanmar, 86 per cent of the more than two million jobs in the clothing and footwear industries may be at risk over the next decade due to automation and disruptive technologies.[8] The country has emerged as an attractive manufacturing hub for global technology companies — supplying smart phones and electronic devices and parts — with exports in electronics surging in recent years to become the biggest export revenue source for the government. Yet statistics show Vietnamese suppliers make up only 20 per cent of businesses in supporting industries that supply to the sprawling high-tech manufacturing sector — compared to up to 40 per cent in neighbouring Malaysia and Thailand.[9] These numbers suggest that, without serious investments devised to help the country move up the value chain, Vietnam will only reap limited benefits from its current growth model. Public institutions, long modelled for a Soviet-style centrally planned economy, have not always kept pace with the demands of a more open, market-driven economy.

The leadership wants Vietnam to become a "basic industralized nation" and have in place the foundation of a "socialist-oriented market economy" by 2020,[10] and understands that comprehensive economic restructuring is critical in order for Vietnam to maintain the level of six to seven per cent growth rates into the future, hence preserving party legitimacy. Across the political spectrum, however, officials and intellectuals alike remain confounded over what it means to build a socialist-oriented market economy, and, as a result, how much state control to ease in different areas of the economy. This dichotomy will be an important fault line in Vietnamese policymaking in the coming years.

Prime Minister Phuc, known as an avid administrator, surprised observers when, shortly after assuming office in April, he began to advocate for the concept of "constructive government" (*chính phủ kiến tạo*), a spirit he urged government officials at all levels to adopt towards the populace and business community.[11] In his speeches Phuc pointed out that the government has too often hindered, rather than aided, businesses and people's lives, a mindset which he said must change. In the context of official Vietnamese discourse, the idea that government ought to be guided by a distinct characteristic — in this case, constructiveness — in dealing with its constituents is fascinating to say the least. This is because in the traditional parlance of Hanoi politics, the party, the state, and the people are very often sub-groups of the same entity, or interchangeable. Phuc's new discourse has prompted a lively debate among intellectuals and on social media on how best to interpret "constructive government", which has no ready equivalent in the English language, and what it says about the trajectory of state–society relations in Vietnam.[12] According to a respected Vietnamese scholar, the fundamental difference between "constructive government" and previous modes of governance is that while the latter places an emphasis on managing or ruling the citizenry and business community, the latter focuses on creating opportunities for them.[13] In addition, the Prime Minister has, since taking office, made multiple surprise visits to local markets and shops under the guise of inspecting food safety and interacting with ordinary citizens, in a fashion akin to politicians in, for example, democratically governed Indonesia. It remains to be seen, however, whether Phuc's mantra will reverberate across Vietnam's officialdom.

Six months after coming into office, the government in October approved a blueprint for economic restructuring for the 2016–20 period, which is built on three guiding objectives. They are: (1) gradually allowing market mechanisms to play a leading role in the economy and allocation of resources; (2) developing higher-value-added industries to gradually become the engine of the economy, taking the place of current low-value-added ones (e.g., garment manufacturing, electronics assembly); and (3) actively undertaking international integration (i.e., in trade and investment) and improving Vietnam's international standing.[14]

In order to implement this agenda, Hanoi settled on five major areas of reform for the current term. First, the government agreed that it needs to help accelerate the growth of the domestic private sector and continue to attract foreign direct investment (FDI). Second, there needs to be concerted efforts in reforming the state-led sector, including revamping SOEs and the mechanisms governing public investment and public spending. Third, reform of the financial sector, including credit institutions and the development of capital markets, should be given greater importance. Fourth, the government needs to modernize its economic thinking and planning in ways that would help boost productivity. And fifth, the leadership needs to allow market forces to decide on important factors of production such as land use, labour, and science and technology.[15] The five-year endeavour was estimated to cost nearly $500 billion, or 10,000 trillion Vietnamese dong, and would include the cost for resolving bad debts at domestic banks that have accumulated since the early 2000s.[16]

Vietnam stands at a juncture where the success of economic reforms and reforms in politics and governance are mutually reinforcing. For Trong, tackling corruption and vested interests in the still sprawling network of SOEs ultimately requires scaling down the role it plays in the economy, as SOEs still account for about 40 per cent of Vietnam's economic output. Logically, this also means strengthening the role of the domestic private sector across all sectors of the economy, and encouraging foreign investors to participate in sectors prone to corruption, such as infrastructure. For instance, the government has been working to speed up the sale of its remaining stakes in large and more profitable SOEs, such as dairy company Vinamilk — the goals of which are to attract capital and improve corporate governance at these companies. Likewise, attracting FDI in sectors deemed strategic for economic restructuring — including infrastructure, high-tech manufacturing, industrial support industries, information and communications technology, and seafood and agricultural processing — is due to be accorded greater priority in the coming years as part of the concerted efforts to reshape Vietnam's economic growth model.[17] The government is also in the process of preparing for the first time legislation on supporting small and medium-sized enterprises.[18]

The uncertainty surrounding the future of the Trans-Pacific Partnership (TPP) trade agreement, which Vietnam signed with eleven other Pacific Rim countries in February, nonetheless had the effect of muddling Vietnam's economic outlook. U.S. president-elect Donald Trump's announcement shortly after his election victory in November of his plan for to United States to withdraw from the TPP came as a disappointment to those in the Vietnamese leadership who had been looking for a robust reform catalyst, especially those who had worked hard over the past few years to convince the collective elite of the TPP's merits. Senior leaders, including Party Chief Trong, have spoken on the importance of meeting the requirements of "new-generation free trade agreements" that Vietnam has signed on to, including with the European Union, South Korea, and the Russia-led Eurasia Economic Union, as a pillar for further economic reforms.[19] The TPP was seen as a prime game changer, and its uncertain road ahead forced questions on the momentum behind Vietnam's reform efforts in areas such as governance, trade, investment, and labour. Lacking clarity from Washington surrounding the future of the TPP, some in Vietnam's leadership have suggested the country could engage in talks on a new bilateral trade agreement with the United States, and welcome such talks with "open arms".[20] Vietnam exported more than $35 billion of goods to the U.S. market in 2016, making the United States consistently the largest export market for Vietnam's trade-dependent economy.[21] As a bilateral trade agreement concluded in 2000 with the United States, and which went into effect the following year, helped Vietnam's economy to begin to take off at the time, there is a unanimous recognition across the political spectrum in Hanoi of the importance of trade with and investment from the United States in Vietnam's future development.

Evolving Social Contract

The government confronted its first major test shortly after assuming office when hundreds of tons of dead fish began in early April to mysteriously wash ashore along four provinces on the central coast, where locals depend heavily on fishing for their livelihoods. What followed was nothing short of a turning point in state–society relations in Vietnam.

Local government officials initially attempted to dismiss concerns about food and environmental safety, even as images of the environmental disaster — believed to be the largest to hit Vietnam in recent decades — were circulated on the Internet and social media. Speculation quickly arose that industrial waste produced by the Taiwanese-invested Formosa Plastics steel complex nearby was the cause, a claim that authorities refuted at first. It was unclear for weeks whether the senior leadership recognized the scale of the disaster as it unfolded, or had any concrete plans to deal with it. Meanwhile, an affront by a representative of the steel plant on Vietnamese media, "You have to decide whether to catch fish and shrimp, or to build a modern steel industry",[22] sparked outrage among large swathes of the population towards both the company, for its arrogance, and the government, for being blatantly out of touch in the face of widespread popular dissatisfaction. The grass-roots response was swift and defiant, as individuals took to the streets and social media to make clear their message: "I choose fish".

Authorities responded to what by June had morphed into large weekly street protests in cities across Vietnam with heavy-handed tactics, arresting demonstrators at rally sites and accusing anti-communist exile forces of propping up the protest movement.[23] The elite has long associated most forms of popular expressions of opinion with possible attempts to subvert the state, for fears that pro-democracy and anti-government forces might find ways to infiltrate grass-roots movements and seek to cause political unrest. Government efforts to suppress protesters and media coverage, however, neither stopped demonstrations nor alleviated the growing sense of anger within society. The clash of expectations between the state and society was striking throughout this episode. The government, had it had any critical information on the environmental disaster or an action plan in the wake of the crisis, did not find it necessary to communicate with the population. Protesters and critics, meanwhile, adopted grass-roots activism, not to incriminate the government but rather to make their sentiments heard in the hope of prompting the authorities to make a more forceful response.

The Prime Minister's office eventually announced at the end of June, breaking weeks of silence, that industrial discharge containing the toxin cyanide into the ocean by Formosa was the cause of the massive death of marine life. It also announced that the government was seeking $500 million in compensation from the company.[24] The Prime Minister himself has since become involved with managing the aftermath of the crisis, ordering the government to draft clear mechanisms for the compensation of households and businesses affected by the disaster. Smaller protests, however, dragged on to as recently as October 2016.[25]

The social contract in Vietnam is slowly being rewritten. It is no longer enough for the ruling elite to deliver only on economic growth. The initial reaction by the government to the environmental disaster shows, however, that top leaders were in many ways out of touch with the sentiment of large swathes of the citizenry. This may present a predicament for the leadership in the future. On the one hand, the current leadership wants to regain the public's trust in the party-state apparatus, which has been eroding in recent years. On the other hand, top leaders by default cannot help but view public participation in politics or grass-roots activism of any form as potential threats to the political system. If the fish-kill incident were an indicator, Vietnamese society at large remains uninterested in the granularity of the current political structure, yet expects increasingly higher standards and accountability in governance and environmental issues — areas the state has long neglected.

The debate over the massive fish-kill took on an added layer, when street protesters and ordinary citizens alike began to openly question the wisdom of attracting foreign investment in manufacturing at all costs and doling out incentives for large investors at the expense of the environment and local economies. This shift is notable because discussions over the merits of government policy towards FDI has long been confined to a small group of intellectuals, many of whom served as former government advisors during the *doi moi* period. It remains to be seen whether the grass-roots chain reaction caused by the Formosa incident will affect the thinking of the leadership in future policymaking.

Shifting Grounds in Foreign Policy

There has been a growing awareness among the top leadership on the role that foreign policy, including defence diplomacy, plays in Vietnam's quest for international integration. Vietnam this year published for the first time a Diplomatic Blue Book that fulfils two objectives: highlighting the diplomatic sector's contributions to national development in 2015, and reaffirming international integration as a "strategic guideline" for its foreign policy over the next five years.[26] The Political Report approved at this year's Party Congress went as far as calling international integration the "pursuit of the whole people and the political system".[27]

While the past five years had focused on broadening, or in some cases redefining, Vietnam's key foreign partnerships, Hanoi is expected to work on deepening Vietnam's engagement with key foreign partners over the next five years. Such partners include ASEAN member countries, the United States, Japan, India, and Australia, in addition to traditional ones such as China, Russia, Cambodia, and Laos. Against the backdrop of a fluid regional environment, China's increasing aggressiveness, and the resurgence of great power politics in Southeast Asia, Hanoi continues to focus on pursuing more strategic options in the conduct of its foreign policy, shifting from a historically cautious stance towards security cooperation with larger powers in general. A key question confronting Vietnamese policymakers, however, will be how far to tap into the newfound strategic partnerships with countries such as the United States, India, and Japan without provoking China.

Hanoi's use of the strategically located deep-sea port at Cam Ranh Bay in central Vietnam overlooking the South China Sea — after it opened the upgraded facility to foreign naval ships early in 2016 — exemplifies this calculus. In the lead-up to a visit by two U.S. Navy warships at the international Cam Ranh port in October — given that Washington has called access for its naval ships to Cam Ranh Bay "a key component" in bilateral U.S.–Vietnam relations[28] — Hanoi had invited visiting warships from Singapore, France, Australia, and Japan to take turns docking at the port. The timing was an effort to alleviate concerns by Beijing over the pace of U.S.–Vietnam defence cooperation in recent years. A few weeks after the brief visit by the U.S. warships, which marked the first time the U.S. Navy had returned to Cam Ranh Bay since the end of the Vietnam War, Hanoi again opened its facility in October 2016 to welcome three Chinese naval ships for four days of meetings and exchanges between the two countries' navies.

Despite its best efforts, however, Vietnam's attempts to strike a balance in its South China Sea approach — a major focus of its foreign policy — have also encountered growing uncertainties. Washington's increasingly active posture in the

South China Sea and a more robust Chinese presence in the sea — especially since Beijing neared completion of its reclamation and construction in the Spratly Islands — have had the effect of reducing manoeuvrability for smaller regional countries. It remains unclear whether or how the incoming U.S. administration, which will walk into many of the policies put in place by the Obama administration, will modify the U.S. stance on the South China Sea dispute. Meanwhile, closer to home, Philippine president Rodrigo Duterte's willingness to cut bilateral deals or reach an understanding with Beijing over Scarborough Shoal, despite the Philippines' legal victory granted by a UN arbitral tribunal against China, undercuts Vietnam's long-held position that disputes in the South China Sea, with the exception of those over the Paracel Islands, should be addressed through multilateral mechanisms. These dynamics will force Vietnam to reflect on the long-term viability of its security ties with the United States, and what its regional role in helping manage the South China Sea situation, including through ASEAN, should be.

The current leadership has continued to invest in rebuilding trust in bilateral China–Vietnam relations, which reached a historic low in the wake of the 2014 oil rig crisis, when China deployed the HY981 oil drilling rig to waters claimed by Vietnam in the South China Sea. The year 2016 witnessed a succession of high-level visits between Hanoi and Beijing. Prime Minister Phuc and party executive secretary Huynh have both visited China since taking office, while a number of Politburo members of the Chinese Communist Party visited Hanoi throughout the year. In a sign of improving ties, Phuc signed wide-ranging agreements on economic cooperation that would commit China to helping Vietnam build industrial capacity and financing infrastructure projects during his visit in September.[29] During Huynh's meeting with Chinese President Xi Jinping in October, he reportedly called the advancement of China–Vietnam relations a "consistent strategy and policy choice".[30] Meanwhile, the two countries' coastguards also stepped up the pace of their joint fishery patrols in the Gulf of Tonkin this year.[31]

The year 2016 marked the culmination of the progress made in U.S.–Vietnam relations under the Obama administration's policy of rebalancing to the Asia-Pacific region. During Obama's visit to Vietnam in May 2016, Washington announced its decision to fully lift the decades-long U.S. ban on the sale of lethal weapons to Hanoi, after it partially eased the ban in late 2014.[32] For the two former foes, the removal of the ban signalled the full normalization of ties between them. While Hanoi continues to attach importance to securing technical assistance from Washington on issues of maritime security, the uncertain future of the TPP for the time being effectively makes it more difficult for Vietnam's leaders to consider moving much closer to the United States militarily. Absent a clearer sense on what the future holds and the extent of U.S. commitment to its economic and security leadership in Asia by the next administration, the U.S.–Vietnam partnership may risk carrying yet more symbolism than substance in the coming years.

Notes

1. See The World Bank and the Ministry of Planning and Investment of Vietnam, *Vietnam 2035: Toward Prosperity, Creativity, Equity, and Democracy* (Washington, DC: World Bank, 2016) <https://openknowledge.worldbank.org/handle/10986/23724>.

2. David Brown, "Viet Party Conference Surprisingly Dumps Dung", *Asia Sentinel*, 22 January 2016 <http://www.asiasentinel.com/politics/vietnam-party-conference-surprisingly-dumps-dung/>.

3. "Resolution on Party Building to be Translated into Deeds", *VietnamPlus*, 1 November 2016 <http://en.vietnamplus.vn/resolution-on-party-building-to-be-translated-into-deeds/101559.vnp>.

4. "Vietnam's Former Minister to be Disciplined for Wrongful Promotion of Son, Wanted Ex-provincial Leader", *Tuoi Tre News*, 25 October 2016 <http://tuoitrenews.vn/society/37711/former-minister-warned-for-wrongful-promotion-of-son-wanted-exprovincial-leader>.

5. "Former Minister of Trade Stripped of Title", *Viet Nam News*, 24 January 2017 <http://vietnamnews.vn/politics-laws/350221/former-minister-of-trade-stripped-off-title.html#IDbiXP85eq4JaWP4.99>.

6. Ibid.

7. For an account of internal reforms of the Vietnamese Communist Party in the early years of *doi moi*, see Lewis M. Stern, *Renovating the Vietnamese Communist Party: Nguyen Van Linh and the Programme for Organizational Reform, 1987–91* (Singapore: Institute of Southeast Asian Studies, 1993).

8. Aradhana Aravindan, "Millions of SE Asian Jobs May Be Lost to Automation in Next Two Decades: ILO", Reuters, 7 July 2016 <http://www.reuters.com/article/us-southeast-asia-jobs-idUSKCN0ZN0HP>.

9. Atsushi Tomiyama, "Vietnam Buckles Down to Build Up Its Parts Industry", *Nikkei Asian Review*, 15 February 2016 <http://asia.nikkei.com/Politics-Economy/Policy-Politics/Vietnam-buckles-down-to-build-up-its-parts-industry?page=2>.

10. "Báo Cáo Chính Trị của Ban Chấp hành Trung ương Đảng khóa XI tại Đại Hội Đại Biểu Toàn Quốc Lần thứ XII của Đảng" [Political report of the Party Central Committee at the 11th Congress of the 12th National Congress], *Nhan Dan Newspaper*, 25 March 2016 <http://nhandan.com.vn/chinhtri/item/29115302-bao-cao-chinh-tri-cua-ban-chap-hanh-trung-uong-dang-khoa-xi-tai-dai-hoi-dai-bieu-toan-quoc-lan-thu-xii-cua-dang.html>.

11. Nguyen Ha, "Thủ tướng: "Sẽ Là Chính Phủ Kiến Tạo và Phục Vụ" [Prime Minister:

The government will create and serve], VnEconomy, 5 May 2016 <http://vneconomy.vn/thoi-su/thu-tuong-se-la-chinh-phu-kien-tao-va-phuc-vu-20160504105050759.htm>.

12. It is worth noting that some have interpreted the concept to mean "developmental state", as in the context of other East Asian states, but Phuc does not use the phrase along these lines.

13. "Chính Phủ Kiến Tạo Là Phải Hành Động Chứ Không Thể Ngồi Trên Dân" [The government is to create and not sit on the people], Voice of Vietnam, 3 September 2016 <http://vov.vn/chinh-tri/chinh-phu-kien-tao-la-phai-hanh-dong-chu-khong-the-ngoi-tren-dan-546178.vov>.

14. "5 Trọng Tâm, 10 Nhiệm Vụ ưu Tiên Tái Cơ Cấu Kinh Tế Giai Đoạn 2016–2020" [Focus 5: 10 priority tasks of economic restructuring in the period 2016–20], Voice of Vietnam, 20 October 2016 <http://vov.vn/kinh-te/5-trong-tam10-nhiem-vu-uu-tien-tai-co-cau-kinh-te-giai-doan-20162020-561862.vov>.

15. Ibid.

16. "Vietnam Needs VND10,000 Trillion for Economic Restructuring", Voice of Vietnam, 30 October 2016 <http://english.vov.vn/economy/vietnam-needs-vnd10000-trillion-for-economic-restructuring-335201.vov>.

17. Government Portal of the Socialist Republic of Vietnam, "Thủ Tướng Nguyễn Xuân Phúc Trình Bày Báo Cáo Tình Hình KT-XH Năm 2016 và Nhiệm Vụ 2017" [Prime Minister Nguyễn Xuân Phúc presents the socio-economic development plans for 2016 and 2017], 20 October 2016 <http://baochinhphu.vn/Hoat-dong-cua-lanh-dao-Dang-Nha-nuoc/Thu-tuong-Nguyen-Xuan-Phuc-trinh-bay-Bao-cao-tinh-hinh-KTXH-nam-2016-va-nhiem-vu-2017/289458.vgp>.

18. Government Portal of the Socialist Republic of Vietnam, "Thiết Lập Đồng Bộ Chính Sách, Chương Trình Hỗ Trợ DN Nhỏ và Vừa" [Set up sync policies, programmes supporting small and medium-sized enterprises], 9 November 2016 <http://baochinhphu.vn/Ky-hop-thu-hai-QH-khoa-XIV/Thiet-lap-dong-bo-chinh-sach-chuong-trinh-ho-tro-DN-nho-va-vua/291133.vgp>.

19. "CPVCC Issues Resolution on International Economic Integration", VGP News, 16 November 2016 <http://news.chinhphu.vn/Home/CPVCC-issues-Resolution-on-international-economic-integration/201611/28982.vgp>.

20. "US Trade 'More Important Than Ever' to Vietnam", Voice of Vietnam, 3 January 2017 <http://english.vov.vn/trade/us-trade-more-important-than-ever-to-vietnam-340228.vov>.

21. "Vietnam's Exports to US Soar", Vietnam Customs Newspaper, 22 December 2016 <http://customsnews.vn/vietnams-exports-to-us-soar-2152.html>.

22. "Beleaguered Taiwanese Firm Tells Vietnam to Choose between Factory and Marine Life", Tuoi Tre News, 26 April 2016 <http://tuoitrenews.vn/society/34498/beleaguered-taiwanese-firm-tells-vietnam-to-choose-between-factory-and-marine-life>.

23. James Hookway, "Vietnam's Dead Fish Breathe Life into Protest Movement", Wall

Street Journal, 19 May 2016 <http://www.wsj.com/articles/vietnams-dead-fish-breathe-life-into-protest-movement-1463692409>.

24. Richard C. Paddock, "Taiwan-Owned Steel Factory Caused Toxic Spill, Vietnam Says", *New York Times*, 30 June 2016 <http://www.nytimes.com/2016/07/01/world/asia/vietnam-formosa-ha-tinh-steel.html>.

25. Mike Ives, "Outrage over Fish Kill in Vietnam Simmers 6 Months Later", *New York Times*, 3 October 2016 <http://www.nytimes.com/2016/10/04/world/asia/formosa-vietnam-fish.html>.

26. "VN Issues First Diplomacy Bluebook", *Viet Nam News*, 23 September 2016 <http://vietnamnews.vn/society/343252/vn-issues-first-diplomacy-bluebook.html#deyPhGRPLYFyPghC.97>.

27. "Báo Cáo Chính Trị của Ban Chấp hành Trung ương Đảng khóa XI tại Đại Hội Đại Biểu Toàn Quốc Lần thứ XII của Đảng" [Political report of the Party Central Committee at the 11th Congress of the 12th National Congress].

28. US Department of Defense, "Media Availability with Secretary Panetta in Cam Ranh Bay, Vietnam" (news transcript), 3 June 2012 <http://archive.defense.gov/transcripts/transcript.aspx?transcriptid=5051>.

29. The State Council of the People's Republic of China, "Premier Li Holds Talks with Vietnamese Prime Minister", 12 September 2016 <http://english.gov.cn/premier/news/2016/09/12/content_281475440476351.htm>.

30. "Xi: China, Vietnam Should Value Positive Momentum in Relations", Xinhua, 20 October 2016 <http://news.xinhuanet.com/english/2016-10/20/c_135769271.htm>.

31. "Vietnam-China Coast Guards Wrap up This Year's 2nd Joint Fishery Patrol", *People's Army Newspaper*, 10 November 2016 <http://en.qdnd.vn/defence-cooperation/vietnam-china-coast-guards-wrap-up-this-years-2nd-joint-fishery-patrol/427412.html>.

32. Matt Spetalnick, "U.S. Lifts Arms Ban on Old Foe Vietnam as China Tensions Simmer", Reuters, 23 May 2016 <http://www.reuters.com/article/us-vietnam-obama-idUSKCN0YD050>.

THE 2016 LEADERSHIP CHANGE IN VIETNAM AND ITS LONG-TERM IMPLICATIONS

Alexander L. Vuving

On 27 January 2016, the 12th Central Committee of Vietnam's ruling Communist Party (VCP) re-elected the seventy-two-year-old Nguyen Phu Trong as its General Secretary, breaking the rule that limits the age of candidates for this position to sixty-five. More strikingly, Trong's rival in the race to this top post was Prime Minister Nguyen Tan Dung, who has been perhaps, as a country expert has noted, "Vietnam's most powerful politician over the past thirty years, since the demise of General Secretary Le Duan."[1] Unlike any previous contenders to this job, Dung fought until the last minute, reportedly gathering nomination votes from nearly twenty per cent of the delegates of the 12th VCP Congress, which elected the Central Committee on 26 January.[2] However, the fate of this contest was substantially sealed five weeks earlier, at the 13th Plenum of the 11th Central Committee (14–21 December 2015).[3] Following this momentous event, the 14th Plenum, held one week before the 12th Congress, finalized the 11th Central Committee's recommendations for the top posts in the party-state: General Secretary Nguyen Phu Trong would stay party chief, Minister of Public Security Tran Dai Quang was named the next state president, Deputy Prime Minister Nguyen Xuan Phuc the next prime minister, and Vice-chair of the National Assembly Nguyen Thi Kim Ngan the next National Assembly chair. A few months later the National Assembly would formally appoint the three individuals to these posts for the next five years.

The 11th Central Committee also prepared the lists of nominees from which the 12th Congress and the 12th Central Committee respectively would select a

ALEXANDER L. VUVING is Professor at the Daniel K. Inouye Asia-Pacific Center for Security Studies in Honolulu, USA.

two-hundred-strong new Central Committee (which is the 12th CC) and a nineteen-strong new Politburo.[4] In Vietnam's party-state, the VCP Central Committee is the country's highest decision-making body between the Party Congresses, while the Politburo takes on this role when the Central Committee, which meets about twice a year, is not in session. As "the Party leads and the State manages" (*Đảng lãnh đạo, Nhà nước quản lý*) in this party-state, the Party General Secretary is the supreme leader of the country and the Commander-in-Chief of the military, even though the titular head of state is the State President, who is empowered by the Constitution to have the highest command (*thống lĩnh*) over the armed forces.

What are the long-term implications of the leadership changes ushered in at the 12th VCP Congress for Vietnam's economic reforms, political developments, and relations with major powers and regional states? How to make sense of the stunning outcome of the race for the country's top job? What characterizes the new constellation and what does it mean for Vietnam's domestic and foreign policies in the years to come? To answer these questions, this chapter first investigates plausible explanations for the downfall of the powerful Prime Minister Nguyen Tan Dung, whose defeat in an unusually vigorous bid for the top job paved the way for General Secretary Nguyen Phu Trong to stay in power. Next, the chapter examines the new leadership constellation with regard to its policy tendencies. Finally, and based on this appraisal, the chapter explores major long-term implications of the new leadership arrangements for Vietnam's domestic politics, economic reforms, and foreign policy, especially its policy regarding China, the United States, and the South China Sea.

Explaining the Outcomes of a Power Contest

Although every VCP congress is a time of intense power struggles, the 12th Congress was especially partisan. Never before has politics in Vietnam been so reduced to a stark choice between two individuals. These two leaders were General Secretary Nguyen Phu Trong and then-Prime Minister Nguyen Tan Dung. Trong's and Dung's personalities are polar opposites. At their core, Trong is a Confucian, who is loyal to his principles, while Dung is a capitalist, who is loyal to his profits. Although personality might play a part in their conflict, it was politics that was the main cause.

A few months into his first term as VCP General Secretary, Trong realized that, in his own words, "corruption is threatening the survival of the Party". At the 4th Plenum of the 11th Central Committee in December 2011, he launched a major campaign to "rectify the Party". Learning from the failure of the previous anti-graft measures, which were lambasted as "beating from the knee down" and "bathing without washing the head", Trong applied a top-down approach to his fight against corruption. Sitting at the apex of a massive network of rent-seeking interests, Dung soon became the main target of Trong's campaign.[5] But Dung was far from an ordinary Prime Minister. More than any of his predecessors, Dung harboured strong ambitions to become the country's supreme leader. The conflict between the two men represented a larger battle in which political campaigns were inseparable from election campaigns. The tide of the battle seesawed throughout four full years, from 2012 through 2015, until a decisive blow struck in December 2015 resulted in Dung's ouster and Trong's re-election at the 12th Congress.

Dung's failure to secure the top job surprised many observers. A May 2015 analysis predicted that "a key factor that is likely to shape the outcome of the next leadership transition is the growing power and influence of Prime Minister Nguyen Tan Dung".[6] By early November 2015, China's Vietnam hands apparently maintained a similar view, as visiting Chinese President Xi Jinping extended an invitation to Premier Dung to visit China in the future but did not similarly invite party chief Trong or State President Truong Tan Sang.[7]

Explaining Dung's defeat, an Associated Press analysis noted, "[the] successful leader in Vietnam needs to be faceless". The report argued that Dung was ousted "because he was seen by party bosses to have become too big for his boots".[8] Similarly, a study by two Vietnam scholars, written before the 12th Congress, contended that "past support for Dung may not translate into support for his general secretary candidacy".[9] The reason is that when the Central Committee cast its confidence vote for Dung in June 2013, it had quite different motives and calculations than when it decided who should be the next party chief. Although Trong was generally able to secure the Politburo's support, the Central Committee sided with Dung against Trong at more than one major juncture. At the 6th Plenum (1–15 October 2012), the Central Committee dismissed the Politburo's proposal to censure Dung. The 7th Plenum (2–11 May 2013) rejected Trong's recommendations that two reformers in his camp, VCP Internal Affairs Department head Nguyen Ba Thanh and VCP Economics Department head Vuong Dinh Hue, be promoted to the Politburo. Instead, the Central Committee elected National Assembly Vice-chair Nguyen Thi Kim Ngan and Deputy Prime Minister Nguyen Thien Nhan to the Politburo. Neither Ngan nor Nhan was a rent-seeker, but they were thought to maintain friendly relations with Dung. At the 10th Plenum (5–12 January 2015), Trong's hope that the Central Committee would cast a no-confidence vote on Dung backfired, with Dung reportedly winning the lion's share of the votes.[10] As the hypothesis goes, the Central Committee rescued Dung from attacks by the Trong camp because it wanted to preserve a division of power at the top, but selecting a strong General Secretary would undermine the Central Committee itself. Dung's ambition to centralize the leadership would mean a diminished role for the provincial officials, government ministers, and party functionaries who made up most of the Central Committee.

This hypothesis may or may not take into account the fact that about 40–45 per cent of the Central Committee were slated to retire at the 12th Congress.[11] In an ideal world, the 55–60 per cent of the Central Committee members who would stay would be united by their collective interest in a strong Central Committee, making the views of the retiring 40–45 per cent irrelevant. But in the real world, Central Committee members act on the basis of a more diverse pool of interests. Many of the retiring members might have wanted a strong leader to lead the country, while many of the staying members might have believed that the pragmatic Dung, rather than the moralistic Trong, would deliver more resources for them. Why these motives did not prevail over others remains unclear.

Another puzzle with the "weak leader" hypothesis is that the Central Committee failed to support a third candidate who would have been weaker than both Dung and Trong. In fact, Trong was not the first choice of his camp for the next General Secretary post. Already two years above the age limit when first elected in 2011, he was supposed to serve only one term — until 2016. In 2013 he endorsed party boss of Hanoi City Pham Quang Nghi as his successor. After Nghi was defeated in 2014, Trong turned his attention to Public Security Minister Tran Dai Quang and head of the Party Central Propaganda Department Dinh The Huynh. However, neither of the two was able to amass sufficient support in the Central Committee for candidacy to the top post. Re-electing Trong required breaking the rule on the age limits. With Dung gone and Trong victorious, the General Secretary would be stronger than ever before. It remains puzzling why a Central Committee that preferred a weak leader favoured these risks over the easier case of supporting an even more faceless leader.

Dung's downfall may be explained by his aggressiveness and the resourcefulness of his opponents. As a Vietnam scholar put it, "the Prime Minister's aggressive politics have turned many party members against him.... He made almost everyone his enemy."[12] Indeed, in addition to party chief Trong, State President Sang was also Dung's arch-rival. It is worth noting that the party chief, the State President, the Prime Minister, and the National Assembly chair are dubbed as the "four pillars" (*tứ trụ*) of the top tier in Vietnam's political hierarchy. By late 2014 Dung's relationship with National Assembly Chair Nguyen Sinh Hung had been a mixture of temporary rivalry and temporary alliance. But in late October 2014 the police arrested the boss of OceanBank, Ha Van Tham, a private tycoon close to Hung. Like Dung, Hung was a rent-seeker who was financially and operationally backed by business bosses under his patronage. Tham's arrest would kill two birds with one stone. It would help the Dung camp to expand its control of the banking sector, and it would provide evidence about Hung's possible corruption, which would hold Hung hostage to the possessor of the evidence. The negotiation between the Dung camp and the Hung camp appeared to last several months, but eventually Dung's hard line put Hung into a corner, pushing him firmly over to the Trong camp. How critical Hung's pivot to the Trong camp was for the overall balance of power remains, however, unclear. What is more certain is that Dung was relatively isolated in the Politburo. In 2012 Trong was able to convince the Politburo to reprimand Dung, and in 2015 Dung failed to gain the Politburo's support for his General Secretary candidacy. It was reported that among the sixteen members of the Politburo, only Nguyen Thien Nhan sided openly with Dung.

While the Trong camp was able to maintain some sort of hegemony in the Politburo, it failed several times to steer the Central Committee in its preferred direction. Some tricks may have helped the Trong camp eventually keep the Central Committee in line. On 9 June 2014 the Central Committee issued Decision No. 244 on intra-party elections.[13] The decision severely restricts the delegates' rights to nominate and self-nominate. Specific to the race for the top post, Decision 244 forbids all Politburo members to nominate candidates outside the list that has been approved collectively by the Politburo. In Central Committee sessions, Politburo members are not allowed to self-nominate or accept nomination from other Central Committee members. With this regulation in place, anyone who is not endorsed by the Politburo would be ousted from the contest, even if he or she obtained some support from the Central Committee. Of course, the Politburo does not work in isolation from the Central Committee. It might feel the need to change its nomination in response to new developments in or pressure from the Central Committee.

One possibility that might explain shifts in the balance of power is the emergence of new information. Although it eventually backfired, the arrest of OceanBank boss Tham was an attempt to obtain information about Nguyen Sinh Hung and then use it to blackmail Hung into siding with Dung. New information has been a critical factor affecting leadership changes. In the run-up to the 8th VCP Congress in 1996, the conservatives' candidate for Prime Minister, Nguyen Ha Phan, was foiled at the last minute due to new information about his alleged treason in the war period. New information about Dung might have been introduced in the last months prior to the 12th Congress, helping to turn the tide of the battle, not least by turning some of his supporters into his detractors. Chairwoman of the National Assembly Social Affairs Committee Truong Thi Mai, who would later gain a seat on the 12th Politburo, reportedly reversed her support for Dung after finding out something new about him.

The New Constellation

The ascent and eventual downfall of Nguyen Tan Dung neatly illustrates the evolution of the communist state in the reform era. The single most important feature of Vietnamese politics in the post-1986 period is the rise and crisis of a rent-seeking state.[14] Underlying this development is an evolving mixture of four policy currents that characterize contemporary Vietnamese politics.[15] The first current is driven by the conservatives, who advocate regime preservation and tend to embrace an anti-Western worldview. The second is represented by the modernizers, who champion national development, which leads them to promote domestic reforms and integration into the Western-led international system. The cohabitation of the conservatives and the modernizers has led to the emergence of the moderates and the rent-seekers as two major policy currents. Moderates take a position in the middle between the conservatives and the modernizers, trying to bridge the diametric differences between regime preservation and national modernization. Rent-seekers blend elements of communism and capitalism in an extractive way, promoting crony capitalism and nurturing authoritarian politics while pursuing a money-first foreign policy.

A popular narrative depicts Vietnam's high politics as a power struggle between a faction of pro-China conservatives led by Trong and VCP Executive Secretary Le Hong Anh and a faction of pro-Western reformists and technocrats led by Dung, buffered by a reform-oriented moderate group led by State President Sang and National Assembly Chair Hung.[16] This characterization does not match the evidence and is misleading at best. An examination of these leaders' behaviour throughout the years demonstrates that Trong is a conservative with moderate tendencies; Anh a moderate; Sang a former moderate who turned rent-seeker but eventually became a modernizer, probably an effect of his rivalry with Dung; Dung a modernizer turned rent-seeker; and Hung a moderate modernizer turned rent-seeker.

Neither Dung nor Trong fit the pro-China/anti-U.S. vs. pro-U.S./anti-China framework. Dung's approach to China combines nationalist rhetoric and dramatic action with economic engagement. The former part of his approach boosted his image as a nationalist hero, while the latter part tightened Vietnam's dependence on China.[17] Several signs indicate that Dung might have been Beijing's choice for Vietnam's next leader. When Chinese President Xi Jinping visited Vietnam in early November 2015, he invited Dung but not Trong or Sang to visit China in the future. China deployed the giant HYSY-981 oil rig near Vietnamese waters the week after the 13th Plenum of the VCP Central Committee (14–21 December 2015), which saw Trong defeat Dung in the race for the top job. Beijing moved the platform closer to Vietnam a few days after the 14th Plenum (11–13 January 2016), which reinforced Dung's downfall. But even if Dung was Beijing's choice, he remained friendly to the West and was a strong supporter of Vietnam's international openness.

Trong's general approach to foreign policy is "soft outside but firmer inside". He had some naive hope towards China, even after the cable-cutting incident of 2011 when China's vessels cut the cables of a Vietnamese survey ship within Vietnam's EEZ. But the oil rig crisis of 2014 changed his perceptions and convinced Trong that he had to reach out to the United States. In early 2015 he yielded to U.S. pressure and made a major concession to allow independent labour unions, paving the way for Vietnam to sign the Trans-Pacific Partnership (TPP), a U.S.-led economic bloc designed to counterbalance China's influence.[18]

Although the key choice at the 12th Congress was between two individuals, the key contest was between two broad coalitions. Dung's allies included mostly rent-seekers, modernizers, and moderates. Trong was backed by an even more heterogeneous coalition that comprised conservatives, modernizers, and moderates, with some rent-seekers in the mix. Illustrative of the Trong camp's ideological diversity are the three individuals who ventured out to the public in support of Trong at the 12th Congress. They included two modernizers (Vice-chair of the VCP Propaganda Department Vu Ngoc Hoang and General Secretary of the Fatherland Front Vu Trong Kim) and a conservative (Senior Lieutenant General Vo Tien Trung, Director of the National Defense Academy).

The end of the Trong–Dung rivalry ushered in a new era. Vietnamese politics remains a mixture of four policy currents represented by party conservatives, nationalist modernizers, moderates, and rent-seekers, but the mixture has changed shape. Compared to the previous configuration, the influence of rent-seekers has decreased while that of modernizers has edged higher. Conservatives are also less strongly represented in the new leadership. Moderates have overtaken rent-seekers as the most influential policy group. Estimates by several keen watchers consulted by the author put the number of moderates in the 16-strong 11th Politburo between 4 and 7, the number of rent-seekers also between 4 and 7, the number of conservatives between 2 and 5, and the number of modernizers

FIGURE 1
Trajectories of Vietnam's Policy Currents, 1986–2016

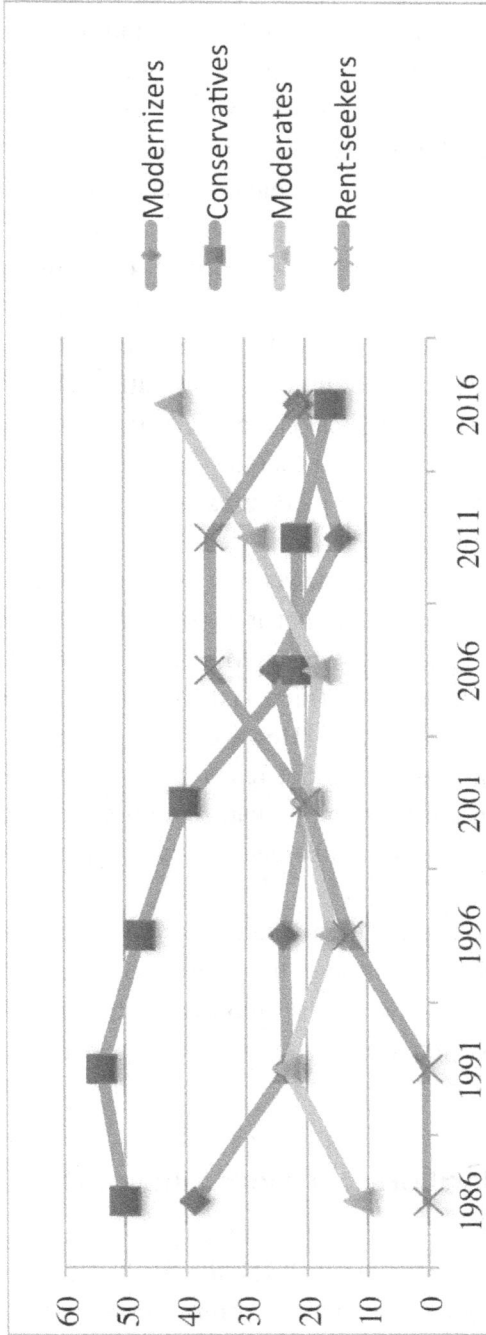

Note: This chart features the percentages of four policy currents as represented in the VCP Politburo.
Source: Author's estimates

between 1 and 3. In the 19-strong 12th Politburo, the estimated number of moderates ranges between 4 and 11, the number of rent-seekers between 3 and 6, the number of modernizers between 2 and 8, and the number of conservatives between 2 and 5. Averaged and translated into percentages, these estimates see the influence of moderates in the Politburo grow steadily from nearly 30 per cent in 2011 to around one third in 2013 to over 40 per cent in 2016. From 2011 to 2015 the influence of rent-seekers remained around the 35 per cent level, but it plunged sharply to just over 20 per cent as a result of the 12th Congress. During the same period, the influence of modernizers dropped marginally from 14.3 per cent in 2011–13 to 12.5 per cent in 2013–15, but the 12th Congress boosted it to over 20 per cent. Finally, the influence of conservatives declined steadily from over 20 per cent in 2011 to a little below 20 per cent in 2013 to about 16 per cent in 2016, making conservatives the least influential policy group in the Politburo. Thus, if moderates and rent-seekers shared the pride of place in the previous Politburo, moderates are now clearly the dominant force in the current Politburo.

Dung's defeat in his bid for power has swept rent-seekers away from the top ranks in the cabinet. The government is now headed by a modernizer — Prime Minister Phuc — and five Deputy Prime Ministers (Truong Hoa Binh, Vuong Dinh Hue, Pham Binh Minh, Vu Duc Dam, and Trinh Dinh Dung) who are believed to be modernizers and moderates. However, Dung's last-minute defeat ensured that the purge of rent-seekers did not reach below the top echelons. As a result of their dominance in the previous period, rent-seekers are still a powerful force at the ministerial level and in the bureaucracy that manages the day-to-day work of the government.

All this creates a constellation where the chief of the party is a conservative with moderate tendencies, the head of the government is a modernizer, the country's collective leadership is dominated by moderates, but these leaders have to rely on a structure heavily influenced by rent-seekers for policy recommendations and implementation.

Long-term Implications for Domestic and Foreign Policy

The rearrangement of Vietnam's ruling elite will impact the way the party-state exerts and maintains power. The survival and resilience of Vietnam's communist regime relies on a varying combination of repression, co-optation, legitimacy, and external factors. The recent power struggle in the leadership suggests that the ruling elite will continue to be characterized by diverse identities and interests.

Coupled with the dominance of the moderates, this will moderately reduce repression and increase co-optation and legitimacy as major tools of the state in its interaction with society. More specifically, the party-state will have to rely more on legitimacy to stay in power. This will push the government to be more responsive to popular demands.

The new constellation suggests that the party and government leadership is now more united in fighting corruption and promoting economic reforms. But how this will work out will depend a great deal on the response from the rent-seekers who have pervaded the party-state. Rent-seekers can now choose from among three major strategies: sabotage and resistance, co-optation, and transformation. Thus, some rent-seekers may sabotage reforms and resist efforts aimed at uprooting corruption, others may entice moderates and modernizers into adopting rent-seeking behaviour, and still others may try to turn themselves into moderates or modernizers. The central fault line of Vietnamese politics in the coming years is likely to be drawn between the rent-seekers and the modernizers.

The dominance of modernizers at the top echelons of the government bodes well for economic and institutional reforms. But the extent to which the Cabinet leadership can advance reform remains a big question mark. Two major factors may interfere to put a break on reform. First, with the party chief remaining a conservative with moderate tendencies, reform is likely to progress step by step rather than by leaps and bounds. Secondly, the pervasive nature of rent-seeking in the government means that reform efforts will meet with strong resistance and be sabotaged to a significant extent by the very people whose job it is to implement them.

On the foreign policy front, Vietnam will likely veer farther, but not too far, from China and closer, but not too close, to the United States. The declining power of party conservatives and rent-seekers and the rising influence of nationalist modernizers suggest that Vietnam will try harder to reduce its economic dependence on China. As U.S.–China rivalry intensifies, Hanoi will strengthen efforts to avoid choosing between the two great powers. This would mean that much of Vietnam's energy and attention would be directed to relations with major regional powers, including Japan, India, Russia, and ASEAN to a large extent, and South Korea and Australia to a lesser extent.

Vietnam's approach to China and the United States is a combination of cooperation and competition (*vừa hợp tác vừa đấu tranh*). But it is a changing, not a constant, combination, with a shifting emphasis that evolves with the changes in the mix of influential groups in the leadership. This combination of cooperation and competition spans six distinct strategies. Ranging from hard to soft approaches, these strategies include hard balancing, soft balancing, enmeshment, engagement, accommodation/deference, and solidarity.

Vietnam's approach to China since the renormalization of relations in 1991 has gone through four major phases. In the 1990s, accommodation and soft balancing, followed by solidarity and enmeshment, were the most salient components of Hanoi's strategy. In the 2000s, engagement was increasingly added to the mix, becoming the strongest component by the second half of the decade. During the same period, solidarity morphed into deference, and enmeshment faded relative to the other components. Starting in the late 2000s, China's aggressive actions in the South China Sea increasingly strengthened both hard and soft balancing while discrediting solidarity and enmeshment.[19] Sino–Vietnamese relations passed a point of no return with the HYSY-981 oil rig crisis of 2014.[20] This crisis shifted the emphasis of Vietnam's strategy towards the balancing end, hollowing solidarity and making engagement highly suspicious. The dominance of moderates in the top leadership suggests that Vietnam will retain all six strategies, regardless of their mutual contradiction. On the other hand, the rising influence of modernizers and the declining impact of conservatives and rent-seekers in foreign policy making will reinforce the shift towards the balancing end, edging away from solidarity, deference, and engagement. This shift will be gradual, barring major events that dictate otherwise.

The evolution of Vietnam's relations with the United States since renormalization in 1995 has undergone two turning points. Until mid 2003, Hanoi emphasized soft balancing, but the perception of U.S. superior power, demonstrated in the 2003 invasion of Iraq, caused a re-evaluation of Vietnam's international outlook. Following the 8th Plenum of the 9th Central Committee in July 2003, Vietnam pursued a dualist policy, emphasizing both soft balancing and engagement in relations with the United States.[21] The other turning point in Vietnam–U.S. relations was triggered by the 2014 oil rig crisis with China. Following this crisis, Hanoi accelerated its rapprochement with Washington, culminating in the protocol-breaking visit by VCP chief Trong to the White House in July 2015.[22] As Washington proved to be a valuable partner in the South China Sea dispute, the emphasis of Vietnam's U.S. policy shifted decisively to engagement, illustrated by Hanoi's embrace of the TPP and its unusually warm reception of U.S. President Barack Obama's visit in May 2016. With the moderates dominating and the nationalist modernizers rising, Vietnam is poised to continue the trend set by the recent U.S.–Vietnam rapprochement.

Nationalist modernizers owe their growing influence in part to China's aggressive behaviour in the South China Sea. At the same time, the South

Alexander L. Vuving

China Sea dispute remains a key issue in Vietnam's regional and international outlook. In recent years, Vietnam's security strategy to address the China threat has been based on three major prongs. The first of these is to develop minimal deterrence through force modernization and defence posturing. This is paralleled by continuous attempts to maintain peaceful relations with China, including maintaining bridges of communication when relations are in crisis. These two prongs are buttressed by efforts to reach out to the outside world for international support and assistance.[23] This security strategy has provided a broad framework for Vietnam to deal with China, but it needs major elaboration. Dominated by moderates, Vietnam's leadership will have a hard time determining the right priorities and the right balance among the possible elements of this framework. On the other hand, the declining influence of conservatives and rent-seekers will provide a positive atmosphere for consensus building. If the modernizers continue to grow in influence, the coming years may witness the emergence of "middle power politics", which will proactively seek to redress the worsening balance of power in the region by reducing Vietnam's dependence on China, strengthening Hanoi's ties with regional powers such as Japan and India, working with fellow ASEAN states to unite the group, and creating some new elements in the regional architecture.

Conclusion

Every VCP Congress produces some leadership changes, but the 12th Congress represented a turning point in the trajectory of Vietnamese politics. It marked a dramatic downturn of the rent-seekers and a reinvigoration of the modernizers. It also established the dominance of the moderates and furthered the conservatives' decline. The 12th Congress put an end to the rent-seekers' dominance, but it did not herald the end of the rent-seeking state. What it ushered in is the twilight of a form of governance that has dominated Vietnam over the last twenty years.

The leadership changes at the 12th Congress suggest that economic and institutional reform will move forward, but it will advance incrementally rather than at full speed. The regime will have to rely more on legitimacy to maintain power, and the government will have to be more responsive to popular demands. If the current trends continue, Vietnam may enter a second reform era in the coming decade. Vietnam will further integrate into the outside world. With respect to relations with the major powers in the region, Vietnam will continue to edge away from China, while moving closer to the United States, Japan, and India, but it will aim for a position of complex balances, not one of partisanship.

These trends are not irreversible, however. They can be accelerated, disrupted, or reversed by major changes in the international and domestic environment. If developments such as the Philippines' pivot to China under President Rodrigo Duterte and the United States' withdrawal from the TPP under President Donald Trump are part of a larger trend, this will cause the Vietnamese to seriously rethink their regional and international outlook and will significantly impact Vietnam's strategic trajectory. On the other hand, an escalation of tensions in the South China Sea and increased rivalry between China and the United States in the future will also leave its mark on Vietnam's political development. A possible big event that may occur in the next decade is a financial crisis in China that plunges the country into a prolonged slowdown or recession. The effects of such a crisis are too complex to forecast, but in any event such a development will likely throw Vietnam into a whirlwind with unforeseeable consequences. Finally, domestic events such as a banking crisis, an environmental disaster, or political turmoil triggered by such a development will also have the potential to change the course of Vietnamese politics.

Notes

1. Le Hong Hiep, "Vietnam's Leadership Transition in 2016: A Preliminary Analysis", *ISEAS Perspective 2015*, no. 24, 18 May 2015, p. 6.
2. It was reported that Dung was nominated by 270 delegates out of a total of 1,510. Người Đưa Tin, "Thủ tướng Nguyễn Tấn Dũng là người được giới thiệu nhiều nhất với 270 phiếu" [Prime Minister Nguyen Tan Dung was nominated with 270 votes, the highest vote], *Ba Sàm*, 24 January 2016 <https://anhbasam.wordpress.com/2016/01/24/6712-thu-tuong-nguyen-tan-dung-la-nguoi-duoc-gioi-thieu-nhieu-nhat-voi-270-phieu/>.
3. Alexander L. Vuving, "Who Will Lead Vietnam?", *The Diplomat*, 16 January 2016.
4. The 12th Central Committee has 180 regular members with voting rights and 20 alternate members without voting rights. The 180 regular members would populate key leadership positions in the country's governance structure, which includes the central party institutions, the provincial party organizations, the central and provincial governments, the military at the national and regional levels, the security forces, and key mass organizations such as the Fatherland Front, the Youth League, the Women's Union, the Labour Union, and the Peasants' Union.
5. Alexander L. Vuving, "Vietnam in 2012: A Rent-Seeking State on the Verge of a Crisis", in *Southeast Asian Affairs 2013*, edited by Daljit Singh (Singapore: Institute of Southeast Asian Studies, 2013), pp. 330–35.
6. Hiep, "Vietnam's Leadership Transition in 2016", p. 12.
7. Vuving, "Who Will Lead Vietnam?"

8. Vijay Joshi, "Analysis: Successful Leader in Vietnam Needs to Be Faceless", Associated Press, 29 January 2016.

9. Paul Schuler and Kai Ostwald, "Delayed Transition: The End of Consensus Leadership in Vietnam?" *ISEAS Perspective* 2016, no. 2, 14 January 2016.

10. The only publicly available numbers of confidence votes at the 10th Plenum are from the blog *Chan dung Quyen luc* (Portraits of Power), which is clearly pro-Dung and anti-Trong. According to this blog, Dung received the highest number of votes for high confidence, followed by State President Truong Tan Sang, while Trong ranked 8th among the 20 members of the Politburo and Secretariat. See Chân dung Quyền lực, "Kết quả bỏ phiếu tín nhiệm Bộ Chính trị, Ban Bí thư tại Hội nghị Trung ương 10" [Results of the Politburo Secretariat confidence vote of the 10th Party Central Committee], 16 January 2015. Some well-informed sources dispute the credibility of these numbers, however.

11. "Tiêu chuẩn nhân sự Ban Chấp hành Trung ương Đảng khóa XII" [HR standards of the 12th Party Central Committee], Zing.vn, 19 January 2016 <http://news.zing.vn/tieu-chuan-nhan-su-ban-chap-hanh-trung-uong-dang-khoa-xii-post620434.html>.

12. Alexander Vuving, quoted in John Boudreau, "Vietnam Signals Leadership Shift as Premier's Prospects Fade", Bloomberg, 24 January 2016.

13. See Quyết định số 244-QĐ/TW ngày 9/6/2014 của Ban Chấp hành Trung ương về việc ban hành Quy chế bầu cử trong Đảng [Decision 244-QD TW dated 9/6/2014 of the Central Committee on the issue of voting regulations in the Party], 9 June 2014 <http://moj.gov.vn/qt/cacchuyenmuc/daihoidaibieu/Pages/van-ban-cua-dang-cap-tren.aspx?ItemID=15>.

14. Vuving, "Vietnam in 2012."

15. Alexander L. Vuving, "Vietnam's Search for Stability", *The Diplomat*, 25 October 2012; Vuving, "Vietnam: The Tale of Four Players", *Southeast Asian Affairs 2010*, edited by Daljit Singh (Singapore: Institute of Southeast Asian Studies, 2010), pp. 367–91.

16. Chanh Cong Phan, "Vietnam after 2016: Who Will Lead?", *The Diplomat*, 10 July 2015.

17. Vuving, "Who Will Lead Vietnam?"

18. Ibid.

19. Alexander L. Vuving, "Power Rivalry, Party Crisis and Patriotism: New Dynamics in the Vietnam-China-U.S. Triangle", in *New Dynamics in U.S.-China Relations: Contending for the Asia-Pacific*, edited by Li Mingjiang and Kalyan M. Kemburi (London: Routledge, 2015), pp. 273–78.

20. Alexander L. Vuving, "A Tipping Point in the U.S.-China-Vietnam Triangle", *The Diplomat*, 6 July 2015.

21. Alexander L. Vuving, "How Experience and Identity Shape Vietnam's Relations with China and the United States", in *Asia's Middle Powers? The Identity and Regional*

Policy of South Korea and Vietnam, edited by Joon-Woo Park, Gi-Wook Shin, and Donald W. Keyser (Stanford: Shorenstein Asia-Pacific Research Center, 2013), pp. 53–71.

22. Vuving, "A Tipping Point".

23. Alexander L. Vuving, "Vượt thác ghềnh, ra biển lớn" [Overcome obstacles to reach the sea], *Thế giới và Việt Nam*, 25 August 2016 <http://baoquocte.vn/vuot-thac-ghenh-ra-bien-lon-34910.html>.